A DAY'S MARCH NEARER HOME

Roger Parkinson

A DAY'S MARCH
NEARER HOME

The War History from Alamein to
VE Day based on the War Cabinet
papers of 1942 to 1945

David McKay Company, Inc.   New York

A DAY'S MARCH NEARER HOME

First American Edition, 1974

LIBRARY OF CONGRESS CATALOG CARD NUMBER: 74-78663

ISBN: 0-679-50471-0

MANUFACTURED IN THE UNITED STATES OF AMERICA

Contents

Maps

Some Major Figures Involved

ALEXANDER, Albert V. (later Lord Hillsborough), First Lord of the Admiralty from 12 May 1940, after Churchill, until May 1945, when Bracken took the post until Alexander returned in July 1945, under Attlee.

ALEXANDER, General (later Field-Marshal) Sir Harold R. G., GOC-in-C Middle East; C-in-C Allied Armies in Italy; Supreme Allied Commander Mediterranean from November 1944.

AMBROSIO, General, Chief of Italian General Staff, February 1943, after Cavallero.

AMERY, Leopold S., Secretary of State for India and Burma, 1940-July 1945, replaced by Lord Pethick-Lawrence.

ANDERS, General Wladyslaw, Commander, Polish Forces USSR, 1941-1942, Middle-East and Italy, 1942-1945.

ANDERSON, Sir John, Lord President of the Council, after Chamberlain, until 28 September 1943, succeeded by Attlee; Chancellor of the Exchequer, after Kingsley Wood, until July 1945, replaced by Dalton.

ANDERSON, General K. A. N., Commander, British 1st Army during 'Torch'.

ANTONOV, General, leader of Soviet Delegation at Yalta, senior member of Soviet General Staff, Moscow.

ARNOLD, General Henry, Chief of US Army Air Forces.

ATTLEE, Clement, Deputy Prime Minister under Churchill; Dominions Secretary until 28 September 1943, succeeded by Cranborne; Lord President of the Council, after Anderson, until May 1945, succeeded by Woolton.

AUPHAN, Admiral Paul, French Deputy Chief of Naval Staff and Vichy French Minister of Marine, 1942.

BADOGLIO, Marshal P., Chief of Italian General Staff; Prime Minister 1943-1944.

BEAVERBROOK, Lord, Lord Privy Seal from 28 September 1943, after Cranborne, until July 1945, succeeded by Arthur Greenwood.

BEVIN, Ernest, Minister of Labour and National Service from 13 May 1940, until May 1945, succeeded by R. A. Butler; replaced Eden as Foreign Secretary, July 1945, under Attlee.

BOISSON, P., Governor, French Equatorial Africa, 1939-1940; French West Africa, 1942-1943.

BRACKEN, Brendan (later Lord), Minister of Information from 20 July 1941, after Duff Cooper, until May 1945, succeeded by Geoffrey Lloyd, then First Lord, replacing Alexander, until latter took office again in July 1945 under Attlee.

BRADLEY, Lieut.-General Omar N., Commander of US 2nd Army Corps, North Africa, in 1943; Commander of US 12th Army Group, North-West Europe, 1944, 1945.

BROOKE, General (later Field-Marshal Lord Alanbrooke), Sir Alan F., CIGS from December 1941 after Dill.

BUTLER, R. A. (later Lord), President of Board of Education July 1941-May 1945, known as Minister of Education after Education Act, August 1944, succeeded by R. K. Law; Minister of Labour and National Service after Bevin, until replaced by Isaacs in July 1945, after Attlee's victory.

CADOGAN, Sir Alexander, Permanent Under-Secretary of State for Foreign Affairs, 1938-1946.

CAMPBELL, Sir Ronald Ian, Minister at Washington, 1941-1945.

CASTELLANO, General G., Chief of the Military Office of General Ambrosio, 1943.

CATROUX, General Georges, French Delegate-General, Syria and Lebanon, 1941-1943; Commissioner for Moslem Affairs, FCNL, 1943-1945; French Ambassador to USSR from January 1945.

CAVALLERO, Marshal, Chief of the Italian General Staff until January 1943, succeeded by Ambrosio.

CHENNAULT, Major-General Claire, Commander US 14th Air Force, Burma-China-India front.

CHERWELL, Lord (previously Professor F. A. Lindemann), scientific adviser to Prime Minister.

CHIANG Kai-shek, General ('Generalissimo'), C-in-C Chinese armed forces, President of Executive Yuan, 1939-1945, and of Nationa Government of China from 1943.

CIANO, Count Galeazzo, Mussolini's son-in-law, Italian Foreign Minister, 1936-1943.

CLARK KERR, Sir Archibald, Ambassador to USSR, 1942-1946.

CLARK, General Mark Wayne, Commander, US 5th Army.

COOPER, Alfred Duff, British representative with FCNL, 1943-1944; Ambassador to France, 1944-1948.

CRANBORNE, Lord, Secretary of State for Dominions until 19 February 1942, succeeded by Attlee; Lord Privy Seal until 20 September 1943, succeeded by Beaverbrook; Dominions Secretary again, after Attlee, until July 1945, succeeded by Viscount Addison in Attlee's Government.

CRIPPS, Sir Stafford R., Minister of Aircraft Production, November 1942, after Llewellin, until May 1945, replaced by Ernest Brown.

CUNNINGHAM, Admiral Sir Andrew (later Admiral of the Fleet, Viscount, of Hyndhope), member of British Mission to Washington and the CCS from November 1942, to 20 February 1943; C-in-C Allied Naval Forces, Mediterranean.

DAMASKINOS, Archbishop of Athens, 1938-1949; Regent of Greece, 1944-1946.

DARLAN, Admiral J. F., Vichy Vice-President of the Council and Minister for Foreign Affairs, Marine and Interior, 1941-1942; C-in-C French Forces, 1941-1942.

DAVIES, Joseph E., US Ambassador to Moscow, 1936-1938.

DEVERS, General J. L., Deputy Supreme Allied Commander, Mediterranean, from December 1943 to September 1944, succeeded by Lieut.-General J. T. McNarney; Commanding-General, 6th Army (US) Group, AEF, North-West Europe.

DILL, Field-Marshal Sir John G., Head of British Military Mission to Washington until his death in November 1944, succeeded by Maitland Wilson.

DOENITZ, Admiral Karl, C-in-C German Navy from January 1943, after Raeder; Hitler's successor, May 1945.

DOUGLAS-HOME, Sir Alec—see DUNGLASS, Lord.

DUNGLASS, Lord (later Sir Alec Douglas-Home), Conservative MP

1931-1945, later Foreign Secretary, Prime Minister, and Foreign Secretary again.

EDEN, Anthony (later Lord Avon), Foreign Secretary from December 1940, after Lord Halifax, until July 1945, replaced by Bevin.

EISENHOWER, General Dwight David, C-in-C Allied Forces, North Africa and Mediterranean; 1944, Supreme Commander, Allied Forces Europe; later US President.

ESTEVA, Admiral, Vichy French Resident-General, Tunisia, 1942.

EVILL, Air Vice-Marshal (Air Marshal, 1944) Sir Douglas, Vice-COAS.

FLANDIN, P. E., French Foreign Minister, 1940-1941.

FRANCO, General Francisco, Spanish Head of State and Generalissimo of National Armies from 1936.

FREDENDALL, Major-General Lloyd R., Commander of Centre Task Force, 'Torch'.

FREYBERG, Lieut.-General Sir Bernard, V.C., GOC New Zealand Expeditionary Force in North Africa, Crete and Italy.

FRIEDEBURG, Admiral Hans von, C-in-C German Navy, May 1945, after Doenitz.

GAULLE, General Charles de, Leader of Free French movement and Head of National Committee, 1940-1943; President, Committee of National Liberation, 1943-1944, and of Provisional Government, 1944-1946.

GEORGE II, King of Hellenes.

GEORGE VI, British Sovereign, 1936-1952.

GIRAUD, General Henri, French C-in-C North Africa, November-December 1942, after Juin; French High Commissioner, North Africa, December 1942-June 1943; Co-President, FCNL, with de Gaulle, 1943; French C-in-C, 1943-1944.

GODEFROY, Admiral, commander of French naval squadron, Alexandria, 1941-1943.

GOEBBELS, Paul J., Nazi propaganda chief, committed suicide, May 1945.

GOUSEV, Feodor, Soviet Ambassador to Britain from 1943, after Maisky, until 1946.

GRIGG, Sir James, Secretary of State for War until July 1945, succeeded by J. J. Lawson under Attlee.

HALIFAX, Lord Edward, Ambassador to America, 1940-1946.

HARRIMAN, William Averell, American Ambassador to USSR, 1943-1946.

HARRIS, Air Chief Marshal Sir Arthur, C-in-C Bomber Command, RAF.

HIMMLER, Heinrich, chief of Nazi SS and Gestapo; committed suicide, 23 May 1945.

HOARE, Sir Samuel (later Viscount Templewood), Ambassador at Madrid, 1940-1944.

HOPKINS, Harry, adviser and special assistant to President Roosevelt, 1941-1945.

HORE-BELISHA, Leslie, Secretary of State for War in Chamberlain's Government from 1937 to 5 January 1940; Minister of National Insurance, May-July 1945, replaced by James Griffiths under Attlee.

HUDSON, R. S., Minister of Agriculture and Fisheries until July 1945, replaced by Thomas Williams under Attlee.

HULL, Cordell, American Secretary of State until November 1944, succeeded by Stettinius.

INÖNÜ, General Ismet, President of the Turkish Republic, 1938-1950.

ISMAY, Major-General Sir Hastings L. (later Lord), Deputy Secretary, Military, to War Cabinet and Churchill's representative on COS Committee.

JODL, General Alfred, Hitler's Chief of Staff; executed at Nuremberg, October 1946.

JOHNSTON, Thomas, Secretary of State for Scotland until May 1945, succeeded by Roseberry.

JUIN, General Alphonse, French C-in-C North Africa, 1941-1942, succeeded by Giraud.

KEITEL, Field-Marshal Wilhelm, Chief of the German Armed Forces High Command; executed at Nuremberg, October 1946.

KESSELRING, Field-Marshal Albert, Commander of German armies in South Italy, 1943; replaced Rundstedt as commander of Army Group G in north-west Europe, March 1945.

KING, Fleet Admiral Ernest J., Chief of US Naval Operations and C-in-C US Fleet.

KING, W. L. Mackenzie, Prime Minister of Canada, 1935-1948, and Secretary of State for External Affairs, 1935-1946.

KOENIG, General M. J. P. F., Assistant Chief of Staff Algiers, 1943-1944; Commander, French forces of the Interior, and delegate to SHAEF, 1944.

LABORDE, Admiral de, Commander of the French Mediterranean Fleet, 1942.

LASKI, Professor Harold, Chairman of the Labour Party, 1945.

LAVAL, Pierre, Head of the Vichy Government, Minister for Foreign Affairs, the Interior and Propaganda, 1942-1944.

LAYCOCK, Major-General R. E., Chief of Combined Operations from October 1943, after Mountbatten.

LEAHY, Fleet Admiral William D., American Ambassador to Vichy, 1940, until May 1942, then Chief of Staff to President until 1949.

LEATHERS, Lord, Minister of War Transport until July 1945, succeeded by Alfred Barnes under Attlee.

LEEPER, R. W. A., Ambassador to Greece, 1943-1946.

LEESE, Lieut.-General Sir Oliver W. H., Corps Commander in 8th Army, 1942, 1943; Commander, 8th Army after December 1943, in succession to Montgomery; C-in-C Allied Land Forces, SE Asia Command from November 1944.

LEIGH-MALLORY, Air Chief Marshal Sir Trafford, C-in-C air forces AEF, north-west Europe from 1944.

LINLITHGOW, Victor, 2nd Marquis of, Viceroy of India, 1936-1943, succeeded by Wavell.

LYTTELTON, Oliver, Minister of Production after March 1942, after Beaverbrook, until July 1945; no successor.

MACK, W. H. B., Foreign Office Political Liaison Officer with Eisenhower, 1942-1943.

MACMILLAN, Harold, Minister Resident, Allied Forces HQ, Algiers, 1942-May 1945; Secretary of State for Air, after Sinclair, until July 1945, succeeded by Viscount Stansgate under Attlee.

MAISKY, Ivan, Soviet Ambassador to Britain, 1932-1943, succeeded by Gousev.

MALLABY, Major-General A. W. S., Auchinleck's Director of Military Operations, India, 1943.

MALLET, Sir Victor, British Minister to Sweden, 1940-1945.

MARSHALL, General George C., Chief of Staff, US Army, from 1939.

MIHAILOVIĆ, General Draza, Yugoslav Chetnik leader, Minister for War and C-in-C, 1942-1944.

MIKOLAJCZYK, Stanslaw, Polish Minister of Interior, 1941-1943; Prime Minister, 1943-1944; Minister of Agriculture and Deputy Prime Minister, Polish Provisional Government, 1945-1947.

MOLOTOV, Vyacheslav, Soviet Foreign Minister, 1939-1949.

MONTGOMERY, General (later Field-Marshal) Sir Bernard Law; Commander, 8th Army, succeeded by Leese, December 1943; C-in-C, 21st Army Group, after Paget.

MORAN, Lord (formerly Sir Charles Wilson), personal physician to Churchill from May 1940.

MORGAN, Lieut.-General F. E., Chief of Staff to the Allied Supreme Commander, 1943.

MORGENTHAU, Henry J., American Secretary of Treasury, 1934-1945.

MORRISON, Herbert S., Home Secretary and Minister for Home Security after Anderson, until May 1945; succeeded by Sir Donald Somervell.

MOUNTBATTEN, Lord Louis (of Burma), Chief of Combined Operations until October 1943, succeeded by Laycock; Supreme Allied Commander, S.E. Asia.

MOYNE, Lord, Deputy Minister of State Resident in Middle East until his assassination in January 1944, when the office lapsed.

MURPHY, Robert D., Chief Civil Affairs Officer, AFHQ, Algiers, and Roosevelt's special representative in North Africa, 1942-1943; political adviser AFHQ, 1943-1944.

NICOLSON, Harold, M.P., Governor of the BBC; diarist.

NOGUÈS, General A. P., French Resident General, Morocco, 1936-1943.

NYE, Lieut.-General A. E. (later Sir Archibald), Vice-CIGS.

PAGET, General Sir Bernard, C-in-C Home Forces until July 1943, succeeded by Franklyn; C-in-C Army Group until December 1943, succeeded by Montgomery; commander, Middle East Command, after Wilson.

PAPANDREOU, Georgios, Greek Prime Minister, 1944.

PATTON, General George S., commander of the US 3rd Army; died after car accident in Germany, December 1945.

PAULUS, Friedrich von, German Field Marshal, surrendered his army at Stalingrad, 1943; survived Soviet captivity.

PEIRSE, Air Chief Marshal Sir Richard, C-in-C Allied Air Forces, SE Asia Command, until November 1944; succeeded by Air Marshal Sir Guy Garrod.

PÉRON, Colonel Juan D., military dictator, Argentina, until 1955.

PÉTAIN, Henri P., French Marshal, Vichy Head of State, 1940-1944; later sentenced to death for treason, but died in prison, 1951.

PETER II, King of Serbs, Croats and Slovenes.

PEYROUTON, M., French Governor-General, Algeria, 1943.

PORTAL, Air Chief Marshal Sir Charles, COAS from October 1940, after Newall.

POUND, Admiral of the Fleet Sir Dudley, First Sea Lord and CHS until 15 October 1943, succeeded by Cunningham.

RADESCU, General N., Prime Minister of Roumania, 1944-1945.

RAMSEY, Admiral Sir Bertram, C-in-C Allied Naval Expeditionary Forces, AEF north-west Europe, 1943 to January 1945, succeeded by Admiral Sir Harold Burrough.

REYNAUD, Paul, French President of the Council, March 1940, and Minister of Defence, May 1940.

ROKOSSOVSKY, Marshal K., Soviet army leader serving at Stalingrad, Kursk, Klim, Orel and in East Prussia.

ROMER, Tadeusz, Polish Ambassador to USSR, 1942-1943; Minister of Foreign Affairs, 1943-1944.

ROMMEL, Field-Marshal Erwin; commander of German forces in North Africa, afterwards serving in Italy and France.

ROSEBERY, the Earl of, Secretary of State for Scotland, May-July 1945, after Thomas Johnston, replaced by Joseph Westwood.

RUNDSTEDT, Field-Marshal Gerd von, C-in-C German armies in the West, February 1942, replacing Field Marshal von Witzleben, succeeded by Kesselring, March 1945.

SALAZAR, Dr Antonio, Portuguese Prime Minister and Foreign Minister, 1932-1968.

SANDYS, Duncan, Churchill's son-in-law; Parliamentary Secretary to Minister of Supply, 1943-1944; Chairman of 'Crossbow' Committee, 1943-1945; Minister of Works, May-July 1945 after Lord Portal, succeeded by George Tomlinson under Attlee.

SARACOGLU, Sukru, Turkish Foreign Minister, 1938-1942 and June-September 1944; Prime Minister, 1942-1946.

SCOBIE, Lieut.-General R. M., GOC British troops in Greece, 1944-1946.

SIKORSKI, General Wladyslaw, Polish Prime Minister and C-in-C, 1939-1943; succeeded by Mikolajczyk and Sosnkowski.

SINCLAIR, Sir Archibald, Liberal leader; Secretary of State for Air from May 1940, after Hoare, until May 1945; succeeded by Macmillan.

SMITH, Bedell, Major-General Walter, Chief of Staff to General Eisenhower.

SOMERVELL, Sir Donald, Attorney-General until May 1945, when succeeded by Sir Donald Maxwell Fyfe; Home Secretary until July, replaced by James Chuter Ede under Attlee.

SOMERVILLE, Admiral of the Fleet Sir James, commander of the Eastern Fleet from April 1942 to October 1944; Head of British Admiralty Delegation, Washington, after Admiral Sir Percy Noble.

SOSNKOWSKI, General K., Polish C-in-C, 1943-1944.

SMUTS, Field-Marshal J. C., Prime Minister of South Africa and Minister of External Affairs and Defence, 1939-1948.

STANLEY, Oliver, Colonial Secretary until July 1945, succeeded by G. H. Hall under Attlee.

STIMSON, Henry L., American Secretary of State for War.

STETTINIUS, Edward R., American Under-Secretary of State, 1943-1944; Secretary, after Hull, from November 1944 to 1945.

STILWELL, Lieut.-General Joseph W., Chief of Staff at Peking; Deputy Supreme Commander, South-East Asia Command; commander of all US forces in China-Burma-India theatre from 1944.

TEDDER, Air Chief Marshal Sir Arthur W., AOC Middle East until 11 January 1943, succeeded by Douglas; Deputy Supreme Allied Commander, AEF, north-west Europe.

TITO, Marshal Josip, Yugoslav partisan leader; President, National Committee of Liberation, 1943-1945; Prime Minister, 1945- .

TRUMAN, Harry S., Vice-President of America, 1945; President, 1945-1953.

TSOUDEROS, Greek Minister of Foreign Affairs and Finance, 1941-1943.

VANSITTART, Sir Robert, Chief Diplomatic Adviser to the Foreign Secretary, 1938-1941.

VORONOV, Marshal of Artillery Nikolai, Soviet victor at Stalingrad.

VYSHINSKY, Andrei, Soviety Deputy Foreign Minister, 1940-1949.

WAVELL, General (Field-Marshal and Viscount, 1943) Sir Archibald P., C-in-C India, 21 June 1941 to June 1943, succeeded by Auchinleck; Viceroy of India after Linlithgow.

WEDEMEYER, Major-General A. C., Commander, US forces in China, serving under Mountbatten.

WILLINK, H. U., Minister of Health from 17 November 1943, after Ernest Brown, until July 1945, replaced by Aneurin Bevan under Attlee.

WILSON, General (later Field-Marshal) Sir Henry Maitland, GOC Persia-Iraq until 16 February 1943; GOC-in-C Middle East after Alexander until December 1943, succeeded by Paget; Supreme Allied Commander, Mediterranean, until November 1944, succeeded by Alexander; Head of British Joint Staff Mission to Washington from January 1945, after Dill.

WINANT, John G., American Ambassador to Britain, 1941-1946.

WINGATE, Major-General Orde C., Long-Range Penetration Group Leader, Burma; killed 24 March 1944.

WOOD, Sir Kingsley, Chancellor of Exchequer after Simon, from May 1940 until his death in September 1943, succeeded by Anderson.

WOOLTON, Lord, Minister of Food from 3 April 1940 to 11 November 1943; succeeded by Llewellin; Minister of Reconstruction until May 1945, when office closed.

ZHUKOV, Marshal Gregory, Soviet army leader, Commander, southern front; C-in-C Germany, 1945-1946.

Abbreviations and Code Names

AEF — Allied Expeditionary Force.

CCS — Combined Chiefs of Staff.

CIGS — Chief of the Imperial General Staff.

C-in-C — Commander-in-Chief.

CNS — Chief of Naval Staff.

COAS — Chief of Air Staff.

COS — Chief(s) of Staff.

COSSAC — Chief of Staff to Supreme Allied Commander.

FCNL — French Committee of National Liberation.

GOC — General Officer Commanding.

IB — Incendiary bomb.

JIC — Joint Intelligence (Sub)Committee.

JPS — Joint Planning Staff.

KKE — Greek Communist Party.

LCI — Landing Craft, Infantry.

LCT — Landing Craft, Tank.

LRPG — Long-Range Penetration Group(s).

LSI — Landing Ship, Infantry.

LST — Landing Ship, Tank.

SEAC — South East Asia Command.

SHAEF — Supreme Headquarters, Allied Expeditionary Force.

SOE — Special Operations Executive.

Anakim — initial plan for recapture of Burma: re-opening of Burma Road and recapture of Rangoon.

Anvil — *see* Dragoon.

Argonaut — Washington Conference, 1942, also Crimea Conference, 1945.

Armpit — operations in the Adriatic, 1944.

Avalanche — invasion of Salerno and Naples from North Africa and Sicily, September 1943.

Axiom — mission sent to Washington by Mountbatten to urge 'Culverin' in February 1944.

Baytown — 8th Army assault on south Italy, September 1943.

Bolero — Build-up in UK of US forces and supplies for 'Round-up' and 'Overlord'.

Bullfrog — abortive plan for amphibious attack on Akyab, 1943, 1944.

Buccaneer — abortive plan for operations against Nicobar and Andaman Islands, 1943.

Brimstone — capture of Sardinia.

Caliph — operation to assist 'Overlord' by invasion of south and central France by Bay of Biscay or Mediterranean.

Capital — advance across Chindwin into Central Burma, previously known as Champion.

Champion — see Capital.

Crossbow — German V-weapons and allied measures against them.

Culverin — operations against North Sumatra and Malaya; not carried out.

Dragoon — allied landings in south of France, August 1944, previously called 'Anvil'.

Habbakuk — scheme for airfields of ice for use in Atlantic or English Channel.

Hercules — plan to capture Rhodes, 1943.

Husky — invasion of Sicily, July 1943.

Manna — plan to aid Greece following German withdrawal, 1944.

Market Garden — allied operation to establish bridgehead over Rhine in Holland.

Octagon — Second Quebec Conference, September 1944.

Overlord — allied invasion of France, previously 'Round-up'.

Pigstick — abortive plan for landings south of Mayu Peninsula on Arakan coast, 1944, behind Japanese lines.

Pointblank — combined bomber offensive from Britain.

Priceless — overall invasion of Italy, 1943, to include 'Avalanche' and 'Baytown'.

Quadrant — First Quebec Conference, August 1943.

Ravenous — part of 'Anakim'.

Round-up — *see* 'Overlord'.

Sextant — Cairo Conference, November-December 1943.

Shingle — Anzio landings, January 1944.

Sledgehammer — limited invasion of France prior to 'Round-up'.

Sunstar — planned landings in Istria, October 1944.

Symbol — Casablanca Conference. January 1943.

Tarzan — planned advance on Indaw-Katha area, Burma, 1944.

Terminal — Potsdam Conference, July 1945.

Thunderclap — plan for intensive bombing in Germany, 1944.

Torch — allied landings, North Africa, November 1942.

Trident — Washington Conference, May 1943.

Tube Alloys — atomic bombs.

Vanguard — capture of Rangoon from the sea, later known as 'Dracula'.

Veritable — Rhineland attack from Nijmegen area, February-March 1945.

Introduction

Hundreds of volumes of War Cabinet papers can now be studied by the public. They include minutes and memoranda of a multitude of committees, apart from Churchill's War Cabinet. They also include directives, reports, signals and a host of other material essential for any examination of the central direction of the Second World War. This book only deals with a small proportion of the mass of files; inevitably a great many stones must be left unturned, both for reasons of space, and also as a result of the aim of the book itself. *A Day's March Nearer Home* is intended as the third in the triology, following *Peace for Our Time*, and *Blood, Toil, Tears and Sweat*. The series attempts to deal with Grand Strategy, and especially with the handling of these supreme strategic matters by Churchill, his Cabinet, the British Chiefs of Staff, and the Combined Chiefs of Staff. Other subjects, of lesser strategic relevance although important and fascinating, have to be left untouched: in this volume, for instance, no mention is made of the hours of Cabinet discussion on Palestine.

Nor does the book delve into events at the battlefronts in any great detail. Again, this was not the brief set for the trilogy. But these 'sharp end' events are linked with the discussions back home at the 'blunt end'; in this way it is perhaps easier to understand how and why those events actually took place, and the reasoning and decisions which lay behind the crucial stepping-stones of the war. The method used in the book, as in the previous two, has been to link the official documents with memoirs and especially diaries written by the participants. The two types of material complement each other: the official papers, written in cold, official language, could never reveal the human emotions behind the decisions; the contemporary diaries, often passionate and biased, could never reveal the still-secret discussions. Using the two sources presents a far more complete picture than hitherto possible.

Although this book is the third in a trilogy, it can also stand alone. The period covered, from Alamein to the atomic bombs, can with hindsight be seen as a definite stage of the war. Churchill inevitably predominates, and with him the Chief of the Imperial General Staff, Sir Alan Brooke. The partnership formed by these two great men stands at the centre: Churchill, romantic, ebullient, usually supremely optimistic; Alan Brooke, hard-headed, careful, usually extremely pessimistic. The two characters formed a most efficient contrast, especially during these months. The period is important for another reason. The years reveal the increasing strain imposed upon Churchill, Brooke and their colleagues; exhaustion which had both physical and mental effect, and which led to such desperate discussion as the possible introduction of gas and bacteriological warfare. The juxtaposition of the official documents and the diaries reveal the extent and nature of the almost intolerable decision-making burden.

Once again, the book has been written on an almost day-to-day basis, to give a clearer indication of the multiple problems confronting the allied leaders and their staffs at any particular time. The method imposes greater hardship upon the reader – and the writer – in having to follow so many different threads simultaneously; this is a pale reflection of the difficulties facing Churchill and his colleagues. Moreover, it allows a closer examination of the inter-action of one problem upon another.

As with previous works I have taken extensive quotations from the following diaries and memoirs: Bryant's fascinating revelation of Brooke's private thoughts in *The Turn of the Tide* and *Triumph in the West*; the detailed *Diaries of Sir Alexander Cadogan*, edited by Dilks, containing many cryptic entries which are explained when compared with the official documents; Lord Avon's *The Reckoning*; Ismay's typically modest *Memoirs*; Kennedy's *The Business of War*; Nicolson's *Diaries and Letters*; Hull's fiery *Memoirs*; Macmillan's *The Blast of War*. And any book on the Second World War owes a tremendous debt to Churchill's history. Details of the quotations and of other books consulted are to be found in the source lists and bibliography.

My thanks go to the staff of the Public Record Office and the London Library. I also express my gratitude to Bob Macdonald, for his unfailing generosity. And with my wife Betty, mere words could never describe my heartfelt appreciation of her help, advice, encouragement in all forms, during this book and with all others.

1

Lighted 'Torch'

Litter of war soon began to gather in the dusty ditches as soldiers filed up the tracks and through the scarlet and golden yellow of the vineyard leaves: canteens, cans, broken equipment, mortar shell cases, scattered cartridges, and, too soon, slumped corpses. Young American dead lay near the bodies of French enemies; among the French were veterans of the disastrous fighting against the Germans, two and a half years ago; the GI slain were among the first American army casualties in this western war and many were raw recruits, straight from training camps. Troops advanced from the scorching beaches and into the North African hills; behind them gangs of men rolled Summerfelt track over the dunes to allow passage for tanks, lorries, jeeps. Stores piled up; signal lines snaked through the sand; bulldozers ground through the uneven scrub; and beyond, along the shimmering Mediterranean horizon, lay the massive invasion fleet. 'Torch', the Anglo-American landings in French North Africa, had begun the previous night, Friday, 7 November 1942.

Winston Churchill's Ministers read the daily situation report provided for them in the Cabinet War Room, Whitehall: 'CWR RECORD for the 24 hours ending 0700, 8 November 1942. *French North Africa.* Operations commenced early this morning to occupy French Morocco and Algeria in order to provide a base for an advance on Tunisia by combined British and US Forces. Landings are taking place at ALGIERS and ORAN covered by strong British

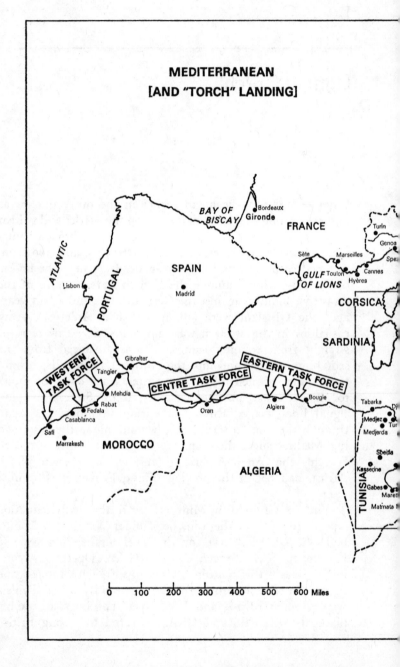

MEDITERRANEAN
[AND "TORCH" LANDING]

ATLANTIC

BAY OF BISCAY

Bordeaux
Gironde

FRANCE

Turin

Genoa

Spez

SPAIN

Sète
Marseilles
Cannes

GULF OF LIONS
Toulon
Hyères

Lisbon

PORTUGAL

Madrid

CORSICA

SARDINIA

WESTERN TASK FORCE

Gibralter

Tangier

CENTRE TASK FORCE

EASTERN TASK FORCE

Mehdia

Rabat

Bougie

Tabarka

Dj

Fedala

Oran

Algiers

Medjez
Tur

Casablanca

Medjerda

Safi

Marrakesh

MOROCCO

Sbeitla

Kasserine

TUNISIA

Gabes

ALGERIA

Mareth

Matmata

| 0 | 100 | 200 | 300 | 400 | 500 | 600 Miles |

AUSTRIA Vienna
Budapest
HUNGARY
Trieste Ljubljana
Istra
Ravenna Fiume
Rimini YUGOSLAVIA
Pesaro Zara CROATIA Belgrade
ence Aneona
Ortone SERBIA
LY MONTENEGRO
ome ADRIATIC
SEA Bari
Cassino Foggia
Naples Salerno
ALBANIA
mo Messlna
SICILY Reggio GREECE
elleria Pindus Mts.
Patras Corinth
MALTA Athens

RUSSIA
RUMANIA
CRIMEA
Danube R. Yalta
Danube R. BLACK SEA

BULGARIA

Salonika
AEGEAN
SEA
TURKEY
Dardanelles
Castel Furni
Rosso Leros
Lispoi Samos
Patmos Cos
Rhodes

MEDITERRANEAN
CRETE CYPRUS

See page 49

OLITANIA Martuba
Benghazi
BYA
Agheila CYRENAICA
Alexandria
EGYPT Alamein
Cairo

Naval forces and at CASABLANCA by US forces. Landings at ALGIERS were reported as being successful, but no reports have so far been received from Oran and Casablanca ... *Egypt*. Throughout the night of the 5th/6th and on the 6th the pursuit of the enemy continued.... Owing to the speed of our advance, accurate details are not yet available.'[1]

Months of Anglo-American debate, argument and acrimonious cross-Atlantic signals, had resulted in the largest amphibious operation so far in the history of war, as the three mighty Task Forces were thrown against the French African shore. In the west, 35,000 US troops under Major-General George S. Patton had sailed direct from America, to brave the Atlantic swell at Casablanca; the centre force, sailing from Britain under Major-General L. R. Fredendall, and amounting to 39,000 US troops, had been aimed at Oran; Algiers would be dealt with by the eastern force, also from Britain, spearheaded by an Anglo-American assault and followed by the British 1st Army under General K. A. N. Anderson. The ultimate object was to drive the Germans and Italians from North Africa by striking east for Tunis; the overall commander was General Dwight D. Eisenhower, now at his Gibraltar HQ. Moreover, far to the east in Egypt, the area of General Alexander's Middle East command, the British 8th Army under General Montgomery had clashed with Rommel's Afrika Korps on 23 October at the battle to be known as El Alamein; four days before, on Wednesday 4 November, the 'Desert Fox' had been beaten, and German units had begun their retreat over the Egyptian wastes towards the Tunisian frontier. Axis forces were threatened from east and west, by the British 8th Army and by 'Torch'.

American hopes had been high that the French would co-operate in the 'Torch' invasion of their colonial Moroccan and Algerian territory. And yet on this Sunday, 8 November, these hopes faded. France had been bewildered and split in opinion since her terrible defeat by the Germans in spring, 1940. The Germans occupied half the homeland; the Government at Vichy under Pétain and Laval wished to co-operate with the conquerors, while 'Fighting French' under de Gaulle demanded continued resistance from overseas; de Gaulle

himself, autocratic, aloof, disdainful, was disliked and even
hated by many of those who themselves wished to carry on
the struggle. Divergences in French opinion and allegiance
were now reflected amongst officers and men in Morocco and
Algeria. The already difficult situation had been further complicated by the unexpected presence in Algiers of Admiral
Darlan, C-in-C of all French forces, anti-British, and firm
exponent of the belief that France's best hope lay in working
with the Germans – at least until he saw the size and scope
of American participation against the Axis. Viewed in
Britain as one of the worst of the contemptible collaborators
with the Nazis, Darlan was especially detested for his refusal
to allow the French fleet to come to British waters in 1940
and thus save it from falling into German hands. His decision
had led to bloodshed and tragic deaths in fighting between
Royal Navy and French sailors in July 1940, even though
the Germans had still to take over these French warships.
Now, on this 8 November, Frenchmen took up arms against
British and American troops at Algiers, Oran and in the
Casablanca area. At Algiers, the most important target,
resistance ended at 7 p.m., but futile fighting would continue
elsewhere. In London, Churchill stayed closeted with his
Chiefs of Staff during the Sunday morning before lunching
with de Gaulle. In Berlin, Adolf Hitler made a wild speech
threatening air reprisal on Britain. In Washington the
American President, Roosevelt, studied signals from Eisenhower at Gibraltar, anxious lest disaster should face the
landings which he and Churchill had urged his reluctant
military advisers to undertake. America had thrown her
ground forces into the war against Hitler; at last, after years
of setback and disaster, the western allies had made their
bold bid for the initiative.

Winston Churchill had especially needed a victory, and
the boost provided by Alamein had come none too soon.
Thirty months had passed since he took over from Neville
Chamberlain at 10 Downing Street in the dark days just
before Dunkirk. His magnificent speeches had lighted the
way through the perilous period of threatened invasion and
the Battle of Britain, and his ability to rally the people and

to represent the spirit of defiance had ensured him immortality. But then had come the most drab days of war, when War Cabinet meetings had consistently opened with news of fresh disasters and disappointments: British troops had been thrown from Greece, then Crete; they had been pushed back in the western desert almost to the flimsy doors of Cairo; Singapore, Hong Kong, Burma and Borneo had fallen to the Japanese. These months of 1941 and 1942 had called upon greater Churchillian strength and resilience than even the acute dangers of 1940, and Churchill had bounced back after each setback; yet each time his strength had been less and his explanations more unconvincing.

Now a major turning-point in the war had been reached, in Churchill's words 'the end of the beginning'. In some ways strain would even be increased. With America's entry into the western ground war, Germany's defeat must be considered inevitable; but again in Churchill's words: 'Between survival and victory there are many stages. Over two years of intense and bloody fighting lay before us all. Henceforward however the danger was not Destruction but Stalemate.' Churchill, almost 70 years of age, would require all his powers of endurance to pull him through the planning and decision-making needed to avoid such a stalemate. These demands, coupled with the toll taken by the length of time in his arduous office, would nearly break him. General Sir Alan Brooke, Chief of the Imperial General Staff, and Anthony Eden, Foreign Secretary, who themselves came near to collapse, increasingly feared for Churchill's health. The CIGS wrote in his diary: 'I am afraid he (Winston) is losing ground rapidly. He seems quite incapable of concentrating for a few minutes on end and keeps wandering continuously.'[2] Others reached similar verdicts; Harold Nicolson, one of Churchill's most devoted followers, would write in June 1944: 'I fear that he is losing such judgement as he ever had in foreign affairs and is unhappily authoritarian. I wish he could die now quite suddenly. I dread any clouds coming over that superb sunset.'[3] Even the cold official War Cabinet minutes reveal a certain mental deterioration, with Churchill sometimes seemingly unable to reach a decision or even express his opinions in a coherent manner.

But the Prime Minister survived; for two reasons. Apart from his own personal resilience, Churchill now had the added and essential power given by a smooth-running war machine, hardened by disasters and grim experience. He himself retained the Defence Minister's post; the supreme bodies dealing with decision-making remained the War Cabinet, the Defence Committee of the Cabinet, and the Chiefs of Staff Committee chaired by Brooke. Long months of conflict had resulted in subtle yet significant changes of emphasis between these three, which would be further accentuated. Churchill had begun his Premiership with a five-member War Cabinet, and with only one member, the Foreign Secretary, having a Departmental post – Churchill aimed to free his Cabinet colleagues from Ministerial responsibilities. But by August 1943, the War Cabinet had grown to eight members: the Prime Minister, Lord President of the Council, Foreign Secretary, Ministers of Labour and Production, Home Secretary, Dominions Secretary, and Minister of State Resident in the Middle East. Five of the eight therefore held departmental posts. By 1944 the last two members had gone, but the Chancellor of the Exchequer and the Minister of Reconstruction had entered, and the proportion of Ministers with heavy administrative duties had therefore further increased. But this reversal from original ideas, caused in part by the increasing number of post-war subjects, became linked with two other developments. First was the growth of the Cabinet Committee system; the second was the gradual decline in the part played by the War Cabinet in strategic and even diplomatic decisions. The first development helped Ministers shoulder their individual burdens; the second decreased the corporate burden of War Cabinet business. Meetings, which had been daily in spring 1940, dwindled to a total of 174 in 1942, 176 in 1943 and 1944, and 79 up to the end of July 1945.

Already, in June 1940, the Lord President's Committee had been created to deal with detailed domestic, Home Front and economic questions, and the influence of this Cabinet Committee steadily increased under Sir John

Anderson's chairmanship. On the strategic side, Churchill had created the Defence Committee soon after taking office, and this, split into Supply and the more important Operations section, played a prominent part in the early years of war. Defence Committee (Operations), chaired by Churchill as Defence Minister, comprised the Foreign Secretary, Lord President, Minister of Production and the three Service Ministers, with the Chiefs of Staff in attendance. Yet the Defence Committee also declined in importance. Whereas the Defence Committee (Operations) met 76 times in 1941, the total fell to 20 in 1942, and only 4 by the end of August 1945. Churchill in fact streamlined the system. The War Cabinet had handed over strategic discussion to the Defence Committee, which in turn passed it to the Chiefs of Staff Committee. By the end of 1942 the COS had assumed tremendous power: 573 meetings were held during the year; 472 in 1943; 416 in 1944. Churchill preferred dealing direct with this compact body; more important or controversial discussions took place at specially summoned Staff Meetings or Conferences, another Churchill innovation, attended by the COS and certain Ministers.

Inevitably, the system radiated from Churchill; yet the result was by no means dictatorial. Churchill treated his Chiefs of Staff with respect; he would never overrule them on a military decision, and they could persuade him not to follow through his ebullient ideas, even though the process of discussion might be bitter, prolonged and extremely exhausting. Churchill remained conscious of the supreme position held by Parliament, and the War Cabinet, whilst less directly involved, suffered no decrease in prestige – Ministers could still seek War Cabinet approval for particular problems, a practice which Eden used – and War Cabinet sanction was often sought for the most important questions, even though members had not been concerned with background discussions. The War Cabinet therefore retained general supervision and overall control, and the shedding of some of the load enabled Ministers to stand back and view decisions from a wider angle; thus members concerned themselves more with the relationship of civil and diplomatic affairs with strategy, rather than with detailed examination of each. In addition, the wide difference of temperament amongst its members gave the War Cabinet added strength. In early November 1942, these Ministers included the handsome, suave Anthony Eden as Foreign Secretary who, wrote Ismay, 'bore a close resemblance to Churchill in methods and hours of work', and who retained rigid and individual principles; in sharp contrast to Eden's aristocratic manner was 'Ernie' Bevin, Minister of Labour, intensely outspoken and socialistic; his Labour colleague in this Coalition War Cabinet remained Clement Attlee, Deputy Prime Minister and Dominions Secretary, extremely business-like in committee. Sir John Anderson, ex-Governor of Bengal and now Lord President, added cool, impersonal Civil Service efficiency to the proceedings. Stafford Cripps, regarded by Churchill as his greatest rival for Premiership, would remain in the War Cabinet as Lord Privy Seal for a few more days; soon to enter the War Cabinet was the lively Cockney politician, Herbert Morrison, as Home Secretary. Few Cabinets can have had a membership more diverse in character and in political and social outlook, and this variety itself prevented the body from becoming too subservient to the Prime Minister, despite his domineering personality and unique power.

The streamlined system enabled the best possible coordination with the American allies. Churchill usually dealt directly with his close friend Roosevelt; the Chiefs of Staff dealt with their American counterparts via the British Mission in Washington, and, linking the two countries in superb fashion was the Combined Chiefs of Staff Committee, with members from both countries and with the power to formulate and execute allied strategy, responsible directly to the President and Prime Minister. When the British and American COS met, they did so as the Combined Chiefs of Staff; otherwise the British element on the CCS was led by Field-Marshal Sir John Dill, Brooke's predecessor as CIGS. Reticent and modest, Dill accomplished his task with brilliant success, establishing a close relationship with General George C. Marshall, Chief of Staff to the US Army. Marshall was described by Churchill as 'the noblest Roman of them all'; he remained a pillar of strength, rugged, unflappable – and close to Roosevelt. 'His views,' commented Stimson, US War Secretary, 'guided Mr Roosevelt throughout.'

This, then, remained the British and the allied structure for collaboration and decision-making: as simple as possible in the acutely complex area of planning and execution of a World War. Both Roosevelt and Churchill were ably served and their burdens eased. Yet the war killed Roosevelt; Churchill barely managed to endure the final months. Moreover, while Churchill's path was smoothed by his partnership with the COS, the latter became subjected to similar strain as war dragged on. Under most pressure was Brooke, and he too almost gave way. Few indications of this were revealed at the time; Brooke remained apparently unemotional and controlled. Intensely quickwitted, he seemed impatient of those who might be slower; he expounded his beliefs in strong, positive fashion, talking at an incredible speed in emphatic sentences. Sir Ian Jacob, a member of the War Cabinet Secretariat, commented: 'I have never met a man who so tumbles over himself in speaking. He cannot make his brain move slowly enough to fit his speech.' Ismay wrote: 'He was apt to speak so fast that the Americans found difficulty in following his arguments, and were at first inclined to think that he was trying to bounce them.'[4] Representing the RAF on the COS was Air Chief Marshal Portal, youngest of the service chiefs and, in Ismay's view, academically and scientifically the best educated. Like Dill with Marshall, Portal established a close link with his US opposite number, 'Hap' Arnold. The Americans found Portal easier to work with than the blunter Brooke. Admiral Sir Dudley Pound, Chief of Naval Staff and First Sea Lord, represented the Royal Navy until his death in September 1943; Andrew Cunningham became his successor – warm-hearted, intensely practical, and with minute knowledge of the Royal Navy. Mountbatten, who had enjoyed a meteoric rise, sat on the COS Committee as head of Combined Operations until his appointment as Supreme Commander, South-East Asia. General Hastings Ismay, Military Secretary of the War

Cabinet and a COS member, occupied a very special place; as Chief of Staff to Churchill, the Defence Minister, he held an important although background position between the various bodies. Infinite tact, patience, thick skin and gentleness were required – Ismay possessed them all. Upon these very few men therefore rested this colossal responsibility. All eyes were focused upon the results of their decisions and yet, paradoxically, only one or two of them would receive instant recognition from ordinary men and women in the street. The COS remained an unknown body to the public as a whole, and Brooke found himself unrecognized in the victory parade; he wrote in May 1945: 'The public has never understood what the Chiefs of Staff have been doing in the running of this war.'[5]

In autumn 1942 this public had long awaited a victory. Civilians had suffered the Blitz, threatened invasion and fear for loved ones, and in return had only been given news of multiple disasters. Hardships had increased. About 100,000 Britishers were living in houses officially condemned as unfit before the war; two and a half million occupied bombed houses which had received only temporary repairs. All healthy women under 40 were obliged to undertake war work, unless prevented by heavy family responsibilities or engaged in looking after billeted war workers. The peak of rationing had been reached the previous August. For the decision-makers at the top existed the stimulating, although exhausting, business of conducting the war; in Churchill's phrase, 'the inward excitement which comes from prolonged balancing of terrible things'. For lesser mortals daily drudgery seemed everlasting. For both strata, the conflict had reached its most telling time; with Alamein and 'Torch' a turning point had indeed been reached; but the way stretched tortuously ahead. With clarity provided by hindsight, the relevance of Churchill's phrase 'the end of the beginning' for this period is easily proved; yet at the time it took a man of Churchill's unique discernment to pick out this feature from the confusion of current events. Churchill and his colleagues had to deal with a multitude of simultaneous subjects, large and small, even apart from 'Torch' and the

Egyptian offensive: affairs in India and Burma, Ireland, the critical shipping shortages, oil and manpower resources, food, bombing policy against Germany, results of bombing against Britain, Parliamentary affairs, post-war subjects, including long hours spent in Cabinet debating the Beveridge report. All these demanded attention in those frosty days of early winter, 1942. Yet from them three main subjects emerged predominant: the handling of North African affairs; dealings with the French; strategic planning for 1943. These three were closely related – and each revealed acute disagreement between British and American points of view. So another type of tension is fully revealed in the official documents: the strain on Anglo-American relations during the second half of the war. And even now, in the actual execution of 'Torch', when Anglo-American military co-operation was inevitably closer than ever before, diplomatic relations were strained over the French.

This diplomatic issue became closely involved with the military question of ensuring the success of 'Torch'. The 560 mountainous miles between Algiers and Tunis had to be travelled in minimum time to prevent the Germans regaining the initiative; French hostility, or even non-co-operation, could impose a disastrous delay. Britain had long since pledged support for General de Gaulle as a means of keeping French resistance alive after the fall of France, and at the time of 'Torch' this prickly Frenchman was in effective control of all the Empire, except North and West Africa, Indo-China and the Caribbean. But the Americans distrusted both his methods and his political objectives: de Gaulle's ideas for a Provisional Government in exile were vigorously condemned by Roosevelt and his Secretary of State, Cordell Hull, on the grounds that France had temporarily ceased to exist, and no single French authority should come into existence until the people could speak for themselves after liberation.

And now, contrary to American hopes and even expectations, the French had opposed the North African landings. All depended on local negotiations. Britain had championed de Gaulle for such an eventuality, but the Americans preferred a choice of their own. General Henri Giraud had been captured by the Germans during the defeat of France; he had suffered similar incarceration in the First World War, and both times had made a dramatic escape. Here, believed the Americans, was a gallant Frenchman who could help unlock the French North African door. They accordingly gave him the code-name of 'King-pin', and just before the landings Giraud had been flown from the south of France to confer with Eisenhower at Gibraltar during the afternoon of 7 November. Giraud, a dapper figure with neat moustache, immediately demanded supreme command of all Allied forces; General Eisenhower, he added, must be content with responsibility for logistics and reinforcements. He claimed he had been led to expect such a position and would accept none other. Giraud refused to change his mind after hours of discussion, during which 'Torch' fleets sailed steadily towards the North African shore. Talks continued next morning, 8 November, as allied soldiers fought the French on the North African beaches. Eventually a compromise was reached: Eisenhower immediately signalled the wording to the Combined Chiefs of Staff in Washington: 'Giraud is recognized as the leader of the effort to prevent Axis aggression in North Africa, as the C-in-C of all French forces in the region and as Governor of the French North African Provinces. Eisenhower, as C-in-C of the Allied American-British forces, will co-operate with Giraud to the fullest possible extent.'[6] Giraud made ready to fly to Algiers. Meanwhile in London the Prime Minister lunched with de Gaulle this Sunday and, to his surprise, secured a promise from the Free French leader that he would serve under Giraud. All seemed well. Only gradually did the dramatic rumours filter through that Darlan was in Algiers. The presence of this anti-British, pro-Vichy Frenchman came as an acute shock and London and Washington anxiously awaited confirmation. Sir Alexander Cadogan, Permanent Under-Secretary at the British Foreign Office, who should have been one of the first to receive this startling information, could only comment in his diary on the evening of the 8th: 'PM hears that Darlan is under "protective arrest" in N. Africa, but I don't know where he got this from.'[7] Eisenhower infers in his memoirs that he did not receive definite news until early next morning, 9 November.[8]

General Alphonse Juin, C-in-C French North Africa, had previously had promising talks with Robert Murphy, US political representative. Now Juin insisted that Darlan's presence completely overrode his authority. Moreover, when Giraud finally landed at Algiers on the morning of the 9th he found himself completely ignored; his broadcast announcing assumption of leadership of French forces and directing these troops to cease fighting had no effect. Giraud hurried into hiding. Fighting against the French was continuing at Oran and Casablanca, and the Germans were recovering from their initial surprise: Vichy approval was demanded and obtained for the dispatch of German troops into Tunisia, where Admiral Esteva, French Resident-General, accepted Vichy instructions, and the first *Luftwaffe* units flew into Tunis from Sicily during the day. Settlement of the tangled Anglo-US relations with the French was clearly becoming even more imperative. And it had become equally clear to those on the spot that this could only be reached by dealing with Darlan himself. General Mark Clark flew to Algiers as Eisenhower's deputy and started negotiations with Darlan during the afternoon of the 9th, and the two men agreed to meet again the following morning. Meanwhile, at his mountain retreat at Berchtesgaden, Hitler had determined upon ruthless action against the French, and he summoned Laval, the Vichy French leader, to an urgent conference.

Winston Churchill was allowing his lively thoughts to range ahead, drafting a memorandum to the COS during the 9th on the next great strategic steps. 'It would be most regrettable to make no more use of the success of 'Torch' and Alamein in 1943 than the occupation of Sicily and Sardinia.... The effort for the campaign of 1943 should clearly be a strong pinning down of the enemy in Northern France and the Low Countries by continuous preparations to invade, and a decisive attack on Italy, or, better still, Southern France....' Churchill even hinted that forces in Morocco and Algiers should be restricted in number. 'If French North Africa is going to be an excuse for locking up great forces on the defensive and calling it a "commitment", it would be better not to have gone there at all.'[9] This memorandum marked the latest step in a continuing dialogue between the Prime Minister and his COS; one which had already generated heated disagreement and which, within a few days, would become of paramount importance. Hitler tried to deal with more immediate problems. Next morning, Tuesday 10 November, Pierre Laval arrived at Berchtesgaden to be told by the Führer that Unoccupied France would now be taken over, with German forces moving forward from French territory already held on the following day; and the Axis would immediately establish a bridgehead in Tunisia. The Franco-German armistice was in effect torn up. General Mark Clark had meanwhile renewed his pressure on Darlan; also on this Tuesday, Oran surrendered to US armoured units. And, under the weight of Clark's arguments including the threat of arrest and US fighting strength, Darlan agreed to a cease-fire throughout French North Africa 'in the name of the Marshal'. Marshal Pétain disowned this cease-fire decision later in the day, leading to an attempt by Darlan to rescind his order, but Clark applied his arguments again – this time fortified by the preliminary news that the Germans had ordered the invasion of unoccupied France.

But even as skies lifted over Morocco and Algeria and a rapid allied advance towards Tunisia seemed possible, first trouble clouds started to descend over London. During this 10 November, de Gaulle asked the British for help in sending a mission to confer with General Giraud; Eden agreed and informed the American Ambassador, Winant. As Cadogan wrote in his diary: 'Think we should now help de G. all we can – seeing he has played up well.'[10] Within hours, Eisenhower would wire that he thought it best to postpone such a mission while the uncertain situation continued – and the refusal of de Gaulle's request would cause renewed upset with the touchy Free French leader. Yet the military situation continued to improve. In Egypt, Montgomery's 8th Army was in full pursuit of Rommel's retreating forces, reaching Sollum on the 11th; in Algeria, British troops from General Anderson's 78th Division had now been despatched by sea to make a landing at Bougie, 300 miles west of Tunis. 'Events moving fast,' wrote Brooke in his diary.[11] Churchill promised the House of Commons that great events would happen in the next few days.

Diplomatic events suddenly deteriorated. Darlan met Giraud during the evening of the 11th, and the Admiral confirmed the General as C-in-C of French forces in North Africa – in return for Giraud's recognition of Darlan as the supreme civil authority. Thus Darlan, so hated in Britain, had apparently been handed North African political power without prior consultation by Eisenhower with London or Washington. Churchill had made no mention of the Admiral in a telegram sent to Roosevelt during the day on the subject of French political power. 'You will I am sure realize that HMG are under quite definite and solemn obligations to de Gaulle and his Movement. We must see they have a fair deal. It seems to me that you and I ought to avoid at all costs the creation of rival French *emigré* Governments, each favoured by one of us.' But Roosevelt included Darlan's name in his reply early on the 12th. 'The principal thought to be driven home to all three of these prima donnas is that the situation is today solely in the military field, and that any decision by any of them, or by all of them, is subject to review and approval by Eisenhower.' The British War Cabinet, meeting at 6 p.m. on this Thursday, heard these telegrams and approved Churchill's wording; Ministers did not realize that a tentative agreement was already being reached in Algiers, which would push Darlan into power and which would correspondingly eclipse de Gaulle.[12] Earlier in the day the Foreign Office had warned Mack, British Civil Liaison Officer with Eisenhower, against co-operating too much with Darlan; now, during the evening of the 12th, news reached London from Eisenhower of the Giraud-Darlan bargain. Cadogan's consternation was revealed in his diary on the 13th: 'Americans are playing with Darlan, Noguès (pro-Vichy French Resident-General in Morocco), Giraud and Juin. What a party! Telegraphed to Mack to try and find out what is going on.... Where are we? And what is going on' De Gaulle can *never* work with that crowd.' Eden emerged from his bed, suffering from 'flu, to signal Lord Halifax, British Ambassador in Washington: 'I think you should make it plain to the President or Mr Hull that the inclusion of Darlan in the French administration in North Africa would be most unpopular here, unless he had delivered the goods in the shape of the French navy.'[13]

British parachutists had dropped on Bône on the 12th, the same day that 8th Army units reached Tobruk and Montgomery told his troops: 'There are no German and Italian soldiers on Egyptian territory except prisoners. In three weeks we have completely smashed the German and Italian Army.'[14] Eisenhower explained his reasons for a Darlan deal in a signal to the CCS on 14 November, with the cable transmitted to London early next morning: 'Can well understand some bewilderment in London and Washington ... it is extremely important that *no* precipitate action at home upsets such equilibrium as we have been able to establish. Foremost is the fact that the name of Marshal Pétain is something to conjure with here.... The civil governments, military leaders and naval commanders will agree on only one man having an obvious right to assume the Marshal's mantle in North Africa. That man is Darlan ... Giraud himself understands.... Giraud is honest and will watch Darlan.'[15] And, also on 14 November, after hearing a verbal account from General Bedell Smith, Eisenhower's Chief of Staff, Churchill signalled his reluctant and qualified agreement. 'Anything for the battle, but the politics will have to be sorted out later on.'[16] Further talks at Chequers on this Saturday, 14 November, with Eden and Smuts, the South African leader, led to another cable from Churchill to Roosevelt early next morning. This confirmed acceptance of the Darlan agreement, but British 'doubts or anxieties' remained; Cadogan summed up the Foreign Office view in his diary entry for the 15th: 'This is going to present us with awful problems, and is dirty.'[17] Eden arranged to see de Gaulle the following morning, Monday, 16 November.

Churchill had to switch his attention to other even more fundamental matters. At 11 a.m. on Sunday a Staff Conference began at Chequers in an attempt to solve acute

differences of opinion between the Prime Minister and his
military advisers over future strategy. The memo sent by
Churchill to the COS on 9 November, warning against force
being tied down in North Africa and urging early operations
against German-held Europe, had been written as a result of
a long report produced by the British Joint Planners on 30
October and approved by the COS. Churchill condemned this
paper as 'unduly negative'. The debate forms an example of
the almost constant clash between the confident and politi-
cally-minded Prime Minister and the more cautious service
chiefs. The argument centred around agreements with both
Washington and Moscow: should a Second Front be opened
in Europe in 1943? The COS fervently believed not; Churchill believed the opposite. The 16-page COS report declared:
'Despite the fact that a large-scale invasion of Europe would
do more than anything to help Russia, we are forced to the
conclusion that we have no option but to undermine
Germany's military power by the destruction of the German
industrial and economic war machine before we attempt
invasion.' The European war must be fought by bomber
forces for the moment, while in the Mediterranean a successful advance by 'Torch' force and by the 8th Army might
make possible the occupation of Sardinia and Sicily. Churchill,
in his elation over the ability of 'Torch' landings to complete
their bridgeheads, had reacted violently against this cautious
document, and he continued to urge the COS to admit the
possibility of carrying out 'Round-up' – the cross-Channel
invasion – in 1943. Indeed in August Churchill had confided
to Stalin that this invasion would still take place in 1943.
The Prime Minister repeated his opinions at the Sunday
morning Chequers meeting, 15 November, and after two
hours of discussion the COS did at least agree to a paragraph
in a paper presented by Churchill: 'The paramount task
before us is, first, to conquer the African shores of the
Mediterranean and open an effective passage through it for
military traffic; and secondly, using the bases on the African
shore, to strike at the underbelly of the Axis in effective
strength in the shortest time.'[18] Thus the COS agreed in principle to Churchill's suggestion of a push north from the

Mediterranean, possibly into the south of France, but the larger plan for 'Round-up' still remained at issue.

On Monday, 16 November, Churchill therefore had two major problems on his mind, one immediate and the other longer term: General de Gaulle, and plans for a European Second Front. At 1 p.m. the Prime Minister lunched with de Gaulle at 10 Downing Street, together with Eden; at 6 p.m. he described the meeting to the War Cabinet. Churchill said he had told the General that his own position was 'unassailable' and he need not be alarmed; 'he would be well advised not to make any strong public protest against what had been done'. De Gaulle had nevertheless decided to issue a declaration, dissociating his French National Committee from events in Algiers, but Churchill added: 'No objection could be raised to the terms of the communiqué.' Ministers accepted the military necessity for the Darlan agreement, and, in Cadogan's opinion: 'No one very excited.' The War Cabinet were also told the latest military situation. 'German strength in Tunisia might now be about 6,000 to 8,000. Reinforcements were continually arriving. Our forces had just crossed into Tunisia from Algeria.... As a result of our operations in French North Africa, the Germans had moved seven to nine divisions from occupied to unoccupied France and the Italians had moved in between two to three divisions.' On the other North African front: 'Our forces in Libya had reached Martuba ... the pursuit of the defeated enemy continued.'[19] During the day Maisky, the Soviet Ambassador, had informed Eden of Soviet anxieties over the Darlan agreement; the Foreign Secretary stressed that Britain was not committed to anything more than a temporary arrangement.[20] Eden also successfully urged Churchill to send a signal to Roosevelt later in the evening, stressing this temporary aspect;[21] the telegram, drafted by Cadogan, declared: 'I ought to let you know that very deep currents of feeling are stirred by the arrangement with Darlan. The more I reflect upon it, the more convinced I become that it can only be a temporary expedient.... Darlan has an odious record.'[22]

Churchill turned to the second of his pressing problems –

the continued debate with the COS over future strategy. He told a Defence Committee meeting at 10 p.m. that he criticized the COS view for three main reasons. 'First, nowhere in the paper was it stated that the creation of this enormous bomber force of 4,000–6,000 aircraft (for the air war against the Germans in Europe) would involve the move to this country of some one and a quarter million American ground personnel. This would present a transportation problem of sufficient magnitude to rule out other large-scale military operations. Secondly, the paper took little account of the effect on Russia of a failure to open land operations against Germany next year.... During his visit to Moscow in August he had promised Operation "Round-up" for 1943, but the COS in their paper were offering nothing better than a series of small-scale amphibious operations during the period while we were building up this gigantic bomber force. Thirdly, the arguments as now presented would probably encourage the "Japan first" elements in America.' Portal, Chief of Air Staff, replied to Churchill's first criticism by saying that the figure of one and a quarter million US air personnel had still to be checked, and might possibly be halved. But the Prime Minister received support at this meeting from Smuts and Eden; according to the South African leader: 'The COS paper tended to give the impression that no large-scale land operations were in course of preparation or were even intended.' The Foreign Secretary commented: 'Although it might be the right strategy to concentrate on the creation of a large bomber force, it would be very difficult to convince the Russians of this, if this was unaccompanied by land operations on our part.' Brooke supplied the general COS reply. 'Shortage of personnel shipping was exercising a stranglehold on our strategy. It was, for example, very doubtful whether the Americans, even if they were so inclined, would be able to find sufficient shipping to go off to the Pacific.' But the CIGS continued: 'It would seem, however, that the COS paper had given a misleading impression. It was the firm intention of the COS to enter the Continent at the first opportunity with the strongest force which could be made available. But to make our re-entry too early and to suffer a reverse might easily add a year or more to the length of the war.' The Defence Committee agreed the COS should redraft their paper; Brooke wrote in his diary that as a result of the discussion Mediterranean strategy was 'now fairly clear'. The CIGS would soon suffer disillusionment.[23]

Churchill's telegram stressing the temporary nature of the Darlan agreement seemed well received by Roosevelt. Heeding this message, and bowing to hostile domestic criticism, Roosevelt issued a statement at his press conference on 17 November. 'I thoroughly understand and approve the feeling in the United States and Great Britain and among all the other United Nations that in view of the history of the past two years no permanent arrangement should be made with Admiral Darlan.' Churchill immediately wired: 'Your public statement about Darlan has settled the matter in the best possible way.'[24] Unfortunately, in attempting to appease Washington and London, Roosevelt created renewed anxiety in Algiers. Fears grew that Darlan might tear up his agreement and that the French might renew hostilities. Admiral Sir Andrew Cunningham, British naval commander of the 'Torch' operation, signalled the First Sea Lord in London: 'I gravely fear repercussions.... With our forces strung out as at present in the race for Tunisia we simply cannot afford a renewal of hostile feeling.' Darlan protested: 'I am only a lemon which the Americans will drop after they have squeezed me dry.' Eisenhower soon attempted to soothe local feelings by broadcasting that Darlan should be congratulated for rallying to the cause, and the French should set aside 'small differences of ideas'. In turn this broadcast inevitably created fresh anger in London: it had 'caused deep offence to the Fighting French', Eden told Churchill, 'who regard it as a slight on their attitude'.[25]

The Prime Minister must have turned with relief to renewed considerations of the equally controversial, but so far less emotional problem of strategic planning. On 18 November he fired another minute at the COS, demanding full plans for 'Round-up' in 1943. 'I must repeat that "Torch" is no substitute for "Round-up".... My own position is that I am still aiming at a "Round-up" retarded till August....

I never meant that the Anglo-American Army be stuck in North Africa. It is a springboard and not a sofa. It may be that we should close down the Mediterranean activities by the end of June with a view to "Round-up" in August.' The Prime Minister pointed out that 48 divisions, British and American, were originally planned for the cross-Channel attempt in 1943; only 13 divisions were being used for 'Torch', leaving 35 which, he inferred, should still be available. Churchill paid no attention to Brooke's warning, given at the Defence Committee meeting 48 hours before, over limitations imposed by shipping shortages, except to comment: 'Allowance should no doubt be made for the larger distances from here to "Torch" compared with those across the Channel.'[26]

But if Churchill disregarded the allied shipping situation, Hitler did not. On 17 November, the day before the Prime Minister's minute, the Führer had held a naval conference to examine enemy shipping resources tied up by 'Torch'. Hitler decided the Tunisian bridgehead must be held as long as possible in order to strain those resources; and this decision, while ultimately resulting in heavy Axis losses in Tunisia, meanwhile activated against Churchill's demand for Mediterranean activities to be closed 'by the end of June'. Moreover, Eisenhower had already heard rumours from London that a reduction in Mediterranean strength might be proposed, and this information – fed to him by his Chief of Staff, Bedell Smith – resulted in an irritated cable from the allied commander. 'Unalterably opposed to reducing contemplated "Torch" strength.... In Tunisia it is touch and go.... Rather than talk of possible reduction we should be seeking ways and means of speeding up the build-up to clear out North Africa ... for God's sake let's get one job done at a time.'[27] Brooke, although agreeing with Eisenhower's sentiments, was becoming increasingly concerned about the African military situation, and by Eisenhower's handling of 'Torch' affairs; the CIGS admired Eisenhower as a man, but never considered him to have strong military ability, believing the American commander to be too involved in the political problems. He wrote later: 'It must be remembered that Eisenhower had never even commanded a battalion in action when he found himself commanding a group of armies in North Africa. No wonder he was at a loss.'[28] Anderson's British advance guard, moving from Tabarka, was checked by an improvised German battle-group on 18 November, and not until the 25th would Anderson feel strong enough to mount a sustained attack towards Tunis down the Medjerda valley. And, over to the east, Montgomery's forces had been held up by heavy rain from the 15th to 17th as they moved across the desert to cut off Rommel's units before Agheila. Anxiety spread in London. Harold Nicolson noted on the 19th: 'I find that a reaction has set in after our victories.'[29]

On 21 November this military situation affected War Cabinet discussion of the final signature of the agreement with Darlan, due to take place at any moment. Eden, supported by Cranborne, Colonial Secretary, objected vigorously to some of the agreement's phrasing, and in fact an argument had been taking place between the Foreign Secretary and Churchill throughout the previous 24 hours, with Eden noting in his diary: 'I cannot get W. to see the damage Darlan may do to the Allied cause if we don't watch it. He can make rings, diplomatically, round Eisenhower. At a moment of the shouting match W. said : "Well D. is not as bad as de Gaulle, anyway."'[30] According to Cadogan, Churchill expressed similar anti-de Gaulle views at the Cabinet meeting, declaring: 'He (de Gaulle) has been battening on us and is capable of turning round and fighting with the Axis against us.'[31] But Churchill's chief weapon at the meeting was the military situation. 'You can't pull this man (Eisenhower) about while he's fighting a battle.' Brooke, fearing for the conduct of the campaign, clearly agreed: 'In the present military situation we ought not to take any risks. We were dependent on French support for communication.... Time was of the essence in the matter, as it was important to avoid giving the enemy an opportunity to establish himself strongly in Tunisia.' Churchill would only agree to inform Roosevelt that Britain could not support an agreement in the form of an official, formal, diplomatic document. Cranborne revealed the strength of political feeling against the agreement when he informed Ministers of a paper put down for debate in the House of Lords: this, by Lord Vansittart, ex-diplomatic adviser to Neville Chamberlain, asked 'whether any other Quislings ... were being imported into North Africa'. The War Cabinet agreed 'it was undesirable that such a motion should be debated at this juncture.... Representations should be made to Lord Vansittart to this effect.'[32]

The so-called Clark-Darlan Agreement was duly signed in Algiers next day, Sunday, 22 November, thus creating provisional administrative machinery. London newspapers reacted violently with such headlines as 'De Gaulle Banned: Darlan Uplifted'. De Gaulle sent a circular to his chief officials making clear he would not co-operate with any French authority in North Africa until those 'guilty men' who had taken orders from Vichy had been eliminated. Darlan immediately despatched a message to all French diplomats abroad, interpreting Roosevelt's emphasis on the temporary nature of the agreement to mean 'until the liberation of France is complete'. 'He *is* a card!' commented Cadogan. 'Darlan has made *rings* round Eisenhower.... What a man!' At least Churchill believed military affairs could now be conducted more smoothly in North Africa, but the Prime Minister had another preoccupation this Sunday; Cadogan also commented in his diary: 'PM reshuffling his Cabinet, which makes him excitable.'[33] Stafford Cripps left the War Cabinet but stayed in the Government, as Minister of Aircraft Production – a post he would keep until the end of the war; Morrison came in as Home Secretary; Cranborne became Lord Privy Seal, not in the War Cabinet; Oliver Stanley became Colonial Secretary, again not in the War Cabinet itself. Eden took over Cripps's other duty, Leader of the House of Commons, and soon found this burden coupled with his Foreign Office task to be almost intolerable.

Russian pincer movements had punched forward at Stalingrad during this Sunday, closing round General von Paulus's 6th Army; Hitler had forbidden a breakout from the beleaguered city. The Russian offensive would soon transform the Eastern Front situation. But Brooke feared for the North African theatre. 'Operations in Tunisia not going as fast as they should,' he wrote next day, 23 November, 'and, on the other hand, Monty's pursuit of Rommel is badly delayed by weather. As a result Rommel given more time than I like to re-establish himself.' Next day he added: 'Am still very worried.' But Rommel, who had reached El Agheila on 23 November, realized he could never stand against the crushing east-west advance unless he received a dramatic increase in strength. On 24 November he decided he must fly to East Prussia to plead with Hitler.

Also on 24 November, allied discussions took place on the next objective in the Mediterranean after Rommel's defeat. Should the target be Sicily or Sardinia? The Joint Planning Staff declared on the 24th that regular Mediterranean convoys would not be safe until Sicily had been taken; on the other hand the establishment of air bases in Sardinia would give tremendous advantage through air cover for these sailings. Sicily would present a far harder invasion task.[34] On this same Tuesday, Eisenhower signalled his views: he favoured Sardinia, but the best date he could give for the assault appeared to be early March; he hoped to occupy Tunisia by mid-December, but the operation might take much longer, and a further advance in Tripoli would be impossible before mid-February.[35] The JPS report, and Eisenhower's gloomy assessment, were added to the COS agenda for their meeting the following morning, 25 November. Meanwhile another shot had been fired in the cross-Channel skirmish between the COS and Churchill. In the midst of this debate, with the Prime Minister still insisting upon 'Round-up' in August 1943, and the COS advocating a delay until 1944, a startling letter had reached London from Major-General Russell P. Hartle, Deputy C-in-C US Army, European Theatre, which seemed to indicate American coolness towards 'Round-up' for either 1943 or 1944. Hartle's communication, dated 19 November, declared that the US War Department had prepared a statement of the modifications to the US build-up in Britain for 'Round-up' – this build-up had the code-name 'Bolero' – necessitated by current 'Torch' operations. According to this statement the programme for 'Bolero' must be limited to 427,000 men, instead of 1,100,000 as previously envisaged. Construction of hospital and storage facilities etc. in the UK for any number in excess of 427,000 'must be accomplished entirely by your own labour and with your own materials'. The letter was referred to the Defence Committee on 23 November, when it was pointed out that 'General Marshall was not prepared to send very large forces to the UK, unless there was an unconditional plan for their employment on the Continent'. The Defence Committee agreed a large-scale 'Bolero' was essential 'in order that we should at any time be able to take advantage of a favourable opportunity for a return to the Continent. The war could not be won without an invasion of Europe, and this might well be possible in 1943 or early 1944.' The Prime Minister accordingly sent a strong signal on 24 November repeating to the President views previously expressed to the COS. 'We had no knowledge that you had decided to abandon for ever "Round-up" and all our preparations were proceeding on a broad front under "Bolero".... "Torch" is no substitute for "Round-up".... All my talks with Stalin ... were on the basis of a postponed "Round-up", but never was it suggested that we should attempt no Second Front in Europe in 1943, or even 1944.'[36]

The British COS remained in adamant opposition to Churchill's optimistic timing for 'Round-up'. On this Tuesday they produced a revised draft of their report of 30 October, as requested by the Defence Committee on 16 November, and they refused to alter their opinion that the cross-Channel operation seemed out of the question until early 1944. 'At the present time, North-West Europe must be likened to a powerful fortress, which can be assaulted only after adequate artillery preparation. To make the assault before the time is ripe would be suicide for ourselves and of no assistance to Russia. Our aim must be to intensify the preliminary bombardment for which purpose Anglo-American air forces will take the place of artillery.' Churchill, in a vigorous minute, reacted against the 'practical abandonment of any resolute effort to form a second front in 1943'.[37] Until this basic issue had been settled, no firm decision could be taken on immediate operations in the Mediterranean after North Africa had been

cleared, specifically as to whether Sicily or Sardinia should
be the next target. As Brooke commented in his diary on
25 November: 'A very difficult and long COS at which we
tried to clear up future operations.'[38] For the moment planning continued for both Sicily, 'Husky', and Sardinia, 'Brimstone'. Confusion was increased still further by the Hartle
letter, which in itself stemmed from the Anglo-American
debate at the time of the 'Torch' decision the previous summer. The Americans had insisted that agreement for 'Torch'
ruled out prospects of 'Round-up' in 1943; one or the other
had to be chosen. Brooke and his colleagues agreed; as the
CIGS had told the War Cabinet on 24 July: 'There was
complete unanimity between the British and American Chiefs
of Staff ... both the British and American COS believed that
it was unlikely that "Round-up" would be carried out in
1943.'[39] The British COS were now even more convinced that
this must be the case if the Mediterranean situation were
properly exploited and the ground prepared for 'Round-up'
in 1944. All depended upon the length of time needed for
this exploitation and preparation, and as far as the first was
concerned, Marshall indicated to a meeting of the US COS
on 25 November that he, like Churchill, believed resources
would be better switched back to 'Bolero' from the Mediterranean. Clearance of the Mediterranean for sea traffic would
involve the occupation of Sicily, Sardinia and Crete, he
claimed. 'A careful determination should be made of whether
or not the large air and ground forces required for such a
project could be justified in view of the results to be expected.'[40]

Next day, 26 November, Roosevelt replied to Churchill's
signal of the 24th regarding Hartle's communication. 'We
of course have no intention of abandoning "Round-up".' But
the President continued: 'In view of our requirements for
the initiation and maintenance of "Torch" our studies indicated that we could not afford to send forces and material
to the UK at this time in excess of that stated by General
Hartle.... North Africa must naturally take precedence. We
are far more heavily engaged in the South-West Pacific than
I anticipated a few months ago. Nevertheless we shall con-

tinue with "Bolero" as rapidly as our shipping and other resources permit.'[41] Roosevelt's reply therefore underlined Marshall's view: either the Mediterranean or 'Bolero' must be chosen – and the message also hinted at a possible move towards the Pacific. Planning remained in a state of dangerous uncertainty; agreement over the next strategic decisions had plainly become urgent. And Roosevelt's letter contained a suggestion for the means to reach such agreement. 'I believe that as soon as we have knocked the Germans out of Tunisia we should proceed with a military strategical conference between Great Britain, Russia, and the United States.' The President believed such a meeting could take place in about a month or six weeks in Cairo or Moscow. Churchill immediately disagreed with the idea of entrusting such vital matters to the professionals, especially in view of the chasm between himself and the British COS; he cabled back on the same day suggesting a conference, perhaps in Iceland in January, attended by Roosevelt, Stalin and himself.[42] Also on 26 November another problem emerged which could complicate strategic planning still further. The War Cabinet, meeting at 6 p.m. this Thursday, heard that British manpower shortages threatened even those plans provisionally agreed upon for 1943. Sir John Anderson produced a memorandum which declared: 'The stated demand of the Service and Supply Departments to meet the planned strengths in programmes up to the end of 1943 totalled 2.5 million men and women. Against this demand the total foreseeable supply was 1.6 million, giving a prospective deficit of at least 900,000.' This unsettling situation was deferred for further discussion.[43]

Eden had meanwhile been growing increasingly concerned over the arrangements with the French; during the day he sent an anxious minute to Churchill: 'The situation seems to be deteriorating and the tone of the French authorities in North Africa to be hardening. Admiral Darlan makes it clear that he interprets the word "temporary" to mean "until the liberation of France is complete".... Darlan has also made it clear that he regards himself as holding his authority from the Marshal (Pétain).... I do not think we can safely allow

this state of affairs to continue.... In Europe as a whole the
"filthy race of quislings", as you once so aptly called them,
will take heart.'[44] Churchill preferred to wait longer before
taking action, but the need for some decision was underlined
by the War Cabinet discussion next morning, Friday, 27
November. Ministers were informed that a notice of motion
had been put down in the Commons which declared: 'That
this House is of the opinion that our relations with Admiral
Darlan and his kind are inconsistent with the ideals for
which we entered and are fighting this war....' While Ministers thought it unlikely this notice would attract much
support, they agreed upon the existence of 'an undercurrent
of anxiety among a number of persons well disposed to the
Government but who were not in possession of the full facts',
and the War Cabinet decided that the Leader of the House,
Eden, should say the Government agreed to make a statement in secret session.[45] At least Darlan had tried to carry
out one part of his bargain: he had attempted to persuade
Admiral de Laborde, Commander of the French Mediterranean Fleet, to bring his warships over from Toulon.
Laborde, fanatically anti-British, had refused. Admiral
Auphan, French Minister of Marine, had however insisted
upon a free zone around Toulon harbour to prevent a German
takeover; the Germans responded with an attempted *coup
de main* on 26 November, but French officers courageously
scuttled their vessels: 73 warships sank, including a battleship, 2 battle-cruisers, 7 cruisers, 29 destroyers and 16 submarines. The tragedy of the French fleet was almost at an
end; on 30 November the War Cabinet discussed the situation
regarding remaining warships at Alexandria, where the
French naval squadron had been immobilized since July
1940. Admiral Godefroy, squadron commander, had asked
for facilities to communicate with Pétain, but the War
Cabinet decided this request should be refused. Godefroy
eventually declared the warships would not be handed over
until the allies had conquered Tunisia: only then would
their power to liberate France be proved.[46]

Fighting in French North Africa reached a climax at the
end of November. Anderson's thrust towards Tunis, launched

on the 25th, reached Djedeida, 15 miles from the city, on the 28th. The Germans bolstered their defences with everything they could find and the momentum of the allied advance faltered. And now came winter rains to sluice the improvised allied airfields and prevent effective air cover and supply. On 29 November Churchill gave a broadcast combining optimism and warning. 'The dawn of 1943 will soon loom red before us, and we must brace ourselves to cope with the trials and problems of what must be a stern and terrible year. We do so with the assurance of evergrowing strength, and we do so as a nation with a strong will, a bold heart, and a good conscience.' The Prime Minister referred his listeners to Italy. 'If the enemy should in due course be blasted from the Tunisian tip, which is our aim, the whole of the south of Italy ... will be brought under prolonged scientific and shattering air attack.' Count Ciano, the disillusioned Italian Foreign Minister, commented: 'I do not see what means are at our disposal today to frustrate his programme of scientifically demolishing our country.' Ciano felt especially depressed by the news that Rommel had left North Africa to see Hitler. 'Rommel does not consider it possible to hold Tripolitania and would like to withdraw into Tunisia at once.'[47] The Desert Fox had in fact confronted an irate Hitler on the 28th. 'I began to realize that Adolf Hitler simply did not want to see the situation as it was.'[48] Rommel was ordered back to the battle: he must stand and fight, despite acute shortages; time must be gained. British 8th Army forces had reached Afrika Korps positions at El Agheila two days before this Rommel-Hitler confrontation. Next day, 27 November, the confident British commander sent his thoughts on future strategy to the CIGS; Montgomery apparently enjoyed even greater optimism than Churchill, informing the unsympathetic Brooke that the best hope for 1943 lay in a cross-Channel attack, and 'given a large number of Americans I believe the invasion of Western Europe could be brought off successfully next summer, about June, when the weather is good.' The CIGS signalled a stern reply: 'Paras 2 and 6 of your letter are not quite in accordance with future possibilities owing to your not being in possession of full picture.'[49]

With divisions of opinion as strong as ever over strategic planning for 1943, Stalin re-entered the debate. On 24 November Churchill had sent the Soviet leader a *résumé* of the advantages of the Mediterranean operations and had stressed, somewhat surprisingly, the benefits outlined by the COS of a large-scale bomber offensive against Germany in 1943. Stalin replied on the 28th: 'I hope that this does not mean that you have changed your mind with regard to your promise given in Moscow to establish a second front in Western Europe in the spring of 1943.'[50] Churchill remained in a bitter mood from this unnecessary reminder when he continued COS discussions on 30 November – his 68th birthday; and to add to his general concern Darlan published an arrogant decree on this Monday, which fully supported Eden's fears: 'We, Admiral of the Fleet, High Commissioner of French Africa acting by virtue of powers conferred upon us by the Marshal of France, Head of State, order....'

The morning COS conference considered the prospect of 'Round-up' for the following year. Brooke complained in his diary: 'We examined most recent ideas of PM for re-entry into Continent in 1943, and where he is again trying to commit us to a definite plan of action. After lunch interview with Secretary of State (Grigg) on new proposed manpower cuts of PM. He never faces realities: at one moment we are reducing our forces, and the next we are invading the Continent with vast armies for which there is no hope of ever finding the shipping. He is quite incorrigible and I am quite exhausted.' Brooke had to rush from his interview with Grigg to a War Cabinet meeting starting at 5.30 and lasting until 8 p.m., at which he gave Ministers the latest military reports. 'The allied forces are closing in on Bizerta and Tunis.... German forces are now back at El Agheila. The administrative situation of the 8th Army is satisfactory.... At Guadalcanal the Japanese have suffered heavily and their morale is low.'[51] And in Berlin next day, 1 December, the German Naval Staff completed a memorandum which supported Rommel's gloomy assessment: the Axis had been

thrown on to the defensive, and the report added that
Germany and Japan would in future tend to fend for themselves, rather than attempting to combine in a global strategy.
Yet on the same day the Germans counter-attacked south-
east from Tunis against Anderson's rain-washed unit; the
allies were forced back, despite American reinforcements,
and within a few days would return to Medjez; not until
22 December would a renewed advance be attempted.

This disappointment strengthened Brooke's position in his
argument with Churchill: delay in clearing North Africa
would tie up resources needed for 'Round-up' in 1943. On
3 December the COS completed a powerful paper, stating:
'Resources in manpower, shipping and landing craft are
wholly inadequate to build up "Torch", reopen the Mediterranean for military traffic, and carry out the operations which
we contemplate in the Mediterranean next spring and summer, in addition to "Round-up" in July, 1943.'[52] Undaunted,
Churchill presented another paper to the COS at their morning meeting this Thursday, which repeated that the Russians
had been led to believe a second front would be opened in
1943, and Russian successes meant that 'before the end of
1942 it may be possible for us to draw with certainty at
least the conclusion *that no important transfers of German
troops can be made in 1943 from the Eastern to the Western
theatre*'. German forces in France would be further stretched
by their takeover of the unoccupied part of the country.
'The whole position must be completely re-surveyed, with
the object of finding means for engaging US and British armies
directly upon the Continent.'[53] The COS attended a Staff
Conference with Churchill at 5.30 p.m., with Eden and Lord
Leathers also present. The Prime Minister repeated his arguments: attacks on Sicily and Sardinia would not constitute
sufficient army activity in 1943, and, Churchill added, 'we
promised Stalin' that a Second Front would be created. Brooke
later wrote: 'I replied: "No, *we* did not promise." He
(Churchill) then stopped and stared at me for a few seconds,
during which I think he remembered that, if any promise
was made, it was on that last evening when he went to say
goodbye to Stalin and when I was not there. He said no

more....' The meeting merely decided to instruct the Joint Planners to present two assessments: first, a forecast of the strength of the largest force which could be built up in the UK by July if all projected operations in the Mediterranean were cancelled; second, the strength of the largest force which could be built up by autumn 1943 if the main weight of the allied offensive in 1943 remained in the Mediterranean.[54] Also on 3 December, Roosevelt replied to Churchill's suggestion for a summit meeting made on 26 November; the President agreed, and proposed a conference somewhere south of Algiers or at Khartoum, to start about 15 January. Churchill replied the same day, expressing delight, and perhaps with the COS attitude in mind he added: 'All prospect of attack in 1943 depends on early decision.' The Prime Minister sent off the invitation to Stalin.[55]

Behind the strategic discussion lurked the possibility of slicing Italy away from the Axis. Success in the Mediterranean could bring about an Italian defeat, either through subsequent military action or through collapse inside Mussolini's demoralized regime. And on this Thursday the subject of Italy received War Cabinet attention at a 12.15 p.m. meeting; Ministers considered two papers, one circulated by Eden on 20 November, and the other written by the Prime Minister on 25 November expressing partial disagreement with the Foreign Secretary's views. Eden, while discounting the possibility of Italy suing for peace – which the Germans would anyway nullify by occupying the country – suggested Britain should concentrate on provoking an internal collapse, both by military action and by political warfare. The capture of Sardinia, and even more of Sicily, 'would have tremendous and even possibly decisive effect'. The Foreign Secretary therefore endorsed Brooke's views. But Churchill disagreed with Eden over the possibility of Italy suing for peace. This could happen, even without the capture of Sardinia or Sicily: 'When a nation is thoroughly beaten in war, it does all sorts of things which no one can imagine beforehand.' Defeat in North Africa might be sufficient; moreover, the Prime Minister hoped that the Italians themselves would prevent a German occupation of the country. The War

Cabinet agreed Britain must adopt a 'wait and see' attitude. Ministers were informed 'of certain tentative enquiries which had recently been made by individual Italians regarding the possibility of a separate peace. No special importance was to be attached to any of these approaches; but they were straws showing which way the wind was blowing.'[56]

Eden still feared for French affairs. On 4 December he repeated his anxieties to Churchill, and the Prime Minister now agreed to instructions being sent to Lord Halifax: the Ambassador must inform the President that the allies should insist on the dismissal of pro-Axis officials in Darlan's administration and the release of allied sympathizers. In addition, Roosevelt's approval was sought for the despatch of US and British political representatives to Algiers.[57] This latter idea stemmed from growing dissatisfaction in London with the Algiers situation, and more especially with the dearth of information from Eisenhower's HQ. On 4 December the COS requested more news from Eisenhower, stating they found much difficulty in following accurately the course of operations; and the Foreign Office had similar criticism over diplomatic developments. Within 24 hours the allied commander replied with a personal telegram to Churchill, in which he took the opportunity to re-state his position as regards Darlan: 'Here he is entirely necessary...' But Eden confided in his diary on the 5th: 'I am much troubled by Darlan developments. Americans seem completely to ignore political issue at stake, and we risk running into grave trouble.'[58]

Next day Stalin ruined Churchill's hopes for a Three-Power summit. 'I will not be in a position to leave the Soviet Union.' And the Soviet dictator added: 'I am awaiting your reply to the paragraph of my preceding letter dealing with the establishment of the Second Front in Western Europe in the spring of 1943.'[59] Stalin evidently intended to keep up the pressure; Churchill, in turn, intended to continue his confrontation with the COS. Meanwhile North African news continued to be disappointing, threatening delays which would react still further against 'Round-up' in 1943. War Cabinet Ministers, meeting at 5 p.m. on Monday, 8 December, heard that Anderson's forces had still to resume their Tunis advance; Brooke commented in his diary: 'Eisenhower's far too busy with political matters.'[60] Churchill saw Eden before and after the Cabinet meeting, arguing for a postponement of a Commons secret session debate on North Africa scheduled in three days' time, 10 December. Eden disagreed: the House would resent such a move, he said, and suspicions of Darlan would be increased.

Lord Halifax lunched with Roosevelt next day, 8 December, and reported to London that the President did not contemplate early action to dispense with Darlan's services, and that he had in mind some kind of Anglo-Franco-American Commission upon which the Admiral would serve with reduced status. Roosevelt did however agree with the idea of sending political representatives.[61] Also on the 8th, Eden and Cadogan dined at the Savoy with de Gaulle; Cadogan wrote afterwards: 'De G.'s one remedy is "Get rid of Darlan". My answer is "Yes but how?"'[62] A solution would come in dramatic fashion in 16 days' time. Eden, dissatisfied with Roosevelt's attitude, successfully pressed Churchill to send a personal telegram; this signal, dated 9 December, declared: 'I have been disturbed by reports received during the last few days from North Africa'; Churchill described the behaviour of Vichy sympathizers and 'kindred Fascist organizations' against pro-Ally French. 'Not only have our enemies been thus encouraged, but our friends have been correspondingly confused and cast down.'[63]

The debate on North Africa opened in Parliament next day, 10 December: Churchill, forgetting his previous desire to postpone this hearing, wrote in his memoirs that 'mounting pressures ... led me to seek refuge in Secret Session'. He spoke for an hour, and according to Harold Nicolson had never been 'more forceful, informative or convincing'. 'I do not at all wonder that this Darlan business has caused a good deal of concern,' declared the Prime Minister. 'The question, however, which we must ask ourselves is not whether we like or do not like what is going on, but what are we going to do about it.' Churchill then gave one of the first indications that Britain must soon take second place to

America as the most powerful anti-Axis nation. 'This is an
American expedition in which they will ultimately have perhaps two or three times as large ground forces as we have,
and three times the air force ... neither militarily nor
politically are we directly controlling the course of events.'
The Prime Minister stressed the temporary nature of the
Darlan agreement, then he exhorted MPs: 'Let us get on
with the war....' Those who concentrated too much on the
Darlan aspect at the expense of these great military events
were condemned as having 'a jaundiced outlook and dis-
organized loyalties'. Churchill sat down to prolonged cheers
– but disappointment and unease would remain.

While Churchill had been addressing the Commons,
General Marshall had been holding another Washington
conference to discuss North Africa; in his speech the Prime
Minister had agreed that 'Torch' was 'an American expedition under the ultimate command of the President of
the United States' and, in Washington, Marshall seemed determined to exercise rigid US control. He told this meeting
that the North African campaign must be closed down as
quickly as feasible, thus switching forces back to the UK
possibly for an emergency operation against Brest or
Boulogne in 1943.[64] The US Chief of Staff repeated his views
to Dill, who wired them to Churchill on the 11th: Marshall
was 'getting more and more convinced that we should be
in a position to undertake a modified "Round-up" before the
summer if, as soon as North Africa is cleared of Axis forces,
we start pouring American troops into England instead of
sending them to Africa for the exploitation of "Torch". Such
an operation would, he feels, be much more effective than
either "Brimstone" (Sardinia) or "Husky" (Sicily), less costly
in shipping, more satisfying to the Russians, engage many
more German air forces....'[65] Churchill reacted with
pleasure; Brooke with corresponding depression. 'I think he
is wrong,' wrote the CIGS in his diary on the 11th, 'and that
the Mediterranean gives us far better facilities for wearing
down German forces.' Next day the Joint Planners produced
their assessment requested by the Staff Conference on the
3rd, and the report gave decisive support to the COS view:

even if all Mediterranean operations were suspended, only five extra divisions would be released for a 1943 invasion of North-West Europe; moreover, a far larger number of German divisions would be released for service on the Eastern and Western fronts. Next morning, 13 December, the COS began to prepare their most emphatic statement to date; this would be presented to the Prime Minister on the 16th. But military events in North Africa had once again exploded into action. The Battle of Agheila began on the 13th: twice in previous years British forces had been thrown back from these positions; this time Montgomery was determined to outmanoeuvre the battered Afrika Korps. The British attack had been put forward 48 hours from the original plan as a result of reports that Rommel had already begun to pull units back; his retreat accelerated as the British advanced, with Rommel knowing he could never stand against the 8th Army while his resources remained so slender. His weary army managed to filter through the enveloping New Zealanders; nevertheless by 15 December Montgomery had at last won possession of the Agheila positions.

Brooke told the War Cabinet on Monday evening, 14 December, that Rommel's forces were now in full retreat. Latest military information otherwise continued to be gloomy; as Cadogan wrote: 'Tunisia is not going well, so PM on his usual (and to me well-found) complaint that, out of about 110,000 men there, there are only about 10,000 fighting men. It does seem rather hopeless.'[66] During the day Eisenhower tried to reassure Churchill over the deteriorating French situation. 'Admittedly the political situation is confused and difficult. I think you shall continue to receive disturbing reports. Our main effort has been to maintain sufficient control of the situation to enable us to fight a battle.'[67] And yet the battle had still to be fought in Eisenhower's area; both the Foreign Office and the British COS therefore remained unconvinced, and the former urged the rapid appointment of a senior political adviser who could perhaps relieve Eisenhower's non-military burden. Also on the 14th, Stalin renewed his pressure for the Second Front, repeating to Roosevelt his 'confidence' that the 'promises

about the opening of a Second Front in Europe ... in regard
to 1942 and in any case in regard to the spring of 1943'
would be fulfilled.[68] Roosevelt cabled to Churchill on the
same day: 'In spite of Stalin's inability to meet with us, I
think we should plan a meeting at once with our respective
military staffs. I should like to meet in Africa about January
15.' Churchill hurried to reply: 'Yes, certainly. The sooner
the better. I am greatly relieved. It is the only thing to do.'[69]

Daily the need for this Anglo-American summit seemed
more apparent. Sir Archibald Clark Kerr, Ambassador to
Moscow and now spending a few days in London, gave the
COS a grim 60-minute warning on the 15th. Stalin was 'ex-
pecting something formidable from us and the Americans
early next year. He had been temporarily consoled by the
unexpected success and size of "Torch" but he did not regard
it as a Second Front. If he now failed to get what he expected,
he would probably turn very sour. Moreover, it was impossible to say whether, faced by the knowledge that there
would be no Second Front, Russian morale would hold ...
he (Kerr) did not exclude, under certain circumstances, the
chance of (Stalin's) making a separate peace with Hitler.' But
Brooke wrote in his diary: 'I refuse to believe such a thing
possible.' And, at this same COS meeting attended by Kerr,
the COS completed their paper refuting Churchill's arguments
for a Second Front in France in 1943.[70] Brooke threw down
the COS gauntlet at a meeting with Churchill on the following evening, 16 December. Eden also attended. First, the
CIGS listed limitations to the US build-up in Britain, 'Bolero',
including shipping and the capacity of British ports, railways and installations. Then he explained Axis difficulties
in containing an allied thrust from the Mediterranean. The
railway network in Europe limited north-south troop movement: only two lines, both vulnerable to air attack, led into
Italy and only one into Greece. On the other hand, the magnificent lateral rail system made it easy for troops to be
transferred from Russia to France. The allies should therefore take advantage of enemy difficulties in reinforcing the
Mediterranean front; if 40 German divisions could be held
down in North-West Europe by fear of cross-Channel attack,

and if at the same time Italy could be forced from the war and perhaps the Balkans entered, more relief could be given to the Russians than a hazardous 'Round-up' attempt in 1943. Brooke expected a renewed outburst from the Prime Minister; he wrote: 'As the paper we put in went straight against Winston ... I feared the worst.' No outburst came; Churchill had given in. He declared: 'Unless the Americans could vastly improve on the estimates given in the (COS) memorandum, he could see no alternative to the strategy recommended by the Chiefs of Staff.' Thus the meeting agreed that: 'Large-scale amphibious operations would have to be undertaken in the early part of the summer, aimed at Sicily or the southern part of Italy or both, with the object of knocking Italy out of the war, preparing the way for an entry into the Balkans, and bringing Turkey into the war on our side. This, together with "Bolero" on the largest scale that the above operations would permit, could be offered to the Russians as our contribution to the war in 1943.'[71]

Brooke emerged from the meeting with a massive load apparently removed. 'I think he (Churchill) is now fairly safe', although his diary entry added: 'I have still the Americans to convince first and then Stalin.'[72] Churchill's sudden acquiescence was in fact typical of his partnership with the COS: he might bluster and bully for meeting after meeting, he might blast and bombard his advisers with minutes and memoranda, but, when he had become absolutely clear in his mind that his advisers would stick rigidly to their convictions, he would concur. And yet this did not prevent him from sometimes taking a backward view, with an abrupt attempt to reverse the decision, if the time seemed opportune. For the moment the British were therefore re-united in strategic policy, although argument would continue over Sardinia or Sicily as targets. Allied planning remained to be hammered out. Meanwhile, Axis plans were discussed at a sombre conference at Rastenburg between 18 and 20 December, with the Italians represented by Ciano. 'The atmosphere is heavy,' recorded the Italian Minister. 'To the bad news there should perhaps be added the sadness of that damp forest and the boredom of collective living in the

Command barracks ... Kitchen odour, smell of uniforms, of boots.' The conference began in this 'troglodyte' existence.[73] Hitler reacted violently to any idea of a separate peace with Russia in order to stop the allies in Africa: any Soviet peace would simply be a truce; Soviet supplies would be sent to the allies; additional Axis troops for Africa would require additional Italian shipping – a doubtful factor. The most that the participants at the conference could decide was to increase the emphasis on submarine warfare against the allies; Axis troops in Tunisia would have to endure with resources already despatched. And, two days after the Rastenburg conference, General Anderson renewed his attack towards Tunis. His forces moved forward during the night of 22 December, and achieved initial success under cover of darkness. But with dawn came torrential rain; within hours the attack had bogged down. Eisenhower called a conference for Christmas Eve – and the outcome was to cause the British COS renewed alarm.

Meanwhile the French situation rapidly imposed additional strain upon Anglo-American relations. Cordell Hull, aged US Secretary of State, wrote later: 'De Gaulle's propaganda machine in England ... was now grinding out violent attacks against the French set-up in North Africa, with scarcely veiled assault against us for being responsible for it. A new hair-trigger situation was fast developing.' Hull saw Lord Halifax on 21 December and inferred that Churchill and his Ministers were encouraging de Gaulle. On this same Monday, before Halifax's report of the conversation reached London, Churchill raised the French subject at the 5.30 p.m. War Cabinet meeting, and seemed to urge an even greater determination by de Gaulle to stand against Darlan. 'He (Churchill) doubted whether de Gaulle realized that the French Administration in North Africa under Admiral Darlan might develop in such a way that it would overshadow the Fighting French movement. He thought that it was neither in the public interest, nor wise on de Gaulle's part, to maintain his present aloof attitude.'[74] At least one development allowed scope for political improvement: on 15 December Roosevelt had appointed Robert Murphy as his personal representative in North Africa, and during the evening of the 22nd Churchill asked Harold Macmillan to accept the post of Minister Resident at Algiers, reporting direct to 10 Downing Street; in this way some of the political muddle and misunderstanding might be cleared. But whereas Murphy was already a full member of Eisenhower's staff as Civil Affairs Officer, Macmillan would only be answerable to his Prime Minister, thereby creating another potential source of friction with Eisenhower.

And while political affairs in North Africa resulted in tension over present Anglo-American relations, a communication now arrived from Washington which threatened still more disruption over future strategic planning. On 16 December Brooke and his colleagues had at last managed to convince Churchill that the Mediterranean area should receive most attention in 1943; now, on 23 December, the British Mission in Washington forwarded a strategic appreciation by the US COS which advocated the closing down of Mediterranean operations. No attempt should be made to take Sicily or Sardinia; instead, Axis forces should merely be expelled from North Africa and air operations launched against Italy. Excess allied forces should be taken from North Africa 'in preparation for a land offensive against Germany in 1943'.[75] The memorandum, clearly the result of Marshall's influence, therefore coincided with Churchill's attitude before he had acquiesced in the COS line; and the Prime Minister, studying the US document over Christmas, began to shift back again: the end of the month would see another, final, tussle.

Black clouds continued to boil over Tunisia. General Anderson's offensive had remained swamped. On the day this attack had started, 22 December, Eisenhower had begun a journey from Algiers to Anderson's HQ; the terrible weather had prevented him flying and he had had to make his way over rutted, flooded tracks, only managing to arrive at the drenched British headquarters on the morning of 24 December. Preliminary moves were being made for a renewed offensive, but the rain continued to pour upon the miserable troops. Guns, tanks, vehicles were stuck in the mud. Eisenhower conferred with Anderson and decided the attack must be called off—and should not be remounted until weather conditions improved, which, Eisenhower warned the Combined Chiefs of Staff, would probably be 'not less than two months.... Evidence is complete, in my opinion, that any attempt to make a major attack under current conditions in Northern Tunisia would be merely to court disaster.'[76] Also on 24 December, General Alexander reported from Cairo that although the port of Benghazi was discharging 1,900 tons of supplies a day, upon which the 8th Army depended for its continued being, this figure must be unreliable in view of the winter weather: the warning proved correct and the 8th Army remained immobilized before Buerat. Added to these military upsets came news of a dramatic North African political upheaval.

A young Frenchman, Bonnier de la Chapelle, stood unnoticed near the *Palais d'Eté*, Algiers. This 20-year-old believed his mission to be the rescue of France from evil leadership. A car drove up; out stepped a sprightly, uniformed figure; Bonnier de la Chapelle pulled a revolver from his coat, fired, and Admiral Darlan staggered into the arms of his aide. Darlan died within the hour; his assassin suffered death from a firing squad soon after dawn on 26 December. On 14 November, Sir Alexander Cadogan had jotted a flippant entry in his diary: 'We shall do no good till we've killed Darlan.'[77] Indeed, charges would now arise that 'interested parties' had been involved; as Churchill wrote later: 'Darlan's murder, however criminal, relieved the Allies of their embarrassment at working with him, and at the same time left them with all the advantages he had been able to bestow during the vital hours of the Allied landings.'[78] Yet although the burden of Darlan's presence had thus been removed, immediate dangers existed of civil disorder in North Africa behind the military front: Eisenhower, informed of the news at Anderson's HQ, immediately hurried back to Algiers. And to whom would the mantle of French leadership now pass? Choice rested upon de Gaulle or Giraud, the first favoured by London, the second by Washington. In the first hours after the assassination it seemed the problem might find a smooth solution, when de Gaulle told the Foreign Office on the 24th that he saw no obstacle to co-operation between himself and Giraud, now Darlan had gone.[79] On Christmas Day de Gaulle sent a message to Giraud proposing a meeting; Giraud was appointed High Commissioner – a logical step approved by the British. But complications began to creep forward. De Gaulle had given his message to the US Embassy in London's Grosvenor Square for despatch to Giraud, but transmission from the Embassy did not take place until next afternoon, Boxing Day, and the message was not handed to Giraud until early morning, 28 December, three days after it had left de Gaulle. The latter's suspicions of the delay were increased by a message to him from Roosevelt, postponing – for a second time – a proposed visit by the Fighting French leader to America; at the same time de Gaulle knew Giraud's representatives were already conferring with Hull's State Department.

Churchill described latest events to the War Cabinet at 5.30 p.m. on Monday, 28 December. He had seen de Gaulle the previous day. 'De Gaulle thought it of first importance to create a strong, united, national French authority. He was quite ready to work with General Giraud, but regarded him as qualified for a military rather than a political role. He had suggested an early meeting with Giraud.' Churchill then disclosed Giraud's reply, which must have only just been received – and which had only taken a day to come from Algiers, compared with the 36 hours needed for de Gaulle's communication. Giraud, while agreeing in principle to a meeting, thought the moment was not opportune. Churchill also told Ministers of Roosevelt's decision to postpone de Gaulle's visit to America until the North African situation had been clarified. But Ministers agreed that 'the political situation in North Africa should not be allowed to drift', and approved a telegram from Churchill to Roosevelt urging an early meeting between de Gaulle and Giraud. The War Cabinet then turned to a delicate discussion of Eisenhower's handling of the military situation; and this section of the official minutes was afterwards headed 'No Circulation'. Churchill referred to Eisenhower's decision to postpone the

Tunis attack, possibly for two months, and added: 'In the meantime the enemy was continuing to reinforce his forces in Tunisia, which might also be reinforced by the bulk of Rommel's army from Tripolitania.... There were indications in General Eisenhower's telegram that matters were not running too smoothly between ourselves and the Americans in North Africa. Furthermore, units were being split up....' Churchill said he would discuss the situation with the COS.[80] As a result the COS drafted a highly critical message for the US COS, to be sent via Dill, warning that Eisenhower's forces were overextended along a wide front, and that the Germans were likely to reinforce faster than the allies. A later signal to Dill, on 5 January, instructed him not to hand over this message in view of the forthcoming summit.

In the midst of these fears over current military events, the COS turned to discussion of strategic planning for 1943; and on 28 December Churchill made his last attempt to persuade the COS to change their minds, overlooking all the arguments exhaustively examined during previous weeks. 'Unless ... during the summer and autumn (of 1943) we also engage the enemy from the West, we shall not be able to bring the most important part of our forces into play.' The whole subject received Defence Committee attention at 10.30 p.m. on Tuesday the 29th. Ministers considered the COS paper embodying their oft-repeated arguments – approved by Churchill at the time of his acquiescence on 16 December – together with proposed amendments by the Prime Minister. But now, at last, full approval was given to the COS view: Churchill once again gave way and approved the COS paper. This document presented a fundamentally different view to that favoured by the US COS, proposing the following activities for 1943: defeat of the U-boat menace; expansion of bombing against Germany and Italy; exploitation of allied positions in the Mediterranean with a view to (i) knocking Italy out of the war, (ii) bringing in Turkey, (iii) giving the Axis no respite for recuperation. Supplies to Russia would continue to be sent, and, for the Far East, the paper advocated limited offensive operations in the Pacific 'on a scale sufficient only to contain the bulk of Japanese forces in that area', and operations to reopen the Burma road to China. Finally the document declared: 'Subject to the claims of the above (there should be) the greatest possible concentration of forces in the UK with a view to re-entry on the Continent in August or September 1943, should conditions hold out a good prospect of success, or anyhow a "Sledgehammer" (limited cross-Channel attack) to wear down the enemy's air forces.' The Prime Minister's influence amounted to more than this sentence: the wording and general attitude of the paper owed much to his aggressive approach, and the result once again underlined the value of the Churchill-COS partnership; as Michael Howard aptly commented in his official history: 'Its (the paper's) realism was due solely to the Chiefs of Staff; but the positive, offensive spirit which inspired it was largely the work of the unwearying and merciless interventions of the Prime Minister.'[81]

Also on 29 December, Eisenhower explained his immediate military policy to the Combined Chiefs of Staff: he intended to pursue an 'aggressive defensive' in Northern Tunisia, using British forces, and to launch an offensive further south towards Sfax with American troops, taking advantage of the easier going. He proposed to take charge of the Tunisian front himself. Dill transmitted this information to London, where it caused renewed COS apprehension. The COS replied to Dill on the 31st: the Sfax operation would not only reduce the weight of the main Northern attack, further delaying the capture of Tunis, but it would also 'expose the Northern Forces to risk of defeat'. The Sfax plan seemed to increase possibilities of a counter-thrust by the Germans from the north and also a move by Rommel from Tripolitania; and the COS added: 'We are much alarmed at the idea of Eisenhower leaving the centre and summit where he alone can cope with Giraud and make sure the front is properly supplied.'[82] Eisenhower had still to find favour among the British COS. Eisenhower for his part had considerable doubts over the proposed despatch of Harold Macmillan to Algiers; his reservations were concealed beneath his customary politeness in a signal to the COS on the 31st: 'I am delighted to work with anyone who can help in the present confused situation, but I am uncertain as to the definition of my relationship with Mr Macmillan and your instructions are requested.' American suspicions of the British attitude towards the French situation had continued unabated; also on 31 December, Cordell Hull called Sir Ronald Campbell to his office, with Campbell representing Halifax in the latter's absence. Hull expressed 'serious concern ... over the course of what seemed to be British policy, more or less, to back up de Gaulle publicity aimed directly at this Government'. Hull warned that matters could not 'drift on in this manner much longer without unfortunate results'.[83]

Two days before, Cadogan had written in his diary: 'Americans becoming impossible at all points.' The Americans clearly reciprocated this opinion. French affairs; the current military situation; future strategy – acute differences existed on all three. As 1942 closed, omens seemed dark indeed for the forthcoming summit conference, scheduled to start at Casablanca within a fortnight.

Casablanca

Other shadows darkened this New Year, 1943. The U-boat war in the grey Atlantic and squall-whipped Mediterranean had continued with ferocious intensity: in September 1942 the total of Allied tonnage sunk had been 485,413, and by November this had soared to 729,160. Shortage of shipping had become acute, with the situation aggravated by North African demands. Imports had plummeted, and stock-piled resources would drop to the lowest point of the war in spring, 1943. Bombing raids were increased in an attempt to beat down the U-boat threat: between January and May 1943, Bomber Command would drop 5,429 tons of high explosive and 3,704 tons of incendiary bombs on the Biscay ports – but the resulting damage would be insufficient.[1] German bombing of Britain had lessened – yet hardly one 24-hour period would go by without at least one raid somewhere in Britain, and sudden tragedy would still strike; Herbert Morrison, Home Secretary, would tell the War Cabinet on 20 January that a bomb landing on a Catford school earlier in the day had killed at least 37 children.[2] People, politicians and service chiefs – all were weary. Eden had written in his diary on 26 December: 'Tired. There is always a reaction after these long periods of work and strain, and the spring seems to uncoil more and more.' Brooke's diary reflected a mixture of exhaustion and hope. 'Age or exhaustion will force me to relinquish the job before another year is finished. It has been quite the hardest year of my life, but a wonderful one in some ways.... The PM was desperately trying at times, but

with his wonderful qualities it is easy to forgive him all.…
And now, at least the tide has begun to turn a little.'[3]
Churchill, Eden, Brooke and the others would need all the
strength which hope could give them: 1943 would be the
most physically wearying of all. The year would be one of
conferences – Casablanca, Washington, Quebec, Moscow,
Cairo, Tehran. Churchill, in his 69th year, would be called
upon to travel over 40,000 miles.

The new year began with the same subject predominant
which had closed the old: French affairs. On 2 January,
Churchill sought to reassure Eisenhower over Macmillan's
appointment: 'Although not formally a member of your
staff he fully accepts your supreme authority throughout the
theatre and has no thought but to be of service to you.'[4]
On the same day Macmillan arrived in Algiers, and learnt
to his dismay that Eisenhower was extremely annoyed
because neither Washington or London had officially informed him of Macmillan's appointment in the first place. In
fact the future Prime Minister and future President soon
struck up a firm and valuable friendship. But the other,
greater point at issue with regard to the French still remained,
and also on 2 January Roosevelt cabled Churchill with an
uncompromising statement of the US position. 'The people
of France will settle their own affairs after we have won
the war. Until then we can deal with local Frenchmen on a
local basis wherever our armies occupy local French territory.'[5] This piecemeal policy clashed strongly with the
British view: full support had been given to de Gaulle,
representing the best chance of unifying French strength,
although the Foreign Office agreed that co-operation between
de Gaulle and Giraud remained essential. Eden therefore
instructed Halifax during the day that Britain now proposed
the establishment in Algeria of a single authority which
would combine de Gaulle's French National Committee in
London with Giraud's local administration; this authority
would be recognized not as a provisional government –
which would be usurping the right of the French people to
choose their own – but only as a *de facto* administration until

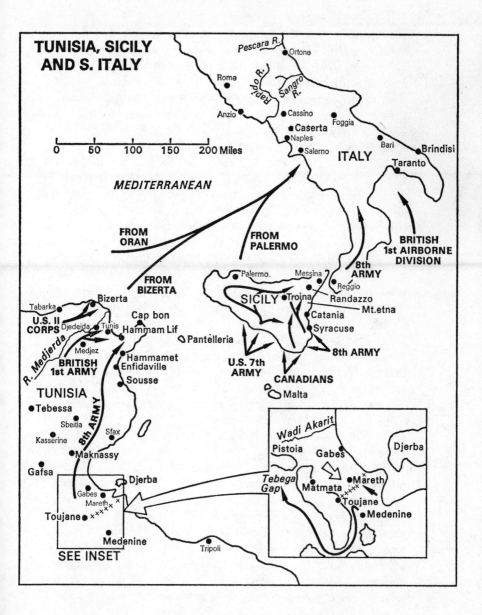

TUNISIA, SICILY AND S. ITALY

Pescara R.
Ortone
Rome
Rapido R.
Sangro R.
Anzio
Cassino
Foggia
Caserta
Naples
Bari
Brindisi
Salerno
ITALY
Taranto

0   50   100   150   200 Miles

MEDITERRANEAN

FROM ORAN

FROM PALERMO

Palermo.
Messina
8th ARMY
Reggio
Randazzo
Mt.etna

FROM BIZERTA

SICILY
Troina
Catania
Syracuse

BRITISH 1st AIRBORNE DIVISION

Tabarka
Bizerta
U.S. II CORPS
Djedeida
Tunis
Cap bon
Hammam Lif
Pantelleria

R. Medjerda
Medjez
BRITISH 1st ARMY
Hammamet
Enfidaville
Sousse

U.S. 7th ARMY
CANADIANS
8th ARMY
Malta

TUNISIA
Tebessa
Sbeitla
Kasserine
Sfax
8th ARMY
Maknassy
Gafsa
Djerba
Gabes
Mareth
x x x x
Toujane
x x x x x
Medenine
Tripoli

SEE INSET

Wadi Akarit
Pistoia
Gabes
Djerba
Tebega Gap
Matmata
Mareth
x x x x
Toujane
Medenine

the establishment of a French-elected Government.[6]

Cordell Hull completely disagreed with such a scheme: the attempted organization of a central French authority would lead to political squabbling and manoeuvring which would hamper the French military effort; the US Secretary continued to complain vigorously over British support for de Gaulle, and over the latter's actions. On this Saturday the French leader gave a broadcast and issued a statement, ascribing North African confusion to the lack of his Committee's representation. Hull angrily declared that de Gaulle had made 'a wholly unjustified attack on the United States Government'. Britain, it seemed, had done nothing to stop him. In fact, Cadogan had spent most of the day unsuccessfully endeavouring to make the Frenchman change his mind over the announcement; Cadogan wrote in his diary on Sunday, 3 January: 'De G. won.... By that, he's probably done for himself.'[7] An unsettling report of the situation in North Africa was now given to the COS by Brigadier Jacob, of Ismay's staff, just returned from a visit to the area. At a meeting with the COS on Monday morning, 4 January, Jacob confirmed Eisenhower's assessment that rains would prevent operations in the north. 'Further south the ground was more favourable and an alternative plan had therefore been worked out, which aimed at cutting the Axis communications between Tunis and Tripoli.... We should be able to reach this objective (Sfax). Whether we could maintain a force there was more doubtful, but if 200 tons a day could be brought in by sea from the Middle East, it should be possible.'[8] Later in the day, at 6 p.m., the War Cabinet were informed that although the dispositions of British troops in Tunisia remained unchanged, lines of communication and supply were being strengthened; Ministers were also informed that the 8th Army was continuing to close up on Rommel's forces.[9] But next day, 5 January, came a depressing signal from Alexander in Cairo: 'Administrative situation of 8th Army makes it impossible for its main body to move forward before night 14/15 January.'[10] Disappointed by this news of the eastern threat to the German forces in North Africa, Brooke returned to criticism of Eisenhower's

schemes for Tunisia in the west. The CIGS told the COS at
their evening meeting that he remained apprehensive, since
the two attacks which Eisenhower contemplated in the north
and further south, were not co-ordinated. 'It should be possible
to speed up the attack in the north and to make it coincide
with that from the south and with pressure from the 8th
Army.'[11]

Also on 5 January the British Ambassador at Washington
saw Hull and attempted to explain how the Foreign Office
had tried to stop de Gaulle's broadcast; Lord Halifax received
a stern reply. 'It is reported here,' declared Hull, 'that the
entire British press and radio and many British leaders of
public thought devoted the better part of two days following
de Gaulle's broadcast to shouting their approval.... The
impression spreading in the United States, that Britain is
supporting de Gaulle in his movement for political prefer-
ment at the expense of the prosecution of the African battle,
would soon create real differences between our two
countries.'[12] Yet also on the 5th de Gaulle received a reply
to a second proposal made to Giraud for a meeting: Giraud
claimed lack of free time before the end of the month. Eden
read Halifax's report of his talk with Hull, and hastened to
pacify the US Secretary: Campbell called on Hull on the 7th
with a memorandum from the Prime Minister and Foreign
Secretary which insisted they could do no more in their
attempt to persuade newspapers not to aggravate matters; to
go further would be to threaten the freedom of Parliament
and Press. Hull retorted: 'Where there is a plain and palp-
able interference with the prosecution of the North African
campaign by pure brazen politics, it is high time, in my
opinion, that this should receive the serious attention of the
British Government.'[13]

On the same day, 7 January, another Washington discussion took place which indicated that allied agreement in
another sphere – future strategy – might be more easily
reached than previously feared. Like the British planners,
US staff officers had produced pessimistic calculations over
the feasibility of 'Round-up' in 1943; and at a White House
meeting on this Thursday, General Marshall admitted 'there

was not a united front on that subject'. Ironically, this same conference saw the introduction of a subject which was to prove controversial for both the Americans and British: the idea that the allies should demand unconditional surrender from Axis powers. Roosevelt told the US COS that he believed such a policy should be adopted, and the subject would be thrust into prominence at the close of the Casablanca conference. Preparations for this summit now approached completion: Churchill would leave for North Africa on the 12th. Meanwhile, on the 8th, Stalin's reasons for not being able to leave Russia became fully apparent – a climax had been reached at Stalingrad. The Soviet offensive had encircled the 6th German Army under von Paulus; an attempt to break through by Manstein in December had driven a bloody 40-mile dent into the Soviet line, but the desperate German thrust had been beaten back 50 miles from Stalingrad. Germans in the city suffered appalling hardship: starvation, terrible cold, typhus. Now, on 8 January, von Paulus rejected an ultimatum to surrender; the last phase began on the 9th. Also on the 9th, Churchill devoted attention to the perpetual complications surrounding despatch of convoys to help Russia. Arctic sailings had been disrupted by the needs for 'Torch' and further shipping shortages had led to an Admiralty decision to reduce subsequent convoys. News of these reductions leaked to Maisky, Soviet Ambassador, who complained bitterly to Eden. On the 9th Churchill sent an angry minute to the Foreign Secretary: 'Maisky should be told that I am getting to the end of my tether with these Russian naggings, and that it is not the slightest use trying to knock me about any more.'[14] The same problem remained constant: too many tasks, too few resources, too little time to gather strength. On 11 January War Cabinet Ministers were told: 'In Tripolitania, where the weather was bad, we had been building up our resources.... Tunisia: both sides were engaged in building up their forces.' Ministers were also informed that 'the resistance of the 6th German Army at Stalingrad was becoming weaker'.[15]

Next day, Tuesday 12 January, Churchill left by air for North Africa in an attempt to settle the spread of these resources for the forthcoming year. While the Prime Minister flew south, British troops in the desert received stirring orders from Montgomery; the offensive against Rommel would be launched in three days' time. Monty declared: *'The 8th Army is going to Tripoli....* Nothing has stopped us since the Battle of Alamein began on 23 October 1942. Nothing will stop us now....'[16] Churchill and the COS reached the Casablanca suburb of Anfa early on 13 January; Eisenhower would fly in from Algiers; the US COS arrived with their advisers, and Roosevelt would reach the rendezvous the following day. Churchill strode happily on the beach, paddling in the foam and admiring the massive rollers crashing in from the Atlantic – the same surf which had bedevilled 'Torch' landings at Casablanca three months before. Brooke and his colleagues plunged straight into work; and a COS meeting at 4.30 on the 13th heard a report from Dill which confirmed the Anglo-American divergences of opinion on fundamental strategy. Dill, who had flown in with the Americans, gave no indication that Marshall and his colleagues might be hesitant over their European policy – as revealed by the US Chief at the Roosevelt conference on the 7th; instead, the opening of the Anglo-American COS talks next day could be expected to result in considerable dissension. Dill warned that the Americans suspected Britain to be lukewarm over the Pacific campaign; once Germany had been defeated, they believed, Britain would be unlikely to co-operate with much enthusiasm in the final stages of the Japanese war. Marshall had strong reservations about continuing operations in the Mediterranean, claimed Dill, especially when these could be countered by a German thrust through Spain, and Marshall instead sought an initial operation against France in 1943 to prepare the way for a larger offensive in 1944.[17] At 6 p.m. the COS met Churchill for further talks, and this meeting seemingly secured approval for Brooke's preference of Sicily, rather than Sardinia, as the next Mediterranean target. Brooke retired to his room to prepare his address to the first Combined Chiefs of Staff session scheduled for 10.30 the following morning. And when he wrote his paper Brooke bore in mind instructions given by

Churchill at the evening conference: no attempt should be made to hurry the CCS talks or force agreement; instead the policy should be 'the dripping of water on a stone'. Churchill would adopt this method with Roosevelt.[18] The strategy, similar to that successfully adopted by the British in securing reluctant US approval for 'Torch' the previous year, would be helped by the fact that the CCS meetings would follow no set programme; instead discussions would be allowed to continue until everyone had gradually exhausted their views. And the British had one strong advantage in this marathon exercise: they came to Casablanca having reached firm and full agreement between themselves and with the Prime Minister; the Americans on the other hand, as Marshall had admitted on the 7th, lacked 'a united front'. Admiral King, unbending and tough, was inevitably preoccupied by the unremitting Pacific struggle, and was anxious to ensure that uncertainties in the West did not endanger his plans by upsetting or diverting resources: the Admiral was therefore more concerned with reaching firm agreement either for the Mediterranean or 'Round-up' rather than having prolonged confusion. General Arnold, head of the USAF, was more flexible than Marshall: he, like Portal, appreciated the value of air bases in the Mediterranean.

So on Thursday morning, 14 January, the British 'drip by drip' strategy began in an attempt to form unified allied planning. Marshall opened this first CCS meeting by discussing the allocation of resources between the West and the Far East, and suggested a proportion of 70 per cent for the former and 30 per cent for the war against Japan. Admiral King immediately complained that 'we were at present engaging only 15 per cent of our total resources against the Japanese.... This was not sufficient to prevent Japan consolidating herself and thereby presenting ultimately too difficult a problem.' Brooke suggested it would be wise to weigh up the enemy situation, and gave the British assessment. The Japanese were definitely on the defensive, while Germany continued to impose the greatest threat. 'The security of the US and the UK had always been basic factors in our strategy.' The CIGS believed maximum

effort should be directed against the German threat, especially
as 'Germany's situation was undoubtedly developing favourably from our point of view'. To gain full advantage, the
British COS felt 'we should first expand the bomber offensive
against the Axis to the maximum and operations in the
Mediterranean offered the best chance of compelling Germany to disperse her resources. With this end in view we
should take as our immediate objective the knocking out of
Italy. At the same time we should try and bring in Turkey
on our side. By these means we should give Germany no
respite at all in 1943 and we should give the best aid to
Russia.' He added: 'We must be in a position to take advantage of a crack in Germany in the late summer. There were
already indications of considerable German withdrawals from
France to the eastwards.' Brooke turned to the Far East,
expressing pessimism over the reconquest of Burma. 'Operations in the north of Burma presented very difficult logistic
problems owing to the absence of roads. The complete conquest of Burma was a much bigger problem, and naval
supremacy in the Bay of Bengal would be required for it.'
Portal described the air situation. 'The present state of the
German air force is critical.... Our greatest need is to force
the Germans to extend the use of their aircraft to as many
areas as possible and thus destroy and bleed them.' Marshall,
always full of vigorous ideas about Burma in order to help
China, took exception to Brooke's doubts: Burmese operations would weaken the Japanese defensive front, and the
Americans were therefore most anxious to undertake
'Ravenous' – a proposed advance into Upper Burma across
the Chindwin. By this time the morning session had almost
finished; Marshall had still to put forward his ideas for the
1943 strategy against Germany, and merely stated: 'The
US COS are concerned as to whether operations in the
Mediterranean area would bring advantages commensurate
with the risks involved.'[19]

The CCS assembled again at 2.30 p.m. Brooke continued
the same tactics, keeping discussion concentrated as far as
possible on the Far East – Jacob wrote in his diary that the
British COS 'felt that "Uncle Ernie" (King) would take a

less jaundiced view of the rest of the world if he had been able to shoot his line'.[20] Brooke therefore asked for King's views, and the Admiral obliged at great length, repeating his complaint that only 15 per cent of the total war effort was being applied to Japan. Brooke and Portal continued to ask detailed questions; Marshall, King and Arnold provided the answers. Debate took place on 'Ravenous' and on 'Anakim' – a seaborne assault on Rangoon. Brooke argued that 'it would be well worth while taking a risk on "Ravenous" since it would not cut across the main effort against Germany, whereas "Anakim" would'. The CCS finally agreed to ask the Combined Planners to report on minimum holding operations required in the Pacific in 1943.[21]

Roosevelt had arrived during the afternoon, and all leading participants dined together that evening. Eastwards, over troubled North Africa, the British 8th Army had moved into battle positions. Against some 700 British tanks, Rommel could only scratch together 91 – two-thirds of them Italian. Next day, 15 January, Montgomery's attack began; once again Rommel could only retreat, and Tripoli now lay just over the horizon. While 8th Army tanks pressed forward across the desert and along the coast on this Friday morning, the British CIGS took a pre-breakfast stroll along the Casablanca shore. 'Delightful hour and a half,' wrote Brooke, the devout ornithologist, 'during which we saw goldfinch, stonechat, warblers of all sorts, white wagtail and several kinds of waders....'[22] Thus fortified, Brooke began his second day of the summit talks. The British COS gave Churchill details of the previous day's discussion, then sat down with the Americans for the third CCS session, starting at 2.30 p.m. The conference heard a report from Eisenhower on the North African situation, with the allied commander repeating his plans for an attack on Sfax, scheduled for 24 January; he was 'faced with the dilemma of either allowing the troops in the north to deteriorate by remaining inactive in the mud, or suffering some losses to them through keeping them more active. In his opinion the latter was the less of two evils.' Brooke remained unconvinced, and the subject for discussion reverted to strategic planning for 1943. Two broad policies

were possible, declared Brooke. First, the Mediterranean
theatre could be closed down immediately after the North
African coast had been cleared and the Mediterranean sea
routes had been opened, devoting all effort to 'Bolero'. The
other broad possibility would be to maintain Mediterranean
activity while building up a maximum air offensive against
Germany, to undertake a comparatively small operation such
as seizing the Cherbourg Peninsula, and to concentrate
greater effort in the Mediterranean. 'If Italy could be knocked
out, Germany would be involved in large new commitments
... our best policy would be to threaten Germany everywhere in the Mediterranean....' For the moment the
Americans contented themselves by saying Germany might
move into Spain to sever communication lines at Gibraltar.
The CCS then argued over the relative merits of Sicily or
Sardinia as a target: Brooke still preferred the former, but
other CCS members pointed out that an attack on this island
would require more resources and would take longer to
prepare.[23]

Churchill had meanwhile been employing gentle persuasion upon Roosevelt. Then, at 5.30 p.m., the CCS, Eisenhower,
Churchill and Roosevelt met for the first plenary meeting of
the conference. Also attending was Alexander, who had just
flown from Cairo – and who created a very favourable impression on Roosevelt with his 'easy smiling grace' and 'con-
tagious confidence'.[24] Alexander was, of course, a strong
supporter of the Mediterranean strategy. And at this Friday
evening meeting, the President gave a definite impression of
favouring this line of action.[25] Nevertheless, Brooke continued to worry over Eisenhower's immediate plans for the
Sfax thrust, and these anxieties were fully expressed at a
60-minute conference next morning, 16 January, attended
by Eisenhower, Alexander and Brooke. Rommel's forces were
still falling back before the 8th Army; Alexander declared
Tripoli would probably be taken within 11 days, but added
that no further advance would be possible until Tripoli port
had been cleared – and this might take up to six months.
Rommel would therefore be allowed breathing space to react
against a US move upon Sfax. Brooke feared that the various

allied attacks could be dealt with and defeated in detail; nor could the 8th Army be in a position to take advantage of any US success. After more discussion Brooke hurried to the 10.30 a.m. CCS session – and he had the pleasure of starting proceedings by saying Eisenhower had agreed to postpone the Sfax offensive until it could be co-ordinated with the renewed advance by 8th Army from the south.

Discussion returned to the central issue. Brooke repeated the main Mediterranean arguments: with the limited ground forces available, the allies would be unable to impose a sufficient threat in northern France for the removal of much German air power from the Russian front; operations in northern France could not be undertaken until very late in the summer, when the weather would be deteriorating; 'since therefore we cannot go into the Continent in force until Germany weakens, we should try to make the Germans disperse their forces as much as possible'; forces must however continue to be built up in Britain ready for a suitable invasion opportunity. Arnold voiced American disappointment. 'It looked very much as if no Continental operations on any scale were in prospect before the spring of 1944'; to which Brooke could only reply: 'We should definitely count on re-entering the Continent in 1944 on a large scale.' After further restrained discussion the Committee agreed to direct the Combined Planners to give further examination to the British plan for an attack on Sicily.[26] Despite the long hours of discussion the Americans therefore still declined to enter a definite commitment; moreover, Marshall seemed to be tending towards another, dangerous attitude: if 'Round-up' had to be ruled out in 1943, greater priority should be given to the Pacific, not the Mediterranean. Brooke began to feel the strain. 'It is a slow and tiring business which requires a lot of patience,' he wrote in his diary. But he added: 'I think we are beginning to make some progress and that they are getting interested.'[27]

Churchill had been conferring with Roosevelt on the other delicate issue – French representation. And on the 16th Roosevelt agreed with the Prime Minister's suggestion that the two French leaders should come to Casablanca; Eisen-

hower, returning to Algiers, would issue an invitation to
Giraud; Churchill cabled Eden, asking the Foreign Secretary
to hand de Gaulle this message: 'I shall be very glad if you
would come to join me here by first available plane, which
we shall provide, as it is in my power to bring about an
unassailable meeting between you and General Giraud under
conditions of complete secrecy and with the best of prospects
... Giraud will be here on Sunday (17 January), and I hope
weather permitting you to arrive Monday.' The Prime
Minister told Eden not to mention Roosevelt's presence at
Casablanca.[28] Eden arranged to see de Gaulle at noon the
following day, Sunday. In Casablanca, Churchill and
Roosevelt discussed possible terms for a French agreement:
these, at the President's wish, did not include the immediate
fusion between de Gaulle's National Committee and Giraud's
administration, as the Foreign Office had proposed, but were
limited to a reconstruction of each of the two bodies to
include representatives of each.[29]

The CCS met again at 10.30 a.m. next day, the 17th, and
found themselves in deadlock – this time over Far East affairs.
The British insisted operation 'Anakim' against Rangoon
would be impossible during the dry season of 1943/44,
owing to lack of naval cover and the time required to assemble
landing craft. Marshall, conscious of the need to help China,
expressed his concern over the delay. The meeting revealed
acute differences of opinion between British and American
staff planners over the Burma question as a whole, and the
CCS adjourned to allow separate consultations with their
staffs. The British COS therefore met their planners in the
afternoon, and found the main difficulty centred on the
apparent US belief that Japan should now be defeated before
Germany – yet this cut right across the fundamental assumption that Germany must be considered the primary enemy.
As Brooke complained in his diary: 'A desperate day. We
are further from obtaining agreement than we ever were.'[30]

In London, Cadogan's diary entry for this Sunday expressed
similar despair. 'He (de Gaulle) is a species of mule; he refuses
to go.' Eden described his noon clash with the French general
in a telegram to Casablanca. De Gaulle had been given

Churchill's message to read. 'When he had finished he expressed no pleasure. He had wanted to meet Giraud after Darlan's assassination but Giraud did not agree. Time was not now so opportune, and he was reluctant to meet Giraud under auspices of Allies, who might press him to compromise. ... There were only two alternatives, Fighting France and Vichy. Giraud, who tried to balance between them, held no position at all. We made a mistake in going into North Africa without de G. We were in difficulties now and asking him to come and help.... He said he would meet Giraud next week at Fort Lamy, alone.' At 5 p.m., continued Eden, de Gaulle had returned with a message to Churchill, which declared: 'I have telegraphed several times to General Giraud since Christmas, urging him to meet me. Although the situation has moved since Christmas in a direction which now renders an understanding less easy, I will gladly meet Giraud in French territory anywhere he likes and as soon as he likes.... Allow me to say, however, that the atmosphere ... of an exalted Allied forum around Giraud-de Gaulle conversations, as well as the suddenness with which those conversations have been proposed to me, did not seem to me to be best for an effective agreement.' This telegram reached Casablanca during the night of the 17th/18th. Roosevelt cabled Hull early next day. 'We produced the bridegroom, General Giraud, who co-operated very nicely on the proposed nuptials and was prepared to go through with it on our terms, I am sure. Our friends, however, could not produce de Gaulle, the temperamental bride. She has become quite high-hat about the whole affair and doesn't wish to see either of us, and shows no intention of getting into bed with Giraud....'[31] Macmillan suggested Giraud should invite de Gaulle himself – Giraud had, after all, refused de Gaulle's previous requests, but Churchill decided to send Eden another telegram. The Foreign Secretary was meanwhile reporting to the War Cabinet during this Monday morning; he had felt 'some difficulty' over Churchill's statement that de Gaulle should not be told of Roosevelt's presence at Casablanca, and had dropped some broad hints. But he claimed de Gaulle was seeking excuses not to go. 'He seemed to have no consideration for the general advantage of the meeting to the Allies. It was difficult to escape the view that he was looking forward to a state of affairs in which he would be virtual dictator of France after the war.' The War Cabinet agreed 'it must be recognized that although none of the other French leaders had a prestige and position comparable with that held by de Gaulle, if General de Gaulle adhered to his present attitude it would be impossible for us to continue our present relationship with him'.[32]

The Combined Chiefs of Staff had meanwhile reached the stickiest point in their strategic debate. 'A very heated CCS meeting,' commented Brooke, 'at which we seemed to be making no progress. King still evidently wrapped up in the war in the Pacific at the expense of everything else.' This session, from 10.30 a.m. to 1 p.m. on 18 January, agreed plans and preparations for 'Anakim' in 1943 should be made, but the actual decision to mount the operation would be delayed until summer. Brooke then stressed the basic question: who should be defeated first, Germany or Japan? Marshall immediately launched into attack: the British wanted to delay 'Round-up', yet wanted to continue the build-up of troops to the UK intended for this cross-Channel invasion; the minutes continued: 'He inferred that the British COS would prefer to maintain such a force in the UK, dormant and awaiting an opportunity, rather than having it utilized in a sustained attack elsewhere. The US COS knew that they can use these forces effectively in the Pacific theatre.' Brooke declared: 'The British COS believed that the defeat of Japan first is impossible and that if we attempt to do so we shall lose the war.' If defeat of Germany came first, 'the immediate question is whether to attempt to do so by the invasion of northern France or to exploit our success in North Africa. The British COS considered that an all-out Mediterranean effort is best but it must be "all-out".' Marshall denied any disagreement over the concept of defeating Germany first. 'On the other hand it is the view of the US COS that the war should be ended as quickly as possible.' He advocated an attack on the Continent, but opposed immobilizing a large force in the UK, and remained anxious lest the allies were committed to 'interminable' Mediterranean operations. King claimed: 'We had on many occasions been close to a disaster in the Pacific.' And so the argument continued.[33] Brooke left the morning meeting and walked miserably to his room. 'It's no use,' he despaired to Dill. 'We shall never get agreement with them.' The CIGS insisted he would not move an inch from the declared British view. 'Oh yes you will,' retorted Dill. 'You know ... you cannot bring the unsolved problem up to the Prime Minister and the President. You know as well as I do what a mess they would make of it.'[34] Prompted by this chilling thought, Brooke agreed Dill should have a quiet discussion with his friend Marshall, but while the CIGS and Dill still sat in Brooke's bedroom, Portal entered with a proposed draft agreement which he and his colleague Slessor had been working on during this lunch-break. This, similar to views already expressed by Dill, contained a compromise statement: 'Operations in the Pacific and Far East shall continue with the forces allocated with the object of maintaining pressure on Japan, retaining the initiative and attaining a position of readiness for the full-scale offensive against Japan ... as soon as Germany is defeated. These operations must be kept within such limits as will not, in the opinion of the CCS, prejudice the capacity of the United Nations to take any opportunity that may present itself for the decisive defeat of Germany in 1943.'[35] Brooke and Portal decided to adopt the document and took it the next CCS meeting, starting at 3 p.m., without having had time to consult the third COS member, Pound.

And the new document found immediate favour with the Americans. 'I could hardly believe our luck,' commented Brooke.[36] During the evening the CCS attended a meeting with Roosevelt and Churchill, when Marshall and Brooke each made policy statements acceptable to the other. Allied unity had suddenly been restored: with this compromise on the correct attitude towards the Pacific went tacit American agreement that 'Round-up' must be considered impossible for 1943 under existing circumstances, but that 'Bolero' should be continued, and meanwhile the Mediterranean should receive priority.

De Gaulle still remained to be wooed. At 5 p.m. the War
Cabinet met in London to discuss the situation; before them
lay a telegram from Churchill, dispatched the previous day
after his talks with Macmillan, and containing a fresh message to be given by Eden to de Gaulle. The Prime Minister
allowed the War Cabinet to make any changes in the text
of the message 'so long as its seriousness was not impaired'.
Ministers made one or two alterations 'bearing in mind that
if de Gaulle maintained his refusal ... the Prime Minister's
message would almost certainly have to be published in due
course'. The note, described by Cadogan as 'pretty hot',
declared: 'I am authorized to say that the invitation to come
here was from the President of the United States of America
as well as from me. I have not yet told Giraud, who ... is
waiting here, of your refusal. The consequences of it, if persisted in, will, in my opinion, be gravely prejudicial to the
Fighting French movement.... The fact that you have
refused to come to the meeting proposed will in my opinion,
be almost universally censured by public opinion. There can,
of course, be no question of your being invited to visit the
US in the near future if you reject the President's invitation
now. My attempt to bridge the differences which have existed
between your movement and the US will have dismally failed
as a result of your refusal, and I should certainly not be able
to renew my exertions in this direction while you remain the
leader of the movement. The door is closed....'[37] Eden sent
the note to de Gaulle and waited for a reply during the 20th;
in Casablanca, Macmillan again urged an irate Churchill that
Giraud should invite de Gaulle, but the Prime Minister
once more turned the suggestion down – the Foreign Office
later thought this to have been unfortunate.[38]

The CCS, meeting at 10 a.m. on the 20th and again at
2.30 p.m., made excellent progress. Agreement was reached
on the difficult question of the command system in North
Africa after the meeting of the 8th and 1st armies from the
east and west. The CCS decided to appoint Eisenhower as
Supreme Commander, with Alexander his deputy. Tedder
would be supreme Air Commander. The system suited
Brooke: his doubts over Eisenhower's military ability were

to some extent removed by having him elevated to Supreme Commander position and thus dealing with political and inter-allied problems, while Alexander, as his deputy, would deal with the primarily military situations.[39] At the afternoon session the CCS turned to a memorandum by the British Planners on 'Husky' – the attack on Sicily – and this received US support.[40] 'The back of the work here is broken,' wrote Brooke, 'and thank God for it! It has been one of the most difficult tasks I have had to do.... They are difficult, though charming, people to work with.'

And de Gaulle had decided with bad grace to show co-operation. Eden gave his report to the War Cabinet at 10 Downing Street at 5.30 p.m. The General had been to see him 30 minutes before. 'He had been rather grudging but had said that in the circumstances he could not refuse the invitation.' Eden had already signalled Churchill and had included a starchy message from de Gaulle: 'Until now the whole Allied enterprise in North Africa has been decided, prepared and executed without any official participation by Fighting French.... Now President Roosevelt and yourself ask me to take part on the spur of the moment in consultations on the subject (of North Africa), consultations of which I am unaware, both of the programme and of the conditions, and which you will bring me to discuss with you at short notice, problems which involve in all respects the future of the French Empire and that of France.' De Gaulle's remarks had certain justification; British Ministers could find no quarrel with the content of the message, and they refrained from further discussion of the French at this 5.30 meeting. Instead, they considered a long telegram from Churchill, dispatched earlier in the day, which described the CCS progress. The Prime Minister had then added a paragraph which was soon to be connected with a new, unexpected controversy. 'I shall be glad to know what the War Cabinet think of our inclusion in this (Press) statement (of) a declaration of the firm intention of the US and the British Empire to continuing the war relentlessly until we have brought about the "unconditional surrender" of Germany and Japan. The omission of Italy would be to encourage a break up there. The Presi-

dent liked this idea.' Ministers expressed no objection to the
'unconditional surrender' declaration in principle, but
thought that 'the omission of Italy was liable to be mis-
interpreted in, for example, the Balkans. Generally, the War
Cabinet thought that it was a mistake, at any rate at this
stage, to make any distinction between the three partners
in the Axis.' A telegram to this effect was sent after the
meeting.[41]

This long War Cabinet session then dealt with another
difficult item. Churchill had sent a further signal saying the
question of Turkey had been raised with Roosevelt. 'It was
agreed that we play the hand in Turkey, whether in munitions
or diplomacy, the Americans taking the lead in China and
of course in French North Africa.' Churchill proposed to
fly to Cairo after a short rest at Marrakesh, and he then
wished to take advantage of the 'playing the hand' bargain.
'Is not this the opportunity and the moment for me to get
into direct touch with the Turks?' He wished to meet Turkish
leaders 'at any suitable place, possibly Cyprus'. Eden told the
War Cabinet that he thoroughly disagreed with the idea of an
invitation to meet the Turks; the Foreign Secretary believed
Churchill would merely suffer a rebuff which would be diplomatically damaging. Other Ministers objected to Churchill
flying to Cairo. 'They doubted whether there were any
matters of sufficient importance in Cairo to justify the Prime
Minister incurring the risks of the further flights.' Attlee
and Eden therefore drafted a signal mentioning these points
and tactfully stating: 'Parliament and public would wish
to welcome you back and to hear from you as soon as
possible what you are able to tell them of meeting with
President. We think it important not to leave the field to
the President alone.'[42]

News of de Gaulle's acquiescence reached Casablanca at
midnight on the 20th; next morning Churchill learnt that bad
weather had postponed de Gaulle's flight, and the French
General did not arrive until the following day, 22 January.
Meanwhile the CCS continued to make good progress, discussing on the 21st the final report to be made to Roosevelt
and Churchill. Then, in the evening, Brooke received a stiff

setback: he heard at a British COS meeting that the British Joint Planners now favoured Sardinia instead of Sicily as the next target, and yet, as Brooke commented: 'All my arguments with Marshall had been based on the invasion of Sicily and I had obtained his agreement.' Mountbatten also supported Sardinia rather than Sicily, and Brooke believed Portal and Ismay were beginning to waver. 'I had a 3-hour hammer and tongs battle to keep the team together.' The CIGS refused to return to the CCS with an admission that the British had changed their minds, and anyway he disagreed with the opinion that Sardinia would be better than Sicily.[43] Brooke had his way: the CCS confirmed next morning, Friday, 22 January, that Sicily would be the target: 'Husky' would be launched in the summer. The afternoon session on the Friday approved a paper by the Combined Planners on the invasion of the Continent, recognizing that any large-scale invasion in 1943 against unbroken opposition was out of the question, although limited operations might be feasible; plans should nevertheless be made to seize a bridgehead in 1943, with these contingency preparations designed to take advantage of an unexpected favourable situation; the allies should prepare for 'an invasion in force' in 1944. The CCS agreed a British officer should start work on the initial planning – this post, Chief of Staff to the Supreme Allied Commander, or COSSAC, would be filled by Lieutenant-General F. E. Morgan.[44]

Churchill had received the telegram containing War Cabinet disapproval of his proposed trip to Cairo and of his plans to meet the Turks. He cabled regretting this decision, but apparently accepting it. Two days later this meek submission would switch to true Churchillian obstinacy. By then the Prime Minister had been considerably ruffled: at midday on 22 January de Gaulle arrived and with him came renewed depression and upset. The flight had done nothing to soothe the disgruntled General; now he seemed determined to wreck any chance of agreement with Giraud. He began discussions during the afternoon of the 22nd with a violent diatribe against Darlan and his successors, while Giraud listened in shocked astonishment; de Gaulle insisted upon some kind of

'Political Committee' which could develop into a French
Government. He himself would be the political leader;
Giraud could be commander of the Liberation Army. But
a French Provisional Government remained anathema to
Roosevelt and the State Department; yet neither the President
nor Churchill could shake de Gaulle, despite mounting
threats from the Prime Minister. De Gaulle recognized Giraud
as being anti-German – but not anti-Vichy. Macmillan and
his US counterpart Robert Murphy therefore spent hours
drafting one possible agreement after another, having them
approved by Roosevelt and Churchill, and having them rejected by de Gaulle. 'It was typical of Giraud,' wrote Macmillan, 'who had no political sense or interests in larger
issues, that he accepted each of them in turn without a
murmur.'[45] And so the dance continued for the next two
days, with Churchill becoming increasingly furious and
tending towards complete rejection of the would-be French
supremo. 'His country has given up fighting,' exclaimed the
Prime Minister. 'He himself is a refugee, and if we turn
him down he's finished. Well, just look at him! Look at him!
He might be Stalin.' On 23 January Churchill reported events
to the War Cabinet. 'I had a long talk with de Gaulle ... and
told him plainly that ... it was the duty of any Frenchman
who became an obstacle to French unity, or to the relations
between the various French sections and the two Great Allies,
to efface himself, and that certainly no individual would be
allowed to obstruct the necessary forward march of the war.
... The President, whom he saw after dinner, was much more
kindly and paternal.... De Gaulle did not make a bad
impression, though the President was somewhat concerned
at the spiritual look which he sometimes had in his eye.'[46]

Leading troops of the 8th Army filed into Tripoli at 4
a.m. on Saturday, 23 January, exactly three months since the
beginning of Alamein. Rommel prepared his forces for a
defensive battle along the old French frontier position at
Mareth, designed originally to cover Tunisia against an
Italian attack from the west. The final fight for Tunisia and
North Africa could soon begin. The CCS, meeting at 10
a.m. this Saturday, continued talks on the next stage of the

war. The Committee approved British proposals for limited cross-Channel operations in 1943, and put final touches to their report to the President and the Prime Minister. This report was presented at 5.30 p.m.; Roosevelt and Churchill made some suggestions which were incorporated into the CCS document at a final meeting beginning at 9.30 p.m. The last session closed with mutual congratulations; Admiral King, whose preference for the Pacific had complicated the opening stages, described the conference as 'the biggest step forward to the winning of the war'.[47] Thus British and American thoughts were now apparently unified in a clear document which gave no indication of the turmoil behind its creation. The report recorded the CCS conclusion 'to attack Sicily in 1943 with the favourable July moon as the target date'; plans and preparations would be made for three types of amphibious operations across the Channel in 1943: '(i) Raids with the primary object of provoking air battles.... (ii) Operations with the object of seizing and holding a bridgehead and, if the state of German morale and resources permit, of rigorously exploiting successes; (iii) A return to the Continent to take advantage of German disintegration.' The paper listed objectives in the Pacific and operations in support of China; the latter would include a limited advance from Assam subsequent to the current operations aimed at the capture of Akyab, and operation 'Anakim' with a provisional date of 15 November 1943.[48]

The de Gaulle–Giraud issue had still to be settled. After working throughout the night of 23/24 January, Macmillan and Murphy realized agreement must be considered impossible, and yet some piece of paper, however flimsy, had to be signed by both Frenchmen or the confrontation would clearly have been a complete catastrophe. Macmillan and Murphy were still desperately trying to find a solution when Roosevelt and Churchill started their press conference on the morning of Sunday, 24 January – until this moment the presence of the American and British leaders at Casablanca had been a well-kept secret. And, at the moment of this dramatic revelation, when the President and Prime Minister strode into the sunlit garden to meet the press, Macmillan and Murphy pushed de Gaulle and Giraud into two extra chairs alongside Roosevelt and Churchill. The Frenchmen were then obliged to shake hands, with a waxwork pose, and the cameras clicked. A shot-gun wedding had been performed. And afterwards, when Roosevelt and Churchill had left the conference camp, the two Frenchmen were prevailed upon to issue a terse joint statement. 'We have met. We have talked. We have registered our entire agreement. The end to be achieved, which is the liberation of France and the triumph of human liberties by total defeat of the enemy ... will be attained by the union in war of all Frenchmen.' Such brevity had one great advantage – the erroneous impression was inevitably given of much more lying behind the empty words. Disputes would continue between de Gaulle and Giraud, between the British and Americans over the French – and between the British and de Gaulle: War Cabinet Ministers were told by Churchill on 3 March that de Gaulle had asked for facilities to visit Free French troops in North Africa; 'when it had been suggested to him informally ... that this was not a suitable moment to make this journey, he had asked whether he was to regard himself as a prisoner'; the War Cabinet agreed 'it would be necessary to take special security measures to ensure that he did not leave the country'.[49]

The Casablanca press conference on 24 January had an importance far beyond the theatrical French affair. Roosevelt concluded his remarks with a momentous announcement: 'The elimination of German, Japanese and Italian war power means the unconditional surrender by Germany, Japan and Italy.' The demand for 'unconditional surrender' would henceforth be a basic war aim. The enemy would be given no quarter; they would have no diplomatic avenues of escape from military destruction. No terms would be offered. And henceforth the argument would burst open as to whether this drastic demand prolonged fighting, and over the question, in Michael Howard's words, 'whether total victory is necessarily the surest foundation for a lasting peace'.[50] Roosevelt said later that the phrase slipped out on the spur of the moment.[51] Yet the phrase appears in the notes from which he spoke, and the subject had been discussed both at the White House and at Casablanca. Bevin, future Foreign Secretary, told the House of Commons on 21 July 1949, that this policy had aggravated difficulties in rebuilding Germany after the war, and he claimed that neither he nor the War Cabinet had been consulted at the time. The War Cabinet minutes for 20 January 1943, show this to be untrue; nor did Bevin or any other Minister record any other objection to the proposal than to disagree with the omission of Italy – and Roosevelt had included Italy in his announcement. Churchill was clearly surprised by Roosevelt's sudden declaration, but he immediately endorsed the President's remarks. And a number of short-term advantages could perhaps be gained from a declaration of this drastic policy: public opinion demanded such a war aim; American suspicions might be lessened that Britain would be lukewarm in the war against Japan once Germany had been beaten; above all, Stalin's fear might be removed that the Western Allies would contemplate a compromise peace. Stalin now needed gentle handling: the Casablanca decisions would be extremely unpopular – no Second Front in 1943.

The mass exodus from Casablanca began. Churchill and Roosevelt drove 150 miles over the desert to Marrakesh; Brooke flew to this oasis during the afternoon, contemplating with pleasure two days of rest, one to be spent partridge shooting. The CIGS felt weary and sapped. Churchill still had enough strength to resurrect his proposed visit to Cairo and for a meeting with the Turks, and now began to bombard the War Cabinet. 'I trust that you (Eden) and my colleagues will give me strict latitude in my personal movements which I deem necessary to the public interests.' The War Cabinet, meeting on the 24th, remained adamant: Ministers were told of the difficulties of sending more equipment to the Turks, as Churchill wished, and the War Cabinet agreed that if Churchill's offer of a conference were refused by President Inönü, or if the meeting were to be held without achieving the desired results, the position would have been worsened. A telegram was sent mentioning these points; Churchill replied on the 25th: 'Neither the President or I are at all convinced by arguments put forward.... I ask most earnestly that telegram in question (the invitation to Inönü) should be sent.' The War Cabinet therefore met again at noon on the 25th, and succumbed to Churchill's pressure.[52] A telephone call summoned Brooke to Churchill's bedside: the confident Prime Minister, who had still to receive the War Cabinet's reluctant approval, had already decided to leave for Cairo that night, 25 January. Roosevelt left for home during the day; Churchill flew triumphantly over the Atlas mountains to Cairo, sending a gleeful note to Attlee and Eden: 'You can imagine how much I wish I were going to be with you tomorrow on the Bench, but duty calls...'[53] Brooke had been robbed of his partridge shooting.

Roosevelt and Churchill had agreed upon a telegram to Stalin, dispatched the following day and outlining the decisions taken 'with a view to achieving an early and decisive victory in the European theatre'. The signal laid stress on the bomber offensive from the UK against Germany, which by midsummer 'should be more than double its present strength', and added: 'We have no doubt our intensified and diversified bombing offensive, together with other operations which we are undertaking, will compel further withdrawals of German air and other forces from the Russian front.' Stalin would not be hoodwinked; on 30 January he requested more details: 'Taking your decisions with regard to Germany and settling the task to smash her in 1943 by way of a Second Front in Europe, I would be grateful to you for telling me what concrete operations and at what time they are envisaged.'[54]

Meanwhile, Churchill's mission to the Turks had been arranged. The War Cabinet met on the 27th at 12.15 p.m. to discuss telegrams from the Ambassador at Ankara: the Turkish President agreed to a meeting with Churchill, and suggested the Turkish capital. British Ministers disagreed strongly with this *venue* on security grounds.[55] After more telegrams between London, Cairo and Ankara, agreement was reached for a rendezvous on a special train at Adana, on the coast near the Turkish-Syrian border, on 30 January. Churchill was delighted, both by Turkish acceptance of the invitation and the cloak-and-dagger nature of the location. 'This is big stuff!' he declared. Security precautions seemed completely inadequate: although the party boarded the train at Adana, where they had flown from Cairo, and the train was then pulled into an open plain, it soon appeared that news of the visit was rife – and German agents were scattered thick throughout the country. After opening speeches Churchill started talks with Inönü and Foreign Minister Saracoglu, while Brooke and his colleagues discussed military matters with Field Marshal Çakmak and his staff. Churchill tried to remove Turkish fears of suffering the same fate as their Greek neighbours if they made a premature entry into the war; moreover, the Turks were apprehensive over the future of non-Communist Europe if Stalin won a resounding victory against the Nazis, to which Churchill replied that Turkey had all the more reason for being closely associated with Britain and America.[56] Brooke meanwhile tried to find details of military equipment required, but the CIGS gained a poor impression of Çakmak's ability and his attention wavered. 'I could see out of the window behind him, and suddenly spotted what I thought was a pallid harrier quartering the plain.... I was consequently very intent in looking out of that window much to Çakmak's discomfiture, who kept looking round and possibly thought I had spotted someone getting ready to have a shot at him.'[57] Discussions ended next morning, after which Churchill suddenly decided to fly to Cyprus instead of direct to Cairo; after a night on the island at Government House, the Prime Minister and party returned to Egypt the following afternoon, 1 February.

Nothing definite had emerged from the Turkish talks but nor had the venture been the failure which Eden had feared. The Turks had been honoured and slightly reassured by Churchill's visit; moreover, the discussions had prompted the Prime Minister to give attention to another important subject, in complete contrast to the topics filling his mind at Casablanca. As he lay in bed on the morning of his second day with the Turks, Churchill's lively thoughts pondered post-war problems, and his contemplation resulted in an interesting memorandum titled 'Morning Thoughts', dated 1

February. 'No one can predict with certainty that the victors will never quarrel among themselves, or that the United States may not once again retire from Europe, but after the experiences which all have gone through and their sufferings, and the certainty that the third struggle will destroy all that is left of the culture, wealth and civilization of mankind and reduce us to the level almost of wild beasts, the most intense effort will be made by the leading powers to prolong their honourable association....'[58] The development of atomic weapons would underline Churchill's prescience, and indeed, these fearful instruments of war had been mentioned at Casablanca. Churchill, back in June 1942, had agreed with Roosevelt during the Washington talks that British and American information and work on atomic weapons – code-named 'Tube Alloys' – should be pooled. But the following months had seen deteriorating allied co-operation; General Leslie Groves, executive agent of the US Military Policy Committee, which handled all atomic research construction work, became increasingly concerned over the security aspect, and Dr James Conant, Chairman of the National Defense Research Committee, deplored the fact that the US effort now amounted to 90 per cent of the whole. Thus, on 13 January, Dr Conant had completed a paper which proposed the British should be given no more information about electro-magnetic separation, about heavy water production, fast neutron reaction, or about the actual manufacture of the bomb. In London, the subject of 'Tube Alloys' was dealt with by Sir John Anderson, who had informed Churchill: 'This development has come as a bombshell and is quite intolerable.' The Prime Minister therefore raised the matter with Harry Hopkins, Roosevelt's assistant, during the Casablanca conference; the British awaited some reply.[59]

Churchill, after the Casablanca and Turkish exertions, now amused himself with one of his favourite occupations: visiting the troops in the field. The Prime Minister declined to seek War Cabinet approval for his trip. An apprehensive Brooke went with him: 'It is high time we started turning homewards.' Churchill and his party flew from Cairo on the morning of the 3rd, over the desert and the Alamein position and along to Tripoli and Montgomery's HQ. Churchill addressed officers and HQ staff of the 8th Army: 'Ever since your victory at Alamein, you have nightly pitched your moving tents a day's march nearer home....' Next day, 4 February, Churchill motored slowly down the ranks of the victorious 51st Division assembled in Tripoli; then the division marched past Churchill and Brooke, bagpipes playing, and the Prime Minister and CIGS stood rigid to attention with tears upon their faces. 'For the first time,' wrote Brooke, 'I was beginning to live through the thrill of those first successes that were now rendering ultimate victory possible. The depth of these feelings can only be gauged in relation to the utter darkness of those early days of calamities.'[60] The party continued to Algiers on the 5th; the irrepressible Churchill wished to fly to Malta after talks with Eisenhower, and could barely be persuaded to change his mind. And so, at 10 a.m. on Sunday, 7 February, Churchill and his weary travellers landed in two aircraft at Lyneham, Wiltshire, after spending the previous night at Gibraltar. Cadogan expressed his opinion of Churchill's touring methods: 'I won't be dragged around the world again in these conditions, which are filthy.'[61] Churchill refused to rest before giving War Cabinet Ministers a description of his travels at a 5.30 p.m. meeting. 'It was highly satisfactory that the Americans had agreed to our playing the Turkish hand. The Turkish attitude at Adana had been realistic and encouraging....' He wished to appoint General Wilson as Alexander's successor at Cairo when Alexander became Eisenhower's deputy. Churchill had been 'most impressed with everything he had seen in Tripoli.... He had received from Alexander a message saying the directive given him on 10 August 1942, had been fully accomplished.'[62] Churchill took two hours to make a statement to Parliament on Thursday, 11 February: 'I thought I had a good tale to tell,' he wrote afterwards. Refusing to be hampered by a cold, the Prime Minister waxed eloquent about his time in Casablanca, the talks with Inönü, and his Tripoli visit. He took care to qualify the unconditional surrender declaration: 'We shall not stain our arms by any cruel treatment of whole populations', but justice would be exacted 'upon the wicked and the guilty'. The highlight of his speech, as intended, proved to be his quotation of Alexander's signal a few days before: 'The orders you gave me on 10 August 1942, have been fulfilled. His Majesty's enemies, together with their impedimenta, have been completely eliminated from Egypt, Cyrenaica, Libya and Tripolitania. I now await your further instructions.' Cheers greeted these words from the normally reticent British commander; in fact Alexander and Churchill had composed the telegram together during the Prime Minister's visit.

A period of relative calm settled over the War Cabinet and COS after the frenzy of Casablanca. Churchill, more exhausted by his journey than he had realized, suffered a cold and sore throat which deteriorated into pneumonia on the 16th; the Prime Minister remained inactive until the end of the month, reading *Moll Flanders* rather than minutes and memoranda, and Attlee took charge of the War Cabinet. Meanwhile the tempo of fighting increased at the battle fronts, and momentous news arrived from Moscow and the Pacific. The Japanese had finally been driven from Papua on 22 January, leaving 13,000 dead – the Australians lost 2,165 and the Americans 913 – and on 9 February, after a costly naval battle, the Japanese abandoned Guadalcanal; Ministers were informed in London on the 15th that 'it had been estimated the US forces had killed over 6,000 Japanese'.[63] The Russians had even more impressive feats to report. By 17 January the Red Army had battered forward to within 10 miles of Stalingrad, and next day the War Cabinet had been told: 'The position of the 6th German Army at Stalingrad must now be considered as hopeless.'[64] A renewed Russian thrust had been made on the 22nd, and the Germans had been forced into a hellish oblong four miles deep, eight miles long. Von Paulus had been captured on 31 January. And on 2 February the jubilant Marshal Voronov reported all German resistance ended: 90,000 prisoners had been taken; of the quarter of a million men under Paulus's command, over half must have died, many through starvation and cold. Russian armies were meanwhile stabbing south and west over the Upper Don, threatening the Dnieper crossings upon which the remaining

German forces in Russia relied for supplies, and on 6 February Hitler had to agree to a shortening of the German line. The Russians pressed on until they became overextended, and the Germans counter-attacked on 22 February. Spring rains and subsequent mud brought mobile operations to a halt in mid-March – but the Germans had been forced back to their June 1942 positions. Reports of the Russian victories were received with rapture in Britain. The poet A. P. Herbert had already written lines of praise in September: 'And now the sons of Stalingrad enact another Iliad...' Celebrations were held on 20 and 21 February, with a massive performance at the Royal Albert Hall; Gielgud spoke 'the Voice of Moscow Radio'. Churchill sent his congratulations to Stalin on 2 February.

But high-level American-British-Soviet relations were in fact going through a delicate period. Stalin, in his telegram to Churchill and Roosevelt on 30 January, had sought more details of 'concerted operations' for a 1943 Second Front in Europe; the final CCS report of the Casablanca Conference had only mentioned one limited operation 'against the Cotentin peninsula with resources which will be available' and with a 1 August target date – even this operation would depend on availability of shipping and on the condition of likely opposition. Roosevelt and Churchill sent a cautious cable on 9 February: 'We are pushing preparations to the limit of our resources for a cross-Channel operation in August....'[65] No reply had been received by 14 February when Churchill sent further congratulations over latest Russian victories. A cool signal reached London from the Soviet leader on the 16th, claiming that because North African operations had slowed down 'for some reason', the Germans had transferred 27 divisions from Western Europe to the Soviet Front. Stalin once again pressed for a Second Front in 1943, and his final words underlined Russian military activity: 'Many thanks for your very warm congratulations on the liberation of Rostov. Our troops today captured Kharkov.'[66] Maisky, Soviet Ambassador, added to the pressure when he saw Eden on 22 February: he also stressed the importance of a German collapse coming about through simultaneous pressure from east and west. 'In such conditions the prospects for future collaboration between our two countries would be the best possible. If on the other hand almost the whole military burden had been borne by Russia and Germany was defeated by military blows alone, obviously the political position would be less satisfactory, not only for ourselves, but, he believed, for Russia also.' This veiled warning over post-war difficulties led to a Defence Committee meeting at 10 p.m. next day, 23 February. Maisky had stressed drawbacks to the proposed allied operations in the Mediterranean in 1943 and the consequent delay to a second front in Europe: equipment would be lost, amphibious operations were always difficult to execute, and the Germans might make use of the present delay to reinforce Sicily. Thus 'the whole summer might pass without British and American forces being engaged on the Continent'. The Committee decided to leave the matter until Churchill had recovered sufficiently to consider the question; in fact Churchill sent a short note to Stalin next day: 'The battle in Tunisia is all right. The enemy have shot their bolt and will now be brought into the grip of the vice.'[67]

Yet also on 24 February, Maisky contacted Eden again: the Russians, believing their partners to be unco-operative, were clearly determined to act in similar fashion. This time the Soviet Ambassador handed over a note concerning RAF squadrons established in North Russia to provide air cover for Arctic convoys. The Russians had previously agreed to find accommodation for the RAF personnel, but Maisky now said facilities could not be provided and suggested the British aircraft should be flown by Russian pilots. After COS consultation the Foreign Secretary saw Maisky again on 26 February and rejected the suggestion; he also complained about recent Russian action in ordering some British naval wireless transmitters in North Russia to close down – these were needed for convoy communications. Maisky was warned that unless the Soviet Government reviewed the situation, Britain would have to reconsider the whole convoy question. The threat proved sufficient to reopen the transmitters, but the Russians still refused to receive the RAF squadrons, and eventually the British Air Ministry agreed to Russian pilots being employed. Meanwhile, further

attempts had been made to soothe Stalin – and the sensitive
convoy issue soon came to the forefront again, bringing with
it a further threat to Anglo-Soviet relations.

Roosevelt tried to reassure the Soviets early in March; on
the 11th Churchill added his contribution. Both stressed the
importance of the forthcoming Mediterranean operations.
Stalin replied on the 15th, still complaining over apparent
setbacks in North Africa, and still stressing the need for a
European Second Front in 1943. Nothing could bridge this
allied gap: not even Churchill's skill in persuasion – ironically, Churchill had the same task which the COS had been
obliged to undertake before the Casablanca conference, when
Churchill, like Stalin now, had been the prime advocate for
a cross-Channel operation in 1943; equally ironically,
Churchill would soon be condemned by the Americans for
his rigid Mediterranean views. In mid-March came the added
convoy complication. Churchill summoned a Defence
Committee meeting on Tuesday, 16 March, at 10.30 p.m.:
he wanted the Committee to consider a disturbing minute,
received earlier in the day from the First Lord of the
Admiralty, proposing the cancellation of the March convoy
to Russia. Churchill 'expressed surprise at the sudden change
of plan, which was all the more unexpected since, within
the last 2-3 days, he had been expressly invited by the COS
to inform Mr Harriman that not only the March, but also
the May, convoys would be sailing'. Admiral Sir Dudley
Pound explained the position. The Germans had concentrated
three heavy warships in north Norway, the *Tirpitz*, *Scharnhorst* and *Lützow*; convoys would therefore have to be protected by comparable surface vessels, yet these would be
vulnerable to U-boat and land-based aircraft attack in the
Barents Sea, and, with the Home Fleet weakened by their
absence, German battle-cruisers might break out and create
havoc among the Atlantic convoys. Churchill recalled the
situation the previous year, when disaster had met PQ-17:
despite the threat of surface attack, the losses to this convoy
had been caused by submarines and air action after the
Royal Navy surface vessels had withdrawn. Might not the
same happen again? Moreover, continued Churchill, the

March convoy 'would provide a challenge to bring about an action with the enemy fleet, by making use of it as bait'. Pound disagreed: battle would not be accepted by the Germans until the British warships had been attacked by U-boat and aircraft, but Churchill still suggested the convoy should be used 'to tease the enemy and keep them in suspense'. The Committee eventually agreed that the convoy should sail as arranged on 27 March and should steam north for 4-5 days, when a final decision could be taken.[68] Almost within hours, news reached London of heavy casualties inflicted by U-boats on two convoys in mid-Atlantic. Moreover, the proposed invasion of Sicily would bring even greater demands for escort vessels. Churchill changed his mind, and agreed not only upon the March cancellation, but the complete stoppage of convoys until autumn when Sicily should have been taken. 'The strain on the British navy,' signalled Churchill to Roosevelt on 18 March, 'is becoming intolerable', and he told Eden, then in Washington: 'I think we might just as well be hanged for a sheep as for as lamb.'[69] Churchill therefore informed Stalin on 30 March and waited apprehensively for his reply.

Churchill's troubles with his ally paled in comparison to Hitler's difficulty with his Axis partner. Italy had been suffering growing disillusionment for months and opposition to the Germans had become so strong by the beginning of March that Mussolini, to safeguard his own position, had felt obliged to dismiss Cavallero, Chief of the General Staff, believed to be dominated by Berlin. At the same time Mussolini attempted to protect himself from German reaction; he called Ciano to his room at 4.30 p.m., 5 February. 'I perceive that he is very much embarrassed,' wrote Ciano in his diary. The Foreign Minister, Cavallero's strongest critic and suspected by the Germans, must go. Ciano asked to become Ambassador to the Holy See, commenting: 'The future, never so much as today, is in the hands of God.' But Mussolini told him: 'Your future is in my hands, and therefore you need not worry.' Within months Ciano, Mussolini's son-in-law, had been thrown into jail and was soon afterwards shot.[70] Ciano's dismissal in February did nothing to appease

the Germans; and in Italy the thoughts of many turned
increasingly to ending the war. On 18 March the War Cabinet
were informed that the Special Operations Executive – SOE
– had been in touch with two senior retired Italian Marshals,
Badoglio and Caviglia. 'The former, who was prepared at a
due moment to establish a military government, wished to
send an emissary, General Pesenti, to Cyrenaica, to discuss
with us co-ordinated action.' Cadogan pointed out that 'this
was the first time we had been in touch with influential
circles in Italy'. Eden strongly favoured the idea; Ministers
agreed, provided no commitments were entered into without
reference to the War Cabinet.[71] And while nothing definite
came from this approach, the Italians were nevertheless taking
the first hesitant, stumbling steps along the path to peace.

During these weeks of early spring, while rains swamped the
gigantic Soviet and German armoured columns on the
Russian plains, while lengthening daylight deprived lonely
Arctic convoys of cover of dark, and while winter storm
clouds rolled away from Tunisia and tracks dried for the
allied tanks, plans for future operations intensified in
Washington, New Delhi, China, Algiers, Cairo and London.
A handful of men had made the Casablanca decisions; a
multitude of men had to put those decisions into effect, and
the results would affect whole nations and peoples.

    But in the Far East doubts soon began to cloak the Casa-
blanca conclusions. The CCS had agreed a limited advance
should be made from Assam after operations then in progress
for the capture of Akyab; air transportation to China would
be improved; the CCS approved 15 November as the provisional date for 'Anakim' – the seaborne assault on Rangoon.
All these were designed to help China. General Arnold and
Sir John Dill arrived in New Delhi on 1 February and began
a 4-day conference with General Wavell, C-in-C India, and
General 'Vinegar' Joe Stilwell, US Chief of Staff in Peking.
Stilwell reacted unfavourably to the 'Anakim' postponement,
and believed the new British proposals to be pure bluff. The
American's suspicions soon seemed justified. Shipping short-
ages led the COS to the conclusion on 2 March that if further

resources could not be found 'Anakim' must be cancelled.[72] The Prime Minister scrawled on this COS report: 'I do not accept this'; but Brooke and his colleagues received support from Wavell – only the day after the COS report, the C-in-C India held a conference which dwelt on the military difficulties of the operation, especially the danger inherent in landings on a shore dominated by hostile land-based aircraft. Wavell cabled that other schemes – for example against North Sumatra – should be prepared in the event of an increase in Japanese strength in Burma. The Joint Planners in London agreed with this assessment. Churchill would eventually become one of the fiercest advocates of a North Sumatra operation, but he now scribbled in red ink across Wavell's report: 'A poor tale!' Nevertheless, by the end of March it seemed 'Anakim' might soon be shelved. Moreover, another of the Casablanca decisions had foundered: the capture of Akyab. Fanatical opposition by the Japanese blocked the attempted advance and by 22 March the enemy had regained all territory lost in terrible fighting since the beginning of the year. On 9 April Wavell and his colleagues were summoned home for urgent consultations.[73]

Complications had also arisen over another of the Casablanca conclusions: to attack Sicily 'with the favourable July moon as the target date'. To this decision the CCS had added a footnote: they agreed that 'an intense effort will be made during the next three weeks to achieve by contrivance and ingenuity the favourable *June* moon period as the date for the operations'. Churchill put his weight behind this endeavour. 'The effort to bring "Husky" forward to June,' he told the COS on the day after his return to London, 'is now the first task of the COS Committee.' The Joint Planning Staff believed this earlier date might be possible, and after a long COS meeting on the morning of 10 February, Ismay reported to Churchill that the June target might well be met.[74] But Brooke remained pessimistic. 'I feel we are running grave risks of wrecking the whole show by trying to rush it,' he wrote in his diary.[75] And next day, 11 February, Eisenhower sent a gloomy report to the CCS in Washington: inadequate training time, the period

required to absorb new forces, the 10 weeks needed to re-
deploy air forces after the capture of Tunisia and the month
to establish air superiority – all these meant a June assault
would be unlikely to succeed.[76] Churchill reacted vigorously.
'It is absolutely necessary to do this operation in June. We
shall become a laughing-stock, if, during the spring and early
summer, no British and American soldiers are firing at any
German or Italian soldiers.'[77] The COS discussed the matter
on 15 February and again on the 18th; Brooke agreed with
Eisenhower's assessment. On 13 March Eisenhower called a
conference of his commanders in Algiers. The meeting
decided to alter the role of the airborne forces taking part
in the invasion: the drop would take place just before midnight, with the seaborne landings just before dawn, and the
airborne troops would need moonlight at this time, which
would be most likely in the moon's second quarter. Such a
moon period would occur around 10 July, and Eisenhower
signalled that this would be his target date. The COS in
London and Washington had to agree to this decision.[78]

Planning went ahead accordingly. Meanwhile, another of
the Casablanca decisions had already been put into operation
– intensified bombing raids upon Germany. On 4 February
a grim directive was issued to the British and US Bomber
Commands in the UK. 'Your primary object will be the
progressive destruction and dislocation of the German
military, industrial, and economic system, and the under-
mining of the morale of the German people to a point
where their capacity for armed resistance is fatally weakened.'[79] The British offensive, directed by Air Marshal Harris
and undertaken at night – as opposed to the US daylight
precision bombing method – was aimed from March to July
at Germany's industrial heart in the Ruhr; and on Tuesday,
6 March, War Cabinet Ministers were informed that this
new battle had been opened the previous night by 442 RAF
Bomber Command aircraft striking at Essen, dropping over
1,000 tons of high explosives and incendiaries in just over 30
minutes. 'Things simply cannot go on like this,' moaned
Goebbels in his diary that day. 'Damage is colossal and
indeed ghastly.' Things did go on. The COAS told the War

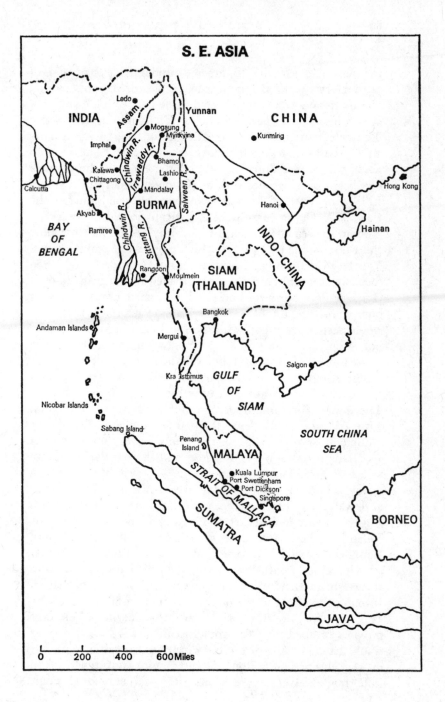

S. E. ASIA

INDIA

Ledo

Assam

Yunnan

CHINA

Mogaung
Myitkyina

Kunming

Imphal

Bhamo

Kalewa
Chittagong

Lashio

Calcutta

Mandalay

Chindwin R.

Irrawaddy R.

BURMA

Hanoi

Hong Kong

Akyab

Salween R.

Hainan

BAY
OF
BENGAL

Ramree

Sittang R.

INDO-CHINA

Rangoon
Moulmein

SIAM
(THAILAND)

Andaman Islands

Bangkok

Mergui

Kra Isthmus

Saigon

GULF
OF
SIAM

Nicobar Islands

SOUTH CHINA
SEA

Sabang Island

Penang
Island

MALAYA

Kuala Lumpur
Port Swettenham
Port Dickson
Singapore

STRAIT OF MALLACA

SUMATRA

BORNEO

JAVA

0   200   400   600 Miles

Cabinet on 8 March: 'Bomber Command has had a most satisfactory week, dropping 2,600 tons of bombs. Berlin, Hamburg and Essen have been attacked. The attack on Essen is considered the best of the war.'[80] And on the 15th: 'Bomber Command has carried out four big night attacks on Nuremberg, Munich, Stuttgart and Essen. The raid on Essen was outstandingly good and the effect of the damage has been to bring the work at Krupps virtually to a standstill. 3,200 tons of bombs have been dropped during the week....'[81] On 20 March the Americans joined in, sweeping in from the sea at Bremen; by mid-July, sorties flown against the Ruhr totalled 18,502, of which 2,070 were against Essen. Yet the British could still suffer, and did so on 3 March: 180 men, women and children were crushed to death in Bethnal Green underground station, rushing to shelter from German bombs. Morrison told the War Cabinet on the 8th that 'it would seem that this disaster had not been started in panic, but simply by one or two people having fallen down the steps and others having fallen on them in the dark.'[82]

The 8th Army had crossed the frontier into Tunisia on 4 February after its advance of 1,200 miles from Alamein. The Army now came under Eisenhower's overall command, with Alexander his deputy. By this time the Axis forces occupied the eastern half of the Tunis bulge, comprising the 1st (Italian) Army under Rommel and the 5th Panzer Army under Arnim. Facing them in the west was the allied 1st Army, while the 8th Army lay over in the east. Eisenhower and Alexander hastily prepared for the next push forward. But the enemy moved first, lashing out at the 1st Army on St Valentine's Day, and although twin thrusts by Arnim and Rommel were weakly co-ordinated, their impact and initial success caused confusion among the allied troops and consternation in London and Washington. Arnim's tanks sliced through the US II Corps position at the southern end of the 1st Army line, heading west towards Sbeitla; on 15 February a report reached the CCS from Eisenhower – the allied wing would have to pull back. This withdrawal became confused; on 18 February both Rommel and Arnim converged on the important Kasserine pass, and Rommel surged through next day. Stiffening allied resistance and shortage of resources brought him to a halt on 21 February; Axis armour began to pull back on the 22nd. To ordinary men and women back at home, sticking pins in maps on living-room walls with news of each communiqué, reports from North Africa were appalling, despite the censor's caution. Harold Nicolson wrote on the 21st: 'I am worried, deeply worried, by the news from Tunisia ... it looks as if the 1st Army may be defeated before the 8th arrives. I sleep badly.'[83] Anxiety accumulated for those at the top, with full information at hand. The King expressed his fears in a letter to Churchill on the 22nd; the Prime Minister sent a reassuring reply the same day: 'I do not feel seriously disturbed by the course of events in North Africa, either politically or militarily, although naturally there is much about both aspects which I would rather have different.'[84] And on 26 February the Axis armies moved on to the offensive again. Arnim advanced towards the British V Corps at the northern end of the 1st Army, and managed to pin down these units for the next month; Rommel was switching his forces over to the east ready to move against Montgomery's 8th Army. On 27 February General Alexander sent a depressing signal to Churchill: 'Regrouping, sort out and reorganization is now under way, but is being somewhat delayed by enemy action in north. Broadly speaking, Americans require experience and French require arms.... I am frankly shocked at whole situation as I found it.... Hate to disappoint you, but final victory in North Africa is not just around the corner.'[85]

Early in the morning of 6 March, Rommel launched three Panzer divisions against Montgomery's line at Medinine. But British defences were well-prepared; Montgomery had been given ample time to make ready while the Germans had been engaged with their Kasserine offensive late the previous month. The morning attacks were beaten back; Rommel tried again in the afternoon; by evening this attack had also failed. Rommel, the greatest tank commander of them all, was finished in North Africa. Weary, sick, bitter, he left Tunisia for good three days later. Messe and von Arnim took over for the final struggle.

Into the Under-belly

Bernard Montgomery, cautious as ever, bided his time.
Ahead lay the Axis positions along the Mareth Line: Rommel
had believed units should withdraw to better defensive terrain 40 miles further north – Mareth could perhaps be
threatened by a southern outflanking movement through
the mountains. But Rommel had gone, and on 11 March
von Arnim ordered no withdrawal would take place. He
disregarded the possibility of the outflanking movement: the
mountainous route would indeed be difficult, but Montgomery, aided by advice from General Catroux who had
helped design and defend the Mareth fortifications, had
determined to try such a manoeuvre. On the night of
17/18 March units of Montgomery's right wing began a
limited thrust in an attempt to cover the outflanking move
by 27,000 New Zealanders through the mountains on the
left. Fighting at the right of the British line proved desperate;
and early on 20 March, Montgomery realised the enemy
had discovered the New Zealand forces waiting to strike on
the left, and he therefore ordered the abandonment of all
attempts at concealment – the New Zealanders must 'go
like hell'. Alexander had promised to inform Churchill of
the start of the main battle; on 21 March this codeword
reached 10 Downing Street: 'Zip'. Yet fighting remained
desperate, and on 22 March the enemy launched a frenzied
counter-attack with 15 Panzer Division and infantry. Units
of 30 corps had to pull back during the night. But even this
upsetting situation still seemed satisfactory to Montgomery;

he gave orders for the attack on the British right to be held, thus tying up German reserves, and at the same time an additional push would be made by the 4th Indian Division against the Germans in the centre; Montgomery also dispatched the 1st Armoured Division to rush through the hills and join the New Zealand outflanking movement. Results proved to be typical Montgomery tactics: block on the right, punch on the left.

Reports were nevertheless received with alarm in London. Just as during Alamein, the setbacks in the middle stages of the clash seemed to indicate a deteriorating situation – and, as with Alamein, Montgomery failed to keep London fully informed of his intentions. Brooke had been away from work suffering from 'flu and general strain; he returned to his office on 24 March to be greeted by the depressing news from the front. On the same day Churchill and the COS discussed the possibility of sending more men to Tunisia: Alexander was authorized to take 56th Division from Palestine, previously earmarked for 'Husky'.[1] Next day, unaware of this decision, Montgomery requested such a reinforcement. 'Enemy fighting desperately and much heavy fighting lies ahead. Essential I should be able to maintain momentum.... Request reinforcement from Egypt ... and consider this must be done at expense of "Husky".... If we do not finish this business properly there will be no "Husky".'[2] Gloom in London correspondingly increased. Yet the following day, 26 March, saw the successful climax of the grim struggle in the Matmata mountains. On 17 March forces led by Patton had begun their advance through Gafsa to the north-east of Arnim's forces, and had taken Maknassy on the 21st to threaten the German rear; on 24 March von Arnim urged his superior that withdrawal should begin, in view of this threat and the 8th Army outflanking offensive. And, on 26 March, this 8th Army movement began the final assault. Tanks of the 1st Armoured Division reached the New Zealand Corps in front of the crucial Tebaga Gap during the day; at 3.30 p.m., 20 minutes after the last tank arrived, squadrons from the Western Desert Air Force streaked in from the huge setting sun to blast enemy defences. The

enemy had expected a night attack – this had been the 8th
Army method until now. But at 4.15 p.m., while pande-
monium from the bombing continued and smoke and dust
swirled high, wave upon wave of British tanks squealed
forward. British units battered their way through the Tebaga
gap and forced open the door to the plain beyond, thus
threatening to encircle the German army. On 28 March
a welcome signal reached Churchill from Montgomery:
'After seven days of continuous and heavy fighting 8th Army
has inflicted a severe defeat on enemy. Enemy resistance ...
is disintegrating.'[3] Messe, the Italian General in command
of this front under Arnim, managed to pull back the bulk
of his forces to the 'Chott' position along the Wadi Akarit,
north of Gabes; the men of the 8th Army, weary, filthy, but
triumphant, moved forward again. Churchill and Brooke
celebrated with a *tête-à-tête* supper in the drawing room at
10 Downing Street: plovers' eggs, chicken broth, chicken pie,
chocolate *soufflé*, champagne, port and brandy.[4]

At 5.30 p.m. next day, 29 March, Brooke told the War
Cabinet: 'The latest information was that, threatened by
the advance of an outflanking force which had reached El
Hamma, the enemy had evacuated the Mareth positions and
that we had captured Mareth, Toujane and Matmata. Over
6,000 prisoners have been taken since 20 March.' Churchill
commented: 'The 8th Army had again performed a very
fine piece of work.'[5] Over in the north-west, British units in
V Corps ended a month's slogging match by restoring the
position in the coastal sector; on 31 March Patton's troops
renewed their thrust down the Gasfa-Gabes road and thereby
imposed a northern threat on the enemy's positions at Wadi
Akarit, causing a dispersal of units. The allies prepared for
the next offensive.

Latest successes in North Africa uplifted spirits in London –
and in Moscow may even have mellowed stern Stalin, despite
Churchill's telegram of 30 March regretting there would
be no Arctic convoys until the autumn. On 2 April Stalin's
reply reached London, read by Churchill to the War Cabinet
on the 5th: 'I understand this unexpected action as a cata-

strophic diminution of supplies of arms and military raw materials to the USSR on the part of Great Britain and the USA.... You realize of course that the circumstances cannot fail to affect the position of the Soviet troops.' Churchill commented that 'in the circumstances Premier Stalin's reply was courageous and not unsatisfactory'.[6] Next day, 6 April, the Prime Minister sent another soothing signal to Moscow, stressing recent intensification of bombing raids, and adding: 'This present week the general battle in Tunisia will begin.'[7]

Montgomery had decided to employ two new tactics: attacking in dark dead of night, rather than moonlight or daylight, and striking at the enemy centre. Messe had expected a delay until the period of full moon around 15 April. The 8th Army struck; and by the evening of 6 April, despite courageous fighting, the enemy were in full retreat from the Wadi Akarit area – leaving 7,000 prisoners. Montgomery sent Churchill a jubilant report: 'My troops are in TREMENDOUS form.' On 7 April advancing 8th Army units linked with troops from Patton's II Corps striking from Gafsa, and British forces from Egypt thus met Americans landed in 'Torch' at Casablanca. 'Hello Limeys!' shouted the dust-covered GIs, regardless of the fact that the troops they greeted were Indians. Sick Mussolini dragged himself to Hitler at Klessheim near Salzburg; he pleaded for concentration in the Mediterranean, at the expense of the Eastern Front; Hitler stressed the impossibility of any disengagement from the Russian front, but Tunisia would be held 'at whatever cost'.

In London on this Wednesday, discussions were being held on future stages of the war. March arguments had now been settled: target date for the attack on Sicily had been established as 10 July. Now planning had to be cast even further ahead. A number of alternatives existed: invasion of Italy; invasion of Corsica and Sardinia; operations in the Eastern Mediterranean. The first would eliminate Italy as an Axis partner, would help Yugoslav partisans, and would provide airfields for bomber offensives on Europe. But operations might be costly and prolonged if Corsica and Sardinia were not taken first – the latter would also enable a threat to be imposed on Southern France; operations in the Aegean could bring Turkey in and help Russia. Churchill had called for urgent study in a telegram drafted to Roosevelt on the 3rd: much depended, he said, on the German attitude towards Italy; if strong reinforcements were sent an invasion of Italy should not be attempted, and operations should be tried in the Eastern Mediterranean. Churchill did not therefore favour a Sardinian invasion. Nor did the Joint Planners, who submitted a report to the COS on 7 April stressing shipping shortages and relating the Mediterranean to the Far East: reports from the latter had thrown doubts on the Rangoon assault, 'Anakim', and the Planners therefore recommended the scrapping of this operation, thus sparing resources for an Italian invasion, or, in the event of a German collapse in 1943, for a cross-Channel attempt. Corsica and Sardinia should be left alone, unless Italy suffered radical disintegra-ion. But the COS refused to be so categorical: an attack on Sardinia and the consequent acquisition of air bases might knock Italy out of the war without a mainland invasion. The COS therefore directed on 8 April that a Sardinian assault should still be studied, together with operations to secure a bridgehead in the foot of Italy.[8] Also on 8 April the COS discussed a disturbing telegram just received from Eisen-hower, concerning the more immediate operation to take Sicily. Eisenhower, and apparently Alexander and Cunning-ham, warned of 'scant prospect of success if the region con-tained substantial, well-armed, and fully-organized German ground forces.... By the term substantial is meant more than two German divisions.' Churchill was already intensely annoyed by recent Far East news, about which he minuted to the COS during the day: 'This campaign goes from bad to worse.... Luckily the small scale of the operations and the attraction of other events has prevented public opinion being directed upon this lamentable scene.' To this irate minute, the Prime Minister added scorching sentences to condemn Eisenhower's signal. 'I trust the COS will not accept these pusillanimous and defeatist doctrines.... We have told the Russians that they cannot have their supplies by the Northern convoy for the sake of "Husky" and now "Husky" is to be abandoned if there are two German divisions (strength unspecified) in the neighbourhood. What Stalin would think of this, when he had 185 German divisions on his front, I cannot imagine.' The COS agreed, and decided at their meeting on this Thursday that 'the views expressed by General Eisenhower, which were tantamount to saying that amphibious operations could not succeed against organized German resistance, should not be accepted'. The COS informed Washington: 'We feel bound to record our view that the abandonment of the operation at any stage solely because the number of Germans in Huskyland had reached a small predetermined fraction of our own strength would be unthinkable.'[9] The US COS expressed similar views in a snappy signal to the unfortunate Eisenhower, dated 10 April.

Sfax fell to the advancing allies on the 10th; on 12 April the town of Sousse was seized. The 8th Army was now rounding up 1,000 enemy prisoners each day. Also on the 12th, Eisenhower sent a cool reply to Washington regarding 'Husky'. 'No thought here except to carry out our orders to the ultimate limit of our ability, while we believe it our duty to give our considered and agreed opinion of relative chances.'[10] On the same day Alexander informed Churchill of his plans for the final assault in Tunisia; the offensive would be launched into the Tunis plain 'to start earliest date and not later than 25 April'.[11] And Churchill also received an exceptionally friendly note from Stalin: 'The speedy development of the Anglo-American advance in Tunis constitutes an important success in the war against Hitler and Mussolini.... We are delighted.'[12]

Yet this Monday saw the emergence of further complications with Russia, this time over relations with Poland; and from now until the end of the war the Polish problem would thread its way through diplomatic and military affairs. The Polish Government in Exile in London had established an uneasy relationship with Moscow after Hitler's invasion of Soviet territory, but had continued to press for the return of Polish citizens interned during the time when Soviet and German armies had overrun the country. Moreover, the advance of the Soviet armies behind the retreating Germans now pushed another aspect to the forefront: the question of the Russo-Polish frontier. On 25 February the Polish Government in London had issued a statement maintaining their claim to their pre-war frontiers. In turn, the Soviet Government demanded the Curzon line as their eastern boundary with Poland: this, proposed by Lord Curzon immediately after the First World War, ran much farther to the west, thus giving the Russians a considerable slice of Polish territory; in exchange, the Poles would be given areas in Germany. The British had so far insisted no frontier questions could be settled until after the war. Now, on 12 April, Eden told the War Cabinet that 'difficulties between the Russians and the Poles were acute. He would like to send instructions to our Ambassador at Moscow to take this matter up with the Russians, as otherwise he feared that the Poles might adopt some extreme course, such as withdrawing their Ambassador from Moscow.'[13] Next day, 13 April, German radio announced the discovery in the Katyn Forest of evidence that the Russians had murdered some 10,000 Polish Officers; the broadcast added a demand for an international inquiry. The Polish Government in London believed the reports – and supported the German proposal for an inquiry.

Britain was forced further into being a broker in this tragic episode; nor, apparently, could much help be expected from America on the Polish problem in general. Eden had visited the United States from 12 March to 4 April, and on the 13th he reported on his talks. 'The public attitude towards Russia,' he told the War Cabinet, 'was on the whole less friendly in the US than it was in this country.... There was, however, general support for the view that no harm could come to the US for endeavouring to come to terms with the USSR.' Roosevelt had asked Eden whether he believed Russia 'would want to communize all Europe after the war'; Eden had replied that he did not think so, and one of the best ways of avoiding the danger was 'to do what we could to keep on good terms with Russia'. Eden continued: 'The President seemed to have reconciled himself to Russia retaining the Baltic States after the war. His view was that he did not see who was going to turn her out.... The

President thought that if Poland absorbed East Prussia and received compensation in Silesia, she ought to be satisfied with the Curzon line as the boundary.... The President thought that one way of handling the matter would be that this country, the US and Russia should settle between themselves what they regarded as fair terms as between Russia and Poland, and that we should then unite in persuading the Poles to accept this settlement.' Britain would later be harshly criticized by the Americans for attempting such a method of settling the internal affairs of particular countries, above the heads of the countries concerned. Eden, in his report on the 13th, mentioned other topics discussed with the Americans. 'Mr Hull clearly hated de Gaulle.... For the most part, however, discussion had related to the future handling of the French. On this it seemed that there was one point of difference between the US and ourselves. The US did not want to see the establishment at this stage of a single French authority.... The Foreign Secretary had made it clear that we should greatly prefer to deal with one authority.' The President had also referred to a suggestion, made earlier to Churchill, that after the war only the four great powers should retain armed forces. 'He had, however, been reminded that, even if it were possible to impose such terms on enemy countries it would hardly be practicable to disarm neutral countries, and it seemed unlikely that this suggestion would be seriously pressed.'[14]

Polish-Russian relations continued to deteriorate. General Sikorski, Polish Prime Minister, lunched with Churchill on the 15th and alleged he had proof of Soviet guilt in the Katyn massacre; Churchill warned the Poles against provoking the Russians, but said Britain would be prepared to intervene on their behalf; as far as frontiers were concerned, Churchill said the eastern frontier should be strengthened at the expense of the west, but he did not go into details. On the Katyn charges, Churchill was reported to have commented: 'Alas, the German revelations are probably true. The Bolsheviks can be very cruel.'[15] Despite the plea to the Poles to avoid provocation, Eden and Cadogan were informed next day, 16 April, that the Poles were about to appeal to the International Red Cross for a Katyn investigation. The Foreign Office persuaded the Poles to dilute this statement by also referring to German atrocities, and the announcement was made on the 17th. On the 24th Maisky, Soviet Ambassador, saw Eden, after which the Foreign Secretary called in Sikorski and informed him that the Russians were about to sever relations with Poland; Stalin would refrain if the Poles withdrew their application to the Red Cross and blamed Germany for Katyn. The Poles refused. Cadogan noted in his diary: 'This heavy Russian plunge is, I think, indicative of a bad conscience. It's a bad move, anyhow, and Goebbels must be happy.' Messages passed between Stalin and Churchill, with the former accusing the Poles of collusion with the Germans over the Katyn announcement. The issue was discussed by the War Cabinet on the 27th; Churchill warned that 'recent developments in the situation ... might have serious consequences. Unless the breach could be healed, there was a risk that the differences between the Russians and the Poles might extend to other issues.' Churchill and Eden had just seen Sikorski. 'The Polish Government had intended to issue a communiqué that evening, in terms which would have exacerbated the situation. The General had agreed to defer issue of the communiqué and consider the matter further.' A further meeting had been arranged for the following afternoon. Churchill told Ministers he had emphasized to the Poles that 'the right line was to ignore what had happened, or might have happened ... and that what now mattered was to concentrate on improving relations.' Eden said he agreed, but 'General Sikorski would be under very strong pressure'.[16]

More developments were described to the War Cabinet on 29 April. Ministers had before them the text of an announcement issued by the Polish Government that morning, as modified after discussions with Churchill and Eden on the 28th; the War Cabinet also had the copy of a telegram sent by Churchill to Stalin, dated the 28th: this drew Stalin's attention to Goebbels's suggestion that Moscow intended to set up a Polish Government on Russian territory, and added that no such Government could be recognized by Britain.

Eden reported on an interview with Maisky that morning: Maisky had made it clear 'he did not like the Polish Government's announcement, in particular the statement that the Polish Government still adhered to the frontiers of 1939. Maisky said that the Polish Government had let it be known that we endorsed their announcement. Did this mean that we also endorsed the Polish claim to their 1939 frontiers?' Ministers at the meeting believed 'we should make it clear that we would not agree to these territorial questions being settled until the end of the war', although 'it might be necessary to reach a settlement of this question before the end of the war'.[17] Stalin replied to Churchill on 6 May, denying there was any intention of setting up an alternative Polish Government, but pressing for the reconstitution of Sikorski's Government; the telegram added that Russia had never prevented the families of Polish soldiers from leaving Russia, as alleged. Cadogan believed this reply to be 'not too bad', but Eden warned the War Cabinet on the 7th that he was 'increasingly disturbed about the position'.[18]

Meanwhile, strategic subjects had become predominant again. And three days before this War Cabinet meeting on 7 May, Churchill had embarked upon another voyage, to attend the second of the great summits in 1943. While the Prime Minister had been lending his thoughts and efforts to the Polish problem during May and early June, he had also been heavily involved with the continuing complex planning for operations in the Mediterranean, in Europe, and in the Burmese jungles. Questions had arisen which could only be answered by another Anglo-American meeting of minds.

Chiefs of Staff discussion in April saw the introduction of a new code-word: 'Crossbow'. The name cloaked a sinister enemy development – the possibility of a German secret weapon which might be launched upon Britain; and a relatively clear picture had now emerged through intelligence reports of German work upon pilotless missiles. The Joint Intelligence Committee circulated a paper on 11 April describing progress which the Germans might have made, and the Vice-COS advocated the appointment of a single person to take charge of investigations. The COS told Churchill on 14 April: 'You should be made aware of reports of German experiments with long-range rockets. The fact that five reports have been received since the end of 1942 indicates a foundation of fact even if details are inaccurate.' Selected for the appointment of 'Crossbow' investigator was Duncan Sandys, Churchill's son-in-law and then Under-Secretary at the Ministry of Supply. Sandys set about preparing his first report, to be presented to the War Cabinet in May.

The COS turned back to their studies of the Mediterranean and the Far East; and at a meeting on 13 April it became clear that the invasion of Sicily, 'Husky', could only be attempted if sacrifices were made elsewhere. Admiral Ramsay, commander of the Naval Task Force covering the British landings, had reported in February that he would need more assault craft. Some would have to be brought from UK reserves to meet the demand, but this in turn would jeopardize remaining chances of a limited cross-Channel operation in 1943, and although the Casablanca conclusions had specified that this operation could only be launched 'with resources which will be available', the idea had been a sop both to Churchill and Stalin. Churchill reacted strongly at the meeting on the 13th, while Brooke stressed the COS view that 'it would be wrong to stint the "Husky" plan for the sake of being able to mount a comparatively small-scale cross-Channel operation'. The COS met Churchill again in the evening. 'Started by being stormy and then improved,' wrote Brooke in his diary; Churchill finally gave his reluctant agreement to this abandonment of a cross-Channel attempt in 1943.[19] Two days later, 15 April, the COS took the final decision to scrap another operation – 'Anakim'. Shortage of resources and lack of enthusiasm by Far East commanders led the COS to agree with the recommendation of the Joint Planners that this assault on Rangoon should be cancelled for the 1943-44 season. Wavell, due to arrive in London for discussion in the next few days, would be asked to suggest an alternative.[20] Once again Churchill had to agree, at a meeting on Monday, 19 April, when he commented that he

'could not view the operation with enthusiasm. The plan
envisaged large-scale diversion of forces with problematical
chances of success at many of the points of attack.' Churchill
added: 'The operation could, in fact, be likened to a man
attacking a hedgehog by pulling out bristles one by one.'[21]
Churchill had once more bowed to the military arguments;
the Prime Minister nevertheless continued to leap upon any
stray strategic idea, either for the Mediterranean or the Far
East, which might have immediate appeal: on 17 April he
telephoned Brooke to enthuse over a signal from Marshall,
just received, which apparently proposed that 'Husky' should
be launched while the Tunisian campaign still continued.
'Quite mad and quite impossible,' confided Brooke in his
diary, 'but PM delighted ... had half an hour's row with
him.'[22]

Churchill seemed inexhaustible. On 19 April, the day he
gave his agreement to the 'Anakim' cancellation, and while
he was deeply involved with the Polish problem and with
studying urgent reports from North Africa, he found time
to address a minute to the Minister of Agriculture. 'I understand you have discontinued the small sugar ration which
was allowed to bees, and which in the spring months is most
important to their work throughout the whole year....'[23]
While the Prime Minister penned his lament for the bees
on the 19th, the final terrible offensive opened in Tunisia.
Alexander planned for the 8th Army to start the general
attack by assaulting enemy positions at Enfidaville, thereby
drawing in enemy forces before an advance on Tunis was
launched via Hammamet; attacks would be made on 21 and
22 April by 1st Army; on the 23rd the US II Corps, commanded by Omar N. Bradley and transferred to the Allied
left, would strike south-east aiming at Mateur. Desert veterans
in the 8th Army now had to push through heavily defended
mountains; the men were already tired and suffering from
prolonged campaigning. The enemy fought back with the
knowledge they could retreat no further. The battle inevitably became a grinding, gruelling clash. Montgomery
massed his guns to pound through the enemy defences, but
the latter were well dug into the mountains and remained

extremely tough, and the 8th Army advance moved painfully
and soon began to slow. Yet Montgomery flew to Algiers
on the 19th, not to discuss the present battle, but the next:
the 8th Army commander had severe criticism to make to
Eisenhower and Alexander over 'Husky' planning. 'I myself,
and my Army HQ Staff, know very little about the operation
as a whole, and *nothing whatever* about the detailed planning.... If we go on in this way much longer we might have
a disaster.'[24] Next day, 20 April, while the 8th Army units
found the going increasingly hard in Tunisia, and while their
commander worried over 'Husky', the COS in London gave
further attention to the operation to follow this conquest of
Sicily. A decision had still to be taken on the three main
alternatives: full invasion of Italy, an attempt at Sardinia,
or the Eastern Mediterranean. The COS, unlike Churchill
and the Joint Planners, still refused to rule out Sardinian
possibilities and decided at their meeting on the 20th to
instruct the Planners to give the matter further study.[25]
The 1st Army main attack went in on 22 April; meanwhile
the 8th Army offensive had virtually ceased. On all sides the
enemy fought with desperate courage and determination;
allied progress proved slow, casualties mounted – but all
enemy reserves were being bled.

Wavell and his colleagues reached London on 22 April
for Far East talks. 'Anakim' had been dropped; discussions
now took place on an alternative. The Joint Planners agreed
that an attack on North Sumatra followed by a landing in
Malaya, as tentatively suggested by Wavell, was desirable
'but is quite beyond our resources in 1943-1944'. Conferences
would continue the following week. Unknown to Wavell, he
was coming to the end of his appointment as C-in-C India:
a new Viceroy of India had to be found following the retirement of the Marquess of Linlithgow; Churchill at first considered Eden, but the Foreign Secretary – and the King –
disagreed.[26] The battle for Tunisia thundered on, and on
23 April the US II Corps launched its offensive in the north
towards Mateur. On 27 April von Arnim reported his troops
were nearing total exhaustion; on the same day the War
Cabinet discussed latest military reports, and in reply to a

question by Churchill, Brooke said he 'would inquire why General Montgomery had found it necessary to go to Cairo at this juncture, and why news of his visit had been published'.[27] Montgomery was in fact back at his HQ in Tunisia, having returned from Cairo the previous day: he now had to retire to his bed in his famous caravan, suffering from 'flu and tonsilitis, while his troops battled on; next day, 28 April, Alexander reported to London that Montgomery's forces were 'undoubtedly tired, and the 4th Indian Division and the 7th Armoured Division are the only veteran ones which can be considered from now onwards as capable of full offensive action'.[28] But on the same day reports were sent from von Arnim's HQ that the fuel situation was 'catastrophic'.

The COS returned to their study of Far East problems on the 28th, and the War Cabinet meeting at noon next day heard a detailed report of the Burma situation and the results of the COS discussions. Churchill told Ministers that the Arakan operations had been 'very disappointing, and the general conditions of warfare in Burma favoured the Japanese. The mountainous jungle country forbade the use of modern weapons and hampered the operations of aircraft. Communications were few and difficult, malaria was prevalent, and the morale of our troops was reported to be less high than it should be.' Increased shipping demands meant 'we should probably have to relinquish the ideas of reconquering Burma during the coming winter'. An invitation had been received from the US COS for the three C-in-Cs, India, to visit Washington on their journey from London. 'It was open to doubt', continued Churchill, 'whether this invitation should be accepted, in view of the natural urge which existed in America to devote resources to the war against Japan.... On the other hand, if the invitation were rejected, and things did not go well, it would afford a pretext to the Americans for saying that we neglected an opportunity for making a combined plan.' Wavell filled in details of the Burma fighting, after which Churchill commented: 'It could not be said that the conquest of Burma was an essential step in the defeat of Japan, though the Americans were in favour of such an attempt.... We must not let the Americans drift away from the concept of Germany as the major enemy.'[29] The idea of the three commanders being allowed to experience Washington temptations did not therefore appeal to Churchill; he had told the War Cabinet that 'the matter would have to be carefully considered'. This he now proceeded to do, and he found a typical answer. Another War Cabinet meeting was called for 3 p.m. on this Thursday, when Churchill told Ministers: 'Our Commanders-in-Chief ought to go, but they ought to go with political support. I have therefore reached the conclusion that I ought to go, and will take with me the COS.' Discussions with the Americans would include the Far East, 'Husky', and the operation to follow the latter. 'I ask the Cabinet's permission to make the necessary arrangements.' He proposed to travel by sea, since his doctors considered it unwise for him to fly at a great height. The official minutes continued: 'The First Lord of the Admiralty asked the Prime Minister to look at the U-boat map of the Atlantic before deciding to make the journey by sea. Various Ministers asked whether it was really necessary that the Prime Minister should undertake this journey, about which they showed no enthusiasm. But when the Prime Minister made it clear that he was sure he ought to go, the War Cabinet's assent was given.'[30] Brooke opposed the idea at a meeting with Churchill at 5 p.m. 'I told him we were not ready to discuss plans on the far side yet,' and the CIGS tried to postpone departure. Churchill argued that he wished to leave the following Sunday, 2 May; in the event this had to be delayed three days because the *Queen Mary*, used as a troop transport, was found to be full of vermin.[31] Churchill wired Roosevelt during the evening, seeking an invitation which came almost immediately.

Montgomery was still ill in bed; Alexander therefore flew to him on the 30th to discuss present Tunisian operations, and heard his criticisms of tactics being employed by the neighbouring 1st Army – 'it was more of a partridge drive than an attack and had no hope of success'. Montgomery urged the regrouping of the 1st and 8th armies to enable a maximum thrust for Tunis. Alexander cabled the results of this conference to Churchill: units from the 8th Army would be switched to the 1st to give added weight for the main offensive and 'a very strong attack with all available air and artillery support will be launched by V Corps probably on 4 May, on the axis Medjez-Tunis'.[32] Churchill left for America on the eve of this *coup de grâce*, boarding the *Queen Mary* in the Clyde and sailing at 5.30 p.m. on Wednesday, 5 May.

With the Prime Minister went a party of about 150, including the COS, Averell Harriman, Lord Beaverbrook, Lord Leathers, Lord Cherwell, Wavell – who spent some of the time on board working on his poetry anthology – the Joint Planners, and a vast variety of other experts filling 21 offices in addition to the VIP suites. *Queen Mary* remained bug-ridden, apart from the select portion used by the British delegation; also on board were 300 German prisoners of war. The journey would take seven days, and for Churchill and his COS they would be busy ones: once again the British had to present a united front – and once again American opposition seemed likely to be stiff. The COS therefore met daily, and Churchill showered them with minutes and directives; Brooke spent long hours with the Prime Minister, explaining, going over details, arguing. Meanwhile the *Queen Mary* sailed on a southerly course towards Cape Finisterre, chosen to make a short right-angle crossing of the 'submarine Piccadilly' – the passage used by U-boats to link bases with operating areas.

Burma remained the principal subject, but from this one topic spread a multitude of others, all connected by the need to find the best use for limited shipping resources; thus the Far East could not be discussed without the Mediterranean, or 'Round-up', and the British still feared the Americans might switch priority to the defeat of the Japanese. Recent discussions in London had underlined the lack of progress in the Akyab operations; the decision had been taken – but not yet officially passed to the Americans – to cancel 'Anakim'. An alternative to the latter had still to be found, and the Joint Planners made a number of suggestions during the voyage; they viewed with some favour an operation against Northern Sumatra, provided this was followed by attacks on Malaya and Penang, but they stressed these would not help China, deemed essential by the Americans. The latter would require a concentration on Upper Burma, including the development of air facilities in Assam, limited land operations from Assam, and attempts to capture Ramree Island and Akyab. The COS accepted the idea of emphasis being placed on Upper Burma, but immediate opposition came from Churchill. Lying in his bed in his stateroom, resplendent in Chinese-pattern dressing gown and surrounded by scattered grey cigar ash, Churchill completed a long paper, dated 8 May. 'Going into swampy jungles to fight the Japanese is like going into the water to fight a shark. It is better to entice him into a trap or catch him on a hook and then demolish him with axes after hauling him out on to dry land.' The shark could be trapped by seizing strategic points 'which will force the Japanese to counter-attack under conditions detrimental to them and favourable to us'. These points would be located in the crescent from Moulmein to Timor, and Churchill listed a number of possible targets: the Andaman Islands, Mergui with Bangkok as the objective, the Kra Isthmus, assault on Northern Sumatra, the southern tip of Sumatra and Java. 'All the alternatives should be examined in a hopeful spirit, resolute to overcome the real difficulties and brush away the still more numerous imaginary difficulties...'[33] The COS discussed this magisterial paper at 5.30 p.m. on the 8th; Wavell seemed to support the spirit of the document, but Brooke vigorously disagreed with the content. He complained to his diary: 'PM had been writing a long paper on our future actions against Japan in which he forgot to take into account the basic limitations of our strategy, namely shipping!'[34] The COS agreed with Brooke that 'we could not embark on a major operation in the Far East while fully engaged in Germany'. Argument with Churchill continued on Monday, 10 May, just before the *Queen Mary* reached New York; the Prime Minister demanded further studies of amphibious operations in the Far East should be made, but a temporary compromise was reached with the decision that care would be taken in

Washington not to go into details regarding Burma.[35]

Shipboard discussions also dealt with the Mediterranean. Agreement had still to be reached on the next target after Sicily: the COS, at a meeting on 4 May, still refused to shelve Sardinia. They feared the dangers of drawn-out campaigning if a direct assault were made on Italy before the acquisition of additional stepping-stones; they also wished to give further consideration to the possibilities of operations in the Eastern Mediterranean. Churchill maintained his disagreement with the inclusion of Sardinia in the operational programme, but agreement was finally reached on a suitable compromise: immediate preparations should be made for establishing a bridgehead on the toe of Italy, which would be used and exploited if Italy seemed on the point of collapse or if the Germans did not send strong reinforcements. If the Germans did divert large forces to Italy – itself helping the Russians – then operations should be launched at Sardinia and Corsica. Possibilities of operations in the Eastern Mediterranean should also be borne in mind.[36] The COS were well aware that shipping for further Mediterranean operations would have to come from 'Bolero' or from the Pacific. And Churchill declared: 'We want them (the Americans) to agree to the exploitation of "Husky" and the attack on the underbelly taking priority over the build-up for "Bolero".'[37] Marshall's fears of the Mediterranean sucking in more and more troops and resources were already apparently justified: US forces in the area, totalling 180,000 at the end of 1942, had now risen to 388,000; and this had been at the expense of 'Bolero', thus affecting chances for 'Round-up'. As Marshall told his colleagues, if 'Round-up' was to be further delayed 'a readjustment of landing-craft and troop shipping should be made in favour of the Pacific'.[38]

A major clash between the US and British therefore seemed inevitable. The Americans believed the abandonment of 'Anakim' might increase the need for added pressure in the Pacific. They considered cross-Channel operations in 1943 to have been ruled out by Mediterranean operations, and while the British agreed, Brooke and his colleagues firmly rejected the US corollary: that operations in the Mediterranean after 'Husky' should only be undertaken if they involved a reduction, rather than a possible increase, in Allied forces. Dangers of the Americans going their own way and shifting priority to the Pacific had therefore increased dramatically. As the *Queen Mary* sailed serenely into New York harbour on Tuesday, 11 May, the outlook seemed indeed stormy. But half a world away in Tunisia, the horizon hourly brightened. On 6 May, the day after the *Queen Mary* slipped down the darkened Clyde, Alexander had launched IX Corps on a narrow front down either side of the Medjez-Tunis road, and this spearhead tore a gaping wound in the Axis defences. Infantry broke through and held open the gap for the tanks to crash onwards, while over 2,500 sorties a day were flown by the Allied air forces – the enemy were only able to attempt 60 in reply. At 4 p.m. on Friday, 7 May, British troops reached Tunis; these units, transferred from the 8th Army, had been present at the beginning of the battle for North Africa many weary months before, and were now in at the kill. The Americans surged forward towards Bizerta. The 6th Armoured Division swung east, then south, to link with the 8th Army.

'CWR RECORD for the 24 hours ending 0700, 8 May, 1943.... *Tunisia.* Advanced elements of British and US forces entered TUNIS and BIZERTA yesterday afternoon. This morning it is officially reported that we have occupied both towns....'[39] 'All London is drunk with victory,' moaned Goebbels on the 9th. 'Our losses there are enormous. We are indeed experiencing a sort of second Stalingrad....'[40] Yet War Cabinet Ministers meeting on the 10th, with Attlee in the chair, were cautioned that the end had still to come. 'The enemy is putting up a stiff resistance in the neighbourhood of Hamman Lif, and we have made little progress against them up to the previous evening. There have been no reports of the retreat of the 1st Italian Army, which was facing the front of the 8th Army.' But the Vice-CIGS continued: 'The administrative situation of the enemy is desperate, and they will have extreme difficulty in maintaining themselves in the Cap Bon peninsula.'[41] And as Churchill arrived in New York on the 11th he received a welcome telegram from Alexander. 'I expect all organized resistance to collapse within the next 48 hours, and final liquidation of whole Axis force in the next two or three days. I calculate that prisoners up to date exceed 100,000, but this is not yet confirmed.'[42] An incident which occurred while the *Queen Mary* lay off Staten Island seemed fitting. The COS, generals, air marshals and admirals, all glittering with medals, were waiting for a launch to take them inshore; and now, as they stood on deck, a shabby file of men walked slowly past them – the German soldiers, captured in North Africa, who had been sailing on the same vessel. One member of Ismay's staff wrote: 'The two groups stared across the gap, steadily and in silence.'[43] News from North Africa continued to flash across the Atlantic as the Prime Minister and his massive entourage took the train to Washington, where Roosevelt waited on the station platform.

Brooke had written in his diary the previous day: 'I do not look forward to these meetings; in fact I hate the thought of them.... It is an exhausting process, and I am very *very* tired and shudder at the useless struggles that lie ahead.'[44] These struggles would begin on Thursday, 13 May; meanwhile the British COS met on the 12th to discuss final details of their position, and to hear likely US views from Dill, after which the British and American staffs attended a 2.30 p.m. White House meeting with Roosevelt and Churchill. The Prime Minister declared: ' "Torch" was over, Sicily was near; what should come next? ... We had the authority and prestige of victory. It was our duty to redouble our efforts and to grasp the fruits of our success.' The only outstanding questions between the two staffs, continued Churchill, were questions of emphasis and priority – but he then proceeded to show the difficulties inherent in this search for a solution by stressing the importance of the Mediterranean, and, while he emphasized Britain's earnest desire 'to undertake a full-scale invasion of the Continent from the UK as soon as a plan offering reasonable prospects of success could be made', he also mentioned the drawbacks. In reply the President pointed to the surplus of manpower which would be available after 'Husky'; this, he added, should be used to build up

'Bolero' and should start at once. Thus, even in these polite opening remarks, the differences in British and American views were being uncovered.[45]

Churchill and Brooke had last stood in the White House study eleven months before, when news had been brought of the fall of Tobruk, and for the first and only time in the war, Ismay had seen Churchill wince with shock. And now the tremendous, drawn-out North African campaign reached its victorious conclusion; the Prime Minister received another signal from Alexander: 'The end is very near. Von Arnim has been captured, and prisoners will most likely be over 150,000. All organized resistance has collapsed....'[46] Next day, 13 May, General Messe surrendered. Another signal flashed from Alexander to Churchill, reaching Washington at 2.15 p.m. 'Sir. It is my duty to report that the Tunisian campaign is over. All enemy resistance has ceased. We are masters of the North African shores.'[47] Over 238,240 prisoners had been taken. At 5.30 p.m. on this Thursday, Attlee held a War Cabinet meeting in London, and Ministers decided that 'at church services on Sunday, 16 May, special prayers of thanksgiving would be offered for the victory in Africa, and that, wherever practicable, church bells should be pealed....'[48]

But as Churchill had said in the White House: 'What should come next?' The Combined Chiefs of Staff had their first meeting of the Washington conference, code-named 'Trident', at 10.30 a.m. this Thursday, 13 May. Admiral Leahy, US Ambassador to the Vichy Government from early 1941 until July 1942 and now Roosevelt's Chief of Staff, was voted into the chair; he welcomed the British; Brooke reciprocated. But Ismay wrote later: 'There was an unmistakable atmosphere of tension.'[49] Leahy read a basic memorandum introducing the US views: 'The concept of defeating Germany first involves making a determined attack against Germany on the Continent at the earliest practicable date ... all proposed operations in Europe should be judged primarily on the basis of the contribution to that end. Similarly ... all proposed operations now or later in the Pacific should be judged primarily on the basis of a con-

tribution to defeating Japan in the shortest practicable time.
... A cross-Channel invasion of Europe is necessary to an
early conclusion of the war against Germany, and an early
opening of communications with China is necessary in order
to keep China in the war and bring a successful conclusion to
the war with Japan.' The statement had admirable simplicity;
but behind the simple sentences lurked a number of traps,
at least according to the British. Brooke read a very much
longer, more specific – and more controversial – paper, giving
the British views. 'The main task which lies before us this
year in the European theatre is the elimination of Italy. If
we could achieve this, it is our opinion that we should have
gone a very long way towards defeating Germany. We therefore consider it essential that we should follow up a successful 'Husky' by amphibious operations against either the
Italian islands or the mainland, backed up, if possible, by
operations in other parts of the Mediterranean. Only in this
way can we reap the full benefits of our victories in Africa.'
Brooke warned: 'The provision of shipping required to deliver
a second amphibious blow in the Mediterranean this year
will affect "Bolero".' Some delay would be caused to the UK
build-up, 'but we believe that this disadvantage will be greatly
outweighed by the fact that successful Mediterranean operations, and still more the elimination of Italy, will ease the
task confronting an army landing in Europe from the UK.'
Brooke turned to the Far East: the British believed 'Anakim'
should be cancelled; moreover, a successful 'Anakim' would
not offer immediate help towards reopening the Burma
road.

Leahy and King expressed fears of forces being diverted
from a cross-Channel assault for the Italian offensive; Brooke
replied: 'If we did not continue operations in the Mediterranean, then no possibility of an attack into France would
arise. Even after a bridgehead had been established, we
could get no further. The troops employed would for the
most part be inexperienced. The force available, some 15-20
divisions, was small, and could not be regarded in the same
category as vast Continental armies, which were counted in
50s and 100s of divisions. Before undertaking operations

across the Channel it was essential that we should create the
right situation to ensure its success.' Marshall now intervened;
the discussion, he said, was coming to the heart of the
problem. 'The Tunisian campaign had sucked in more and
more troops. Operations invariably created a vacuum in
which it was essential to pour in more and more means.'
He felt 'deeply concerned' that the invasion of Italy would
establish such a vacuum. 'If further Mediterranean operations
were undertaken, then in 1943 and virtually all of 1944
we should be committed, except for air attacks on Germany,
to a Mediterranean policy.' And he added: 'This would
entail a very serious state of affairs in the Pacific. It would
mean a prolongation of the war in Europe, and thus a delay
in the ultimate defeat of Japan, which the people of the
United States could not tolerate. We were at the crossroads –
if we were committed to the Mediterranean, except for air
alone, it meant a prolonged struggle, and one which was
not acceptable to the United States.' Brooke retorted: 'To
cease Mediterranean operations at the conclusion of "Husky"
would lengthen the war. The seizure of the Brest Peninsula,
which was all that we could now achieve, would merely
lock up 20 divisions.... Only by continuing in the Mediterranean could we achieve the maximum diversion of German
forces from Russia.'[50] Already, at this first 'Trident' session,
stark deadlock had been reached, and Brooke wrote that
evening: 'I am thoroughly depressed with the prospects.'[51]
A meeting of the British COS, starting at 5.30 p.m., failed
to find any means for reaching agreement with the
Americans.

Churchill had meanwhile been spending time this Thursday on another Anglo-American source of conflict – the
French. Three days before, Hull had handed a stiff memorandum to Roosevelt: 'De Gaulle's active political propaganda,
directed from London, immediately threatens the military
success against the Axis Powers to which we have dedicated
our every effort.... The real French contribution was given
by French forces under General Giraud, while throughout
the period of the battle de Gaulle ... caused nothing but
disturbance and concern.' Hull sought an interview with

Churchill on the 13th and repeated his grievances. He warned: 'If this de Gaulle matter is allowed to go forward as it has been, it will undoubtedly bring about serious friction between our two Governments.' He accused Britain of aiding de Gaulle; Churchill, according to Hull's account, replied that 'he personally was utterly disgusted with de Gaulle' and that the British 'were not aiding him as much as I (Hull) seemed to think'.[52] British relations with de Gaulle had indeed been passing through a sensitive period since the refusal to allow him to visit troops in North Africa at the beginning of March.

Brooke opened the second 'Trident' meeting on Friday, 14 May, by disagreeing with a number of points in the US paper on global strategy read by Leahy the previous day. He referred first to a US proposal for 'an extension of pressure against Japan', and he then applied Marshall's criticisms of the Mediterranean policy to the situation in the Far East: 'Such an extension might well cause a vacuum.' Brooke then declared that the British held a different view of 'Round-up' and its possibilities. 'It was their firm intention to carry out "Round-up" at the first moment when the conditions were such that the operations would contribute decisively to the defeat of Germany. These conditions might arise this year, but in any case, it was the firm belief of the British COS that they would arise next year. They could be created only by the Russian army. Our action, therefore, must consist of a) continuing our increasing bombardment of Germany; and b) drawing off from the Russian front as many forces as possible. On the basis of this definition of "Round-up" the British COS had put forward their views on operations in the Mediterranean.' The US reply came from the chairman, Leahy; he was unable to see that the US conception of global strategy differed materially from that set out at Casablanca. 'The intention was now, and was then, to prepare for cross-Channel operations. The African venture was undertaken in order to do something this year while preparing for cross-Channel operations.... The North African campaign was now completed. If we launched a new campaign in the Mediterranean, then we should continue to use our resources in that area. This would again postpone help to Russia, since we should not be able to concentrate forces in the UK and thus cause a withdrawal of German forces in Western Europe.'

With disagreement as wide as ever, the CCS turned to the Far East. Brooke explained the British reasons for wishing to cancel 'Anakim', and briefly mentioned possible alternatives. The Americans had apparently expected an 'Anakim' cancellation, and made no objections; King was attracted towards a Bangkok operation although he admitted this would not be of direct assistance to China, where morale was weakening. 'If China went out of the war, the task of the United States in defeating Japan would be terrific.' Wavell, Somerville and Air Chief Marshal Peirse entered the meeting, and Wavell explained the situation on behalf of his fellow C-in-Cs. Stilwell and Chennault gave the American views, which differed substantially from the British with a strong preference for Upper Burma. And so, with both the Far East and Europe, the CCS could only resort to seeking room for manoeuvre: Combined Staff Planners were asked to submit papers on both areas. With Europe, the Planners were asked to submit plans for the defeat of Germany, a) by concentrating on the biggest possible invasion force in the UK as soon as possible; and b) by accepting the elimination of Italy as a necessary preliminary. The first would be prepared by US planners in consultation with the British, and the procedure would be reversed for the second. With the Far East, the CCS directed the planners to report on the potentialities of the air route from Assam to China, and on the most promising operation for the opening of a land route to China. All these papers would be considered by the CCS on Monday morning, 17 May.[53] A further meeting took place at the White House at 2 p.m., at which Roosevelt and Churchill were present: this concentrated upon Burma, and Brooke came away thoroughly depressed. 'By the time we left, what is not a very simple problem had become a tangled mass of confusion.' The British CIGS was especially irritated by Stilwell who, he claimed, 'had little military knowledge and no strategic ability of any kind. His worst failing was, however, his deep-rooted hatred of anybody or anything British.'⁵⁴ The British COS met at 5.30 p.m. and could find no ground for optimism.

Next day, Saturday 15 May, the US COS invited the British chiefs and Wavell and his colleagues to be their guests at Williamsburg in Virginia; the First Sea Lord enjoyed himself swimming, Wavell took photographs, Brooke studied Virginian birds, and the party returned refreshed on the Sunday afternoon, in time for the British to hold a brief meeting to prepare for the next day's work. 'I wish the next week was over,' wrote Brooke. Churchill had spent the weekend with Roosevelt at the latter's Maryland mountain refuge, spending the time admiring the President's stamp collection, fishing, drinking and talking; they returned to Washington's stifling heat on the Monday. Next time Churchill visited America he would bring with him a young RAF pilot, by then famous, and the reason for the invitation and the fame had come about during the Sunday night, 16 May: while the Prime Minister and President talked together in the peaceful mountain retreat, Wing-Commander Guy Gibson was braving the flak in the dark sky above the Möhne and Eder dams.

Visiting America to press China's case were the Chinese leader's wife, and his brother-in-law, Dr Soong. Roosevelt had tried to arrange a meeting between Churchill and Madame Chiang Kai-shek for the Monday but she had felt unable to leave New York. Meanwhile, also on the Monday, Dr Soong delivered a solemn warning to the CCS. 'Anakim' was considered by the Chinese as a 'definite US/British commitment, and he must therefore ask for its fulfilment.... If not undertaken, they would believe themselves abandoned by the allies.' Yet the British and, tacitly, the Americans had already agreed to scrap the operation; nor had they reached any agreement over an alternative. Studies which the CCS had asked the planners to prepare for this Monday, on Burma and on Europe, had still to be completed. Instead the CCS turned to another subject, upon which they could at last find agreement: they decided to recommend to the President and to Churchill that the Azores should be 'acquired' by the allies as soon as possible. This decision would soon cause anxiety back home in London.[55]

The British paper on Europe was presented to the CCS next day, 18 May. Respective rates of allied and Axis build-up in Northern France were analysed, to show the Germans could reinforce far faster than the British and Americans. 'It seems clear that unless Russian action or allied action elsewhere reduces the enemy potential in France from the figures in paragraph 10 (35 divisions) to something approaching those given in paragraph 12 (22 divisions) we are unlikely to be able to retain a foothold in France until our rate of build-up gives us superiority over the enemy.' This enemy reduction could be brought about through an Italian collapse, which, claimed the British planners, 'would create a situation which will make the difference between success or failure of a re-entry into North-West Europe in 1944.' The paper claimed Mediterranean commitments would not delay a 'Round-up' date for spring, 1944. Discussion on this British paper was deferred until the next morning, Wednesday, 19 May, when the document prepared by the US planners was also ready for consideration. The Americans stressed their belief that Italy's elimination was not a prerequisite for a favourable 'Round-up' situation. The US planners agreed that the enemy could build up rapidly to counter an allied cross-Channel invasion – indeed, the US figures were even more pessimistic than those put forward by the British – but the Americans gave greater importance to allied air superiority over the battle area. Mediterranean operations were irrelevant to the early defeat of Germany; they would use up valuable resources – and, even more important than numbers of men diverted to the Mediterranean, these soldiers would be veterans and hence far more valuable. Thus the American paper concluded: 'Operations in the Mediterranean subsequent to "Husky" should be limited to the air offensive, because any other operations would use resources vital to "Round-up" and present the risk of limitless commitment of US resources to the Mediterranean vacuum, thus needlessly prolonging the war.'

Brooke, in the subsequent CCS discussion on the Wednesday morning, criticized the American paper for its neglect of any provision for allied action to take advantage of Italian disintegration. Secondly, the US proposal apparently accepted 6 or 7 months' inactivity after 'Husky', yet 'this year was the most critical time for Russia, and we must take all possible steps to assist her.... Without crippling "Round-up" in 1944, we could ... with the forces now available in the Mediterranean, achieve important results and provide the greatest measure of assistance to Russia in this critical period, and at the same time create a situation favourable for cross-Channel operations in 1944.' Marshall countered by saying 'it would take some time to mount any operation subsequent to "Husky" which itself might not be completed until September', and the British proposals gave insufficient weight 'to the devastating effect of our air bombardments' in connection with 'Round-up', nor did they give sufficient importance to the psychological value of a bridgehead – and the effect such a European bridgehead would have on the U-boat campaign by provision of airfields. Moreover, Marshall believed the British underestimated the difficulties of an Italian campaign. 'It must be remembered that in North Africa a relatively small German force had produced a serious factor of delay to our operations. A German decision to support Italy might make intended operations extremely difficult and time-consuming.'[56]

Agreement seemed impossible – Brooke was becoming increasingly concerned over the effect of failure on the alliance. But so too was Marshall, and now, at the end of this morning session on the 19th, the US Army Chief made a simple suggestion which would make a dramatic difference to proceedings. He believed the CCS should hold 'Off the Record' talks between themselves alone, and thus without the attendants who normally crowded into the CCS sessions. Both the Americans and the British had gradually increased the numbers of staff officers, until the room was now filled by up to 30 people besides the COS. Brooke wrote: 'I felt that frequently Marshall did not like shifting from some policy he had been briefed on by his staff lest they should think he was lacking in determination.'[57] Brooke and his colleagues therefore accepted Marshall's suggestion and staff officers filed from the room, leaving the six Chiefs of Staff, Leahy, Dill and a secretary, surrounded by empty chairs; and in Brooke's words: 'We then had a heart to heart talk.' In this less stifling atmosphere, the CCS came with remarkable speed to a compromise – weighted towards the British proposals. The session broke for lunch, after which the British and Americans held separate meetings to discuss draft proposals. The CCS met again at 4.30 p.m. in full conference, and agreed upon these conclusions: 'Forces and equipment shall be established in the UK with the object of mounting an operation with target date the 1st May 1944, to secure a lodgement on the Continent from which further offensive operations can be carried out....' The Allied C-in-C North Africa 'should be instructed to mount such operations in exploitation of "Husky" as are best calculated to eliminate Italy from the war and to contain the maximum number of German forces. Each specific operation will be subject to the approval of the CCS.' Forces would comprise those available in the Mediterranean, except for 4 US divisions and 3 British which would be held in readiness from 1 November for withdrawal to the UK. Naval vessels required would have to be approved by the CCS, and the CCS would review the situation at a July meeting, or early August, in the light of the 'Husky' result and the Russian situation.[58] Thus the British objective of eliminating Italy and maintaining Mediterranean pressure had been endorsed; but the Americans had succeeded in restricting these operations, both in the forces available for them and in overruling the British plea that they should have superiority over 'Bolero'. Moreover, the CCS would continue to keep tight control; this, Marshall hoped, would prevent the Mediterranean from sucking in more troops. Both the British and Americans had reason for satisfaction. The latter had now received a full British commitment to an invasion of Europe in spring, 1944 – although the date had been delayed one month; the British had received full US confirmation that Germany would continue to be regarded as the primary enemy.

Thunderstorms broke over Washington that Wednesday

evening to cool the heavy air; sweet-smelling rain swept the dust from the sidewalks and garbage from the gutters. Churchill had addressed the US Congress earlier in the day: 'It behoves us therefore to search our hearts and brace our sinews and take the most earnest counsel one with another....' In London, Churchill's prayer was matched by those given by the crowds flocking to bomb-battered St Paul's for a Thanksgiving Service. Montgomery, in London for talks, was not invited to attend this service to mark the ending of the North African campaign – he was informed afterwards that 'it was desired to keep my presence in England a secret'. Wherever he walked, a multitude mobbed him.

The CCS switched again to Far East discussions. Papers had been completed by the Combined Planners, requested the previous week and examining the potentialities of the air route from Assam, together with Burmese operations to secure an overland route to China. Brooke made a number of criticisms at a CCS morning meeting on 20 May. The Americans favoured full-scale operations to capture Mandalay; these, said the CIGS, 'were not possible of achievement' in view of military difficulties and administrative problems. Instead, the British advocated a more cautious policy of building up the air route, undertaking limited protective operations from Ledo and Imphal, and operations on the coast to secure Akyab and Ramree Island. The Americans continued to press for more ambitious plans; agreement could not be reached, and the meeting broke up. The CCS assembled again at 2.30 p.m., but this time in closed session, and once again this procedure proved successful: agreement had been reached within an hour – substantially on the basis of the British proposals. Thus the CCS agreed upon the 'concentration of available resources as a first priority within the Assam-Burma theatre' for building up air traffic to China, and for intensifying air operations against the Japanese. Secondly, the CCS agreed upon 'vigorous and aggressive land and air operations from Assam into Burma via Ledo and Imphal ... as an essential step towards the opening of the Burma Road'. Amphibious operations would be launched to capture Akyab and Ramree

Island, and Japanese sea communications into Burma would be disrupted.[59] Brooke was extremely pleased: 'We finally reached agreement and obtained practically exactly what we had originally put forward.'[60] Next day the British consented to American plans for the Pacific, covering operations to eject the Japanese from the Aleutians, seizure of the Marshall and Caroline Islands, the Solomons, the Bismarck Archipelago and Japanese-held New Guinea, and the intensification of operations against enemy lines of communication. The most contentious items had therefore been fully discussed and agreement reached. Remaining CCS discussions during this busy week would cover subjects such as propaganda and the anti-U-boat war; on the following Monday the CCS would turn to last discussion of the final report to the President and Prime Minister.

Meanwhile, on Friday, 21 May, War Cabinet Ministers in London discussed a disturbing telegram from Churchill. The Prime Minister and President had received the formal statement from the CCS stressing the 'extreme importance' of acquiring the use of the Azores at the earliest moment in order to help the Battle of the Atlantic. Churchill fully supported such a policy; moreover, he believed a military operation should not be preceded by a diplomatic request to the Portuguese for the use of the island facilities: such a diplomatic approach, he claimed, would be rejected and the Portuguese would thus be warned of the forthcoming invasion. Churchill therefore asked 'to be empowered to state ... that, if the President agreed to share the responsibility, we would authorize the CCS to make and execute a plan to attack the islands at the earliest possible moment'. Eden thoroughly disagreed. The value of the Azores was indisputable; without the use of these islands, and in order to gain greatest possible air protection, Atlantic convoys had to follow a northerly route affected by weather and ice. The Azores would provide airfields allowing cover for a more southerly route, would give naval fuelling facilities, and would also provide a valuable air staging post. But Britain and Portugal were allies, through a treaty signed in 1373 – the oldest alliance in Britain's history and viewed with pride by the Portuguese. War Cabinet Ministers now agreed with Eden that 'the Prime Minister's proposal seemed to involve making an attack, without warning, on the territory of our oldest ally, whom we had recently been providing with arms to defend themselves against aggression'. Ministers were informed that 'our Ambassador at Lisbon thought that there was some prospect of persuading Dr Salazar to yield to a request for facilities on the island, if made by way of a diplomatic approach'. Eden believed difficulties would be increased if the Americans took a substantial part in proceedings: public opinion in Portugal was strongly pro-British. A telegram therefore left London expressing War Cabinet opposition to Churchill.[61] Cadogan noted in his diary: 'Everyone (except Morrison) against PM – which they wouldn't have been if he'd been here!'[62]

Despite Cadogan's cynicism – shared by Eden – the decision proved that the War Cabinet still had a part to play. And two days later Ministers again felt obliged to defy Churchill, this time over the delicate problem of General de Gaulle. Churchill now wanted to be rid of the troublesome French leader. Ministers met at 9 p.m. on Sunday, 23 May, to consider a telegram in which the Prime Minister reported that 'a very stern situation was developing' in America about de Gaulle, and Churchill believed 'urgent consideration should be given to the question whether de Gaulle should not now be eliminated as a political force, the French National Committee being told that we would have no further relations with them, nor give them any money, so long as de Gaulle was connected with them'. Another telegram enclosed a memorandum handed to the Prime Minister by Roosevelt, making various allegations against de Gaulle and his National Committee. Once again Eden disagreed with the Prime Minister and received War Cabinet support – as the Foreign Secretary wrote in his diary: 'Everyone against it and very brave about it in his absence.' De Gaulle had now been invited to Algiers, explained Eden, and would probably accept; Ministers agreed 'it was extremely difficult to see how we could break with de Gaulle at the moment, when he was on the point of reaching agreement with General

Giraud. If de Gaulle made trouble after an agreement had been reached, we should be in a stronger position to insist upon his withdrawal should this latter prove necessary.' Attlee pointed out that if action were taken against de Gaulle he would receive support from many Frenchmen who were now opposed to him, and the War Cabinet agreed that if the break were made during or immediately after Churchill's visit to America, the inference would be drawn that Britain had done so under US pressure. 'It must be recognized that US policy towards the French had not met with success and there was increasing recognition of this fact within the US itself. This was probably responsible for some of the pressure which was now being exercised in favour of getting rid of de Gaulle.' Attlee and Eden sent a telegram to Churchill: 'We had no idea that de Gaulle situation was rankling so much.... We are fully conscious of the difficulties which de Gaulle has created for us, and of your position under heavy pressure from Americans. We do not however consider that the policy which you so strongly recommend is practicable....' Among accusations made against de Gaulle was his alleged intention to favour the Russians in any future settlements, as opposed to Britain and America, and even Germany might be preferred. This led to another message from the War Cabinet: 'We find it incredible that de Gaulle would ever have said that he would base his policy solely on Russia and perhaps on Germany. He uses the Russians in his political game, but a permanent association with communism would be alien to his whole nature. Incidentally he is a devout Catholic. There is surely no warrant for suggesting that he has ever contemplated dealings with the Germans.' Another telegram from Attlee and Eden, despatched late on the 23rd, added further arguments: 'We must remember that during the 18 months before the US came into the war, when de Gaulle represented all there was of French resistance, we entered into a number of agreements with the General. To break with de Gaulle would mean the automatic cancellation of the agreements.... We are sorry not to be more helpful, but we are convinced that the Americans are wrong in this and advocate a line which would not be

understood here, with possible evil consequences to Anglo-
American relations.'[63]

Churchill signalled the War Cabinet next day, Monday,
24 May. He agreed to stand down over the de Gaulle question
for the moment – action could await the outcome of the
de Gaulle-Giraud negotiations. But Churchill refused to give
way completely over the Azores, and the War Cabinet met at
3 p.m. to hear his new suggestion: 'The expedition should
be prepared and sailed at the earliest convenient date, and
that, not more than 36 hours before its arrival off the islands,
the Portuguese should be informed that a descent in overwhelming force was imminent.... If however this bluff failed,
and the Portuguese refused our request and made it clear
that they would back their refusal by armed resistance, then
the expedition could be called off at the last moment.'
Ministers displayed considerable distrust: 'If the plan now
suggested by the Prime Minister were adopted, it was most
unlikely that the expedition would, in the event, be called
off, even if the Portuguese showed that they would resist.'
Another telegram left for Washington; as a result the Prime
Minister consented to reserve the British decision until his
return home.[64]

Churchill seemed docile. Yet during this Monday he made
proposals in Washington which threw Brooke into fresh
despair and which, according to the CIGS, threatened to
sour Anglo-American relations after all the days of patient
negotiations. The CCS held their long meeting in the morning
to settle remaining points in their final report, which they
took to the President and Prime Minister at 4.45 p.m.
Churchill raised immediate objections: no specific mention
had been made in the report of an invasion of Italy after
'Husky', and the wording on this point seemed to Churchill
to be too vague. The CCS compromise agreement 'to plan
such operations in exploitation of "Husky" as are best calculated to eliminate Italy from the war' might, in Churchill's
view, allow an attack on Sardinia which he opposed. He
asked for more specific plans. Brooke complained in his
diary: 'He had no idea of the difficulties we had been
through, and just crashed in.... As a result he created a

situation of suspicion in the American Chiefs that we had been behind their backs.' The CIGS discussed the position with Ismay the following morning, 25 May. 'I discovered ... that the PM had produced an impossible addition to our agreement, which would have crashed the whole discussion.'[65] But Harry Hopkins, Roosevelt's trusted aide, told Churchill: 'If you wish to carry your point you will have to stay here another week, and even then there is no certainty.'[66] Churchill gave way, and merely asked for the inclusion of the words 'as a matter of urgency' in Eisenhower's instructions to plan next Mediterranean operations; this amendment was approved at a short, final CCS meeting on Tuesday morning, 25 May. But Churchill, while ostensibly agreeing to moderate his last-minute demand, had merely changed his tactics; he still believed greater emphasis should be given to Mediterranean operations leading to an invasion of Italy. He had already decided not to travel home immediately and would instead fly to North Africa for consultations with the military commanders. And now he decided General Marshall should fly with him: the US chief would perhaps soften his opinions when he had been subjected to a hard-sell tour of the area. Roosevelt gave his permission. Early next morning, 26 May, the Prime Minister and his party boarded a flying boat berthed on the Potomac; at 8.30 a.m. the Clipper left in heavy rain on the first stage of the flight to Algiers.

'Trident' had been a success. The basic programme now seemed settled: exploitation of 'Husky' in the summer and autumn; 'Round-up' in spring 1944, with 1 May set as the target date. Talks in Washington, like those at Casablanca, had managed to bridge the Anglo-American gap. But Brooke, for one, had doubts; these summits were 'the most exhausting entertainments imaginable ... they fall short in so far as our basic convictions remain unaltered.... Compromises emerge and the war is prolonged, while we age and get more and more weary.'[67] This time the talks had fallen very close to failure; discussions suffered from the hot-house Washington atmosphere, and never again would a CCS summit be held in either one of the capital cities. Agreement had only been reached through moving into closed session, and through the tireless efforts of men like Sir John Dill working behind the scenes. Dill was in fact a very sick man, suffering from an infection following a hernia operation, yet he remained in constant demand as an intermediary between Marshall and Brooke. Moreover, agreement had only been reached through the very nature of the alliance: the British and Americans might argue, lose their tempers, reach apparent deadlock, yet the basic quality of their relationship remained undamaged and the strength of this carried them through.

Churchill's flying boat travelled the 2,300 miles from the heat of Washington to the bitter cold of Botwood, Newfoundland; at 9 p.m. the aircraft left again for the 3,260-mile flight to Gibraltar. Churchill was awoken from his sleep in an extra-wide 'bridal' bed by a sharp crack caused by lightning striking the Clipper, but the aircraft droned safely on to land at Gibraltar on the 27th; next day the Prime Minister arrived at Algiers. The next 8 days were to prove extremely refreshing and Churchill wrote later: 'I have no more pleasant memories of the war.'[68] But first the Prime Minister addressed himself briefly to perhaps the oldest – and stalest – problem: the French. De Gaulle was expected to reach Algiers on the 30th and agreement with Giraud was now expected, yet Churchill wished Eden to be on hand. 'It seems to me important,' he cabled Attlee on the 29th, 'that Eden should come here for a few days. He is much better fitted than I am to be best man.'[69]

The Prime Minister turned back to military affairs. 'I was determined to obtain before leaving Africa the decision to invade Italy should Sicily be taken,' he wrote in his memoirs.[70] At 5 p.m. on the 29th he held his first conference at Eisenhower's villa, with Eisenhower presiding. The allied commander revealed that in 13 days' time an operation would be launched for the capture of Pantelleria Island: seizure of the island would provide airfields for 'Husky' and would be a step towards clearing the Sicilian Narrows. Then, after details of 'Husky' operations had been given, discussion touched the crucial issue: invasion of Italy. Churchill launched into his exposition; as Eisenhower wrote later: 'Mr Churchill was at his eloquent best.'[71] Yet Eisenhower refused to commit himself, suggesting instead that plans should be made for possible operations against Corsica, Sardinia, and the mainland; he added that he would not submit his recommendations as to which he preferred until after 'Husky' had started. Marshall agreed with this caution.[72] Brooke described the conference as 'good value'; Churchill expressed similar optimism – he believed that among the field commanders – Alexander, Cunningham and Tedder – there would be strong support for his own wish to sweep on over the Mediterranean and into Italy. 'The desire of all the leaders to go forward on the boldest lines was clear, and I felt myself that the reservations made on account of the unknowable would be settled by events in accordance with my hopes.'[73] The Prime Minister reapplied pressure at a second meeting two days later, 31 May, after circulating a document which declared: 'Compelling or inducing Italy to quit the war is the only objective in the Mediterranean worthy of the famous campaign already begun and adequate to the Allied forces available and already in the Mediterranean basin.... For this purpose the taking of Sicily is an indispensable preliminary, and the invasion of the mainland of Italy and the capture of Rome are the evident steps. In this way the greatest service can be rendered to the Allied cause and the general progress of the war, both here and in the Channel theatre.' Despite Churchill's appeal the conference on the 31st failed to come to a definite conclusion. Nor could it; as Brooke wrote in his diary: 'We did not get very much further at the meeting, and the situation is on the whole very much as we settled it in Washington, which is as it should be.'[74] But at least Marshall might now be carried along with the Algiers enthusiasm – only time would tell. Churchill, Brooke and Ismay left for a two-day tour of Tunisia. Before departure Brooke was appalled to hear the Prime Minister now intended to fly to Moscow, to inform Stalin of the Washington talks; Brooke offered to go instead, but nothing came of the suggestion. Instead Churchill

enjoyed himself among the troops, addressing them amidst
the ruins of Carthage amphitheatre. 'I have no idea what I
said, but the whole audience clapped and cheered as doubt-
less their predecessors of two thousand years ago had done
as they watched gladiatorial combats.'[75]

Another gladiatorial struggle had apparently reached a
successful conclusion: de Gaulle had arrived in Algiers
and had found himself able to reach agreement with Giraud,
although the confrontation had nevertheless been complicated and had called upon all those skills already displayed by Macmillan and Murphy. Eden stayed in the
background. Matters had reached such a pitch on 1 June
that Giraud had become convinced de Gaulle was intending
a 'putsch' against him and insisted upon alerting some of
his troops. Finally, on 3 June, agreement was achieved for a
new French Committee of National Liberation with de Gaulle
and Giraud as co-Presidents. FCNL powers would be surrendered to a provisional government which would be constituted as soon as liberation of France allowed, and
discussions would now take place on all measures necessary
for the administrative fusion of the de Gaulle and Giraud
groups.[76] The Prime Minister cabled Roosevelt: 'I consider
that the formation of this Committee brings to an end my
official connection with de Gaulle as the leader of the Fighting
French ... and I propose, so far as is necessary, to transfer
these relationships, financial and otherwise, to the Committee
as a whole.'[77] But only 5 days later de Gaulle resigned from
the Committee and the whole French problem had landed
squarely back in the British lap.

The Prime Minister left for Gibraltar and home on 4 June.
The Germans made a futile and tragic attempt to kill him
en route – agents had mistakenly reported his presence on
board a passenger aircraft from Lisbon and this was intercepted and shot down, killing 13 people, including the actor
Leslie Howard.[78] Churchill arrived in London at 6 a.m. on the
5th; at noon he addressed the War Cabinet. The Washington
visit had been amply justified, he claimed. 'It had again
demonstrated the need for personal exchanges of view at
intervals, in order to preserve the harmony of Anglo-

American co-operation.' He continued: 'Public opinion in the United States was much concerned about the war against Japan – it was almost true to say that the American public would be more disturbed if China fell out of the war than if Russia did. Although this was not the view of the President and the leaders of the administration, they could not fail to be influenced to some extent.' Churchill described the 'marked difference of opinion' between the two staffs at the outset of the talks. 'As the conversations proceeded, however, initial antagonisms were broken down by personal contact.' The Prime Minister turned to the Mediterranean question. 'In the course of the discussions at Washington it had become clear that Eisenhower was somewhat disinclined to concentrate the forthcoming attack against the mainland of Italy. The Prime Minister was strongly of the opinion that, if we struck boldly for the main objective, the secondary objectives would fall automatically into our possession.' The North African visit had been 'most successful'. Full and frank conversations had taken place, 'at the end of which Eisenhower had indicated his complete agreement with the Prime Minister's view. Moreover, General Marshall, who had not previously been specially enthusiastic about operations in the Mediterranean, had been greatly influenced by what he had seen and heard ... and it seemed likely that he would return to the US a convinced supporter of the projected operations in this theatre.'[79] Ministers welcomed Churchill's optimistic assessment.

Efforts were now made to settle differences of opinion between Churchill and his Ministers over the Azores. The Prime Minister and Eden attended a COS meeting on the 7th; Churchill did not believe facilities would be granted without at least a military threat, but the COS were reluctant to stretch shipping resources still further.[80] Eden commented: 'So diplomacy had its chance.' Diplomacy proved successful, but only after considerable negotiations spreading over the summer; on 2 August the Prime Minister complained at a Defence Committee meeting that Salazar was deceiving Eden, and that the island could now have been in allied hands if Churchill's policy had been adopted.[81]

Two weeks later an agreement was signed, with 8 October accepted as the date for British entry into the Azores.

After the 'Trident' summit grand strategic planning now entered a lull, two-thirds of the way through the war. On his return to London in June the Prime Minister could do no more, for the moment. Nor could Brooke and his colleagues; they could merely await the outcome of 'Husky', with the gigantic operation to be launched in just over a month's time. Meanwhile, the COS had a period of relative relaxation, and at the same time lower-level detailed planning gradually intensified for the most crucial operation of all: 'Round-up' – now increasingly referred to by its final majestic code-name, 'Overlord'. During those early summer months Brooke formed the British units which would invade France into the new 21st Army Group, led by General Sir Bernard Paget. And, for a while, Brooke even believed he might soon receive the greatest command of the war: on 15 June the Prime Minister disclosed that he wanted Brooke to be 'Overlord's' Supreme Commander.

One allied campaign, in North Africa, had ended; another was about to begin. Hitler remained under pressure on all fronts. His U-boat war had suddenly deteriorated, due to the bold decision by the British anti-U-boat command to move on to the offensive even at the risk of defence for convoys. Aided by improved patrolling zones in the Atlantic, these hunters now dealt dramatic destruction to U-boat packs. In Russia, the great battle of Kursk was about to be fought. And massive allied bomber fleets continued to batter the German homeland: on 10 June the CCS issued a new directive, with emphasis on attacking German fighter forces and the aircraft industry, and in the second quarter of 1943 a total of 35,000 tons of bombs was dropped on the Ruhr – almost three times the tonnage suffered by London in the Blitz.

Goebbels had written on 22 May: 'We must try to develop counter-measures as fast as possible, especially reprisal attacks. Otherwise, sooner or later, the war in the air will become unbearable for us.'[82] The Germans were indeed struggling to find a counter-measure. The Führer visited the 'secret weapon' experimental centre at Peenemünde on the Baltic coast early in June, and on the 10th told his military chiefs that London would be levelled by the end of the year; Britain would capitulate; Germany had merely to hold on. On 11 June Duncan Sandys requested the Air Staff to intensify reconnaissance flights over Peenemünde and recommended the bombing of the area. His long report of 'Crossbow' findings to date was put before the Defence Committee on the 29th. 'The rocket was a fact,' declared Sandys. 'Nearly all the reports agreed on its range as from 90-130 miles.... Remarkable photographs had been obtained (of Peenemünde), and showed quite clearly specimens of the rocket lying on the ground close to what appeared to be the apparatus from which they could be discharged.... It was said that Hitler was pressing hard for the rocket to be used at the earliest possible moment.' Sandys added: 'It had been suggested by some that the whole affair was a fantasy or a hoax. If it were a hoax, it was a hoax on an extremely big scale.' Terrifying estimates had been made by the Minister of Home Security which showed that 'up to 4,000 casualties, killed and injured, and very heavy damage, might be caused by the explosion in London of one such rocket'. And 'one report spoke of 30 projectors being constructed, of which 15 were completed'. Some experts disagreed with this appalling assessment, including Lord Cherwell, Churchill's scientific adviser, who detailed to the Defence Committee a number of technical objections to Mr Sandys' report. 'The evidence could not be conclusive either one way or the other, but the impression he had formed was that the rocket story was a well-designed cover plan', and he believed estimates of possible damage had been exaggerated. Cherwell nevertheless agreed that Peenemünde should be bombed and a radio watch should be maintained. The Defence Committee decided the experimental station should be attacked with the heaviest raid possible on the first suitable occasion.[83] The raid would eventually be launched on 17 August with 571 bombers taking part, but the experts continued to be divided, especially over whether the 'secret weapon' consisted of a rocket or a pilotless aircraft. Hitler's scientists meanwhile continued their urgent development of both.

Added to this threat for the future was another, which also received anxious attention during these weeks: manpower. Lack of manpower had been drawn to the attention of the War Cabinet the previous November; now shortages had clearly become acute, aggravating problems of planning for 'Overlord'. One example illustrates the demands which this huge operation entailed: more men were needed to man landing-craft than the total pre-war personnel of the Royal Navy. Shortages were especially severe in the aircraft industry, affecting the outflow of bombers; Lord Cherwell wrote to Churchill on 23 June to say that the RAF only had a first-line strength of 864 heavy bombers as opposed to the 4,000 originally planned. More workers would have to be allocated to the Ministry of Aircraft Production to remedy this deficiency, but this in turn would cause further strain elsewhere. Churchill took the problem to the War Cabinet on 9 July. 'It was clear that our resources in manpower were now strained to the utmost and would not enable us to meet all our needs.' Bevin, Minister of Labour, said a gross intake of 80,000 workers a month was needed for aircraft production; this meant the intake of tradesmen into the services would have to be cut to negligible figures; requirements of REME for technical officers would have to be very substantially reduced; Fleet Air Arm demands for aero-engine and airframe fitters would have to be cancelled. On manpower figures in general, the First Lord of the Admiralty warned he was 'gravely perturbed at the allocation proposed for the Royal Navy': total naval deficiency would be equivalent to personnel required to man 47 cruisers, or 195 destroyers; there would be a deficiency in landing-craft personnel 'which would have the effect of reducing by one-third the total lifting capacity for operation "Overlord".'[84] After War Cabinet discussion on 22 July, a total of 115,000 men and women were allocated to aircraft production with corresponding reductions elsewhere, and with cuts in the army's planned strength of the equivalent of 4 divisions; the RAF lost 57 squadrons in 1943 and would lose another 89 in 1944.[85]

'Crossbow' and manpower problems were both typical of the insidious and possibly crippling threats which lurked beneath the surface of day-to-day war-making during summer, 1943. The other main category of subjects discussed by the War Cabinet consisted of those which remained on the fringe of impending great events, but which could have an indirect influence upon these landmarks of war. And typical of this second category remained the problem of the French, and especially de Gaulle. Churchill had told Roosevelt that the new arrangement between de Gaulle and Giraud brought to an end his official connection with the former. But on 7 June, two days after Churchill's return from the Mediterranean, first signs of further complications appeared; the Foreign Office received a request from the new French Committee of National Liberation for official recognition of their status as 'qualified to ensure the conduct of the French effort in the war, within the framework of Allied co-operation, as well as the administration and defence of all French interests'.[86] Churchill told the Commons on the 8th that the question of the 'degree of recognition' would be studied, and if 'things went well' a solution might shortly be reached. But things were not going well; as Churchill spoke to the Commons in London, discussions were taking place in Algiers on the command, organization and control of the French armed forces. Tempers flared; de Gaulle wanted to be Minister, or Commissioner, of Defence, following the British model; Giraud took this as a threat to his authority as C-in-C, and two days later de Gaulle resigned both from his position as co-President and as member of the new French Committee. Anger against de Gaulle could be expected to mount rapidly in Washington. 'American hatred is keen,' wrote Eden in his diary on the 11th, and the Foreign Secretary discussed the situation with Churchill during the day, as a result of which a signal left London for Macmillan. 'There can be no question of our giving recognition until we know what it is we have to recognize.... You are quite right to play for time and let de Gaulle have every chance to come to his senses and realize the forces around him. We play fair with him if he plays fair with us and with France.'[87] Macmillan tried again to persuade de Gaulle to co-operate, and the two men went to the coast for a long talk. Macmillan took the opportunity for a swim. 'I bathed naked in the sea at the far end of the Roman city; de Gaulle sat in a dignified manner on a rock, with his military cap, his uniform and belt.'[88] Macmillan, who had considerable sympathy for 'this strange – attractive and yet impossible – character' believed de Gaulle to be essential for the French movement; he also believed his opinion was shared to some extent by Eisenhower and his Chief of Staff. 'Both of them, as well as Murphy, were beginning to feel that Giraud was really no good. He was stupid and vacillating.'

But the Washington attitude remained very different. Dislike of de Gaulle intensified, and Hull was now satisfied that the British were swinging over to the US view.[89] The Americans disagreed strongly with proposals by the French in Algiers – presumably de Gaulle supporters – to form an inner Cabinet of the National Committee responsible for the French conduct of the war and a Commissariat for the discharge of business. Roosevelt suspected that de Gaulle intended to use the consequent increase in Committee numbers to swell his followers; and US suspicions of the FCNL meant that recognition of this body would be further delayed; on the other hand, Roosevelt had clearly reached the end of his patience with the arch-trouble-maker, de Gaulle. On 17 June Churchill received a copy of a signal despatched by Roosevelt to Eisenhower. 'The position of this Government is that during our military occupation of North Africa we will not tolerate the control of the French Army by any agency which is not subject to the Allied Supreme Commander's direction. We must have someone whom we completely and wholly trust.... We are not interested moreover in the formation of any Government or Committee which presumes in any way to indicate that, until such times as the French people select a Government for themselves, it will govern in France.'[90] So de Gaulle must go. And Churchill, who on 23 May had urged the War Cabinet to agree to such

a step, apparently shared the President's view. The Foreign
Secretary had doubts, describing Roosevelt's telegram in his
diary on 18 June as 'pretty hysterical'.[91] Eden persuaded
Churchill to dilute the draft of his reply to Roosevelt,
supported by Attlee; this left London on the 18th and
declared: 'I am not in favour at this moment of breaking
up the Committee of Seven or forbidding it to meet. I should
prefer that General Eisenhower should take your instructions
as his directive, and that Murphy and Macmillan should
work towards its fulfilment.'[92]

The next move lay with Eisenhower, who immediately
conferred with Macmillan. 'It was a difficult dilemma for
the Allies to resolve,' wrote the British Minister later. 'De
Gaulle was strong, but uncertain; Giraud was reliable, but
weak.' Eisenhower and his British and American advisers
decided to concentrate on the military and short-term aspect,
covering immediate operations, and from this point of view
Giraud must remain C-in-C of the French forces. The two
French generals were invited to Eisenhower's villa at 10 a.m.
on Saturday, 19 June. Two days later, War Cabinet Ministers
in London were informed of the result. 'General Eisenhower
had informed the two generals that, in view of his responsibility and the impending operations, he must insist on
effective control of the French forces being in the hands
of General Giraud, with whom he had worked during recent
months.... De Gaulle had taken the view that this demand
constituted a breach of French sovereignty.' It had been
agreed Eisenhower's statement should be put into written
form, and this was being studied by the French Committee
at that moment. War Cabinet discussion revealed a considerable wavering of Ministerial opinion; according to the
official minutes: 'The view was expressed that while it was
understandable that the US Government should lose patience
with de Gaulle, it must not be overlooked that he exercised
a considerable influence among those in Metropolitan France
in whom the spirit of resistance had not been quenched. To
force a break with him now would not restore American
prestige in France and might damage ours.... On the other
hand, it was the general view of the War Cabinet that we

could not conscientiously assure the US Government that, if de Gaulle were in control of the French Army in North Africa, the allies could rely confidently upon his loyal co-operation in the Allied military operations now impending.' Ministers agreed 'it was vitally important to prevent this issue from clouding our relations with the President and the US Administration.' The War Cabinet decided to defer further discussion until news arrived of the FCNL's consideration of Eisenhower's statement.[93] The FCNL came in fact to the best decision in the circumstances, one which they persuaded de Gaulle and Giraud to accept. A permanent Military Committee would be established, to include both generals and to be responsible for the unification, training and organization of French armed forces. The FCNL would exercise general direction of the French war effort and control over all French forces; Giraud would be C-in-C in Africa, as demanded by Eisenhower, but de Gaulle would be C-in-C in other parts of the French Empire.[94] The arrangement could only be considered temporary; squabbles continued, and the major question of recognition of the FCNL remained. But for the moment French affairs slipped into second place. Giraud left Algiers for Washington on 2 July and conflict between the two generals would cease for a while – Giraud confessed to Macmillan that he felt 'like a schoolboy leaving for the holidays'.[95] De Gaulle felt equally pleased: during his rival's absence he would enjoy supreme position in French North Africa.

Churchill had been anxious lest the French situation should ruffle Anglo-American affairs. Relations with Russia were under even greater strain. A communication had been sent to Stalin on 2 June, signed by the two Western leaders and giving the military results of the 'Trident' conference – including the decision to postpone a cross-Channel invasion until 1944. Stalin replied to Roosevelt on 11 June: postponement would cause 'quite painful difficulties for the Soviet Union', making a 'painful impression' on the Red Army, and Stalin's frigid message concluded: 'As far as the Soviet Government is concerned, it cannot join in this decision, which may have grave consequences for the further course

of the war, and which moreover was taken without its participation, and without any attempt to consider together
the question of such tremendous importance.'[96] Sir Archibald Clark Kerr, Britain's Ambassador to Moscow, urged an
early meeting between the three Heads of State; Churchill
told Kerr that although he would send a 'soft answer' to
Stalin, he was 'getting rather tired of these repeated scoldings
considering that they have never been actuated by anything
but cold-blooded self-interest and total disdain of our lives
and fortunes'.[97] Churchill repeated the arguments against a
1943 second front in a telegram on the 19th and also suggested
a summit meeting at Scapa Flow. On the 24th, Churchill
was informed by Harriman that Roosevelt had made a
suggestion to Stalin in May for a meeting between themselves,
i.e. without Churchill; next day, Churchill received another
angry cable from the Soviet leader, in reply to which Churchill
again repeated the strategic argument. He suggested to
Roosevelt on the 29th July that a US-Soviet summit might
indeed be desirable. Roosevelt proposed that he and Churchill
might meet beforehand, perhaps at Quebec. In early August
a sullen silence fell over the Churchill-Stalin dialogue; the
Prime Minister seemed prepared to let Stalin simmer.[98]

Threaded throughout this debate were the complications
caused by the Polish question. The Russians had continued to
press for changes in the Polish Government in London; an
answer had still to be found to the frontier problem – and at
the beginning of June, the Soviet Ambassador warned the
Foreign Office that if an understanding could not be reached,
the Russians would advance to their 1941 frontiers and stay
there.[99] General Sikorski, Polish Prime Minister, remained
stubbornly independent over both issues; then, early on
Monday, 5 July, reports reached the Foreign Office that the
General had been killed in an aircraft accident at Gibraltar
the previous night. 'This is a great blow,' wrote Cadogan in
his diary. 'There's *no one* to take his place.'[100] Goebbels's
propaganda machine immediately claimed the British had
removed an inconvenience in order to smooth relations with
Russia. The charge apparently went unnoticed in London,
or was considered unworthy of attention; War Cabinet

minutes do not even include discussion of Sikorski's death. Talks began between the Poles and the Foreign Office over Sikorski's replacement, and eventually the Polish President appointed Mikolajczyk, Deputy Prime Minister, to be Premier, while General Sosnkowski became C-in-C. The former was viewed by the Foreign Office as an advocate of easier relations with Russia, but Sosnkowski was considered distinctly hostile. Further trouble seemed inevitable.[101]

Complications were also arising over two more countries. And these, like the Polish problem, would soon increase in importance both for their immediate relevance to the war and for their implications for future, post-war Europe. Yugoslavia and Greece had both been overrun by the Germans yet in neither had the spirit of resistance been completely stamped out by Nazi jackboots. Nearly three years had passed since the Germans had launched operation 'Punishment' upon Yugoslavia, slaughtering 17,000 civilians. A guerrilla movement had begun in 1941 consisting mainly of Serbs under Mihailović and known as the Chetniks; these rebels were loyal to King Peter and his Government, now in exile in London, and British liaison officers had been sent to help. But the Chetniks never seemed very active, and later reports resulted in suspicions that they might be collaborating with the enemy, especially with the Italians. Tito and his partisans had begun their much more vigorous operations in autumn, 1941, but not until 29 May 1943 was a British officer – Captain F. W. Deakin – sent to Tito's HQ. The Middle East Defence Committee at Cairo urged a complete shift of support from the Chetniks to Tito; the Foreign Office objected, both because of Tito's communism and also because of approval given to Mihailović by King Peter. The COS agreed with Cairo. 'It is clear from information available to the War Office,' reported the COS on 6 June, 'that the Chetniks are hopelessly compromised in their relations with the Axis.'[102] The Middle East Defence Committee added further pressure the following day: 'The Partisans are now the most formidable anti-Axis element in Yugoslavia and our support of them is therefore logical and necessary.'[103] The COS informed the Foreign Office on the 17th: 'We should supply

Croatian guerrillas and Communist partisans with war material in as much as these groups represent the most formidable anti-Axis elements existing outside Serbia.'[104] Discussions and arguments continued, and soon, as a result of great events in the central Mediterranean, this local matter in the Eastern Mediterranean would assume very much greater importance.

The same applied to Greece. And, as with Yugoslavia, purely military matters were complicated by internal political divisions which also reflected the wider clash with communism. Soon after Greece's capitulation in April 1941, the National Liberation Front, EAM, had been formed and became increasingly active. EAM, under the control of the Communist Party, announced the formation of the more militant ELAS in spring 1942; early in 1943 ELAS began to attack rival guerrilla bands, and Greece seemed threatened by full-scale civil war. Trouble spread to regular forces evacuated to the Middle East in February 1943, and in an attempt to quieten the situation the King and the Tsouderos Government decided to move to Cairo from London. A Cabinet reshuffle resulted in a number of republicans being brought into the administration, and early in July agreement between rival guerrillas – ELAS, EDES and EKKA – resulted in a joint committee. At the same time, politicians who had remained in Athens requested the King to state publicly that free elections would be held after the war to determine whether Greece should in future be monarchist or republican. On 4 July the King made a broadcast agreeing to this request, and for the moment the threat of widespread civil fighting seemed to have been averted. British arms and assistance had continued to reach Greece during these disturbances, and on 23 June, after strong representations by Churchill, the COS agreed these supplies should be further increased.[105]

'It is of decisive importance,' Hitler had declared on 19 May, 'to hold the Balkans.' The Führer therefore cast anxious eyes upon the growing resistance activities in Yugoslavia and Greece: an allied move in this direction could expose the whole southern flank of his military empire and, linked with the Soviet thrust further north, might be decisive. Renewed attempts were made to wipe out the guerrillas: on 15 June reports reaching Hitler from his units in Yugoslavia spoke of 12,000 partisans dead. Tito had been wounded, but resistance continued in the bleak mountains and thick forests. Yugoslavia and Greece thus formed part of the backcloth for the mighty military events which were now to take the stage. Already, during these weeks of early summer, preliminary moves had been made. On 7 June General Alexander had appeared before the War Cabinet to explain plans for 'Husky'. 'It was estimated that there were some 9 Italian divisions in the island, 5 mobile and 5 second class. In addition, there was the equivalent of 1 German division. So far there had been no signs of other German reinforcements. The success of the operation depended on our ability to get our troops ashore in fighting trim. Once that had been done he was very confident of the outcome.' Alexander concluded: 'Our troops were training hard and were in terrific heart. We had never had such a good army as we had today.'[106] Next day, 8 June, concentrated bombing attacks had started upon the small island of Pantelleria, lying in the Channel between Tunisia and Sicily. This short offensive marked the most spectacular display of air power so far: after three days, and after 5,258 sorties had dropped 4,656 tons of high explosives, the island surrendered.[107] Over 11,000 prisoners were taken. Military activity died again, but only for a few more days.

'People are becoming impatient with this long lull,' noted Harold Nicolson on 28 June. Sir Alexander Cadogan wrote a few days later: 'Not v. much work and v. little news. This period of waiting (now drawing to a close) has been trying....' General Sir Alan Brooke agreed: 'It has been getting more and more trying waiting for operations to start.'[108] But the last preparations for 'Husky' were now complete; and on the Russian front another giant convulsion of conflict was about to erupt.

4

Splintered Axis

For 21 days bombers had roared over the Mediterranean heading for the Sicilian triangle; raids were increased on 3 July prior to the offensive. 'Husky' would be the first major landing in the Second World War of seaborne troops against full-scale opposition; air superiority was essential. War Cabinet Ministers in London read daily reports of the growing numbers of sorties against the island. In Rome, Mussolini's Ministers waited with growing trepidation for the onslaught and on 4 July General Vittorio Ambrosio, Chief of the Italian General Staff, addressed a melancholy minute to the Duce: 'If we cannot prevent the setting up of such a front, it will be up to the highest political authorities to consider whether it would not be more expedient to spare the country further horror and ruin, and to anticipate the end of the struggle.' Hitler had every reason to feel anxious for his Axis partner, but the Führer had another preoccupation, one which he admitted made his 'stomach turn over'. On 15 April Hitler had issued a fatal order to his forces in Russia: 'This offensive is of decisive importance. It must be carried out quickly and shatteringly.... The victory of Kursk must be a signal to the world.' And now, for this Battle of Kursk, the Germans had accumulated some 3,000 tanks, 900,000 men and 2,000 aircraft; only one figure could be counted more impressive than these: just under two million German soldiers had been lost on the Eastern front in the 12 months ending 30 June 1943. To wipe out the effect of these losses and to regain ground lost, Hitler intended to thrust 50 divisions against the Kursk salient. German troops were issued with dry rations and vodka for 5 days and at 3 p.m., 5 July, massive artillery bombardment began. But the Russians were prepared. And 48 hours after this largest-ever tank battle began at Kursk, the greatest amphibious operation so far launched began to creep across the Mediterranean. The initial 'Husky' assault alone involved 160,000 men, 14,000 vehicles, 600 tanks and nearly 2,000 guns; this allied armada of 2,600 vessels, under the command of Admiral Sir Andrew Cunningham, surged towards the Sicilian shores, having been gathered from Gibraltar, Malta and virtually every North African port from Casablanca to Suez. Latest reports were taken into Churchill during the evening of the 7th as he entertained the King at a 10 Downing Street dinner party.

Operational plans for 'Husky' had been completed early in June. Montgomery, who had described the original scheme to Brooke as 'a dog's breakfast', felt more confident: instead of two widely separated landings at either end of the island, the offensive would now be better concentrated and integrated. General Eisenhower, Alexander and Admiral Cunningham had established their HQ at Malta; Tedder directed air operations from his HQ near Carthage. The assault would begin early on Saturday, 10 July. Churchill would spend the weekend at Chequers, anxiously awaiting results; Brooke remained at his War Office desk. The invasion fleet sailed on.

But disturbing reports began to reach London during the 9th. Weather news from the Mediterranean had deteriorated: a *tramontana* – equivalent of the French *mistral* – had begun to blow, and Mediterranean waves were being whipped high. Eisenhower stayed in conference with Cunningham, debating whether to postpone the attack; he would be faced with a similar problem the following year with an even bigger Armada. At 8 p.m. the Admiralty in London asked Cunningham whether a decision had been taken; Cunningham replied: 'Weather not favourable. But operation proceeding.' The winds rose higher until midnight then began to lessen: Italian troops in Sicily believed the *tramontana* would have postponed the expected offensive. But Brooke wrote in his diary as he went to bed: 'Tonight the attack on Sicily starts and thank heaven the suspense will be over.'[1]

'CWR Record for the 24 hours ending 0700, 10 July 1943. MEDITERRANEAN OPERATION. Allied forces under the command of General Eisenhower began landing operations on Sicily early this morning. The landings were preceded by Allied air attacks. . . .'[2] First reports to reach waiting London during this Saturday seemed a mixture of good and bad. Some gliders in the airborne attack at the British front had met disaster, partly through the gale and partly through faulty handling, and parachutists in the US brigade had also encountered difficulties. But seaborne landings were developing well, against only moderate opposition: airfields were taken and the port of Licata fell within a few hours. Churchill celebrated at Chequers; Hitler anxiously studied reports from Rome and from Kursk – and found time to issue another, different directive: immediate large-scale production must begin of both pilotless flying bombs and long-range rockets for launching against London and southern England. Eisenhower arrived in Sicily on the 11th to find the enemy were pulling back, probably to strengthen defences in the critical Catania region. Counter-attacks against the US 7th Army had been shattered by artillery and naval fire. Brooke spent this Sunday at home 'repairing the Pook's goat-cart to keep my mind occupied' and, returning to London next day, 12 July, gave a cautious assessment to the War Cabinet at 6 p.m. 'The air position would be difficult until we could operate fighters from the captured aerodromes. . . . The landings had been carried out according to plan, with only slight casualties. All the first, and some of the second objectives had been secured. . . . During the next phase the major problem was likely to be that of landing munitions and supplies sufficient to enable our forces to maintain their operations.' Churchill, like Brooke the previous day, had also apparently been seeking ways of taking his mind off Sicily; during these tense hours he had been giving thought to a new and totally irrelevant idea, which he now insisted should have War Cabinet consideration. He referred 'to the advantages that might follow if Basic English were widely used as a

means of interchange of thought throughout the world'. The
Prime Minister suggested the BBC should broadcast lessons,
and thus enable simple English to become a standard, world-
wide language, and he urged the War Cabinet to agree to a
'preliminary examination ... by a committee of Ministers'.
Approval was given for such a committee, but in September
Churchill would be 'shocked' to find that urgent pressure of
other business had prevented this group from holding even a
preliminary meeting.[3] Meanwhile, by the close of 12 July
over 80,000 men, 7,000 vehicles and 300 tanks had been
poured into Sicily and Italian units were surrendering in
scores. At Kursk, the Russians struck back; during the day
about 850 Russian tanks moved out to clash with 700
Panzers. 'The battlefield seemed too small for the hundreds
of armoured machines,' wrote the official Soviet war historian.
      Eden dined with Churchill after the War Cabinet meeting
on the 12th, and found himself involved in fierce argument
with the Prime Minister over the French. The two men sat
in the deserted Cabinet room and continued their confrontation until 2 a.m. Two days before Roosevelt had told
Churchill that he would 'accept' but not recognize the new
French Committee. Eden strongly disagreed with this attitude; Churchill maintained matters must be allowed to rest
for a while, and according to Eden's account he 'admitted
that if we broke on this I (Eden) should have much popular
support, but warned he would fight vigorously to the death'.
Eden tried to assure him he had no intention of resigning.
The two men left to put their respective ideas on paper,
and in his memorandum, dated 13 July, Churchill complained about 'the preposterous conduct of General de Gaulle'
and urged more time before FCNL recognition. 'I am afraid
lest the anti-de Gaullism of the Washington Government may
harden into a definite anti-France feeling. If however de
Gaulle is gradually merged and submerged into the Committee, and the Committee comports itself in a reasonable
and loyal manner, this dangerous tendency on the part of the
US may be deflected and assuaged.'[4] Eden's paper, also completed on the 13th, claimed there were grounds 'for believing
that some at any rate of the governing authorities in

Washington have little belief in France's future and indeed do not wish to see France again restored as a great imperial power'. Eden saw Churchill during the day and found him 'formal'. 'He said he didn't like my paper and thought we might be coming to a break.' The Foreign Secretary feared Churchill to be suffering from strain; Cadogan condemned the Prime Minister as 'making rather an ass of himself'.[5] French affairs were considered by the War Cabinet at 12.15 the following day, 14 July, and Churchill now seemed to agree that the Americans might be going too far. Ministers discussed recent telegrams from Washington indicating that statements 'which had recently been allowed to leak out in the American Press were part of a campaign to break up the committee of National Liberation and to get rid of de Gaulle'. Ministers believed 'it was unfortunate that these public statements should be made at a time when the position and authority of the Committee were increasing, and the civilian elements of the Committee were becoming more influential. There was a risk that the course of action taken by the US Administration might have the result of strengthening de Gaulle's position at the expense of the Committee.'[6]

Opposition in Sicily had begun to stiffen, and Hitler had confirmed orders the previous day, 13 July, for reinforcements to be rushed to the island. Attacks by the 8th Army against enemy positions covering Catania on the 14th were beaten back. Yet the initial success of 'Husky' had already given impetus to Churchill's cherished schemes for the next stage: invasion of mainland Italy. On 3 July the COS had finally voiced full agreement with Churchill in a telegram to the CCS; Sardinia should not be attempted, instead 'we wish to assert our conviction that the full exploitation of "Husky" will be best secured if offensive action be prosecuted on the mainland of Italy with all the means at our disposal towards the final elimination of Italy from the war'.[7] The COS advocated attacking the 'toe and heel of Italy'; Churchill, in a memorandum to Ismay on the 13th, urged more ambitious anatomical moves: 'Why should we crawl up the leg like a harvest-bug from the ankle upwards? Let us

rather strike at the knee.'[8] Next day the Joint Planners
supported Churchill's policy in a paper presented to the
COS: 'Provided the German air forces in Italy are harassed
on the ground and brought to battle in the air without respite
during the interim period, operations against the Italian
mainland will, if they take place within the next 5-7 weeks,
be as ineffectively opposed by the enemy close-support units
as have been our operations in Sicily.'[9] Churchill enthused
to his great friend Smuts: 'Not only must we take Rome
and march as far north as possible in Italy, but our right
hand must give succour to the Balkan patriots.... I shall go
to all lengths to procure the agreement of our Allies. If not,
we have ample forces to act by ourselves.'[10] Yet a mere
seven months before, the COS had had to argue long hours
to obtain Churchill's agreement for continued emphasis on
Mediterranean operations.

During this Thursday, 15 July, discussions were held at
the Foreign Office over latest reports of Italian units wishing
to surrender in the Balkans; and in Berlin, General Jodl
warned Hitler of treacherous elements in the Italian officer
corps – to send further German reinforcements to Italy
would be to expose them to risk of annihilation. Hitler staked
even more upon his 'secret weapon' to batter the British
into submission. In London, the COS met the Prime Minister
at 10 Downing Street for a 10.30 p.m. meeting, also attended
by Morrison, Home Secretary, who urged the provision of
additional shelters to meet the threat of these new German
weapons. The meeting also agreed upon the use of 'Window'
– strips of tinfoil dropped to confuse German radar readings
– to increase the effectiveness of RAF attacks. The device
would soon render deadly results. The Staff Conference then
discussed the possibility of another summit conference.
Roosevelt had suggested a meeting between himself and the
Prime Minister at Quebec; the COS, while enthusiastic about
Quebec in view of poor communication facilities and the
likelihood of a Canadian wish to participate, were prepared
to accept the President's preference. The suggested month,
September, was considered too late.[11] Churchill accordingly
cabled Roosevelt next day, 16 July, proposing mid-August:

there would be a need, he said, to settle 'the larger issues which the brilliant victories of our Forces are thrusting upon us about Italy as a whole'.[12] And possibilities of firm Anglo-American agreement on these 'larger issues' now seemed excellent: General Marshall urged the CCS during this Friday to adopt a policy of 'boldness and taking justifiable risk' with regard to Italy, and Eisenhower should be asked to study 'the possibilities of a direct amphibious landing operation against Naples in lieu of an attack on Sardinia if the indications regarding Italian resistance makes risks worthwhile'.[13] Churchill's policy of taking Marshall to North Africa after 'Trident' seemed successful. Yet fighting on Sicily grew even more intense during the day in the struggle to reach Messina, and advances were slow and laborious in the face of determined German defences amongst the rugged terrain; soon, more allied troops would have to be brought from Tunisia.

Ambassador von Mackensen, the Führer's envoy to Rome, arrived at Hitler's HQ on Saturday, 17 July, in answer to an urgent summons. Mackensen gave a gloomy report on Italian morale, and Admiral Doenitz believed the Italian Navy and Army to be 'rotten'. Surely, declared Hitler, 'some capable people must be left ... everything could not suddenly have turned evil', and he asked Rommel which Italian officer could be trusted. 'There is no such person.' Hitler decided to meet Mussolini within the next few days. He turned anxiously back to his maps of Russia, Sicily, and, despite the threatened attack on Italy, to maps of Greece and the Aegean, still fearing an allied assault towards the Balkans. On this Saturday, Churchill heard of Marshall's agreement with the policy of attacking Italy and immediately wired: 'I am with you heart and soul.'[14] And next day, 18 July, Eisenhower finally confirmed his support for such a plan, although he warned that the stiff German resistance in Sicily meant 'Husky' would probably not be completed before mid-August. Eisenhower also recommended that an attack on the toe and heel of Italy should be accompanied by a landing in Salerno Bay, aiming at Naples – Marshall had already tentatively suggested such an idea, which matched Churchill's 'strike at the knee' plea. Next day, 19 July, the British COS spent the morning discussing this operation, code-named 'Avalanche', and Brooke and his colleagues discovered the difficulties involved: air cover would be bad; the rate of allied build-up would be much slower than the arrival of German reinforcements.[15] The COS arranged to meet again during the evening for a full conference attended by Churchill and Eden. Meanwhile the War Cabinet met at 6 p.m. to hear excellent reports from Sicily and from the Eastern Front. 'News from Russia is very reassuring,' said the CIGS. 'The Russians are making two attacks, north and east of Orel, and have regained all the ground lost in the recent German offensive north of Kursk. The Russians have also launched two more offensives, one in the Rostov area and the other in the Taman Peninsula....' Ministers were then diverted into a long, rambling discussion by the Prime Minister, illustrating the manner in which his active mind took him down strange highways and byways. 'The Germans, by keeping a very large number of Frenchmen of military age as prisoners for several years, had undoubtedly taken action which would affect the French population.' Churchill thought 'it was for consideration whether some corresponding action should not be taken against the Germans at the end of the war: that is to say, that a large number of young German males should be segregated from their womenfolk.' According to the official minutes, Ministers believed that 'while there was much to be said for this idea from the point of view of abstract justice, it was very difficult to believe that such a measure could be enforced for any appreciable time, and that it would be better to leave any retributive action to be taken by the Russians....' Sinclair, Air Secretary, summed up the suggestion with one caustic comment: the only way to be certain of the required result would be to shoot millions of German women.[16]

Two hours later Churchill, Eden, Attlee and Lyttelton met the COS for resumed discussion on the Naples operation. The meeting agreed that planning for 'Avalanche' and for operations in the far south of Italy should proceed together; the decision as to which should be adopted would be made on the spot in the light of existing circumstances.[17] Brooke wrote in his diary: 'Winston on the whole very open to reason and on the right lines.' In the event both operations were launched, with Montgomery's south Italy landings just preceding 'Avalanche' at Salerno. Mussolini had been meeting Hitler while these discussions took place on the future of his country. Hitler agreed to send further German units to Sicily, but only if the Italians carried through 'far-reaching measures in the military and civil spheres' and if they did more to protect lines of supply. According to one of those present, von Rintelen, the atmosphere was one of 'leaden weariness'; Mussolini sat pale and sweating and barely spoke – except to give a trembling announcement which showed how difficult this added protection to supply lines would be. A message had been handed to him: Allied aircraft had bombed Rome, for the first time, and in daylight. Mussolini's capital had been plunged into panic. This air strike had in fact only been undertaken after considerable heart-searching by the British War Cabinet; on 14 July representations had been made by Lord Fitzalan, on behalf of Roman Catholics, despite assurances by Eden that all efforts would be made to spare the Vatican City. According to the minutes of the 14 July War Cabinet meeting, 'the feeling ... was that in present circumstances the balance of advantage might lie against bombing Rome. Although General Eisenhower had been authorized to order the bombing of the marshalling yards at Rome at the moment which he thought best ... he had also been instructed to give 48 hours' notice of his intention.... The War Cabinet would, therefore, have an opportunity of reconsidering the matter.'[18] Two days later, 16 July, Churchill had read Ministers a telegram from Eisenhower tentatively fixing the 19th as the date for the Rome attack, and the Prime Minister had urged his colleagues to remove their objections. 'This operation might well be of considerable military importance in stopping the flow of reinforcements passing from north to south Italy.' Tedder had signalled that 'the run up to the targets could be so arranged as to reduce to a minimum' the risk of hitting non-military features. Ministers agreed authority should be given.[19]

And now the smoke plumed above the marshalling yards and Roman citizens wept with shock; morale slumped ever lower. Next day, 20 July, General Vittorio Ambrosio offered his resignation as Chief of the Italian General Staff. Mussolini refused to accept this offer; Ambrosio thereupon considered other means of extricating Italy from the hopeless conflict. In London on the 20th the COS continued discussions on plans to invade Italy, expressing anxiety over slender resources available for the direct attack at Salerno, 'Avalanche'. It had been agreed at 'Trident' that some landing-craft would return to the UK for 'Overlord' or would be moved to Burma once their part in 'Husky' had been played; now, however, the British COS decided to recommend a change in these agreements so painfully worked out at Washington, sending a disturbing signal to the US COS: since Italy 'might be within measurable distance of collapse ... it would be a profound mistake to allow anyone or anything which General Eisenhower might need to move from the Mediterranean area until we know the outcome of the examination on which he is engaged'. The British did not wait for an American reply before taking action; Admiral Sir Dudley Pound, First Sea Lord, signalled Cunningham in the Mediterranean to inform him of this message: 'In view of the effect this proposal will have on "Overlord" and "Bull-frog" (the operation against Akyab) there may be objections from Washington, but meanwhile you should hold everybody and everything you think may be required for "Priceless" (overall invasion of Italy).'[20] Brooke added a rueful note in his diary concerning likely American reactions: 'This will not be greeted with great joy.'[21]

Once again strategic planning seemed to threaten an allied split; and Anglo-American differences now emerged more strongly in the other, political, source of contention – the French. Eden and Churchill had re-established their easy relationship; the Foreign Secretary saw Churchill after dinner on the 20th and was asked to read a message which the Prime Minister proposed to send to Roosevelt regarding recognition of the French Committee. 'He remarked,' wrote Eden in his diary, 'that he seemed now to have swallowed my thesis whole, to which I said that it would be truer to say that he was asking Americans to face up to realities.'[22] Churchill's message, described by Eden as 'admirable', detailed the pressures exerted upon the Prime Minister by the Foreign Office and War Cabinet. 'Macmillan tells us repeatedly that the Committee is acquiring a collective authority and that de Gaulle is by no means its master. He tells us further that if the Committee breaks down, as it may do if left utterly without support, de Gaulle will become once again the sole personality in control of everything except the power exercised by Giraud...' Churchill therefore hoped Roosevelt would agree to recognition. 'If I do, Russia will certainly recognize (them), and I fear lest this might be embarrassing to you.'[23]

Mussolini, whatever his private opinions, assured the Germans on 21 July that Sicily would be defended to the last man. Palermo fell to Patton's tanks next day. In Rome, Mussolini was confronted by Dino Grandi, former Ambassador to Britain and now Foreign Minister; Grandi warned the Duce that he intended to propose the formation of a National Government and the restoration of the King to supreme army command. In London, the COS finally agreed, in Brooke's words, that the Salerno operation 'was a gamble, but probably one worth taking'.[24] Churchill sent a powerful signal to Alexander: 'You can use both your right and your left hand like a boxer and strike or feint as you choose....' The signal described the 'marvellous' resistance being put up by Tito in Yugoslavia and by the guerrillas in Greece. 'Great prizes lie in the Balkan direction.'[25] The Prime Minister's exuberance was however damped by a signal from Roosevelt concerning the French: the President was moving towards 'limited acceptance' of the FCNL but wanted to avoid the word 'recognition'. The Foreign Office feared this proposal would anger rather than mollify the French.[26]

In the midst of elation over Mediterranean prospects, the COS now had to tackle dismal discussion of the Far East. Wavell had become Viceroy of India on 18 June; his successor as C-in-C, India, General Auchinleck, had been sending gloomy reports to London on the plans decided upon at

'Trident'. Operations from Assam were dependent upon a precarious line of communications, he warned, and so many difficulties confronted the 'Bullfrog' attack on Akyab that the operation could not be mounted before January 1944, and resources allotted by the CCS would be inadequate. If the same shipping for 'Bullfrog' had then to be used for the proposed attack on Ramree, a further 3-4 months' delay must follow. Major-General Mallaby, Auchinleck's Director of Military Operations, flew to London to explain the position to the COS on 23 July, and Brooke and his colleagues felt considerable sympathy. They refused, however, to accept the delay of 3-4 months in the Ramree assault and informed Auchinleck accordingly.[27] This signal crossed an even more depressing message from Auchinleck, doubting the value of attacking Ramree at all.[28] 'The kind of paper we have just received from General Auchinleck,' minuted Churchill angrily to the COS on 24 July, 'would rightly excite the deepest suspicions in the US that we are only playing and dawdling with the war in this theatre.... A more silly way of waging war by a nation possessing overwhelming sea power and air power can hardly be conceived.' The Prime Minister outlined 'the proper course for the campaign of 1944', with proposals including maximum air aid to China and amphibious operations against Sumatra. Moreover, Churchill had been stimulated by the exploits of Brigadier Orde Wingate: on 3 May Wingate and the survivors of his Long Range Penetration Group had emerged from the jungle after 3 months harassing the Japanese; Churchill wanted 'maximum pressure by operations similar to those conducted by Wingate in Assam and wherever contact can be made on land with Japanese forces'.[29] The subject of Far East operations would be brought before the Defence Committee on the 28th.

Meanwhile, on 24 July, the day Churchill sent his stinging memorandum to the COS on the subject of Burma, the US COS answered the British suggestion that Mediterranean resources should be temporarily frozen and not diverted to Burma or 'Overlord'. As expected, this attempt to reverse the hard 'Trident' bargaining met with determined opposition. A full reply would arrive from Washington on the 26th, but a preliminary message from the British Mission gave a clear indication of the unwelcome content. Marshall had indeed advocated an attack on Naples via Salerno, but only with resources which had not been designated for other theatres, and he feared '"Avalanche" might well be a first step to similar further demands'.[30] Brooke's reaction seemed typical: 'Marshall absolutely fails to realize the strategic treasures that lie at our feet.'[31] Within hours, the lid on this treasure-trove would be dramatically lifted. Meanwhile another operation took place on the night of Saturday, 24 July, which revealed the horrors now to be heaped upon the German people – and which gave further warning to the Italians.

'CWR RECORD for the 24 hours ending 0700, 25 July 1943 ... *Last night,* 857 aircraft were dispatched: HAM-BURG 791 (12 missing), LEGHORN 33 ... At HAMBURG visibility was good, marker bombs were accurately placed, bombing was very concentrated, and there were extensive fires over the whole target area.' More information came in the Cabinet War Room record next morning, 26 July: 'A record total of 2,319 tons of bombs was dropped on Hamburg; at 1815 hours yesterday, the city was completely obscured by smoke up to 20,000 feet.'[32] Beneath this smoke, hell had erupted. Following the COS decision of the 15th, the main raid had incorporated the use of 'Window' – foil strips dropped to jam radar; another raid took place on the 25th, undertaken by 68 US Flying Fortresses. Hamburg would again be struck on the 26th; meanwhile Essen experienced the bombers on the 25th and 35,000 people were rendered homeless. A third raid on Hamburg followed on the 29th. Over 7,000 tons of bombs were dropped on the city during these few days, devastating 12 square miles and driving three-quarters of the inhabitants from their homes; a German report described the first raid on Saturday the 24th: 'Human beings were thrown to the ground or flung alive into the flames by winds which exceeded 150 miles an hour. The panic-stricken citizens knew not where to turn. Flames drove them from the shelters, but HE bombs sent them scurrying back again. Once inside, they were suffocated by carbon-monoxide poisoning and their bodies reduced to ashes....'³³

Churchill had motored to Chequers to spend the weekend relaxing in the gentle July sunshine. A telephone call interrupted his Sunday evening; the Prime Minister immediately contacted Eden at his country home: Mussolini had been thrown from power. Dino Grandi had called a meeting of the Grand Council at 5 p.m. the previous day, 24 July, and his resolution had been carried, calling upon the Crown to assume more power. Mussolini had seen the King at 5 p.m. on the Sunday, 25 July, to be informed 'you are the most hated man in Italy'; he found himself under arrest as he left the Palace and his position usurped by Marshal Badoglio. Hitler, hearing the news at the same time as Churchill at Chequers, screamed out frantic orders: airborne troops must be dropped on Rome to arrest the conspirators, units must be pulled back from Sicily.... 'It's bare-faced treachery,' he shouted. Hitler amended his orders next day, 26 July, and once again his fear for the Balkans affected his planning; Sicily and the toe of Italy must be held until troops could be brought from Russia – this, he hoped, would buy time for further defensive measures in Greece and for operations to be intensified against the guerrillas. But he believed allied landings were now to be expected on the Aegean islands, the Peloponnese peninsula, and on the west coast of Greece. Also on 26 July, a cable from Roosevelt to Churchill seemed to indicate US willingness to contemplate Balkan operations: 'If any (peace) overtures come we must be certain of the use of all Italian territory and transportation against the Germans in the north and against the whole Balkan peninsula.' This signal crossed a message from 10 Downing Street to the White House. 'Changes announced in Italy probably portend peace proposals. Let us consult together so as to take joint action.'³⁴

War Cabinet Ministers met at 5.30 p.m. on the 26th to consider the implications of Mussolini's downfall. Brooke assessed the military situation: 'The Germans might find it difficult to continue operations in the south with a passive, or even hostile, Italian population, and might decide to cut their losses and hold the line of the river Po. They would

find it difficult to spare troops from the Russian front for
Italy – particularly as they would have to reinforce their
garrisons in the Balkans.' Ministers agreed Italian peace
moves were likely. Churchill said he had met the COS
during the afternoon, and approval had been given to a
memorandum on Italy by the Prime Minister, written as long
ago as November 1942. In addition to complete surrender
of Italian forces, Churchill had written, the allies should
also demand of the Italians that the Germans in the country
should lay down their arms: this could lead to fighting
between the Italians and Germans, and 'we should provoke
this conflict as much as possible' even helping the Italians
by armed assistance. The question of terms to be demanded
from the Italians had been under discussion for some weeks,
both in London and Washington, but firm agreement had still
to be reached. 'The main points of difference,' Eden told the
War Cabinet on the 26th, 'was whether or not any kind of
Italian administration could be allowed to act – our view
being that it would be greatly to our advantage to have the
country run for us as long as possible.' The Americans sought
stiffer demands, and Roosevelt, in his signal to Churchill on
the 26th, had declared: 'We should come as close as possible
to unconditional surrender.' But Eden commented: 'There
were signs that the Americans were coming round to our
view.' Ministers agreed upon 'the great military prizes to be
gained by securing a docile Italy, or even one hostile to
the Germans; there would be no objection to agreeing
upon terms of surrender with an Italian administration now
that Mussolini had been deposed and the Fascist regime
broken up.'[35]

'One worry after another piles up on us,' moaned Goebbels
in his diary. 'We hardly know how to meet them.' The Joint
Intelligence Committee advised the British COS next day,
27 July, that Italian surrender overtures must be imminent.
Clearly, a dramatic change had come over the whole future
of military operations in the Mediterranean, but now, on
the 27th, the COS considered the unpleasant full-length
reply received from the US COS, declaring 'Trident' decisions
should be maintained, and resources allocated to 'Overlord'

and to the Far East should not therefore be retained in the
Mediterranean. 'The US COS adhere to their previous recommendations – that General Eisenhower be instructed to
prepare a plan as a matter of urgency for direct attack on
Naples using the resources that have already been made
available.' The COS decided to play for time: a signal left
for Washington pointing out that since the departure of
Mediterranean forces for 'Overlord' and Burma would not
be necessary until early August, the British COS were maintaining their 'freeze' order in the Mediterranean until the
matter had been considered at the Quebec Conference.[36]

Eisenhower was primarily concerned with exploiting the
Italian situation to greatest possible military effect. He cabled
armistice proposals to the CCS on the 27th: these dealt with
conditions of ceasefire and surrender, but also included the
demand to be made to the Italians that there should be
'immediate acknowledgement of the overriding authority of
the Allied C-in-C to establish a Military Government'.[37]
This added another complication to the armistice discussions,
which were rapidly sliding into confusion. The British and
Americans had still to agree over diplomatic and political
terms – soon to be known as the Long Terms – and now
Eisenhower had injected his military demands, known as
the Short Terms, which also raised diplomatic and constitutional issues. The allies might find themselves in the
awkward situation of having no official document prepared
when the Italians sued for peace. And, on the evening of the
28 July, Badoglio's Government decided to contact the allies.
Members of the Defence Committee were meeting in London
as Badoglio took this crucial decision in Rome. British
Ministers objected to a proposal made by Eisenhower that
the allied terms should be broadcast – the Italians should
first ask for them. Moreover, Ministers disagreed with an
announcement of these mainly military Short Terms without the civil Long Terms. At this point in the meeting
Churchill left the room to telephone Roosevelt – a call which
the Germans intercepted and recorded: '*Churchill*: "We do
not want proposals for an armistice to be made before we
have been definitely approached." *Roosevelt*: "That is right."

Churchill: "We can also wait quietly for one or two days."
Roosevelt: "That is right...." ' The Defence Committee confirmed the British desire not to remove Mediterranean
resources for the moment.[38] The intercepted Churchill-
Roosevelt conversation convinced the Germans that the
Italian Government had started unofficial surrender talks;
already, earlier on the 28th, orders had been issued for
operation 'Axis' – German moves to ccunteract an attempted
Italian ceasefire: all areas held by the Italians would be
taken over; those Italian forces who refused to continue the
fight would be interned if necessary. Eisenhower knew full
well the Germans would attempt such an operation; hence
his desire to take rapid steps to exploit the military situation
while time still remained. Thus, as Churchill elaborated the
Defence Committee conclusions to Roosevelt on the 29th –
'terms should cover civil as well as military requirements' –
Eisenhower wired the Prime Minister to plead his case. 'I
urged that we do not allow ourselves to get in a position
where military opportunity may slip out of our fingers.'
Cables from Roosevelt and Macmillan supported this view.
War Cabinet Ministers were therefore called from their beds
at 1.30 a.m., 30 July, to discuss the situation, and after a
two-hour meeting, agreed to accede to the American view
over the Short Terms; if Eisenhower were approached he
could present his terms, dealing with military matters, and
the Long Terms would be presented later despite the risk of
consequent confusion.

But differences of opinion remained over the content of the
Long Term document. Roosevelt had declared in a broadcast on the 28th: 'We will have no truck with Fascism in
any way, shape or manner.' American propaganda dealt abuse
at the Badoglio administration and the King of Italy, and
Roosevelt admitted in a signal to Churchill on the 30th:
'There are some contentious people here who are getting ready
to make a row if we seem to recognize the House of Savoy
or Badoglio.' The Prime Minister hurriedly replied: 'Once
Mussolini and the Fascists are gone I will deal with any
Italian authority which can deliver the goods.'[39] He asked
Roosevelt to consider 'our most carefully drafted' terms of

surrender 'which we sent a fortnight ago' and added: 'We are rather puzzled to know why you never refer to this document.'[40] Roosevelt avoided a direct answer; instead he sent another cable to Churchill reaching London next morning, 31 July. Cadogan noted in his diary: 'A (Eden) rang up, in an awful flap, about a telegram from Pres. suggesting, apparently, *new* armistice terms. Ye Gods!'[41] So the muddle continued until, on 3 August, Churchill and Roosevelt agreed the matter should be left until the two leaders met at Quebec.

Long Terms, Short Terms, Yugoslavia, Greece, Sicily, Burma, the French ... and yet Churchill could still find time for other detailed and apparently unimportant matters. 'Prime Minister to President of the Board of Trade. 1 August 1943. Thank you for your note about shortage of playing cards. What happened to the 1,950,000 produced over and above the 1,300,000 issued in the last 12 months? ... I must know what has happened.'[42]

Top-level discussions on an Italian armistice might be rendered useless unless allied troops showed their ability to step on to the Italian mainland; Sicily had to be conquered in minimum time. On 25 July Alexander had given orders for a new combined assault, to be launched by regrouped forces towards the formidable enemy defensive positions based on Mount Etna, in the north-east quarter of the island and blocking the road to Messina. This final drive began on 1 August; during the same day German staff officers drew up first plans for quitting the island, but the existence of this evacuation scheme made no difference to the stubborness of the defences. Late on the 1st, units from 8th Army attacked the important hill town of Centuripe and the port of Catania, fanatically defended by the Herman Göring Division; War Cabinet Ministers were informed next day, Bank Holiday Monday: 'The battle for Catania began the previous night. No reports of its progress have yet been received. In the fighting before the battle the Germans suffered heavy casualties: prisoners now amount to 100,000, mostly Germans.' Ministers also heard good news of the progress in the Battle of the Atlantic: 91 U-boats had been sunk during the last 92 days. Churchill gave this meeting a report on Hitler's 'secret weapon'; dissension had continued among experts. 'While it seemed clear that some rocket development was in hand, the balance of opinion among experts doubted whether the Germans had in fact achieved so remarkable a technical advance as would be implied in the firing of a heavy rocket over a range sufficient to attack London from northern France.'[43]

Members of the Defence Committee met at 10.30 p.m. on this Monday to discuss another aspect of the war against Italy; and once again British and American views were directly opposed. A telegram had just been received from the British Mission containing a message from Marshall to Eisenhower: proposals had been received by the US Government through the Vatican that Rome should be made an open city, and Eisenhower was told to avoid bombing the capital while the appeal was being considered. The British Mission had approved these instructions. The Defence Committee now expressed 'unanimous and complete disagreement with the instructions issued to General Eisenhower, and their surprise that these should have been agreed to by representatives of the British COS without reference to London'. Members decided it was 'out of the question to entertain any proposal for the declaration of Rome as an open city'. To do so would be entirely inconsistent with speeches both of Churchill and Eisenhower, promising 'the most powerful air attacks which we could possibly make' after the lull granted on Badoglio's accession. The meeting adjourned while a telephone call to Marshall explained this British attitude; Marshall agreed to rescind the directive to Eisenhower.[44] Fighting had meanwhile continued in the steep cobbled streets and among the shattered houses of Centuripe. Last pockets of German resistance were wiped out during the morning of the 3rd; Montgomery's units pressed on to Catania. One of Patton's leading divisions was advancing east from San Stefano; another had encountered fierce resistance at Troina. 'The offensive has opened well,' signalled Alexander to the COS during the day, but he warned: 'Progress may be slow ... the country must be seen to be believed. Only a few mountain roads, which pass through gorges and round cliffs.'[45] Churchill, while studying reports from Sicily, had also increased pressure for operations in the Aegean: on 27 July he had asked for plans for a quick occupation of Rhodes if the Italians on the island asked for an armistice; General Wilson had replied from Cairo that a plan had been prepared, but this would involve drawing heavily on central Mediterranean resources – and the operation would take 6 weeks to mount. Six weeks might be far too long; the COS met on the 3rd to discuss the situation and before them lay a minute from Churchill dated the 2nd. 'Here is a business of great consequence, to be thrust forward by every means.... There is no time for conventional establishments.' Brooke and his colleagues decided to urge Wilson to profit by any favourable opening, enlisting local help if feasible. Supplies to Turkey would be diverted to speed planning and execution.[46]

Time was indeed precious; on 4 August the newly arrived Counsellor of the Italian Legation in Lisbon came to the British Embassy, and while making no mention of a possible armistice, D'Ajeta explained that Badoglio and the King sought peace: they had to make a pretence of continued fighting to prevent a German takeover. D'Ajeta begged the allies to suspend bombing of Italian cities, yet while this initial contact was taking place at Lisbon, Ministers in London confirmed their opinion that Rome should not be spared allied air attacks. This Defence Committee session, starting at 1 p.m. on the 4th, discussed telegrams from Washington: the President considered it would be difficult to refuse the Vatican request; the British Mission had set out conditions which the US War Department had suggested should be met before open-city status was given – these included the removal from Rome of all agencies concerned with the conduct of the war, and of all Italian and German armed forces. Ministers pointed out that the Americans had not favoured an open-city policy for Rome when the proposal had been put forward seven months before. 'To declare the city open now, would be regarded as a success for the Badoglio Government. It would also seem likely to give rise to an outcry in this country.' Brooke said the COS believed the policy would be militarily 'catastrophic'. Churchill read a draft telegram to Roosevelt, repeating British objections and asking for a decision to be deferred until the Quebec meeting.[47]

Another subject had thus been added to Quebec's long list; and at 10 p.m. Churchill left London for the Clyde to board the *Queen Mary*. In the Prime Minister's personal party travelled Mrs Churchill, his daughter Mary, Wing-Commander Guy Gibson, and, as a very late addition, Brigadier Orde Wingate, still in crumpled tropical outfit. Churchill had dined Wingate during the evening and suddenly decided to dazzle the Americans with the Chindit leader's exploits. Brooke had written on the 3rd: 'I hate going and dread the conferences in front of me; the work will be never-ending and very trying.'[48] The *Queen Mary* sailed at midday on the 5th; in Sicily Catania fell and the German evacuation of the island began; in the massive Eastern Front conflict, Soviet tanks occupied Orel and the Red Army closed upon Kharkov.

Churchill would reach Halifax on 11 August, after which he would spend some days with Roosevelt at Hyde Park before moving to Quebec for the first plenary session of the 'Quadrant' conference on the 19th. The Combined Chiefs of Staff would begin talks on the morning of the 14th. Meanwhile as the *Queen Mary* sailed the Atlantic, events moved to a climax in Sicily, Patton's 1st Division took Troina on the 6th and the US commander ordered his 9th Division to leap-frog forward; his tanks entered Cesaro on the 8th. Out-flanking amphibious operations helped the US 45th Division in the advance along the north coast and Cape Orlanda was reached on the 10th. Randazzo fell three days later and the defenders began to stream back on to mainland Italy. On the Eastern Front, the Russians continued their advance upon Kharkov, and threatened the city on three sides by 11 August. The German armies in Russia had been shattered at the gigantic battles of Kursk, Orel and now Kharkov; Hitler's hopes for enslaving the Soviets turned to fear for the future of

Germany in the face of the advancing Red Army. And to this threat from the east had to be added the danger of an allied invasion of the Balkans and the collapse of Italy. On 6 August Hitler sent a strong delegation to Rome – with instructions not to eat any food unless they had seen their hosts sample some first. The new Italian Ministers immediately criticized the influx of German troops into the country, and the Germans left even more depressed. 'The Italians are going ahead with their negotiations at full speed,' commented Hitler.[49] Indeed, also on 6 August the Italians opened contact with the British Ambassador at Tangier, when the diplomat Alberto Berio stated that Badoglio wished to talk peace and only the threat of a German *coup* prevented him from doing so openly; Berio would however act as his representative, and the Italians again sought an end to the allied bombing. The Foreign Office in London considered this development to be more favourable than the D'Ajeta affair; Eden immediately signalled Churchill on the *Queen Mary*: 'We are entitled to regard it as an offer by the Badoglio Government to negotiate on terms.... Should we not insist on unconditional surrender?' Churchill still had doubts over this policy, and scrawled in the margin of Eden's signal, 'don't miss the bus'. But after COS consultations he cabled on the 7th: 'We agree with the course you have taken.'[50] Eden sought War Cabinet approval at 5.30 p.m. on Monday, 9 August – only two other Cabinet Ministers, Attlee and Lyttelton, attended this meeting. 'Looking at the (armistice) matter from a political point of view,' said Eden, he favoured 'the continuance of heavy air attacks on Northern Italy. As regards propaganda ... we should keep hammering at the point that the present Italian Government had said that the war continued, that from the allied point of view war was therefore continuing and that the Italian Government was responsible for this state of affairs.' Eden added: 'We should stand by our demand for unconditional surrender.'[51] Instructions were sent to Tangier on 12 August for the British Consul to tell Berio that the allies demanded unconditional surrender; once the Italian Government had placed themselves in allied hands, 'honourable' terms would be presented.[52]

At least Anglo-American agreement had therefore been reached on the immediate procedure for dealing with the Italians. Details of the Long Terms would have to be taken up in the Churchill-Roosevelt talks, together with the other outstanding diplomatic problem – the French. Views remained as divergent as ever over recognition of the FNCL. Macmillan wrote after having seen Giraud on the 27th: 'I'm afraid that his visits to Washington and London have had a disastrous effect upon him.... He thinks (perhaps with some justice) that the Americans have promised their material to him personally.... Of course, they are only interested in him as a convenient instrument to a) injure de Gaulle, b) break up the French Union.' Compromise was at least reached between de Gaulle and Giraud on 31 July: de Gaulle would be sole FCNL President, but he and Giraud would sign all orders jointly. Giraud would remain C-in-C but would cease to be part of the Government if he took any active operational command. De Gaulle would thus concentrate on political aspects and Giraud upon the military. Macmillan believed the compromise to be a good one and that recognition must soon follow. 'I do not see how the President can hold out now.'[53]

Churchill and the COS spent their time on the *Queen Mary* in intensive discussions on Anglo-American strategic problems. These centred upon two questions: what should follow the fall of Sicily, especially in view of a likely Italian collapse? Secondly, what effect, if any, should the Mediterranean situation have upon 'Overlord', scheduled for 1 May 1944? British insistence, on 20 July, that Mediterranean resources should be frozen for the moment, had aroused acute suspicions and immediate hostility in Washington; once again the British seemed to be shying away from 'Overlord' and from Burmese operations. The Americans would have been even more concerned had they known that Churchill, in a minute to the COS on 19 July, had once again returned to his favourite idea for an operation against Norway, 'Jupiter', which he had advocated so hard earlier in the war.

The COS vehemently disagreed and tried to persuade the Prime Minister not to raise the subject at the forthcoming conference.

Yet the British COS – with Churchill's broad agreement – thought along lines by no means dissimilar to those followed by the Americans: discussions on the *Queen Mary* on the 6th and 7th underlined the COS adherence to 'Overlord', with the operation to be launched as soon as possible. While the British believed 'Husky' and an Italian collapse should be exploited as much as possible, they nevertheless viewed Mediterranean operations not as a substitute for 'Overlord', but as an essential and integral part of the whole scheme. A direct assault on North-West Europe must be undertaken. On the other hand, such an assault could be disastrous unless correct conditions were prepared beforehand, including a weakening of German opposition. At this point the British and American views began to vary. The British believed the necessary conditions for 'Overlord' could best be fulfilled by operations in Italy, and believed their position had been strengthened by the first operational plan for 'Overlord', completed on 30 July by the Chief of Staff, Supreme Allied Command, COSSAC. This laid down three conditions for 'Overlord' success: German fighter strength must be substantially reduced prior to the assault; German reserve formations must be limited to 12 first-class divisions, and the enemy must not be allowed to transfer more than 15 first-class divisions from the Eastern Front during the first 8 weeks after the landings; thirdly, the problem of supplying the invasion forces over open beaches must be overcome. The latter condition would be partially met by development of artificial 'Mulberry' harbours, and discussion on this scheme took place on the *Queen Mary*, complete with demonstrations in Churchill's bath. The British COS believed the first two conditions could be met by post-'Husky' operations in the Mediterranean: German divisions could be diverted by this thrust from the south, and 65 per cent of German fighter production remained situated in an area which could be best attacked from North Italy. Thus the COS decided upon three main recommendations, approved by Churchill. '1.

"Overlord" should be carried out, on the basis of COSSAC's plan, as near the target date as possible. 2. To procure conditions for the success of "Overlord", General Eisenhower should exploit his victories to the full, aiming at the Milan-Turin area. 3. Resources diverted to the Mediterranean campaign should be limited to those necessary to produce conditions essential to the success of "Overlord".' But the COS admitted that divisions due to return for 'Overlord' might have to be retained in the Mediterranean, thus perhaps postponing 'Overlord' from 1 May to June or even July 1944.[54]

Discussions on the *Queen Mary* on 8 and 9 August mainly centred on Burma and the Far East. The Prime Minister considered that Auchinleck's latest report, which he had vigorously condemned on 24 July, showed 'how vital and urgent is the appointment of a young, competent soldier, well-trained in war, to become Supreme Commander (South-East Asia) ... so as to infuse vigour and audacity into the operations.' Mountbatten, at present Chief of Combined Operations, seemed a perfect choice; Brooke had some doubts: 'He had never commanded anything more than destroyers.... He had boundless energy and drive, but would require a steadying influence in the nature of a very carefully selected Chief of Staff.'[55] The COS approved Churchill's suggestion, but opposed him over plans for Far East operations. The Prime Minister wished to abandon assaults on Akyab and Ramree, but he urged even more ambitious schemes including the operation against the northern tip of Sumatra. Wingate's proposals for the reconquest of Upper Burma should be accepted, he declared. The COS argued that to abandon the Akyab landings would shake US confidence still further, while operations against Sumatra would alert Japanese defences against a subsequent move upon Singapore and would use up valuable resources; Wingate's operations would have to be followed by more extensive campaigning. Satisfactory conclusions had still to be reached by the time the *Queen Mary* arrived at Halifax.[56]

The American Chiefs had also been preparing their position. This time they were determined to face the British with a united, stubborn front. 'We must go into this argument in the spirit of winning,' said Marshall.[57] Too often, believed the American COS, the British had slid away from a compromise, back to their original positions, and proof of this intransigence had apparently been given by the freezing of Mediterranean resources, despite the 'Trident' decisions. Above all, the Americans continued to doubt British enthusiasm for 'Overlord'. Henry Stimson, US War Secretary, had visited London during the summer and, on the day Churchill reached Halifax, submitted a damning report to Roosevelt at a conference also attended by the US COS. An American commander must be chosen for the cross-Channel invasion, because the British were half-hearted towards such an operation. 'The shadow of Passchendaele and Dunkirk still hang too heavily.... Though they have rendered lip-service to the operations, their hearts are not in it.' The British favoured 'a series of attritions in northern Italy, in the Eastern Mediterranean, in Greece, in the Balkans, in Rumania and other satellite countries'. Stimson added: 'The time has come for you to decide that your Government must assume the responsibility of leadership in this great final movement on the European war.'[58] The irony, and tragedy, of the situation lay in the fact that Stimson's report was indeed an accurate assessment of British fears and feeling – up to a point. The British did not consider the Mediterranean operations to be an end in themselves; they would not be a substitute for 'Overlord', but an essential prerequisite to the cross-Channel attempt. Stimson and his colleagues failed to grasp this factor in British thinking, and on 8 August the British Mission had wired a depressing document to the COS on the *Queen Mary*. 'We felt that before your arrival in Canada you should realize some serious difficulties may lie ahead in "Quadrant".... Mediterranean. There is apparent in all the US COS a feeling that the British are not standing firm enough to considered decision of "Trident".... They seem particularly to take exception to British "standstill" order.... Burma. There is an increasing feeling with the US Chiefs that we do not mean business in Burma, and have never meant business.... Pacific. We think it fair to say that for some time past it has been Admiral King's determination to effect such progress before "Quadrant" regarding operations in the Pacific that his position will be impregnable....'[59] A major clash lay ahead, not so much through differences between British and American proposals, but through the American conception of this British outlook. And even before this Anglo-American conference started, tentative arrangements were being made for another summit, this time with Stalin. On 8 August the Soviet leader had finally informed Roosevelt that he could not leave Russia during summer and autumn; but on the 10th Stalin agreed with Churchill that 'a meeting of the heads of three Governments is absolutely desirable' and next day the War Cabinet in London approved a message from Eden to Churchill stating: 'This is better than I (Eden) dared to hope for and a great relief. Should we not now at once agree a meeting in principle, time, place, personnel and agenda to be decided later.... Joe is unaccountable.'[60]

After a day's fishing, the British COS started business in their HQ at the plush Château Frontenac Hotel, Quebec, on the morning of Friday, 13 August. Full Combined discussions would start next morning. Churchill remained with Roosevelt four hundred miles away on the banks of the Hudson River, sweltering in the heat and discussing the tricky problem of choice of 'Overlord' Supreme Commander. The Prime Minister had previously promised the position to Brooke; now, bearing in mind his own desire to have Mountbatten as Supreme Commander, South-East Asia, he proposed Marshall; moreover, a US commander for 'Overlord' could result in a British Supreme Commander in the Mediterranean as exchange. Roosevelt, bearing in mind Stimson's report, gladly accepted. Brooke would soon hear of this decision, which would throw him into added despair. Meanwhile, on this Friday the British COS examined a preliminary paper provided by the Americans to describe their basic position. The document began in uncompromising, hostile fashion. 'We must not jeopardize our sound overall strategy simply to exploit local successes in a generally-accepted secondary theatre, the Mediterranean, where

logistical and terrain difficulties preclude decisive and final
operations designed to reach the heart of Germany.' 'Overlord' must have 'whole-hearted and immediate support'. These
opening statements reflected the US interpretation of the
British attitude, yet once the paper passed beyond this stern
beginning and concentrated more upon details, the content
proved similar to British thoughts. Operations should continue in the Mediterranean with available resources, but
'Overlord' should have priority; efforts should be made to
bring about the Italian collapse, to create diversion of German
forces, and to seize Sardinia and Corsica. The British COS
criticized the paper's lack of emphasis on the importance of
obtaining North Italian bomber bases, its inflexibility, and
the apparent US failure to appreciate 'Overlord' dependence
on Mediterranean operations; nevertheless, the COS believed
the paper to be an excellent starting point. 'I am delighted,'
wrote Brooke, 'and feel that at last they are beginning to
see some daylight in the problem confronting us.' But he
added: 'We still have several difficult points to settle.'[61]

British and American chiefs therefore met at 10.30 a.m.,
Saturday, 14 August, in the sunlit room 2208 at the Château
Frontenac Hotel. Red-coated mounties guarded the doors.
As 'Quadrant' was taking place on British soil, Brooke took
the chair, and with memories of the excellent progress made
in 'Trident' closed sessions, the CCS agreed that numbers
attending should be limited to about 12 on each side. Brooke
opened with an exposition of the European situation; the
Germans were obviously suffering in Russia, and 'though the
number of German divisions remained almost constant, it
was believed that their strength both in personnel and
equipment, was only some 60 per cent of their authorized
strength. The manpower of Germany was now stretched to
its limits.' Mediterranean operations contributed to this
sapping of German strength. 'The German air force was now
completely on the defensive,' said Portal, but he warned:
'Their fighter forces ... were growing fast, and had achieved
the remarkable increase of 22 per cent during the year 1943.
All this had been absorbed on the Western Front.' Portal
stressed that 'the key to the situation from the air point of

view would be the placing of strong offensive air forces in northern Italy. From there all south Germany would be within comfortable range and above all the largest German aircraft factories, which between them produced nearly 60 per cent of the German fighters.' Pound, now under almost intolerable strain from a brain tumour, claimed the Battle of the Atlantic had swung in favour of the allies. Marshall asked for British opinions on operations against Sardinia and Corsica; Brooke replied: 'It would not pay us to attack these islands at this stage. There were indications, as yet inconclusive, of German withdrawals from Sardinia', and if Italy collapsed the Germans would probably pull out completely.[62] The CCS adjourned for lunch and assembled again at 2.30 p.m. to start talks on the war against Japan. Just before this session began, the British received a depressing signal from Auchinleck: extensive flooding west of Calcutta would affect the despatch of supplies to Burma, hindering operations. As Brooke commented, this 'put us in a difficult position in view of the pressure put on us by our American friends to carry out a Burma campaign'.[63] But discussion at this afternoon meeting centred upon the Pacific, with King complaining that operations directed at Rabaul were being delayed by lack of means. 'He had said at Casablanca, and he must now repeat, that lack of means was in his opinion caused by failure to consider the war against all three Axis powers as a whole.' King urged greater percentage of resources devoted to the Far East, but the session failed to find a solution.[64]

Sunday, 15 August, was for Brooke one of the saddest, most dismal days of the war. Churchill arrived at Quebec and asked to see the CIGS just before lunch; he took him on to the balcony overlooking the St Lawrence and told him of the decision to appoint Marshall as Supreme Commander. Brooke felt 'swamped by a dark cloud of despair'. He returned to another of the CCS sessions which by now he thoroughly disliked, and he wrote after this meeting: 'It was most painful and we settled nothing.'[65] Brooke began this afternoon session by referring to a message sent from Washington to Eisenhower the previous day, ordering no more bombing raids on Rome, pending clarification of press reports that the Italian Government had declared the capital an open city. Brooke remained firmly opposed to Rome being considered a non-military area, especially through a unilateral Italian decision. The allies might wish to use Rome themselves, or at least might consider more bombing raids militarily necessary, and the message to Eisenhower should be revoked. Some support came from King, who agreed 'if we were in any way a party now to its being declared an open city our hands would be tied'. But Leahy felt 'it would be impossible to reach a decision until the matter had been discussed with the President', and he could not see any disadvantage in refraining from bombing. Marshall also believed Presidential clearance must be obtained before cancellation of the message, although he agreed the allies must not be tied to the Italian declaration. Marshall and Leahy had their way; the CCS decided to advise Roosevelt and Churchill that the two Governments 'should in no way commit themselves'. After this inauspicious start, discussion turned to European strategy. Brooke attempted to smooth the path; the British 'believed that there was a great similarity of outlook between themselves and the US COS.... Such divergencies as there were did not appear to be fundamental. The British COS were in entire agreement that "Overlord" should constitute the major offensive for 1944 and that Italian operations should be planned with this conception as a background.' Brooke then discussed the three conditions which COSSAC deemed necessary, and continued: 'It was essential ... to ensure that the Germans had available to them the minimum possible number of divisions in France and that their rate of reinforcement should be as slow as possible. Operations in Italy, therefore, must have as their main object the creation of a situation favourable to a successful "Overlord".' He considered the US statement that 'Overlord' should have a priority of resources over the Mediterranean to be too binding. 'Sufficient forces *must* be used in Italy in order to make "Overlord" a possibility.' The Americans only envisaged allied forces pushing north to the Apennines across the neck of Italy; Brooke believed 'this should be regarded as the first stage only, and that if possible the north-west plain should be seized.'

But Brooke's protestations concerning British support for 'Overlord' fell on barren ground; American suspicions were already too deep-rooted. Admiral King opened the American attack: he believed 'the British COS had serious doubts as to the possibility of accomplishing "Overlord".' Brooke wearily replied that the three COSSAC conditions must be met. King retorted 'he did not believe that the achievement of the necessary conditions were dependent solely on operations in Italy. The necessary conditions might be produced by many other factors, such as operations in Russia, the result of those already taking place in Sicily, and the air offensives from the UK.' Marshall stated: 'Unless a decision were taken to remove the 7 divisions from the Mediterranean and unless overriding priority was given to "Overlord" ... "Overlord" would become only a subsidiary operation.... If "Overlord" was not given overriding priority then in his opinion the operation was doomed, and the US forces in Britain might well be reduced to the reinforced army corps necessary for an opportunist cross-Channel operation.'[66] Brooke wrote in his diary: 'It is quite impossible to argue with him (Marshall) as he does not begin to understand a strategic problem. He had not even read the plans worked out by Morgan (COSSAC).' Discussion would be continued next day. Brooke dined alone 'as I wanted to be with myself', then conferred with Dill. 'Dill had been for a private talk with Marshall and had found him more unmanageable and irreconcilable. Even threatening to resign if we pressed our point.'[67]

While this frustrating debate had been continuing over future operations in Italy, the Italians had taken another step towards surrender. The British COS had just sat down next morning, 16 August, to discuss the plan of action for the next CCS session, when they were summoned to Churchill's bedside. The Prime Minister showed them a signal from Eden, forwarding a message from Sir Samuel Hoare, British Ambassador in Madrid. General Giuseppe Castellano, a senior member of Ambrosio's staff, had reached Madrid via Lisbon the previous day. 'Castellano informed me,' reported Hoare,

'that he had come officially and with full authority from
Marshal Badoglio.... Italy was in a terrible position. Practi-
cally the whole country was in favour of peace, the Italian
Army was badly armed, there was no Italian aviation and
German troops were streaming in by the Brenner and the
Riviera. Feeling against the Germans was intense. The
Italian Government however felt powerless to act until the
Allies landed on the mainland. If and when however the
allies landed, Italy was prepared to join the allies and fight
against Germany.' Hoare had asked Castellano for his
Government's reaction to a demand for unconditional
surrender. 'We are not in a position to make any terms,'
the Italian emissary had replied. 'We will accept unconditional surrender provided we can join the Allies in fighting
the Germans.' Hoare had been impressed; in London the
Foreign Office had more doubts, and Eden pointed out in
his covering note to Churchill that once the allies landed the
Italians would probably co-operate anyway.[68] Eden would
arrive at Quebec within 48 hours. Meanwhile the COS agreed
with the contents of a message to Roosevelt, still at Hyde
Park, which Churchill had drafted; the Italians should be
told that the allies 'cannot make any bargain about Italy
changing sides, nor can we make plans in common at this
stage. If however serious fighting breaks out between the
Italian Army and German intruders a new situation would
be created.' The COS sent a memorandum to the US Chiefs,
recommending Eisenhower should be instructed to send a
British and an American staff officer to Lisbon to present
the Short Terms.[69]

Allied troops had been plunging forward over the Sicilian
lava slopes towards the north-east corner of the island.
Demolitions on the narrow, precipitous coastal road from
Catania had slowed the 8th Army and now, on 16 August,
Patton's dusty troops triumphed in the race for Messina.
On the same day Hitler ordered Rommel to hurry troops
south into Italy. In Quebec, at 2.30 p.m., the CCS met
again to continue their arguments over the next strategic
steps, and agreed to hold the discussion in closed session.
The Americans had already handed a stiff memorandum to

the British, which insisted that Mediterranean and North
European theatres were separate and must remain so. 'The
discussion in the CCS meeting yesterday made more
apparent than ever the necessity for decision now as to
whether our main effort in the European Theatre is to be
in the Mediterranean or from the UK. The US COS believe
that this is the critical question.... We propose the following:
"The Combined Chiefs of Staff reaffirm the decisions of the
'Trident' Conference as to the execution of 'Overlord',
including the definite allotment of forces thereto and assign
to it an overriding priority over all other preparations in
the European Theatre." The US COS believe that the
acceptance of this decision must be without conditions and
without mental reservations....'[70] Brooke, according to his
account, began this closed session 'by telling them that the
root of the matter was that we were not trusting each
other. They doubted our real intentions to put our full hearts
into the cross-Channel operation next spring, and we had
not full confidence that they would not in future insist on
our carrying out previous agreements irrespective of changed
strategic conditions.' The CIGS produced 'countless arguments to prove the close relation that exists between cross-
Channel and Italian operations', and, after three exhausting
hours, Brooke believed his arguments had had 'some effect'
on Marshall.[71]

Roosevelt reached Quebec the following day, and agreed
with Churchill's proposals concerning Castellano's offer. The
US COS supported the British recommendation that Eisenhower should send two staff officers to Lisbon. And during
the afternoon a short signal reached Churchill from
Alexander: 'By 10 a.m. this morning, 17 August 1943, the
last German soldier was flung out of Sicily and the whole
island is now in our hands.'[72] Moreover, the CCS now
managed to reach agreement in the great strategic debate at
Quebec. They met again in closed session at 2.30 p.m. this
Tuesday, and to Brooke's immense relief the Americans
accepted the British proposals. The joyful CIGS wrote: 'All
our arguing had borne fruit.' The CCS agreed on a statement
to be submitted to the President and Prime Minister, which

closely followed the paper handed by the US COS to the
British prior to the opening of the conference – and which,
in general, the British had approved. But two major alterations had been made: the US paper had originally declared:
'As between the operation "Overlord" and operations in the
Mediterranean, when there is a shortage of resources
"Overlord" will have an overriding priority'; the last six
words were now struck out and the following substituted:
'available resources will be distributed and employed with
the main object of ensuring the success of "Overlord".
Operations in the Mediterranean Theatre will be carried out
with the forces allotted at "Trident" except in so far as these
may be varied by decision of the CCS.' Secondly, the statement stressed that Italian operations would be aimed at
creating 'conditions required for "Overlord"'. The meeting
then agreed upon an American paper on Pacific operations
in 1943/1944, after which Wingate was invited to explain his
views of long-range penetration groups acting in conjunction
with main forces in north Burma. 'Quite a good meeting,'
commented Brooke.[73]

But Burma still remained to be settled, and the subject
received full CCS attention next afternoon, Wednesday, 18
August. Considerable differences of opinion were revealed
between the US policy of vigorous offensive operations, and
the British hesitations over the feasibility of such operations
especially in view of the recent floods.[74] And next morning,
19 August, Churchill injected another complication; he told
Brooke at a private meeting that he still insisted upon an
operation against North Sumatra. Brooke complained that
this might easily clash with any general plan agreed upon
by the British and American chiefs. 'He refused,' wrote
Brooke, 'to accept that any general plan was necessary,
recommended a purely opportunist policy.... Got nowhere
with him.' The CIGS had therefore been placed in an even
more difficult position for his talks with the Americans,
which resumed at 2.30 p.m. The British COS were caught
midway between US pressure for maximum attempts to push
back the Japanese in Burma, especially in the north, and
Auchinleck's pessimistic on-the-spot assessments: the General

had signalled on 13 August with a plea to abandon all offensive operations in Burma for the coming season, and in a signal reaching Quebec this Thursday, listed military objections to Wingate's proposals.[75] Confusion surrounding the British position therefore aggravated the Anglo-American clash, and the afternoon CCS meeting on the 19th proved heated and inconclusive.[76] Mountbatten provided a moment of comic relief. He had become extremely enthusiastic for a scheme to make aircraft carriers from artificial icebergs; this project, code-named 'Habbakuk', relied upon the manufacture of ice strengthened by sawdust to make it resilient. Mountbatten urged Brooke for permission to demonstrate samples at this CCS session; Brooke, under pressure, had at first snapped: 'To hell with Habbakuk', but had then relented. Mountbatten brought his equipment into the room and showed the strength of the material by firing a revolver at a large cube. The shot echoed round the conference room; a bullet ricocheted from the block, nicked King's trousers and, in Brooke's words, 'buzzed round our legs like an angry bee'. Staff officers waiting outside heard the explosion; one exclaimed: 'Good heavens, they've started shooting now.' General Arnold attempted to smash the cube with an axe, bringing his weapon down with full force, then he yelped with pain from the impact, clutching his wrist while Mountbatten's sample remained intact.[77]

The CCS gathered their papers and met Roosevelt and Churchill for the first plenary session of the Quebec conference. Their agreed document on 'Overlord' and the Mediterranean was accepted by the two leaders, but difficulty was encountered with Far East strategy. Churchill emphasized his Sumatra scheme, code-named 'Culverin', which he claimed could be the 'Torch' of the Indian Ocean; the Americans still tended towards the main assault through Burma into China.[78] The subject occupied Brooke's time until after midnight, first through discussions, with Marshall, then Mallaby, Director of Military Operations in India, then Dill. 'I feel cooked,' wrote the CIGS. 'It is quite impossible to run a Conference such as the present one with the PM chasing hares in the background.'[79] Churchill was meanwhile

taking further steps towards another, even more critical conference: during the day he had joined with Roosevelt in a
message to Stalin urging a summit meeting immediately after
the Quebec talks. 'The Prime Minister will remain on this
side of the Atlantic for as long as may be necessary.'[80]
Crucial talks were taking place at Lisbon during the night
of 19 August. Bedell Smith, Eisenhower's Chief of Staff, and
Brigadier K. W. D. Strong, British head of his Intelligence
Section, had been hastily fitted with civilian clothes and
had reached the Portuguese capital earlier in the day, to open
discussions with Castellano at 10 p.m. The meeting lasted
until 7 a.m., 20 August. The Short Terms were explained
in detail and Castellano agreed to take them back to Rome;
if the Italian Government accepted the terms they were to
signify the fact by 30 August, and Castellano would then fly
to Sicily to meet allied representatives on the 31st. The
Italian General left Lisbon, joining other Italian officials in
order to avert German suspicions, and travelled back to
Rome by rail: the journey would be dangerously slow.[81]
And, as Churchill had warned Alexander in a signal on the
19th, quick action remained imperative. 'Our greatest danger
is that the Germans should enter Rome and set up a Quisling-
Fascist Government'; Alexander replied on the 20th: 'Everything possible is being done here to put on "Avalanche"
(invasion at Salerno) at the earliest possible date. We realize
here very clearly that every hour gives enemy more time.'[82]
On the same day Montgomery received detailed orders for
8th Army's part in the invasion further south, 'Baytown', on
the toe of Italy. His army would advance if the enemy withdrew, exerting maximum pressure to relieve the Americans
at Salerno; it was not, however, envisaged that the 8th Army
would push forward more than about 60 miles.[83]
In Quebec, Churchill sent an unsettling minute to the COS
this Friday. 'We are not yet agreed among ourselves about
the policy to be pursued in Akyab, "Culverin", etc., and in
my opinion the whole matter has been insufficiently studied.
... In the meanwhile it is not possible to come to any decision
with the Americans.... I hope the COS will beware of
creating a situation where I shall certainly have to refuse to

bear any responsibility for a decision which is taken on their level. This would entail the whole matter being referred to the War Cabinet at home after our return....'[84] Churchill thereupon departed for a fishing trip with Roosevelt, leaving Brooke with his hands tied for the CCS meeting at 2.30 p.m. He could only declare that the British 'had not had sufficient time to arrive at a definite conclusion'.[85] The meeting closed. 'I then went for a walk,' wrote Brooke, 'which was badly needed as I was in a foul temper.'[86] He returned for more discussions with the British Planners, Dill and Portal, which finally resulted in a compromise statement to be put before the COS formally next day.

Eden had been engaged in an attempt to settle Anglo-US differences over the French. The Foreign Secretary had arrived with Cadogan on the 18th, and on the 20th he broached the subject of FCNL recognition with Hull. 'We both got quite heated,' wrote Eden. 'I like the old man but he has an obsession against Free French.' 'Conversation had become a trifle sharp,' remembered Hull, 'although Eden and I had more than enough respect and friendship for each other to keep our voices calm and our manner friendly.' Eden finally suggested Britain and America should each take their own course over the recognition problem; Hull said he would regret such a divergence but 'if the British could stand it, we could too'. Cadogan complained to another member of the British delegation that Hull was 'as vindictive as an old woman about whom someone had been spreading scandal'.[87]

But at least progress proved possible on the 21st towards Anglo-American agreement on Far East strategy. Brooke presented his compromise document to his COS colleagues during the morning, received approval, then took it to Churchill – who also acquiesced. The statement avoided details, concentrating instead upon broad strategic aims, and after a brief tussle in the afternoon, this received approval from the Americans.[88] During the Saturday evening Brooke left with his colleagues – and 300 other British, American and Canadian participants at 'Quadrant' – for an overnight pleasure cruise down the St Lawrence and up the Saguenay. Roosevelt, Churchill, Eden and Hull held a conference on the Sunday to discuss Hull's proposal for a Four-Power Declaration; the most important clause stated: 'They (the Four Powers) recognize the necessity of establishing at the earliest possible practicable date a general international organization ... for the maintenance of international peace and security.' The American and British leaders agreed to seek Russian and Chinese support; Eden and Cadogan then picnicked in the country, with Cadogan still wearing his Whitehall suit.[89]

American and British Chiefs of Staff resumed work on Monday, 23 August. A short CCS meeting in the afternoon put last touches to the final report, presented to the President and Churchill in plenary session during the evening. The CCS proposals were 'approved by the almighty', in Brooke's words, but not without intervention from Churchill; he expressed doubts over the idea, now put forward by the Americans, for operations in the South of France, and he insisted upon further emphasis on conditions essential for a successful 'Overlord'. Minor amendments were made to the report next day, 24 August. This confirmed 1 May 1944 as the target date for 'Overlord'; the Mediterranean campaign would comprise three phases: the elimination of Italy as a belligerent and the establishment of air bases in the Rome area and, if feasible, further north; secondly the seizure of Sardinia and Corsica; thirdly 'the maintenance of unremitting pressure on German forces in Northern Italy, and the creation of conditions required for "Overlord", and of a situation favourable for the eventual entry of our forces ... into Southern France'; Balkan operations would be limited to supplies to guerrillas, to minor Commando forces and to bombing. The report avoided details in its section on the war against Japan. 'We have found it impracticable during "Quadrant" to arrive at all the necessary decisions for operations against Japan in 1943/44. We therefore propose that, as soon as the necessary examinations have been made, a CCS conference should be held ... unless agreement is reached through the ordinary channels.' Plans for the capture of Upper Burma recognized that operations depended upon 'logistic considerations as affected by recent floods', and preparations for an amphibious operation in spring, 1944, were mentioned: studies would be made of an offensive against North Sumatra, operations southward from Northern Burma, and the capture of Akyab and Ramree. The CCS had approved proposals for a new command system in South-East Asia, including the appointment of a Supreme Allied Commander.[90]

'We have not really arrived at the best strategy,' wrote Brooke, 'but I suppose that when working with allies, compromises, with all their evils, become inevitable.' The CIGS felt flat and miserable, and described his weariness in his diary on the 24th. 'After Casablanca, wandering alone in the garden ... if it had not been for the birds and the company they provided, I could have almost sobbed with the loneliness. Tonight the same feelings overwhelm me, and there are no birds.'[91] Brooke revived; he changed into plain clothes and left with Portal on a 60-mile drive for a two-day fishing expedition in the Canadian bush. He returned to Quebec on the 27th and left by air for England the following day. Churchill also showed signs of strain as the conference closed, and his doctor expressed fears for his health to Eden. 'When W. arrived,' wrote Eden, 'I admit that he confirmed CW's diagnosis. He did not look at all well and was a bad colour.' The Prime Minister left for a few days' rest near the Lake of Snows on the 25th; first he sent a report to the War Cabinet in London. 'Everything has gone off well.... Unanimous agreement is expressed in a masterly report by the CCS.... I am feeling rather tired, as the work at the conference has been very heavy and many large and difficult questions have weighed upon us.' Among these problems had been the subject of 'Tube Alloys' – atomic bombs – and an agreement had been signed which restored full wartime co-operation between the two countries.

Churchill also mentioned the French question in his report to the War Cabinet. 'On this last we all had an awful time with Hull, who has at last gone off in a pretty surly mood.' Britain and America decided to adopt two different recognition formulas, which were wired to Algiers on the 25th and presented by Macmillan and Murphy to de Gaulle and

Giraud the following day. The French leaders made no complaints and the declarations were published during the evening. Thus the British recognized the FCNL as 'administering those French overseas territories which acknowledge its authority' and noted 'with sympathy' the desire of the Committee to be regarded as the body qualified to ensure the administration and defence of all French interests; the British intended 'to give effect to this request as soon as possible'. The Americans, while proposing to co-operate with all patriotic Frenchmen and welcoming the establishment of the FCNL, emphasized that their statement 'does not constitute recognition of a Government of France or of the French Empire'.[92] Eden left for England with Brooke's party on the 28th. Cadogan remained with Churchill, and clearly the Prime Minister had soon recovered his strength. 'WSC in terrific form,' wrote Cadogan on the 29th, 'singing Dan Leno's songs and other favourites of the Halls of 40 years ago....'[93] Churchill would broadcast to the Canadians on the 31st and then leave for a few days at the White House on 1 September, waiting for a possible favourable reaction from Stalin to a Three-Power meeting – but Stalin was otherwise engaged.

Meanwhile, stumbling, complicated and theatrical steps were being made towards an Italian surrender. By 26 August the Prime Minister, President, Eden and Hull had reached formal agreement on Long Term conditions: the Italian Government would continue to have responsibility for financial and commercial dealings; the arrangement thereby preserved Italian honour, and instead of complete subjugation, the Italians would merely have to agree to allied forces occupying certain parts of Italian territory. Nevertheless, the terms were couched in complicated and detailed fashion. Already, on 22 August, Eden had informed the Foreign Office that the allied leaders wished to have this document communicated to the Italians: these demands, and not the Short Terms handed to Castellano on the 19th, were to be considered definitive. The news caused disquiet at Eisenhower's HQ: reports were accumulating of growing German strength in Italy, and insistence upon the Long Terms might result in disastrous delay – final preparations were being made for Salerno landings, 'Avalanche', which would be preceded by Montgomery's assault on the toe of Italy. No news had come from Castellano. On the 26th yet another Italian emissary surfaced at Lisbon: General Zanussi, from the staff of General Roatta, Chief of the Italian Army Staff. He had come without proper credentials, but had brought instead the famous British POW, General Carton de Wiart, as sign of his good faith. Almost simultaneous with his arrival came the text of the Long Terms from the Foreign Office in London, and following the Quebec instructions, the British Ambassador handed them to Zanussi. The Italian expressed 'regret and alarm' at the decision to force Italy into making a public surrender, and he warned this would place Italy at German mercy. He urged that the Short Terms might remain prominent: these constituted a military armistice which the Italians might more easily accept, and he asked that Castellano's deadline, 30 August, should be retarded. Zanussi did however agree to take the Long Terms back to Rome the following morning; his aircraft would fly via Gibraltar where a refuelling stop would be made. But also on the 27th, the details of the Long Terms had been received at Algiers and anxiety at Eisenhower's HQ multiplied when the document was read – all 42 clauses. 'It was formidable,' wrote Macmillan. Eisenhower, who also suspected Zanussi's intentions, took matters into his own hands: on 28 August Zanussi was intercepted at Gibraltar and 'kidnapped' to Algiers. Macmillan and Murphy interviewed the Italian and his associate, Di Trabia. 'They were really quite an engaging couple. We bathed with them before dinner and spent a very agreeable evening in their company.'[94] Zanussi was persuaded to send a message to Rome, urging the Italians to sign the Short Terms as soon as possible; in direct contradiction to the wishes of the Foreign Office, endorsed by the War Cabinet, he was not however permitted to transmit the Long Terms.

Eisenhower's irregular methods received approval from Roosevelt on 30 August. On the same day a message reached Algiers from Rome that Castellano would appear at the appointed rendezvous in Sicily the following day, and he arrived as arranged at Alexander's HQ. Talks soon reached deadlock: the Italians were reluctant to surrender until the allies landed in strength near Rome; the allies initially considered such landings out of the question, and even the Salerno operation would be rendered far more hazardous without prior Italian surrender – and 'Avalanche' was now scheduled for 9 September. Castellano returned to Rome. But just before his departure Alexander did however decide to recommend the adoption of part of Castellano's proposals, that an airborne division should be landed outside Rome to help the Italians defend the capital. Despite the risks involved, Eisenhower gave his approval on 1 September, fearing the Italians would otherwise be unwilling to accept and announce the immediate armistice terms. War Cabinet Ministers were informed on 2 September that Roosevelt and Churchill had signalled Eisenhower to say: 'We highly approve your decision to go on with "Avalanche" and to launch an airborne division near Rome.' Portal reported to the War Cabinet that the COS believed 'in the present circumstances the proposed landing ... was justified'.[95]

Castellano returned to Sicily on the 2nd. Montgomery's assault across the Messina Straits would begin within 24 hours – and yet Castellano now declared he still had no authority to sign the armistice. Macmillan asked Alexander to intervene, and a few minutes later the General appeared in full dress uniform – clean cut tunic, breeches, medals, glittering boots, gold spurs and gold peaked cap. A guard of honour presented arms with brilliant precision. Alexander proceeded to threaten the Italians, with icy awesome dignity, and demanded to know whether they had come to negotiate – or to spy. With this threat he remounted his car and disappeared, leaving the Italians considerably shaken. Alexander stopped his vehicle round the corner, dashed behind the tent, sweated through an olive-grove and scrambled over a wall, creeping unseen to the negotiating stage – all in his curiosity to know how successful his dramatic entrance had been. And the Italians agreed to ask for immediate authority to sign, contacting Rome through the secret radio-link now established

by Special Operations. At 4 p.m. next day, 3 September, a
message came through from Rome. 'General Castellano is
authorized by the Italian Government to sign acceptance of
the armistice conditions.' Formalities were completed, and
the negotiators agreed Eisenhower and Badoglio should announce the armistice at 6.30 p.m. on the day before the
Salerno landings. The Italians were not given the exact date
for this 'Avalanche' offensive, but were told to listen to the
BBC: 24 hours before the Salerno operations two talks would
be broadcast about Nazi propaganda in the Argentine; this
would be the signal. Meanwhile, texts would be interchanged
of the Eisenhower and Badoglio announcements.

As these delayed talks took place in the early evening of
3 September, British troops were already clambering ashore
on to the toe of Italy. Montgomery's 8th Army assault over
the Straits of Messina, 'Baytown', had begun at 4.30 a.m.
Initial opposition seemed slight: the Germans had evacuated
Reggio. Four years to the day since Britain's entry into the
Second World War, the allies had re-entered mainland
Europe.

Talks at Tehran

First vessels for the Salerno landings steamed from North Africa as Montgomery's 13th Corps established its Reggio bridgehead on 3 September. The Germans had been preparing urgent defensive measures for the expected invasion, and by this Friday enemy troop deployment had been completed, under Rommel in the north and Kesselring further south. The allies had one important advantage: the Germans believed the landings would be aimed further north than Salerno. Montgomery's assault at Reggio continued to meet minimum resistance. 'The Germans are fighting their rearguard action more by demolition than by fire,' signalled Alexander to London on the 6th; on the same day Brooke gave an optimistic report to the 5.30 p.m. War Cabinet meeting: 'Our forces in southern Italy have made good progress and have now advanced some 20 miles north-east and south-west from the landing beaches; 3,000 Italian prisoners have been captured. No German troops have been met so far. The immediate object of securing a bridgehead to allow the passage of our ships through the Messina straits has been obtained.' Brooke added: 'In the Smolensk area the Russians have made good progress.... The Germans are strongly resisting in the Kharkov area but their counterattacks have been unsuccessful.'[1] Increased pressure was being exerted upon the Reich from the east and from the south. Moreover, Hitler had recently received another serious setback: on 17 August the RAF had bombed the 'secret weapon' site at Peenemünde, and despite the loss of 41 aircraft sufficient damage had been caused to disrupt Hitler's plans for the counter-offensive upon London – rockets or flying-bombs would not be available until spring, 1944. But with the Führer's desperation might come another appalling development, discussed by the War Cabinet on the 6th. Reports had been received that the Germans had threatened to use poison gas against the Italians if they turned against the Axis. Ministers agreed that if the Germans were to use gas against the Italians after the armistice 'we should almost certainly retaliate'.[2] Ministers thus agreed in principle to use gas on behalf of the Italians, even though they were still at war with Britain; and in fact the complex armistice negotiations had run into further difficulties.

Talks with Castellano in Sicily on the evening of 3 September had led to agreement over the dispatch of airborne troops to Rome: the Italians would hold back the Germans from four airfields in the area, to permit an allied assault a few hours before the seaborne landings at Salerno. These and other plans for Italian co-operation were sent by Castellano to Rome on 5 September, where they caused consternation. Castellano's superiors doubted whether the Italian Army would or could switch allegiance overnight. Moreover, Castellano had tried to guess at the Salerno landing date and had come to incorrect conclusions: in his message of the 5th he declared: 'I presume that the landings will take place between the 10th and 15th September, possibly the 12th.' The Italians therefore believed they had longer to make up their minds and continued to hesitate. An American emissary, General Maxwell Taylor, was smuggled into Rome on the 7th in an attempt to speed events; the Salerno landings were due to start in 24 hours' time. Ministers met in London at 3 p.m. on the 7th, still believing that an armistice announcement would be made; thus the War Cabinet were informed that 'at 17.30 hours on the following day, BST, an announcement was to be made by Eisenhower to the effect that the Italian Government had surrendered unconditionally. Marshal Badoglio's announcement of the armistice ... would be issued at the same time.'[3] But Ministers were hurriedly summoned at 3.15 p.m. the following day, 8 September;

convoys for the allied landings were gathering off the Gulf of Salerno; the assault would start within a few hours. Yet a message had just reached Whitehall from Eisenhower's HQ, containing the following signal from Badoglio in Rome: 'Owing to changes in the situation which has broken down, and the existence of German forces in the Rome area, it is no longer possible to accept immediate armistice ... the capital would be occupied and the Government taken over forcibly by the Germans.' The airborne operation at Rome was 'no longer possible because of lack of forces to guarantee airfields'. Both the War Cabinet and the COS immediately agreed the armistice should nevertheless be announced by the allies 'since this might weaken Italian resistance and help operation "Avalanche"'. A telegram was drafted to inform Eisenhower, but before this could be sent another signal came from the General: 'I ... am determined not to accept the Italian change of attitude. We intend to proceed in accordance with the plan for the announcement of the Armistice. ... Marshal Badoglio is being informed through our direct link that this instrument entered into by his accredited representative with presumed good faith on both sides, is considered valid and binding.'[4] Roosevelt and Churchill agreed in a telegram reaching Eisenhower at 5 p.m.: 'No consideration, repeat no consideration, need be given to the embarrassment it might cause the Italian Government.'[5]

At 6.30 p.m. Eisenhower therefore issued his message on Radio Algiers. 'The armistice was signed by my representative and the representative of Marshal Badoglio and becomes effective this instant. Hostilities between the armed forces of the UN and those of Italy terminate at once....' Ten minutes later Radio Algiers issued the agreed text of Badoglio's message, handed to the allies following the talks on the 3rd. 'The Italian Government ... has requested an armistice from General Eisenhower.... This request has been granted. The Italian forces will, therefore, cease all acts of hostility against the Anglo-American forces.... They will, however, oppose attacks from any other quarter.'[6] Now the Italians could only acquiesce: the Radio Algiers message presented evidence of collusion, about which the Germans could be expected to show no mercy. At 7.30 Badoglio gave the agreed announcement on Rome radio; the Italian Royal Family, senior Ministers and senior officers fled the capital in confusion; Italian forces were swamped by infuriated Germans. Only the Italian navy managed to slip away during the evening of the 8th, heading towards Malta. Contrary to the hope lying behind this whole armistice negotiation, no Italian army help was therefore given for the allied landings at Salerno, and allied troops came ashore against determined, undistracted German opposition.

Kesselring's 16th Panzer Division had moved into the Salerno area at the end of August. Announcement of the Italian armistice resulted in the immediate disarmament of Italian units and the takeover of defence posts by the Germans. Beach positions were covered by well-sited machine gun posts and by mobile 88-mm batteries in the surrounding hills; tanks were moved up close behind these shore defences. Even before the armistice declaration the Germans at Salerno had been placed on alert: a report had been received of 36 ships with destroyer escorts steaming 25 miles south of Capri. And so, as General Mark Clark's two US and two British divisions attempted to land before dawn on 9 September, they encountered increasing, stiffening resistance: well-sown minefields on the beaches, multiple machine-gun nests in the dunes, heavy gun emplacements in the nearby hills. When darkness fell on the 9th none of the attacks had penetrated more than three miles inland. But one report from Italy gave especial cheer in London: Admiral Cunningham's warships had sailed unopposed into Taranto to land troops and take this valuable port.

Churchill and Roosevelt spent the evening of the 9th in discussion with the CCS at the White House, and once again the Prime Minister's thoughts were leaping ahead. The Italian fleet had continued to sail towards Malta despite Luftwaffe attacks which had sunk the battleship *Roma*, and Churchill had sent a minute to Roosevelt which declared: 'Assuming we get the Italian fleet we gain not only that fleet but the British fleet which has hitherto contained it. This very heavy addition to our naval power should be used at the earliest possible moment to intensify the war against Japan. I have asked the First Sea Lord to discuss with Admiral King a movement of a powerful British battle squadron ... to the Indian Ocean.' Admiral King now expressed doubts over this offer: weather, port facilities and lack of escorts would prove limiting factors when adding to capital strength in the Far East. 'However, the US Navy were fully aware of the political value.' King would express similar opposition, in even stronger form, to later British proposals on the same lines. Churchill turned to the highly sensitive subject of future operations in Italy, and the enthusiastic Prime Minister, with Brooke far away in London, now threatened to ruffle the uneasy calm which the 'Quadrant' compromise had created. 'We are I presume agreed to march northwards up the Italian peninsula until we come up against the main German position ... and I should hope that by the end of the year at the latest we should be confronting it in full strength. If sooner, then better.' But Churchill hastily added: 'There can be no question of whittling down "Overlord". We must not forget at this juncture our agreement to begin moving seven divisions away in succession (from Italy) from the beginning of November.' The Prime Minister had been contemplating the 1944 campaign: the allies should not advance beyond the narrow part of the Italian peninsula, but should perhaps dig in if the Germans did likewise. 'Of course, if the Germans retreat to the Alps, another situation is presented.' Churchill switched to another of his favourite subjects: the Balkans. 'When the defensive line across Northern Italy had been completed, it may be possible to spare some of our own forces assigned to the Mediterranean theatre to emphasize a movement north and north-eastward from the Dalmatian coast.' Roosevelt agreed in principle with Churchill's proposal for digging in across North Italy, but 'operations in the Balkans would be largely a matter of opportunity. However ... we should be prepared to take advantage of any opportunity that should present itself.'[7] During the day Churchill had pressed Alexander for firm action against Rhodes. 'This is the time to play high. Improve and dare.' But the Germans had clamped down their tight control, and the island remained in enemy hands.[8] Churchill continued to urge determined action in the Eastern Mediterranean, and secured CCS agreement in principle on the following day, 10 September, for small-scale lightning operations to take advantage of the Italian armistice. In London the British COS also agreed in principle, but signalled Churchill to warn that operations must 'not, in any way, prejudice our main effort in Italy. We must guard against being drawn into a fresh campaign with inadequate forces.'[9]

The Prime Minister also concerned himself with summit diplomacy during these days at the White House. Stalin had suggested a conference of Foreign Ministers, and on 5 September Churchill proposed London as a venue; three days later Stalin asked for Moscow to be chosen. Churchill agreed in a signal on the 10th, and at the same time took up Stalin's suggestion for a Three-Power summit later in the year. 'I am ... prepared to go to Tehran.'[10] Also on the 10th, Eden wrote in his diary: 'Felt depressed and not very well all day, partly, I think, because of exasperating difficulty of trying to do business with Winston over the Atlantic.... Roosevelt has had his way again and agreed to Moscow for the Foreign Secretaries conference with alacrity. His determination not to agree to a London meeting for any purpose, which he says is for electoral reasons, is almost insulting considering the number of times we have been to Washington. I am anxious for good relations with US, but I don't like subservience...'[11] Yet Churchill was accorded a unique honour by Roosevelt next day, 11 September. The President had left Washington for his Hyde Park home; Churchill remained in the capital, at full liberty to use the White House as his home and his office, and with permission to summon the US COS for a meeting. The British Prime Minister accordingly chaired a meeting of the CCS at 11 a.m. this Saturday. Marshall reported that 'the battle in the Naples area was going to be very difficult for the next few days. However, he had great confidence in the effectiveness of allied air support.' Churchill urged 'we should do anything we possibly can to expedite the build-up in Italy and, if necessary, repay any losses incurred by "Bolero" out of the windfall which has come to us in the form of additional (Italian) shipping ... the attack was a critical one.... Even the acceleration of one division by a fortnight might make a big difference.' Marshall must have suspected his fears were being confirmed that Italy would suck in additional resources; nevertheless he 'assured Churchill that everything possible would be done'.[12] And Churchill's point concerning the valuable acquisition of the Italian fleet received a boost during the day, when a short, poetic and very naval signal flashed from Cunningham to the Admiralty in London. 'Be pleased to inform their Lordships that the Italian battle fleet is anchored under the fortress guns of Malta.'[13]

Troops at Salerno had now battled 10 miles inland; they found the narrow lanes covered by a network of enemy machine-gun arcs of fire. Alexander had already sent an anxious signal to Montgomery – 'it was of the utmost importance that he should maintain pressure upon the Germans so that they could not move forces from his front and concentrate them against "Avalanche"'.[14] Reinforcements were sent to Salerno during the 11th after the COS in London had wired their approval. Next morning, Sunday, 12 September, German gliders floated down in the mountains at Abruzzi, Central Italy. Ninety German soldiers jumped out, and moments later a light aircraft carried the sick, shocked Benito Mussolini away from Italian captivity. Hitler had ordered this 'rescue'; now he would install the Duce as leader of a Fascist Government in Exile on the shores of Lake Garda.

In London, Brooke had become increasingly anxious over Churchill's absence, but on the 12th he did at least receive some reassurance that the Prime Minister had restrained himself in Washington; Dill wrote: 'The PM left last night on his way to Hyde Park and so home.... His conduct has been exemplary.... He has been active but never too wild ... no harm has been done.'[15] Churchill nevertheless continued to seek more vigorous action, both at Salerno and in the Dodecanese, and at one point threatened to fly to Salerno himself instead of sailing home in the *Renown*. On the 13th he pressed for attacks on Rhodes and on other Eastern

Mediterranean islands. 'This is the time,' he signalled Wilson at Cairo, 'to think of Clive and Peterborough and of Rooke's men taking Gibraltar.'[16] But Rhodes was now lost; instead, British troops were landed on islands to the north during the 13th and 14th – Cos, Leros, Samos, Lipsoi, Patmos, Furni and Castel Rosso – yet, without Rhodes, the fate of these garrisons would remain uncertain.

Members of the War Cabinet, meeting in London at 5.30 p.m. on Monday the 13th, discussed another, unexpected aspect of the Italian situation. Stafford Cripps, Minister of Aircraft Production, reported on a weekend visit to a number of factories. 'In all of them he had been impressed with the very serious effect on the war effort of the announcement that Italy had signed an armistice. In many factories, work was proceeding almost as if the war was over.' Ministers asked the Minister of Information to make some form of announcement. Eden then drew the War Cabinet's attention to the fact that the Italians had still to sign the Long armistice terms, and he warned that 'this might lead to some embarrassment'. He also referred Ministers to the agreement to hold the Foreign Secretaries Conference in Moscow; he 'deprecated the American attitude that no important conference, attended by US representatives, could be held in London. Sooner or later, we should have to take a firm stand on this point.'[17] News from Salerno continued to cause disquiet in London; Brooke wrote in his diary that evening: 'It is hell to have to face the chance of being driven out of Salerno at this juncture.'[18] And now Kesselring launched his counter-attack, spearheaded by the 16th Panzer Division and aiming at the gap between the US and British sectors. Over 600 tanks smashed into the flimsy allied bridgehead; the allies remained desperately short of armour and used any possible type of artillery, regardless of calibre, to keep the Panzers at bay. Warships sailed close inshore to pound the enemy with giant 15-inch guns. Enemy artillery thundered in reply, and so deadly were these salvoes on 14 September that unloading on to the beaches had to be halted. 'News about Salerno is going from bad to worse,' wrote Brooke. Montgomery received another appeal from Alexander to press north –

despite lack of resources following the original assumption that the 8th Army would advance no more than 60 miles from Reggio.

But 14 September also saw the last German reinforcements arrive at Salerno: German strength would remain static, while allied power would steadily increase. Between 12-15 September allied air sorties dropped over 3,000 tons of bombs – the actual target areas received an average bomb density of 760 tons per square mile.[19] Thus the allies smashed and bombed their way forward to secure the immediate hinterland, and Churchill signalled Alexander from the *Renown*: 'My feeling is you are going to win.'[20] On 16 September, the 5th and 8th Armies joined hands, the latter having marched 300 miles in 17 days over appalling terrain, arriving a few hours late for the main battle. Churchill reached the Clyde on Sunday, 19 September, and received another signal from Alexander: 'I can say with full confidence that the whole situation has changed in our favour and that the initiative has passed to us.'[21]

Two days later Alexander completed his appreciation for the next stages of the Italian campaign. This envisaged four phases: first would be the consolidation of the Salerno-Bari line, already almost complete; second would be the capture of Foggia and Naples; third would be the capture of Rome and its airfields, perhaps by the end of the year; fourth would be the capture of Florence and Leghorn. The COS agreed with this programme on the same day.[22] Also on 21 September, the Prime Minister gave a marathon Parliamentary performance. 'Winston came in beaming genially with a "Here I am again" look,' observed Harold Nicolson. His speech lasted 120 minutes, with an interval for lunch; he concentrated upon criticisms of the long delay in attempting the Salerno landings and in allied dealings with the Italian Government. He warned the Commons of German experiments with 'a new type of aerial bomb' and added: 'We must expect that the terrible foe we are smiting so heavily will make frenzied efforts to retaliate.' Churchill also gave a warning to the Germans. 'I call this front we have opened, first in Africa, next in Sicily, and now in Italy, the Third

Front. The Second Front, which already exists potentially and which is rapidly gathering weight, has not yet been engaged, but it is here, holding forces on its line.' Yet he told MPs: 'The bloodiest portion – make no mistake about it – of this war for Great Britain and the United States lies ahead of us.' Nicolson commented: 'He sat down, leaving the House stunned by the magnitude of his performance.'[23]

And now a brief lull fell after the quarrels at 'Quadrant' and the tension of Salerno. The old routine began again in Whitehall after the Prime Minister's six-week absence. First of all Churchill had to address himself to two changes in personnel, one Ministerial and the other naval. Kingsley Wood, Chancellor of the Exchequer since 1940, died suddenly on 21 September. Churchill chose Sir John Anderson to replace him, and Attlee took Anderson's previous office, Lord President of the Council, although Anderson retained his seat in the full War Cabinet. Lord Cranborne became Dominions Secretary in place of Attlee, but without a War Cabinet seat, and Beaverbrook became Lord Privy Seal, again without a War Cabinet seat. The other main change resulted from the resignation of Admiral Sir Dudley Pound; Pound had been ill for a considerable time, longer than his colleagues on the COS had realized, and had clearly deteriorated during 'Quadrant'. His participation in the CCS conference at Quebec had been minimal, and an ambulance had met him on arrival back in London. He had sent his resignation to Churchill almost immediately. The Prime Minister initially considered Admiral Fraser, C-in-C Home Fleet, as his successor as First Sea Lord and Chief of the Naval Staff, but followed the advice of Alexander, First Lord of the Admiralty, and appointed Admiral Sir Andrew Cunningham, illustrious commander in the Mediterranean. Pound died on 21 October, Trafalgar Day.

Immediately after his return to London, Churchill reapplied pressure for greater activity in the Aegean. On 22 September General Wilson signalled details of a proposed attack on Rhodes, scheduled for 20 October, but stressed he would need additional escorts and landing craft – yet available Mediterranean resources were already stretched to the limit. Two days later Hitler told a conference at his HQ that the Aegean islands must be held at all costs. Churchill sought help from Eisenhower in two telegrams on the 25th: 'I feel I ought to place before you the priorities which I assign in my own mind.... Four-fifths of our effort should be the build-up in Italy. One-tenth should be our making sure of Corsica ... and in the Adriatic. The remaining tenth should be concentrated on Rhodes.' He therefore asked Eisenhower to transfer some resources from the central to Eastern Mediterranean. The 25th also saw the end of the second phase of Italian operations, as specified in Alexander's directive: the Germans evacuated the Foggia airfields. Eisenhower, in his reply to Churchill the following day, believed 'minimum' requirements for Rhodes could be met.[24]

Churchill also concerned himself with Greece, believing British troops must be ready to take full advantage of a German withdrawal – and also to foil an attempted Communist *coup*. On 29 September the Prime Minister sent a minute to the COS which contained the first definite proposal for an intervention by British forces, and the minute thus marked the beginning of a long and painful story. 'Should the Germans evacuate Greece we must certainly be able to send 5,000 British troops with armoured cars and Bren gun carriers into Athens.'[25] Resources were likely to be spread extremely thin. And in a minute to the COS on 28 September, Churchill again brought up his project for an operation against Sumatra, which might mean men and landing craft being switched from the Mediterranean to the Far East. The Prime Minister asked for the Akyab, Ramree, Rangoon and Sumatra operations in 1944; the COS believed these would be impossible with existing resources unless Germany were defeated by the end of the current year, 1943. Churchill refused to alter his requirements at a meeting with the COS during the evening, despite discussion lasting until 1 a.m.[26] But Brooke saw Churchill after the COS session next morning, 29 September, and found him more co-operative: 'He started by saying that he was just as anxious as I was about our Mediterranean strategy and for not doing anything that might draw forces away from the Mediterranean.' Brooke's diary entry continued: 'I think he felt that he had been in an unpleasant mood the previous evening and wanted to make amends.'[27] The COS discussed the Sumatra operation again on the 30th, and remained unable to find any way in which the plan could be executed without drawing resources from the Mediterranean; yet Churchill resumed the attack on 1 October in a 60-minute COS confrontation. Brooke wrote: 'I was refusing to impair our amphibian potential power in the Mediterranean in order to equip Mountbatten for ventures in Sumatra.' Events in the Eastern Mediterranean would soon divert Churchill's mind back from the distant Far East jungles, and Sumatra remained shelved, yet the argument proved typical: a comparatively small number of landing-craft held a disproportionate value in critical and far-reaching decision-making.

The Italians at last signed the complete armistice document. Macmillan and Murphy had flown to Brindisi on 27 September and opened final negotiations with Badoglio and Ambrosio. Badoglio protested over the title of the document – 'Instrument of Surrender' – and the first clause: 'The Italian Land, Sea and Air Forces ... hereby surrender unconditionally.' Moreover, many of the clauses had been rendered out of date by intervening events. Badoglio signed on the 29th, on board HMS *Nelson* in Malta harbour, but only on the understanding that his appeals for textual changes would be handed to the Allied Governments by Eisenhower with strong recommendations that they should be accepted. Eisenhower gave him a formal letter admitting the terms were 'based upon the situation prior to the cessation of hostilities' and 'developments ... have altered considerably the status of Italy, which had become in effect a co-operator of the UN.' Eisenhower carried out his part of the bargain in a signal to the CCS on 30 September, agreeing with Badoglio's objection to the unconditional surrender. 'We all feel that our Governments have much to gain and will have lost nothing by granting Badoglio's request.' After further discussion, Britain and America agreed to a protocol, eventually signed on 9 November, which changed the document's title to 'Additional Conditions of Armistice with Italy', and adopted

Eisenhower's suggestion stating the terms had been 'accepted unconditionally', thus removing the offensive 'unconditional surrender'.²⁸ In the midst of this flurry of activity at the end of September and beginning of October, Churchill also had to broach another difficult diplomatic-military subject. Convoys to Russia had been suspended during 'Husky'; on 21 September Molotov requested they should now be resumed. Churchill told a Defence Committee meeting on Tuesday evening, 28 September, that this request should be granted. In addition, the massive German surface raider, *Tirpitz*, had been severely damaged by Royal Navy midget submarines, and with this threat removed, the Defence Committee agreed a 35-ship convoy should be assembled for sailing by 15 November; further 35-ship convoys should leave in December, January and February.²⁹ But before Churchill could send this news to Stalin, he received from Eden a list of grievances concerning the treatment of British personnel in North Russia. These complaints were added to Churchill's message to the Soviet leader, dated 1 October, including the refusal of visas for additional personnel and for relief of existing personnel, severe restrictions on movement, and censorship of mail by the Russian authorities. Moreover, the Prime Minister qualified his convoy news by stipulating 'this is no contract or bargain, but rather a declaration of our solemn and earnest resolve'.³⁰ Stalin would take almost a fortnight to compose an extremely offensive reply.

Anglo-American units of the 5th Army entered Naples on 1 October; Montgomery's 8th Army consolidated its hold on the Foggia plain; the Germans withdrew from Sardinia and Corsica and continued to pull back in the Italian mainland. But the position suddenly deteriorated in the Eastern Mediterranean. Hitler remained determined to keep the allies from his Balkan doorway, and at dawn on 3 October, German parachutists billowed upon Cos. The island fell on 4 October; Brooke found Churchill 'in a great flutter'. With this island gone, neighbouring Leros had been placed in greater danger, needing further reinforcement. But resources for the proposed attack on Rhodes, scheduled for 23 October, might now be insufficient. The Chiefs of Staff met on 6

October to discuss this dilemma, and believed extensive
Aegean operations could not be carried out in view of the
shortage of strength and the Italian commitment.³¹ The
Prime Minister remained determined that the attack on
Rhodes, 'Accolade', should go ahead, and a heated argument
took place at a staff conference at 3.15 p.m. this Wednesday,
without firm conclusions being reached. On the same day
Hitler issued a fresh directive: he was unsure where the
allies would undertake a Balkan push, but declared: 'The
enemy may be expected to direct his main operation against
the south-east area from Italy.... It cannot yet be determined
whether he will cross from southern Italy into Albania,
Montenegro and Southern Croatia.' Hitler therefore ordered
further reinforcements to be moved into the Balkans as well
as Northern Italy. Next day, 7 October, the British arguments
continued at a 3 p.m. staff conference, and broke out again
at another evening discussion until, at 11 p.m., Churchill
informed the shocked CIGS that both of them would fly to
Tunis the following Saturday, two days away, to discuss the
situation on the spot.³² Churchill also appealed to Roosevelt:
'I am much concerned about the situation developing in the
Eastern Mediterranean.... The Germans evidently attach the
utmost importance to this Eastern sphere.... What I ask for
is the capture of Rhodes and the other islands of the
Dodecanese.... Rhodes is the key.' Churchill added: 'Even
if landing-craft and assault ships on the scale of a division
were withheld from the build up of "Overlord" for a few
weeks without altering the zero date, it would be worthwhile.'³³ The thought of 'Overlord' plans being affected, even
if the target date remained unaltered, caused dismay in
Washington; agreement to this appeal might merely result
in further calls for more, and Churchill received a cold reply
from Roosevelt next day, 8 October. 'I am opposed to any
diversion which will in Eisenhower's opinion jeopardize the
security of his current situation in Italy, the build-up of
which is exceedingly slow.... It is my opinion that no diversion of forces or equipment should prejudice "Overlord" as
planned. The American Chiefs of Staff agree.' But another
signal left Downing Street for the White House. 'I am

willing to proceed to Eisenhower's HQ with the British COS immediately, if you will send General Marshall.'[34] 'I can control him no more,' despaired Brooke in his diary this Friday. 'He has worked himself into a frenzy ... even at the expense of endangering his relations with the President and the Americans and the future of the Italian campaign...'[35] Even before a reply had been received from Roosevelt to his second appeal, Churchill added a third, dispatched the same night. 'The effect on "Overlord" ... is limited to a delay of about 6 weeks in sending home 9 landing-craft which were to have started from the Mediterranean this month, nearly 6 months before they would actually be needed for "Overlord".'[36] 'The Americans are already desperately suspicious of him,' wrote Brooke, 'and this will make matters worse.' These US suspicions were revealed in a polite message from Roosevelt on the 9th. 'As I see it, it is not merely the capture of Rhodes, but it must mean of necessity, and it must be apparent to the Germans, that we intend to go farther.... This in turn involves the necessity of drawing for the means ... from some other sources, which inevitably must be Italy, "Overlord", or possibly Mountbatten's amphibious operations.'[37]

Eisenhower had called a conference on this Saturday, 9 October; Churchill signalled Wilson as a last resort: 'You should press most strongly at the conference for further support for "Accolade".... I am doing all I can.' But the meeting opened with discussion of disturbing news from Italy, indicating the Germans were now about to establish themselves in strong positions before Rome, further south than had been expected. Main German defences would be based at a point which would soon receive terrible notoriety – Cassino. During the evening Eisenhower sent a personal message to Churchill. 'We sincerely regret that current situation in Italy, aggravated by drastic changes of the last 48 hours ... does not permit, at this moment, diversion necessary to successful "Accolade".'[38] Churchill wrote in his memoirs: 'With one of the sharpest pangs I suffered in the war I submitted.... Rhodes remained a thorn in our side. Turkey, witnessing the extraordinary inertia of the allies near her shores, became much less forthcoming, and denied us her airfields.' The episode marked the closest that Churchill ever came to directly overruling the Chiefs of Staff; he added in his memoirs: 'The American Staff had enforced their view; the price had now to be paid by the British.'[39] Vulnerable Leros would fall on 16 November.

Brooke agreed with the Prime Minister that the American COS had a blinkered attitude to 'Overlord' which prevented them agreeing to proper uses of resources. But while Churchill urged for these resources to be employed in the Eastern Mediterranean, Brooke believed they should give added strength in the Italian campaign itself. American reluctance to see the real value of the Italian operations – an essential adjunct to 'Overlord' – had led to half-hearted exploitation of the Italian collapse; Hitler had made full use of the extra breathing-space, and now the Germans would offer determined resistance south of the capital. In addition, Brooke feared further American inability to see Italy's importance could lead to a setback in the next stage, with consequent detriment to the aim of fulfilling 'Overlord' conditions.[40] Already the rigid timetable laid down at Quebec might have to be altered. Italy declared war on Germany on Wednesday, 13 October, and the 5th Army resumed the offensive. But grim fighting clearly lay ahead.

Anthony Eden had meanwhile been preparing for the Moscow meeting. An important section of the conference would be concerned with post-war affairs, and Eden therefore drafted a paper on the British position which he brought before the War Cabinet on 5 October. Churchill, preoccupied with the Aegean and Italy, showed little enthusiasm for this discussion over future peacetime topics; Cadogan wrote in his diary: 'Perfectly *hopeless*. PM didn't want to discuss the question at all ... so took semi-humorous-critical line.... A. (Eden) lost his temper – quite rightly – and said if he couldn't get *any* guidance he'd rather not go.... I never witnessed such deplorable proceedings.'[41] Cadogan would later have increasing cause for complaint over Churchill's attitude to post-war subjects; the Prime Minister's lack of application to peacetime problems became acute as war neared its exhausted end. Churchill told the War Cabinet at this meeting on the 5th that the importance of the Moscow Conference lay primarily in its opportunity for ascertaining Russian views. 'It would be a mistake to try to define too clearly, at this stage, our own attitude ... on the future of Germany, and he deprecated in particular any attempts to reach binding conclusions.' Eden retorted that it would be helpful to know his colleagues' opinions. The War Cabinet eventually agreed that 'while we should like to see a united Germany give place to a number of separate states and should certainly encourage any separatist movements which might develop, it was impossible to foresee at this stage whether it would in the event be practicable to bring about such a solution.' Ministers doubted the feasibility of forcing a solution on these lines upon an unwilling Germany; one view advanced was that 'the increasing power of Russia might make it inexpedient to carry too far a policy of breaking up the unity of Germany'.[42] Armed with this somewhat vague brief, augmented by a declaration of basic principles drafted by Churchill, Eden therefore departed for Moscow via Cairo on the 9th. Hull had left Washington two days before, despite fears that this 72-year-old Secretary of State would be unable to stand the strain of travelling – he had never flown before. Eden had suggested a pre-Moscow meeting with Hull at Cairo; Hull had refused in view of Soviet suspicions. 'It might look as if Britain and the United States were forming a common policy in advance.'[43] Eden spent 4 days in Egypt, discussing military questions with Wilson and Montgomery and attempting to deal with renewed problems over Greece. On 8 October renewed civil fighting had broken out in this unhappy, occupied country; expectation of an allied invasion had led the ELAS guerrilla group to make a bid for supremacy, ready for an allied arrival, and attacks in strength had been launched on rivals. Eden saw Tsouderos, Prime Minister of the Greek Government in Exile, on the 15th, and attempted to find some way to clear the confusion but without success.

Churchill shouldered the added burden of Foreign Secretary. In this capacity he informed the House of Commons on 12 October of the successful agreement at last reached with Portugal for facilities in the Azores; on the same day he signalled Clark Kerr, Ambassador at Moscow, with a reminder that Stalin had still to reply to the telegram concerning the convoys.[44] The Soviet answer left Moscow within 48 hours. Meanwhile Churchill crammed other problems into his crowded schedule on the 13th, devoting attention to a report by Lord Cherwell on 'the undoubted superiority of the German explosives charges', and directing the Minister of Production to examine this development. And on this Wednesday – the day Italy declared war on Germany – Churchill had also to turn to domestic political affairs. The Conservative and Labour parties had suspended the issue of nationalization of the coal-mines while war continued, but 'a lot of rumblings' on this point now led Churchill to make a long Commons speech, stressing the general need for national unity. 'What holds us together is the prosecution of the war. No Socialist or Liberal ... has been in any way asked to give up his convictions. That would be indecent and improper.' But the Prime Minister warned: 'We must be careful that a pretext is not made of war needs to introduce far-reaching social or political changes by a side-wind.' Churchill brought up this question of coalition co-operation at a War Cabinet meeting next day, 14 October; he referred Ministers to the recent Labour Party conference decision that 'if the Party called on a Labour Minister to withdraw from the Government after the war, these Ministers would resign office'. Churchill claimed this attitude injected a 'a new factor in the situation.... There were obvious objections to formulating post-war policy and still more to giving effect ... in legislation, if there were no assurance of the continued co-operation of the Labour Ministers after the war.' The Prime Minister also described his own feelings towards peacetime policies. 'We were approaching the grimmest climax of the war. In these circumstances he found the greatest difficulty in giving that close attention which he would like to be able to give to the great social changes which were involved in the discussion of post-war policy.'[45]

Ivan Maisky, Soviet Ambassador to London since 1932,

had recently been recalled to Moscow. His successor, Feodor
Gousev, previously a butcher, then Ambassador to Canada,
had failed to establish the relatively easy relationship which
Maisky had enjoyed with the British Foreign Office;
Cadogan had condemned him on 6 October as 'quite stupid
and inarticulate'.[46] Gousev was now about to experience his
first interview with Churchill, and the moment could not
have been less auspicious. Stalin's reply concerning the
convoys reached London during Thursday night, 14 October,
and Cadogan took it to Churchill the following morning. 'I
warned him before he read it,' wrote Cadogan, 'that he'd lose
his temper.' Churchill's offer of convoys had lost its value,
according to Stalin, 'by your statement that this intention ...
is neither an obligation nor an agreement, but only a statement, which, as it may be understood, is one the British
side can at any moment renounce regardless of any influence
it may have on the Soviet armies at the front. I must say that
I cannot agree.... Supplies from the British Government to
the USSR ... cannot be considered otherwise than as an
obligation.' Stalin refused to accept any foundation for
Churchill's criticisms of treatment of British personnel in
North Russia. Churchill snapped: 'I'll stop the convoys.'
Cadogan persuaded him against hasty decisions; Eden could
take the matter up when he reached Moscow on the 18th.[47]
Also on the 18th the unfortunate Gousev was summoned for
his meeting with Churchill. The Prime Minister thrust
Stalin's message back to the Ambassador and bundled him
out of the room before he could try to return it again. The
situation was described to the War Cabinet 30 minutes later
and Ministers approved Churchill's action: firm, and designed
to impress the Soviet Government, but stopping short of an
open break.[48] Cadogan commented 'he seems to have done
it v. well.... Poor A. is to settle the matter.'

With this wound in Anglo-Soviet relations still to be healed,
Churchill also plunged into renewed strategic debate – and
once again ran the risk of disturbing the Anglo-American
alliance. On 14 October the British COS voiced their fears over
the relationship between the Italian campaign and 'Overlord'.
Inadequate resources and time for the former might prevent

conditions for the latter being adequately met. A meeting on
this Thursday therefore recorded 'a feeling of uneasiness ...
that the rigidity imposed by the "Quadrant" decisions on
our military dispositions is hampering the proper exploitation
of our successes in the Mediterranean'.[49] This unease continued, despite an optimistic signal from Dill on the 17th.
'I do not believe it was ever possible to make the Americans
more Mediterranean-minded than they are today. The
American COS have given way to our views a thousand times
more than we have given way to their's. Of course this has led
to compromises which are always dangerous, but inevitable
when one is dealing with a strong ally.'[50] Churchill called a
Staff Conference to discuss the situation at 10.30 p.m. on
the 19th, and the Prime Minister shared COS apprehension.
'It was unsound to miss present opportunities for the
sake of an operation which could not take place for
another seven months, and which might, in fact, have
to be postponed to an even later date.' Churchill expressed
fears for the 'later stages' of 'Overlord' rather than the
initial landings. 'By landing in North-west Europe we
might be giving the enemy the opportunity to concentrate, by
reason of his excellent road and rail communications, an
overwhelming force against us and to inflict on us a military
disaster greater than that of Dunkirk.' Smuts agreed that
the present fluid situation had changed the Quebec decisions.
'We were standing pat on an agreement which was already
out of date and were missing great opportunities.' Brooke
obviously agreed: 'It was quite wrong to try to wage war on
the principle of a series of "lawyer's contracts"', but Portal
warned against pushing the Americans into a position whereby they might shift to the Pacific. Churchill was prepared to
take this risk; he wanted to reopen discussions with the
Americans, because he 'felt so strongly that our strategy, as
at present agreed, was wrong in that it exposed our forces
in the various theatres to defeat in detail, and at the same
time led to our missing great opportunities'. If, as a result of
further discussions the Americans wished to transfer the bulk
of their forces to the Pacific, Churchill said 'he would be
prepared to accept this provided they would leave the forces

already in this country and would build up their air force
for operations against Germany as already promised. He did
not however think the shipping position would permit them
to employ the greater part of their army in areas other than
Europe.'[51] 'I am in many ways entirely with him,' wrote
Brooke after this meeting, 'but God knows where this may
lead us as regards clashes with the Americans.'[52] Or with the
Russians; also on the 19th the Foreign Secretaries Conference
opened in Moscow with a demand by Molotov 'that the
Governments of Great Britain and the US take in 1943
such urgent measures as will ensure the invasion of northern
France in 1943'.[53] Even 'Quadrant' had stipulated that 'Over-
lord' could not be launched until May 1944.

Churchill sent an anxious signal to Roosevelt on the 23rd,
based on the Staff Conference discussion. After mentioning
increased German strength in Italy, the Prime Minister
declared: 'Our present plans for 1944 seem open to very
grave defects. We are to put 15 American and 12 British
divisions into "Overlord" and will have about 6 American and
16 British or British-controlled divisions on the Italian Front.
Unless there is a German collapse Hitler, lying in the centre
of the best communications in the world, can concentrate at
least 40-50 divisions against either of these forces while
holding the other.... It is arguable that neither the forces
building up in Italy nor those available for May "Overlord"
are strong enough.... Personally I feel that if we make serious
mistakes in the campaign of 1944, we might give Hitler the
chance of a startling comeback.' Churchill concluded: 'My
dear friend, this is much the greatest thing we have ever
attempted, and I am not satisfied that we have yet taken the
measures necessary to give it the best chance of success....
For these reasons I desire an early Conference....'[54] Churchill
also sent a personal message to Marshall: 'We are carrying
out our personal contract, but I pray God it does not cost us
dear.'[55]

'We shall have to have an almighty row with the Americans,'
wrote Brooke on 25 October, 'who have put us in this position
with their insistence to abandon the Mediterranean operations.... It is quite heartbreaking when we see what we might

have done this year if our strategy had not been distorted by the Americans.'[56] The CIGS was in fact approaching collapse under the strain; and reports from Italy continued to reveal that the Germans were able to reinforce faster than the allies. At least news from the Moscow conference seemed excellent; Cadogan believed talks were going 'suspiciously well' and Churchill told the War Cabinet on the 25th that 'it looked as if we should receive satisfaction in regard to the treatment of British personnel (in North Russia)'.[57] Also on the 25th the Defence Committee had another discussion on the threat from Germany's 'secret weapon'; experts remained divided, and Lord Cherwell still felt that 'at the end of the war, when we knew the full story, we should find that the rocket was a mare's nest'. Cripps on the other hand was 'forced to the conclusion that they contemplated being able to use the rocket operationally, and that the threat should be regarded seriously'.[58]

Next day, 26 October, Churchill and the COS suffered even greater consternation over Italy. A long signal arrived from Eisenhower, embodying a review by Alexander which specified that in mid-September 13 allied divisions in Italy had faced 13 German; now the figures were 11 versus 25. The allies might be so reduced during the winter that the Germans could withdraw forces from Italy with which to oppose 'Overlord'. Maximum pressure must therefore be maintained, said Alexander; Eisenhower had given his approval to this appreciation on the 24th. The COS hurriedly prepared a wire for Washington which received Churchill's approval in the afternoon. 'We consider that Eisenhower and his C-in-Cs must be backed to the full so that momentum of offensive can be restored until Roman airfields to the north have been captured. For this they must have the resources they require, even if "Overlord" programme is delayed.'[59] At 6.44 p.m. the same day, 26 October, a signal flashed from Churchill to Eden in Moscow. 'I send you in my immediately following a very serious telegram from Eisenhower reporting Alexander's appreciation.... You should show this to Stalin.... The reason why we are getting into this jeopardy is because we are moving some of our best divisions and a large proportion of vital landing-craft from the Mediterranean in order to build-up for "Overlord".... This is what happens when battles are governed by lawyers' agreements made in all good faith months before, and persisted in without regard to the ever-changing fortunes of war. You should let him know if you think fit that I will not allow, while I am responsible, the great and fruitful campaign in Italy which has already drawn heavy German reserves into action, to be cast away and end in a frightful disaster, for the sake of "Overlord" in May ... it is no use planning for defeat in the field in order to give temporary political satisfaction.'[60]

War Cabinet Ministers heard full details of these distressing developments at 6 p.m. next day, Wednesday, 27 October. Churchill declared: 'An attempt to carry out "Overlord" in May, regardless of its effect on other operations, would prevent us from reaping the fruit of our successful Mediterranean strategy.' He had 'high hopes' that Roosevelt would be impressed by the arguments put to him. 'It was essential that there should be another meeting of the CCS in the near future.' Brooke claimed he had foreseen the latest developments even at the time of 'Quadrant'. He had stated 'that he thought that we should not be able both to carry the operations in Italy through to a successful conclusion and also to carry out operation "Overlord" at the date which had been agreed in the "Trident" conference'. He had then expressed the view 'that our power to carry out "Overlord" successfully depended upon the success of operations in Italy'. Portal pointed out that the Americans were now sending air forces to the Mediterranean to an extent which would hamper their 'Overlord' build-up. 'This seemed to be inconsistent with their withdrawal of land forces and landing craft from the Mediterranean in order to ensure the carrying out of "Overlord" in May.' Smuts commented: 'But in a nutshell, to insist on "Overlord" in May would mean defeat of all our operations against the underbelly.' Brooke mentioned signs of a German division being withdrawn from Italy to meet the continued Russian advance; Churchill remarked that 'this provided a strong argument against taking any action which would reduce the pressure we were bringing against the enemy in the south'. The War Cabinet 'warmly endorsed' the line taken by Churchill.[61] Cadogan commented in his diary: 'Winston will fight for "nourishing the battle" in Italy and, if necessary, resign on it. Most useful discussion.'[62]

The Americans declined to send detailed replies to the British pleas; instead, signals were speeding between London, Washington and Moscow over a possible Three-Power meeting place: Stalin continued to insist upon Tehran; Roosevelt was reaching reluctant agreement. Churchill hoped the British and American Chiefs could meet immediately before this momentous summit, but late on the 27th a message from Roosevelt added another complication; the President suggested Stalin should be invited to send a military representative to attend future Anglo-American staff conferences. Churchill reacted with alarm: apart from other long-term considerations, the consequent renewed insistence for an early cross-Channel offensive would reduce still futher any hope of the Americans agreeing to bolster the Mediterranean front. The American and Russian representatives would merely join against the British. Churchill sent a hasty reply to Roosevelt during the night of the 27th, and the message also contained a grim warning. 'I deprecate the idea of inviting a Russian military representative.... Unless he understood and spoke English the delays would be intolerable.... I regard our right to sit together on the movements of our own two forces as fundamental and vital. Hitherto, we have prospered wonderfully, but I now feel that the year 1944 is loaded with danger. Great differences may develop between us.... The only hope is the intimacy and friendship which has been established between us and between our High Staffs. If that were broken I should despair....'[63] Roosevelt backed down, but more complicated arrangements had to be made before the allies could finally settle for an Anglo-American meeting at Cairo, starting 23 November, followed by a meeting with the Russians at Tehran on the 28th, after which the British and Americans would meet again at the Egyptian capital.

For the moment strategic plans had to stay in abeyance, and Brooke continued to despair. 'When I look at the

Mediterranean,' he wrote on 1 November, 'I realize only too well how far I have failed. If only I had had sufficient force of character to swing those American COS and make them see daylight....' Brooke added after the war: 'Reading between the lines I think I cannot have been far off a nervous breakdown.'[64]

At least the Moscow Conference ended with highly satisfactory results. The Russians even seemed reassured over the Second Front question, mainly due to a long exposition by Ismay on 20 October; Churchill's telegram to Eden, dispatched after the receipt of Eisenhower's signal of the 26th and warning of a possible postponement to 'Overlord', seemed to be received calmly by Stalin when Eden saw him on the 27th. The Soviet leader reserved his comments for the forthcoming summit. Eden also settled the convoy problem, exacting promises of better conditions for British personnel and arranging in return that the next convoy should leave in November. Diplomatically, progress was made on a number of important items, although Poland – a matter of special concern in view of the rapidly advancing Red Army – received scant attention. The conference agreed to the establishment of an Advisory Council and Allied Control Commission for Italy; most important of all, the European Advisory Commission was created, to meet in London and plan for the armistice with Germany and its enforcement. The conference recognized 'the necessity of establishing at the earliest practicable date a general international organization ... for the maintenance of international peace and security'. Eden and Ismay left Moscow on 3 November, well-satisfied. 'I had hitherto,' wrote Ismay, 'been inclined to think that (Eden) was one of fortune's darlings, ... and that his meteoric success had been primarily due to charm of manner and a lucky flair for diplomacy. I now saw how wrong I had been. His hours of work were phenomenal.'[65] The Foreign Secretary continued to make full use of his time. He arrived in Cairo on the evening of the 4th and immediately entered into three days of talks with the Turkish Foreign Minister over the use of air bases in his country. The Turks continued to express fears of the German reaction – and of the threat from Russia after the war. On 7 November Eden turned from Turkey to Greece. Fighting between the ELAS and its main rival EDES had intensified, and EAM, the political group controlling ELAS, had launched a propaganda attack on Britain, the Greek King and the Greek Government, and disturbing reports continued to arrive from Athens as Eden started for home on the 8th. The Foreign Secretary reported to the War Cabinet at 6 p.m. on Wednesday, 10 October, and received Ministerial congratulations. He also received news of another diplomatic crisis, this time with the French. Back in 1941 the Free French had announced the limited independence of Syria and the Lebanon, and after strong British pressure, elections had been held in summer 1943. The new Nationalist Government in the Lebanon attempted to drive the French from the country; the French Committee reacted by arresting Lebanese Ministers and dissolving the Assembly. Fighting broke out. Meanwhile, Giraud had resigned from the French Committee on 8 November, although remaining C-in-C; this left de Gaulle sole President. Britain insisted upon the reinstatement of the Lebanese Government, and the situation received War Cabinet attention on Friday, 12 November, when Ministers read a draft message from Churchill to Roosevelt suggesting that if de Gaulle did not co-operate, he should no longer receive allied support. Ministers hesitated to take such a strong step, but at a further meeting on the 15th agreed that if the French would not meet British demands, British troops would have to move in to assume responsibility for law and order.[66] The French Committee eventually agreed to restore the Lebanese administration, but the episode resulted in even further distrust between the French, especially de Gaulle, and Churchill's Government.

Eden had again been concerning himself with Greece, drafting a drastic memorandum for submission to the War Cabinet. '1. We should break with the present leaders of EAM-ELAS. 2. We should invite the King ... to make a declaration that, at the moment of liberation, a Regency Council would be nominated and that he himself would remain outside Greece

until the constitutional issue had been settled.' Thirdly, Eden
proposed that Archbishop Damaskinos of Athens, who had
behaved courageously under German occupation and was on
good terms with all Greek parties, should be authorized to
appoint this Regency Council. The paper received War
Cabinet attention on 16 November, when Eden admitted
that 'if the matter was regarded solely from the military
point of view, there was a case for continuing to support
EAM-ELAS. This organization operated in the area east of
the Pindus Mountains, through which the main communications ran; operations to interrupt these communications were
of considerable value to us. On the other hand, it was quite
certain that if we continued to support this movement, which
was Communist led, we should be faced with acute difficulties, and the Greek Government would resign and the King
of Greece would abdicate.' Brooke believed that to close down
support for EAM-ELAS would be 'definitely contrary to our
military interests', despite their being Communist, but he
added that he had wired to Cairo for the latest appreciation.[67]
General Wilson replied three days later; he agreed with Eden
that the future value of ELAS was likely to decrease – Eden
had pointed out that these guerrillas were unwilling to risk
serious engagement with the Germans. The C-in-C Middle
East therefore recommended the adoption of a plan put
forward by Leeper, British Ambassador to the Greek Government in Exile: the King should be told that Britain would
withdraw support from ELAS on the understanding that he
would not return to Greece until invited to do so by a
representative Greek Government after liberation.[68] The
War Cabinet approved this policy at a meeting on Monday,
22 November.[69]

Next day, Eden left London for Cairo after less than a
fortnight at home, and the summit conference began this
Tuesday. Churchill had sailed for the Middle East on the
12th, handing over the War Cabinet chair to Attlee. Military
events in November had meanwhile continued to feed his fears
for the Mediterranean; solutions to the Italy-'Overlord'
strategic problem had become even more urgent.

*   *   *

Pressures for reinforcements in Italy and amphibious landings on the Italian coast to speed forward movement, had arrived at a time when naval resources were scheduled to be moved to Britain for 'Overlord'. These resources amounted to about 80 per cent of the Tank Landing Ships (LSTs) and Infantry Landing Ships (LSIs): the 'Quadrant' programme had specified that during the six weeks between 2 November and 12 December a total of 56 British and 48 American LSTs would leave the Mediterranean for the UK. Eisenhower had already agreed with the British that this rigid timetable should be rendered more flexible, and on 31 October he had told the CCS that if the 56 British and 12 American LSTs could be held in the Mediterranean until 15 December, they could be used for an amphibious assault by one division and could transfer one-third of six bomber groups proposed to operate from Italy. If the landing-craft could be held until 5 January, the whole programme could be completed; the vessels would then sail to arrive in Britain before the end of February.[70] Eisenhower's signal formed the subject of a staff conference at 3 p.m. on 4 November, when Churchill vigorously attacked the whole Italian situation. 'In these operations we were handicapped at every turn by the disinclination on the part of the Americans to agree to a relaxation of the decisions.... In view of the preponderance of the British troops and effort in the Mediterranean theatre and the correspondingly high rate of casualties which we were suffering compared with the Americans, the present situation could no longer be tolerated.' Overlooking the fact that this British presence in the Mediterranean resulted from British, rather than American insistence, Brooke said the COS agreed with Churchill: Eisenhower should be empowered to retain the necessary landing craft. Churchill said he considered the matter to be 'of such high importance' that a Cabinet decision should be taken and a telegram dispatched to Roosevelt; first, the COS should send their views to the US COS 'as a matter of urgency'.[71] The War Cabinet therefore met at 6 p.m.; Brooke told Ministers that Eisenhower had warned he would be unable to carry out amphibious outflanking attacks if landing craft were withdrawn. 'We should have to depend on a series of frontal attacks; and if we had to rely on these methods we should not get the desired line covering Rome and its airfields until some time in January, and we should not secure it until some time during February.' Brooke then read the telegram from the British COS to the Americans urging an immediate decision; he added: 'This was not a matter of bargaining.' Churchill read a signal which he proposed sending to Roosevelt, and this draft received War Cabinet approval.[72] 'We very much regret,' declared Churchill's message, 'that the urgency of the matter does not permit us to wait another three weeks until the next Staff Conference.' The Prime Minister added that 'by various intense efforts' an additional 75 LSTs would probably be produced in the UK by the date fixed for 'Overlord', so reducing the number required from the Mediterranean.[73]

Eisenhower was informed by the CCS on 6 November that he could keep the 56 British and 12 American LSTs – but only until 15 December. Yet the difference between this date and 5 January might mean the difference between partial and total success; as Alexander told Churchill and Brooke on 9 November: 'The retention of LSTs will do a great deal to help my plans, and am most grateful for them. December 15 will not however allow me to carry out the whole of my plan.' The COS gave further consideration to the problem on the 9th; later in the day Brooke told Alexander in private that he should plan on the assumption that the LSTs would remain in the Mediterranean until 15 January.[74] Official American approval would have to await the CCS conference at Cairo.

The hot Italian summer had ended; rains had swept down from the north at the close of October and by 9 November the country lay waterlogged. British criticism increased over American half-heartedness in supplying resources since the start of the campaign; Montgomery wrote: 'We now began to pay dearly for the loss of time in Sicily.'[75] But on 8 November Eisenhower could issue a firm directive for the winter, with the capture of the Rome area still predominant. The 5th Army paused to regroup for the next offensive. Brooke and his colleagues saw the landing-ship issue as merely a section of the whole Mediterranean question, reflecting the fundamental differences between British and American views. And the Anglo-American divergence of approach was emphasized by a COS paper completed on the 11th which laid down the British position for the Cairo conference, code-named 'Sextant'. 'The point at issue is how far what might be termed the "sanctity" of "Overlord" is to be preserved in its entirety, irrespective of developments in the Mediterranean theatre. This issue is clouding the whole of our future strategic outlook, and must be resolved....' The paper pointed to major developments since 'Quadrant': the victorious Russian advance; the elimination of Italy; the possibility of Turkey entering the war. Readjustment of the 'Trident' and 'Quadrant' decisions was 'not only fully justified but positively essential'. The COS continued: 'We emphasize that we do not in any way recoil from, or wish to side-track, our agreed intention to attack the Germans across the Channel.... We must not, however, regard "Overlord" on a fixed date as the pivot of our whole strategy on which all else turns.' The COS therefore urged the nourishment and maintenance of the Italian offensive until the Pisa-Rimini line had been secured; intensified support for guerrillas in Yugoslavia, Greece and Albania; 'we should aim to open the Dardanelles as soon as possible'; 'we should undermine resistance in the Balkan States'.[76] 'I cordially agree,' wrote Churchill next day, 12 November. And during the afternoon of this Friday the Prime Minister sailed from Plymouth on HMS *Renown*, heading for Malta, Cairo and Tehran. With him travelled Ismay and the First Sea Lord; Brooke and Portal would fly from Northolt for Malta at 1 a.m. on the 17th. The CIGS had written in his diary on the 11th: 'I feel that we shall have a pretty serious set-to which may strain our relations with the Americans, but I am tired of seeing our strategy warped by their short-sightedness.'[77]

Churchill spent most of his time on the *Renown* in his cabin suffering from a heavy cold, sore throat and the after-effects of typhoid and cholera inoculations. His illness failed to prevent him drafting a hard-hitting paper on the Mediterranean which reinforced the COS document; like the COS, the Prime Minister also urged adoption of a unified command in the Mediterranean instead of the present division between Eisenhower and Wilson; Churchill also complained of 'the shadow of "Overlord" '.[78] Roosevelt had sailed from America with his COS on the 13th; and US discussions during this trans-Atlantic voyage highlighted the wide gap between American and British lines of thought. Each of the allies had now become saturated with suspicions of the other. Roosevelt and his advisers decided that to secure the correct emphasis on 'Overlord', General Marshall should be proposed as Supreme Commander of all operations against Germany, from the Channel right down to the Aegean. The suggestion had become known to the British at the beginning of November, and the COS had reacted with horror; Churchill had wired to Dill, asking him to inform Leahy that he would never consent to such an idea.[79] Now the proposal seemed likely to re-emerge. Just as the British believed the Americans to be half-hearted over Italy, the Americans believed the British to be likewise over 'Overlord'; thus the US COS considered that 'while the Prime Minister invariably gave his most enthusiastic and eloquent approval to "Overlord" in principle, he steadfastly refused to accept it as a scheduled fact, preferring to believe that German power could be worn down by attrition to the point of collapse, whereupon the Anglo-American forces in the UK could perform a triumphal march from the Channel to Berlin with no more than a few snipers' bullets to annoy them'.[80] On the contrary, the British believed that without this attrition elsewhere, the Germans would be able to prevent the 'march from the Channel to Berlin' from struggling further than the bridgehead.

The Prime Minister held a staff conference at Malta on the 18th, with participants clustered around his bed. Brooke wrote: 'PM gave a long tirade on evils of Americans.... He was not at all at his best, and I feel nervous as to the line he may adopt.'[81] Leros had fallen 48 hours before, underlining the lack of resources in the Mediterranean – and, for Churchill, stressing wasted opportunities. The Prime Minister, still sick, spent much of the time at Malta trying to recover sufficiently for Cairo. In London, other fears had been voiced for his health; the War Cabinet had been warned on the 15th that the Mena House Hotel, rendezvous for the Cairo Conference, lay in an 'extremely distinctive position' close to the Pyramids, and Ministers agreed it might be wiser if the Prime Minister slept in Cairo, 'which the enemy were much less likely to bomb, and where his position would not be so accurately known'. Attlee signalled this suggestion to Churchill.[82] The Prime Minister refused to alter arrangements and settled himself in a villa by the Mena House on 21 November. Roosevelt arrived early next day.

From the start another complication was added to the already difficult situation; one which would drive Brooke and his colleagues to new heights of desperation and frustration. Roosevelt had proposed that Chiang Kai-shek should travel to Cairo to join the Anglo-American summit; Churchill had felt obliged to agree, and the Chinese leader therefore arrived on the 22nd. The Far East would thus have to be given prominence, and yet the British were acutely anxious to come to some arrangement over the Mediterranean before the British and Americans travelled to Tehran to meet Stalin on the 28th. Brooke suspected the Americans of deliberate stalling. The CCS had only six days in which to sort out the Mediterranean muddle; time would have been severely restricted even without the necessity of dealing with the Chinese first; at Tehran the Americans could expect full support from the Russians, at the expense of the British. 'We should never have started out the Conference with Chiang,' wrote Brooke. 'By doing so we were putting the cart before the horse. He had nothing to contribute towards the defeat of the Germans, and for that matter of that uncommonly little towards the defeat of the Japanese.'[83] The first day of the CCS conference at Cairo proved disastrous, with British and American service chiefs almost coming to blows.

The first plenary session assembled at the President's villa before the CCS met; also present were Chiang, Madam Chiang, Mountbatten and Stilwell. Mountbatten urged an amphibious attack on the Andamans, 'Buccaneer', which the Supreme Commander, like the Americans and the Chinese, wished to launch in March 1944. The American position had been declared in a memorandum dated 18 November. 'Since the US cannot furnish the required assistance for "First Culverin" (attack on Sumatra), it is agreed that operation "Buccaneer" should be mounted as early as practicable.' The Americans believed the operation would be a practical pledge of support for Chiang Kai-shek. The British on the other hand, with lesser enthusiasm for China, were doubtful over the part 'Buccaneer' could play in the context of the wider strategy for the war against Japan, but were prepared to agree that the operation could be launched in March 1944 – if a postponement of 'Overlord' from May to July enabled necessary assault shipping to be transferred to the Indian Ocean. Without such a postponement, the British COS feared 'Buccaneer' would deplete still further Mediterranean resources; hence the British desire to discuss the war against Germany before moving on to consideration of the war against Japan. But Chiang now insisted on 'Buccaneer' priority. 'The success of the operation in Burma depended ... not only on the strength of the naval forces established in the Indian Ocean, but on the simultaneous co-ordination of naval action with the land operations.' Churchill avoided a British commitment; instead he stressed added naval strength in the Indian Ocean owing to the surrender of the Italian fleet, and pointed out that naval operations need not necessarily be connected with a land campaign.[84] The short plenary session ended with a decision to refer discussion to the CCS. The British and American chiefs therefore met after lunch to examine Far East proposals in detail, despite the British anxiety to deal with European affairs. Almost immediately angry arguments broke out. Stilwell stressed China's importance and Mountbatten gave details of 'Buccaneer' with Admiral King giving full support. But Brooke maintained European plans must be finalized before the operation could be considered. General Arnold wrote afterwards: 'It became quite an open talk, with everybody throwing his cards on the table, face up.' General 'Vinegar Joe' Stilwell's recollections were more descriptive: 'Brooke got nasty and King got good and sore. King almost climbed over the table at Brooke. God, he was mad! I wish he had socked him.'[85] The official CCS minutes gave no hint of this depth of feeling, and by the time the Chinese were invited into the room at 3.30 p.m. sufficient calm had been restored for a compromise: a 'final decision' on 'Buccaneer' would be suspended until the plan could be considered in relation to other operations. Chinese attendance at this CCS meeting on the 23rd proved extremely unfruitful; Chiang's representatives merely sat mute while Brooke explained the basic proposals and refused to proffer opinions of their own.[86] The British and American chiefs met informally in the evening to celebrate King's sixty-ninth birthday, and the atmosphere proved in complete contrast to the afternoon confrontation. 'Good food, good wine, splendid service and good conversation', reported the amiable Arnold.[87]

Churchill managed to focus attention on the war against Germany in his speech to the second plenary session next morning, 24 November – not attended by the Chinese. The Prime Minister sought allied approval for the further delay of LSTs from the Mediterranean, with these craft staying in the area until mid-January; he stressed continued support for 'Overlord', and concluded: 'To sum up, the programme he advocated was Rome in January, Rhodes in February, supplies to the Yugoslavs, a settlement of the Command arrangements and the opening of the Aegean subject to the outcome of an approach to Turkey; all preparations for "Overlord" to go ahead full steam within the framework of the foregoing policy for the Mediterranean.'[88] Churchill's speech would receive CCS attention on 26 November; meanwhile, on the afternoon of the 24th discussion was resumed on South-East Asia. No progress seemed possible, and when the Chinese again joined the session they seemed incapable of adding to the debate. Brooke wrote in his diary that they 'spent an hour asking the most futile questions'. The CCS also considered a proposal made by the Americans for a new committee to include Chinese and Russian representatives, titled the United Chiefs of Staff; this would 'furnish adequate and satisfactory machinery for discussions by the principal allies at the COS level'. Brooke, on behalf of the British COS, disagreed: the United COS would be 'superimposed on the

CCS which would be undesirable', and he suggested that the
Russian and Chinese representatives should instead be asked
to attend all future conferences to discuss matters directly
concerning them. The Americans agreed to adopt this
alternative.[89]

Only four days remained before talks with the Russians,
and the British and Americans had still to settle their strategic
differences. But next day, 25 November, came a partial breakthrough, and once again this resulted from the CCS moving
into closed session. Brooke described the British position,
based on the COS paper of the 11th which urged continuing
active operations in the Mediterranean at the expense of an
'Overlord' postponement; surprisingly, the Americans
accepted this proposal, including plans for the opening of the
Dardanelles, the capture of Rhodes and a unified Mediterranean command. Significant progress had apparently been
made.[90] But next afternoon, 26 November, the British found
they had a stiff price to pay. The Americans revealed their
conditions for agreement; Brooke and Marshall thereupon
had, in Brooke's words, 'The father and mother of a row'.[91]
The Americans insisted upon tying Mediterranean operations to 'Buccaneer'; Leahy said the US COS 'tentatively
accepted' the British paper for the Mediterranean 'as a basis
for discussion with the Soviet Staff', but continued: 'It was
the understanding of the US COS that the British proposals
would include the opening of the Dardanelles and the capture
of Rhodes for which the retention of landing-craft in the
Mediterranean was essential, but that the retention of these
landing-craft would in no way interfere with the carrying out
of operation "Buccaneer".' Marshall said he understood
'Overlord' might have to be delayed, but 'it was essential to
do operation "Buccaneer" for the reasons that, firstly, not only
were the forces ready, but the operation was acceptable to
the Chinese; secondly, it was of vital importance to operations
in the Pacific, and, thirdly, for political reasons it could not be
interfered with.' Brooke pleaded for a 'Buccaneer' postponement, since 'by so doing the full weight of allied resources
could be put to bear on Germany, thus bringing the war as a
whole to an end at the earliest possible date'. Portal felt 'the

Russians might well say that not only did they agree with the proposed course of action outlined by the British COS and tentatively accepted by the US COS, but also that they required operation "Overlord" at the earliest possible date. In this case we must surely consider the possibility of putting off operation "Buccaneer". He did not believe this operation essential to the land campaign in Burma.' King retorted: 'The land campaign in Burma was not complete without operation "Buccaneer". Our object was to make use of China and her manpower, and the delay of a year in achieving this object must most certainly delay the end of the war as a whole.' Marshall declared that the US COS 'had gone far to meet the British COS views, but the postponement of "Buccaneer" they could not accept'. Leahy wished it to be clearly understood that 'the US COS were not in a position to agree to the abandonment of operation "Buccaneer". This could only be decided by the President and the Prime Minister.'[92] Further discussion would soon confirm British suspicions that Roosevelt had made some commitment while he had been closeted in private conversation with Chiang.

Anglo-American discussions would be resumed at Cairo after the meeting with the Russians. Brooke and his colleagues had been prepared for a Mediterranean versus 'Overlord' conflict; instead the clash had been between the Mediterranean and 'Buccaneer'. They advocated a postponement of 'Overlord', and while they believed such a delay would allow resources to be shifted for 'Buccaneer', they insisted that the Mediterranean must have priority. Whereas the British had full faith in the giant cross-Channel operations provided the necessary conditions could be met through Mediterranean activity, they believed 'Buccaneer' to be a minor plan, irrelevant to the main struggle against Germany and of minimum importance in the main struggle against Japan. Brooke privately considered Chiang to be 'shrewd but small. He was certainly very successful in leading the Americans down the garden path.'[93] The Americans, on the other hand, believed China to be a vital factor in the war against Japan, and with this conviction they believed that the Mediterranean operations must take second place; if 'Overlord' had to be delayed, then this postponement should allow 'Buccaneer'. Talks at Cairo had therefore led to more complications rather than allowing agreement prior to Tehran. And still further difficulties had been encountered through an American paper on the 25th which resurrected the proposal for a single Supreme Commander, together with a proposal that American and British strategic air forces throughout Europe should also be united in a single command. The British COS warned on the 26th that a single air command would raise serious technical and administrative problems, while opposition to the larger scheme for a single Supreme Commander remained as strong as ever. In a reply to the Americans on the 26th, the British stressed that such an individual would have to refer the multitude of political, economic, industrial and domestic problems to both the US and British Governments, and 'instances will occur in which the Supreme Commander has issued orders and the troops have marched in accordance with these orders, only to be followed by a reversal of the order by the CCS, and consequent confusion'. The Supreme Commander's position would be a 'sham' yet he would have official responsibility from Britain to the Balkans.[94] Churchill added his arguments in a paper handed to Roosevelt. 'The British would have available against Germany in May decidedly larger forces than the US. It would therefore appear that the Supreme Command should go to a British Officer. I should be very reluctant ... to place such an invidious responsibility upon a British Officer. If, on the other hand ... the Supreme Command were given to a US Officer and he pronounced in favour of concentrating on "Overlord" irrespective of the injury done to our affairs in the Mediterranean, HMG could not possibly agree.'[95] This warning effectively closed discussion for the moment.

On 27 November the exodus from Cairo began and the various dignitaries descended upon Tehran. Security precautions were almost non-existent at this rendezvous; cars carrying Churchill and Roosevelt from the airport had to push through a jostling throng to the British Legation and to the American Embassy. The latter was situated a mile from the imposing Soviet Embassy, where talks would be held, and Molotov claimed the Soviet Secret Police had unearthed a plot to kill one of the 'Big Three'; Roosevelt, being the most exposed, should therefore move into the Soviet buildings. 'If anything like that were to happen,' said Molotov, 'it could produce a most unfortunate impression.' Roosevelt obliged; Ismay commented: 'I wonder if microphones had already been installed in anticipation.'[96] Other British suspicions centred on the fact that Roosevelt and Stalin would now be in closer contact, leaving Churchill on the outside. Rumours of dark deeds increased dramatically on the 28th when Roosevelt became 'indisposed' during dinner and disappeared – stories immediately circulated that the President had been poisoned. Talks began in this hectic, melodramatic and rumour-riddled atmosphere on the 28th. Arguments had taken place this Sunday morning over the correct hour for the first plenary meeting: the British wanted the early afternoon, the Americans the evening, the Russians very late at night. Four o'clock was eventually chosen as a compromise. Brooke spent most of the morning catching up on his sleep, while Churchill still suffered from his cold and sore throat and could hardly speak. 'Lord Moran, with sprays and ceaseless care, enabled me to say what I had to say – which was a lot.'

So, at 4 p.m. the historic summit began with Roosevelt, Churchill and Stalin sitting round an ornate, specially-carved oak table at the sycamore-shaded Soviet Embassy. General Marshall had gone on a sight-seeing tour of Tehran, having misunderstood the time. Roosevelt opened with a review of the war in the Pacific and north Burma, before warning that if full-scale operations were launched in the Mediterranean, a cross-Channel operation might have to be delayed for perhaps three months, or even cancelled completely. Churchill reserved his remarks, and Stalin therefore spoke next. Almost immediately he gave a categorical assurance that Russia would eventually declare war upon Japan: 'The moment for their joining friends in this theatre would be at the moment of Germany's collapse; then they would march together.' Stalin then stressed the importance of 'Overlord': Italy was not a suitable jumping-off ground for the invasion

of Germany. Churchill now attempted to describe the relationship between the two theatres, and also to stress continued
British support for 'Overlord' itself; the operation would
definitely be launched, he declared, in the late spring or
summer 1944. Rome should be taken by January 1944, and
the allies would then stand on a line Pisa-Rimini; they
might thereafter attack southern France or might, as Roosevelt himself had mentioned in his opening remarks, move
north-east from the head of the Adriatic towards the Danube.
Meanwhile, Churchill continued, pressure must be maintained to bring Turkey into the war, after which it would
be possible to take the Dodecanese with 2-3 divisions and to
open the passage to the Russian ports in the Black Sea.

Stalin immediately tossed questions at Churchill; and from
the very start these revealed the Russian attitude which
would be maintained throughout the conference. Stalin
obviously wanted 'Overlord' as soon as possible; the British
and Americans had expected such a demand. But he also
insisted that an operation against southern France should be
launched by remaining forces in the Mediterranean, rather
than a move north-east towards the Danube; nor did he
apparently consider it worth while to attempt to bring Turkey
into the war. Stalin's interest in southern France took the
British and the Americans by surprise. Such a move had been
mentioned by the Americans at Quebec and had been
included in the final report, despite Churchill's reservations:
thus pressure would be maintained in Italy to create conditions necessary for 'Overlord' 'and of a situation favourable
for the eventual entry of our forces, including the bulk of the
re-equipped French Army and Air Force, into southern
France'.[97] Since then the idea had received minimum
attention, although Eisenhower had produced a report on
27 October which had given qualified approval. Stalin now
proceeded to bring the scheme to the forefront: militarily,
he believed a stroke against southern France would be best
able to combine with 'Overlord' – attacks upon the Germans
from north and south could act as the two arms of a pincer
movement. But Brooke, for one, believed Stalin had other
reasons: allied troops moving into the Dardanelles would

clash with his political aims: 'He had by then pretty definite ideas as to how he wanted the Balkans run after the war', while the southern-France scheme 'fitted in with his future political plans'.[98]

Stalin, to Brooke's disquiet, then advocated an early closing down of the Italian campaign – after Rome had been taken and before the Pisa-Rimini line had been reached. He thought 'it would be a mistake to disperse forces by sending part to Turkey and elsewhere, and part to southern France. The best course would be to make "Overlord" the basic operation for 1944 and, once Rome had been captured, to send all available forces in Italy to southern France. These forces could then join hands with the "Overlord" forces when the invasion was launched. France was the weakest spot on the German front.' Churchill 'entirely agreed with Marshal Stalin's observations about the undesirability of dispersion, but all that he suggested was that a handful of divisions – say two or three – would be very well employed in making contact with Turkey'. Stalin repeated that '"Overlord" was a very serious operation and that it was better to help it by invading the south of France'. Roosevelt now intervened, and by doing so revealed the differences of opinion between the British and Americans – differences which the Soviets would soon probe. 'Any operations undertaken in the eastern Mediterranean would probably put off "Overlord" until June or July. He himself was opposed to any such delay if it could possibly be avoided. He therefore suggested that the military experts should examine the possibility of operations against southern France on the timing put forward by Marshal Stalin, i.e. two months before "Overlord", the governing factor being that "Overlord" should be launched at the pre-scribed time.' Roosevelt's suggestion received Stalin's support; Churchill was obliged to agree.[99]

Stalin's insistence upon southern France had therefore added an even further complication; moreover, his desire to close the Italian campaign after the fall of Rome clashed directly with British views – and such a closure would mean that an invasion of southern France would have to come in from the sea, rather than by land via north Italy, hence calling upon

even greater landing-craft resources. As Brooke commented:
'We sat for three-and-a-half hours and finished up the conference by confusing plans more than they ever have been
before.' Admiral Leahy believed the opposite: 'The Soviets
and Americans seemed to be nearly in agreement as to the
fundamental strategic principles that should be followed.'[100]
And to add to British discomfort, Churchill and his COS
learnt during the day that Roosevelt had indeed struck a
bargain with Chiang Kai-shek at Cairo, pledging the allies
into undertaking 'Buccaneer' with all the additional strain
upon landing-craft resources which this operation would
entail. Churchill immediately addressed a minute to the
COS, dated 29 November: 'The Prime Minister wishes to
put on record the fact that although operation "Buccaneer"
is at present to be carried out solely by British forces, he has
never been consulted upon it, and that he specifically refused
the Generalissimo's request that he should undertake an
amphibious operation simultaneously with the land operations
in Burma.'[101] Also on this Sunday, the 8th Army resumed
their offensive in Italy after a six-day delay caused by rain,
mud and swollen rivers; Montgomery had been ordered to
push across the river Sangro. The 5th Army, regrouped west
of the Apennines, would begin to march north on 1
December – against Cassino.

Brooke wearily began the second day of the Tehran conference on the 29th; before him lay seven hours of discussion.
Staff talks began at 10.30 a.m., attended by Brooke, Marshall,
Leahy, Voroshilov and Portal. Voroshilov began by delving
into Anglo-American differences: he wanted to know
whether Brooke considered 'Overlord' to be an operation 'of
the first importance', or whether it might be replaced by
another operation if Turkey came into the war. Brooke
doggedly repeated the British case: operations in the
Mediterranean were designed to give 'Overlord' the best
chance of success. Voroshilov dug deeper. He asked Brooke
'if he could say a little more precisely whether he regarded
operation "Overlord" as the most important operation, as he
understood the US to think so and, from the Russian point
of view, it was an operation of vital importance'. Brooke

agreed the operation to be of 'vital importance' but added that 'he knew the strength of Northern France and of its defences and he did not want to see the operation fail. In his opinion, in certain circumstances, the operation would be bound to fail, i.e. if the circumstances were not right.' The Russian Marshal agreed with the need for other operations to divert troops from the Russian Front and from north France but, this being so, 'if "Overlord" were considered to be the most important operation, other auxiliary operations must be so planned as not to interfere with operation "Overlord".' He added: 'Operations should be undertaken in southern France; operations in Italy and elsewhere in the Mediterranean must be considered as of secondary importance, because, from those areas, Germany could not be attacked directly with the Alps in the way.' The meeting adjourned at 1.30 p.m.; Brooke had been cross-examined for three hours.[102]

The British COS had a 45-minute meeting in the afternoon before rushing to the Russian Embassy at 3.30 p.m., when Churchill handed over the Stalingrad sword – a magnificent sword of honour presented on behalf of the British people – to Stalin. The Soviet leader kissed the scabbard and handed it to Voroshilov, who fumbled and the weapon slipped with the pommel thumping his foot. At 4 p.m. the second plenary session began. 'Bad from beginning to end,' commented Brooke.[103] Churchill repeated his arguments for the Aegean and for continued pressure in Italy prior to 'Overlord'; Stalin insisted upon 'Overlord' in May, supported by a landing in the South of France on 1 April. Roosevelt agreed on 'Overlord' in May, and the Americans and Russians remained united. But the British position remained unaltered: Churchill warned he could not agree to a definite date for 'Overlord' to be launched in May, and he did not believe that 'the very great possibilities in the Mediterranean should be ruthlessly sacrificed and cast aside as if they were of no value', merely to save a month or so in the launching of 'Overlord'. The Prime Minister repeated his plea for pressure upon Turkey and for Aegean operations to fill the gap before 'Overlord' could be launched, during which time allied armies north of

Rome would continue to hold considerable German forces. Churchill proposed that a military committee should meet the following day, 30 November, to consider the nature and timing of the subsidiary operations in support of 'Overlord', and this suggestion was approved. The session ended with Stalin staring at Churchill across the table and declaring: 'I wish to pose a very direct question to the Prime Minister.... Do the Prime Minister and the British Staffs really believe in "Overlord"?' Churchill replied: 'Provided the conditions previously stated for "Overlord" are established when the time comes, it will be our stern duty to hurl across the Channel against the Germans every sinew of our strength.'[104]

Brooke was almost in total despair. 'After listening to the arguments put forward during the last two days I feel like entering a lunatic asylum or nursing-home.'[105] To close down operations in Italy would allow the Germans to transfer divisions elsewhere; an allied landing by 6 divisions in the south of France would mean re-starting the whole difficult and dangerous process of finding assault resources, establishing a bridgehead against a determined enemy, and exploiting this initial step. If the operation were launched on 1 April, as suggested, the Germans would be able to concentrate forces upon the landings before 'Overlord' in May and while allied pressure in Italy had been relaxed; if the operation coincided with 'Overlord' it would fail to attract significant enemy from the cross-Channel attempt. Moreover, the other condition for 'Overlord' would not have been met: reduction of enemy air strength, which the British hoped to be able to achieve by acquisition of airfields in northern Italy. And the need for landing-craft for the south of France might itself delay 'Overlord'. This confusion confronted the British COS when they met at 8.45 a.m. next day, 30 November. In an attempt to clear a way, the COS listed a number of points to put before the Americans at a CCS conference due to start at 9.30; these included: 'a) an operation shall be mounted for the south of France. Timing and scope to be decided later – maybe after "Overlord". b) We advance in Italy to Pisa-Rimini line.... d) Operations in Aegean are entirely dependent on the entry of Turkey into the war. In any event no more landing-craft will be kept away from "Overlord" for the specific purpose of operations in the Aegean. e) in view of (b) we must keep landing-craft in Mediterranean till 15 January. f) Because of (e) earliest date of "Overlord" cannot now be before 1 June. g) Is "Buccaneer" affected by Marshal Stalin's statement about Russia coming in against Japan once Germany is out?' These points represented the British attempt at compromise: a delay of the southern France operation until after 'Overlord' would remove the threat to Italian resources during the critical pre-'Overlord' period, yet would still allow Stalin's 'pincer-movement' aim; by tying the Aegean with Turkey's entry into the war, the COS effectively downgraded these operations – about which they had never been so enthusiastic as Churchill; above all, these measures would allow Italian operations to continue, and thus fulfil 'Overlord' conditions.[106] Brooke developed these points at the CCS meeting. Admiral Leahy then struck at the central problem, and by doing so indicated the start of the path to allied compromise. 'As far as he could see, the date of "Overlord" was the only point confusing the issue. If this matter were settled, everything would be fixed. If "Overlord" was to be done by the date originally fixed, other operations could not be carried out.' Leahy added: 'It was entirely agreed ... that the operations in Italy must be carried on'. This last statement therefore removed Brooke's chief fear. And eventually, by a circuitous route which delved into details of dates for the return of landing-craft to the UK, the CCS reached their solution. Brooke pointed out the advantages of linking 'Overlord' with the 1944 Russian offensive – and no Russian offensive had so far been launched as early as May. Moreover, the date of 1 May for 'Overlord' had been selected at 'Trident' merely as a compromise. 'Unless we could give the Russians a firm date,' warned Brooke, 'there would be no point in proceeding with the conference.' He believed 1 June might be possible, and he hinted that 'Buccaneer' should be sacrificed to bring this about. 'It would be better to use the landing-craft allocated to "Buccaneer" for this main effort against Germany'; the Americans refused to give way to this appeal, and Brooke admitted that 'a political background' existed with the 'Buccaneer' question. But the CCS, after three arduous hours, did manage to reach agreement on three important points. The rigid 1 May date for 'Overlord' should be abandoned, with a date 'during May' chosen instead, but this delay had only been granted by the Americans in return for agreement that the CCS should also recommend 'Overlord' being undertaken 'in conjunction' with a supporting operation against southern France, 'on the largest scale that is permitted by the landing-craft available at that time'. This threatened operations in the Aegean, and the official minutes declared: 'The CCS were unable to reach agreement on the question in the Aegean until they had received further instructions from the President and Prime Minister.' And the CCS agreed that 'we should continue to advance in Italy to the Pisa-Rimini line. This means that the 68 LSTs which are due to be sent from the Mediterranean to the UK for "Overlord" must be kept in the Mediterranean until 15 January.'[107]

Churchill had meanwhile been deep in private conversation with Stalin. The Prime Minister still felt far from well, and the strain of the conference had begun to tell: this Tuesday, 30 November, was his 69th birthday. Churchill had attended a dinner the previous night, at which Stalin had been host, and the Prime Minister had been irked by Stalin's semi-joking reference to the need to shoot 50,000 German officers after the war. When Elliot Roosevelt, the President's son, had intervened to pledge support for this proposal, Churchill had huffed out of the room in outraged indignation; Stalin had come after him to assure him it was all a joke, and had persuaded him back again with the misunderstanding cleared. And now Churchill wished to clear up further, more important, misunderstanding over his attitude towards 'Overlord'. He blamed 'Buccaneer' for present difficulties. 'If we had the landing-craft needed for the Bay of Bengal in the Mediterranean we should have enough to do all we wanted there and still be able to keep to an early date for "Overlord".' The Prime Minister insisted he was in no way 'lukewarm' about the cross-Channel invasion. 'I wanted to get what I needed for the Mediterranean and at the same time keep to the date for "Overlord" ... a great battle was impending in Italy.' Churchill apparently convinced Stalin and, gradually, the conference air had begun to clear.[108]

The British and American COS reported to their respective leaders at 12.30 p.m., after which Churchill, Roosevelt and Stalin met for lunch in the American quarters. The Soviet leader heard that the CCS recommended an 'Overlord' launching 'during the month of May' and that Churchill and Roosevelt accepted this recommendation. Stalin received the news well, and after a short interval the last plenary session opened at 4 p.m. Brooke read out the results of the morning CCS session, then listened while the three leaders made 'pretty speeches'.[109] Churchill suggested a short communiqué should be issued – 'the note to be sounded was brevity, mystery, and a foretaste of impending doom for Germany'. The statement therefore declared: 'The Military Staff of the Three Powers concerted their plans for the final destruction of the German forces. They reached complete agreement as to the scope and timing of the operations which will be undertaken from East, West and South....'[110] Military discussions were over – until the return to Cairo.

The British and American COS left Tehran at 7.30 a.m. next day, 1 December, for a day's sightseeing in Jerusalem before the third round of the conference marathon in Egypt. Churchill, Roosevelt and Stalin used this Wednesday to discuss diplomatic issues. Eden and Cadogan had been relatively unoccupied until now; 'I am bored by this Conference,' wrote Cadogan on the 29th. 'Have little to do and am wasting my time.'[111] Talks now began on the permanent problem of Poland, Roosevelt taking minimum part: Eden wrote: 'President Roosevelt was reserved about Poland to the point of being unhelpful.... He told the Marshal that for electoral reasons he could not take part in any discussion of Poland for another year.... This was hardly calculated to restrain the Russians.'[112] Stalin demanded the Curzon line as the eastern frontier, but subsequent talks revealed differences of opinion as to where this line should be drawn on the map. 'I began to fear greatly for the Poles,' stated Eden.[113]

The three leaders also considered Germany's future, and discussion led to divergence of views between America and Russia on the one hand, and Britain on the other. Churchill's proposal included the disbandment of the German general staff and German aviation, the supervision of industry, the inclusion of Bavaria, Austria and Hungary in a 'broad, peaceful, cow-like confederation', and the isolation of Prussia. Stalin and Roosevelt believed these ideas to be insufficient. The President suggested a five-part division: Prussia, Hanover and the north-west, Saxony and Leipzig, Hesse-Darmstadt and Hesse-Cassel and the area west of the Rhine, and a grouping of Bavaria, Baden and Württemberg. As Churchill commented, Roosevelt 'said a mouthful'; the plan was new to the Prime Minister, and he raised a number of immediate objections: small units would be unable to exist independently, and although agreeing to the detachment of Prussia, he believed the south Germans to be less belligerent. Stalin supported Roosevelt. The three leaders finally agreed a special committee should study the question.[114] Churchill later remarked that the summit underlined how small a nation Britain actually was. 'I sat with the great Russian bear on one side of me, with paws outstretched, and on the other side the great American buffalo, and between the two sat the poor little English donkey who was the only one ... who knew the right way home.'[115]

And now the donkey would have to bray again in sultry, sticky Cairo. Churchill and Roosevelt rejoined their military staffs on Thursday, 2 December. On the same day the last 8th Army units crossed the Sangro river – but winter weather had closed in again, troops were tired, and administrative problems loomed large; also on 2 December, British and American units in Clark's 5th Army successfully attacked German positions near the river Garigliano – but ahead loomed sullen Cassino. Brooke and his colleagues met on the morning of Friday, 3 December, to settle their plans for the resumed CCS talks at Cairo. Three main problems remained for urgent solution; first an early appointment of a Supreme Commander for 'Overlord'; second, Turkey and the Aegean; third, and most controversial, the CCS would have to decide upon resources for the Italian campaign, for 'Overlord' during May, and for the south of France operation, code-named 'Anvil' – and for the bedevilling 'Buccaneer' in the Bay of Bengal. The first point would have to be settled by Roosevelt, since Churchill had agreed an American would be selected, and with the second the COS were inclined to pass responsibility to Churchill, since Aegean operations were linked with Turkey entering the war and since Churchill, rather than the COS, had laid emphasis on the Aegean area. Talks between Churchill, Eden and the Turkish leaders during this Cairo conference confirmed that Turkish entry was an extremely unlikely event. The third question therefore remained predominant, and the British COS now formally recommended that either 'Buccaneer' should be scrapped, or its equivalent in assault shipping for the Mediterranean should be supplied by the Americans.[116]

The British confronted the Americans at 2.30 on this Friday, 3 December. Almost immediately the meeting became cluttered with disagreements: Brooke mentioned a 2-divisional assault on the south of France; King intervened to say no figures had been given, to which Brooke replied that a 2-divisional attack must be regarded as the minimum. And so discussions continued, until Leahy suddenly 'dumbfounded' the British COS by announcing the early American departure from Cairo; the Admiral 'believed the US COS would have to leave Cairo on the morning of Monday, 6 December, or possibly the morning of Sunday, 5 December'. Brooke declared: 'It would be a calamity if the CCS broke up without fully agreeing on all the many points still to be resolved' but Leahy 'saw no hope of postponing their departure'.[117] Brooke wrote a furious entry in his diary: 'No apologies – nothing! They have completely upset the whole meeting by wasting all our time with Chiang Kai-shek and Stalin.... And now, with nothing settled, they propose to disappear into the blue.... It all looks like some of the worst sharp practice that I have seen for some time.'[118] Churchill dined with Roosevelt and tried without success to persuade the President to change his mind over the main stumbling block, 'Buccaneer'. And next morning, 4 December, Churchill called in the COS

to discuss the latest telegram from Mountbatten in India
on this proposed operation against the Andamans: Mountbatten now estimated 'Buccaneer' would need up to 50,000
men, instead of the 14,000 which Roosevelt had hoped.[119]
At 11 a.m. Roosevelt and Churchill met the staffs in plenary
session, with the President beginning by formally announcing
that the conference must end on the 6th – 48 hours away.
He saw no difficulties; the main remaining problem seemed
to be the distribution of some 18-20 landing-craft, and he was
sure the staff would not be beaten 'by a small item like that'.
Churchill stressed the need to reconsider 'Buccaneer',
especially in view of the increased demands which had just
reached him. Brooke complained about the unsatisfactory
nature of the conference as a whole: the preliminary Chinese
involvement, the rush to Tehran, and now the rush to finish.
But Roosevelt asked 'whether he was correct in thinking that
there was general agreement on the following points: a)
nothing should be done to hinder "Overlord"; b) nothing
should be done to hinder "Anvil"; c) by hook or by crook we
should scrape up sufficient landing-craft to operate in the
Eastern Mediterranean if Turkey came in to the war; d)
Admiral Mountbatten should be told to go ahead and do
his best with what had already been allocated to him.'
Churchill refused to consent to (d) until means had definitely
been found for (a) (b) and (c). The two leaders could only
invite the staffs to discuss the issue further.[120]

The CCS accordingly met at 2.30 p.m. King now made a
welcome announcement: all new landing-craft and ships
completed in the US between 1 March and 1 April would be
sent to Europe instead of the Pacific. Yet the British did not
apparently realize the full significance of this news, presumably resulting from their demand that 'Buccaneer'
resources should be provided by the Americans rather than
going from the Mediterranean. Figures of the craft involved
were probably not given at this session, yet 24 LSIs and 26
LSTs could be sent to the Mediterranean as a result of the
switch, which would be sufficient for shortages caused by
'Anvil' and would allow 'Buccaneer' craft to be moved. Brooke
continued to oppose plans for the same reason that Marshall

had previously opposed Italian operations: more and more resources would be drawn in, despite the original assessments. Thus Brooke declared that 'Anvil' remained an outline plan, and the exact numbers of craft involved had still to be determined, and the British therefore continued to press for the abandonment of 'Buccaneer'. Moreover, this session also considered a report on the Far East just completed by the Combined Staff Planners, declaring 'the main effort against Japan should be made in the Pacific'; the British COS therefore stressed the comparative unimportance of the Bay of Bengal. The CCS agreed to exchange papers on the relation of operations in south-east Asia to those in Europe, for discussion next morning, 5 December. This meeting on the 4th also studied the US proposal to unite the air war in Italy and in Europe under one commander. Portal declared he 'would like to go on record as advising most strongly against the arrangements ... in his view, they would not attain the objects desired, were unnecessary and would prove inefficient'. Arnold retorted that whereas in other theatres 60-70 per cent of available aircraft were being used in operations, in the UK the figure was about 50 per cent, and only once in the last month had 600 aircraft taken part in operations in one day. 'A sufficient weight of bombs was not being dropped on the targets to destroy them, nor was the proper priority of targets being followed.' Necessary drive and ideas were coming from Washington, claimed Arnold, and more aircraft were being sent to Britain than were being effectively used. Unless better results could be achieved no more aircraft should be sent. The CCS deferred the subject for further discussion.[121]

At least one problem had been solved. Churchill told Brooke at dinner that Roosevelt had now decided Eisenhower should command 'Overlord'; Marshall could not be spared from Washington. Brooke suggested General Maitland Wilson, then at Cairo, to be Eisenhower's successor in the Mediterranean, Alexander as C-in-C Italian Land Forces, Paget to take over from Wilson at Middle East Command, Montgomery to command 21 Army Group – the British contingent for 'Overlord' – and Oliver Leese to take command of the 8th Army. This discussion also led to Brooke fearing for Churchill's health. 'I found the PM very tired that evening, and it was with difficulty that I could get him to absorb all the intricate points.'[122] Anxiety would soon multiply.

Sunday, 5 December, proved decisive despite an inauspicious beginning. The CCS met at 10.30 and agreed to defer the question of a unified European air command for still further study. The British and Americans presented respective papers on south-east Asia operations versus Europe, and deadlock clearly remained. Leahy stressed that the Americans believed operations in north Burma, 'Tarzan', and operations against the Adamans, 'Buccaneer', were essential. The British continued to insist upon the scrapping of the latter; Brooke suggested 'the CCS were in agreement militarily and only in disagreement on the political aspect', but Leahy refused to accept even this measure of common ground: 'The US COS believed that the abandonment of the amphibious operation ("Buccaneer") would mean either the failure or the abandonment of "Tarzan". In the latter case, there would be serious military repercussions throughout the Pacific.' King declared: 'Operation "Buccaneer" was as much a part of "Tarzan" as "Anvil" was of "Overlord".' Military implications had been overstated, insisted Brooke, and the CCS could only decide to send a memorandum to the President and Prime Minister setting out various points of agreement and disagreement.[123] This CCS document, presented to the two leaders in plenary session at 11 a.m., began with statements agreed by both parties. ' "Overlord" and "Anvil" are the supreme operations for 1944. They must be carried out during May 1944. Nothing must be undertaken in any part of the world which hazards ... success.' The agreed statements continued: 'Operations in the Aegean, including in particular the capture of Rhodes, are desirable, provided that they can be fitted in without detriment to "Overlord" and "Anvil".' The paper then included short sections by the British and American COS each declaring their positions over south-east Asian operations. 'We fully realize,' said the British, 'that there are political and military implications in postponement of "Buccaneer".... As regards the military disadvantages, these are overridden by the far greater advantages to be derived from a successful invasion of the Continent and the collapse of Germany.' The Americans put their view. 'Political and military considerations and commitments make it essential that operation "Tarzan" and an amphibious operation in conjunction therewith should take place. Apart from political considerations, there will be serious military repercussions if this is not done, not only in Burma and China, but also in the South-West Pacific.' But Mountbatten, in pressing for 50,000 men for 'Buccaneer', had raised difficulties unforeseen by Roosevelt; and the Americans therefore added: 'The Supreme Commander, South-East Command, should be told that he must do the best that he can with the resources already allocated to him.' Moreover, this plenary session on the 5th agreed upon the need to examine a possible alternative to 'Buccaneer', and this in turn at least meant an American shift away from the rigid preference for the operation. So, when the CCS met again at 3 p.m., they discussed this question of other possible operations; General Wedemeyer, recently sent by Mountbatten to urge a stronger 'Buccaneer', was asked if he could see any other amphibious operation of a hit-and-run nature using fewer forces. Wedemeyer could, although 'this would not be as effective'. The CCS decided to send a telegram to Mountbatten asking for suggestions in the event of 'Buccaneer' being ruled out before the monsoon.[124] The Americans had thus begun to bend under the pressure. And they finally broke, before dinner on this Sunday. Roosevelt had been reconsidering the 'Buccaneer' problem during the afternoon; deadlock could only be broken by going back on his promise to Chiang Kai-shek. Yet the President made his decision, and a joyful Churchill received a terse message: ' "Buccaneer" is off.'[125] Churchill telephoned Ismay with instructions to pass the good news to Brooke, but the British COS only received the message, 'to our joy', next morning.[126]

The end of the toughest Anglo-American summit so far now seemed in sight. But Churchill's health had faltered. 'At times he seems almost played out,' wrote his doctor, Lord Moran, on the 5th. 'I went into his bedroom tonight and found him sitting with his head in his hands. "I have never felt like this before," he said. "Can't you give me something so that I won't feel so exhausted?" Nevertheless, he still talks of going to Italy to see Alex.' Moran sent a warning 'in the strongest possible terms' to Churchill's good friend Smuts.[127] The President and Prime Minister spared no words of comfort for Chiang Kai-shek. 'We have reduced the scale of operations scheduled for March in the Bay of Bengal to permit the reinforcement of amphibious craft for the operations against southern France.'[128] The CCS agreed at their 11 a.m. meeting on the 6th that all preparations should be made 'to conduct "Tarzan" as planned, less "Buccaneer", for which would be substituted naval carrier and amphibious raiding operations....' Alternatively, 'Tarzan' would be postponed and replaced with heavier air activity; the final decision would be taken after reports from Chiang and Mountbatten.[129] Churchill and Roosevelt accepted the CCS Final Report at the last plenary session, held at 7.30 p.m. on the 6th; Brooke felt 'very satisfied at the final results'. 'Overlord' had been pushed back to enable the Italian campaign to continue; the Americans would send more landing-craft; landing-craft due to return to the UK would remain in the Mediterranean until 15 January; 'Buccaneer' had been pushed to one side. Words expressed next morning, 7 December, must have been heartfelt; according to the CCS minutes: 'Sir Alan Brooke said he would like to express on behalf of the British COS their deep gratitude for the way in which the US Chiefs had met their views.... General Marshall said that he very much appreciated Sir Alan Brooke's gracious tributes. He felt that it was most important that during the next month or so the British and US COS should both study how best the magnitude of future conferences could be reduced. They would undoubtedly in future have to take place at shorter intervals.'[130] Yet a longer interval in fact took place between 'Sextant' and the next allied conference than had existed between any since America had entered the war. Roosevelt left early on the 7th, his departure delayed after all, and his Chiefs of Staff followed next day.

Programmes had thus been settled. 'Overlord' and probably 'Anvil' in May 1944; meanwhile continued advance by the

5th and 8th armies to take Rome and push to the Pisa-Rimini line. In view of the 'Overlord' date, the Italian offensive would have to make good progress – yet on 6 December the War Cabinet Ministers could only be told that 'after a week's hard fighting, the 8th Army offensive had gained between 7-9 miles'.[131] This in fact would mark the limit of the 8th Army's advance in 1943, and by the end of the year the 5th Army had come to a halt south of Cassino. Lack of progress threw existing plans for Italy into confusion: these centred upon an amphibious movement forward to Anzio, 'Shingle', designed to speed the offensive by a leap-frogging stroke, and which had been scheduled for 20 December. An essential part of the scheme lay in the ability of the 5th Army to be within supporting distance of the Anzio bridgehead, now, with the 5th Army delayed, lack of support would in turn delay the 'Shingle' launching. On 18 December General Clark reported that even an alternative date of 10 January for 'Shingle' could not be met. Once more the careful allocation of assault shipping had been complicated: 68 LSTs retained in the Mediterranean, largely for 'Shingle', were due to return to the UK on 15 January for 'Overlord'. The bulk of remaining landing-craft would be needed for 'Anvil'. And so within a fortnight of the ending of the laborious 'Sextant' conference, fresh problems would arise. Acute difficulties would also occur over south-east Asian business which had been left unfinished at Cairo. On 11 December Mountbatten submitted a new plan for a smaller seaborne attack, 'Pigstick', on the southern Mayu peninsula, designed to replace 'Buccaneer'. Still no firm reply had come from Chiang Kai-shek by the third week in December; and the CCS would then find Mountbatten had virtually taken matters into his own hands. One other 'Sextant' item did receive a satisfactory ending: on 5 December the US COS had produced a revised arrangement for their proposal to unify the European air command: the commander of the US strategic air forces would come under the Chief of Air Staff in London for the control of all US bombing operations against Germany, until the CCS transferred his allegiance to the 'Overlord' Supreme Commander; better arrangements were made for co-operation with the Mediterranean Command. After final consultations the directive was issued on 4 January 1944.[132] The other American proposal, for a single Supreme Commander for all operations against Germany, quietly faded away.

But a sudden dark shadow lay across deliberations after the Cairo Conference: Winston Churchill fell critically ill; at one point his doctor believed him to be dying.

6

Winter Ills

Smuts tugged Brooke's sleeve and pulled him to one side at
the British Embassy dinner on 8 December. 'He was not at
all happy about the condition of the PM,' wrote the CIGS.
'He said he was beginning to doubt whether he would stay
the course....'[1] Churchill, wearing grey zip-suit and huge
Mexican hat, lunched alone with Brooke next day and complained of feeling very flat, exhausted, and of pains across
his loins. His desultory and wandering conversation was
punctuated by the sharp smack of his fly-whisk as he swatted
fly after fly on the green card-table, pushing each body to
join the growing pile on the edge. Brooke described the
lunch as 'a bad nightmare.... I felt desperately anxious
about him.... I began to wonder how near he was to a
crash.' Two days later Churchill and the CIGS left Cairo to
fly to Tunis, where they landed at the wrong airfield and
with no one to meet them. Churchill climbed slowly from the
hot aircraft and sat on an upturned box; the wind fluttered his
wispy hair and his pale face shone with sweat. The aircraft
went on to Carthage, and the grey-cheeked Churchill collapsed
into a chair. 'All day he has done nothing', wrote Moran.
'He does not seem to have the energy even to read the usual
telegrams. I feel much disturbed.' Churchill complained of a
pain in his throat, yet still seemed determined to fly on to
Italy to confer with Alexander. 'He seemed to be going from
bad to worse,' remembered Brooke. 'I felt that a trip to Italy
in December ... would finish him off.' By 12 December the
Prime Minister was clearly suffering from acute pneumonia

combined with general exhaustion, and a signal left Carthage
asking Mrs Churchill to fly out immediately. Brooke flew
alone to Italy on the 13th, worried 'about leaving the PM in
his present state'. Ismay, Churchill's faithful lieutenant, also
ill, was sailing home with other members of the British
delegation.

Eden had arrived back in London on Saturday, 11 December, reporting to the War Cabinet on the 13th on the general
course of 'Sextant' and describing Churchill's 'patient persuasion' in overcoming the 'Buccaneer' difficulty. The Foreign
Secretary added that Stalin 'obviously regarded the state of
France as rotten', and said Stalin and Roosevelt 'had been
rather of the same mind in thinking that France should not
have all her possessions restored to her. Thus President Roosevelt seemed to have it in his mind the idea that the US might
take over Dakar, and that it would be a good thing if we
took over Bizerta.'[2] Ministers in London were meanwhile
becoming increasingly concerned over the health of the far-
away Prime Minister; nor did reports reaching home reveal
the full picture. Mrs Churchill arrived on the 14th. 'The PM
received the news of her arrival with considerable emotion,'
noted Moran. In spite of a temperature of 101 degrees,
Churchill insisted upon sending a long telegram to the War
Cabinet concerning command changes following Eisenhower's appointment. This signal left open the choice of
Alexander or Montgomery as C-in-C Italy under Wilson;
Brooke, on the 4th, had advocated Alexander. Whichever of
the two was not chosen would lead the British contingent
in 'Overlord', and would also command the American ground
forces in the initial assault and build-up stage. Churchill concluded: 'I very much regret that on account of my illness
and fever which continue, I have not been able to visit the
Italian Front. I still hope to do so.' At 5.30 p.m. on the 15th
the War Cabinet therefore discussed whether Alexander or
Montgomery should be C-in-C Italy or commander of the
'Overlord' expeditionary army. Most Ministers supported
Montgomery for 'Overlord' 'both on merit and from the
point of view of the reception by public opinion', although
some favoured Alexander, 'having regard not merely to his

achievements, but also to the capacity which he had shown
to work smoothly with the Americans'. Montgomery had
shown no such capacity – nor would he do so in the future.
Montgomery subsequently received the 'Overlord' appointment and Alexander stayed in Italy; all other changes suggested by Churchill, which were the same as those recommended by Brooke on the 4th, were accepted by the War
Cabinet without discussion, and the appointments were
announced on Christmas Eve.

Churchill's illness reached a climax on the 15th. At 6 p.m.
he suffered a minor heart attack; Macmillan wrote next day:
'Lord Moran tells me that he thought the PM was going to
die last night. He thinks him a little better as regards the
pneumonia, but is worried about his heart.'³ The Prime
Minister lay immobile in his bed. Brooke was still in Italy,
spending the 15th at Alexander's forward camp after visiting
Montgomery on the Sangro. 'My impression of the day,' he
wrote in his diary, 'is that we are stuck in our offensive here
... I have an impression that Monty is tired and that Alex
has not fully recovered from his jaundice. The offensive is
stagnating badly, and something must be done about it as
soon as I get back.' Next day he motored close to Cassino
and discussed with Alexander 'the very nasty nut we should
have to crack'.⁴ But at least good news started to come from
Carthage: Churchill's temperature remained high but the
pneumonia seemed to be clearing. By 18 December the Prime
Minister could signal Roosevelt: 'I have harkened unto the
voice of Moran and made good progress, but I am fixed here
for another week.' Churchill's output of telegrams began to
soar again as his temperature fell and he fretted to be back
in full action – in his words: 'Here I was at this pregnant
moment on the broad of my back amid the ruins of ancient
Carthage.'⁵ Brooke returned to Churchill and reported on his
Italian trip. 'I said nothing to him about the depressing
impressions I had gained whilst in Italy. I knew from experience that he would only want to rush into some solution
which would probably make matters worse.'⁶ Brooke would
leave for home next day; meanwhile, to add to his misgivings
about Italy, Eisenhower had completed a plan for 'Anvil'

against the south of France, sent to the CCS on the 17th, which imposed another threat to the arduous Cairo arrangements: instead of an initial assault force of two divisions, Eisenhower insisted at least three would be required to establish a broad and deep bridgehead, and 'Anvil' thus called for even larger resources; as Eisenhower commented: ' "Anvil" has become an operation of major proportions.' Within three weeks it had mushroomed to a commitment enjoying priority second only to 'Overlord' and demanded three times its original strength.[7] Yet Italian operations remained deadlocked; and on 18 December General Clark's recommendation reached Alexander that the amphibious operation against Anzio, 'Shingle', could not be attempted for the moment – and yet the landing-craft were due to return to the UK in less than a month's time. The CIGS, on leave until the end of the month, would be spared most of the frantic telegraphic debate between the COS and the convalescent Churchill; Brooke's tactful description of his Italian visit to Churchill had failed to fool the Prime Minister.

On the day Brooke left, Churchill wired a probing minute to the COS. 'I am anxiously awaiting a full list of all landing-craft of all types in the Mediterranean.... The stagnation of the whole campaign on the Italian front is becoming scandalous. The CIGS's visit confirmed my worst forebodings....'[8] Churchill began to exert pressure for renewed Anzio plans, despite the 15 January date for the departure of essential landing-craft. The COS met on 20 December to discuss Churchill's telegram; before them lay depressing reports of lack of progress in the Italian fighting. The Germans had continued to make best use of their defensive positions on the 80-mile front; Canadian units in the 8th Army reached Ortone during this Monday, but would not be able to clear the town until after Christmas. Clearly some means would have to be found to shatter the stalemate. The COS saw Brooke on the 21st, then sent a reply to Churchill on the 22nd supporting his plan for a bold amphibious operation. 'We are in full agreement with you that the present stagnation cannot be allowed to continue.... The solution, as you say, clearly lies in making use of our amphibious power to strike at the enemy's flank and open up the way for a rapid advance on Rome.' The answer, according to the COS, would be to increase the strength of the Anzio amphibious force to make it less dependent upon support from the main army, which would not be within striking distance. 'We think the aim should be to provide a lift for at least two divisions.' Thus strengthened, 'Shingle' could exist without the 5th Army; but a stronger 'Shingle' would itself mean a larger number of landing-craft, and the question again arose as to where they could be found. A 2-division attack would need 246 vessels, comprising 96 landing ships and 150 landing craft. The critical shortage, as usual, involved LSTs, of which 88 would be needed; 105 LSTs remained in the Mediterranean in December, but 68 would depart for 'Overlord' on about 15 January. Of the remaining 37, 10 would be refitting and 10 would be departing for 'Anvil' against southern France. Fifteen LSTs were on their way from South-east Asia, but they had been earmarked for an attack on Rhodes, 'Hercules', if Turkish negotiations proved successful. A total of 71 out of the 88 LSTs required for 'Anzio' would thus have to be found from one source or another. The CCS suggested two methods in their signal to Churchill on the 22nd: cancellation of the attack on Rhodes, and abandonment of amphibious operations in south-east Asia, planned as an alternative to 'Buccaneer', thus allowing more LSTs to be concentrated in the Mediterranean.[9] The gap would still not be fully bridged – and the remaining means of doing so would be to retain LSTs scheduled to leave for 'Overlord', with the consequent danger of affecting the sacrosanct May date for this operation.

Only a week before, Moran had feared the PM to be close to death. Now Churchillian energy was exerted upon the problem, with the Prime Minister pondering telegrams, dispatching signals, summoning commanders to his bedside. Alexander told him he fully supported the proposal for a 2-divisional Anzio operation; Bedell-Smith, Eisenhower's Chief of Staff, was asked if he believed the LSTs scheduled for 'Overlord' should be delayed a further month. 'He replied he just could not bear asking for a third extension,' wrote Churchill. 'I had no such compunction.' First, Churchill agreed the Rhodes operation should be cancelled; he also cast his eyes upon 'Anvil'. 'You will observe,' he signalled the COS on 23 December, 'in no case can we sacrifice Rome for the Riviera. We must have both.' Churchill invited Eisenhower to a conference at Carthage, scheduled for Christmas Day, and meanwhile told the COS: 'I wish to keep all the issues open for the next three or four days.'[10] But as Churchill sent his signal, the COS in London were shocked to find Mountbatten seemed intent upon blocking at least one source of LST supply. Without seeking CCS permission, he had informed the Chinese on 21 December that his idea of an alternative to 'Buccaneer' would be mounted – 'Pigstick' against the Mayu peninsula. The COS had discussed the 'Pigstick' idea on the 20th, and had agreed that 'at first glance' the operation 'looked attractive, although it was recalled that we were in no way bound to undertake an amphibious operation of this scope'. The COS had agreed at this meeting on the 20th that full discussions must await the Prime Minister's return. On the 22nd the COS had decided that landing-craft for 'Pigstick' should now be used for the Anzio operation; within 24 hours Mountbatten, unaware of this decision, had committed Britain to the Mayu assault. Next day, 23 December, the COS discussed the disturbing development at a 10.30 a.m. meeting. 'It was pointed out that by committing us to operation "Pigstick" ... it might be found impossible to undertake the amphibious assault on Rome on the required scale, and might also prevent "Anvil" from being mounted on the scale thought necessary by Eisenhower. If this was so, to carry out operation "Pigstick" would contravene the "Sextant" decision.'[11] Churchill was immediately informed, yet the Prime Minister reacted calmly; his reply received COS consideration on the 24th, together with a report on 'Pigstick' by the Joint Planning Staff. The latter declared that while the operation seemed attractive, 'it was inevitable however that further demands would be forthcoming which would interfere with operations in the Mediterranean, and it should not therefore be approved'. The COS agreed. On the other hand Churchill had said in his telegram 'that the President would be averse to giving up an amphibious operation in the south-east Asia area, and that landing-craft from "Pigstick" would in any case arrive too late for "Shingle"'. Churchill preferred another solution rather than scrapping the Mayu idea; the COS were told that 'the Prime Minister saw no reason why the return to the UK of any landing-craft needed for this operation ("Shingle") should not be delayed up to 15 February, as they would still be in time for "Overlord" if they left a month later'. The COS had doubts: time would be needed for training and the 15 February date would leave an extremely tight programme. The COS agreed to inform Churchill accordingly.[12]

Within hours, the Prime Minister had apparently found a way round this latest difficulty. He had continued discussions with Wilson, Alexander, Tedder, and Captain M. L. Power, Deputy Director of Plans in the Mediterranean. And the latter pointed out that the Mediterranean LSTs were manned by highly-trained crews, unlike those in Britain, and would hence need minimum training; thus they need not join the 'Overlord' assault forces more than three weeks before the date of the operation, allowing the Anzio assault to be launched about 20 January. Churchill informed the COS at 12.30 p.m. on 25 December. During Christmas Day, Churchill conferred with Eisenhower and other commanders; all agreed upon an Anzio operation launched by two divisions, and next day Churchill wired Roosevelt direct for permission to retain the LSTs; bowing to continued COS doubts, Churchill cut this extra period from a month to 5 February. 'Nothing less than this will suffice,' said Churchill. 'By various expedients it is believed that the lost three weeks can be recovered and the existing prescribed build-up for "Overlord" maintained. ... If this opportunity is not grasped we must expect the ruin of the Mediterranean campaign of 1944.' And again with reference to COS feelings, Churchill added: 'It may well be that "Pigstick" will require to be moderated into "Pigstuck".'[13] He insisted to Roosevelt that the May 'Overlord' date would not be 'prejudiced' – and yet within a few hours the Prime Minister suggested to the COS that a delay in the cross-Channel event might still occur; this signal, dated 26 December, made first mention of an historic date: 6 June

1944. He told the COS 'in strictest secrecy' that both Eisenhower and Montgomery had 'expressed themselves entirely dissatisfied with what they have heard of the present plan for "Overlord".... I should think it very likely that when they have examined the plan they will propose a delay. Our contract is "during May", but I do not know whether if responsible commanders required the June moon around 6 June, and could show better prospects then, the extra week might not have to be conceded.'[14]

In London the COS continued to hesitate over Churchill's proposed tight programme for landing-craft; and they too believed that the 'Overlord' date might have to be changed, as well as 'Anvil'. After meetings at 6 p.m. on the 26th and 11 a.m. on the 27th they signalled Churchill: 'From past experience, we feel that a programme so tight as this cannot be accepted unless we are prepared to face the probability of a postponement of "Overlord" and "Anvil".'[15]

Churchill left Carthage on 27 December for a rest period at his favourite Marrakesh. So weak was he after his illness that he found difficulty in walking to the aircraft. Good news cheered him on his way: just before departure he received a telegram from the Admiralty to say the giant German capital ship *Scharnhorst*, the only heavy enemy warship left in Northern waters, had been sunk in attempting to attack the December convoy to Russia. And on the 28th Churchill received more excellent news, this time from Washington: the President agreed to the retention of the landing-craft in the Mediterranean until 5 February. But he only did so 'on the basis that "Overlord" remains permanent and will be carried out on the date agreed to at Cairo and Tehran'. The Prime Minister had already indicated to the COS that this date might be delayed; the COS had expressed a similar view, although for different reasons. Churchill made no mention of the possible alteration when he replied to Roosevelt, less than 60 minutes after receiving the President's agreement: 'I thank God for this fine decision which engages us once again in whole-hearted unity.'[16]

On the same day, Churchill received Alexander's appreciation for the Anzio operation: an American and a British division would be used, with the attack commanded by an American officer. The assault would be launched on 20 January, 10 days after an offensive against Cassino to draw off enemy reserves. 'I was well content,' wrote Churchill. He sat back to enjoy his stay at Marrakesh, and the New Year opened with the bright Africa sunshine warming his tired body, and with the mists seemingly rolling away from the grand strategic vista for 1944 – 'Shingle', 'Anvil', and above all 'Overlord'.

'The attack will come,' warned Hitler. 'There's no doubt about that any more.... If they attack in the West, that attack will decide the war.' General Ismay wrote: '1944 will always live in my memory as the year of destiny. Our fate, nay the fate of the whole free world, depended upon the outcome of "Overlord".'[17] Yet tremendous tasks had to be accomplished before the gigantic cross-Channel operation could take place; detailed tactical plans had to be completed, landing-craft had to be gathered and personnel trained, the railway system between France and Germany had to be severed by massive air attacks, air superiority had to be won and Luftwaffe factories smashed, a multitude of weapons, vehicles, ammunition stocks, supply stores had to be manufactured, accumulated and distributed. And while these background activities continued, an apparent lull would fall over the dramatic events, and for those without full access to information, this resulted in further strain upon morale. 'Altogether the war is passing through a bad phase,' commented Harold Nicolson. 'We have been held up in Italy "by the weather", which is rather a lame excuse considering what the Russians are doing.'[18] Alan Moorehead summed up a general feeling: 'The truth was that we were very tired ... we could neither remember the beginning nor see the end.... No matter how far you advanced – a thousand, two thousand miles – there was always the enemy in front of you, always another thousand miles to go.'[19] Only in Italy could military success liven the inevitable lull before 'Overlord', but the New Year opened with the 5th Army blocked beneath Cassino and the 8th Army halted between the rivers Sangro and Pescara.

In the war against Japan, Mountbatten gave way with good grace over 'Pigstick' and this operation became, as Churchill had quipped, 'Pigstuck'. Landing-craft were withdrawn during the first week in January, but as the Supreme Commander later wrote: 'Our projected operations had now been reduced to four: an offensive without landing-craft in Arakan, an advance from Ledo, operations by Long Range Penetration Brigades, and a limited advance across the Chindwin River. None of these could result in a big strategic victory.'[20] So, for the moment, the public at home had to stay starved of choice items of war news, and instead suffered the same dull diet of restrictions, dreary bulletins, dull wartime routine. The country experienced a wave of winter strikes. A Gallup poll revealed that only one person in twenty wanted a Conservative Government after the war, and by-elections, especially one at Skipton, Yorkshire, underlined the unpopularity of the Tory Party.

Churchill, far away in North Africa, remained anxious to push forward the great strategic events, but instead had to turn his attention to diplomatic affairs – the French, Yugoslavs and Poles. Another French row had blown up in December, with de Gaulle and his followers determined to deal rigorously with former French leaders who had collaborated with the Germans. Trouble especially centred round the arrest and imprisonment of Peyrouton, Boisson and Flandin. Peyrouton, ex-Governor of Algeria, had been persuaded by the Americans to leave the safety of South America and had been landed by them at Algiers early in 1943; Boisson, ex-Governor-General of French West Africa, was held in high regard by Roosevelt; Flandin, ex-Vichy Minister, had been Churchill's pre-war friend. By 22 December Churchill was ringing Macmillan at almost hourly intervals to demand an end to this Gaullist behaviour. 'I am sure it is bad for him,' wrote Macmillan. 'He was in such a passion on the telephone today that I thought he was going to have an apoplectic fit.' Next day, with Churchill still 'roaring like a bull', Roosevelt threatened military action: he signalled Eisenhower: 'You shall direct the FCNL immediately to set free and discontinue the trial of Peyrouton, Boisson and

Flandin.' Macmillan spent Christmas with Churchill, attempting to soothe the situation, and, when he returned to Algiers
on the 26th he found that Roosevelt had withdrawn his
instructions to Eisenhower. Moreover, de Gaulle agreed on
the 27th that the accused Frenchmen would be well treated
in house arrest, and the trial would be postponed until after
the liberation of France.[21] But suspicions had been revived;
Roosevelt still seemed anxious that de Gaulle should be
pushed from power; Churchill's anger was rekindled by the
offhand manner with which de Gaulle delayed acceptance
of an invitation to Marrakesh.

Yugoslav affairs had also been thrown into further disorder during the past weeks. On 29 November Tito had
established a Council of National Liberation, and on 17
December a Tito broadcast had demanded recognition for
the Council and had attacked the Yugoslav Government.
Eden advised a meeting between Churchill and Tito, to bring
the Yugoslav leader into a 'better frame of mind', and the
Partisan leader opened the way for direct contact when he
sent a warm message of good wishes to Churchill at the time
of the Prime Minister's illness. Eden nevertheless advised
caution, signalling Churchill on 1 January: 'I am doubtful
whether we should tell Tito now that we are prepared to
have no further dealings with Mihailović.'[22] The Prime
Minister disagreed: 'I have been convinced by the arguments
of men I know and trust that Mihailović is a millstone tied
round the neck of the little King, and he has no chance till
he gets rid of him.'[23] And Churchill's reply to Tito on the
8th gave the self-styled Marshal unequivocal support: no
more help would be given to his rival, although the British
Government would continue to maintain contacts with King
Peter. 'It would not be chivalrous or honourable for Great
Britain to cast him aside.' Churchill hoped this would mean
'an end to polemics'.[24]

Poland burst into prominence again at the start of the
year. Reports were reaching London that the Red Army had
crossed the frontier; the Polish Government in Exile wished
to make a public statement emphasizing their position, and
after consultations with Eden this was issued on 5 January:

the Polish Government declared themselves to be 'the sole
and legal steward and spokesman of the Polish nation'.[25]
Hopes for a favourable Soviet reaction were not encouraged
by a message from Stalin to Churchill on the 7th: 'These
people are incorrigible', yet a Soviet statement four days later
revealed a relatively friendly attitude: despite an attack on
the Polish Government in Exile, the announcement referred
to interest in 'solid friendly relations', and the Poles suggested
talks with the Russians on the frontier question; the Russians
rejected this approach on the 17th. And so the problem continued.

Churchill had concerned himself with these complicated
long-distance issues while officially resting at Marrakesh. The
effort took its toll. 'I passed 18 hours out of the 24 prone,'
he wrote later. 'I never remember such extreme fatigue and
weakness in body.... Every temptation, inducement, exhorta-
tion, and to some extent compulsion, to relax and lie down
presented itself in the most seductive form.' But Churchill
added: 'Events continued to offer irresistible distraction.'[26]
Brooke had returned from leave on 31 December, chairing his
first COS meeting in London since leaving for Cairo on 17
November. 'Not a very arduous one, mainly concerned with
putting straight telegrams from PM, who is now becoming
very active.'[27] Next day, 1 January, Brooke's promotion to
Field-Marshal was announced; he plunged into detailed
matters concerning the Anzio landings, and into planning for
'Overlord'. Montgomery reached London on the 2nd and
established his HQ at St Paul's School, Kensington, where he
had been a schoolboy. Churchill, at Marrakesh, also busied
himself with detailed questions of Anzio planning: forces
to be used, landing-craft for the assault; and an increasing
barrage of signals bombarded the COS in London, taking up
most of a COS meeting on the 5th. Brooke wrote: 'Most of the
difficulties are caused by the PM at Marrakesh convalescing
and trying to run the war from there.'[28] Another signal from
Churchill, reaching London late on the 5th, suggested
Brooke should fly out to the Prime Minister's villa. The COS
opposed the idea at a meeting on the 6th: unless Marshall
were also present the Americans would suspect the British

of exercising unilateral control of Mediterranean events. This meeting then turned to a telegram from Washington 'expressing concern' over the cancellation of 'Pigstick'; the COS agreed upon a cable which repeated British reasons for this cancellation, including the belief that 'requirements for any operation are bound to increase once the commanders get down to detailed planning'.[29]

Also on the 6th, Churchill sent a potentially explosive cable to Washington, following talks with Bedell-Smith on 'Overlord' the previous day: the Prime Minister told Roosevelt that it seemed 'very probable that the June moon will be the earliest practicable date. I do not see why we should resist this if the commanders feel they have a better chance then.'[30] The Americans were unlikely to treat this alteration to the Tehran date, albeit by a few days, with such unconcern; and, on this same Thursday, the British COS were handed a paper which would soon cause further Anglo-American disruption. The paper concerned operations against the south of France, originally proposed by the Americans and urged with such insistence by Stalin at Tehran. COSSAC, the Chief of Staff for 'Overlord', now declared this 'Anvil' scheme should be scrapped, to give extra resources for 'Overlord'. 'Operation "Anvil" as at present planned, if successful, could do little more to assist the main operation than the pinning down of two or three divisions of the German mobile reserves. It is too remote from any German vital interests to be likely to cause a greater diversion.' COSSAC added: 'I feel that the same effect could equally well be achieved, and with much less diversion of resources, by a threat.' Such a threat to the south of France would involve the use of one assault division, as originally conceived for 'Anvil', rather than an actual assault of two or three divisions which Eisenhower had urged on 17 December.[31] Next day, 7 January, the COS informed the Americans that they were considering the COSSAC paper on 'Anvil'/'Overlord' as a matter of urgency'. Yet despite the threat which 'Anvil' imposed upon Mediterranean resources, a COS meeting on the 7th showed considerable opposition to the COSSAC conclusion that this south-of-France operation should be reduced to a mere threat rather than an actual assault. Brooke pointed out: 'No mention was made in the memorandum of the fact that there were in the Mediterranean certain forces which could not be returned to the UK (in time) to take part in "Overlord".... Though COSSAC referred to a 2 or 3 division assault, he made no mention of the fact that it was the intention ultimately to build up a force of some 10 divisions.' Cunningham pointed out that whilst the threat might hold the enemy forces already in southern France, a landing would almost certainly make him divert reserves; Portal said he understood the bottleneck in the build-up of American forces in France would be the capacity of French ports; if it were possible to obtain possession of ports in southern France, the build-up rate would be increased. The COS therefore instructed the Joint Planners to review the COSSAC paper and report as soon as possible.[32]

'Winston sitting in Marrakesh is now full of beans,' wrote Brooke. 'As a result a three-cornered flow of telegrams in all directions is gradually resulting in utter confusion. I wish to God that he would come home and get under control.'[33] Rather than obliging, Churchill had summoned a conference which began this Friday and continued on the 8th, attended by Beaverbrook, Wilson, Admiral John Cunningham, Alexander, Bedell-Smith and General Devers, Deputy-Commander in the Mediterranean. The meeting covered the Anzio landings, 'Anvil' and 'Overlord', with discussion centring upon the first. Churchill had still to be informed of the COSSAC paper advocating a downgrading of 'Anvil' and seeking additional resources for 'Overlord'. Meanwhile, his conference 'thrashed out in full detail' all aspects on the Anzio operation, 'Shingle', and Churchill had informed Roosevelt on the 8th that the conference had agreed unanimously on an assault by two divisions with a third following. 'It should be possible to do this, barring accident, without conflicting with requirements of "Overlord" or "Anvil", and still have sufficiency of landing-craft to maintain the force up till the end of February....'[34] Churchill and the Mediterranean commanders therefore insisted upon a strong 'Shingle' against Anzio; COSSAC insisted upon a strong 'Overlord' at the expense of 'Anvil' – a view strongly shared by Montgomery;

yet on 13 January the Joint Planners reported to the British COS that they advised both a strong 'Overlord' and a strong 'Anvil', despite COSSAC's opinion that the latter should be downgraded. Brooke seemed perfectly justified in his criticism of the 'three-cornered' situation causing 'utter confusion'. Meanwhile the Americans had signalled the COS on the 12th, after having received the COSSAC report: they told the British that Eisenhower would soon return to London and should study the question further, submitting a final report by 1 February; Eisenhower, author of the 'Anvil' plan yet Supreme Commander for 'Overlord' – and also deeply involved with Italian operations – had therefore been placed in the most awkward position of all.

The Joint Planners report of the 13th declared both 'Overlord' and 'Anvil' should be undertaken, if possible, but warned that increased estimates for these operations as submitted by Eisenhower for 'Anvil' on 17 December and COSSAC for 'Overlord' in his paper of 6 January, would result in considerable extra resources: some 60 LSTs, 200 merchant ships, 200 transport aircraft, long-range fighters and naval forces. These would be in addition to resources already allocated. Yet the Joint Planners' report received considerable support at a British COS meeting, also on the 13th. Cunningham maintained that an 'Anvil' assault would most certainly divert enemy forces; 'furthermore, the abandonment of "Anvil" would give rise to very great difficulties with the French who had already been informed of the outline plan and approximate area of the operation, in which it was intended that the bulk of their forces should participate.' Portal felt 'the correct strategy would be to strengthen "Overlord" and try to undertake "Anvil" as well and that, if necessary, forces should be diverted from the Pacific'. Brooke agreed with Portal, but feared 'we might skimp both operations with the resulting possibility of failure. We should be running grave risks if we did not give "Overlord" all the forces we could.' But he added: 'We should at the same time endeavour to undertake "Anvil". We should maintain our offensive in Italy, where it might perhaps prove possible to employ the French troops who must, in any case, be given battle experience before undertaking operations in France.'[35]

The COS signalled Churchill next day, informing him of the COSSAC paper, the Joint Planners' report, and their own opinions – which amounted to a wish for both a strong 'Overlord' and 'Anvil'; they also warned Churchill of the additional resources which would be required, and they added that any increase in 'Overlord' might mean its postponement until June.[36] Yet also on 14 January, Roosevelt sent Churchill a discouraging reply to his signal of the 6th, which had suggested a possible June date for the cross-Channel attempt. 'It is my understanding that in Tehran Uncle J. (Stalin) was given a promise that "Overlord" would be launched during May and supported by strongest practicable landing in the south of France at about the same time, and that he agreed to plan for simultaneous Russian attack on Eastern Front. I do not believe that we should make any decision now to defer the operations, certainly not until the responsible commanders, Eisenhower and Wilson, have had full opportunity to explore all possibilities.'[37]

Clearly, Churchill's place in this chaotic situation was at 10 Downing Street, and on the 14th he left Marrakesh for Gibraltar on the first stage of his journey home. At 10 a.m. two days later, the COS and War Cabinet assembled at Paddington to welcome the Prime Minister. After a call upon the King at Buckingham Palace he drove to the House of Commons; few MPs were aware of his long-delayed arrival. He shuffled into the House still weak and walking slowly. Harold Nicolson reported: 'Winston, very pink, rather shy, beaming with mischief, crept along the front bench and flung himself into his accustomed seat. He was flushed with pleasure and emotion, and hardly had he sat down when two large tears began to trickle down his cheeks. He mopped at them clumsily with a huge white handkerchief.'[38] Churchill had been away two months. At 12.15 he apologized to the War Cabinet for having been absent so long, and then reported on his recent discussions. 'He had taken the opportunity of taking General de Gaulle to task for not conducting matters in a way which would lead to early and friendly relations', but he added: 'The French Committee of National

Liberation was now by no means a one-man show and contained some new and powerful figures.' Turning to Germany, Churchill said that recent intelligence reports showed Hitler's position to be still very strong. 'If operation "Overlord" did not achieve considerable success, many people would no doubt start objecting to the demand for unconditional surrender.'[39]

'The PM is starting off in his usual style,' wrote Brooke next day. During this overcast Wednesday, Churchill occupied himself with the Poles, the Russians, the Japanese, and planning for 'Overlord' and 'Anvil'. The Anzio assault, 'Shingle', would take place in 4 days' time; already, on the 17th, the 5th Army had launched an offensive to draw off German reserves, and had now reached the foothills beyond Garigliano plain. First of all on the 19th, Churchill saw Eden to discuss the Poles and the Russians. Moscow had rejected negotiations over the Polish frontier: Eden had told the Soviet Ambassador that this reaction was 'like a blow in the face'. Then, on 17 January, *Pravda* had published a story from its 'Cairo Correspondent' of an alleged meeting of British representatives with Ribbentrop to discuss a separate peace. The Foreign Office found *Pravda* had no Cairo Correspondent, and that the Russians had sent instructions to foreign embassies that this lie should be given wide publicity. Eden commented in his diary on the 19th: 'The Russian business ... seems to get worse and worse.' The Foreign Secretary and Churchill agreed they would see the Poles, which they did next day but without making progress, and that Churchill should complain to Stalin over the damaging effect of reports such as the *Pravda* fabrication.

The British XVth Corps began its advance down the Arakan coast in Burma during this Wednesday; Churchill once again pleaded for a revival of his plan to attack Sumatra in November. 'Culverin' had been shelved through shortage of resources, but Churchill believed the existing 1944 programme to be insufficient. He told a Defence Committee meeting at 10.30 p.m. that he was 'dismayed at the thought that a large British army and air force would stand inactive in India during the whole of 1944.... "Culverin" would provide an important

diversion and contain substantial Japanese forces in the
Malayan area. If, of course, a superiority of 6 or 8 to one was
demanded on all occasions amphibious operations became
impracticable.... Nothing that had been said had convinced
him that "First Culverin" should be discarded.'[40] Mountbatten had also been considering future operations – and
strongly favoured 'Culverin'. Stilwell disagreed: the very large
assault forces required would be unlikely to arrive in 1944
even if Germany were defeated by October, and he urged
instead a concentration on opening the Ledo Road to China;
Mountbatten believed that even if this route could be opened,
the capacity carried would not make the effort worthwhile.
This divergence between Mountbatten and Stilwell led to a
decision by the former to take the issue to higher authorities:
on 20 January, the day after Churchill's plea for 'Culverin',
the Supreme Commander told Ismay he was sending a mission
to London and Washington. This mission, code-named
'Axiom', would reach Britain on 11 February; meanwhile
Stilwell had decided to send a delegation of his own to
Washington, without informing the Supreme Commander.[41]

Far East complications might soon match those surrounding the European theatre. And Churchill, at a Staff Conference at 5.30 p.m. on the 19th, showed himself even more
ambitious than the COS, urging maximum strength for
'Overlord' and elsewhere regardless of lack of resources. He
declared himself 'in agreement with the views expressed by
the CCS and thought that the strategy was absolutely sound.
He was strongly in favour of broadening the front for the
"Overlord" assault and instructing General Wilson (in the
Mediterranean) to develop the maximum possible threat
along the 400 miles stretch of coastline between Genoa and the
Spanish frontier, using for this purpose such amphibious resources as were available after strengthening "Overlord". It
was an essential part of our strategy that our forces in the
Mediterranean should engage and hold the enemy forces
opposite them. A successful "Shingle" would give us an
opportunity of deploying large forces in northern Italy, and
perhaps forcing the Germans to withdraw behind the Alps.
It would then be open for us to turn left into France, or to

pursue the Germans towards Vienna, or to turn right towards the Balkans....'[42] To Churchill's optimistic mind, opportunities seemed endless – providing resources could be found; one indication of Churchill's future position was however revealed in this Defence Committee minute: he merely mentioned the 'maximum possible threat' along the Mediterranean coast, rather than an actual assault – the latter should be saved for 'Overlord' and Italy. Nothing definite could be discussed until Eisenhower had produced his recommendations and, by 21 January, the Supreme Commander had reached his conclusions. They did nothing to solve the dilemma of resources: he agreed with COSSAC, and with Montgomery, that 'Overlord' should be strengthened; but he disagreed with both COSSAC and Montgomery on the consequent desirability of downgrading 'Anvil' against the south of France. Discussions with the British COS were arranged for 24 January and meanwhile Eisenhower prepared to send his conclusions to the American COS.

War began to increase in intensity on all fronts: Burma, Italy – and London. On 21 January, Londoners experienced the first of a new series of heavy air raids in the 'Little Blitz'. Thirteen major attacks would be directed upon the capital before the end of March, seven of them in February which killed nearly 1,000 civilians. But as the sirens wailed in London during this Friday, 21 January, deep in the underground war room below Whitehall yellow lights blazed upon a huge map of the Mediterranean; approaching the coast of Italy, 35 miles south of Rome and 60 miles behind the German lines at Cassino, were a multitude of markers identifying the Anzio assault convoys. Ships carrying 50,000 men under the command of the American general, Lucas, sailed undisturbed by enemy reconnaissance flights; five minutes after midnight 21/22 January the convoys arrived off Anzio; at 2 a.m. on the 22nd the first troops crossed the beaches. Complete surprise had been achieved. Twenty-four hours later the Cabinet War Room record declared: 'The landings were virtually unopposed, though some of the beaches were heavily mined. Our troops quickly got ashore and pushed on to their initial objectives about four miles inland. The harbour of Anzio was in our hands by 1400 hours.'[43] Hopes were high that the Germans on the Gustav line at Cassino would be thrown off balance by this threat to the rear and the allies would roll forward for Rome; Anzio would then have played its part in the 'Anvil' 'Overlord' programme by sapping enemy strength. This great strategic programme formed the subject of Eisenhower's signal to the CCS on 23 January, detailing his belief that 'Anvil' should be attempted on the increased scale he had proposed on 17 December, despite added resources required for 'Overlord' under COSSAC's latest plans. 'I deem "Anvil" to be an important contribution to "Overlord" since I feel that an assault will contain more enemy formations in southern France than a threat ... an actual landing by them will increase co-operation from elements of the resistance in France.' Eisenhower did however add that 'as a last resort', if resources could not be found 'Anvil' should be reduced to one division to give 'Overlord' sufficient strength.[44]

Ninety per cent of the cargo had been unloaded in the Anzio assault area by the night of 23 January. But this very success brought dangers. 'Shingle' had been launched on the assumption that opposition would be stiff and that the bridgehead must support itself for some weeks before the 5th Army could join up from the south. General Lucas now declined to alter plans to fit the new circumstances, and preferred to consolidate his position rather than exploit initial enemy weakness; he presumably hoped the mere presence of the Anzio force would achieve the purpose of drawing off Germans from the Cassino area. But on 24 January Hitler issued fresh orders: 'The Gustav Line must be held at all costs.' Reserves were rushed down from Rome and from North Italy: while this would fulfil one of the aims of the Italian campaign – reducing opposition in France for 'Overlord' and 'Anvil' – it would hinder further Italian advance, and would threaten the Anzio forces. For the moment, optimistic reports continued to reach London, and War Cabinet Ministers were informed at 6 p.m. on Monday, 24 January, that the bridgehead seemed reasonably secure.

Brooke, Portal and Cunningham had held their discussions

with Eisenhower during the day on 'Overlord' and 'Anvil' plans, and the excellent reports from Italy played their part in the subsequent decision. Eisenhower stressed the need to strengthen 'Overlord'. 'In the present "Overlord" plan the assault was mounted on too narrow a front. He believed that an increase in the number of assault divisions from 3 to 5 was essential.... In recommending at the same time that "Anvil" should be carried out with 3 divisions assaulting, he was presenting the CCS with the difficult problem of finding resources for both the new "Overlord" and the stressed the British support for both 'Overlord' and 'Anvil', was to produce a threat in southern France to contain German forces there which might otherwise be used to reinforce their defence against "Overlord".' Eisenhower believed the initial 'Anvil' assault should comprise three divisions, if possible, but two divisions should still be successful. He continued: 'If we could not find the resources to provide for an "Anvil" on this scale we should have to devote all our Mediterranean resources to an energetic offensive in Italy. The main disadvantage of this course of action was that we should be developing a threat more distant to "Overlord".' Brooke stressed the British support for both 'Overlord' and 'Anvil', provided these operations were strong enough. ' "Overlord" must under no circumstances be skimped. But he also believed that, to be of any effect, "Anvil" should not be skimped either. He was not convinced that a 2-division "Anvil" assault had a reasonable chance of success, and he was sure that nothing less than a total force of 10 divisions would achieve the results we desired.' And Brooke added that he 'would prefer the vigorous campaign in Italy to a weak "Anvil". The launching of a force of 10 divisions and its subsequent maintenance represented a very heavy commitment, including the establishment of new bases in France.' Cunningham suggested Brooke had perhaps underestimated the effect that even a relatively weak 'Anvil' would have on the Germans. The COS eventually 'agreed to give strong support to the general policy outlined by Eisenhower' in his telegram to the CCS.[45] Next day, 25 January, the COS discussed a draft telegram to Washington, which left London on the 26th:

'Anvil' would be useful if two divisions could be used, but if resources could not be found there should be greater concentration in Italy where progress still seemed good; 'Overlord' should therefore be increased to five divisions, whatever the cost to 'Anvil'. The COS, also with Eisenhower's concurrence, added that 'Overlord' should definitely be postponed to early June instead of during May, to allow time for the increased forces to be trained and organized.[46] A week later the US COS would send an extremely discouraging reply, but by then the Italian situation had suffered severe deterioration.

Serious news arrived in London on the 27th and 28th: troops in the Anzio bridgehead had been unable to take the important nearby towns of Campoleone and Cisterna; German defences at Cassino had stiffened. Churchill summoned an urgent staff conference at 4.30 p.m. on the 28th and expressed doubts over Lucas's handling of 'Shingle'. 'I had some job quietening him down again,' wrote Brooke. 'Unfortunately this time I feel there are reasons for uneasiness.'[47] By the close of January the 3½ allied divisions at Anzio were faced by the equivalent of 5 German divisions, and, on 3 February, the enemy counter-attacked in force. No further advance would be possible; the only hope remained in a push from the south, but first Cassino had to be taken. The British COS decided on the 3rd that the latest situation reinforced their previous opinion: a weak landing in the south of France should be scrapped and all forces concentrated in Italy; this conviction was no longer based on hopes for a rapid Italian advance, but on the realization that good use could be made of the renewed enemy resolve to fight it out. Italy, and not a weak thrust at south France, would thus be of far greater benefit to 'Overlord'.[48] But by now the American COS had replied to the British signal of 26 January urging such an Italian concentration: the Americans were prepared to provide an additional 3 landing-ships and 57 landing-craft for 'Overlord' to meet new demands, yet they reminded the British that the Russians had been promised an attack against southern France, not a mere threat; nor did they see any reason for

postponing 'Overlord' until June.[49] The British COS met on
3 and 4 February to list objections: the offensive in Italy
must be maintained in order to render 'Anvil' unnecessary;
nothing must be done which would harm 'Overlord' preparations or strength; and as for the 'Overlord' date, moon and
tide conditions dictated a period in early or mid-May or early
in June. Of these three, only the latter would be feasible. The
COS drafted a reply which received Churchill's approval on
the 4th. The Americans would clearly be displeased, and
Churchill suggested that Marshall and his colleagues should
be asked to discuss the situation in London.[50] The British
and American roles had apparently been reversed: the
former were now arguing that no efforts should be spared
for 'Overlord', and all resources should be used for this main
operation except for those which could not be spared from
Italy, or which could not be returned to the UK in time; the
Americans were pressing for a diversionary operation which
the British – and Eisenhower – feared might be at the expense
of 'Overlord' itself. A further complication existed. The
Americans were struggling at this time over the formation of
a Pacific policy, with the prolonged debate taking up time,
energy, and resources.

The British also had other preoccupations; in addition
to considering 'Overlord', 'Anvil' and 'Shingle', Churchill
and the COS had to devote attention to the threatened
German counter-attack upon the UK – 'Crossbow'. Discussion
on Hitler's secret weapon had taken up COS time in the past
weeks, and on 3 February Churchill introduced a staff report
to the Defence Committee. The COS considered that 'a scale
of attack by pilotless aircraft equivalent to 400 tons of bombs,
spread over a period of 10 hours, was the worst likely to be
experienced by mid-March'. This estimate, although well
below previous figures, was still pessimistic, according to Lord
Cherwell; Churchill said he felt 'much easier regarding the
"Crossbow" threat'.[51]

Even before a reply from Washington concerning 'Overlord', Churchill had decided to proceed further with his suggestion made to the COS on the 4th for an Anglo-American
conference; as Ismay had commented to the Prime Minister

on the 5th: 'We are now within less than four months of
decisive events and yet our plans are still indeterminate. Nor
is the situation likely to improve unless there can be a meeting
of minds.'[52] Next day Churchill accordingly asked Roosevelt
if such a meeting could be arranged, and on 7 February the
need was further underlined by the receipt of the US reply
to the COS signal of the 4th. The Americans continued to
insist upon 'Anvil', although they now apparently agreed to
a postponement of 'Overlord': they proposed a target date of
31 May, on the understanding Eisenhower should have
latitude for a few days either way. A day in the first week of
June was thus taken by the British as D-Day. Yet indecision
over the 'Anvil'/'Overlord' relationship remained; Brooke
commented: 'Nothing left but to ask them to come over to
discuss. Time now too short for any other course.'[53] Within
a few days Brooke received the American refusal for the
proposed conference, with Marshall suggesting instead that
Eisenhower should speak for them in discussions in London.
Meanwhile, news from the Anzio bridgehead continued to
worsen, and Ministers heard a depressing COS report at the
5.30 p.m. War Cabinet meeting on Monday, 7 February:
allied troops were pressed tight into the defensive perimeter;
German divisions had accumulated. Churchill seemed 'in
the depths of gloom' over the Italian situation when Brooke
saw him during this Monday, and attempted to cheer him
up by saying Anzio was at least drawing off German strength.
Next day Churchill signalled in this sense to Marshall: 'We
have a great need to keep continually engaging them, and
even a battle of attrition is better than standing by and
watching the Russians fight. We should also learn a good
many lessons about how not to do it which will be invaluable
in "Overlord".'[54] Conversely, the ease with which the Germans
summoned up strength from the rear to block the unexpected
Anzio assault underlined enemy efficiency and mobility, and
augured ill for the cross-Channel assault.

With the argument still continuing over 'Anvil', Churchill
now added another complication, caused by his restless desire
to speed events. He called a staff conference at 10 Downing
Street at 6 p.m. on the 8th to discuss his idea for an entry

into France through Bordeaux, operation 'Caliph', which would make use of the two armoured divisions assigned to 'Anvil' should the latter operation be cancelled. Brooke raised objections to an assault on Bordeaux: 'The defences at the mouth of the river Gironde were strong, and the port could not be captured until these defences had been overcome'; moreover, he explained that the British COS did not object to 'Anvil' itself as much as the clash over resources for 'Overlord' which this operation would bring about. 'The main conflict between ourselves and the Americans lay in the fact that, whereas we held the view that only after the requirements of "Overlord" had been met should we consider what to do with forces remaining at our disposal, the Americans took the opposite line of laying down at this stage the resources to be allotted to both "Overlord" and "Anvil".' Churchill continued to insist that if 'Anvil' were scrapped, forces should not 'be allowed to remain idle', and the conference finally agreed: '1. That the full requirements of "Overlord" should in any event be met. 2. That when a decision had been reached on the balance of forces that would remain available in the Mediterranean ... alternative plans should be prepared. 3. That the decision and the adoption of any such plan was dependent on the course of the war in Italy.'[55] Churchill again pressed for 'Caliph' at a meeting with the COS the following evening, 9 February, but Brooke continued to argue that full figures for 'Overlord' demands must first be settled; he added that the COS would meet Eisenhower next day for further discussions. Churchill hoped that 'in planning "Overlord" the lesson of the "Shingle" campaign would be taken to heart, where over 18,000 vehicles had already been crammed into the congested bridgehead. There was a strong tendency in all our plans to allow a large margin against accidents.'[56] Dill reported to Brooke during this Wednesday: 'I have been in and out of Marshall's room lately trying to get him to see your point of view regarding "Anvil"–"Overlord" and trying to get his point of view'; but Dill added: 'The US COS are engaged in a fresh battle regarding Pacific strategy.'[57]

The British COS met Eisenhower at noon on the 10th,

and this long session succeeded in making considerable progress: Eisenhower presented a paper on his requirements for the cross-Channel operation and the COS found themselves in agreement. All participants agreed that 'Anvil' would probably have to be shelved; Eisenhower 'agreed that allied action in the Mediterranean must be largely determined by events in Italy', and he even added that he believed 'General Marshall was of this opinion also'. 'All seems to be going well at present,' wrote Brooke.[58] But Anzio remained as an example of how 'Overlord' should not be undertaken, with Alexander reporting on Friday, 11 February: 'The first phase of operations, which started so full of promise, has now just passed, owing to the enemy's ability to concentrate so quickly. The battle has now reached the second phase, in which we must now at all costs crush his counter-attacks, and then, with our own forces regrouped, resume the offensive.'[59]

Far away in the jungles of New Guinea, Australian and American troops at last managed to clear the Japanese from the Huon peninsula, where they had clung like leeches throughout a terrible 5-month campaign. Only 4,200 Japanese survived from the original 12,000-man force. Also on the 11th, Mountbatten's 'Axiom' mission arrived in London to open talks on strategy in Burma; the COS would soon have to switch their attention from the European theatre to the equally complicated Far East. Meanwhile, as news reached London that the American corps at Cassino had been forced on to the defensive, and that the German counter-offensive at Anzio seemed imminent, the COS met Eisenhower again to discuss 'Anvil' and especially 'Overlord'. A conference on the 13th examined detailed proposals for increasing the strength of the cross-Channel operation; the British agreed with these proposals, which would give added assault power on a broader front – and which further ruled out 'Anvil'.[60] Next day Mountbatten's 'Axiom' mission attended a staff conference at 10 am., with Churchill in the chair. Wedemeyer, Mountbatten's Chief of Staff, stressed objections to Stilwell's policy of developing the Ledo Road, and proposed instead 'Culverin' to be launched in November. Brooke, like Stilwell, feared that resources would be insufficient for 'Culverin'

against Sumatra unless Germany had been defeated by
October; Portal pointed out that 'in the event of the Japanese
not reacting strongly to "Culverin", we would have committed our fleet to no good purpose', and the COS in general
favoured more studies of the use of the British fleet in the
Pacific. Churchill warned that 'it was his impression that
Admiral King did not wish the British fleet to go into the
Pacific', and Wedemeyer described the maintenance difficulties involved. Eventually the Joint Planners and the 'Axiom'
Mission were instructed 'as a matter of urgency' to examine
the merits of operations either against Sumatra alone, or
against Sumatra and the Netherlands East Indies.[61] This
examination would take almost a fortnight.

The COS were now inundated by signals from Italy, where
events had reached a climax. On 15 February a determined
and controversial attempt was made to snap the Cassino
stalemate. Bombers roared low up the valley to drop their
loads on the ancient monastery dominating the battlefield.
Freyberg, the Corps Commander concerned, had urged such
an attack; Mark Clark, the Army Commander, had hesitated
and had passed the request to Alexander. The latter, using his
own initiative and without involving the COS, had given
permission. Over 450 tons of bombs were now dropped on the
historic target, demolishing the 15-foot thick outer walls. The
Germans moved in to make use of the defensive positions
which rubble now offered; stalemate continued and Cassino
still blocked the allied advance. And away at Anzio the
expected German counter-attack had begun on the 15th with
a fierce onslaught continuing throughout the 16th, and with
German troops ordered by Hitler to spare nothing in cutting
out this 'abscess'. The COS in London believed the allies to
be outnumbered two to one; the COS had to devote attention
to post-hostilities subjects at their three-hour meeting this
Thursday, and as Brooke commented: 'It is not yet easy to
concentrate one's thoughts on after-war matters.'[62] Signals
late on the 17th indicated that the enemy had driven a deep
wedge into the Anzio defences, and early next day the
Germans were pushing against the last allied line. The defenders retaliated with a terrible sea and air bombardment,

and during the night of the 18th, while German bombers
blasted Battersea in the 'Little Blitz', scrappy signals at last
reached Whitehall to say the enemy were beginning to fall
back.

Brooke was dining with Montgomery. 'Very good value,'
wrote the CIGS, and he used information gained at this talk
with 'Overlord''s ground force commander for a further
meeting with Eisenhower next morning, 19 February. The
Supreme Commander had been re-examining his figures to
see if 'Anvil' could after all be undertaken 'if the situation
in the Mediterranean was such that the south of France was
the only suitable area for a diversionary operation'. And he
now believed that a 2-divisional assault could be made, by
paring 'Overlord' requirements to 'the irreducible minimum',
but he added: 'A successful conclusion to the Italian campaign was an essential prelude to a successful "Anvil".'
Brooke warned that preparations for 'Anvil' already seemed
to be interfering with the Italian campaign, for example the
85th American Division was being held back for amphibious
training and could not therefore be employed in Italy, and
he added: 'The trend of operations in Italy was becoming
increasingly unfavourable to the prospects for "Anvil". He
was doubtful if the 10 divisions which it was agreed would be
required to give "Anvil" a reasonable chance of success could,
in fact, be found. Their withdrawal would leave only some
20 divisions for the Italian campaign and any other commitments which might arise in the Mediterranean.... It appeared
that there was a danger that "Overlord", "Anvil" and possibly
the Italian campaign would all be skimped if the proposals
now submitted by Eisenhower were adopted. The forces now
employed in Italy were many of them tired and in urgent
need of rest and refit.... We certainly could not afford to
relax our efforts as long as the forces on the Cassino front
and in the bridgehead remained separated.' Eisenhower
clearly suffered from his in-between position, pressed by the
Americans on the one side and the British on the other, and
once again he shifted his opinion: 'Owing to developments
in the situation in Italy, it might no longer be practicable to
undertake "Anvil". A very early decision was required.' 'I

think the matter is now all right,' commented an optimistic Brooke in his diary.[63]

German bombers continued to batter the British capital: a heavy raid on the 20th shattered windows at 10 Downing Street, the Foreign Office, Admiralty, Horse Guards, and all the windows at the War Office excepting Brooke's. The COS crunched their way through the debris next morning, Monday, 21 February, to hold another long meeting on Far East strategy. Brooke and his colleagues agreed to continue their opposition to 'Culverin' against Sumatra, so strongly urged by Mountbatten and Churchill, and instead to advocate British aid to the American thrust from Australia. 'We shall have very serious trouble with him (Churchill) over this,' wrote the CIGS.[64]

During the night a signal arrived from Washington containing the American reply to a message from Eisenhower sent after the meeting with the COS on the 19th: the US COS still insisted upon 'Anvil', with two divisions for the initial assault; American and French units being 'rehabilitated' from the Italian campaign should be re-equipped and trained for 'Anvil'. The COS met Eisenhower again for a long and difficult session to discuss this telegram, and to hear the Supreme Commander's views; Brooke believed Eisenhower to be sympathetic but 'he is too frightened of disagreeing with Marshall'. The unfortunate American general now made a courageous attempt to 'interpret' the American telegram; he believed the US COS to be saying that 'it was not essential to make a decision cancelling "Anvil" at once', and despite his call at the last meeting for a very early decision, he now said 'it would be wrong to take a decision before the last possible moment. He could not overlook the possibility that the Germans, worn out by the intense fighting on the present lines in Italy, might decide upon a sudden and unexpected reversal of policy, and withdraw slowly.' In this case, 'Anvil' might still be possible, and he believed planning should still proceed. Brooke declared that instructions to Wilson to continue planning for 'Anvil' would interfere with the Italian campaign. 'There had been a tendency to refer to "Anvil" as a two-division operation, which in fact referred only to the assault lift. It should be clearly recognized that this operation entailed the employment of 10 divisions. There were in all some 30 divisions in the Mediterranean, and to withdraw 10 of these for "Anvil" would mean that we should not have the strength to maintain the initiative in Italy.' Discussion would be continued next day.[65]

Meanwhile the COS continued their meeting on the 22nd by hearing an exposition from Wedemeyer on current operations in Burma. Activities were passing through an extremely critical stage: thrusts into Arakan had started a number of weeks before, and these troops were now heavily engaged. Mountbatten had pleaded for more aircraft to drop supplies; permission would reach him on the 24th to divert aircraft being used to fly over the 'Hump' to China, and within a few days the enemy would begin to withdraw, leaving over 5,000 dead.

As the COS spent long hours discussing Burma and Europe on the 22nd, Winston Churchill delivered one of his periodic reviews in the House of Commons. The 'Little Blitz' had deflated public morale still further; grumbling against the Government's direction of the war had become louder, and two weeks before the loyal Harold Nicolson had noted in his diary: 'I fear that Winston has become an electoral liability now rather than an asset. This makes me sick with human nature. Once the open sea is reached, we forget how we clung to the pilot in the storm. Poor Winston, who is so sensitive although so pugnacious, will feel all this.'[66] Churchill rose to address a packed House at noon on this Tuesday. Hampered by a slight cough, he refused to soothe those who needed reassurance, but warned instead: 'This is not a time for sorrow or rejoicing. It is a time for preparation, effort and resolve.' The Germans might soon unlease a 'secret weapon'. He admitted Anzio had been a disappointment: 'The landing was virtually unopposed. Subsequent events did not however take the course which had been hoped or planned', but he added: 'We must fight the Germans somewhere, unless we are to stand still and watch the Russians. This wearing battle in Italy occupies troops who could not be employed in other greater operations, and it is an effective

Scapa Flow

SWEDEN

NORTH SEA

Viborg

BALTIC

Danzig

DENMARK

Rostock Peenemünde
Lübeck Wismar Schwerin
Hamburg Lüneburg Wittenberg
Bremen Soltau Domitz
Amsterdam Herford Celle Berlin
Utrecht Munster Hanover Magdeburg
Kassel
Harz Mts. Leipzig Breslau
Dresden
Weimar Chemnitz

GREAT
BRITAIN

London
Portsmouth
Dunkirk
Bologne
Amiens
Soissons
Paris
St. Malo
Brest
Brittany
Rennes Vitré Le Mans
Verneuil
Rambouillet

See page 409

GERMANY

Frankfurt Schweinfurth
Worms
Mannheim Nuremberg
Strasbourg Karlsruhe Stuttgart
Belfort
Vosges
Munich
Regensburg

Prague
Moldau

CZECHO

Brno

Passau
Linz
Vienna

Danube R.

AUSTRIA

See
page
309

Inn R.
Berchtesgaden
Landeck
Brenner Pass

ATLANTIC

FRANCE

SWITZERLAND

Ljubljana

Vichy

Como

Trieste

Gironde

Bordeaux

Grenoble

Avignon Sisteron

Sète

Arno R.

SPAIN

MEDITERRANEAN

ITALY

Rome

A DAY'S MARCH NEARER HOME—I

EUROPE

0   100   200 Miles

Leningrad

LATVIA

LITHUANIA

Tilsit
Konigsberg

E.
PRUSSIA

Minsk

Moscow.

Smolensk

Orel

Kursk

RUSSIA

Kharkov

Warsaw

POLAND

Lublin

Sandomierz

Dnieper R.

Stalingrad

SLOVAKIA

Budapest

HUNGARY

RUMANIA

CRIMEA

Yalta

BLACK SEA

Belgrade

YUGOSLAVIA

BULGARIA

Sofia

Istanbul

TURKEY

prelude to them.' As Churchill spoke in the Commons, a long telegram from Wilson in Italy was being dispatched to London which warned of future dangers: if the Americans had their way over 'Anvil', allied objectives in the Italian campaign would be disastrously affected. 'To make the necessary preparations for this operation ("Anvil") ... we must start withdrawing service units from the battle in Italy now.... We obviously cannot withdraw combat divisions now and I cannot state when circumstances will allow me to start training. If it is decided to undertake a two or three divisional "Anvil", the effect on operations in Italy will be most serious. ... If, on the other hand, the battle in Italy is continued and combined with feint operations which are already being planned, we may go far, now and after "Overlord" is launched, towards keeping the enemy employed.'[67] Armed with this signal the British COS met Eisenhower for their meeting on the 23rd, and Eisenhower agreed with a British cable to Washington proposing a compromise: the Italian campaign should have complete priority until at least 20 March, when the situation would be reviewed in the light of the position in Italy. Meanwhile, Wilson should make whatever plans and preparations he could for 'Anvil' but without prejudicing Italian operations; if, on 20 March, 'Anvil' was cancelled, all assault shipping needed for 'Overlord' would be withdrawn at once from the Mediterranean. 'We have got all we want,' wrote Brooke, 'but we must word the wire to let the Americans "save face" as much as possible.'[68]

The centre of London received devastating attention from Luftwaffe bombers on the night of the 24th, and a stick of bombs badly damaged Pall Mall and smashed all windows in St James's Palace. The five raids between 18 and 24 February rendered 3,000 Battersea homes uninhabitable. Churchill, in his speech to the Commons on the 22nd, had forecast reprisal upon the Germans, and on 23 February began a week of concentrated day and night attacks on the enemy aircraft industry. The Cabinet War Room record for the 25th declared: 'SCHWEINFURTH (Ball-bearing factories) – total of 392 and 341 aircraft were detailed to attack at 2300 and

0100 respectively. First operation: good visibility – some fires from day attack seen on arrival. Town well covered by IBs, causing good fires. Second operation – large fires visible from 70 miles – existing fires rapidly extended and, at end of attack, appeared to be spread throughout entire town area.'[69] The ball-bearing plants in the city had unfortunately already been dispersed.

Breakthrough at last came in the Anglo-American argument over 'Anvil'. During the 25th Roosevelt and the US COS agreed to the British signal of the 23rd, and Italian operations would thus have priority until 20 March. Yet even as the skies began to clear in the west, clouds swirled lower in the east. Three meetings were held with the Prime Minister on the 25th, totalling almost eight hours; Churchill remained adamant that 'Culverin' offered the best employment for British strength in Burma and the Indian Ocean, while the COS insisted Britain should join with the Americans in the Pacific. The situation had been further complicated by the reported movement of a Japanese fleet towards Singapore, comprising 7 battleships, two fleet carriers, 8 cruisers and 18 destroyers. Churchill opened the first meeting at noon by saying he had only just heard of this reported movement; Cunningham said the Japanese could have a number of motives, including hopes of an easy success in the Indian Ocean, or defensive aims against a British amphibious assault; he added that the consequent decrease of Japanese naval strength further south presented the Americans with 'a great opportunity in the central Pacific'. Churchill commented: 'The Americans appeared to be using steam-hammer methods to crack nuts in the Pacific ... our counter to the Japanese move should be the concentration of as large a force as possible in the Indian Ocean. This would rule out for the time being the dispatch of major British naval units to the Pacific, where the Americans should have plurality of strength.' But he also admitted that while the Japanese fleet remained at Singapore, 'a different view would have to be taken of "Culverin"'. The meeting adjourned until 3 p.m., when Brooke stressed the additional dangers for 'Culverin' under the latest situation. 'The naval commander would be likely to increase his bill for the operation since he would now have to be prepared for the Japanese main fleet.' But Churchill remained convinced that 'Culverin' 'was the only operation which could afford a prospect of employing, during the next 12 months, the large British forces available, in useful activity against the enemy', and at the third session starting at 10 p.m. the Prime Minister attacked the COS proposal to shift to the Pacific: 'It was not a nice prospect for us to tail along at the heels of the American fleet, and when great victories had been won, to be told that all credit was due to US forces.' If 'Culverin' proved impossible, 'it would be better to do "Buccaneer" than nothing at all in the Indian Ocean'. The COS decided to study Japanese intentions further.[70]

Deadlock still existed, and the 'Axiom' mission had now to leave for America. But discussions had also been taking place in Washington, with Stilwell's mission continuing to oppose Mountbatten's plans for 'Culverin', urging operations in north Burma instead; and on the same day that the succession of meetings took place in London, conferences in Washington led to the dispatch of a cable from Roosevelt to Churchill. The President stressed the need to capture Myitkyina in north Burma to protect the air route to China and to advance construction of the Ledo Road. He continued: 'I am gravely concerned over the recent trends in strategy that favour an operation towards Sumatra and Malaya.... I fail to see how an operation against Sumatra and Malaya, requiring tremendous resources and forces, can possibly be mounted until the conclusion of the war in Europe.' Churchill, disappointed but undeterred, replied that nothing would be withdrawn or withheld from the campaign in north Burma on 'Culverin''s account, but added that he still believed the Ledo Road could not be advanced in time to help the Chinese.[71] Complete lack of common ground therefore existed between Churchill, still seeking 'Culverin', the British COS, seeking a switch to the Pacific, and the Americans, stressing north Burma. And the division between the Prime Minister and his military advisers now widened to almost disastrous proportions: February ended and March began with talk of resignation. Brooke's diary described the War Cabinet meeting on the 28th: 'Winston was in an impossible mood with nothing but abuse about everything the Army was doing.... It was all I could do to contain my temper.'

Soon after this 6 p.m. meeting on the 28th, Brooke received news from Alexander which threatened another outburst from the prickly Prime Minister over army inefficiency. Thirteen precious LSTs were scheduled to leave the Mediterranean theatre of 29 February for 'Overlord'; now, late on the 28th, Alexander sent an urgent message through Wilson seeking further postponement to help the Anzio beachhead. Brooke arranged to see Churchill at 4 p.m. next day to discuss the situation; the CIGS conferred with Eisenhower just before this meeting, and a signal was drafted for Washington agreeing with Alexander's request 'in order to prevent the collapse of the bridgehead'.[72] The confrontation with Churchill proved to be explosive, as expected. 'We had hoped to land a wild cat that would tear out the bowels of the Boche,' snapped Churchill. 'Instead we have stranded a vast whale with its tail flopping about in the water.'[73] While the Prime Minister paced the War Cabinet room and threw scorn upon the Anzio operation, troops in the battered beachhead were hurling back latest German attacks. By the end of the 29th the enemy had started to pull back again, leaving 2,500 casualties, and Churchill's description of the 'flopping vast whale' underwent dramatic change in a relieved signal to Roosevelt. 'I am always deeply moved to think of our men fighting side by side in so many fierce battles and of the inspiring additions to our history which these famous episodes will make.'[74]

Decision had still to be reached on Burma-Pacific strategy. The CCS met the 'Axiom' mission in Washington on 3 March to begin a series of conferences, while in London on this Friday, differences between Churchill and the COS bordered upon catastrophe. Churchill circulated a memorandum to members of the Defence Committee, and the seriousness of the situation was fully revealed in the opening words: 'A question of major policy and strategy has now opened on which it may be necessary to obtain a decision by the War Cabinet.' Churchill outlined the alternatives: Proposal A to send British warships to the Pacific, to be followed by British troops; Proposal B to 'keep the centres of gravity of the British war against Japan in the Bay of Bengal for at least 18 months from now', conducting amphibious operations 'on a considerable scale' as resources became available. The COS favoured A, but Churchill continued: 'Admiral Mountbatten and the South-East Asia Command are in favour of "B", which is perhaps not unnatural since "A" involves the practical elimination of the South-East Asia Command.' Churchill referred to the dangers presented by the Japanese fleet move to Singapore. 'To my surprise, the Admiralty do not consider these dangers serious.... The Admiralty would be prepared to divide our Fleet, leaving a certain force in the Indian Ocean and sending all the best ships on into the Pacific.'[75] Brooke reacted angrily at a COS meeting during this Friday. He cleared the room of secretaries and told his colleagues that Churchill seemed to be trying 'to frame up the War Cabinet against the Chiefs of Staff Committee'. He added in his diary: 'It looks very serious and may well lead to the resignation of the COS Committee.'[76] General Ismay, the indispensable go-between, hurriedly stepped in with a minute to Churchill. 'We are faced with the practical certainty of a continued cleavage of opinion between the War Cabinet and their military advisers; nor can we exclude the possibility of resignation on the part of the latter. A breach of this kind ... would be little short of catastrophic at the present juncture.' Ismay urged a series of meetings. 'It is just possible that agreement can thus be reached.' If not, Ismay suggested one way to avoid a complete rift: the COS always tendered their opinions on strictly military grounds, and Ismay therefore asked: 'Would it not be possible and right for you to take the line that the issue cannot be decided on military grounds alone, and that, apart from the military merits of the respective strategies, political considerations must be overriding? I cannot but think that the COS would accept this decision with complete loyalty.'[77]

Churchill half-accepted this suggestion: a staff conference would meet on 8 March. Meanwhile neither side gave ground. On 6 March the COS sent an uncompromising minute to Churchill in response to his Defence Committee memorandum: 'Your definition of Pacific strategy omits its first object, namely to obtain a footing in Japan's inner zone at the earliest possible moment; while your definition of the Bay of Bengal strategy does not bring out that it is contingent upon Germany's defeat, and, therefore, cannot begin until about 6 months after that defeat.'[78] Churchill replied next day, stressing the importance of·the mere threat to Sumatra which could be posed by 'Culverin'. 'The longer we can detain them (the Japanese) in their present position at Singapore, the greater the help we can give the US.'[79] Brooke commented: 'He has produced the worst paper I have seen him write yet.'[80] The following evening, 8 March, while reports reached London of excellent fighting by Mountbatten's units in north Burma, the COS held a discussion to settle their strategy for the 10 p.m. staff conference with Churchill. The CIGS commented in his diary: 'Portal not too anxious to argue against the PM, and dear old Cunningham so wild with rage that he hardly dared let himself speak! I, therefore, had to do most of the arguing with the PM and four Ministers.'[81] Eventually both sides agreed that not enough was known about the implications of supply, either for 'Culverin' or a Pacific strategy, for agreement to be reached. Two days later, 10 March, Churchill sought more ammunition in a message to Roosevelt: 'We have not so far reached united conclusions.... I should be very grateful if you could let me know whether there is any specific American operation in the Pacific a) before the end of 1944 or b) before the summer of 1945 which would be hindered or prevented by the absence of a British Fleet detachment.'[82] The President's reply to this loaded question reached London on the 13th, and seemed to bolster Churchill's position. 'There will be no specific operation in the Pacific during 1944 that would be adversely affected by the absence of a British Fleet detachment ... it does not now appear that such a reinforcement will be needed before the summer of 1945.... In consideration of recent enemy dispositions, it is my personal opinion that unless we have unexpected bad luck in the Pacific your naval force will be of more value to our common effort by remaining in the Indian Ocean.'[83]

Churchill immediately called another staff conference for this same day, 13 March, and received support from Attlee. 'The effect in India and, indeed, in England, of strong operations against Malaya to recapture Singapore, would be very much greater than the effect of operations through New Guinea towards the Philippines, in which by far the greater share would be borne by the Americans. It was in Malaya, Borneo, and the Netherlands East Indies that our reputation had suffered.' Brooke pointed out that under the Pacific Strategy, these areas would be cut off then cleared by British forces, to which Churchill retorted that 'people would find it difficult to understand why, when we could launch direct attacks to retake Singapore across the Indian Ocean, we should elect instead to travel 9,000 miles round Australia'. Eden stressed the importance of boosting morale, and questioned the availability of shipping for the Pacific Strategy; this led to an argument between Cunningham and Lord Leathers, Minister of War Transport, with the First Sea Lord claiming figures had been given to him by officials of the Transport Ministry, and Lord Leathers declaring he 'took exception to statements that papers had been prepared in consultation with his Ministry.... There might have been some talks on an extremely low level, but there had been no proper investigation.' In spite of this lack of investigation, Lord Leathers proceeded to attack the Pacific Strategy: 'It was not only a question of shipping to be provided after the defeat of Germany. The proposal was to use Australia as a base and this meant starting from zero, and building-up while the war with Germany was still in progress all the great stocks of oil, petrol, transportation, equipment and so on.' Oliver Lyttelton believed 'we should consider our position *vis-à-vis* the USA at the peace table. If our operations formed merely a small part of the great American advance we should be swamped.'[84]

The COS were therefore faced by determined Ministerial opposition; moreover, Churchill sought additional help – and the COS were still unaware of the exchange of telegrams with Roosevelt. Late on the 13th Brooke discovered the Prime Minister had called a meeting with the Joint Planners, to which the COS were not invited. 'Heaven knows what he is up to.' This apparent treatment of the Joint Planners as part of the Prime Minister's staff rather than belonging to the COS committee raised important implications; Brooke claimed that the result would have made it 'quite impossible for the COS Committee to function.... To suggest, as the PM was doing, that the Planners were part of his staff ... was the equivalent of depriving the headquarters of command of its operational branch.'[85] In addition, the CIGS found to his consternation that Churchill proposed to fly to Bermuda to meet Roosevelt on the 25th, despite – or because of – lack of British agreement, and despite the risk to his health: Lord Moran told Brooke on the 13th that he was urging Churchill not to go because 'he may become a permanent invalid if he does ... he is liable to bring on a heart attack'.[86]

Heavy allied bombers struck the ruins of Cassino early on 15 March. For three hours the hill lay shrouded by smoke and dust. 'It seemed to me inconceivable,' wrote Alexander, 'that any troops should be left alive.' But allied troops advanced to find defence offered by the 1st German Parachute Regiment just as stubborn as ever. By nightfall on the 15th most of Cassino town had fallen and Indian troops had struggled halfway up Monastery Hill, but the Germans remained far from beaten; contrary to forecasts the weather broke again during the night – and a clear spell had been considered necessary to allow the use of tanks.

Apprehensive reports from Cassino were reaching Whitehall on the 16th, but once again the COS devoted attention to Burma and to the festering conflict with Churchill. The Joint Planners were called in during the morning and discussed Churchill's instructions to them on the previous Monday: these had centred on compilation of evidence to support the 'Culverin' policy.[87] Talks were resumed with the Prime Minister next day, 17 March, while the slogging match continued at Cassino; and now Churchill suggested an alternative scheme for the Bay of Bengal: the island of Simalur should be attacked, rather than Sumatra, requiring fewer resources. The COS still sought a Pacific strategy.[88] Churchill therefore told the CIGS on the 18th that he

remained determined to have a meeting with Roosevelt at
Bermuda, probably at Easter. 'He insists on going, and
proposes from there to fly to Gibraltar and on to Italy, which
will probably be the end of him.'[89] The Prime Minister,
dogged as ever, found time on the 19th to send a school-
masterly minute to the Director of Military Intelligence:
'Why must you write "intensive" here? "Intense" is the right
word. You should read Fowler's *Modern English Usage*....'[90]
    German forces counter-attacked at Cassino during this
spring Sunday and New Zealand thrusts on the 20th were
beaten back. The clash between Churchill and the COS
continued, and Dill wrote to Brooke: 'What the hell of a
time you must be having.' The War Cabinet met to discuss
the Far East at 6 p.m. on the 20th; Brooke described the
meeting, which failed to reach any conclusions, as 'one of
the worst'. Cadogan wrote: 'PM looked flushed and was very
woolly. Hope he's not unwell.' Afterwards the Prime
Minister completed a document addressed to each of the
COS personally, rather than collectively as a committee; he
accused them of reluctance to meet the Americans, and he
continued: 'The Minister and the Defence Committee are
convinced ... that it is in the interest of Britain to pursue
what may be termed the "Bay of Bengal" strategy, at any
rate for the next 12 months.' Churchill, as both Prime
Minister and Defence Minister, therefore made a number
of definite rulings. 'Unless unforeseen events occur, the
Indian theatre and the Bay of Bengal will remain, until the
summer of 1945, the centre of gravity for the British and
Imperial war effort against Japan. All preparations will be
made for amphibious action across the Bay of Bengal.... A
powerful British fleet will be built up, based on Ceylon.'[91]
Yet the COS still refused to be browbeaten, condemning
the document as 'impossible' and deciding on the morning of
the 21st to refuse to accept the contents. They agreed it would
be better to resign than accept Churchill's policy.[92]
Churchill and his COS had therefore come the closest
yet to a complete break; Cadogan's diary entry declared:
'PM this morning confessed he was tired – he's almost done
in.'[93] But Churchill felt that Roosevelt's reply had given him

solid foundations for his determined stand: his paper to the individual Chiefs had declared: 'We now know that there is no obligation (for British forces to go to the Pacific) and that their operations will not be hampered, also that they will not in any case require our assistance ... before the autumn of 1945.' Yet on this 21 March, Churchill found himself mistaken over the American attitude. Granted, Roosevelt had said the British naval forces 'will be of more value to our common effort by remaining in the Indian Ocean', but all depended on the conception of an Indian Ocean strategy, and the US COS remained just as opposed as their British counterparts to 'Culverin'. Talks in Washington with the 'Axiom' mission had done nothing to change American opinion that the main areas for operations against the Japanese should be in north Burma and in the Pacific, and after a last 'Axiom' session on this Tuesday, the US COS signalled London: 'These meetings have more conclusively developed that the greatest contribution which can be made to the defeat of Japan by the South-East Asia Command, is to assist in providing timely direct support of the Pacific theatre to the China-Formosa-Luzon triangle.... It is conclusive to us that the greatest accomplishment that can be achieved by Admiral Mountbatten is to secure Myitkyina with the object of providing an immediate increase of the air transport capacity to China.'[94] The American preference for Upper Burma had been reinforced by Stilwell's success, and by Wingate's Chindits; tragically, Wingate himself died in an aircraft accident during this week.

A three-way split therefore existed: the Americans might oppose the move of the British fleet to the Pacific, but they equally opposed Churchill's 'Culverin'. And in this tense situation renewed Anglo-American arguments concerning 'Anvil' in the south of France seemed increasingly likely. The US agreement of 25 February had allowed temporary priority to be given to Italy, subject to a review around 20 March. On 22 March General Wilson replied to a British COS request for the latest situation: a renewed Cassino offensive would be launched, but Wilson warned that preparations would not be complete before 15 April and allied armies would be unlikely to link with the Anzio bridgehead before 15 May, after which another month would pass before Rome could be reached; on the other hand, continued emphasis on the Italian campaign would allow maximum pressure to be maintained against the enemy, and would aid strategic bombers in their operations from the theatre. Wilson therefore asked for a CCS directive: 'a) To continue the battle in Italy to include the capture of Rome and its airfields; b) Thereafter to carry out intensive operations up Italy, the assault lift of one division plus ... being allotted for this purpose; c) To cancel forthwith "Anvil"...' Eisenhower submitted a report on this same day, 22 March, which reached the same conclusion: 'Anvil' should be abandoned 'in its present conception of a two-division assault building up to 10 divisions'. The COS agreed with these reports at a meeting on the 22nd, and immediately informed the US COS.[95] 'I now hope ... that the American COS will see wisdom,' wrote Brooke. At least one of his fears had been removed: Roosevelt had now wired that a Bermuda meeting with Churchill would be impossible at the moment.

The strain of these difficult days had increasingly begun to tell on all the principal decision-makers. Eden was heavily involved with Poland, Yugoslav affairs, diplomatic planning for D-Day, and also the task involved with his Leadership of the House; Cadogan had written in his diary on the 21st: 'A. can't bear his double burden any longer', and Eden's own diary entry for the 24th read: 'Hate these endless crises, first in Foreign Office, then in House.... I am so weary.'[96] On 26 March the Foreign Secretary's troubles were increased by an announcement issued from the Greek mountains, declaring the official creation of the communist Political Committee of National Liberation – a direct challenge to the authority of the Tsouderos Government. Churchill also seemed to be wilting at last; on the 27th Nicolson commented upon reaction to a broadcast by the Prime Minister the previous evening: 'People seem to think that Winston's broadcast ... was that of a worn and petulant old man. I am sickened by the absence of gratitude towards him. The fact is that the country is terribly war-weary, and the ill-success of Anzio and Cassino is for them a bad augury of what will happen when the Second Front begins.'[97] Brooke described Churchill at this time: 'We found him in a desperately tired mood. I am afraid that he is losing ground rapidly. He seems quite incapable of concentrating for a few minutes on end, and keeps wandering continuously.'[98]

The American reply to the proposal to scrap 'Anvil' reached London on the 27th. Wilson's appreciation and Eisenhower's report, plus the British COS recommendations, had failed to convince Marshall and his colleagues. The Americans agreed 'Anvil' could not be launched early in June, and consented to transfer assault shipping to 'Overlord' as proposed by Eisenhower, but rather than cancelling 'Anvil' completely they suggested the operation should be launched around 10 July. The Americans did however offer to send 26 LSTs and 40 landing-craft from the Pacific to the Mediterranean, to arrive during June – the first time assault shipping had been withdrawn from the Pacific area – but the signal stated this should be 'only on condition that it is agreed by the British COS that preparation for the delayed "Anvil" will be vigorously pressed and that it is the firm intention to mount this operation in support of "Overlord" with the target date indicated'. The British COS discussed this telegram on the 27th and 28th, and agreed that while 'Anvil' might be postponed rather than completely abandoned, it would be a mistake to specify a rigid date for the assault. This decision was immediately transmitted to Washington.[99]

Also on the 28th the COS sent another paper to Churchill on the Far East, reaffirming their conviction that the Pacific strategy would be far more likely to shorten the war against Japan than 'Culverin', but pleading more time to gain data on the relative capacities of Australia and India as bases.[100] 'I have just about reached the end of my tether,' wrote Brooke to Dill on the 30th, 'and can see no way of clearing up the frightful tangle that our Pacific strategy has got into.' Yet also on the 30th, Brooke heard unofficially from Dill that the Americans were refusing to alter their rigid demand for an 'Anvil' date; and the CIGS commented: 'I am giving up hope of getting Marshall to understand what the situation is in Italy.'[101] The Americans had become even more determined after a telegram from Wilson to the CCS announcing the Italian offensive was now unlikely to start until mid-May instead of mid-April, thus increasing US fears that unless 'Anvil' were given a fixed date, the operation would be abandoned by default. Wilson's news had also caused disquiet in London, and conversely had increased British determination not to hinder Italian operations by the need for 'Anvil' preparations; thus when a telegram reached London from Washington on the 31st, giving the latest US decision, the British sent an immediate, anxious reply stressing the importance of the Italian operations, but adding: 'The implication that in (the) British view Mediterranean strategy is any less subservient to "Overlord" than in the American view, is particularly painful to us on the eve of this greatest of our joint ventures.'[102]

Allied planning had fallen into complete shambles, with the Far East and with Europe. Never before had unity been so lacking; the situation during and since the Tehran-Cairo talks had gone from bad to worse – and yet 'Overlord' would be launched in just over two months' time, and in Italy the allies were still desperately trying to break the German lines. Either London or Washington would have to give way, and after hours of discussion on 1 and 3 April, the British COS came to the painful conclusion that American wishes over 'Anvil' must be met. Wilson urgently needed a new directive to maintain the current Italian offensive, and such a directive would only be approved by the Americans if the British co-operated; the absence of a directive would have a disastrous effect on the Italian campaign, deemed by the British to be so essential to 'Overlord'. The British COS therefore submitted a draft to Washington on 3 April; Wilson should be ordered to '... 2(a) Launch as soon as is practicable a co-ordinated, sustained all-out offensive in Italy so as to join the beachhead with the main line. Thereafter through offensive action contain the greatest number of German formations in Central Italy.... (c) Prepare plans for "Anvil" on a basis of at least a two-divisional assault to be launched at the earliest practicable date. *Target date 10 July.* (d) "Anvil" is the most ambitious operation that can be undertaken in the Mediterranean theatre, and plans for this operation should be pressed forward vigorously and wholeheartedly, together with all preparations that do not prejudice the operations specified in (a) above.'[103] Within 24 hours came an American demand for even more from this directive. Four alterations were required in the version proposed by the British, which would lay even greater stress on 'Anvil' at the expense of Italian operations: the American signal stated: '2(a) *last sentence*: Insert "maintain pressure to" after "thereafter". *Delete* "through offensive action". 2(c) *first sentence*: Insert "and preparations" after "plans". 2(d) *Delete* "together with all preparations that do not prejudice the operations specified in (a) above".' The British COS considered these alterations on the 5th and agreed they were 'quite unacceptable'.[104] Complete impasse remained.

Also on 5 April, the COS attempted to solve another dangerous problem, which had been simmering beneath the surface for a number of weeks and which held dire implications for future Anglo-French relations: the choice of bombing policy for 'Overlord'. Should allied heavy bombers be unleashed to attack railways and communication centres in northern France, despite the inevitable French civilian casualties? The latter, according to some estimates, could be as high as 40,000 killed and 120,000 injured. Technical debate had taken place among air authorities since the beginning of the year over the respective roles of this 'Transportation Plan' and the existing policy of attacking German aircraft and petroleum industries – 'Pointblank'. Portal had chaired a meeting on 25 March which had agreed that strategic air forces should be divided between operations involved with both, and four days later Portal reported this decision to Churchill: 'In the execution of this Plan very heavy casualties among civilians ... will be unavoidable.... Eisenhower realizes this and I understand that he is going to propose that warnings should be issued.... I hope you will agree that since the requirements of "Overlord" are paramount, the Plan must go ahead.'[105] Churchill now involved the War Cabinet in greater strategic decision-making than had been the case since 1940 and 1941; he brought the attention of Ministers to the subject on 3 April, and the War Cabinet expressed apprehension over casualties. Portal explained the plan, and Churchill mentioned doubts among the experts over which targets should be attacked; he himself admitted unease. The War Cabinet agreed to refer the question to the Defence Committee.[106] The COS therefore attended a Defence Committee meeting at 10.30 p.m. on the 5th for a long and anxious discussion.

Eden had already expressed opposition to the bombing scheme in a minute to the Foreign Office earlier in the day: 'Does the Department realize that casualties will be greater than total suffered by all in Britain since the war began?'[107] Churchill now voiced a similar view. He felt that 'even if the casualties were not as great as estimated, they might well be sufficient to cause an unhealable breach between France and Great Britain and the USA'. The Prime Minister also attacked the plan on military grounds. 'In Italy, where railway communications were confined to well-defined defiles, the RAF had failed to prevent the enemy moving divisions to the south.... The enemy forces which would be employed to oppose "Overlord" were relatively small, and the distances over which they would have to be moved and maintained relatively short.' He remained unconvinced that the bombing results 'would justify the slaughter of masses of friendly French allies, who were burning to help us when the day came, and who showed their friendly feelings by giving unstinted help to any of our airmen forced down'. Portal admitted he had opposed the idea until he had studied results of bombing in North Africa; he did not claim the plan would entirely sever rail communications: 'It should, however, be possible to canalize them into a few channels which could be blocked at short notice.' Firm support for the plan came from Tedder, Deputy Supreme Commander and co-ordinator of 'Overlord' air operations; but Lord Cherwell warned: 'If we were to stop the enemy deployment, it would be necessary to reduce the present capacity of the railways by 90 per cent or more' and he disbelieved this could be achieved by bombing railway centres. When Churchill asked for individual opinions only Sinclair, Air Secretary, seemed to agree with the plan. Attlee declared himself unsatisfied that results would outweigh 'what we should lose from the antagonism aroused in the French'; Oliver Lyttelton said 'the argument in favour of the policy could not be sustained for one minute in the face of the very serious political objections'; Alexander felt there were more suitable targets, and Grigg, War Secretary, believed that 'in view of the large number of targets and the inevitable inaccuracy of the bombing, it was doubtful if the desired results could be achieved'. Eden dealt with the diplomatic aspects: 'After the war we would have to live in a Europe that was already looking more to Russia than he would wish.' Sir Andrew Cunningham, First Sea Lord, gave qualified support to his Air colleague; he favoured the attacks 'provided that the civilian population was warned and that the attacks did not entail too great a slaughter of the civilian population'. But Brooke opposed Portal; he 'doubted if the success likely to be achieved by bombing justified the effort which would be entailed', and while confirming that the enemy would have to rely to some extent on railways for bringing up troops and maintaining the front, he did not think bombing would result 'in any large-degree canalization of communications'. Brooke's attitude proved important: as Portal declared: 'He (Portal) was of course entirely in the hands of the soldiers. If they said the plan would not materially contribute to the success of "Overlord", then he agreed that it should be dropped.' Brooke had given his soldierly verdict. But so too had Eisenhower, in a signal to Churchill during the day: 'I and my military advisers have become convinced that the bombing of these centres will increase our chances of success in the critical battle.' Opinion therefore remained divided between the soldiers themselves and between the air authorities and British Ministers. The Defence Committee agreed to a temporary compromise: bombing attacks 'should be continued experimentally against those railway centres where there was no great risk of inflicting heavy civilian casualties', but Tedder was asked to review his plan, 'with a view to eliminating those of the less important target attacks'.[108]

Churchill had a private conversation with Eden after this meeting ended in the early hours of 6 April. The Prime Minister, like Cadogan, had become concerned over the Foreign Secretary's health, and now told him he was 'clearly overpressed'; Eden was told to have three weeks' rest. The Foreign Secretary therefore left his office and would not return until 26 April. Churchill, despite his own colossal burden, shouldered Eden's Foreign Office tasks; moreover, these had recently been increased by the deteriorating Greek situation. The British had attempted to take away some of the influence of the recent communist rallying cry by urging the Greek King to agree to the appointment of a Regent, pending a national plebiscite to decide if the Monarch should return. But King George refused, saying the appointment of a Regent would mean delegating his authority before a plebiscite had been held. Disorders broke out in Greece, and these spread to Greek servicemen in the allied forces; on 3 April the Greek Prime Minister, Tsouderos, felt obliged to resign. British troops moved against Greek soldiers in an attempt to quell the mutiny in the Mediterranean, and Greek warships were kept under close observation. The Greek King decided he must fly to Alexandria to quieten the disturbances, while Churchill cabled Tsouderos on the 7th pleading for the politician to stay at his post until the monarch's arrival. Prospects for the future remained stormy, and a civil war following German evacuation of Greece could lead to a complicated British commitment – at the expense of resources needed for the Italian campaign. Churchill tackled the immediate problem with customary energy, even though he seemed as much in need of a rest as his Foreign Secretary: on 7 April he attended a meeting held by Montgomery on current planning for 'Overlord', and Brooke believed Churchill to be 'looking old and lacking a great deal of his usual vitality'. General Kennedy agreed: 'He looked puffy and dejected and his eyes were red.'[109]

Moreover, Churchill would soon be drawn back into the Anglo-American quarrel over 'Anvil'. Dill had reported from Washington: 'Only over his (Marshall's) dead body will you get a change of outlook.' The Americans informed London on 8 April that they would consent to the British draft directive for Wilson, but only on the understanding that the offer to divert assault shipping from the Pacific to the Mediterranean would be withdrawn, since the directive removed the possibility of 'Anvil' as a complement to 'Overlord'. 'This is typical of their methods of running strategy,' wrote Brooke angrily. 'They use some of their available landing-craft as bargaining counters in trying to get their false strategy followed.'[110] Yet the Americans had made their condition clear in their offer on 24 March; nor had the British seemed to take great heed of the resulting extra strength; and now, on 8 April, the COS in London decided the withdrawal of the offer must make no difference to their determination not to alter their draft directive to Wilson; they accordingly put finishing touches to the document ready for presentation to the Prime Minister.[111] Churchill remained entangled by the continued mutiny by troops of the 1st Greek Brigade in Egypt; he telegraphed Paget, Middle East Commander, on the 9th: 'You will have achieved success if you bring the Brigade under control without bloodshed. But brought under control it must be. Count on my support.' He nevertheless found time to study the Anglo-American confrontation over 'Anvil' on 10 April, and he immediately minuted to the COS that further attention should be given to the problem before a final decision; specifically, a further attempt should be made to obtain the landing-craft from the Pacific, and Churchill wished to communicate direct with Roosevelt.[112]

The COS advised against this appeal to the President until talks had been held with General Alexander, who arrived in London for conferences on the 10th and 11th. Brooke and his colleagues were anxious to learn full details of Alexander's plan for Italy, especially after Wilson's signal at the end of March saying the offensive was unlikely to start until 14 May instead of mid-April; if confirmed, this delay must definitely rule out 'Anvil' by 10 July. Alexander explained his reasons for the changed programe. German strength in Italy apparently totalled 23 fully-equipped divisions, 18 south of Rome. These were deployed along the Gustav Line, the Adolf Hitler Line running east from the Liri river to north of Cassino, and thirdly the Caesar Line, between Anzio and Rome and then westwards towards Pescara. The allies therefore had to punch through three defensive barriers. Alexander wished to keep the Anzio forces in reserve, ready for the pursuit on Rome, and to concentrate air power for the attacks by the 5th and 8th Armies against the Gustav and then the Adolf Hitler Lines. Allied strength would amount to 28 divisions, and 18 of them would be west of the Apennines – the bulk of the 8th Army would therefore have to be moved across the mountains to join with the 5th Army offensive. This transfer, plus other essential reinforcement, redeployment and deception measures, would take considerable time: Alexander would not therefore be ready until after 10 May. The COS agreed with this assessment, and thus emerged from the conference even more determined not to allow the impossible 'Anvil' date of 10 July to appear in Wilson's draft.[113]

Churchill met Alexander and the COS on the 12th. After hearing the details he accepted Alexander's dates, but added: 'It seemed worth while making one more attempt to get the Americans to send to the Mediterranean additional landing-craft from the Pacific.... It should be borne in mind that our present lack of success in Italy was due almost entirely to the arrival of 8 fresh German divisions in Italy from other theatres, and to our withdrawal from the Mediterranean of 7 of our best divisions for "Overlord".' Churchill saw no reason why German forces in the south of France 'should not be fastened there during the critical stage of "Overlord" by feints and threats' rather than a full-scale landing. Alexander agreed: 'The maintenance of amphibious threats of two or three divisions should cause the Germans serious concern; the launching of this force and the successful sealing-off of the bridgehead would be a great relief to the Germans.'[114] An appeal from Churchill to

Marshall left London during the day: 'I have not hitherto
intervened in the intricate and lengthy correspondence
which has been proceeding between the US and British COS
about "Anvil".... We should above all defeat the German
army south of Rome and join our own armies. Nothing
should be grudged for this.... Regarding "Anvil".... I
believe that whatever happens on the mainland of Italy,
the enemy forces now detached to the Riviera can in the
meanwhile be fastened there by feints and threats. One thing
alarms me, however, is lest our Directive to General Wilson
should make him fall between two stools. This would mean
that we should be denied the exploitation of any victory
gained south of Rome ... or the power to pin down German
divisions in Italy, and yet on the other hand not be able to
make a major operation out of "Anvil".'[115]

Churchill had to turn back to Greek problems. During the
12th the King of Greece issued a proclamation from Cairo,
stating he would submit himself to the result of a national
plebiscite, to be held when Greece had been liberated. Such
a statement had long been urged by the Foreign Office;
next day Venizelos took office in succession to Tsouderos.
But Greek naval and army units in Egypt stayed in a state
of mutiny; the Greek Brigade, 4,500-men strong with 50 guns,
had deployed itself in defensive positions against British
troops. Churchill cabled the British Ambassador to the
Greek Government, Leeper: 'There can be no question of
making terms with mutineers about political matters....
They must submit to be disarmed unconditionally.' The
situation was described to the War Cabinet on this Thursday,
13 April, and Ministers gave full approval to the Prime
Minister's actions.

Two hours after this War Cabinet meeting finished the
Defence Committee met in the Map Room for another dis-
cussion on the controversial bombing policy for 'Overlord'.
Since the last session on the night of the 5th, bombers had
carried out their 'experimental' raids over French targets.
Portal now brought a revised list of targets, including
estimates of civilian casualties which the attacks would entail.
Centres of lesser importance had been excluded, and Portal's

note declared: 'Whereas the casualties previously estimated for the original list of targets totalled between 80,000 and 160,000 killed, seriously injured and slightly injured, it will be noted that the total for the revised list now amounts to approximately 10,500 killed and 5,500 seriously injured. This figure of 16,000 killed and seriously injured makes no allowance for any scale of evacuation.' Although recent attacks on nine railway centres had resulted in 1,103 deaths – according to Vichy broadcasts – this remained well below original figures; Portal declared: 'Vichy were unlikely to minimize casualties and the fact that, even according to Vichy reports, the number of killed had been less than half that estimated, indicated that either our figures were on the high side or possibly that an evacuation had already started.' Churchill still doubted whether the plan 'would have a material effect on the battle'. Attlee suggested 'we should regard the casualties inflicted in some of the recent attacks as being heavy had they resulted from attacks on similar targets in this country'. Sinclair pointed out that no complaints had so far been received from the Fighting French. The Committee finally agreed with Churchill that as 'the slaughter during the last week had been much less than had been expected', the attacks should be continued for a further week, during which a close watch would be kept on results achieved, casualties inflicted, and world opinion.[116]

Subjects for urgent consideration continued to crowd round Churchill and the Chiefs of Staff: bombing policy, the host of 'Overlord' plans, Greece, Italy and 'Anvil'; the multitude of time-consuming yet less imminent problems such as military occupation of Germany, armistice details, India, postwar conscription, rationing.... And on 14 April the COS had to take up again the troublesome subject of Burma and the war against Japan. Mountbatten had been asked for his views of the US decision, made on 21 March, to give further support for the Ledo Road strategy in north Burma urged by Stilwell; Mountbatten himself remained preoccupied with the clash with the Japanese on the Imphal plain: this, believed the Supreme Commander, represented the crucial shallenge.

He therefore replied to the COS on the 14th that while
Stilwell might be able to take Myitkyina, as part of the Ledo
Road policy, he could not guarantee its retention until the
outcome of the Imphal battle was known. He therefore proposed to halt Stilwell's northern advance in the area
Mogaung-Myitkyina, while his other forces completed the
vital battle and the consolidation of Arakan.[117] Mountbatten's telegram thus clashed with the American policy.
Also on this Friday, 14 April, the British COS studied
another paper in the clash between themselves and
Churchill: this document by the Joint Planners considered
a revised version of the Pacific Strategy, called the 'Middle
Strategy', which proposed a more direct route to Borneo,
Saigon and Singapore from Australia, rather than the more
easterly approach via the Coral Sea. The COS would discuss
the problem for another fortnight before presenting definite
proposals to the Prime Minister, and disagreements with the
Americans would likewise continue.[118] Also on the 14th
the latest signal from Marshall revealed, as expected, continuing disagreement over Mediterranean strategy. Replying
to Churchill's appeal of the 12th, Marshall declared: 'We
appear to be agreed in principle, but quite evidently not as to
method. If we are to have any option as to what we can do
when the time comes, preparations for "Anvil" must be made
now, even though they may be at the partial expense of
future operations in Italy after the beachhead has been
joined.' The Americans refused to transfer landing-craft from
the Pacific, unless they could be assured that 'we are to have
an operation in the effectiveness of which we have complete
faith'. After a Churchill-COS meeting during the afternoon
of this busy Friday, the Prime Minister repeated his arguments to Marshall, again with no success.[119] The British and
Americans could only agree to exchange differences: no
landing-craft from the Pacific in return for no date specified
for 'Anvil'. The directive to Wilson was accordingly issued
on 19 April, containing orders to 'launch, as early as possible
an all-out offensive in Italy; develop the greatest possible
threat to contain German forces in southern France....'[120]
Brooke wrote in his diary on the same day: 'History will

never forgive them (the Americans) for bargaining equipment against strategy, and for trying to blackmail us into
agreeing with them.'[121]

At least one problem had apparently been solved, but
Churchill's burden remained. He reported latest Greek
developments to the War Cabinet at 6.30 p.m. on the 19th,
and the mutiny appeared to be approaching a crisis. Cadogan
wrote in his diary: 'PM, I fear, is breaking down. He
rambles without a pause, and we really got nowhere by 7.40.
N. Chamberlain would have settled it in 6 minutes.... I
really am fussed about the PM.... I really don't know
whether he can carry on.'[122] This War Cabinet meeting
stretched until after 9 p.m.; an hour later Churchill chaired
a Defence Committee meeting for another long discussion
on 'Overlord' bombing. Once again Churchill appeared to
ramble rather than risk a clear decision. Portal, Tedder and
Leigh-Mallory described the damage caused to the enemy
even by the experimental raids on France so far, and claimed
considerably fewer casualties than had been feared: only
about 400 had been killed in Paris, for example, compared
with an originally estimated total of 1,600. Churchill tentatively suggested changing bombing policy in order to attack
enemy oil supplies from Roumania; Tedder replied this had
already been examined and rejected 'as being unlikely to
contribute to the success of "Overlord"'. Portal urged a
definite directive, and added: 'If the plan were abandoned
we should have already wasted a considerable effort and killed
a number of French civilians unnecessarily.' Alexander felt
the scheme should still be scrapped and better targets found;
Grigg and Attlee believed the present half-scale raids should
continue for another week. But Brooke now supported
Portal's view regarding the importance of a clear decision.
'We had already gone a third of the way towards implement-
ing the plan, and he felt that it would be fundamentally
wrong to change now and thus the effort and bombload
already expended and the lives of the French civilians who
had already been killed.' Churchill wavered badly. 'He did
not feel that a firm decision could be taken now, though he
admitted that the longer a decision was deferred the stronger

became the case for continuing the attacks on railway centres. It was true that hitherto the casualties had not been nearly as great as had been expected. On the other hand it was difficult to judge the efficacy of the policy.' Cadogan's criticism of Churchill's rambling seemed fully justified; even the official minutes could barely sort sense from this almost incoherent statement: 'He (Churchill) was not yet prepared to be faced with a Cabinet decision that the policy should be abandoned and with having to inform the President of this decision and that if the Supreme Commander insisted that it was essential to the success of "Overlord", it could only be continued on American responsibility. He did not agree that it was fair to say that having gone so far we must continue the policy to its conclusion.'[123] Eventually the Defence Committee agreed the present level of bombing should continue for another week; Brooke complained in his diary: 'The matter put back for another week's consideration, at a time when we are within five weeks of the attack and definite decisions are required....'[124]

Exhaustion seemed at last to be crippling Churchill's mental powers. Brooke on the other hand would be spared further strain for the moment: he managed to leave for 7 days' leave on the 21 April. And Churchill's load was partially lifted on the 23rd with the surrender of the mutinous Greek servicemen in Egypt. One British officer had been killed. On 26 April the short Premiership of Venizelos ended with the arrival from Athens of Papandreou, who immediately issued an agenda for a proposed conference of all Greek political parties: this would meet in the Lebanon in mid-May. But even as the Greek problem began to slide from the Prime Minister's daily tasks, he plunged into another complicated and time-consuming area of discussion. The issue of Wilson's directive on 19 April had established a clear programme: all-out offensive in Italy, code-named 'Diadem', in mid-May; a limited 'Anvil' threat to the south of France; above all, 'Overlord' in the first week of June. But within this framework, other possible operations might be found. Despite his weariness Churchill cast his thoughts and they alighted again on the idea for a Bordeaux landing,

'Caliph'. The COS had previously opposed the idea in view of shortages of resources, and to a lesser extent on the grounds of military difficulties involved; but only three days after Wilson's directive, Churchill resurrected the idea in a minute to the Chiefs of Staff, believing that the problem of resources might be solved if the operation were launched after 'Overlord' had begun. His staccato questioning now contrasted sharply to his rambling conversation at the Defence Committee on the 19th: 'What is the day when the bulk of transportation for the battle ("Overlord") will be over? In what posture may we reasonably hope to be on D (Day) plus 20? What will be the condition of the German Fighter and Bomber Air Force at that time? Will it not probably be shot to a standstill and largely annihilated? ... I am sure that even if as few as 50,000 troops were landed around Bordeaux by a surprise operation, they would liberate the city and enable reinforcements to sail up the Gironde. The effect upon the enemy would be profound....'[125] Churchill called a staff conference on the evening of the 24th to discuss this minute, and, because 'Caliph' differed from 'Anvil', in that it would be launched well after 'Diadem' and 'Overlord', the Conference agreed the scheme merited serious study. Progress now accelerated: the COS decided to call Wilson home for talks, and informed the Americans on the 27th that they tended towards some form of both 'Anvil' and 'Caliph', to be launched if possible some three weeks after 'Overlord'.[126] Even before talks began with Wilson in London on 3 May, Anglo-American relations had undergone a startling improvement, all the more dramatic and sudden when compared with the tortuous 'Anvil' discussions: with priority now firmly given to 'Diadem' and 'Overlord', the COS in London could show more favour for operations elsewhere. And with this attitude from London, the American position could in turn undergo a thaw: Admiral King told a CCS meeting in Washington on 28 April that if conferences with Wilson produced a definite recommendation for an assault on southern or western France, he would send assault shipping for that purpose from the Pacific.[127] The way at last seemed open for full

allied agreement, stemming from Churchill's minute of the
21st.

Bombers meanwhile continued to fasten upon selected
French targets. Portal told the Defence Committee at 10
p.m. on 26 April that Bomber Command had attacked nine
targets during the last week, dropping a total of 7,880 tons
of bombs, and the RAF had completed 30-40 per cent of its
share of the Transportation Plan programme. On the other
hand the Americans had barely begun. Churchill feared 'lest
by continuing the attacks over a long period we would build
up a volume of dull hatred in France which would effect
our relations with that country for many years to come....
It was unfortunate that the Americans had not played an
equal part with us.' Sinclair thought 'the French regarded
these attacks in the same way as we did, namely as a
horrible necessity of war'. Eden agreed and believed 'we had
now gone so far that we could not cease all attacks on railway
targets without putting a weapon into the hands of German
propaganda. We should therefore continue ... where the
number of casualties inflicted was likely to be small.'
Lyttelton repeated his previous view: the plan was 'in-
supportable' in the face of the political disadvantages, and
Cherwell thought other targets 'such as dumps and lorry
parks' were more suitable. General Nye, speaking in Brooke's
absence, said the CIGS felt 'we had now gone so far that
it would be wrong to abandon the policy'. Alexander agreed
with Cherwell, but Grigg and Cunningham supported the
view that bombing should continue because the plan was
about one-third completed; Grigg commented: 'We should
incur little additional odium.' Defence Committee opinion
had splintered even further during the last week, and
Churchill said he would refer the question to the War
Cabinet at a meeting the following day.[128]

Ministers accordingly met at 12.15 p.m. on 27 April.
Strong opposition to the bombing policy as a whole came
from Churchill, Eden, Attlee, Cherwell and Brendan
Bracken, but the War Cabinet eventually agreed to continue the raids on a limited scale against railway centres
where estimated casualties would not exceed 100-150, and

Ministers also agreed Churchill should cable Roosevelt to say Britain saw grave objections to the overall plan on political grounds. The signal would be shown to General Eisenhower before despatch.[129] Five days later an uncompromising and extremely disturbing message reached London from the Supreme Allied Commander, revealed to the War Cabinet by Churchill at 7.15 p.m. The Transportation Plan was, in fact, merely one part of the allied bombing offensive for 'Overlord', and Eisenhower warned: 'If it is still considered that the political considerations are such as to limit the operations to centres where the casualties are estimated at 100-150, such a modification would emasculate the whole plan.' He added: 'Such a limitation would logically apply to all Air Operations prior to the assault, including essential tactical operations which must begin at least two or three weeks before the assault. It is not perhaps fully appreciated that from D-30 onwards there is an extensive programme of bombing operations against military targets of diverse character over a wide area, extending over 150 miles from the coast. Attack on many of these targets, e.g. MT Depots, will inevitably involve considerable civilian casualties.' This message clearly came as a shock to the War Cabinet. Churchill admitted he 'had not fully realized that our use of air power before "Overlord" would assume so cruel and remorseless a form. It was clear that great slaughter would inevitably result.' He felt these air operations should be governed by 'some laws of war' laid down by the War Cabinet. Lyttelton declared: 'The destruction now envisaged was something new in war', and he considered that devastation on the scale mentioned was unacceptable. Brooke, who had returned from leave the previous day, argued the military case. 'The whole concept of "Overlord" was based on making full use of the terrific air power at our disposal. He doubted if we should have undertaken a task which was almost superhuman had it been anticipated that our use of air power would have been restricted.' Once again, the War Cabinet felt obliged to pass the problem back to the Defence Committee.[130]

Members of the Defence Committee accordingly met at
10.30 p.m. next day, 3 May, for final consideration of this
subject. Leigh-Mallory declared that 'between now and D-
Day some 34-40 per cent of the bomber effort would be
directed against railway targets'. A heavy percentage would
therefore be directed elsewhere, but Churchill had conceived
a method of putting the Transportation Plan into more
acceptable perspective. 'With the exception of railway centres
the targets were of purely military nature and no one could
reasonably object to their being attacked.' Eventually, after
the familiar arguments, Churchill asked Tedder if he would
be 'content' with a plan governed by 'the restriction that
the number of civilians in such (railway) attacks up to D-Day
was not to exceed 10,000.' Tedder believed the number killed
so far to be between 3,000 and 4,000, and was 'hopeful that
the full plan could be implemented without exceeding the
limits suggested by the Prime Minister'. The Defence Committee agreed to recommend this compromise solution to
the War Cabinet.[131] So ended this painful discussion, when
numbers of slaughtered had to be expressed in unemotional
percentages and ratios. The War Cabinet does not, in fact,
seem to have been officially consulted over this final decision.
Churchill sought Roosevelt's opinion in a signal despatched
on 7 May; the President replied on the 11th: 'However
regrettable the attendant loss of civilian lives is, I am not
prepared to impose from this distance any restriction on
military action by the responsible commanders that in their
opinion might militate against the success of "Overlord" or
cause additional loss of life to our Allied forces of invasion.'[132] Five days later – only three weeks before 'Overlord'
– Churchill told the COS and Eisenhower that the War
Cabinet would be content to let the matter rest.[133] Once
again, the War Cabinet does not appear actually to have
been consulted, and Churchill himself continued to worry
over reports of French casualties, writing to Eden on 28 May:
'We will talk about this tomorrow. Terrible things are being
done.'[134] But by then the RAF programme had almost been
completed; 'Overlord' lay just around the corner. And so

the bombs continued to crash down as the allies prepared to liberate bleeding France.

The great operation of the war fast approached, and tension began to mount among those with knowledge of the plans. But as always the COS had to plan ahead. General 'Jumbo' Wilson, Supreme Commander in the Mediterranean, began his talks in London on 3 May, and the COS asked him to study four possibilities: an entry into western France after 'Overlord' was successfully under way, with the object of seizing a port – basically Churchill's 'Caliph' plan; an entry into southern France on the lines of 'Anvil', also after 'Overlord' had successfully started; a seaborne 'left hook' in Italy to accelerate or exploit 'Diadem' operations against Rome; the seizure and development of air bases across the Adriatic. Wilson decided not to count on any help from 'Overlord' resources before the end of June. He disagreed with the idea of 'Caliph' being launched from the Mediterranean: the operation would be better launched from Britain, in view of Eisenhower's knowledge by that time of conditions in the north; Eisenhower agreed. Wilson proposed instead to plan for four possible seaborne operations inside the Mediterranean: an assault on the Gulf of Lions, probably on Sète; an assault east of Toulon in the area already proposed for 'Anvil'; an assault in the Gulf of Genoa, and an attack on the Italian coast north of Rome. Preparations would concentrate initially on the 4 divisions not engaged in the Italian offensive. The COS agreed these conclusions were as definite as possible before the Italian offensive, 'Diadem', had started, and on 7 May the COS accordingly asked the Americans to accept them as fulfilling King's conditions for transferring assault craft from the Pacific. An affirmative answer reached London next day. No more could be done before 'Diadem', scheduled to start in 3 days' time, but the simple solution of postponing events until after 'Diadem' and 'Overlord' had successfully cleared a way through the previous muddle.[135]

Discussions on the war against Japan coincided with these talks on Mediterranean strategy. Results were far less satisfactory. The Joint Planners had continued to study various schemes for the Pacific, titled the 'Middle Strategy' and 'Modified Middle Strategy' depending on the line of the northern thrust from Australia. On 4 May the COS submitted the Planners' paper to the Prime Minister. Meanwhile, lack of decision in London had caused increasing concern to Mountbatten in India. On 3 May he therefore sought some kind of definite plan for the immediate future, and asked whether, on completion of the current Imphal battle, he should 'continue operations in North Burma with all ... available forces and at the expense of any other operations'.[136] On 5 May, Churchill chaffed at the lack of planning progress: 'What with our own differences, and the uncertainty of American opinion, we are not unveiling a creditable picture to history.' But also on this Friday, some progress was reported to the COS by the Joint Planners, following talks with the Prime Minister. 'It could definitely be said that the Prime Minister had accepted the fact that "Culverin" could not be carried out, since it was unlikely that the necessary forces could be made available. The Prime Minister was probably prepared to reach agreement with the COS on the basis of the "Middle Course".' Yet this Pacific advance could not be started before March 1945, and Churchill remained 'determined that an amphibious operation should, if possible, be carried out by SEAC during the autumn/winter of this year.' He apparently still favoured an attack on Simalur. The Directors of Plans continued: 'The Prime Minister had been informed that strategically there was little value to be gained from this operation.... On the assumption, however, that an operation had to be undertaken in SE Asia this year, and provided that the necessary resources could be found, the capture of Simalur was probably the best that could be selected.'[137] The COS could only summon lukewarm enthusiasm for this scheme and a Staff Conference with Churchill on 8 May failed to find agreement over long-term plans. But at least the meeting on the 8th resulted in a draft directive being submitted to Washington next day, regarding Mountbatten's orders for more immediate operations in Burma: this agreed to the attack on Myitkyina, but stressed the need to build up the air route to China rather than the Ledo Road; the Americans acquiesced, and the directive was eventually sent to Mountbatten on 3 June.

But British quarrels over further future operations in the Far East continued. The COS-Churchill confrontation had become a war of attrition, and the former were beginning to weaken. They wearily agreed on Tuesday, 16 May that they had 'represented to the Prime Minister the strategy which, in their opinion and on military grounds, was the best ... but the point was being reached at which it might be better to adopt a less satisfactory strategy rather than to continue to have no strategy at all.... A further discussion with the Prime Minister ... was becoming urgently necessary.'[138] The Directors of Plans informed the COS two days later that the Joint Planning Staff 'had been considering what recommendations to make to the COS for a new approach to the Prime Minister designed to resolve the present conflict of opinion'. The COS agreed with the Planners that 'it would be wise now to base our strategy upon Australia, leaving the choice of the actual operations to be carried out within that strategy to subsequent discussion.'[139] After further private talks between Brooke and Churchill a Staff Conference on the 26th decided Darwin and Fremantle should be developed for future operations, and British representatives would work with the Australian General Staff.[140] As usual with disagreements between Churchill and his COS, Brooke and his colleagues had emerged the winners on points: The Prime Minister had been obliged to stand down from his memorandum of 20 March, virtually amounting to an ultimatum, in the face of the threatened COS resignation. But within weeks the smouldering controversy would break into flames again.

While Churchill toiled with his COS, Eden had resumed his Foreign Office tasks with continuing Greek complications. The Lebanon political conference arranged by Papandreou initially promised well: the delegates signed a Greek Charter on 20 May providing for a united Government and a single guerrilla army; on 24 May the King asked Papandreou to

form a new Government to include communist representatives. But on the same day EAM informed their delegates
that they should not have signed the Lebanon Charter, and
within a few weeks the situation had slipped back to virtual
civil war. Eden attempted to remove outside interference
by Moscow in this sensitive atmosphere, and thereby brought
about another Anglo-American quarrel. On 18 May he
revealed startling news to the War Cabinet. He had recently
'put it to the Russians that if they wished us to allow them
to take the lead in Roumania, they should be prepared to
reciprocate by allowing HMG to do likewise in Greece'.
Eden had just heard officially from the Russian Ambassador
that Moscow agreed HMG should 'play the hand' in Greece.
'They had asked, however, whether the US would mind this,
to which he (Eden) had replied that he was sure that no
difficulty would arise.'[141] Eden would soon be proved far
too optimistic; American apprehensions over 'spheres of
influence' would multiply. Nor did Churchill help to allay
these US suspicions – or even those of some fellow-country-
men – by his growing description of Russian policies given
in the House of Commons on 25 May. 'The terms offered
by Russia to Roumania made no suggestion of altering the
standards of society in that country and were in many
respects, if not at all, remarkably generous.... The victories
of the Russian armies have been attended by a great rise
in the strength of the Russian state and a remarkable
broadening of its values.' Lord Dunglass, who after renun-
ciation of his title in 1963 would be plain Sir Alec Douglas-
Home, was among those who criticized this attitude. Post-
war Europe would be a cauldron of suspicion and civil war,
he warned. 'The Government should tell the people of this
country, if they can, that for many years ahead we shall be
unable to shift the burden of our defence on to somebody
else's shoulders.' Churchill's speech seemed to mark an
abdication of responsibility; as Harold Nicolson declared:
'We are not taking sufficient account of the rights, interests,
and independence of the smaller powers.' One American
newspaper commented: 'Americans share the fear of the
smaller nations that the trend is towards another balance

of power system with British and Russian spheres of influence.'

So, on the eve of the invasion of Europe, Churchill and Eden suddenly found themselves embroiled in confrontation over future, peacetime diplomacy. Lord Halifax, British Ambassador at Washington, was instructed to ask the US State Department whether they agreed to Britain taking the lead in Greece, while the Russians did the same in Roumania; this proposal was based on 'military realities' and would not affect the rights and responsibilities of the Three Powers at the Peace Conference. The British did not apparently foresee any American objections, and in fact a precedent had already been set for this type of 'taking the lead' share-out: as Churchill had reported to the War Cabinet from Casablanca back in June 1943, Roosevelt had agreed 'that we play the hand in Turkey ... the Americans taking the lead in China....'[142] And after Tehran in December, Eden had reported: 'President Roosevelt seemed to have it in his mind the idea that the US might take over Dakar, and that it would be a good thing if we took over Bizerta.'[143] Such previous examples now accounted for Eden's optimism. But when Lord Halifax saw Cordell Hull on 30 May, the US Secretary reacted extremely unfavourably – and he had still to learn that Britain had already proposed such a procedure to the Russians. Next day, 31 May, Churchill disclosed this news in a telegram to Roosevelt urging the British case. 'We do not of course wish to carve up the Balkans into spheres of influence....'[144] The State Department immediately expressed concern to Lord Halifax that the Russians should have been approached first; Hull and Roosevelt prepared a reply to Churchill, and the issue remained unsettled when the gigantic military events swept into the forefront at the beginning of June.

Brooke wrote in his diary on 27 May: 'I never want again to go through a time like the present one. The cross-Channel operation is just eating into my heart. I wish to God we could start and have done with it....'[145] Thousands of soldiers had converged upon the south of England; assault forces massed together for a full-scale rehearsal between 3-5 May; Montgomery, visiting each unit in turn, expressed himself well pleased.

With these last steps to the invasion of France came fresh difficulties over de Gaulle and his French Committee. American suspicions remained as strong as ever, and involved discussions had been taking place between the Foreign Office and State Department, between Churchill and Roosevelt, over the critical question of the administration of France after 'Overlord'. On 5 May Roosevelt had sent draft instructions for Eisenhower: the Supreme Commander should be told to make it clear to the French Committee that arrangements with them 'do not preclude consultation with and assistance from other elements of the French people with whom you (Eisenhower) may feel it necessary or advantageous to deal'. The Foreign Office objected strongly to this draft; three days later Eden supported a suggestion by Duff Cooper, now British representative with the French Committee, that General de Gaulle should be invited to London once agreement had been reached over instructions to Eisenhower; this in turn clashed with the CCS opinion that de Gaulle should not come to London until D-Day, for security reasons. And so the days slipped by towards the launching of the invasion to liberate France, with no formal agreement reached between the allies over the administration of the liberated country.[146]

General Alexander had been quietly making his arrangements in Italy. Early on 11 May a signal from the C-in-C reached Churchill: 'All our plans and preparations are now complete and everything is ready.... We expect extremely heavy and bitter fighting, and we are ready for it. I shall signal you our private code-word when the attack starts.'[147] Within 12 hours the signal reached London, the same code which had announced the start of Alamein so many offensives ago: 'Zip'. The 5th and the bulk of the 8th Armies had been packed into the 15-mile front before Cassino and the Gustav Line; at 11 p.m. on this Thursday, some 1,600 allied guns opened a bombardment upon the entrenched Germans. At dawn on 12 May the allied tactical air force swept in to rake the defences, and during the Friday morning waves of infantry and armour washed forward against the jagged rocks of Cassino. Tactical surprise had been achieved, but after the initial advantage the offensive once again became a tangled maul. In London, Churchill and Brooke waited anxiously for news; the CIGS had written the previous night: 'I pray to God that it may be successful. A great deal depends on it.' But at 11.30 p.m. on the 12th Brooke had still to receive firm information. 'I am now awaiting a message which is being deciphered. It is very trying having to wait....'[148] By Saturday morning the CIGS could stand the tension in London no longer and left for his country home, to spend the Sunday crouched in a hide photographing a marsh-tit. While Brooke soothed his mind amidst the rustling reeds, the 5th and 8th Armies had continued to claw forward in the hell beneath Cassino. The Germans at last began to weaken. Allied units began to filter through the defences: French troops under Juin crawled up the west bank of the Garigliano, the British XIII Corps struggled across the Rapido. By the end of 14 May the enemy's eastern flank had started to collapse, and optimistic reports were on their way to London. The final assault on Cassino was expected soon; the break out from Anzio would take place within a few days. Brooke drove straight from his home on Monday, 15 May, to attend Eisenhower's final run-over of plans for 'Overlord' at St Paul's School, Kensington. Present were the King, Churchill, Smuts, Montgomery and a multitude of senior officers and commanders. Churchill grumbled at the heavy proportion of transport vehicles to be landed in the first 24 hours, and Brooke's impression of the conference strengthened his belief that Eisenhower was 'no real director of thought, plan, energy or direction. Just a co-ordinator, a good mixer, a champion of inter-Allied co-operation, and in those respects few can hold a candle to him. But is that enough?'[149]

News from Italy continued to be excellent. Polish troops attacked north of Cassino monastery on the 17th and occupied ridges overlooking the strategic highway. By nightfall they had reached within a few yards of the monastery

itself; before dawn on 18 May most of the enemy had withdrawn and the Poles probed forward. By noon they had
raised their proud Eagle over the ruins and craters of
Cassino. 'Battle continues to progress satisfactorily,' reported
Wilson. '8th army and Americans have resources to maintain impetus of attack, but those of Juin's corps uncertain
after 8 more days of hard fighting, at present rate of casualties. I discussed this with de Gaulle today.... He has agreed
to send from North Africa one armoured and one infantry
regiment at once, and to follow this up with further reinforcements....'[150] Despite this co-operation on the part of the
French leader, a Staff Conference in London during this
Thursday failed to find a solution over allied relations with
the French regarding 'Overlord'. General Koening, the
French negotiator, had refused to continue talks unless the
cipher ban imposed for 'Overlord' security were removed.
Churchill and the COS agreed conversations with Koening
on civil administration should continue as far as possible,
but no security relaxation should be permitted. Agreement
had still to be reached with the Americans on the wider
issue of instructions to Eisenhower over dealings with
the French. Cadogan, who also attended this meeting, wrote
in his diary: 'PM says, as usual, "Don't ask me to quarrel
with Pres. over de G." No one asks him to but do wish he
would *reason* with Pres. He won't.'[151] 'Overlord' was
scheduled to start in 14 days' time. On 23 May Churchill
attempted to push forward the diplomatic proceedings: he
signalled an invitation for de Gaulle to visit London, although
he made no mention of a specific date, and he also cabled
Roosevelt again explaining the 'strong sentiment in England
in favour of the French'.[152] The Americans refused to
abandon their cautious attitude; de Gaulle doubted whether
he should come to London without receiving assurances that
he would be negotiating with the Americans as well as with
the British.

German forces in Italy had fallen back to the Adolf Hitler
Line, and on 23 May the 8th Army launched its attack on
this position; on the same day VI Corps began its push from
the Anzio bridgehead. Main defences in the Hitler Line had

fallen by noon next day and the Germans pulled back to the Caesar Line defences. By evening on 25 May allied troops from Anzio had made contact with 5th Army units on Route 7 while armoured elements were thrusting swiftly towards the Alban Hills and Rome. 'We have taken over 10,000 prisoners,' reported Alexander. 'We have freed 500 square miles of Italy from the grip of the German aggressor in under a fortnight.' 'Thank Heaven for it!' exclaimed Brooke.

On 28 May subordinate 'Overlord' commanders were informed that D-Day would be 5 June. All personnel committed to the assault were now sealed in their ships or camps; all mail had been impounded. Churchill began to agitate for the opportunity to witness at first hand the Normandy landings. 'I thought it would not be wrong for me to watch the preliminary bombardment in this historic battle.'[153] On Tuesday, 30 May, the Prime Minister informed the King of his intention at their weekly Buckingham Palace lunch; the King immediately replied that he would come with him. Churchill soon saw the folly of the King's presence in the battle area; the King, in turn, persuaded the Prime Minister not to embark on his adventure. Also on the 30th the COS considered a report by the Joint Intelligence Committee on the German situation in Europe with regard to 'Overlord'. 'During the last week there has been little evidence to modify our former conclusion that the enemy appreciated that our main assault was likely to be made in the Channel area, from Boulogne to Cherbourg inclusive. The recent trend of movement of German land forces towards the Cherbourg area tends to support the view that the Le Havre-Cherbourg area is regarded as a likely, and perhaps even the main, point of assault.... The enemy still considers that Allied preparations are sufficiently advanced to permit of operations at any time now, and that from the point of view of moon and tide the first week in June is the next likely period.' According to this JIC report the enemy had therefore correctly judged both the area and timing of 'Overlord'.[154]

Allied troops closed in upon Rome. The last German defence line south of the capital had now been penetrated, but the enemy continued to cling to remaining positions

and the hilly terrain restricted the use of allied armour.
Meanwhile an expectant silence had fallen across southern
England and northern France. 'Overlord' would be launched
in less than a week. Brooke snatched a few days' rest over
the Whit holiday weekend. Churchill stayed in London,
still struggling with the French problem. On 30 May he
informed the War Cabinet that he wished to reinvite de
Gaulle on D-Day; Eden felt he should come sooner – once
the allies had landed in France, de Gaulle would feel obliged
to issue a public statement, and if he did so in Algiers without consulting the Foreign Office, 'it might well be unhappily
phrased'.[155] The COS discussed security aspects again next
day, 31 May, and sent a minute to Churchill saying 'de
Gaulle's departure from Algiers, coupled with the naval
movements which will be in progress, will give the enemy a
very good clue to the imminence of "Overlord".... On the
other hand they readily recognize that political sub-
considerations may outweigh the military risks.'[156] Eden
discussed the dilemma with Churchill during the day, and
the Prime Minister now agreed de Gaulle must be told about
'Overlord' before the operation began, and in this case it
would be safer to tell him in England than in Algiers.[157]
Also on 31 May Roosevelt cabled Churchill with discouraging information: he refused to send anyone to represent him
at talks with the French leader on future political affairs.
The Prime Minister was still determined to persuade the
French leader to come, and arrangements were made for
his reception. The COS were informed on 3 June that these
arrangements were considered by Churchill to be 'on rather
too lavish a scale'; the COS therefore decided to scrap the
idea of a guard of honour.[158]

Weather conditions throughout May had been excellent.
Troops waiting for 'Overlord' had relaxed in continuous
sunshine; seas had been calm and perfect for amphibious
and airborne assaults. But on 31 May reports from Iceland
indicated the beginning of a break and on the morning of 1
June a drizzle started to fall across the English Channel.
Eisenhower and Montgomery anxiously studied latest
information at twice-daily commanders' meetings. 'Overlord'

would only be possible on one of four days in early June if operational requirements were to be met, including suitable tide-level to clear beach obstacles, requisite amount of daylight prior to the early morning landing for naval and air bombardment, about 3 hours of rising tide after the leading landing-craft had arrived, correct moon conditions. The date of 5 June had been chosen as giving the best chance of complying with these needs: if landings started at 6.10 a.m. about 55 minutes of twilight would be given for the preliminary bombardment. The 6th, with a landing at 6.35 and 80 minutes half-light, would also be acceptable, but thereafter the daylight before tide conditions for the landing would be too prolonged, thus reducing night cover for the approaching assault forces. After 7 June correct conditions would be lacking for about 14 days, and delay would bring heavy security risks. Yet clouds continued to gather on Friday, 2 June.

Churchill sent a signal to de Gaulle during the day, urging the French leader to come at once. During the morning the Prime Minister left London with Smuts, Bevin and Ismay for Portsmouth, where he would establish a temporary Governmental nerve centre in a special train parked in a siding near Eisenhower's HQ. 'It's hell here,' complained Ismay on this Friday, 'impossible to get a moment to oneself, and ONE telephone, very inefficiently staffed, in a room four feet by three feet occupied by three people. Apart from the difficulties of working, the personal discomforts are considerable. No bath, except for one very poor shower – damned stuffy; and no privacy. "Master" is "on the ball" all the time. ... Today has been bloody.'[159] First warships sailed from the Clyde during the Friday evening; Eisenhower dined quietly with Montgomery, then attended another conference with the meteorological experts, who expressed fears over a depression still centred on Iceland. These fears increased next day, Saturday, 3 June, while Churchill inspected the armada waiting to sail from the Solent. Eisenhower conferred with Montgomery, Tedder and the weather experts at 9.30 p.m.: the Icelandic depression had begun to spread ominously southwards and the high pressure coming up from the Azores was being pushed back. Eisenhower decided to make no changes for the moment, but arranged to meet the weathermen again at 4.15 a.m. next day. The commanders accordingly made their way through the dark for this early Sunday morning meeting and heard discouraging reports. Admiral Ramsay considered a landing would still be possible on the 5th, but would be difficult; Tedder urged postponement in view of the inability of the air forces to carry out their programme; to Tedder's amazement, Montgomery believed the landings should still be attempted on the 5th. Eisenhower made his decision: D-Day would be postponed for 24 hours. Troops were thus condemned to an extra day cooped in the landing-craft and assault ships.[160]

General de Gaulle, pressed into flying from Algiers by the French Committee, reached Portsmouth in time for lunch on this Sunday, 4 June, and immediately added a new dimension to the tense situation. Churchill came out to meet him with arms outstretched, moved by his sense of history, but de Gaulle, described by the Prime Minister as 'bristling', refused to respond to the embrace. 'The meeting was a failure,' reported Eden. Churchill revealed the forthcoming invasion to liberate France; de Gaulle complained over the cipher ban. Churchill attempted to discuss the administration of liberated territory; de Gaulle retorted that this should have been arranged many months before. The Prime Minister, irritated and over-anxious, snapped that 'if there was a split between the Committee of National Liberation and the United States we should almost certainly side with the Americans'. Eden winced and Bevin whispered his disagreement in 'a booming aside'. General de Gaulle was taken to see Eisenhower, and the 20-minute meeting seemed a success, yet even this would result in further upset: Eisenhower showed the French General a declaration he intended to make to the French people, upon which de Gaulle believed he was asked to comment, but when he did so next day his observations were too late – the declaration had already been issued.[161]

Clouds had continued to clamp down during the Sunday. 'Overlord' ships which had already been in the Channel and which had been recalled, were buffeted and battered as they sought shelter in Weymouth Harbour. Troops on the transports waiting to leave were already chewing their sea-sickness pills. 'We're in the hell of a mess,' commented Ismay. 'But we'll get out all serene if we keep our heads and our tempers. I'm doing my utmost to get "Master" to get back to London tonight. We are hopelessly out of touch here.... How I've hated the last 48 hours.'[162] Brooke described the wait as 'shattering' with 'all the same feelings as I used to get before starting a point-to-point race, an empty feeling at the pit of one's stomach and a continual desire to yawn'.[163] Then, during the Sunday evening, excellent news reached London from the other battle-front: allied troops had pushed into Rome. Leading units of the US 88th Division entered the Piazza Venezia in the heart of the city at 7.15 p.m. On the same day Hitler ordered a further German division to be pulled from northern France and rushed south to reinforce the crumbling Italian front.

Eisenhower held another conference at 9.30 p.m. Weather reports were still bad – but the experts gave some promise of slight and temporary improvement for the morning of the 6th. The Supreme Commander called for another, final meeting at 4 o'clock next morning, Monday, 5 June. Churchill left in his train for London where he arrived 'in a very highly strung condition', according to Brooke. Eisenhower's 4 a.m. meeting on the 5th lasted just 15 minutes, time enough for the loneliest and most crucial decision of his life – 'Overlord' would be launched to take advantage of the promised short spell of finer weather on 6 June. Landings would take place soon after dawn; fleets were ordered to sea.

Monday passed with agonizing slowness as the machinery for invasion moved inexorably forward. Over 4,000 vessels began to move, carrying 150,000 troops for the first assault wave, and 8,000 aircraft prepared to play their part. In London, strain revealed itself in the attitude of Churchill and his Ministers towards the proud, errant de Gaulle. The French leader's behaviour received vigorous condemnation at a 6.30 p.m. War Cabinet meeting: in addition to his other misdemeanours, de Gaulle was believed to have refused to

agree to a broadcast explaining the invasion to the French.
De Gaulle was later discovered to have merely declared his
unwillingness to broadcast so soon after Eisenhower, preferring a short delay. But Churchill now told the War
Cabinet that he was 'extremely dissatisfied' with de Gaulle.
Almost immediately a message came into the Cabinet room
indicating the French leader refused to allow French liaison
officers to go with 'Overlord' as arranged, since a detailed
agreement about their duties had still to be reached.
Churchill burst into a violent tirade: if this refusal took
place 'it would not be possible for us to have any further
discussions with General de Gaulle on civil or military
matters. It might even be necessary to indicate that an aero-
plane would be ready to take him back to Algiers forthwith.'[164] 'It's like a girls' school,' commented Cadogan in
his diary. 'Roosevelt, PM, and – it must be admitted – de G.
all behave like girls approaching the age of puberty.'[165]

Ministers were informed at this meeting, for the first time,
that 'Overlord' had sailed. 'God help us all,' prayed Cadogan.
An endless stream of naval transports pushed across the
Channel, led by minesweepers and protected by a steel curtain of warships. Throughout the night bombers throbbed
over London; soon after 5 a.m. on Tuesday, 6 June, this
throbbing rose to a thunder which rattled remaining windows
in Whitehall. 'I am very uneasy,' wrote the ever-cautious
Brooke. 'At the best it will fall so very far short of the
expectation of the bulk of the people, namely all those who
know nothing about its difficulties. At the worst it may well
be the most ghastly disaster of the whole war.' And he
repeated: 'I wish to God it were safely over.'[166]

D-Day and Beyond

Behind lay Dunkirk and the Blitz and the long chain of disasters stretching through Greece, Crete, Singapore, Hong Kong, before the gradual grim climb back to this June morning. Ahead lay 41 German divisions in northern France and the smoke lying thick over the Normandy beaches. The first troops swept ashore from the jaws of the landing-craft at 6.30 a.m. Three airborne divisions had already swung down behind the dunes and cliffs. By 7.30 a.m. first reports reached London: airborne landings had been successful; first amphibious waves had met moderate opposition. By mid-morning it seemed clear the landings on the British front were proceeding well, but the eastern corps on the American front had run into difficulties at 'Omaha' beach, north-west of Bayeux. While the thin skeins of soldiers crossed the French beaches, the British COS met at 10.30 to consider the latest appreciation of German intentions – and this revealed that the enemy would, after all, have been taken largely by surprise. 'He appears to expect several landings between the Pas de Calais and Cherbourg.... There is evidence that the enemy overestimates the size of the allied forces likely to be employed, not only in the first wave but in the operations as a whole.' Another report by the Joint Intelligence Committee looked further ahead, on the assumption that 'Overlord' would be successful. 'We cannot estimate precisely when Germany's resistance will collapse ... (but) we believe that faced with the situation outlined above Germany's defeat should occur before 1945.'[1]

Churchill addressed the House of Commons at noon.

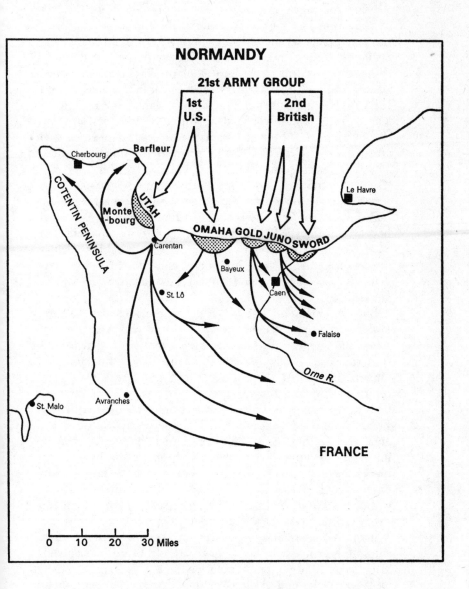

'During the night and early hours of this morning the first of a series of landings in force upon the European continent has taken place.... Reports are coming in in rapid succession. So far the commanders who are engaged report that everything is proceeding according to plan.' This plan envisaged American landings at 'Omaha' and at 'Utah' further west on the Cherbourg Peninsula, and British/Canadian landings at 'Gold', 'Juno' and 'Sword', all to the north-west of Caen. By the evening of 6 June the British had made lodgements in all their three sectors and had pushed inland up to six miles. The US landing at 'Utah' had been successful, but the 'Omaha' attempt had almost encountered disaster: for several hours troops had been pinned to the beach, and by nightfall on the 6th the beachhead had still to be extended beyond 1,000 yards. Now was the crucial moment; as Montgomery later wrote to Brooke: 'We were liable to defeat in detail.... That was Rommel's chance.... If you saw "Omaha" beach you would wonder how the Americans ever got ashore.'[2]

But Rommel had left his HQ the previous day to visit Hitler at Berchtesgaden; and the recent bad weather had lulled the enemy into false security. Montgomery, who had spent most of the day quietly in the garden of his HQ near Portsmouth, sailed for France at 9.30 p.m., and would not return to England for six months. At 9 p.m. BBC listeners had heard the first eye-witness accounts of the battle for France, but Cadogan noted the 'absence of definite news, and calm, rather an anti-climax'.[3] Eden had been struggling with the diplomatic problem of France's administration; he sent a paper to Churchill advising that Britain should discuss civil affairs with the French Committee, with or without US participation in the initial stages, but asking the Prime Minister if he would seek Roosevelt's approval for Winant, US Ambassador, to act on the President's behalf. Churchill, still extremely angry with de Gaulle, disagreed. 'Soon after midnight W. rang up in a rage,' wrote Eden, 'because Bevin and Attlee had taken my view. Argument continued for 45 minutes, perhaps longer. I was accused of trying to break up the Government.'[4]

Reports continued to indicate good progress in the British sectors; units were converging from the three landings. In Italy, the allies were pursuing the Germans up the Tiber valley and through the open country north of Rome. On 7 June the CIGS received an appreciation from Alexander: the Germans had been severely mauled, with only 6 out of 20 divisions probably still fit to fight. The allies, on the other hand, were buoyed up by 'irresistibly high' morale, and 'neither the Apennines nor even the Alps should prove a serious obstacle to their enthusiasm and skill'. Alexander believed he would be in a position to attack the Pisa-Rimini Line by the end of July; if the line were broken and a further advance made to Pistoia and Bologna he could either thrust towards Turin and Genoa and hence into France, or towards Padua and Venice and hence into Austria. Alternatively, he could stand on the Pisa-Rimini line, freeing substantial resources for operations outside Italy.[5] The latter plan would thus allow 'Anvil' or other amphibious operations. Clearly, decisions would soon have to be taken, and a staff conference was arranged for the following day, 8 June; moreover, following a series of requests from the British COS, the US COS now agreed to visit London for talks. Marshall and his colleagues would arrive on 10 June. The next great stage of strategic discussions on Europe, the Mediterranean and the Far East was about to begin, even as 'Overlord' troops battled from the beaches in Normandy.

Meanwhile the diplomatic tussle over the French continued. Churchill hinted at drastic measures to the War Cabinet at 6 p.m. on the 7th; he listed grievances against de Gaulle, including the supposed difficulties over a broadcast, the refusal to send liaison officers – although de Gaulle had now agreed to send 20 – and difficulties over the issue of special French currency notes for Allied forces. The Prime Minister warned the War Cabinet that on 21 May 1943, he had felt obliged whilst in Washington to invite Ministers to consider whether relations with de Gaulle should be terminated. 'The position had not improved ... and he (Churchill) was obliged to say that General de Gaulle had shown a most non-co-operative attitude and had exposed himself to the suggestion that he was primarily concerned with his personal position. He (Churchill) had himself done everything in his power to ease matters.... But it was clear that General de Gaulle still felt most reluctant to work with us.' Ministers agreed de Gaulle should be told Britain wished to discuss civil matters with the Committee, if necessary without US participation although the President would be kept closely informed.[6] Eden's policy had therefore been approved; the Foreign Secretary dined with de Gaulle after this meeting and found him 'pleasant, but politically stiff' and reluctant to agree to talks with Britain alone. Eden advised him to adopt a policy of 'she stoops to conquer', and, in fact, de Gaulle would soon agree to Pierre Vienot, the Committee's Diplomatic Representative, entering into discussions with the Foreign Office. But Roosevelt had still to decide upon a US representative by the time these negotiations began 11 days later.[7]

On 8 June, Churchill devoted attention to another sensitive Anglo-American subject: the subject of British involvement in Greece. The Americans had still to send an official reply to the proposal that Britain should look after Greek affairs while the Russians did likewise in Roumania. Churchill now cabled Lord Halifax with material to be used in reassuring the White House and State Department. 'There is no question of spheres of influence. We all have to act together, but someone must be playing the hand. It seems reasonable that the Russians should deal with the Roumanians and Bulgarians, upon whom their armies are impinging, and that we should deal with the Greeks, who are in our assigned theatre.' Churchill added: 'I have reason to believe that the President is in entire agreement with this line I am taking about Greece. The same is true of Yugoslavia.'[8] Halifax showed this telegram to Hull late on this Thursday; the content immediately caused fresh alarm through the mention of two new countries – Bulgaria to be dealt with by the Russians, and apparently Yugoslavia to be handled by the British. Roosevelt and Hull prepared their reply.[9]

De Gaulle, Greece, 'Overlord' – Churchill's energy took him everywhere, and, at the staff conference during the 8th

called to discuss Italy, the Prime Minister presented a paper
which seemed to Brooke to be over-enthusiastic and premature. Churchill proposed early execution of 'Caliph'
against Bordeaux; the CIGS on the other hand believed that
'we *must* first see what happens to our cross-Channel operation and what the final stage of Alex's offensive leads to'.
A statement by Portal at the conference matched this diary
entry by Brooke: 'If we called a halt in Italy on the Pisa-
Rimini line and began to transfer forces round by sea to
northern France, we should suffer the disadvantage that these
forces would be out of action for many weeks at a critical
stage of the war.' Portal urged instead for consideration to be
given to a further Italian advance into Istria. Churchill
agreed that 'the possibilities open to us of exploiting the
situation eastwards from northern Italy ought certainly to
be examined'.[10] Excellent news arrived from France during
the evening. The British right had joined with the American
left and the allies now controlled a 30-mile stretch of coast
up to 10 miles deep; enemy forces still separated the two
halves of Bradley's US Army, but the vigorous British and
Canadian offensive southwards towards Caen was drawing
off German strength. Montgomery had kept the initiative.
And in Italy, Alexander's advance continued with full
momentum north of Rome. Militarily, the scheduled Anglo-
American strategic talks could not have opened in better
circumstances: Brooke met Marshall, King and Arnold at
Euston at 7.30 p.m., 9 June, and the British and American
COS met in CCS session at 11.30 a.m. next day. Indeed, this
June series of CCS discussions seemed surrounded by optimism; agreement proved easier to reach than at any other
CCS conference so far – perhaps too easy: so smooth were
discussions that they missed possible drawbacks which the
cut and thrust of outspoken argument might otherwise have
revealed. The first meeting on 10 June dealt with current
'Overlord' and Italian progress, and touched upon latest
operations in South-East Asia.[11]

Harold Nicolson wrote next day: 'There is a continual
crowd around the ticker-tape in the House of Commons
corridor. There are all sorts of rumours buzzing through the

smoking-room. And there is the hourly expectation that Winston may make another statement.'[12] Churchill was in fact preparing for a visit to France the following day – his first since his despairing mission to see Reynaud at Tours four years and one day earlier. By 11 June the allied bridge-head in France had been fully established. The next task would be to consolidate the lodgement area for the decisive push forward; Montgomery had firm plans for this allied break-through, signalling Brooke during this Monday: 'My general objective is to pull the Germans on to the 2nd Army so that 1st (US) Army can extend and expand.'[13] Unfortunately, the policy would soon run into Anglo-American misunderstandings.

On the supreme strategic level, Anglo-American co-operation seemed to continue promising when the CCS met for the second meeting on 11 June, this time at Stanwell Place, Middlesex. The US and British COS agreed to stop the Italian campaign at the Apennines or at the Pisa-Rimini Line. Thereafter would be 'an amphibious operation to be mounted from the Mediterranean with target date 25 July ... this operation would be of approximately 3-divisional assault lift ... the objective for the operation would be determined later'. Plans would be made for possible attacks on Sète, Istria or in the Bay of Biscay.[14] Brooke's diary entry showed him to be well satisfied: 'Now at last we had put the south France operation in its right strategic position. By the time we reached the Pisa-Rimini Line, the Italian theatre should have played its part in holding the German reserves away from Northern France. We could then contemplate the landing in southern France to provide a front for French forces from North Africa and to co-operate on southern flank of "Overlord" operations. The Bay of Biscay landings did not attract me.'[15] This had been Brooke's attitude from the start; he had never considered the Italian campaign to be an end in itself, and his objections to other Mediterranean operations had stemmed from the fear that they might detract from the Italian offensive before the latter provided best help for 'Overlord'. The Pisa-Rimini Line would mark an excellent termination point, and to Brooke the CCS decisions on the 11th matched discussions in London with Wilson at the beginning of May. But to the commanders in Italy the situation was no longer the same: the allies were pushing vigorously forward – and Alexander's appreciation on 7 June had made tentative suggestions for a continued campaign either westwards towards France or eastwards towards Austria; Churchill, at the Staff Conference on the 8th, had seemed attracted towards an offensive in Istria. The CCS decisions so easily reached on the 11th might soon encounter fresh complications.

No progress seemed possible with the Anglo-American argument over 'spheres of influence'. A telegram from Roosevelt reached Churchill on the 11th: the proposed Anglo-Soviet agreement over Greece would result 'in the division of the Balkan region into spheres of influence.... We believe efforts should preferably be made to establish consultative machinery.' Churchill hastened to reply: 'I am much concerned to receive your message. Action is paralysed if everybody is to consult everybody else about everything before it is taken.' He proposed the arrangement should have a 3-month trial period.[16] Whilst awaiting Roosevelt's answer, Churchill abandoned diplomatic discussions to visit troops in the operational area; his pleasure was given added spice by the presence of possible danger – Montgomery had signalled Brooke: 'Roads not – repeat not – 100 per cent safe owing to enemy snipers, including women. Much enemy bombing between dusk and dawn. Essential PM should go only where I take him, and you must get away from here in early evening.'[17] Churchill apparently behaved himself during his day's outing on the 12th. 'For once,' wrote Montgomery, 'he was prepared to admit that I was in charge in the battle area.' The Prime Minister's party left for England at 6.15 p.m.; in London the War Cabinet had just assembled to hear the Vice-CIGS give an account of the present military situation. 'US forces on the east side of the Cherbourg Peninsula were outflanking Montebourg and had captured Carentan. Further to the east, the Americans were now advancing south of Colombières, and had captured the Forest of Cerisy. The British, in the neighbourhood of

Bayeux, had reached Hottot and Tilly-sur-Seulles. Canadians advancing on Caen had met considerable opposition in the early stages of the battle, but were now astride the Caen-Bayeux road.'[18]

Hitler now placed increasing reliance on a totally new form of counter-attack. Later that night strange stuttering sounds could be heard over South England; these sounds suddenly ceased and moments later came violent explosions. Hitler had launched his secret weapon, long discussed by the War Cabinet and COS under the code-name 'Crossbow' but now to be called pilotless aircraft and later V-1s. First estimates indicated 27 of these bombs had landed on England during the night of 12/13 June, each travelling at between 350-390 m.p.h. Hitler hoped they would create sufficient damage and panic to force the British people to demand peace; their effect would, he believed, be multiplied by their newness and eerie, automatic abilities. Rumour would feed upon rumour, and already these had begun. 'There have been mysterious rocket-planes falling in Kent,' wrote Nicolson next day, 13 June. 'The thing is very hush at the moment.'[19] The pilotless aircraft would be discussed by the War Cabinet at 6.30 p.m., at the second of two meetings held this Tuesday, and the subject received brief attention at the CCS session which started in the War Cabinet offices at 11.30 a.m.

This CCS meeting then switched back to Italy, and to approval of a directive to Wilson to formally limit the Italian campaign south of the Pisa-Rimini Line. Amphibious operations after this objective had been reached would be decided later, but the CCS tended to favour either an initial landing at Sète designed to lead to the early capture of Bordeaux, or a descent on the west coast of France. Target date would be 25 July, 'always provided that this does not limit the completion of the operation south of the Pisa-Rimini Line'.[20] Respective lines of thought of the British and American COS had therefore continued to run parallel.

Churchill expressed approval over CCS progress, but he took no part in the accompanying COS discussions. His anger over de Gaulle had continued undiminished, and he insisted upon referring the French leader's behaviour to War Cabinet meetings at 4.30 and 6.30 p.m. this Tuesday, 13 June, especially complaining over de Gaulle's attitude towards the issue of currency notes for liberation forces. The British Government had been prepared to allow the French Committee to issue notes from France, but the Americans had refused. Special notes had thus been printed in the States, but de Gaulle now declared these should be replaced by currency issued under the authority of the French Committee. The War Cabinet could think of no way to break through this tangle. But at least an apparent improvement had come about with the other Anglo-American diplomatic difficulty. Churchill told the 4.30 War Cabinet meeting that Roosevelt now agreed to the Anglo-Soviet arrangement for Greece and Roumania for a 3-month period, on the understanding 'that we should be at pains to make it clear that we were not establishing any post-war spheres of influence'.[21] But this telegram from Roosevelt, received during the day, failed to end the dialogue; Roosevelt had sent the signal without informing the State Department, and when Hull returned from a short holiday he immediately revived the issue.

War Cabinet Ministers met again at 6.30 on the 13th to discuss the V-1 attacks the previous night. Portal said 11 pilotless aircraft had been used, not 27 as previously thought. 'The aircraft did not appear to be controlled by wireless and their speed was relatively low. It was possible, however, that the enemy would be able to follow up with a heavier attack.' The Home Secretary shared this attitude of cautious optimism. 'The reports of the damage done by the pilotless aircraft which had landed in London showed that the effect was no greater than a parachute mine and was rather less than an up-to-date 2,000 lb bomb.'[22]

The Combined Chiefs of Staff held their final meeting next afternoon, 14 June. Discussion centred upon the Pacific and South-East Asia, with the Americans underlining drawbacks to proposed British 'Middle Strategy': US operations in the Pacific were advancing so fast that a British contribution might not be required, and the Americans were seriously worried by the growing weight of Japanese attacks in China, and would therefore prefer a continuing concentration on northern Burma. Since the British seemed determined to deploy an assault force somewhere in the Far East, they urged it should be used in operations from the Indian Ocean towards the South China Sea, rather than causing a diversion of strength by shifting to the south-west Pacific. The British COS therefore agreed to re-examine the Indian Ocean strategy, with an immediate target of Sourabaya as a prelude to an attack on Borneo. They did however stress the disadvantages of the latter idea: to attack North Borneo in the late summer, 1945, Sourabaya must be captured by winter, 1944 – and this target would be heavily defended. The COS therefore continued to prefer their previous 'Middle Strategy' plan, and the divergence of views continued. Brooke clashed with Marshall over the importance of North Burma in a meeting next day, 15 June; although attended by respective American and British colleagues, this discussion was not apparently considered a formal CCS session and no official minutes were taken. Brooke commented in his diary: 'I found it quite useless to argue with him.'[23]

The American COS left London on 16 June, with Marshall and Arnold travelling to North Africa and Italy – and to complications which would cloud the decisions reached so easily in London. Meanwhile, German counter-attacks against the 'Overlord' advance had begun to increase. Montgomery had absorbed these piecemeal thrusts, and intended to use them to draw the German weight on to the British and Canadian 2nd Army. Reports were nevertheless anxiously studied in London and, because the 2nd Army had apparently failed in a break-out attempt – although no such attempt had been intended – rumours increased that the advance had faltered. Memories of Anzio were still too fresh. Injected into this tense situation was a sudden increase in V-1 attacks. Late on 15 June the Germans launched the full-scale *Vergeltung* – retaliation – offensive, and during the next 24 hours over 200 of these missiles were thrown across the Channel. Ministers met for a special meeting of the War

Cabinet in the Prime Minister's Room, House of Commons,
at 11.45 next morning. The Home Secretary said first reports
showed about 50 people had been killed and 400 injured, but
warned that later figures would probably be higher. Morrison
added: 'In view of the relatively low speed with which the
(pilotless) aircraft approached, the existing warning system
appeared to be adequate.... The missiles seemed to give
rise to extensive rather than intensive blast damage.'
Air Marshal Sir Douglas Evill, Vice-COAS, gave details of
the V-1's estimated performance. 'Normally the aircraft
appeared to fly from 1,000 to 4,000 feet, so that they were
well within range of light anti-aircraft guns or balloons, and
their speed made them vulnerable to fighter attack.' Ministers
agreed to hold a Staff Conference at 5 p.m.; this second
meeting agreed: 'i) To request the Supreme Commander,
AEF, to take all possible measures to neutralize the supply
and launching sites.... iii) That, for the time being ... the
AA guns both inside and outside the London area should
continue to engage pilotless aircraft.' This latter decision
had been made despite the risk of bringing down aircraft
in the London area which might otherwise have flown
over.[24]

Hitler journeyed to Margival, near Soissons, to confer with
his commanders, Rundstedt and Rommel, on 17 June. Both
urged the Führer to avoid bleeding the German armies to
death in Normandy, and advocated an orderly withdrawal
to the Seine prior to a defensive battle in strong positions.
Hitler refused. On the same day, as Montgomery prepared
plans for the next stage of the 'Overlord' offensive, and as
the Americans completed their occupation of the entire
Cherbourg Peninsula, General Marshall held an important
conference with Alexander and Wilson to discuss next
operations in the Mediterranean. The British commanders
were impressed by the argument that 'Overlord' needed more
ports for the arrival of further divisions from America, hence
underlining the importance of amphibious operations in the
south of France. They nevertheless seized upon complications resulting from the recent CCS discussions in London,
and Wilson, who had previously been prepared to show

favour for the 'Anvil' idea, now agreed with Alexander that all efforts should be made to go beyond the Pisa-Rimini Line and swing east towards the Balkans and Austria. Opportunities had opened which were too good to miss; as Alexander had said on the 7th, his armies were going so well that neither the Apennines nor Alps would stop them; the allies had won the initiative. Moreover, both Wilson and Alexander were perturbed by the withdrawal of troops from the 5th Army, despite the CCS stipulation that no forces would be taken from the Italian battle until German forces south of the Pisa-Rimini Line had been destroyed. On the day Marshall arrived in Italy, 17 June, one US division began to leave under the preparations for landings at Bordeaux or near Marseilles or Toulon; a second would depart on the 24th, a third on the 27th, and a fourth in the first week of July. Alexander took the unusual step of asking a civilian Minister, Harold Macmillan, to travel to London and put the military case to Churchill. Macmillan consented to act as military go-between, and would reach London on 21 June. Meanwhile another conference with Marshall would take place on the 19th.

'Bombers stream over,' wrote Nicolson on 18 June, 'totally disregarding the secret weapons which scream across Kent underneath them....'[25] Montgomery issued orders for the next phase: 1st US Army would take Cherbourg and maintain a line some 10 miles to the north of St Lô; 2nd Army was to take Caen and to reorganize beyond the town to contain the bulk of the enemy forces; these movements should be completed by about 25 June. V-bombs continued to shrill and stutter across the south of England during this Sunday; one dropped on the Guards Chapel, Wellington Barracks, slaughtering 200 Guardsmen attending a service. Churchill ordered that the House of Commons should meet in Church House, offering greater protection than the Palace of Westminster, and the War Cabinet began to reuse the underground chamber known as 'The Hole', just off Whitehall. Ministers met in this gloomy hideaway on Monday, 19 June, to discuss the V-1 offensive; Morrison said total casualties so far reported amounted to 526 killed and 2,200 seriously injured, and he added that the Civil Defence Committee had considered whether evacuation from London should be started. 'The London schools were congested and, if a school were hit while the children were there, there would no doubt be much criticism. On the other hand, there was at present no public demand for evacuation.' Ministers agreed to risk deferring a decision for the moment.[26] Brooke described Churchill as 'in very good form, quite 10 years younger, all due to the fact that the flying-bombs have again put us into the front line'.[27]

Also on the 19th, the front line in France suffered from a disturbing development. High winds from the Atlantic whipped up the Channel into the worst gale for 40 years, and severe weather would continue for another seven days, dispersing convoys at sea and virtually stopping unloading on to 'Overlord' beaches. Supplies and reinforcements to the forward areas dropped drastically and rain bogged down front-line armour. The Germans rushed troops into Caen to take advantage of the delay in the allied offensive. And on this Monday, 19 June, the second half of the Marshall-Wilson conference in Italy failed to remove fears felt by the Mediterranean commanders. Both Alexander and Wilson sent urgent signals to London stressing the need for further operations in Italy. The choice between Italy or the south of France would, believed Wilson, show 'whether our strategy in the coming months was to be aimed at the defeat of Germany in 1944 or in the first half of 1945'.[28] While these difficulties arose in both France and Italy, Soviet forces began their promised summer offensive. Preliminary moves had been made on the Leningrad front on 10 June; Viborg fell on 20 June and thus precipitated negotiations to end the Russo-Finnish war, and over 100 divisions ground forward towards Minsk, which would be taken on 3 July.

Telegrams from Alexander and Wilson reached Whitehall late on the 20th. Churchill called a staff conference for 2.45 p.m. on the 21st, attended by Smuts who had recently returned from a visit to Italy – and who immediately supported the argument put forward by the Italian commanders for a move north-east towards Venice and the Ljubljana

Gap: this would maintain the Italian momentum, would continue to tie up German forces which might otherwise be moved to face 'Overlord', would stimulate the Yugoslav Partisans, and might eventually result in a common front with the Russians against Germany's sensitive south-east flank. This proposal, originally put forward by Alexander, had received full support from Wilson, although the latter had previously considered an amphibious assault on the Istrian peninsula might be preferable, making for Trieste. Discussion at the Wednesday afternoon staff conference failed to lead to definite decisions, despite the meeting lasting two hours. Brooke had been disturbed by the case put forward by the Mediterranean commanders: an upset at this point with the Americans might complicate the primary objective of pushing forward to the Pisa-Rimini Line, and the CIGS had not abandoned his support for the CCS decision that the line would be a good stage at which to terminate the Italian campaign.[29] But as the staff conference drew to a close on the 21st, Harold Macmillan reached Whitehall on his military mission, and at 6 p.m. he began talks with Churchill at 10 Downing Street; Gammell, Wilson's Chief of Staff, had also arrived in London. The stage was being set for renewed intensive debate; another staff conference began at 10.30 p.m. next day, Thursday, 22 June. Churchill still displayed caution and declined to commit himself either for against 'Anvil' or for Alexander's plan, 'Armpit', which was explained in detail by Macmillan. Portal seemed attracted to the idea of a further Italian advance: the air force would stay as a single unit instead of being split between two theatres; moreover, Portal had favoured a further advance in the staff conference discussions on 8 June – and Churchill had inclined towards his views. Brooke remained doubtful and reserved his position. The meeting merely agreed that 'Anvil' was in any event preferable to a landing on or near Bordeaux, 'Caliph', which was far from any base and from the allied line in the north. The COS were asked to undertake detailed studies.[30] Churchill kept Macmillan until 2 a.m. after the meeting, and Alexander's emissary now believed the Prime Minister to be 'getting very worked up and interested in the immense strategic and political possibilities'.[31]

Also on this Thursday, Anglo-American relations received another jolt. Hull in Washington had continued to agitate against the 'spheres of influence' scheme, and had put forward strong opposition when he had belatedly learnt of Roosevelt's 12 June signal apparently accepting the idea. 'Mr Churchill's further exposition on the British case,' he had told Roosevelt on the 17th, 'did not overcome our objections or seem to us to warrant any change in our views.'[32] Then, on 19 June, Churchill had informed Roosevelt that the Russians had already been told of Britain's formal agreement to the plan following apparent US support. In view of Hull's objections, Roosevelt protested on the 22nd over this premature move. Simultaneous with the arrival of this signal came a telegram from Lord Moyne, British Minister of State in Cairo, showing the American Ambassador to Greece had revealed Roosevelt's latest message to the press. 'A slight sense of exasperation on W's part,' noted Eden, 'and on mine.'[33] 'The Russians are the only Power that can do anything in Roumania,' signalled Churchill to Roosevelt, 'and I thought it was agreed between you and me that on the basis of their reasonable armistice terms, excepting indemnities, they should try to give coherent direction to what happened there.... On the other hand, the Greek burden rests almost entirely upon us, and has done so since we lost 40,000 men in a vain endeavour to help them in 1941.' The Prime Minister's tart message ended: 'I cannot admit that I have done anything wrong.'[34] With this Anglo-American diplomatic tangle still to be untied, Churchill now revealed his position in the likely military upset between the two allies: he met the COS in the evening of the 23rd and indicated support for Alexander's proposed advance towards Venice. Brooke pointed to disadvantages even apart from the disagreeable clash with the Americans which would result: the advance beyond the Pisa-Rimini Line would not start until at least the end of September, and the allies would therefore be fighting a winter campaign in the Alps. 'It was hard to make him realize,' wrote the CIGS in his diary, 'that if we took the season of the year and the topography of the country in league against us, we should have three enemies instead of one. We were kept up till close on 1 a.m. and accomplished nothing.'[35]

Churchill began to draft a paper on the 'Armpit' proposal. On the same day the British COS received a memorandum by Eisenhower with a strong intervention in favour of 'Anvil'. 'France is the decisive theatre. The CCS took this decision long ago. In my view, the resources of Great Britain and of the US will *not* allow us to maintain two major theatres in the European War, each with decisive missions.' Next day, 24 June, the American COS signalled their entire agreement. 'The essential requirement is the support of "Overlord".... This demands a rapid concentration of maximum forces against the enemy in the decisive theatre of France. Such a concentration can only be achieved by seizing another major port in France....' The Americans urged 'an "Anvil" at the earliest possible date....'[36] This demand thoroughly alarmed the British CIGS: the 'earliest possible date' might threaten immediate operations in Italy designed to secure the area south of the Pisa-Rimini Line, despite assurances given by the Americans at the recent CCS meetings; Brooke's fears seemed justified that the pressure for 'Armpit' might cause upset even for the attainment of this basic objective. On the other hand the American arguments had been strengthened by the ground situation in France: delay caused primarily by the weather had thrown out Montgomery's programme; German opposition at Caen and Cherbourg remained strong, yet Montgomery had hoped both would fall by 25 July. On 23 July the allies only stood on the line which had been prescribed for the 11th. Montgomery remained confident: German armour continued to be drawn on to the British on the left of the allied line, as he had intended, and he felt he could keep the battle balanced; to him the actual programme seemed of lesser importance. But others believed the failure of the time-table indicated a flagging offensive.

The tactical situation in North-West Europe therefore

became linked with the Anglo-American strategic debate. And now Churchill plunged in with all the power his pen could muster. 'I have laid an egg,' he told Eden on Sunday, 25 June.[37] A copy of his paper was immediately sent by dispatch-rider to Brooke, and the document received full COS attention next morning, 26 June. 'Whether we should ruin all hopes of a major victory in Italy, and all its front,' wrote Churchill, 'and condemn ourselves to a passive role in that theatre, after having broken up the fine allied army which is advancing so rapidly through that peninsula, for the sake of "Anvil", with all its limitations, is indeed a grave question for His Majesty's Government and the President, with the Combined Chiefs of Staff, to decide.... I should greatly regret to see General Alexander's army deprived of much of its offensive power in Northern Italy.' Neither an assault upon Sète or Marseilles would directly influence the present battle in 1944, claimed Churchill.[38] The COS avoided full discussion for the moment, but Brooke remained unconvinced. 'We are up against the same trouble again,' he wrote in his diary, 'namely saving Alexander from being robbed of troops in order to land in southern France.' The main priority must be to reach the Pisa-Rimini Line; pressure from Churchill and Alexander to go further would merely complicate this aim. 'We shall have great difficulty with the Americans, especially as Alex keeps talking about going to Vienna.'[39] A COS signal to Washington, drafted at the meeting on the 26th, therefore made no mention of the dangerous 'Armpit' but concentrated on the first objective now threatened by the withdrawal of troops for 'Anvil'. 'We are convinced that the allied forces in the Mediterranean can best assist "Overlord" by completing the destruction of the German forces with which they are now in contact, and by continuing to engage, in maximum strength, all German reinforcements deployed to oppose their advance. Any compromising of the prospects of the destruction of the enemy Armies in Italy at this crucial phase of the war, without a compensation in the early destruction of equal forces elsewhere would, in our opinion, be wrong.'[40] Brooke and Churchill were thinking along different lines; nevertheless, the COS telegram applied to both their views, even without referring to 'Armpit', and the Prime Minister gave his enthusiastic approval to the COS signal at a meeting during this Monday evening, and it was accordingly dispatched.

The diplomatic tussle over 'spheres of influence' at last seemed to be reaching an amicable end. 'It appears,' signalled Roosevelt next day, 27 June, 'that both of us have inadvertently taken unilateral action in a direction that we both now agree to have been expedient for the time being.' Perhaps with a knowledge of the COS telegram on Italy which by now had reached Washington, the President added: 'It is essential that we should always be in agreement in matters bearing on our allied war effort.'[41] Yet the Soviet Ambassador informed the Foreign Office three days later that, in view of previous US doubts, the Soviet Government thought it better to consider the matter further and would deal direct with America – to which Churchill angrily wrote: 'Does this mean that all we had settled with the Russians now goes down through the pedantic interference of the United States?'[42] But the dispute subsided – to be replaced by another. America had been quarrelling with Colonel Péron's Government in the Argentine for some time, and Hull had made no secret of his desire to overthrow the dictator; the American Ambassador had been recalled earlier in the month and the US State Department pressed Britain to sever diplomatic relations. Eden resisted – Hull's attitude was 'unreasonable': nearly half the British meat ration came from the Argentine, and a large amount of British capital remained invested in the country. Then, at the end of June the British Ambassador was 'recalled for consultation' as a result of US insistence.

So, as June finished, Anglo-American relations were again stumbling through a sticky period. The British COS anxiously awaited the reply to their Washington signal on Italy, and feared the worst. Meanwhile, news from France improved. Cherbourg fell on 26 June, and Montgomery signalled Brooke next day: 'My general broad plan is maturing. All the decent enemy stuff, and his Panzer and

Panzer SS Divisions, are coming in on the 2nd Army front –
according to plan. That has made it much easier for the 1st
US Army to do its task.' And yet Anglo-American differences and misunderstandings had arisen even with the
tactical 'Overlord' situation. Montgomery believed Eisenhower to be complaining to Churchill over the apparent unwillingness to thrust the British/Canadian army into a break-
out offensive; Montgomery in turn believed some American
commanders to be too cautious. 'I tried very hard,' he wrote
to Brooke on the 27th, 'to get 1st US Army to develop its
thrust southwards towards Coutances at the same time as it
was completing the capture of Cherbourg.... But Bradley
didn't want to take the risk; there was no risk really.... I
have to take the Americans along quietly and give them
time to get ready; once they are really formed up, then they
go like hell.'[43]

War Cabinet Ministers assembled in the War Room at 6
p.m. on this Tuesday to hear extremely depressing news of
flying-bomb attacks. The Home Secretary reported that
about 1,600 people had been killed so far, and 4,500 seriously
injured; about 1,500 V-1s had been launched, 600 entering
the London area. Over 200,000 houses had been damaged.
'The Ministry of Works ... were finding it difficult to keep
up with the damage caused. The result was that considerable
numbers of people were homeless. The attacks had led to
serious loss of sleep and the fact that they went on continuously meant that there was no relaxation from the strain
... and, in particular, made parents anxious for the safety
of their children.' Herbert Morrison, himself a Londoner,
gave a severe warning, stronger than any issued during the
Blitz. 'After five years of war the civil population were not
as capable of standing the strain of air attack.... If flying
bombs were supplemented by rocket attacks, which according to reports might do as much damage as had been
experienced in the heaviest 1940-41 raiding, the Civil Defence
machine, which was much weaker in numbers than it had
been in 1940-41, might prove unable to cope ... and there.
might be serious deterioration in the morale of the civil
population.' Attlee and Anderson agreed. Churchill said he

realized the civil population remained under constant strain, 'but the hardships imposed on them must be considered in comparison with what was being suffered by the enemy population who were subjected to our air raids'. Yet he added: 'It would be unwise to rely on any diminution in the scale of casualties and damage even though our defences should improve.'[44]

Next morning, 28 June, the US reply regarding Italy and 'Anvil' reached London; Brooke immediately condemned the content as 'rude', and seemed justified. The harsh signal stated: 'The fact that the British and US COS are apparently in complete disagreement in this matter at this particular moment when time is pressing presents a most deplorable situation. We wish you to know now, immediately, that we do not accept the statement in your paper.... The desire is to deploy as many US divisions in France and as quickly as possible. A successful advance by Alexander's force in Italy does not promote this possibility.' With this reply, a situation now existed which seemed in complete contrast to the atmosphere surrounding the recent CCS talks in London, when decisions had been so easily reached; and yet, basically, the Americans and British COS, especially Brooke, were still advocating those CCS decisions: 'Anvil', and destruction of German forces south of the Pisa-Rimini Line. These decisions had however been clouded and complicated: by the apparent lack of 'Overlord' progress, which made the Americans even more anxious for another port to be obtained through 'Anvil'; by the excellent progress in Italy, which made the Mediterranean commanders, and Churchill, wish to press on for more. The Americans suspected, incorrectly, that the British COS supported the 'Armpit' proposal; while Portal had shown sympathy for it, the COS as a whole had not in fact decided upon such support, but Marshall and his colleagues feared 'Anvil' would be jeopardized, and hence pressed for early withdrawals from Italy – which in turn caused anxiety for the British COS. Once again, lack of clear Anglo-American understanding had resulted in a dangerous muddle. The British COS especially disagreed with the American statement that Alexander's advance in Italy would not help 'Overlord'; on the same day as the US signal reached London, intelligence reports arrived which indicated Hitler now expected the allies to follow up their Italian advantage, and the Führer had therefore decided definitely to hold the northern Apennines. This could only be at the expense of German strength opposing 'Overlord' or the Russian offensive. A signal therefore left London containing the British refusal to withdraw forces from Italy for the moment.[45] Churchill backed this telegram with a long message to Roosevelt: 'The deadlock between our Chiefs of Staff raises most serious issues. Our first wish is to help General Eisenhower in the most speedy and effective manner. But we do not think this necessarily involves the complete ruin of all our great affairs in the Mediterranean, and we take it bad that this should be demanded of us.' Next day, 29 June, a long signal from Roosevelt mentioned that Wilson had previously supported 'Anvil' and insisted that the original plan, as agreed by Stalin at Tehran, must be maintained. The last paragraph of this message, according to Brooke, finally revealed 'the basic reason for the opinions expressed'. This declared: 'Finally for purely political considerations over here I would never survive even a slight setback in "Overlord" if it were known that fairly large forces had been diverted to the Balkans.'[46] The British COS could not argue against this reference to the coming Presidential election. Moreover, American forces in total now comprised the major strength in the struggle against Hitler, and in Brooke's words: 'They (the Americans) therefore consider that they are entitled to dictate how their forces are to be employed.'[47]

Also on 29 June, Alexander signalled for urgent instructions: a decision had now become imperative. Under this pressure Brooke appreciated that the British COS might have to give way, and the CIGS was anyway not completely convinced that the withdrawals would mean 'the complete ruin of all our great affairs in the Mediterranean' as Churchill feared. This might apply to 'Armpit', but not to operations south of the Pisa-Rimini Line; thus Brooke wrote in his diary on the 30th: 'I am not certain that this need cripple

Alexander's power to finish crushing Kesselring.' Churchill had meanwhile ordered an aircraft to be prepared ready for a sudden dash to Washington, but the COS saw him at 10 p.m. on the 30th to express willingness to stand back in the clash. The COS attitude was described by Brooke as 'all right, if you insist on being damned fools, sooner than fall out with you, which would be fatal, we shall be damned fools with you, and we shall see that we perform the role of damned fools damned well'.[48] In official terms, the COS declared in a minute to Churchill that on military grounds they continued to oppose withdrawals from Italy at the moment, but 'we feel that in the broadest interests of Anglo-American co-operation there may be grave objection to laying ourselves open to the accusation that dragging out discussions, and employing delaying tactics, we have made "Anvil" impossible by reason of time alone.' The President had raised political questions which only Churchill could consider. 'We therefore take the view that as a decision must be reached at once and it is clear that the Americans are determined on grounds other than military to carry out "Anvil", and would in the final event withdraw their troops from Italy, the only course is to defer to the President's wishes.' Churchill told the meeting that he opposed 'Anvil' on the grounds that it could not bring early help to 'Overlord'. He had been impressed by Eisenhower's views, which, supported by Montgomery's view that it would be 90 days after a landing had been affected in the south of France before appreciable relief was afforded to 'Overlord', had first given rise to his grave doubts regarding 'Anvil'. Alexander had reported that troops were already being withdrawn, and his army units were having to 'look over their shoulder', causing uncertainty and added strain. Moreover, Roosevelt himself had mentioned operations in the Adriatic during the Tehran conference. But, after more discussion, Churchill agreed to draft a telegram based on the COS minute, and after a further meeting with the COS on the morning of 1 July the Prime Minister accordingly bowed to the American demands. His signal to Roosevelt still seemed belligerent: 'What can I do, Mr President, when your Chiefs

of Staff insist on casting aside our Italian offensive campaign,
with all its dazzling possibilities? ... If you still press upon
us the directive of your COS to withdraw so many of your
forces from the Italian campaign and leave all our hopes
there dashed to the ground, HMG, on the advice of their
COS, must enter a solemn protest.' Roosevelt's final word
reached London next day. 'We are still convinced that the
right course of action is to launch "Anvil" at the earliest
possible date.... I do not believe we should delay further in
giving General Wilson the Directive.... Will you ask your
Chiefs to dispatch it to General Wilson at once.' The directive left London on the same day: 'You will use every effort
to meet a target date of 15 August (for "Anvil").... You
will use all available Mediterranean resources not required
for "Anvil" to carry out your present directive with regard
to operations in Italy.'[49] The target date had therefore been
delayed from that decided upon at the CCS meetings in
London – 25 July.

The Burmese battle of Imphal had finally come to an end;
by the last week of June the Japanese were in full retreat.
Over 13,000 enemy dead had been counted and thousands
more must have died through starvation and disease. And
now the British-Indian 14th Army under Slim remained
determined to keep the initiative; the myth of the 'invincible
Jap' had been shattered, and despite the monsoon the offensive would be continued throughout July to batter the
Japanese back to the Chindwin. At last, after years of toil
and disaster, and terrible deadlock, British and Indian
jungle fighters could look forward with optimism, despite
continuing lack of resources. And June as a whole had been
the most successful month of any so far in the Second World
War – victories in Burma, the Pacific, Italy, France. Rundstedt, overall commander in North-West Europe, had been
asked on 1 July for his answer to the present military pre-
dicament, and had snapped: 'Make peace, you fools.' He
was relieved the same night; his successor, Gunther von
Kluge, would commit suicide seven weeks later.

But Britain still suffered. Herbert Morrison, Home Secretary, gave another grim report to the War Cabinet at 5.30 p.m. on Monday, 3 July. 'The weight of high explosives dropped in London in the two weeks ended 29 June was 650 tons, as compared with 770 tons dropped in London from aircraft in the worst fortnight of the 1940-41 raids.... The main weight had fallen in the boroughs south of the river, Lewisham, Croydon, Greenwich and Southwark having suffered particularly. The total number of casualties to date was 17,328. Although the number of killed was relatively small, about 2,000, the total number of killed and seriously injured in London for the 14 days up to 29 June was 7,403 as compared with 16,456 for the whole month of September, 1940.... The bombs had a high blast effect and many casualties were due to broken glass.' Mr H. U. Willink, Minister of Health, explained that on average the attacks were destroying about 500 houses and damaging 21,000 each day. 'In the first 12 days it had been possible to carry out repairs on about 8,000 houses a day, and, although the rate of repairs had now risen to around 12,000 a day, this meant that arrears were accumulating at the rate of 9,000 houses a day.' Ministers were also informed of the likelihood of increased rocket attacks; up to 50 tons a day might be dropped in London for several months. Churchill commented: 'It was for consideration whether we should not publish a list of, say, 100 smaller towns in Germany, where the defences were likely to be weak, and announce our intention of destroying them one by one by bombing attacks.' Minister agreed this plan should be considered.[50]

But consideration would also be given to a far more drastic form of retaliation – poison gas. Duncan Sandys and Lord Cherwell attended a COS meeting next morning, 4 July; reports indicated fighter aircraft were not proving fast enough against flying-bombs, AA guns were having difficulty finding their targets, and launching sites were difficult to bomb. Later in the day the COS Secretary sent a note to the Joint Planning Staff. 'At their meeting today, the COS instructed the JPS to examine the desirability and practicability of using gas as retaliation for "Crossbow" attacks. The report should consider the use of gas (a) against the

"Crossbow" area alone, (b) as a general retaliation against Germany. It is understood that Combined Operations HQ have a particular interest in the possible German reactions to the use of gas because of the vulnerability of beaches and beach organizations to gas attacks.'[51] The Joint Planners would complete their report within 24 hours.

Meanwhile, General Wilson reached London during this Tuesday, 4 July, to discuss the Italian campaign following his recent directive. Brooke urged greater efforts to smash Kesselring's forces before they reached the Pisa-Rimini Line, rather than looking longingly at 'dreams of an advance on Vienna'. And yet at a meeting between the CIGS and Churchill at 6.30 p.m., the Prime Minister demanded another effort to drag the Americans from their 'Anvil' preference. 'He has prepared a telegram,' wrote Brooke anxiously, 'and I only hope we succeed in stopping him from sending it.'[52] The signal remained safe at 10 Downing Street. But the next few days would be filled with discussions on the three pressing problems of 'Overlord', Italy and the flying bombs. The 'Overlord' break-out attempt had still to be made, and criticism grew in Washington. In Italy, Siena had fallen on 3 July, and by the 5th American forces faced Volterra, while the 8th Army had deployed near Arezzo, but Kesselring had regained full control of his army and now made a stand. Alexander had to pause while he gathered his forces for the next assault.

And still the flying bombs came screeching across the Channel. On 5 July the Defence Committee considered Churchill's suggestion for bombing reprisals on small German towns, and decided against the idea. Brooke believed such retaliation would be insufficient: the Germans must fully realize the advantages being gained from the V-1 offensive – including the diversion of nearly 50 per cent of the British air effort in attempting to stop the attacks – and the loss of successive small German towns would not be enough to make Hitler throw these advantages away.[53] Also on 5 July the COS discussed more deadly measures. Before Brooke and his colleagues lay the JPS report on possible use of poison gas; and once again the suggestion that Britain might initiate this form of warfare, banned by the Geneva Protocol, was turned down on military grounds. The JPS declared that 'the use of gas, even employed continuously and in large quantities against these sites, all of which have not yet been located, would not be likely to have more than a harassing effect.... In our view, it would be impossible to confine the use of gas to attack against "Crossbow" installations, and it would be likely that if we initiated it for this purpose, it would bring about the widespread use of gas in Europe.' The report continued: 'There are three particular reasons why we recommend the rejection of gas as a measure of retaliation against Germany. i) It is unlikely to stop the Germans making use of "Crossbow" weapons. ii) In Europe the use of gas at present would be militarily to our disadvantage, having regard in particular to the possibility of its use by the Germans against the beaches in "Overlord" and "Anvil", and to the general slowing down of operations which is likely to result. iii) The initiation of the use of gas would require the agreement of the American, Dominion and Russian Governments.' Moreover, the Germans might retaliate by the use of gas against London. 'The most likely form of retaliation by the Germans would be the use of a mixture of gas and HE in "Crossbow" weapons', and although casualties would not be high, 'the psychological effect should not be underestimated. Coming upon the top of "Crossbow" attacks which have already continued for three weeks, the strain on civilian morale would be very considerable, and the effect might be serious.' The JPS examined the use of gas against Germany in detail. 'At first attacks would probably be made with phosgene which would achieve greater surprise and a greater initial effect upon morale. As soon as the enforcement of strict defensive precautions made the use of non-persistent gas less effective, we should probably turn to attacks with mustard gas.' Such an offensive 'might well cause serious but not uncontrollable panic'.[54] The COS approved this report, and passed their recommendation to Churchill that gas should not be used. Churchill, despite this COS decision, would soon return to the subject – and subsequent discussion would also bring forward the

possibility of an even more terrible form of retaliation:
bacteriological warfare. On 6 July the Prime Minister gave
a sombre account to the House of Commons. 'We must
neither underrate nor exaggerate. In all up to 6 o'clock this
morning about 2,750 flying bombs have been discharged from
the launching stations along the French coast. A very large
proportion of these have either failed to cross the Channel
or have been shot down and destroyed by various methods.'
Churchill hinted at retaliation. 'The flying bomb is a weapon
literally and essentially indiscriminate in its nature, purpose,
and effect. The introduction by the Germans of such a
weapon obviously raises some grave questions, upon which I
do not propose to trench today.'[55]

Churchill and other Ministers met the COS for a staff
conference at 10 p.m. on the 6th, and strain and exhaustion
broke through. Eden described the meeting as 'really ghastly'
and believed it could not have happened 12 months before.
'We were all marked by the iron of five years of war.' The
main purpose of the meeting had been to discuss the Far
East, but discussion soon expanded to cover European
operations and other subjects, with Churchill attacking
Alexander and Montgomery, and even quarrelling with
Attlee over the political future of India. As far as Italy
was concerned, Churchill had underlined his attitude with
an aggressive minute to the COS earlier in the day. Let the
Americans take all they needed for 'Anvil', he declared, 'but
let us at least have a chance to launch a decisive strategic
stroke with what is entirely British and under British command. I am not going to give way about this for anybody.
Alexander is to have his campaign ... an intense impression
must be made upon the Americans that we have been ill-
treated and are furious. ... After a little we shall get together
again; but if we take everything lying down there will be
no end to what will be put upon us.' Brooke disagreed; with
his lack of enthusiasm for 'Armpit', and his belief that something could still be salvaged from 'Anvil' – and perhaps with
his realization that the present position differed little from
the CCS decisions – a confrontation with Churchill became
inevitable. Now, at the staff conference, the CIGS and the

Prime Minister became involved in one of the most violent arguments they ever had with one another. Some flavour of this outburst emerges from the cold official minutes. Churchill began referring to his minute and to his desire to send a telegram to the President demanding no further Italian withdrawals. 'It might well be that our worst foreboding would be realized and pressure put upon us to withdraw further forces from the campaign in Italy to support the exceedingly unpromising operation which had been forced upon us.... Everything possible should be done to support Alexander at this juncture.' Churchill believed Bologna might be reached by mid-August, and Trieste by mid-September, and forces should be sent from Persia to give added strength. Brooke objected: 'The Prime Minister had underestimated the military task that confronted us in Persia. The maintenance of law and order in that country presented a more difficult problem than had been suggested.' And he disagreed with the idea of demanding an undertaking from the Americans that further forces would not be removed, until it was known for certain that such withdrawals were in fact intended. 'He did not want to put predatory ideas into their heads.' Churchill 'reiterated' that he wanted Alexander's plan to have 'at least the sanctity that the US COS demanded and the CCS had accorded to "Anvil"'. Cunningham warned that the effect of making such a statement to the Americans now 'might well be that the American COS would try and impose restrictions, at this stage, upon the limit of Alexander's advance'. Portal doubted the wisdom of making any bargain. But Churchill stood firm; he intended to draft a telegram to the President 'indicating that we could not expect Alexander to make firm plans unless he was certain of the resources he was going to have, and that we must have an assurance that these resources were inviolate'. The COS could merely bring themselves to 'take note' on the Prime Minister's decision.[56] Diary accounts by Eden and Brooke gave more descriptive versions of the meeting; according to the CIGS, Churchill was very tired after his Commons speech on the flying-bombs. 'As a result he was ready to take offence at anything. He began to abuse

Monty because operations were not going faster, and apparently Eisenhower had said that he was over-cautious. I flared up and asked him if he could not trust his generals for five minutes instead of belittling them.' Eden commented that the Prime Minister's remarks brought 'an explosion from CIGS' which continued when discussion turned to the Far East. During consideration of this subject, which according to Eden was 'meaningless when it was not explosive', Churchill once more reverted to his idea for 'Culverin' against Sumatra, as opposed to the Pacific Strategy proposed by the COS.[57]

Churchill after all decided against a message to Roosevelt concerning Italy. But Brooke's fears over Anglo-American conflict remained strong, especially after a visit to London by Alexander. On the day after the heated staff conference, the C-in-C addressed the War Cabinet, and revealed he had not abandoned his ambitious aims, fully supported by Churchill, to break through the Pisa-Rimini Line into the valley of the Po, thus splitting Kesselring's armies in half, and to establish bridgeheads over the Po from which operations could be launched in any direction which might be decided upon. He wanted to establish control over the quadrilateral Padua/Verona/Parma/Bologna, and then 'advance north-eastwards through the historical entry into Europe', thus threatening the whole of the enemy's position in the Balkans, and aiming at the Danube valley and Vienna. The Prime Minister 'fervently agreed'.[58] This War Cabinet meeting then discussed future world organization; Churchill excused himself – he had to lunch with the King – nor did he seem particularly interested. 'I am rather lukewarm,' he admitted. Cadogan commented in his diary: 'This is hopeless and v. naughty.' The subject had become urgent in view of a conference due to open at Dumbarton Oaks in America, on 21 August, to discuss post-war subjects centring upon the United Nations.[59]

'Overlord' still caused anxiety. Eisenhower now asked Montgomery to thrust forward with the British left in addition to the American right, and Brooke commented: 'Ike has been smouldering.' Montgomery refused to alter his overall plan, and informed Eisenhower on the 8th: 'The great thing now is to get 1st and 3rd US Armies up to a good strength and to get them cracking on the southward front.... Of one thing you can be quite sure: there will be no stalemate.'⁶⁰ And also on the 8th, British and Canadian forces reached the last stage in their bitter struggle to take the key city of Caen, intended as the central pivot for the main American swing into the enemy flank. RAF heavy bombers cracked the defences with over 2,000 tons of explosives; infantry pushed forward. Brooke, resting at home on Sunday, 9 July, received welcome news: 'Leading troops of 2nd Army now in (western) outskirts of Caen and pushing on tonight towards centre of city and the river lines.' On the same day, Rommel answered a question as to how long the German front in the West could be held. 'At the most 14 days to 3 weeks. Then the breakthrough may be expected. We have nothing more to throw in.'⁶¹ Yet another 9 days would crawl by before British and Canadian troops could reach the eastern outskirts of Caen, and Churchill warned the War Cabinet on the 10th against undue optimism. 'While the news from the various battle-fronts was good, the public should not be led to expect that the war against Germany would end this year.' Morrison described latest flying-bomb attacks: 3,197 people had been killed so far. 'There was a certain amount of discontent and tendency to criticize the Government.'⁶²

One major diplomatic concern in Whitehall now began to disappear – the long-lasting and time-consuming conflict between Britain and America over de Gaulle and his Committee. Problems over currency for the allied troops in France had been solved at the end of June within the framework of a mutual aid agreement. De Gaulle had left for a visit to America on 6 July, and Hull found him 'in a much more reasonable frame of mind'; likewise, Roosevelt and Hull adopted a more reasonable attitude towards the French leader and his Committee. De Gaulle's recent visit to France had indicated the strength of support he enjoyed; on the other hand the slowness of the allied advance had removed some of the panic urgency from the question of a civil administration. In this calmer atmosphere, Roosevelt announced on 11 July that America would now recognize the French Committee as the 'de facto' authority in the civil administration of France. Full recognition of de Gaulle's administration as the Provisional Government now appeared a mere formality and would eventually be granted in October. Yet as so often, the removal of one diplomatic problem merely resulted in its replacement by another. Greece came to the forefront again at the beginning of July, accompanied by ominous warnings of a future British military commitment. On the 7th King George of Greece cabled from Cairo seeking official allied support for Papandreou's Government following EAM repudiation of the Lebanon Charter, and he asked Britain to denounce these communist guerrillas.[63] Linked with this problem was the question of 'spheres of influence'; although the Americans had agreed to a three-month trial for the Anglo-Soviet scheme, Moscow's enthusiasm had apparently cooled. Churchill cabled Stalin on 12 July to ask whether the Soviet leader would not accept the trial period. Stalin replied that since the Americans had doubts, it would be better to wait – and later in the month Eden learnt the Russians had sent a military mission to the Greek communists. Yet on 13 July the COS discussed a possible British military mission to bolster Papandreou's non-communist administration, and as Brooke wrote: 'I can foresee a very serious military commitment very rapidly increasing.'[64] In May the Joint Planning Staff had reported to the COS that as many as 10 divisions might be needed for occupational duties in the Balkans, following a German withdrawal.[65] And these could only come from Italy, already being weakened by 'Anvil', itself designed to help the hard-pressed 'Overlord' situation.

British and Canadian troops had continued to pin down German armour around Caen, while Bradley's US units struggled southwards through the thickly-wooded marshy country in order to reach the Périers-St Lô road, where armour could be deployed for the breakthrough. Progress remained slow. Apparent stalemate in France; frustration over flying-bombs; exhaustion from the daily drudgery of decision-making – all these made Churchill now seek new and terrible possibilities to guard against further setbacks. On 10 July the seriousness of the flying-bomb situation had been emphasized by a COS meeting, at which Portal had warned that V-1s were becoming more efficient. 'During the last three days some 86 per cent of those which had not been shot down had reached the London area.' Moreover, Portal continued: 'Information had been received that a large rocket had landed in Sweden. Preliminary reports indicated that it was a very complicated piece of mechanism; that it was radio-controlled or operated, and that it had a warhead of some 12,000 lbs.'[66] This evidence, which had resulted from a trial flight from Peenemünde swinging away in the wrong direction, would prove beyond doubt the existence of the V-2. Now, on Wednesday, 13 July, the Vice-Chiefs of Staff met at 3.30 p.m. to discuss a minute from Churchill, sent individually to each member of the Vice-COS committee as an extra-security precaution. A comprehensive examination should be undertaken 'of the military implications of our deciding on an all-out use of gas, principally mustard gas, or any other method of warfare which we have hitherto refrained from using against the Germans, in the following circumstances: a) as a counter-offensive in the event of the use by the enemy of flying bombs and/or giant rockets developing into a serious threat to our ability to prosecute the war; or, alternatively b) as a means of shortening the war or of bringing to an end a situation in which there was a danger of stalemate.'[67] General Sir Archibald Nye, Vice-CIGS, told the meeting on the 13th that he believed 'the Prime Minister had in mind the possibility of a stalemate in the general military situation, which the introduction of chemical warfare in Europe might break in our favour. The initiation of chemical warfare in Europe might, however, have repercussions in the Far East, particularly if it could not be claimed as a measure of retaliation.' He suggested the examination should be 'confined to strictly military considerations and should exclude ethical and political factors. The effect upon morale should, however, be regarded as a military factor.' The Vice-COS asked the JPS to undertake studies. The official minutes continued: 'It was suggested that the Germans might react to the initiation of gas warfare by the employment of bacteriological warfare. The investigation should, therefore, include consideration of German readiness to undertake bacteriological warfare.' Churchill had himself stated in his minute that 'gas or any other method' should be considered.[68] The Joint Planning Staff completed their chilling report on 16 July. British use of gas in Europe would achieve an initial tactical advantage, but would thereafter restrict allied movements. 'The initial use of gas by us in Italy against the Pisa-Rimini position might hasten a break through the line, but thereafter would delay our advance. We believe that the Russians would lose more than they would gain were chemical warfare to start on the Eastern Front.... Public morale in those areas in England which might be affected (by retaliation) is less resilient than it was and might react unfavourably at first.' Gas was again ruled out. But the Joint Planners hinted that germ warfare might result in allied advantages. The JPS report concentrated on a bacteriological strain code-named 'N' – possibly anthrax. 'There is no known prophylactic against "N". If it can be used in practice, the effect on morale will be profound. It is improbable that the Germans will initiate biological warfare. There is no evidence to show whether they are in a position to retaliate in kind, were we to initiate it.... There seems to be little doubt that the use of bacteriological warfare would cause heavy casualties, panic and confusion in the areas affected. It might lead to a breakdown in administration with a consequent decisive influence on the outcome of the war.' The JPS report stated: 'If the claims of "N" are substantiated, its use could probably make a substantial change in the war situation.' But, for the moment, bacteriological warfare would be out of the question. 'There is no likelihood of a sustained attack being possible before the middle of 1945.' And the report concluded: 'The only military advantage to be gained from the use of gas lies in the surprise and that is a fleeting advantage. On the other hand we do not believe that for us to start chemical or biological warfare would have a decisive effect on the result or duration of the war against Germany.'[69] No further references are made in the official documents to this report or to suggestions that Britain might initiate gas or bacteriological warfare; no reference to this or any other discussion on this subject is to be found in the official histories. Yet, for one brief moment, Britain contemplated the use of these terrible weapons, which the Government had repeatedly declared she would never employ unless the enemy did so first. And the possibility exists that the JPS report of 16 July might have reached a different conclusion if Britain's development of the mysterious 'N' had been a year further advanced.

Churchill still disagreed with the American COS over 'Anvil'; he disagreed with the British COS over 'Armpit'; he seemed to support Eisenhower's view that Montgomery was not pushing forward with sufficient vigour; and the Prime Minister continued to clash with his COS over Far East plans. The latter received further attention at a Staff Conference on 14 July, but nothing definite had emerged after $2\frac{1}{2}$ hours' discussion. Brooke repeated the COS argument for the 'Middle Strategy', but Churchill again advocated 'Culverin' although he seemed reluctant to give a definite ruling. Attlee scribbled on a slip of paper and passed it to Eden: 'Two hours of wishful thinking.' Brooke pleaded with the Prime Minister: 'If the Government does not wish to accept our advice let them say so, but for Heaven's sake let us have a decision.' Churchill promised a definite answer within a week, but three days later he imposed still further delay by calling Mountbatten to London for talks; the Supreme Commander would arrive with Wedemeyer in the first week of August.[70]

Cadogan described the War Cabinet meeting on 17 July: 'PM is evidently ageing, and the rambling talk is *frightful*.' This meeting lasted from 5.30 p.m. to 9 p.m.; the most important topic proved to be the continued flying-bomb offensive, and Duncan Sandys proposed radical new defensive measures including a belt of fighters over the English Channel, a coastal gun system, and an inland fighter belt combined with the existing balloon barrage.[71] These

measures received further discussion at the COS meeting
next morning, 18 July. They involved the movement of 1,000
guns, the laying of 3,000 miles of telephone cable and the
transfer of 23,000 personnel. Yet the bulk of the operation
would be completed within four days – and figures for
downed flying-bombs would soar; as Churchill wrote: 'The
V-1 had been mastered.' But on 18 July, the day when the
COS discussed these V-1 defence measures, Brooke wrote in
his diary: 'The rocket is becoming a more likely starter',
and on the same day the 'Crossbow' Committee was informed
that 1,000 rockets might already be in existence.[72] Hitler's
latest weapon made an early advance in France all the more
imperative. And on this Tuesday Montgomery launched his
3-corps offensive to enlarge the bridgehead over the Orne from
Caen, while the Americans pushed in the St Lô direction. The
British commander did not however intend his Orne offensive to achieve a breakthrough; he still insisted this should
come in the west with the US 1st Army, while the eastern
push threatened Falaise and the open country beyond. But
when bad weather again clamped down on 19 July and
operations slowed, his critics once more complained at the
apparent failure of a supposed break-out attempt by the
British and Canadian 2nd Army. On the same day Churchill's
already shaky relations with Montgomery received another
jolt, when he learnt that the General had forbidden the
arrival of visitors to his HQ over the next few days; Churchill
believed this to be directed at him, and dressed in new blue
and gold dressing-gown he confronted Brooke to demand his
right to visit the Front. The CIGS asked Montgomery to send
a soothing note, and Churchill left for France on 20 July at
the start of a 4-day visit.

Almost a month before Churchill had complained to his
wife about feeling old, weary and exhausted; Mrs Churchill
had replied: 'But think what Hitler must feel like!' Now,
on 20 July, as Churchill inspected Cherbourg, Hitler staggered from the ruins of his conference room at his East
Prussia HQ, victim of an attempted military *putsch*. The
Führer had barely managed to escape an assassin's bomb:
his right arm hung stiff, his ear-drums were damaged, his

hair scorched and his clothes in tatters; but he recovered in time to meet Mussolini in the early afternoon and to give orders for the conspirators to be annihilated. Yet the attempted assassination revealed more forcefully than ever before the extent of German disintegration; and already, three days before, Germany had lost her most brilliant General when Rommel fell victim to an RAF low-level attack. Rommel, although seriously wounded, managed to survive – only to commit suicide in October under orders from Hitler. British War Cabinet Ministers discussed the attempt on Hitler's life on 24 July. 'There seemed little doubt,' said Eden, 'that there had been, and perhaps still was, a movement of considerable force in Germany behind the Generals. It was still impossible to judge what the consequences would be, but, if the German Government were successful in repressing the movement, the result for the time being would be to rivet the Nazi machinery still more firmly on the German nation.'[73] On the other hand political repression merely accelerated possibilities of military collapse, and daily reports reaching the Führer revealed mounting pressure against the Reich from the East, South and West. Red armies were approaching the Gulf of Riga, and further south swept over the Polish border to take Lublin on 23 July; in Italy, Leghorn fell on 19 July and Alexander's armies pressed on towards Forence. And, after a false start on 24 July, the massive break-out began from the right of the 'Overlord' bridgehead in operation 'Cobra'. For the next 48 hours heavy punches were placed against two sectors of a 20-mile front, with Eisenhower demanding still more aggressive action from the British left, and appealing to Churchill 'to persuade Monty to get on his bicycle and start moving'.[74]

In London further reports increased expectations of an early V-2 offensive. Ministers discussed the problem at 6 p.m. on 27 July and decided that 'the evacuation of the priority classes should be stimulated, and these classes should be extended to include mothers with schoolchildren.... Steps should be taken, without publicity, to move patients from the London hospitals.'[75] Ministers also hears excellent reports of the fighting in France: 'Cobra' was clearly going to be successful; the German front opposite the American front had begun to crumble, allowing a way to open for Patton's armour. Eisenhower had continued his campaign for greater British effort, renewing his personal appeal to the Prime Minister at a lunch on the 26th, but Churchill now showed himself ready to give partial support to Montgomery. He referred the War Cabinet to the statement in morning newspapers that there had been a serious setback to British troops on the Orne. 'This statement had been given out by a spokesman of SHAEF at midnight on the previous night. In fact, all that had happened was that on part of the front our forces had had to withdraw about 1,000 yards and that two villages had changed hands twice.' Ministers agreed with Churchill that 'a statement of this kind at the present juncture was unfortunate, more particularly in view of the feeling of disapproval in certain circles that our advance from the Normandy bridgehead had not gone faster'.[76] Churchill conferred with Eisenhower at a dinner immediately after this War Cabinet meeting, attended by Bedell Smith and Brooke, and aimed at smoothing relations. 'It did a lot of good,' wrote Brooke in his diary that night. 'There is no doubt that Ike is all out to do all he can to maintain the best relations between British and Americans. But it is equally clear that Ike knows nothing about strategy.' The CIGS immediately reported both Churchill's 26 July lunch with Eisenhower and his 27 July dinner to Montgomery, and he warned that Eisenhower 'has some conception of attacking on the whole front ... unfortunately this same policy ... is one that appeals to PM. Ike may, therefore, obtain some support in this direction.'[77] Churchill had hinted at such tendencies in a signal to Montgomery earlier in the day: 'It certainly seemed very importance for the British Army to strike hard and win through; otherwise there will grow comparisons between the two armies. ...' Montgomery replied to Churchill and Brooke in the same sense: he still intended to adhere to his policy of the giant sweep from the west, using the Americans; and by 29 July this US advance had acquired massive momentum, with armoured units racing south and west towards Avranches and Brittany.

Now military events in eastern Europe demanded British attention. One of the most tragic episodes of the war was about to begin – the Warsaw Rising. Already the Russian advance into Poland had led to Foreign Office discussion, and soon after the occupation of Lublin, west of the Curzon Line, Stalin had informed Churchill that the Moscow-backed Polish Committee of National Liberation intended to set up an administration 'on Polish territory'. This Committee, in direct rivalry to the British-supported Polish Government in Exile, had for many months been a source of Anglo-Soviet friction, but the Soviet Ambassador in London had hinted to Eden that the Russians hoped for a new body to be created, possibly including Mikolajczyk, Polish Prime Minister. The latter flew to Moscow at the end of the month. But even as these delicate diplomatic discussions started, an acute complication had been injected by the military situation at Warsaw. The Polish Government in Exile and the Underground Movement in Warsaw had prepared extensive plans for a general uprising, and on 26 July sought British assistance. The Foreign Office replied that distances prevented any effective help, and a rising could only be successful if it took place in agreement and co-operation with the Russians. On 29 July the Red Army reached the outskirts of Warsaw. On the same day Moscow radio broadcast an appeal from the Polish Communists to the Warsaw citizens; guns of liberation were now within hearing, declared this message, and 'the hour of action had already arrived ... by direct active struggle in the streets, houses etc., of Warsaw the movement of final liberation will be hastened'. Two days later Russian tanks were rumoured to have pierced German defences east of the city; at 5 p.m. next day, 1 August, the Warsaw Rising erupted. First news reached London next morning, swamped by signals reporting excellent progress in France. Avranches had fallen on 31 July and Patton's tanks advanced into Brittany. St Malo, Rennes and Vitré had been taken by the evening of 2 August. Von Kluge reported to Hitler's HQ: 'The whole Western Front has been ripped open ... the left flank has collapsed.' And on 3 August Montgomery ordered Patton to wheel the newly formed 3rd US Army east to push

hard for Le Mans. Similar heartening news arrived from
Italy, where flanking attacks on the enemy at Florence had
begun early in the month: German divisions disengaged
during darkness on 3 August and pulled back over the Arno,
and next day 8th Army units occupied the southern suburbs
of the city. This success virtually ended the campaign in
central Italy, and a 3-week pause would take place before
the assault on the Gothic Line: the allies had advanced 270
miles in 64 days, despite the withdrawal of troops for 'Anvil',
now code-named 'Dragoon'.

The spate of signals from France and Italy contrasted
sharply with the complete absence of news of Red Army
activity at Warsaw. The Russian thrust of 31 July had
faltered; tanks entering the outskirts proved not a spearhead
but an exposed flank, and on 4 August the Germans counter-
attacked. General Bor-Komorowski, commander of the Polish
Underground, asked the Polish Government in Exile to
appeal for help. Arrangements had already been made for
supplies to be dropped by aircraft from the Polish wing
serving with the allied armies in Italy, but bad weather had
prevented flying on the night of 3/4 August. Churchill
informed Stalin of the Polish request on 4 August, and added
that flights from Italy during the next night would attempt
to drop 60 tons of equipment and ammunition in the south-
west quarter of Warsaw. Of this flight by 15 aircraft, six were
lost and only two succeeded in reaching the city; and next
day Stalin sent an extremely discouraging reply to Churchill's
message. 'I think the information which has been communicated to you by the Poles is greatly exaggerated and does not
inspire confidence.... The Home Army of the Poles consists
of a few detachments which they incorrectly call divisions.
... I cannot imagine how such detachments can capture
Warsaw.'[78] By the end of the first week in August the
Russian forces had advanced no further, and the Germans
had begun to split the city into sectors to isolate the Polish
partisans. The Underground movement intensified their pleas
to the British, but a COS meeting on the 7th emphasized the
difficulties involved in supplying help – and also revealed a
lack of sympathy by Portal for the Poles. 'From the many

approaches made by the Poles in the course of the last few days,' said Portal, 'it appeared that they were trying to pass on to us the responsibility for any failure of the operations of the Polish secret army, which results from these forces having undertaken open warfare prematurely.' He claimed that operations to drop supplies on Warsaw were not practicable and added: 'It would be extremely difficult to locate particular streets and squares in a large city at night. It was one thing to risk heavy losses in getting through if one had a good chance of delivering the supplies, but quite another to risk such losses when it was not expected that the survivors would be able to drop the supplies in the correct place.' Next day, following further appeals, Portal agreed these almost suicidal flights from Italy should continue for the moment.[79]

By now the COS were once again confronting Churchill in the drawn-out argument over Far East policy. Mountbatten had reached London on the 4th with his Chief of Staff, and had had preliminary meetings with the CIGS on the 5th and with the COS on the 7th. The Supreme Commander inevitably concerned himself with more immediate operations against the Japanese, rather than those after the defeat of Germany, and these more immediate plans equally inevitably stemmed from recent activity in central and north Burma: the British/Indian success at Imphal and Stilwell's advance towards Myitkyina. Mountbatten had therefore brought with him details of two main schemes. The first, 'Champion', entailed an advance by Stilwell's force from Myitkyina to the line Katho-Bhamo, simultaneous with British airborne attacks on Kalewa and on the entrance to the Mandalay plain, after which the British would push beyond the Chindwin with Mandalay the ultimate objective. These operations would reopen north Burma sufficiently to provide substantial help to the Chinese, and would provide a base for clearing central Burma as soon as possible. But eventual clearance of central Burma would raise administrative problems which could only be solved by seizure of the port of Rangoon. Mountbatten's second plan, 'Vanguard', had therefore been conceived as an alternative, concentrating on a seaborne and airborne attack on Rangoon. This would force the enemy to withdraw to the south and hence enable the allies to clear north Burma with less difficulty. Stilwell would advance as in 'Champion'. But the drawback to 'Vanguard' lay in the additional forces which would be required. Mountbatten had submitted the outline of these plans to the COS on 23 July; now they had to be considered in the light of COS preference for an eventual Pacific Strategy and Churchill's renewed campaign for 'Culverin'. And, at the preliminary meeting on 7 August, the COS decided Mountbatten's immediate proposal for 'Vanguard' must be accepted, combined with elements of 'Champion'. Brooke explained this decision to a staff conference next day, starting at 11 a.m. and attended by Mountbatten, Wedemeyer, Attlee, Eden and Lyttelton, with Churchill in the chair. The CIGS intended to retain the Pacific Strategy for the future, while concentrating on Mountbatten's schemes for more immediate activity. 'The operations envisaged by Mountbatten would not absorb all the forces available. Considerable naval forces could be spared now, and air forces would become available after the defeat of Germany. His own view was that we should undertake as much of Plan "Champion" as was necessary to maintain our position covering the air route over the "Hump" during the period between the end of the monsoon and March 1945, and should launch a "Vanguard" at the earliest possible moment, which under present conditions would probably be not before March 1945.' Any naval forces which could be spared now should therefore be sent to the Pacific, to work in conjunction with Australian land forces as a British task force. Churchill continued to plead for 'Culverin'. 'An operation for the capture of Rangoon would result in the diversion of Japanese forces ... whereas an operation such as "Culverin" would not', but he preferred 'Vanguard' to 'Champion' since the latter 'appeared likely to commit us to a laborious reconquest of Burma from the north'. On the other hand, Churchill was 'horrified' to learn that 'Vanguard' could not be launched before the spring of 1945.[80] The Prime Minister seemed to be hesitating, yet refused to commit himself; Brooke wrote:

'Winston still hovers back to his tip of Sumatra', and Eden commented: 'W. harks back to "Culverin" always and generally seemed very tired and unwilling to address himself to the arguments. As a consequence Brookie became snappy at times which didn't help much. Portal was the most constructive of the COS.'[81] Two more discussions took place on the 8th, at 6 p.m. and 10.30 p.m., totalling 7 hours of talking, but a firm decision had still to be reached. Churchill said another staff conference would meet at noon the following day, 9 August.

First of all on the 9th the COS met at 10.30 a.m. to discuss another appeal from the Poles. General Sosnkowski had asked for flights from the Mediterranean by the Polish crews of 300 Squadron; Portal pointed out that only half the crews were in fact Polish, that the aircraft were urgently needed for other operations, and that the crews would have to be specially trained. 'Their chances of ever reaching their destination successfully would be very small and he could not recommend that the proposal should be adopted.' The General had also asked for the dispatch of the Polish parachute brigade to Warsaw, but Portal commented: 'It would require 125 Stirlings or over 200 Halifaxes to lift the complete Polish parachute brigade. At the risk of very heavy casualties during the course of their flight over Germany, this operation might be carried out ... provided that the aircraft were permitted to continue the flight and land on Russian airfields.... He did not believe that this was a practicable operation.' Portal summed up the situation: 'The only people who were physically capable of providing air cover for operations in Warsaw were the Russians.'[82]

Churchill and the COS met again for Far East discussions; and at last the marathon seemed to be nearing an end. The Prime Minister was swinging round to 'Vanguard', providing it could be launched sooner, and he had prepared a paper which seemed open to a compromise. The COS had also committed their position to paper, and Brooke suggested Ismay should draft a document combining the two. 'I told him (Ismay) privately,' wrote Brooke, 'that he was to draft it on our paper but with P.M.'s phraseology.' Another meeting began at 10.30 p.m., lasting until 1.30 a.m. and eventually resulting in a number of definite conclusions. Action should be taken along the lines of 'Champion' – 'the necessary steps must be taken to contain the Japanese in northern Burma' – and the 'Vanguard' proposal should be put to the Americans. 'If German organized resistance collapses early, it will be necessary to review the situation and decide between the operations against Rangoon and other operations, principally "Culverin" or a variant thereof....' Churchill had therefore managed to secure a mention for his favourite. Likewise the COS succeeded in obtaining agreement for a British contribution to the Pacific war, although on a reduced scale. 'The greatest offer of naval assistance should be made at once to the US COS, it being impressed upon them that it is our desire to share with them in the main operations against the mainland of Japan or Formosa. ... If this offer is declined in favour of support by the British fleet to General MacArthur's operations, we should propose the formation of a British Empire task force under a British Commander ... to operate under General Mac-Arthur's supreme command.' After further argument over wording and emphasis, a signal embodying these decisions would be despatched to Washington on 18 August, bringing an end to a seven-month debate. Brooke gave his verdict: 'It is not what we started out for and not ideal, but it saves as much as it can out of the wreck....'[83]

Military events in Europe entered one of the most dramatic months of the war. Now, at last, seeds sown at Casablanca, Quebec and Tehran bore fruit on the bloody battlefields of France and Italy, while the Red Army scythed onwards in the east. But mingled with the triumph as Patton's tanks raced into Le Mans on 8 August and the Canadians turned upon Falaise, came increasing pain at Warsaw, a tiny speck on the strategic map of Europe. A Polish representative came to see Brooke on the 9th, in the midst of the Burma talks, to plead for more help. 'I had some difficulty in calming him.'[84] The Polish Prime Minister saw Stalin during this Wednesday and begged for Red Army relief; the Soviet leader seemed sympathetic and promised help: none arrived. Stalin had also seemed responsive over the political and diplomatic questions concerning Poland's future, claiming frontier issues could wait and he had no intention of 'communizing' Poland.[85] But inevitably the lack of Russian military assistance for the Polish patriots in Warsaw became linked to these diplomatic issues: how far were the Russians denying help in order to have Polish nationalists slaughtered? Neither the COS nor the British War Cabinet apparently shared Polish suspicions; they seemed to accept that the Russian thrust towards Warsaw had been genuinely blocked and that the Polish rising had been premature, although British ill-feeling increased over Russian non-co-operation with facilities for aircraft attempting to send supplies.

Churchill gave stimulating war news to the War Cabinet at 6 p.m., 9 August. 'What might prove to be a battle of great importance is now being fought in Normandy. The British and Canadian attack south of Caen is proceeding satisfactorily and our armour is now within 6 or 7 miles of Falaise. The American forces, moving with great daring, are engaged in a wide encircling movement.' In Italy, preparations were being completed at full speed for two complimentary punches in the east and the centre against the Gothic Line: the first would aim up the Adriatic coast to Rimini and the second at Bologna. Alexander had been compelled to alter his plans in view of troop withdrawals for 'Dragoon' ('Anvil') against the south of France, and a small amphibious landing to aid the eastern attack had been cancelled; the British commander nevertheless remained optimistic. And yet Ministers at the 9 August meeting also discussed the despatch of troops to Greece, agreeing that '10,000 troops and 2-3 squadrons should be sent to Greece in the event of a German withdrawal', even though Brooke had long feared such a commitment would be at the expense of Italian strength.[86] Mediterranean matters would still cause complications. And early on Friday, 11 August, Churchill flew to the area to gain first-hand impressions, leaving Attlee in charge of the War Cabinet until he himself flew to the Mediterranean a few days later – the only time in the European war that

both Prime Minister and Deputy Prime Minister were absent
from the country together.

Churchill took with him his worries for Warsaw. Aircraft
again attempted to reach the city from Italy on 9 and 12
August, despite Portal's objections, but only a total of 7
reached the objective out of 36, and a despairing appeal came
from the Poles in the city on the 12th: 'We are conducting
a bloody fight.... We receive from you only once a small
drop.... The soldiers and the population of the capital look
hopelessly at the skies.' Churchill, now at Naples, sent this
appeal on to Stalin and asked: 'Can you not give them some
further help, as the distance from Italy is so very great?'[87]
Larger sorties from Italy on the 13th and 14th resulted in
23 aircraft reaching their targets, but at the cost of 11 lost
and 11 damaged. War Cabinet Ministers discussed the situation on the 14th. Portal said two squadrons had already been
diverted to attempt the flights to Warsaw, and 'it was hoped
that US aircraft would shortly start dropping supplies'. Eden
turned to another aspect of the problem: the Polish Government had pressed him to issue some statement that HMG
recognized the Polish Underground Movement as having
'belligerent status', hence giving the fighters added prestige
and greater theoretical protection under the Geneva Con-
ventions. Eden added he had previously replied that any
such statement would have to be countersigned by Moscow
to be of any value, an attitude which had 'evoked protest
from certain quarters in this country'. Eden therefore wished
to have his view confirmed by the War Cabinet; Ministers
agreed he should continue to maintain his previous position.[88] British and American diplomats in Moscow were
meanwhile pressing for Soviet co-operation: Harriman
wrote to Molotov on the 14th asking that US aircraft should
be allowed to use Soviet landing fields, to enable a shuttle
service over Warsaw from Britain. Vyshinsky replied two
days later: 'I am instructed ... to state that the Soviet
Government cannot go along with this. The outbreak in
Warsaw into which the Warsaw population has been drawn
is purely the work of adventurers.' On the same day Stalin
cabled Churchill to say Soviet arms were already being

dropped – a claim denied by the Poles – but repeating that 'the Warsaw action represents a reckless and terrible adventure'. Ministers in London were told on the 16th that a Russian liaison officer had been parachuted into Warsaw but had been killed. Eden described the general situation as one of 'great delicacy' and added: 'The consequences on Russian-Polish relations and Anglo-Soviet relations ... could not but be most unfortunate.' He felt it essential to press the Russians as strongly as possible, and Ministers agreed Churchill should be asked to cable Stalin – they also agreed it would be best if the Poles in Britain were kept as uninformed as possible.[89] The Prime Minister signalled Roosevelt on the 18th: 'An episode of profound and far-reaching gravity is created by the Russian refusal to permit American aircraft to bring succour.' The two leaders began to draft a joint appeal.[90]

Churchill had also been delving into murky Balkan affairs. On 11 August he had installed himself in 'the palatial though somewhat dilapidated Villa Rivalta' at Naples, and for the next two days enjoyed the view of Vesuvius and the bay while tangling with Tito. The latter seemed unresponsive to Churchill's pleas for a firm reconciliation between his partisans and the Serbs, nor would he agree to meet King Peter in an attempt to discuss Yugoslavia's future, although he commented privately to Churchill that he did not intend introducing a communist system into the country.[91] Yet signs had continued to accumulate indicating an early German withdrawal from the Balkans, increasing the urgency of both a Yugoslav and Greek settlement, and on 14 August General Wilson was asked to prepare plans for the possible dispatch of troops to Greece, following the War Cabinet decision of the 9th. Also on the 14th, Churchill left for Corsica to witness the most disliked operation of all: 'Dragoon', formerly 'Anvil'. On the same day a fresh Anglo-American squib exploded over this inflammable subject. The British Mission handed a note to the US COS: 'The British COS note that the US COS refer to "Dragoon" as a major operation on the same footing as "Overlord". They assume that this does not imply that "Dragoon" is to be regarded, after its launching, as necessarily having priority over the Italian campaign....' The US reply, on 26 August, would make no attempt at conciliation: 'The US COS consider "Dragoon" to be a major operation rendering direct support to "Overlord", and as such to have priority over the Italian campaign.'[92]

Usually Churchill thoroughly enjoyed visiting operational areas. Tuesday, 15 August, seemed an exception. The 7th Army under General Patch had been created for 'Dragoon', plus a mixed Anglo-American airborne division. Over 2,000 allied aircraft battered the shore defences; the enemy had only 200 aircraft with which to attempt a reply, while an allied naval force of 6 battleships, 21 cruisers and 100 destroyers added their massive fire-power. Early on the 15th three divisions were successfully landed between Cannes and Hyères, soon joining with the airborne divisions dropped during the night around Le Muy. The launching of 'Dragoon' provided a signal for French resistance fighters to rise and harass the Germans in the rear; German forces withdrew, and in the words of the British official historian: 'The assault on the Rhine Valley soon became a procession.'[93] And as the secondary action started in the south of France, the main operations in the north began a new and apparently unstoppable advance, which to 'Dragoon' critics seemed to emphasize its superfluity.

American armies thrust forward to surround the fifteen German divisions near Falaise; by 15 August only sixteen miles remained through which the enemy could escape. The battle ended five days later with the virtual destruction of about eight of the German divisions; nearly 30,000 prisoners had been taken and 15,000 enemy had been killed. Further south an American division slipped over the Seine on the night of 19/20 August, only 20 miles from Paris. French policemen rose in revolt and seized the Ile de la Cité, and resistance groups gained control of the capital's centre on Sunday, 20 August. A brief armistice ended with renewed fighting next day. 'Dragoon' forces in the south had reached Sisteron and were making for Grenoble. Also on the 20th, the Russians opened their Roumanian offensive. But the Red

Army had still to push forward at Warsaw, and Churchill, now at Siena, joined with Roosevelt in the appeal to Stalin. 'We are thinking of world opinion if the anti-Nazis in Warsaw are in effect abandoned.... We hope that you will drop immediate supplies and munitions to the Patriot Poles in Warsaw, or will agree to help our planes in doing it very quickly.'[94] Eden described the 'very severe fighting' in Warsaw to the War Cabinet next day, Monday, 21 August, and revealed continued difficulties with the Russians, of which 'the Poles were well aware'. Further Polish appeals had reached London. 'Arrangements had in fact been made for a small number of planes to drop supplies nightly for the present. This would be an encouragement to the Poles.' Ministers agreed that Eden, Sinclair and Evill should meet Polish representatives next day to discuss whether anything further could be done; nothing resulted from this meeting.[95]

While the Russians remained static outside Warsaw yet rolled forward in Roumania, and while allied armies crashed onwards in France, diplomats converged on Dumbarton Oaks in America: the subsequent conference would attempt to give substance to various allied statements of intention to establish an international organization – the eventual United Nations. Sir Alexander Cadogan, who would be first British permanent representative at the UN, now bargained on behalf of Britain. Talks began on 21 August. On the same day Brooke and Portal reached Rome for discussions with the Prime Minister on the next stages of the conflict. Greece formed the main topic, and Churchill agreed to ask the Greek Government to move to Italy from the dangerous Cairo atmosphere. Brooke continued to feel apprehensive over a military commitment; he left Rome to visit forward areas in Italy before leaving for home on the 23rd. Churchill signalled to Eden on the 22nd: 'For reasons which will presently become apparent, I shall be returning to Alexander's army on the night of the 22nd-23rd, and hope to be at Chequers in time for Matins next Sunday....'[96] During the day he received Stalin's reply to the joint appeal over Warsaw: the Soviet leader still refused aircraft facilities and branded the Polish Underground Army as a 'group of criminals'.[97]

So Warsaw's agony reached new heights while France's capital came closer to liberation. General Leclerc, commander of the French 2nd Armoured Division, received orders at 7.15 p.m., 23 August. 'Mission. (1) To seize Paris....' His first detachments moved on the city from Rambouillet early next morning and pierced the faltering German defences. At 9.22 p.m. Fighting French tanks squealed into the square before the Hôtel de Ville. The Germans capitulated; swastikas were torn from buildings. General de Gaulle reached the city during the evening of the 25th, and made his formal appearance before the frenzied crowds next afternoon. The Intelligence Summary issued by Supreme HQ declared in highly optimistic words: 'Two and a half months of bitter fighting, culminating for the Germans in a blood-bath big enough even for their extravagant tastes, have brought the end of the war in Europe within sight, almost within reach. The strength of the German Armies in the West has been shattered, Paris belongs to France again, and the allied armies are streaming towards the frontiers of the Reich.'[98] The 2nd British Army reached the area north of Verneuil; elements of the 1st Canadian Army linked with the 3rd US Army over the lower Seine. 'Dragoon' forces entered Avignon on the 25th; on 23 August King Michael of Roumania had led a successful *coup* against the collaborationist Government and at once opened surrender talks with the advancing Russians; the Bulgarians had also offered to surrender; the Finns sued for an armistice on 26 August. On the 22nd the Joint Intelligence Committee had completed an encouraging report on Germany's capacity to resist: 'Since our last appreciation of German strategy dated 14 July, Germany has suffered new and major disasters, bringing her to the verge of defeat ... if the allied attempts on the three major fronts continue to be pressed home, such a defeat will come about before the end of this year.'[99]

But black war clouds hung low over Warsaw. Terrible eye-witness reports reaching London described the fighting in the streets, the houses and even in the sewers. 'In many cases they (the Germans) have burnt whole streets of houses and shot all the men belonging to them, and turned the women and children out on to the streets, where battles are taking place.... The German forces have brutally murdered wounded and sick people, both men and women.... The food situation is continually deteriorating.... Today there is no water at all in the pipes.... All quarters of the town are under shellfire, and there are many fires.' Churchill in Rome instructed the Minister of Information to give full publicity to the atrocities.[100] Eden told the War Cabinet on the 24th that he had revised previous ideas over the status of the Polish partisans: he requested Ministerial approval for a declaration saying the Polish Home Army must be considered an integral part of the Polish Armed Forces: 'Any reprisals against members of the Polish Home Army violate the rules of war by which Germany is bound. Such reprisals will be taken by Germans at their peril and those who take them will be held responsible for their crimes.' Ministers fully realized that the declaration was unlikely to be of any real help but was 'unquestionably' the 'farthest we could safely go'.[101] The Americans were asked to agree to this declaration, and did so on the 29th. But this, for the moment, also seemed as far as Roosevelt felt he could go: on the 25th Churchill sent him the draft of a further appeal for aircraft facilities, but the President replied next day: 'I do not consider it would prove advantageous to the long-range general war prospect for me to join with you in the proposed message.' The Prime Minister decided against sending the appeal alone.[102] Aircraft from the Polish wing in Italy had continued to embark in the extremely hazardous flight to drop supplies near Warsaw: in operations between 17-27 August a total of 46 sorties were successful, but by 28 August only three aircraft remained available for operations. Portal stressed difficulties to the War Cabinet on the 28th: 'To drop supplies to the Polish Underground Army in Warsaw, it would be necessary for our aircraft to fly at an altitude of about 1,000 feet, and at a very low speed.... Warsaw was very strongly defended by flak.... The AOC-in-C in the Mediterranean was coming to the conclusion that the opera-

tion could scarcely be regarded as an "operation of war".
On the last two nights nine aircraft had been dispatched, of
which one had dropped supplies successfully and four had
been lost.' Ministers agreed 'there was no doubt that the
Russians had suffered a setback; and all the evidence went
to show that they were doing their utmost to reach
Warsaw'.[103]

Forty-eight hours before, on Saturday, 26 August, the
reason for Churchill's prolonged stay in Italy had been revealed. On the 25th the Prime Minister had travelled to
Alexander's forward HQ and had been escorted to a comfortable tent behind Monte Maggiore. At midnight a mighty
gun barrage lit the skyline and the thudding artillery
reminded Churchill of the First World War. Alexander
had opened his offensive against the Gothic Line in the
Adriatic sector. Tactical surprise enabled the coastal drive
to punch through Kesselring's defences; by 28 August
allied units were reaching for German positions inland from
Pesaro. Churchill flew home, well satisfied with his visit
but suffering from a temperature of 103 degrees: he
would only spend seven days in London before embarking on yet another mission. In France the 3rd US Army
prepared to strike across the Marne and the 2nd British
Army towards Amiens. But on the 28th the British COS
discussed a problem caused despite, or even because of,
this allied success; and the problem would soon grow to
painful proportions.

Forces in France consisted of Montgomery's 21st Army
Group, comprising the 1st Canadian Army under Crerar and
the 2nd British Army under Dempsey; and the 12th US
Army Group, comprising the 1st Army under Hodges and
the 3rd Army under Patton. To this would be added the 9th
Army, not yet operational, under Simpson. To the south
were the 'Dragoon' forces. Disagreement had now broken
out over the best use of these armies. On 17 August Montgomery had presented a plan which envisaged a joint move
by both 12th and 21st Army Groups north-east towards the
Pas de Calais, Antwerp, Brussels and Aachen. This would
present 'a solid mass of some 40 divisions which would be so

strong that it need fear nothing'. The movement would pivot
on Paris, while the 'Dragoon' force would be directed on
Nancy and the Saar, but Montgomery insisted that the 'solid
mass' in the north-east must not be dispersed in an attempt
to join the 'Dragoon' thrust. 'The basic object of the movement would be to establish a powerful air force in Belgium,
to secure bridgeheads over the Rhine before the winter began,
and to seize the Ruhr quickly.' The essence of the plan therefore lay in its emphasis on one, massive main punch.
Eisenhower disagreed. On 20 August he expressed his strong
preference for a wider front, entailing a division of resources;
this, he hoped, would ease maintenance problems and would
present the Germans with multiple threats. He therefore
agreed that 21st Army Group should secure the Channel
ports and Antwerp, but the 3rd US Army would move on
Nancy and Metz, supported by the 'Dragoon' force – 6th
Army Group. He decided the time had come to take over
from Montgomery in the direction of land operations because
the two main Army Groups would now be advancing along
divergent lines. Montgomery would command 21st Army
Group and Bradley the 12th. This 'final system of command'
had always been envisaged in the 'Overlord' scheme, and the
British COS voiced no objections. But Brooke expressed
vigorous opposition to Eisenhower's 'wide front' scheme at
the COS meeting on 28 August. 'This plan is likely to add
another three to six months to the war,' he wrote in his diary.
The CIGS flew over to France to consult Montgomery the
following day; he returned in the evening of the 29th slightly
reassured by the news that the 1st US Army would, like the
2nd British Army, move with Brussels as the objective, and
would hence be available to give some support. But this disagreement would continue from now almost to the ending
of the war.[104]

British Ministers were informed on 31 August that
Churchill, back in London but ill in bed, intended to promote Montgomery to Field-Marshal; the suggestion was
made at the War Cabinet meeting that this promotion might
be unfair to Alexander, but Ministers did not press the point
and 'took note' of Churchill's decision.[105] On 1 September

Eisenhower assumed direct command of Army Group Commanders; already his armies were in full advance. The British 2nd Army and the 1st US Army would push forward 250 miles in the next six days, and Brooke announced stirring news to the War Cabinet on Monday, 4 September: 'British forces have crossed the Somme near its mouth and are working along the coast near Boulogne. Further inland a rapid advance has been made and Brussels has been taken. ... The continuing advance of the allied forces in France is now mainly a question of overcoming administrative difficulties.'[106] But Ministers were also told that Russian attacks to the north of Warsaw 'have been held in check'. Eden and Churchill had discussed the Warsaw problem the previous day, 3 September, and had considered the possibility of a ban on convoys to Russia as a protest to Stalin, but such a stoppage would not help the Poles in time. The War Cabinet held a special meeting at 12.30 p.m. on the 4th and heard the text of a harrowing appeal sent to the Pope on 22 August from women in the Polish capital: 'For three weeks, while defending our fortress, we have lacked food and medicine. Warsaw is in ruins. The Germans are killing the wounded in the hospitals. They are making women and children march in front of them in order to protect their tanks. There is no exaggeration in reports of children who are fighting and destroying tanks with bottles of petrol.... Holy Father, no one is helping us....' The War Cabinet believed Churchill should attempt to persuade Roosevelt to allow American aircraft to drop supplies on Warsaw, 'if necessary gate-crashing on Russian airfields'. A telegram should also be sent to Stalin, in the name of the War Cabinet. Churchill dispatched the appeal to Roosevelt later in the day; another signal left for Moscow: 'The War Cabinet wish the Soviet Government to know that public opinion in this country is deeply moved by the events in Warsaw.... Our people cannot understand why no material help has been sent.... The fact that such help could not be sent on account of your Government's refusal to allow US aircraft to land on aerodromes in Russian hands is now becoming publicly known. If on top of all this the Poles in Warsaw should now be overwhelmed by the Germans, as we are told they must be within two or three days, the shock to public opinion here will be incalculable.... Your Government's action in preventing this help being sent seems to us at variance with the spirit of Allied co-operation....'[107] Roosevelt replied next day: 'I am informed by my Office of Military Intelligence that the fighting Poles have departed from Warsaw and that the Germans are now in full control. The problem of relief for the Poles in Warsaw has therefore unfortunately been solved by delay and by German action, and there now appears to be nothing we can do to assist them.'[108]

Roosevelt had been misinformed. Polish fighters continued to cling to the city ruins, and Polish appeals continued to reach London. Also on 5 September, Eden told the War Cabinet at 5 p.m. that the Polish Prime Minister remained unconvinced that Britain and America could not carry out air operations to drop supplies. Sir Douglas Evill, Vice-Chief of Air Staff, said about 182 sorties had been flown from Italy in the last three weeks; of these, 35 aircraft were missing and 88 had made successful or semi-successful drops. 'Taking account of five aircraft so badly damaged as to be no longer serviceable, one aircraft was missing for every 2.5 successes.... The last attempt was made three nights ago, when out of seven aircraft used, four had been lost. No more would be sent during the present moon period.'[109] Ministers could only await the reply to their appeal to Stalin.

Churchill had recovered from his latest attack of pneumonia in time to attend the War Cabinet meeting at 5.30 p.m., 4 September. Brooke described him as 'not looking at all well'. Yet next day the Prime Minister left on the *Queen Mary* for Quebec, for another summit ordeal with Roosevelt and the CCS, and the voyage itself would be strenuous, with daily and sometimes twice daily COS and Staff Conferences; Brooke feared: 'I very much wonder whether he will be up to the strain of this trip.' Winant, the American Ambassador, had written to Hopkins on 1 September: 'Each journey has taken its toll, and the intervals between each illness have been constantly shortened.' Ismay commented on the voyage: 'Mr Churchill had not yet recovered from his illness, but instead of having a rest, he insisted on working harder than ever. Large doses of M & B had wrought miracles with his pneumonia, but had not improved his temper, and although the sea was calm, some of us had a rough passage.'[110]

Back in London, Ministers noted with relief the easing of the V-1 offensive. Already, on 4 September, Ministers had agreed with the Home Secretary that the scheme for priority evacuation from London should be discontinued, and the War Cabinet also decided 'an announcement should be made at an early date that the blackout would not be continued throughout the coming winter'. About 8,500 flying bombs had been launched from sites in France, of which 1,006 crashed soon after launching; 6,184 people had been killed and 17,981 seriously injured.[111] On 7 September Duncan Sandys told the press: 'The Battle of London is won ... except perhaps for a last few shots.' Yet next evening, at 6.34 p.m., the first V-2s landed upon London with sudden unheralded explosions. Ministers assembled at noon next day, Saturday, 9 September, for a special meeting chaired by Attlee, and Morrison reported that 'two missiles had fallen the previous evening – one in Chiswick and one near Epping. From investigation, it appeared almost certain that these missiles were rockets of the type expected. They had caused large craters but there had been few casualties.' Sir Douglas Evill said there had been no radar trace of these rockets, but they had been plotted by sound-ranging devices. Montgomery had been asked to give an estimate of the time it would take to seal off or capture the Rotterdam-Utrecht-Amsterdam area, but the Vice-COAS felt that 'no serious attack could be developed by the enemy, whose organization in Holland must have been hurriedly improvised, and any attacks would probably be of short duration'. Ministers agreed no publicity should be given to the latest offensive for the moment. Two days later the War Cabinet heard that 'two or three further incidents' had been reported, but little damage and few casualties had resulted. The ban on publicity remained.[112]

Morale soared, despite the V-2s. Excellent news continued

to reach London from all fronts, and on 9 September an improvement was even reported on the Warsaw situation, when Stalin told the British that facilities would at last be offered for allied air operations. Although the Soviet leader repeated his denunciation of the 'Warsaw adventure', his reply to the War Cabinet was, in the British Ambassador's word, a 'climb-down'.[113] Preparations were immediately intensified for an American air drop, but moon conditions would rule out a flight until the 18th. Ministers were told on the 11th that 'a Russian offensive north of Warsaw had met with limited success'. Soviet aircraft also dropped supplies over the city, but few of the parachutes opened, and Ministers also learnt on the 11th that even with Russian airfield facilities, RAF flights from Italy would be 'militarily unjustifiable'. Eden commented: 'Could the War Cabinet overrule the military opinion expressed in the (Vice-COAS) appreciation? His own opinion was that this view should not be overruled, but he thought it right to warn the War Cabinet that there was considerable political activity ... and that they would have to defend any decision which they took in Parliament.' Ministers were informed that 20 aircraft had attempted the flight the previous night: 5 had not returned, 5 had managed to drop supplies over Warsaw, 4 had dropped blind. Bomber Command estimated that losses on an operation with 120 aircraft, as urged by the Poles, would be between 10-15 per cent for an actual delivery of some ten tons. The War Cabinet agreed that arguments against operations were 'overwhelming'.[114]

Allied armies continued their victorious advance through France and Belgium. Dunkirk fell on 6 September, and the 1st Canadian Army moved forward over the rusted relics of the British evacuation three and a half years before. By 10 September elements of the 2nd British Army were thrusting into Holland; to their right the 1st US Army had liberated Luxembourg and further south the 3rd US Army had advanced beyond Metz and Nancy into the Vosges mountains. Next day, 11 September, 'Dragoon' and 'Overlord' forces joined hands at Sombernon. But ahead lay the German Siegfried Line. Meanwhile, Alexander's armies had

made good progress, despite the reduction of forces. The
Germans had pulled back into the hills beyond the Arno,
and Wilson informed the COS on 8 September of his confidence that 'the enemy will be driven completely from the
Gothic Line'.[115] The Russians had continued to stab forward: they refused to listen to Bulgarian attempts to withdraw from the war, and attacked the country on 5 September;
the Bulgarians capitulated on the 9th. Soviet forces had also
reached the Yugoslav frontier, hence pushing the future of
the Balkans into even greater prominence.

These successes, and the prospect of more to come, lay
behind Churchill's mission to the 'Octagon' conference at
Quebec. Next stages of the war had to be agreed upon;
diplomatic issues over the future of Europe had to be decided.
And above all, a strategy must be settled for the war against
Japan. Churchill disembarked at Halifax on 10 September
to a tremendous reception of ships dressed overall, screeching sirens, packed ranks of Canadian Mounties and fire-boats
playing their hoses. Next morning the Prime Minister's train
drew into Quebec to enthusiastic greetings from the President and Mrs Roosevelt. But the journey had shown
Churchill to be still unwell and liable to further collapse –
and the voyage had revealed fresh differences between the
Prime Minister and his Chiefs of Staff.

Quebec to Moscow

Brooke continued to fear for Churchill's health. 'He was not looking at all well and was most desperately flat,' wrote the CIGS on the 7th, and added next day: 'He looked old, unwell and depressed. Evidently found it hard to concentrate and kept holding his head in his hands.'[1] Yet concentration and clear-cut decisions were urgently required; ahead lay the conferences with the Americans, but *Queen Mary* discussions showed Churchill and the professional advisers to be divided over future plans both for Europe and the Far East. With the latter, compromise had apparently been reached in August for 'Vanguard' against Rangoon, combined with elements of the 'Champion' plan for North Burma, plus the transfer of British forces, mainly naval, to the Pacific. The British had submitted these proposals to the Americans on 18 August, and Wedemeyer, Mountbatten's Chief of Staff, had visited Washington to provide fuller explanations. The Americans had sent their broad agreement on 1 September, although preferring greater emphasis on 'Champion'. But these operations in north Burma were now condemned by the Prime Minister, despite previous agreement. On 5 September, as the *Queen Mary* sailed from the Clyde, Brooke wrote: 'Winston has agreed to our airborne campaign on Burma but limits his sanction to the capture of Rangoon alone without the clearing of the rest of Burma. This makes the expedition practically useless and, what is worse, converts it into one which cannot appeal to the Americans since it fails to affect Upper Burma where their air route is situated.'[2]

For the next two days, 6 and 7 September, the COS discussed the transfer of forces from Europe to the Far East. Churchill was anxious to avoid premature withdrawal, and cautioned against optimism felt in some professional circles over the duration of the European war. The Joint Intelligence Committee had reflected this optimistic attitude in a report dated 5 September: 'Whatever action Hitler may now take it will be too late to affect the issue in the West, where organized German resistance will gradually disintegrate under our attack, although it is impossible to predict the rate at which this will take place.' The COS had given general support for this assessment on the 6th.[3] But Churchill detailed his disagreements in a paper handed to the COS two days later. 'No one can tell what the future may bring forth.... The fortifying and consolidating effect of a stand on the frontier of the native soil should not be underrated. It is at least as likely that Hitler will be fighting on the 1st January as that he will collapse before then. If he does collapse before then the reasons will be political rather than purely military.'[4] Churchill, usually so optimistic, therefore felt the need to caution Brooke, usually so careful and even pessimistic.

But the COS continued along their line of approach which would take them closer towards the Americans, and further away from the Prime Minister. On 6 September they had agreed that the Italian campaign 'must become of secondary importance as soon as the Pisa-Rimini Line has been broken and Kesselring's forces defeated and driven back'. No more should be attempted, despite pleas by Wilson and Alexander, supported by Churchill. And now, on the 8th, the Americans agreed with a proposal for Burma put forward by the British Mission in Washington, compromising a directive to Mountbatten 'to initiate planning and preparation for ("Vanguard") in mid-March' as long as these did not conflict with prior commitments to 'Champion'.[5]

Disagreements with Churchill over both Burma and Italy came together at a staff conference on the 8th which degenerated into prolonged argument. The Prime Minister sought an operation against Istria to seize Trieste, and complained

over the amount of troops likely to be taken from Europe
for Burma. 'It was hard to keep one's temper with him,'
wrote Brooke, 'but I could not help feeling frightfully sorry
for him.... We made no progress and decided to go on
tomorrow. He finished up by saying: "Here we are within
72 hours of meeting the Americans and there is not a single
point that we are in agreement over."'[6] The meeting with
Churchill on the 9th had to be cancelled when doctors found
the Prime Minister's temperature had soared again; a conference at noon on the 10th failed to find agreement, and on
the 11th Churchill cabled privately to Mountbatten to ask
if he could provide more forces from his own theatre.

As far as the British were concerned, the 'Octagon' conference could not have begun in greater confusion. And yet
the results completely contradicted the dreary opening
prospects: disagreements had existed amongst the British
themselves, rather than between the British and Americans,
and when the summit started on 12 September both the COS
and Churchill showed more flexibility, the former over
Churchill's emphasis on an Istrian campaign, the latter over
Burma and the Pacific. Moreover, also on this Tuesday, 12
September, units of the 1st US Army pierced the Siegfried
Line south of Aachen: the optimistic Joint Intelligence
Committee report might after all be proved correct.

The CCS began their first session by discussing the report
submitted by Eisenhower on the 9th concerning future
intentions, continuing to advocate a 'broad front' strategy.
The Ruhr and the Saar would be the main objectives: the
northern group of armies under Montgomery would capture
Antwerp, break the Siegfried Line and seize the Ruhr, and an
airborne army would support operations over the Rhine;
meanwhile the central group of armies under Bradley would
take Brest, breach the Siegfried Line covering the Saar and
seize Frankfurt. Montgomery had already repeated objections to the wide front scheme in a signal to Eisenhower on
the 4th. 'I consider we have now reached a stage where one
really powerful and full-blooded thrust towards Berlin is
likely to get there and thus end the German war. We have
not enough maintenance resources for two full-blooded

thrusts.... In my opinion the thrust likely to give the best and quickest results is the northern one via the Ruhr.' At a conference with Eisenhower on the 10th, Montgomery had also laid stress on an operation to take Arnhem, standing in the way of the northern advance over the Meuse and Rhine – and also in the way of an advance towards Rotterdam and Antwerp and the V-2 sites. Now, at Quebec on 12 September, the CCS supported Eisenhower's policy in general but agreed to a British proposal which would seek emphasis for Montgomery's thrust. The reply to Eisenhower therefore pointed out 'the advantages of the northern line of approach into Germany as opposed to the southern, and the necessity for opening up the northwest ports, particularly Antwerp and Rotterdam.'

The American and British chiefs turned to Italy and especially to the future use of the US 5th Army. Marshall revealed dramatic news. 'A message had just been received from the US Military *Attaché* in Switzerland, to the effect that a German withdrawal of forces in Northern Italy had already begun.' The information, plus Churchill's policy declared during the *Queen Mary* discussions, led to a complete change of attitude by the British COS. Further advances in Italy might after all be possible. The CIGS now said that 'if the Allied armies could break through to the Plains the enemy forces remaining in northwest Italy would be badly placed. A threat to Verona would cut off these forces and might result in their retirement to the westward.... The attack by the 5th Army was planned to take place on 13 September and a successful advance north of Florence might well result in driving the enemy forces back to the Po and Piave.' Brooke saw 'great advantages' in a 'right swing at Trieste and an advance from there to Vienna'. If German resistance proved strong, allied forces would be unlikely to push through to Vienna during the winter, but 'even the seizure of the Istrian peninsula would be valuable as a base for the spring campaign or as a base from which our forces could be introduced into Austria in the event of Germany crumbling. It had not only a military value but also political value in view of the Russian advances in the Balkans.'

Churchill could not have wished for a better declaration of
his preferred policy. And, with the arguments over 'Dragoon'
now long since passed, support came from the Americans.
Admiral King also 'had in mind' the possibility of
amphibious operations in Istria, and looked favourably upon
the British request to keep assault craft in the Mediterranean
which had previously been used for 'Dragoon'. Marshall
pointed to availability of equipment for winter operations in
the Alps, and said 'there was no intention in the minds of the
US COS to effect the withdrawal of forces from Italy at the
present time'. The CCS therefore asked Wilson to submit
plans, not later than 15 October, for operations against the
Istrian peninsula. Brooke described this first session in his
diary: 'It went off most satisfactorily and we found ourselves in complete agreement with American COS.'[7]

The British COS met alone at 4.30 p.m. on this Tuesday
to discuss another minute from Churchill on Far East
strategy. Brooke and his colleagues were relieved by the
content: although the Prime Minister laid greatest stress on
central Burma and on the eventual reconquest of Singapore,
the paper seemed a suitable basis for compromise. Thus
Churchill declared: 'Our policy should be to give naval
assistance on the largest scale to the main American operations, but to keep our own thrust for Rangoon as a preliminary operation.' Churchill did not specifically rule out
operations in the north, under 'Champion'; moreover the
Prime Minister had himself raised the question of the use of
the British fleet in the Pacific the previous day: Leahy had
told him this offer had been accepted. When the COS met
Churchill later in the evening they found him completely
changed in manner. 'He was all smiles and friendliness,'
wrote Brooke. 'How quickly he changes! An April day's
moods would be put to shame.'[8] Unfortunately, the Prime
Minister's mood would soon undergo another lightning
transition.

For the moment, all continued to go well. Next morning,
13 September, Roosevelt and Churchill met the COS for the
first plenary session, and the Prime Minister's introduction
glowed with optimism and satisfaction. 'Everything we had

touched had turned to gold, and during the last seven weeks there had been an unbroken run of military successes. The manner in which the situation had developed since the Tehran conference gave the impression of remarkable design and precision of execution ... future historians would say that the period since Tehran had shown the successful working of an extraordinarily efficient inter-allied war machine.' Past disagreements and bitter arguments were conveniently forgotten. Churchill congratulated the Americans over 'Dragoon', 'which had produced the most gratifying results'. He stressed the British wish to send the Fleet to the Pacific, and according to the official minutes: 'The President intervened to say that the British fleet was no sooner offered than accepted.'[9] Churchill reported to the War Cabinet: 'The conference has opened in a blaze of friendship.... The idea of our going to Vienna if the war lasts long enough and if other people do not get there first, is fully accepted here....' And he cabled Wilson and Alexander: 'Pray therefore address yourselves to this greatly improved situation in the spirit of audacious enterprise.'[10] Harmony continued at the second CCS session, starting at the Chateau Frontenac Hotel at 2.30 p.m. The British and American chiefs gave their formal approval to a directive for Mountbatten: the Supreme Commander would therefore be ordered to plan for 'Capital' – formerly 'Champion' – to secure the air route and overland communications to China, and 'Dracula' – formerly 'Vanguard'. These would be launched before the monsoon in 1945, with a target date of 14 March.[11] Final touches would be put to the directive next morning, 14 September. But by then complications had begun to arise.

General Ismay telephoned Brooke at 7.30 next morning, Thursday, 14 September. Churchill wanted to see the CIGS at 9 a.m., and Ismay asked if he could talk to Brooke prior to this meeting. Brooke found him 'very upset'. Churchill had received a signal from Mountbatten, said Ismay, in reply to a request for information sent by the Prime Minister on the 11th. Mountbatten's message seemed obscure, but apparently revealed to Churchill the extent of proposed operations in north Burma under 'Champion', now 'Capital'.

According to Brooke's account of his conversation with Ismay: 'As a result Winston had accused us all to Ismay of purposely concealing changes of plans from him.' Ismay had written a letter of resignation and asked for Brooke's advice as to whether he should send it in. 'I told him that this decision must rest with him.' Brooke later believed Ismay did in fact hand in his resignation, which Churchill refused to consider. Either the threat or the actual resignation attempt served to clear the atmosphere; Brooke, to his surprise, found Churchill in an excellent mood at 9 a.m. Mountbatten had also said he could probably spare three divisions for the assault on Rangoon, one of which must be replaced as soon as possible by a division from Europe, and Churchill now agreed with the CIGS that the 2nd Indian Division should be transferred from Italy.[12]

The CIGS hurried to a short COS meeting then to the main conference room in the Chateau Frontenac for the 10 a.m. CCS session. Main item for discussion was the question of using a British Fleet in the Pacific main operations. The offer had apparently been fully accepted by Roosevelt the previous day. Yet doubts had been raised by a memorandum from the US COS handed to the British later in the afternoon: the Americans welcomed the offer of a naval task force but continued: 'The initial use of such a force should be on the western flank of the advance in the South-West Pacific.' Thus the fleet would not, apparently, be deployed in the principal operations against the Japanese, as the COS and Churchill had stipulated, but would instead be relegated to the shadows – as the Prime Minister had warned might happen. Brooke now sought to clarify the issue, and in doing so precipitated a quarrel with Admiral King who in turn found himself opposed by his own colleagues. The CIGS wrote afterwards: 'We had great trouble with King who lost his temper entirely and was opposed by the whole of his own Committee. He was determined, if he could, not to admit British naval forces into Nimitz's command in the Central Pacific.'[13] Brooke began by saying the British COS were 'disturbed' by the US paper. They realized this had been written before the plenary session on the previous day, but

stressed that 'for political reasons it was essential that the
British fleet should take part in the main operations'. Leahy
asked if British fears would be removed by the deletion of
the words 'they consider that the initial use of such a force
should be on the western flank of the advance in the South-
West Pacific'. Admiral Sir Andrew Cunningham agreed. The
matter seemed settled, until King declared 'the practicability
of employing these forces would be a matter for discussion
from time to time', and suggested the British COS should
put forward proposals with regard to the employment of the
fleet. Cunningham immediately repeated the British stipulation that the fleet must be employed in the central Pacific.
King claimed no specific reference to the central Pacific had
been made at the plenary meeting, and was 'in no position
now to commit himself as to where the British fleet could be
employed'. Portal reminded him of the original British
offer, which read: 'It is our desire, in accordance with HMG's
policy, that this fleet should play its full part at the earliest
possible moment in the main operations against Japan
wherever the greatest naval strength is required,' and
Cunningham claimed the Prime Minister and President had
agreed. King retorted that 'it was not his recollection that
the President had agreed to this. He could not accept that a
view expressed by the Prime Minister should be regarded as
a directive to the CCS.' Brooke reminded King that the
offer had been 'no sooner made than accepted by the President'. King's colleague, Leahy, could see 'no objection whatever to this proposal', but the Admiral refused to move. 'The
question of the British proposal for the use of the main fleet
would have to be referred to the President before it could
be accepted.' Leahy replied that 'if Admiral King saw any
objections to this proposal he should take the matter up himself with the President'. According to one irreverent British
observer at this session, the official minutes should have
read: 'At this point Admiral King was carried out.' Instead,
the minutes described the conclusions reached: 'The CCS
a) agreed that the British fleet should participate in the main
operation against Japan in the Pacific....'[14]
'My mind is now much more at rest,' wrote Brooke in his

diary. 'Things have gone well on the whole in spite of Winston's moods.'[15] Churchill had been attempting to deal with a non-military problem – the question of Germany's future. And some Americans were considering an extremely drastic plan, involving harsh treatment of German citizens, which had already aroused considerable apprehension amongst War Cabinet Ministers in London. Anthony Eden was flying with all speed to Quebec to take part in critical discussions, yet would arrive too late to prevent a dangerous agreement between Churchill and Roosevelt.

The latest proposal had been drafted by Henry Morgenthau, US Secretary of the Treasury, and had been presented to Roosevelt early in September. The so-called Morgenthau Plan envisaged the parcelling up and 'pastoralizing' of Germany. 'This area (the Ruhr) should not only be stripped of all presently existing industries but so weakened and controlled that it cannot in the foreseeable future become an industrial area – all industrial plans and equipment not destroyed by military action shall either be completely dismantled or removed from the area or completely destroyed, all equipment should be removed from the mines and the mines shall be thoroughly wrecked.' Cordell Hull had reacted strongly against these radical methods: the plan 'would leave Germany with practically no industry, and would force the population to live entirely off the land, regardless of the fact that there was not enough land on which the large German population could live. Essentially, this was a plan of blind vengeance.'[16] Lord Halifax reported the scheme to London on 2 September, adding it would probably receive attention at Quebec, and on the 11th the War Cabinet agreed a message should be sent to Churchill warning that Roosevelt seemed to be willing to support a policy of 'letting chaos have its way' in Germany, which would involve purposeless suffering rather than just retribution. The draft of this telegram received approval from Attlee, Anderson, Bevin and Eden, but the message was not sent until 14 September and did not arrive in Quebec until the 16th. Meanwhile, on the 15th, Churchill reached agreement with Roosevelt both on the Morgenthau plan and on American aid to Britain during

the period between the surrender of Germany and the surrender of Japan. Hull later claimed agreement for the latter
had been made in exchange for Churchill's acceptance of
the Morgenthau Plan, but no evidence can be found in
British sources that Churchill considered such a deal. Eden
arrived in Quebec on 14 September too late to intervene:
Churchill had already pledged support and the Prime Minister and Roosevelt initialled a drastic document on the 15th,
stressing the ease with which Germany had converted peaceful industry into war use and declaring: 'It must also be
remembered that the Germans have devastated a large
portion of the industries of Russia and of other neighbouring
allies, and it is only in accordance with justice that these
injured countries should be entitled to remove the machinery
they require in order to repair the losses they have suffered.
The industries referred to in the Ruhr and in the Saar would
therefore be necessarily put out of action and closed down.....
The programme ... is looking forward to converting
Germany into a country primarily agricultural and pastoral
in its character.'[17] Eden objected on the 15th. 'It was as if
one were to take the Black Country and turn it into Devon-
shire.' He suggested Cordell Hull's opinions should be sought,
but not surprisingly in view of Hull's violent reactions
already expressed, the idea received short shrift. 'This was the
only occasion I can remember,' wrote Eden later, 'when the
Prime Minister showed impatience with my views before
Foreign representatives.'[18] Churchill cabled both the text
of this agreement and the Lend-Lease agreement to Attlee
during this Friday; the Deputy Prime Minister and Chancellor of the Exchequer replied next day, 16 September, with
warmest congratulations to Churchill and Lord Cherwell for
the Lend-Lease arrangement, but made no mention of the
other agreement for the future of Germany. Presumably
Attlee believed the War Cabinet's views had already been
fully expressed in their telegram sent on 14 September.[19]

'Octagon' closed on 16 September and hence proved the
shortest of the Anglo-American wartime summits. The CCS
had met the previous day to reach agreement over their final
report. Petty difficulties had been encountered by Brooke

when Churchill was shown the draft report during the evening of the 15th: Eden, also present at this meeting, described the Prime Minister as 'in a tiresome mood, fastening on many minor points of wording', and Brooke therefore entered the last plenary discussion on the 16th fearful of a Churchillian intervention, but the session had a smooth passage.[20] The 'Octagon' participants departed their various ways: Churchill to spend three days at Hyde Park before sailing for London on 19 September, arriving on the 25th; Eden flying direct to England on the 17th; the COS embarking on a 4-day fishing expedition before flying home on the 21st. The COS would not see Churchill for 10 days.

While 'Octagon' had once again established a strategic programme for the future, military events would still cause complications. And these events emphasized that bitter battlefield toil still lay ahead: contrary to the optimistic reports, Germany remained far from total collapse.

Polish fighters in Warsaw had continued their hopeless struggle. Insufficient allied help came too late. Eden told the War Cabinet on the 18th, the day of his return from Quebec, that 'the Russians had now sent help by air to the Polish Underground Army in Warsaw, and had also afforded facilities for the USAF.... There had in consequence been a very marked improvement in the relations between Russia and Poland, which we could fairly attribute to our persistence.'[21] This optimism soon faded. On the 18th 110 heavy bombers of the 8th USAF flew from East Anglia to the Polish capital, and dropped 30 per cent of their supplies for the loss of 9 aircraft – but an operation on this scale demanded careful planning and fine weather and could not be repeated immediately. A report from Warsaw reached London on 26 September: 'Food situation among the army and population is catastrophic.... There have been cases of death from starvation and mortality among the children is dangerously increasing.... The rising may collapse because of famine.' 'The people are eating dogs,' said another message of the 26th. 'Soviet droppings of gruel and biscuits are of little help for the quantities are very small and are mostly destroyed

when reaching ground as droppings are effected without parachutes ... we won't be able to hold out for more than 8, at the
most 10 days.' Another plea came next day. 'We urgently
appeal to the Governments of Great Britain, United States
and Soviet Union for immediate and large-scale intervention
of allied aircraft from Soviet bases....' These three appeals
were brought to the attention of the COS at 11 a.m. on Friday,
29 September, but Portal said 'it was quite clear that the
Polish request for a concerted plan of regular deliveries could
not, for technical reasons, be acceded to. The Americans were
preparing one more operation to take place early in October,
but this would be the last, since they were starting to close
down their refuelling facilities in Russia with the approach
of winter.'[22] The planned American flight could not be
arranged in time: resistance had virtually ceased on 2
October. A last broadcast was picked up in London, in words
described by Churchill as 'indelible'. 'This is the stark truth.
... May God, who is just, pass judgement on the terrible
injustice suffered by the Polish nation, and may He punish
accordingly all those who are guilty. Your heroes are the
soldiers whose only weapons against tanks, planes and guns
were their revolvers and bottles filled with petrol. Your
heroes are the women who tended the wounded and carried
messages under fire, who cooked in bombed and ruined
cellars to feed children and adults, and who soothed and
comforted the dying. Your heroes are the children who went
on quietly playing among the smouldering ruins. These are
the people of Warsaw....'[23] An estimated 200,000 Polish
men, women and children died in the rising; the Germans
lost 10,000 killed, 7,000 missing and 9,000 wounded. Warsaw
lay gutted; and the shadow of the city lay over Western
thoughts like a shroud.

While the Warsaw tragedy staggered to its finish, allied
troops in Europe narrowly escaped disaster. A bold stroke
had been launched to secure a dominating position over the
western bank of the lower Rhine. The result brought the
bitterest fighting since the Normandy landings, centred on
the small, hitherto obscure Dutch town of Arnhem.

Despite the CCS advice regarding the northern thrust into

Germany, Eisenhower adhered to his basic plan for a 'broad front' invasion of Germany. But the Supreme Commander did agree to added support for a scheme put forward by Montgomery. The British commander sought permission to strengthen the northern thrust by an ambitious push to secure canal and river crossings over the Maas, Waal and Rhine in operation 'Market Garden'. The plan envisaged an advance by ground forces in conjunction with airborne attacks on the bridges across the three rivers at Grave, Nijmegen and Arnhem. On 12 September Eisenhower allocated Montgomery 1,000 tons of supplies a day for this operation, and he also confirmed Montgomery could use 1st Airborne Corps, of three divisions, from the Airborne Army. This consent did not however change Eisenhower's outlook: 'Market Garden' would be a tactical thrust within the 'broad front' strategic framework; success would not lead to further exploitation of the bridgehead across the lower Rhine; the allies must still advance on two fronts.[24] The Supreme Commander confirmed his Ruhr/Saar objectives in his directive issued on 17 September, and as if to emphasize this broad front, offensives both against Arnhem and Metz were initiated on this same day. Eisenhower still believed Montgomery's demands to be excessive: he had written in his diary on the 12th: 'Monty's suggestion is simply – "Give him everything". This is crazy.'[25]

'Market Garden' almost achieved total success – and almost proved a calamity. Troops of the 1st British Airborne division, supported later by the Polish Brigade, were dropped on the north bank of the lower Rhine to move forward and seize the Arnhem bridge; airborne units of 82nd US Division parachuted down to capture the bridges at Nijmegen and Grave; the 101st US Airborne Division aimed to secure the road from Grave to Eindhoven. During these airborne attacks the 30th Corps of the 2nd Army, led by the Guards Armoured Division, would force up the road to Eindhoven and thence over the captured bridges to Arnhem to link with the parachute units. Shortages of aircraft meant the drops had to be spread over three days, during which time the Germans could be expected to be reinforcing rapidly, and quick relief of the airborne forces by the ground advance was essential. First reports reaching London late on 17 September and early on the 18th were confused; Ministers were informed at the 5.30 p.m. War Cabinet meeting that 'it was as yet too early to get a clear view of the situation, but one report stated that the Guards Division had already made contact with the airborne troops at Eindhoven'.[26] The two American airborne divisions achieved their objects to the north of Eindhoven and at Grave and Nijmegen, but the British element spearheading the attack at Arnhem suffered severe setback. British troops were dropped seven miles from the main target – the bridge over the Rhine – and by the time they reached the river the Germans had been reinforced. Bad weather hampered the fly-in of reinforcements, food and ammunition. Elements of the 2nd Army reached Nijmegen on the 20th, but fierce opposition delayed the advance forward. On 25 September Montgomery had to order the survivors of the Arnhem assault to pull back, this attempt being made during the night of 25th-26th. Only 2,400 out of the original 10,000 managed to escape. Only gradually did the 2nd Army expand the new 50-mile salient into a 20-mile-wide front, and even then the allied position remained vulnerable.

'Market Garden' had a number of depressing implications. The critical check at Arnhem and the consequent failure to outflank the Siegfried Line showed a stiffening of enemy resistance, and this soon became apparent along the whole allied front. 1st and 3rd US Armies found themselves blocked further south, the former at Aachen and in the Ardennes, the latter at Metz and south of Nancy. Montgomery's fears of a dispersal and weakening of effort through the 'broad front' strategy seemed confirmed, and now Montgomery believed three tasks must be fulfilled before the Rhine could be assaulted: the Scheldt must be opened and the use of Antwerp guaranteed; the bridgehead at Nijmegen must be strengthened; the enemy's bridgehead west of the Maas must be destroyed. Eisenhower apparently agreed in a report to the CCS on 29 September: his intention remained to seize both the Ruhr and the Saar, but first Antwerp must be opened 'as a matter of great urgency'. Yet it would take almost four months to complete Montgomery's essential three tasks, and not until April 1945 would British troops again set foot in Arnhem. At the beginning of October 1944 hopes had been finally and emphatically dispelled that the enemy would be brought near to defeat by the winter. War in Europe would probably stretch far into 1945, with all the consequences upon morale at home and upon the war in the Far East.

Moreover, by the end of September over 14,000 men had been taken from the 8th Army in Italy for operations elsewhere, and 7,000 had been cut from the 5th US Army, even though Alexander's forces had achieved brilliant success during the previous month. The main assault on the Gothic Line had been launched on 13 September and within a week German defences had been pierced. But the enemy refused to withdraw further than strictly necessary, and by the end of September still held the 8th Army near Rimini; Alexander explained his difficulties in a signal to Wilson on 26 September: 'My forces are too weak relative to the enemy to force a breakthrough and so close the two pincers.... We shall have to continue the battle of Italy with about 20 divisions, almost all of which have had long periods of heavy fighting this year, and some for several years, against the 20 German divisions committed to the battle front ... we are fighting in country where, it is generally agreed, a superiority of at least 3 to 1 is required.'[27] Prospects of deadlock increased the need for a landing in Istria to assist victory, yet the COS heard on Friday, 6 October, that operation 'Sunstar' also seemed surrounded by difficulties. Gammell, Wilson's Chief of Staff, had opened studies on this amphibious assault and had recently conferred with Brooke. 'From a preliminary discussion with Gammell,' said the CIGS, 'it appeared that there were two serious disadvantages.... First, the area of assault would be dangerously far from the land front in Italy. Secondly, the forces required to seize and hold the beachhead were of the order of one airborne division, two assault divisions, and one follow-up division. It would be difficult, if not impossible, for Alexan-

der to provide these forces.' Amphibious operations to capture successive Yugoslav islands had been considered as an
alternative, 'but it appeared that these operations could not
be mounted before the early spring. In effect, it would
probably be unwise to attempt a large-scale amphibious
operation in the near future.' Wilson nevertheless remained
anxious to keep American assault craft in the Mediterranean,
continued Brooke, 'so as to retain the option on "Sunstar"
or other amphibious operations for the time being'. But he
added: 'It seemed unlikely that Admiral King would agree
to leaving the LSTs in the Mediterranean for an indefinite
period.'[28]

So yet another of the 'Octagon' conclusions had already
been complicated. And the same applied to Burma. The
CCS had decided – with Churchill's reluctant approval – on
'Capital' for north Burma and 'Dracula' for Rangoon. The
latter would require six divisions, of which four must come
from Europe. On 26 September, after reviewing resources,
the COS completed a paper dealing with the transfer of two
divisions from north-west Europe and two from the Mediterranean. But the former included one airborne division, and
on the same day, 26 September, news came which confirmed
the failure at Arnhem and hence the impossibility of sending
such an airborne division to the Far East. Moreover, the
First Sea Lord reported three days later that landing-craft
intended for Rangoon might have to be retained for operations up the Scheldt. And the latest uncertainty in Italy
seemed likely to delay the transfer of the two divisions from
this area. A staff meeting with Churchill had been arranged
for 10 p.m. on 2 October; only a few minutes before this
conference began, Brooke received a signal from Montgomery: 'He could not spare either 52nd Division or 3rd
Division, 6th Airborne Division or 6th Guards Armoured
Brigade or a Corps HQ.' The COS therefore advised Churchill
that the Rangoon operation 'Dracula' should be cancelled,
at least until after the next monsoon. The Prime Minister
agreed. 'In these circumstances he thought it would be wrong
to weaken our effort in France, which was and must remain
the main theatre of operations until Germany was finally

defeated. He therefore reluctantly concluded that "Dracula" must be postponed ... and that in the next dry weather season we should devote all our strength in South-East Asia Command to the vigorous execution of "Capital".' 'We were lucky to find the PM in a very reasonable and quiet mood,' wrote Brooke. 'We might otherwise have failed to obtain any decision from him.'[29] A telegram was despatched to Mountbatten on 5 October, postponing 'Dracula' until November 1945.

A commitment to Greece loomed larger, to add to existing fears for Italian strength. Plans had been worked out at the end of August for a British expedition in the event of a German collapse or early withdrawal; Brooke's apprehension remained over this operation, 'Manna', but Churchill and the Foreign Office were determined to prevent a communist-led takeover. The Prime Minister minuted on 29 August: 'It is most desirable to strike out of the blue without any preliminary crisis. It is the best way to forestall the EAM.'[30] On 13 September Wilson received orders to prepare for the preliminary descent on the Peloponnese, where the Germans were already pulling back northwards to the Corinth area, and 'Manna' troops – totalling over two British brigades plus Greek units – were placed at 48-hour alert. Eden reported to the COS on Thursday, 21 September that 'the King of Greece was much concerned by a message he had received from the Greek Prime Minister reporting that EAM were occupying all those parts of Greece evacuated by the Germans and the Bulgarians, and stating that the only way of safeguarding the position of the Greek Government was by dispatching adequate British forces'. Nye, Vice-CIGS, warned: 'Nothing more could be done unless we were prepared to withdraw forces from the battle in Italy for Greece, which he did not consider was justified.' The Foreign Secretary said: 'The Prime Minister had now agreed to his proposal that we should remind the Soviet Government of our close interest in Greek affairs and warn them in general terms of our determination to send a British force to that country to restore law and order, so as to pave the way for the provision of relief and to assist the Greek Government to re-establish their authority.'[31] Four days later a conference of Greek politicians and guerrilla leaders opened at Caserta. The initial tense atmosphere improved during the day; the following morning, 26 September, an agreement was signed placing all guerrilla forces under the Greek Government and under General Scobie, who was to command the British expedition under 'Manna'. Helped by this improved political situation, British troops occupied Patras in the early hours of 4 October and began working their way along the southern shores of the Gulf of Corinth on the heels of the German withdrawal.

Germany, Italy, Burma, the Balkans – plans were either having to be changed or new commitments made. The war passed through an uncertain, unsettling period; and despite ground gained in France and Belgium, the enemy could still reach out to strike the British homeland. Morrison told the War Cabinet on 18 September that 26 V-2s had been launched during the previous week. The Home Secretary wanted to retain the ban on publicity; other Ministers believed that a statement would not convey any useful information to the enemy, and 'it was a serious matter for the Government to suppress the publication of news'. The War Cabinet decided to leave the subject for discussions next week.[32] By then, 25 September, there had been a dramatic decrease in the past seven days – but 83 flying bombs had been launched from aircraft. Cripps urged that no public statement should be made yet, and Ministers agreed.

But rumours increased; and these weeks saw carping criticism, of Churchill, of the Government, of the conflict in general. Autumn tints on the trees heralded another winter of war; campaigns which had begun with such high hopes and stimulating victories had apparently degenerated into dreary slog. The Prime Minister's attitude – bouncy, irrepressible – which had seemed so suited to the mood of 1940, now seemed tiresome. The *New Statesman* declared on 23 September: 'Temperamental buoyancy and personal enjoyment in the art of war have sustained both Mr Churchill and Mr Roosevelt through the difficult years. Viewed from the heights of Quebec the military prospect is splendid....

But as soon as we turn to the actualities we are impressed by the adolescent irresponsibility of some of Mr Churchill's phrases. What are soldiers in the forgotten outposts of Burma and New Guinea fighting a remorseless enemy in a cruel climate, to think when they are told by the Prime Minister that we do not wish to miss any of the "fun"...?' The Prime Minister returned to London two days after this attacking article; on 28 September he addressed the House of Commons at the opening of a two-day debate on the war situation, and his first task was to announce the failure at Arnhem. Harold Nicolson gave his verdict of the speech. 'He is in fine form at the start, finding his words easily, thumping upon the box. But after three-quarters of an hour his voice gets husky and his delivery hesitant. We adjourn for an hour for lunch, and when Winston resumes, he has not entirely recovered his first brio. He lags a bit, and appears to be tired and bored.'[33] Churchill's speech next day, 29 September, concentrated more upon future, diplomatic prospects. 'I may say that everything depends on the agreement of the three leading European world powers.... I have sedulously avoided the appearance of any one country trying to lay down the law to its powerful allies or to any other state involved.' Lord Dunglass – Sir Alec Douglas-Home – advised caution. 'The question of the political relationship between Russia and Poland could not be left to be settled between those two countries without any intervention by us.... Russia operated under a code of ethics by no means the same as ours ... unless we faced that fact we should look down a long vista of political misunderstanding.' He added: 'We must not shirk plain speaking, for to that alone would the Russians respond.'

On this same Friday, Churchill raised the possibility of a visit to Moscow in a signal to Roosevelt. 'Anthony (Eden) and I are seriously thinking of flying there very soon.... The two great objects we have in mind would be, firstly, to clinch his coming in against Japan, and, secondly, to try to effect an amicable settlement with Poland. There are other points too concerning Yugoslavia and Greece which we would also discuss.' Next day both Roosevelt and Stalin signalled approval. And the Prime Minister left London on 7 October to journey to Russia via the Mediterranean; he had only spent 13 days at home since returning from 'Octagon', and before 'Octagon' only 8 days had separated his return from Italy from his departure to Quebec. This Moscow visit would be in marked contrast to Churchill's last meeting with Stalin at Tehran. Diplomatic issues now rated equal importance with military. War Cabinet and COS discussions during the last few days had been involved especially with one post-war problem liable to complicate East-West relations – the question of Germany's future.

The drastic Morgenthau plan to render Germany 'pastoral' still remained in official existence, but these War Cabinet discussions did not extend to its consideration, and Churchill did not raise the question: perhaps Ministerial opposition expressed in the telegram reaching Churchill at Quebec, combined with Eden's objections, persuaded the Prime Minister to quietly change his mind. The plan was allowed to fade from view; the Prime Minister wrote in his memoirs: 'In the event, with my full accord, the idea of "pastoralizing" Germany did not survive.' Churchill overlooked to mention that he had previously supported the idea.[34] Instead of the Morgenthau Plan, discussions on Germany centred on possible dismemberment and military occupation. The two were interrelated, and the COS had already completed a paper dated 9 September which urged cutting up the country to prevent German rearmament and renewed aggression; such a policy would also provide insurance against a hostile Russia – dismemberment would be less likely to allow a Russo-German combination, and vital British interests would be secured by British occupation of the north-west. On 5 June the COS had stressed that 'when Germany capitulates it will be essential to occupy the country up to the boundary of the Russian zone as quickly as possible, and that will mean the British occupying North Germany and the Americans South Germany.... The argument that we have far greater interest than the Americans in north-west Germany still held.'[35] But a Foreign Office memorandum on 20 September took a different attitude towards dismemberment: the Germans would try to evade such a measure, and British and American opinion would gradually regard the policy as unjust. The Foreign Office disregarded COS fears of a Russo-German combination, and believed the COS policy of a British combination with part of Germany, the north-west, against Russia to be 'fantastic and dangerous'. Such action might lead to a division of Germany with the north-west supporting Britain and the East Germans linked with the Russians. Plans must be made to preserve the Anglo-Soviet alliance and to preserve the unity of the United Nations. The COS discussed this Foreign Office paper on 2 October, yet found no reason to change their views.[36] A meeting between the COS and Eden on the 4th failed to bridge the gap, and Ismay minuted to Churchill that the problem would have to be given further study. On 6 October Churchill replied to the COS that he understood both the President and Stalin were in favour of dismemberment, 'and went even further in the matter than he (the Prime Minister) was inclined to go.' Churchill proposed to discuss the matter with Eden.[37] But the problem had still to be settled when Churchill, Eden and Brooke left England on 7 October: Brooke continued to agree with his colleagues that the Russians, with whom he would now discuss military matters, might eventually prove to be militarily hostile; Eden remained convinced that such pessimism could only increase the dangers of a divided Europe. East-West confrontation must be avoided; and yet, during this first week in October simultaneous moves were made by the Russian troops into Hungary and by British troops into Greece, the latter to bolster an anti-communist Government. And while in Moscow, Eden would learn that Tito of Yugoslavia had secretly visited the Soviet capital.

Churchill and Ismay left from Northolt during the night of 7 October; Brooke and Eden flew from Lyneham and landed at Naples at 7.10 a.m. next day, a few minutes behind the Prime Minister. After breakfast the group gathered for a conference with Wilson and Alexander. The local commanders reported on the latest stalemate situation in Italy.

'I was much distressed by their tale,' wrote Churchill, and Brooke commented in his diary: 'Alex is getting stuck in the Apennines with tired forces.'[38] Yet future planning had been rendered difficult by the number of unknown factors involved – Russian plans in the Balkans; the effect of allied pressure in France on German opposition in Italy; American intentions for some of their resources in the Mediterranean, especially landing-craft. The latter amounted to five-sixths of the assault shipping in the theatre; under existing arrangements the bulk would be moved by the Americans after 15 October. The conference examined two possible ways in which the advance in Italy could be maintained; both would involve operations at the head of the Adriatic and would therefore have political benefits with regard to the Russian advance in the Balkans. First, the allies might launch a sea-borne attack on the Istrian peninsula, aiming at Trieste, under the plan already discussed by the CCS; secondly, they could land south of Fiume and advance northwards, again aiming at Trieste. Choice would largely depend on the Yugoslav situation and on Tito's help – the Russians were already pushing into the country and Tito's partisans were making ground. Despite difficulties which had arisen over the Istrian operation, already discussed by the COS, the conference asked Wilson to report to the CCS as soon as possible.[39]

Churchill and his party left Naples at 11.30 a.m. heading for Egypt. The Prime Minister's aircraft made an appalling landing at Cairo, smashing the undercarriage beyond immediate repair, and the group had to cram into a single machine for the remainder of the journey. This aircraft left Cairo on 9 October, flying over the Crimea and war-torn Soviet soil to reach Moscow at noon. The Soviet capital seemed to be emerging like a chrysalis from the drabness of war: camouflage nets were being undraped from the gold balls on the towers; workmen were painting white and yellow over the khakied Kremlin walls. This confidence seemed to provide a fitting atmosphere during the talks over the next 10 days. Yet Eden had reached Moscow in a pessimistic mood, especially over the likelihood of a Polish settlement. 'The Russians had already grabbed the territory they wanted, so that the Curzon Line was no longer the real issue. It was what happened in Poland that mattered.... I was unhappily conscious that the Soviet Government had every motive to play for time.'[40] The Foreign Secretary and Prime Minister had recently persuaded Polish leaders in London to dismiss General Sosnkowski, Polish C-in-C, who was especially distrusted by the Russians – and who had recently criticized the allies for not giving sufficient help to the Warsaw Poles. Moreover the Polish Prime Minister, Mikolajczyk, had shown himself willing to accept a type of coalition Government, in which the communists would have a fifth of the seats. But Eden still felt the Russians could delay while opposition was broken up in Poland, and while the Soviet-backed Polish Committee of National Liberation, now established at Lublin, consolidated its position. Nevertheless, when Churchill and Eden met Stalin for their first talks at 10 p.m. on the 9th, the Soviet leader agreed with a British suggestion that Mikolajczyk and his colleagues should be invited to join the Moscow talks; the Poles would arrive on the 13th.

Churchill continued the first meeting on 9 October by taking dramatic advantage of Stalin's apparent willingness to be agreeable. As the Prime Minister wrote later: 'The moment was apt for business.' Yet this 'business' seemed a total contradiction of his statement made to the Commons only 12 days before that: 'I have sedulously avoided the appearance of any one country trying to lay down the law to its powerful allies or to any other states involved.' Churchill told Stalin: 'Let us settle about our affairs in the Balkans. Your armies are in Roumania and Bulgaria. We have interests, missions, and agents there. Don't let us get at cross-purposes in small ways.' He scribbled down figures on a half-sheet of paper: these gave percentages of respective Russian and British 'predominance' in the various Balkan countries, indicating 'spheres of influence' in clinical, mathematical form. 'Roumania, Russia 90 per cent, the others 10 per cent; Greece, Great Britain (in accord with the USA) 90 per cent, Russia 10 per cent; Yugoslavia, 50-50 per cent; Hungary, 50-50 per cent; Bulgaria, Russia 75 per cent, the others 25 per cent.' Churchill pushed the paper over the table to Stalin; after a slight pause the Soviet dictator took up his blue pencil and flicked a large tick on the document before tossing it back. 'It was all settled in no more time than it takes to set down,' wrote Churchill. But even the Prime Minister feared this method might appear too heartless. 'Might it not be thought rather cynical,' he asked Stalin, 'if it seemed we had disposed of these issues, so fateful to millions of people, in such an offhand manner? Let us burn the paper.' Stalin shrewdly replied: 'No. You keep it.'[41] Also on 9 October, recommendations agreed by diplomats at Dumbarton Oaks were published, regarding a possible post-war United Nations. This long conference had in fact become bogged down over UN voting procedure, with the Russians claiming 16 seats in the future Assembly – one for each constituent Republic. Diplomats had decided to refer the question to heads of Governments. Churchill had assured Roosevelt that UN topics would not be discussed during the visit to Moscow; Roosevelt in turn had made clear to both Churchill and Stalin that he regarded the British visit as a preliminary to a tripartite meeting, so, on 10 October, the Prime Minister and the Marshal sent Roosevelt assurance that they had not been poaching upon American preserves. 'We have agreed not to refer in our discussions to Dumbarton Oaks issues, and that these shall be taken up when we three can meet together.' The joint message mentioned Balkan discussions – but without giving 'predominance' percentages. 'We have to consider the best way of reaching an agreed policy about the Balkan countries, including Hungary and Turkey.' The signal did however state that Averell Harriman, US Ambassador, would sit as an observer 'at all meetings where business of importance is to be transacted.... We shall keep you fully informed.' Harriman had not been present at the meeting the previous night; nor would he attend similar sessions during the next few days. Churchill also sent a private message to Roosevelt. 'It is absolutely necessary we should try to get a common mind about the Balkans, so that we may prevent civil war breaking out in several countries, when probably you and I would be in sympathy with one side and UJ (Uncle Joe) with with other ... nothing will be settled except preliminary agreements ... subject to further discussion and melting down with you. On this basis I am sure you will not mind our trying to have a full meeting of minds with the Russians.'[42]

Information revealed to Eden on this second day of the visit, 10 October, underlined the necessity for mutual arrangement over the Balkans. The Foreign Secretary reported to the Foreign Office: 'I had a pretty vigorous exchange with Molotov on the Bulgarian situation.... I said that a number of reports had reached us this morning showing that the Bulgarians were behaving with increasing insolence towards ourselves.... Such a state of affairs was intolerable.... Molotov seemed embarrassed by these charges and begged me to believe we should together discuss the whole Balkan situation when he felt sure that agreement could be reached. ... The Soviet Government had no desire to pursue a separate policy.' But Eden's report added: 'He continued that he had a secret to tell me. Marshal Tito had recently been in Moscow. At the Marshal's express request the visit had been kept secret. Its object had been to agree upon joint military action in Yugoslavia.... I replied that we took the strongest exception to Marshal Tito's behaviour and to the fact that we had not been told of the visit.... Molotov hurriedly put all the blame on Marshal Tito. He said he was a peasant and did not understand anything about politics.'[43] Eden had another 2-hour meeting with Molotov during the evening, and the Soviet Foreign Minister immediately attempted to bargain over the percentage figures proposed by Churchill and accepted by Stalin the previous night: Russia should be allowed 75 per cent predominance in Hungary, rather than the 50-50 basis suggested, and should have 90 per cent in Bulgaria instead of 75 per cent. Haggling continued until 9 p.m. with Eden finally declaring: 'I was not interested in figures. All I wanted was to be sure that we had more voice in Bulgaria and Hungary than we had accepted in Roumania, and that there should be a joint policy in Yugoslavia.'[44] The Foreign Secretary reported this unpleasant encounter to Churchill later that night. 'W. rather upset by my report,' wrote Eden. 'I think he thought I had dispelled the good atmosphere he had created night before. But I explained this was the real battle and I could not and would not give way.'[45]

During the day Churchill had been concerning himself with Anglo-American military planning. Two extra British divisions were being sent to help strengthen the Dutch salient, and Churchill believed this reinforcement could be used as a bargaining counter with the Americans for the despatch of additional US troops to the Mediterranean. He therefore signalled Roosevelt: 'Could you not deflect two, or better still three, American divisions to the Italian front, which would enable them to join Mark Clark's 5th Army and add the necessary strength to Alexander?' The Prime Minister added that Wilson would be forwarding his plans direct to the CCS, concentrating on the Istrian scheme. 'This plan will be in accord with the overall strategic objective, namely, the expulsion from or destruction in Italy of Kesselring's army.'[46] Wilson completed his report during this Tuesday, and it made discouraging reading. No troops could be spared from Italy for an amphibious assault in the head of the Adriatic until December at the earliest, thus ruling out an attack on Istria in 1944 if Alexander's current operations were to be sustained. Moreover, if an Italian mainland offensive were to be launched in spring, 1945, additional troops would have to be brought in from elsewhere for an Istria operation: Wilson would need three fresh divisions, including the airborne division, although the latter would probably not be required if the alternative plan for a landing south of Fiume were attempted. Wilson added some gloomy comments on the value of the Italian theatre as a whole: the campaign now seemed unlikely to contribute directly over the next few months to the campaign in western Europe, and 'the Russian advance will be a more decisive factor in influencing the withdrawal of Kesselring's army out of Italy'.[47]

The Eden-Molotov clash brought Churchill's attention back to the Balkans on the night of the 10th; and, perhaps with this quarrel revealing to him the dangers inherent in this method of business, the Prime Minister now apparently suffered second thoughts over his percentage arrangement. On 11 October he drafted a letter to Stalin: 'These percentages which I have put down are no more than a method by which in our thoughts we can see how near we are together, and then decide upon the necessary steps to bring us into full agreement. As I said, they would be considered crude, and even callous, if they were exposed to the scrutiny of the Foreign Office and diplomats all over the world. Therefore they could not be the basis of any public document, certainly not at the present time....'[48] But the atmosphere suddenly improved again, and Churchill's letter remained unsent. Eden met Molotov at 3 p.m. on this Wednesday, 11 October, and 'all was as smooth as it had been rough yesterday and we obtained what we wanted on almost all points'. Eden also learnt with relief that Tito had invited the Yugoslav Prime Minister to meet him in Serbia, thus opening the way to possible political compromise. And the cordial Moscow climate continued: Stalin dined at the British Embassy that night – the first time the British Ambassador had succeeded in making such an arrangement. Next day, 12 October, Roosevelt replied to the joint message sent by Stalin and Churchill after their talk on the 9th: the President seemed to accept the need for the Anglo-Soviet discussion. Nevertheless, even without knowledge of the 'percentage' proposals, Roosevelt hinted that nothing drastic should be done without American consultation. 'I am most pleased to know that you are reaching a meeting of your two minds as to international policies in which, because of our present and future common efforts to prevent international wars, we are all interested.'[49] A signal to Harry Hopkins, dispatched on the same day Churchill received Roosevelt's cable, explained why Harriman had not been invited to sit as an observer at Balkan talks, despite the promise given to the President. 'We have so many bones to pick about the Balkans at the present time that we would rather carry the matter a little further *à deux*.' Also on the 12th, Churchill explained his behaviour to the War Cabinet. 'The system of percentages is not intended to prescribe the numbers sitting on commissions for the different Balkan countries, but rather to express the interest and sentiment with which the British and Soviet Governments approach the problems of those countries.... It is not intended to be more than a guide, and of course in no way commits the US, nor does it attempt to set up a rigid system of spheres of interest. It may, however, help the US to see how their two principal allies feel about these regions.'[50]

The Polish Prime Minister and Foreign Minister reached Moscow that night. And so began five days of 'the stiffest negotiations' which Eden had ever known. Nothing definite had resulted by the time Mikolajczyk and Romer flew back to London on the 17th. Stalin withdrew his earlier concession that the settlement of the frontier question could be postponed, and demanded immediate acceptance of the Curzon Line. The Polish Prime Minister, who, according to Eden, showed 'a calm courage throughout his ordeal', refused to give immediate acceptance despite pressure exerted by Churchill. Moreover, Mikolajczyk insisted upon the settlement of Polish international political questions, saying he could not safely agree to merge his Government with the Soviet-backed Lublin Committee. Churchill told him on the 14th that the Great Powers had spent 'blood and treasure' to liberate Poland, and they could not allow themselves to be drawn into a dispute for the sake of a Polish domestic quarrel. Mikolajczyk retorted that he knew the state of Poland had been settled at Tehran, but the quarrel was not merely between Poles – it included the Soviet Union. Churchill answered that the time was past when the Poles could afford the 'luxury' of indulging patriotic feeling. The Polish Premier told Eden on 17 October that if he accepted the Curzon Line, he would lose control not only of his own supporters in London but of the army and the Polish people; nevertheless he agreed to fly back to Britain and attempt to persuade his Government.[51]

Brooke had been thoroughly enjoying himself; Ismay's staff were working at full stretch to find him enough parties to go to; he watched *Prince Igor* one night, *Eugene Onegin* the next, and a Gala Ballet on another and *Swan Lake* the

next. And in the relaxed atmosphere he gave a brilliant
exposition to a military conference late on 14 October, detailing the situation in France, Italy and Burma, and
answering technical questions fired at him by Stalin. Brooke
believed the Soviet leader had an, 'outstanding' military
knowledge; the Russians in turn seemed extremely impressed
by the British CIGS and responded with a full description
of the Eastern front activities. Brooke wrote in his diary:
'The whole was on a most open and free basis of discussion.
We broke up at 1.30 a.m., well satisfied with our meeting.
We have come a long way for it, and have had a long wait
for it, but it has made up for these inconveniences.'[52]
Churchill, suffering from a mild fever, was unable to attend
the second military conference next day, at which the
Russians gave a firm pledge that they would enter the war
against Japan once Germany had been defeated. Gone were
the days of recriminations over the Second Front question,
and Brooke could speak with the authority and confidence
stemming from the powerful allied presence in Europe.

Yet a discussion in London next day, 16 October, underlined the difficulties which lay ahead in planning for a further
European advance. Wilson's report on the Italian campaign
had been studied by the Joint Planners, who completed a
document on the 14th which criticized his call for additional
resources. On the 16th the COS met with Portal in the chair
to examine both Wilson's appreciation and the JPS comments. The latter stressed the need for operations in Italy
to conform with 'Overlord' needs. Eisenhower might be able
to launch a major offensive in January 1945; the armies in
Italy could best help by continuing to fight hard on the
mainland itself, and thereafter possibly providing troops for
operations in north-west Europe through the withdrawal of
the US portion of the 5th Army. Alternatively, British and
Imperial troops could be pulled out to form a strategic
reserve. The Planners therefore concluded: 'Bearing in mind
the effect on other theatres, we cannot, on our present information, recommend that on military grounds additional
resources should be allotted to the Mediterranean; nor that
the American assault craft should be retained there.' The

COS decided that the Italian theatre must remain secondary to the western front. 'Both theatres were in need of fresh formations, but whereas Eisenhower could absorb and employ all fresh divisions which could be made available, the narrowing front in Italy would prevent Alexander ever employing, in his present advance northwards, much more than half his present force.' The COS decided to send this conclusion to Churchill and Brooke in Moscow.[53] The COS decision therefore cut across Churchill's appeal to Roosevelt, about which Portal and his colleagues had not been consulted, and also on the 16th, the President replied to the Prime Minister. 'Diversion of any forces to Italy would withhold from France vitally needed fresh troops.'[54] The President and the British COS were therefore in agreement, in opposition to Churchill; nevertheless, Churchill would attempt to salvage something in a further conference on his way home from Moscow.

Departure from the Soviet capital was delayed 48 hours, first by the Polish negotiations and then by the Russian wish to stage a Kremlin banquet on the 18th. The extra time allowed opportunity for discussion of the controversial topic of Germany's future. The topic remained sensitive for two reasons: the British had still to agree upon a policy of dismemberment; secondly, Churchill did not wish to be reminded of the drastic Morgenthau Plan. Thus, when Stalin mentioned the latter, the Prime Minister avoided a direct answer and merely said the President and Morgenthau were not very happy about the reception it had received. At a meeting on the 17th Stalin said he favoured dismemberment, and asked for British views. Eden could only reply that the British Government had not yet come to a firm conclusion; in fact, five days before the British COS had once again given support for such a policy of dismemberment – and one of their reasons for doing so lay in their belief that this would offer better protection. Thus the COS meeting on 12 October had decided upon a new paper declaring 'our principal aim in advocating dismemberment was to secure the north-west part of Germany as our ally against a future threat to our security'.[55] Conversely, Eden became even more convinced after his talks with Stalin that dismemberment might be a mistake. 'I became more wary of the advantages the Soviets might seek in a weakened and divided Continent.'[56]

Churchill and his colleagues left on Thursday morning, 19 October, with Stalin bestowing a further honour by coming to say goodbye at the airfield. Stalin and the rest of the Soviet hierarchy had been courteous, expansive, good-humoured; this Moscow conference seemed to mark the summit of Anglo-Soviet relations. Churchill was most impressed. Yet three subjects still chafed beneath this comfortable cloak: Poland, the Balkans, the future of Germany. All would assume increasing importance; all would demand increasing attention after Churchill's triumphant return to London. And to add to the importance of one of them, the Balkans, Russian troops now entered Belgrade, and the Greek Government returned to Athens – where British troops were already finding the communists in a position of almost arrogant authority.

For the moment Churchill attempted to deal with more immediate problems in the struggle against the Germans and Japanese. The Prime Minister had suggested a meeting with Mountbatten at Cairo on his way home, and talks with the Supreme Commander SEAC therefore took place on 20 October. Mountbatten produced revised plans, brought about by the cancellation of 'Dracula' against Rangoon following the events at Arnhem; operations would be severely restricted by the limited resources available. Moreover, 'Dracula' had been considered an essential part of the full-scale launching of 'Capital' in north Burma. Instead, Mountbatten proposed to maintain the offensive in Arakan, and operations would also cover the capture of Akyab, after which two divisions would be available for an amphibious operation against the Kra Isthmus to sever Japanese communications between Burma and Malaya. A larger operation might then be launched against the area Fort Swettenham – Port Dicksom, from which to threaten Singapore, and 'Dracula' would be staged early in 1945.[57] This complicated programme would need careful consideration; on 20 October

Mountbatten was therefore asked to submit detailed studies as soon as possible. Mountbatten flew back to India; Churchill and Brooke flew on to Naples, where a conference opened on the 21st to discuss the Italian campaign. Wilson, like Mountbatten, made a further attempt to cut his coat according to his rationed cloth. Both the Americans and the British COS opposed the dispatch of further troops to Italy, but US landing-craft remained. Moreover, the German position was clearly collapsing in the Balkans as a result of the Red Army advance. Wilson therefore proposed the attack on the Dalmatian coast to capture Fiume, using fewer troops than hitherto suggested. Wilson was asked to send another report to London and the CCS.[58]

Churchill and Brooke flew home next day, 22 October, and the Prime Minister reported to the War Cabinet at 5.30 p.m. on the 23rd, informing Ministers that he intended to make a 'brief statement' to the Commons on the 27th: he would describe his Moscow mission, and would also mention the V-2 attacks without going into detail. The Prime Minister accordingly prepared his speech on the 26th and lay in bed on the morning of the 27th to add finishing touches. Cadogan wrote: 'He due to make it at 11 and didn't upheave himself out of bed till 10.40.' The effort seemed worthwhile: the speech, which also announced full British and American recognition of de Gaulle's Government of Liberated France, met with wide approval. Churchill seemed in peak form. 'He is quite himself again,' wrote Harold Nicolson. 'A few months ago he seemed ill and tired and he did not find his words as easily as usual. But today he was superb. Cherubic, pink, solid and vociferous.'[59] And to match the Prime Minister's mood, next day Eisenhower issued orders for a general offensive.

'The general plan, subject always to prior capture of the approaches to Antwerp, is as follows: a) Making the main effort in the north, decisively to defeat the enemy west of the Rhine and secure bridgeheads over the river; then to seize the Ruhr and subsequently advance deep into Germany.' So far the directive went some way to meeting Montgomery's wishes for a northern emphasis; but Eisenhower continued:

'b) To conduct operations so as to destroy the enemy in the Saar, to secure crossing over the Rhine, and to be prepared to advance.... c) On the right, i.e. the southern, flank, making full use of maintenance available from the Mediterranean, to act aggressively with the initial object of overwhelming the enemy west of the Rhine and subsequently of advancing into Germany.'[60] Thus the offensive would still be maintained along the whole front, despite shortages of ammunition and the bottleneck in sending supplies and men through the few available ports. Brooke did not receive details until 2 November, when he wrote in his diary: 'Found out that Ike's plan as usual entails attacking all along the front, instead of selecting main strategic points. I fear that the November attack will consequently get no further than the Rhine at the most.'[61] The Antwerp approaches were not cleared until the end of the first week in November – not until the 28th could the first convoy reach this valuable port. The precise control of effort and timing between the different sectors had thus been disrupted from the start. Bitter fighting continued throughout November, mostly in the thickening winter weather, and even Brooke's gloomy forecast proved optimistic. Aachen had fallen on 21 October, yet by the end of November the Americans could only manage to struggle forward 8 miles south-east of the town; to the north the 2nd Army pushed slowly to the line of the Maas and Roer, but would only be able to clear the latter's western bank as far as Roermond by the beginning of December. To the south, success seemed more likely when the 1st French Army broke through between Nancy and Belfort on 19 November to reach Strasbourg and the upper Rhine, but the Germans pushed in reinforcements, and by the end of the month allied operations south of the Ardennes had been thrown into a similar impasse as those in the north. The main Siegfried Line defences remained intact; supplies were even scarcer; winter weather fast closed in.

Similar depression resulted from news of the Italian campaign. Heavy rains swept down upon the 8th Army, and attempts by the 5th Army to the left failed to make ground. Further advances were undertaken during brief respites from the foul weather during November, but no major offensive seemed possible. Even Churchill had become disillusioned over Italian possibilities. Wilson completed his report on a Fiume assault on 24 October, and this received COS attention on the 30th: Wilson proposed to pass to 'an offensive defensive' in Italy after the capture of Bologna; he would put in light forces near and south of Zara as soon as the position on the Dalmatian coast allowed, and would prepare to attack overland on Fiume and Trieste in the first week of February, 1945. Wilson therefore seemed to assume that the operation could not be launched until late in the winter. 'One of the absurd things,' minuted Churchill to the COS, 'in all the plans which are submitted by AFHQ, is the idea that if they move in February they will be in time to effect anything. In the three months which they say must elapse before they are capable of movement, the whole of Yugoslavia will be cleared of the Germans.... The Yugoslavs will then occupy Trieste, Fiume and other towns which they claim. So what will be the need of an expedition and all the landing-craft, and so on? The days of these slow-moving, heavy-footed methods are over, but we still cling to them with disastrous results.' The COS considered Wilson's plan and Churchill's minute at their meeting on the 30th, and agreed with the Prime Minister that a 'large-scale operation' in the Balkans should only be attempted if an earlier date could be secured; meanwhile increased support should be given to the Yugoslav guerrillas.[62] The Americans were informed of this decision next day, but did not reply until 17 November, when they questioned the feasibility of a 'large-scale operation' in the Balkans, and reminded the British COS that 'Mediterranean operations have been aimed primarily at furnishing maximum support to the Western Front'. A large Balkan operation would do little to further this aim, and the American COS therefore considered that 'the proper action at this time is to introduce light forces into the Dalmatian ports in order to maintain pressure and harass the German forces withdrawing from the Balkans'.[63] But by the time this US reply reached London the situation had altered still further. The

Germans had managed to consolidate their position in Italy and in western Yugoslavia; no withdrawal through the Balkans seemed likely for the moment; above all, relations with Tito had undergone serious deterioration. No progress had been made on diplomatic matters with Yugoslav partisans, and military co-operation suddenly took a turn for the worse. In October Tito had asked for the help of a British artillery unit, and this element, named Floydforce from its commander Brigadier Sir Henry Floyd, landed on 28 October to operate under the local partisan commander. But partisan treatment of this unit proved hostile, and on 25 November a Titoist broadcast declared no agreement had been signed authorizing the entry of British or American troops into Yugoslavia, 'such as has been signed between Yugoslavia and the Soviet High Command'. Tito had shifted even further into the Soviet sphere. Militarily, this meant virtually no possibility of partisan co-operation with forces landed from Italy, and already, on 22 November, Wilson reported that recent developments obliged him now to concentrate on the Italian campaign. Wilson attended a COS meeting in London on the 28th, and discussions resulted in a new directive. 'The introduction of major forces into the Balkans as recommended by you ... is not favourably considered at this time.... Your first and immediate objective should be to capture Bologna, then to secure the general line Ravenna-Bologna-Spezia.'[64]

Moreover, another complication was pushing rapidly to the front, likely to involve forces in the Mediterranean. Eden had remained in the Middle East after Churchill's return home, and had flown to Athens on 25 October to discuss the general Greek situation with the British Ambassador, Leeper, and British commanders. 'The political situation on the surface at least is fairly satisfactory,' he reported to Churchill, 'but it yet remains to be seen how far the authority of the Government can be established beyond Athens.... EAM is active and we should be unwise in my judgement to underestimate its strength.' On the 30th he signalled: 'I am by no means confident that this little country will be able to regain its stability without other and maybe terrible upheavals.'[65]

The Foreign Secretary returned to London at the beginning
of November; disorder spread in Greece as the communist
EAM sought greater control. And Churchill minuted to
Eden on the 7th: 'Having paid the price we have to Russia
for freedom of action in Greece, we should not hesitate to
use British troops to support the Royal Hellenic Government
under M. Papandreou.... I fully expect a clash with EAM
and we must not shrink from it, provided the ground is well
chosen.' Unsettling reports continued to reach London;
within 24 hours Churchill signalled Wilson: 'In view of increasing threat of Communist elements in Greece and
indications that they plan to seize power by force, I hope
that you will consider reinforcing our troops in Athens
area.'[65] The War Cabinet had discussed Greece on 6 November, without taking any firm decision over the dispatch of
more troops. Nor did the COS take any such decision;
Churchill instead applied pressure on his own initiative,
despite the possibility of increased British involvement.
Wilson reported on 15 November that the communists
seemed likely to bring matters to a head, and he had therefore
instructed Scobie, commander of the troops in Greece, to
hold all units already in the country and to concentrate on
the capital. Athens should be declared a military area, continued Wilson, and the EAM military force should be
ordered to withdraw quietly from it. By now over 30,000
British troops were in Greece – compared with the original
idea of limiting the allied force to 10,000 men. Yet the
increased number of British troops further inflamed the
communists; preparations were intensified for full-scale
opposition, although measures taken by Papandreou, combined with the tightening British military control over the
capital, seemed to restore an uneasy quiet.

The British Foreign Office continued to view the Greek
situation with foreboding. and the same applied to the other
main diplomatic preoccupation – Poland. On his return from
Moscow the Polish Prime Minister had found even greater
opposition than he had expected from his Government to
frontier demands made by Stalin, together with Soviet
requirements for the composition of a Coalition Government.

Romer, the Polish Foreign Minister, called to see Cadogan on 31 October, who wrote in his diary: 'Poles have done *nothing* – simply havering. Now put three questions to us.... Delay is dangerous.' Churchill told Cadogan next day that the situation would be discussed by the War Cabinet at 5.30 p.m., 'meanwhile I was to stop Poles taking any irrevocable decision'.[67] Ministers were told at this War Cabinet meeting that Romer had put certain queries to HMG 'and thought that if favourable answers could be given to them it might facilitate a decision by the Polish Government'. The first question asked: 'Was the attitude of HMG on the territorial compensation which Poland had been promised in the west so decided that even though the US might not agree ... HMG would still consider themselves bound to advocate these at the peace settlement?' Churchill believed an affirmative answer should be given, mainly because he had 'no reason whatever to believe that (the Americans) were not strongly in favour'. The second question asked: 'Is the policy of HMG definitely in favour of extending the Polish frontier up to the Oder?' Again, Churchill believed an affirmative answer should be given, and Ministers decided the Poles should be informed that 'the policy of HMG was definitely in favour ... unless Poland, of her own volition, should desire at a later stage of more restricted territorial compensation in the west'. Thirdly, the Poles asked whether Britain would guarantee the independence and integrity of the new Poland. And this question proved the most difficult to answer, raising as it did the possibilities of future commitments. Churchill believed 'we would be justified in giving the guarantee ... particularly if it was a joint guarantee with Russia, and if the US could thereafter be associated with it'. Beaverbrook, Lord Privy Seal, strongly disagreed. 'We had the lesson of 1939 before us and we should not again give guarantees to Poland which we could not implement.... The great bulk of British public opinion would be opposed to a further commitment of this nature.' The position was not parallel to the 1939 situation, argued Churchill. 'The guarantee now proposed ... would recognize a situation which would be confirmed at the peace conference. If it was joint, we should

have the support of Russia and in due course, it might be
hoped, the USA. Finally, the guarantee had to be set against
the background of the proposed world organization, which
was to ensure the respect of frontiers and maintain peace
and good fellowship.' The Prime Minister, warmed by
the Moscow Conference, had firm faith in future Russian
co-operation; Cranborne, Dominions Secretary, pointed out
that 'if the Russians were to maintain the position they had
taken up at Dumbarton Oaks they could effectively block
any discussion or action, in regard to a breach of the guarantee, by the Council of the World Organization', to which
Churchill retorted that 'our whole position had to proceed
on the assumption that Russia would in fact rank as a partner'. After further discussion Churchill had his way on this
crucial point: the Poles would be told that the guarantee
would be given, if possible jointly with Russia and America,
lasting until the establishment of a world organization, the
United Nations.[68]

The Poles sought to obtain the American attitude, and
received rather vague assurances on 22 November: Roosevelt would accept a frontier arrangement approved by the
Polish, British and Soviet Governments – but he could not
offer an actual guarantee. 'It is not worth much to the Poles,'
commented Eden.[69] Next day, 23 November, Mikolajczyk
felt obliged to resign; Churchill and Eden told him they
thought his decision to be wise, and expected him to return to
office soon, meanwhile they would treat any new Polish
Government coldly, but correctly. Cadogan hoped the resignation would mean 'the end of these silly Poles', and clearly
Churchill also blamed the Polish Government in Exile,
rather than the Russians, for lack of progress in reaching
agreement. He told Parliament that if the Polish Government had agreed to the proposals made in Moscow, 'Poland
might now have taken full place in the ranks of the nations
contending against Germany and would have had the full
support and friendship of Marshal Stalin and the Soviet
Government.'[70]

Behind discussions on the three subjects of Yugoslavia,
Greece and Poland lay one common factor – Soviet policy.

Debate on each of these subjects had to centre upon communist activities: Tito, apparently being drawn closer to
Moscow; the EAM; the Moscow-backed Polish National
Committee at Lublin. Churchill had been overwhelmingly
impressed by Stalin's apparent spirit of co-operation shown
at the Moscow talks, and the Prime Minister retained an
attitude towards the Soviet Union which, with the advantage
of hindsight, seems incredibly idealistic. This attitude was
fully revealed at a War Cabinet meeting on 27 November,
when Churchill referred Ministers to the subject of 'the so-
called western bloc which appeared to be attracting increasing attention'. Discussion on this subject did in fact
contain the seeds of future NATO, but Churchill told
Ministers that: 'It was important that there should be no
misunderstanding in our attitude and in particular that de
Gaulle should not be in a position to suggest in Moscow that
we had made overtures to him to join a western bloc which
he had rejected. He (Churchill) was very doubtful himself
as to the soundness or practicability of a western bloc. In his
judgement the only real safeguard was an agreement between
the three great powers within the framework of a world
organization. He felt himself Russia was ready and anxious
to work in with us. No immediate threat of war lay ahead
of us once the present war was over, and we should be careful
of assuming commitments, consequent on the formation of
the western bloc, that might impose a very heavy military
burden upon us.' Eden assured Churchill that 'nothing more
had ever been contemplated than a special group based on
the proximity of certain states to us ... and finally on the fact
that Stalin had himself in 1941 favoured an arrangement
of this nature.'[71] So Churchill sought to reassure Stalin:
'There has been some talk in the Press about a western bloc.
I have not yet considered this. I trust first of all to our Treaty
of Alliance and close collaboration with the US to form the
mainstays of a World Organization to ensure and compel
peace upon the tortured world. It is only after and subordinate to any such world structure that European arrangements for better comradeship should be set on foot, and in
these matters we shall have no secrets from you, being well

assured that you will keep us equally informed.' Churchill read this telegram and Stalin's reply to the War Cabinet on 4 December. 'As regards the western bloc, Stalin had expressed appreciation of the Prime Minister's message and had added that he would not fail to profit from his good advice and inform him as to developments.' Stalin had referred to de Gaulle's visit to Moscow, which had just begun, and 'had asked the Prime Minister for his advice on two questions likely to be raised by the General. a) The conclusion of a Franco-Soviet pact of mutual assistance similar to the Anglo-Soviet Pact; b) The question of the eastern frontier of France.' Churchill expressed satisfaction 'at the cordial tone of Stalin's message, and at his request for our advice'. He had consulted Eden over the reply to Moscow, and 'was anxious that it should be in cordial terms and should issue without delay'. Eden suggested the message should state that while 'we were wholly in favour' of a Franco-Soviet Pact, a tripartite pact would be better, and Ministers agreed.[72] Stalin would in fact sign a strictly Soviet agreement with de Gaulle on 10 December. Churchill's optimism over future Anglo-Soviet relations would nevertheless increase still further.

This slightly unreal attitude reflected the general atmosphere in November 1944. The cold foggy month seemed to be a time of waiting, of gathering strength, of circular and non-productive discussion. The COS spent many hours debating topics such as ammunition shortages, command networks, personnel changes, post-war problems, and Palestine – and with the latter, War Cabinet Ministers were shocked to hear on 6 November that Lord Moyne, Minister of State in Cairo, had been assassinated the previous day by Jewish terrorists. Meanwhile the COS, and especially Brooke, continued to fear for future battles in Europe and criticized Eisenhower's handling of the situation. These criticisms culminated in a meeting between Brooke and Churchill on 28 November, when the CIGS attacked the Supreme Commander's 'broad front' strategy, describing it as 'sheer madness', and urged Churchill to press for Bradley to be made commander of the Land Forces. 'I think I succeeded in pointing out that we must take control out of Eisenhower's hands,' wrote Brooke in his diary.[73] But arguments continued; a meeting between Montgomery and Eisenhower on 28 November seemed to sort out some differences, but when the British commander wrote to Eisenhower next day, repeating his ideas in writing, the Supreme Commander disagreed again. Brooke secured Churchill's agreement for a plea to the Americans for another CCS meeting; Roosevelt appeared unenthusiastic. So, as December opened, the situation remained unsettled both on the ground in Europe and in the conference rooms of Whitehall and 10 Downing Street. And this situation threatened both military operations and Anglo-American relations. As far as the latter were concerned, both the British and the Americans had suffered a severe loss early in November through the death of the hard-working, dedicated Sir John Dill. Dill's contribution to Anglo-American understanding had been unique; his death on 4 November left a virtually unbridgeable gap. 'His loss is quite irreparable,' wrote Brooke in his diary. 'Without him at Washington I do not know how we should have got through the last three years.' And the CIGS added later: 'To my mind we owe more to Dill than to any other general for our final victory.' Brooke's predecessor as CIGS now received a unique honour for a British soldier – burial in the US Arlington National Cemetery. In London, the COS decided on 7 November to recommend Wilson as Dill's successor, with Alexander taking over as Supreme Commander in the Mediterranean and Mark Clark from Alexander as Army Group Commander in Italy. Churchill eventually agreed, after a brief argument that Alexander should be both Supreme Commander and Army Group Commander – a similar dual function as that held by Eisenhower, and strongly opposed by the British COS.[74]

Brooke described Churchill as 'on the flat side' at the beginning of November. This drop in spirits seemed only momentary. Elation and zest resulting from the Moscow talks received another boost when the Prime Minister, Mrs Churchill, Eden, Brooke, Cadogan and others flew to France for a triumphant entry into Paris on 11 November, Armistice

Day. The Prime Minister revelled in the trip, deriving enjoyment both from sleeping in the same bed as used by Göring
and from the magnificent reception given to him and de
Gaulle by the French people. 'The pent-up emotion of perhaps
half a million Parisians broke loose like a flood,' wrote Ismay.
'Some were cheering: some were laughing: some were
sobbing: all were delirious.... It was a bitterly cold day, and
the tears froze on our cheeks.'[75] Churchill and Brooke
spent two more days touring French military positions and
conferring with Eisenhower, returning to London late on
14 November; on 13 November Eden had described the
Paris visit to the War Cabinet. He had been left 'with the
feeling of a people who had been in a prison camp, and
who were still slightly dazed on recovering their freedom....
As regards personalities, the general impression left on him
had been that the French Government was a young Government, who were dealing capably with a new state of things....
De Gaulle's own position was very strong and the general
feeling seemed to be that he was a man to whom France
could rally.'[76]

The weather turned bitterly cold. Ice froze the boggy
roads of France into iron ruts; oil hardened in tank engines
and rifle bolts; fears were voiced for Churchill's health when
he toured the military positions during the freezing day of
13 November. Two weeks later, on 29 November, Churchill
celebrated his 70th birthday. On the same day, Nicolson
wrote: 'When he (Churchill) came back from his Italian
visit, we had all been horrified by his apparent exhaustion.
But Moscow did him good, and the snowdrifts of the Vosges
did him even more good. He is, or seems, as fit as he ever
was.'[77] And now waiting had ended; activity would erupt,
and not of allied choosing. Churchill would throw himself
further than ever before into the centre of these events,
regardless of risk.

9

Counter-offensive

Reports reaching London on 1 December revealed Papandreou's Government to be breaking up under communist
pressure; ELAS guerrilla groups around Athens were being
reinforced, and the communists were calling for settlement
by force after their rejection of Papandreou's demands made
on 28 November. On 2 December the remains of the Greek
Government attempted to fight back through a decree
dissolving guerrilla units; EAM responded by a call for a
general strike and shifted its HQ from the capital. General
Scobie issued a message to the Greek people: he stood firm
behind the present constitutional Government 'until the
Greek State can be established with a legally armed force and
free elections can be held'. Churchill issued a similar statement in London. On Sunday, 3 December, shots were fired
during a demonstration in Constitution Square, either by
police or ELAS guerrillas, and civil war began. Next day
Scobie ordered ELAS to evacuate Athens and the Piraeus;
ELAS refused and closed in upon key points in the capital,
attacking police stations.

Churchill and Eden sat up late at 10 Downing Street
studying the situation, and the Prime Minister decided to
take direct control of the affair. He wrote later: 'It is no use
doing things like this by halves. The mob violence, by which
the Communists sought to conquer the city and present themselves to the world as the Government demanded by the
Greek people, could only be met by firearms.' At 2 a.m. on
5 December, Churchill and Eden agreed Scobie should be

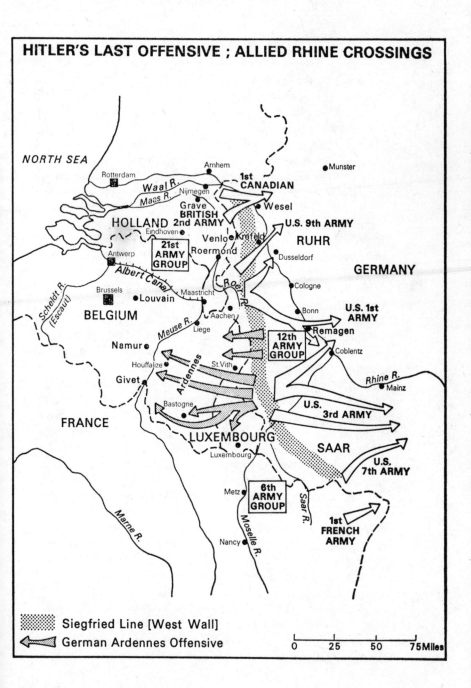

HITLER'S LAST OFFENSIVE ; ALLIED RHINE CROSSINGS

NORTH SEA

Munster

Rotterdam

Arnhem

Waal R.
Maas R.   Nijmegen
Grave   **1st**
CANADIAN

Wesel

BRITISH
HOLLAND **2nd ARMY**

Eindhoven

U.S. 9th ARMY

Venlo   Krefeld   **RUHR**
Roermond

21st
Antwerp   **ARMY**
GROUP

Dusseldorf   **GERMANY**

Albert Canal

Brussels

Scheldt R.
(Escaut)

Louvain

BELGIUM

Maastricht

Roer R.

Cologne

Bonn   **U.S. 1st**
ARMY

Aachen   Remagen

Meuse R.   Liege

12th
ARMY
GROUP

Coblentz

Namur

Houffalize   *Ardennes*   St.Vith

Givet

Bastogne

Rhine R.
Mainz

U.S.
3rd ARMY

LUXEMBOURG

Luxembourg

SAAR

U.S.
7th ARMY

Marne R.

Metz   **6th**
ARMY
GROUP

Saar R.

1st
FRENCH
ARMY

Nancy

Moselle R.

Siegfried Line [West Wall]
German Ardennes Offensive

0   25   50   75 Miles

ordered to open fire. 'There was no time for the Cabinet to
be called,' wrote Churchill, and he himself drafted and
despatched the orders: 'We have to hold and dominate
Athens. It would be a great thing for you to succeed in this
without bloodshed if possible, but also with bloodshed if
necessary.'[1] The message to Scobie left London at 4.50 a.m.;
British Ministers had still not been informed, nor would the
subject receive War Cabinet attention for another six days.
The controversial commitment to plunge British troops
directly into the Greek civil war had therefore been taken
without full War Cabinet authorization – just as the commitment to send British troops to Greece in the fateful 1941
expedition had been made by Eden on the spot, without
prior reference to the War Cabinet, but acting under instructions given by Churchill alone.[2]

The Prime Minister's decision now led to immediate and
bitter criticism, and his announcement to Parliament on 5
December received a rough reception, especially from
Aneurin Bevan. Feeling at the American State Department
was already running high against the British, over the
Foreign Office's handling of a current leadership crisis in the
Italian Government. Hull had recently left the State Department owing to ill-health, but his successor, Edward Stettinius,
issued a highly provocative statement on the 5th: 'Since
Italy is an area of combined responsibility, we have
reaffirmed to both the British and Italian Governments that
we expect the Italians to work out their problems of government along democratic lines without influence from outside.'
And he added: 'This policy would apply to an even more
pronounced degree with regard to Governments of the United
Nations in their liberated territories.' The message seemed
clear: Britain must keep her hands off Italy and Greece.
Neither Eden nor Churchill wavered: the Foreign Secretary
told Lord Halifax that the Stettinius statement showed
'calculated unfriendliness' and he could speak as 'roughly'
as he liked to the US Secretary; Churchill told Roosevelt
that he was 'much astonished at the acerbity' of the
announcement.[3] Also on this Tuesday, the Prime Minister
signalled Leeper at Athens: 'The matter is one of life and

death....'[4] Latest military reports were considered by the COS at 11 a.m. next day, 6 December. A telegram from General Wilson to Churchill, repeated to Brooke, said 'he (Wilson) did not anticipate that General Scobie would have any difficulties in dealing with any disorders which might occur in the Athens area', but a later signal reported a deteriorating situation. The COS discussed a request from Papandreou, passed on by Scobie, that the Greek police might be allowed to use tear gas supplied by the British. The COS decided against, explaining their reasons in a minute to the Foreign Office. 'There are two types of tear gas available in the Mediterranean theatre. One is KSK, which may cause blindness, and the other is an American product causing no permanent harm, which was recently imported in a limited quantity from the US and is specifically intended for use in Palestine. Although the Cabinet agreed to the employment of KSK in Palestine until the arrival of the American product, CAP, the case of Palestine and the case of Greece are not analogous from the point of view of possible enemy retaliation, and it would be unwise to sanction its use against ELAS even by the Greeks. Wilson's suggestion that it should only be employed by Greeks would hardly exculpate Britain effectively.'[5]

This COS meeting had to switch from Greece to Italy. A long exposition from Alexander reported the latest depressing news – Bologna would not be taken until the end of the year. And amidst signals from Athens reporting a strengthening ELAS hold on the city, Churchill still found time this hectic Wednesday to send a long report to Roosevelt on 'the serious and disappointing war situation which faces us'. Churchill declared: 'All my ideas about a really weighty blow across the Adriatic or across the Bay of Bengal have equally been set back.' Concerning north Europe, he commented: 'We have definitely failed to achieve the strategic object which we gave to our armies five weeks ago. We have not yet reached the Rhine in the northern part and most important sector of the front....' Churchill added: 'The question very definitely arises, "What are we going to do about it?"... I feel that if you are unable to come yourself before February I am bound to ask you whether you could not send your Chiefs of Staff over here as soon as practicable.'[6] The COS met at 10.30 a.m. next day, the 7th, to discuss future operations in north Europe. The Directors of Plans gave the JPS opinion of latest proposals put forward by Eisenhower, and could only find very qualified approval: future operations 'would take the form of a main thrust supported by subsidiary operations designed to destroy enemy forces, to force the enemy to divert resources from the main effort, and possibly to develop a second thrust into Germany. Everything depended on the interpretation placed on the term "main object".' The Directors of Plans believed 'the forces allocated to this effort should be sufficient to ensure that its momentum should be maintained and should be the maximum that could be maintained on the line of advance selected for this thrust. Only after these requirements had been met should forces be allotted for subsidiary operations.' The COS agreed.[7] Yet also at 10.30 a.m. on this Thursday a conference took place at Maastricht between Eisenhower and his commanders, and Montgomery came away even more convinced that the main thrust would be sacrificed for the subsidiary operations. While admitting that current operations in all sectors would not prove immediately decisive, Eisenhower claimed they were fulfilling his ultimate aim by grinding down the Germans continuously along an extended front. Moreover, he believed prospects might prove more favourable to the south rather than to the north of the Ardennes – the enemy seemed badly stretched in the Saar region. Eisenhower's orders therefore laid emphasis on the 3rd US Army, which would strike towards the Saar in the hope of capturing this area by Christmas, while the 1st US Army attacked from the Roer and 21st Army Group concentrated for the complementary attack in the north.[8] Montgomery immediately wrote to Brooke: 'I personally regard the whole thing as quite dreadful. I can see no good coming out of this business. Eisenhower and Bradley have their eyes firmly fixed on Frankfurt, and the route thence to Kassel. We shall split our resources and our strength, and we shall fail.'[9]

Brooke despaired over prospects both in north-west Europe and in Greece. Next day, 8 December, Churchill telephoned him to say he wished to reinforce Scobie with two extra brigades; Brooke wrote in his diary: 'One thing is certain, we must get out of the mess that this Greek venture has let us in for. Consequently I agreed to additional forces being sent, since the greater the force, the quicker the job will be done.'[10] Churchill was meanwhile trying to explain himself in a two-day House of Commons debate. The Prime Minister spoke for 60 minutes on the evening of 8 December: the Government was fighting for democracy, and 'the last thing which resembles democracy is mob law, with bands of gangsters, armed with deadly weapons, forcing their way into great cities.... Democracy is not based on violence or terrorism, but on reason, on fair play, on freedom, on respecting the rights of other people. Democracy is no harlot to be picked up in the street by a man with a tommy gun....' Despite Churchill's ringing phrases, violent criticism echoed in the Chamber. Harold Nicolson, a staunch Churchill supporter, believed him to have been 'in one of his boyish moods ... he seemed to me to be in rather higher spirits than the occasion warranted. I don't think he quite caught the mood of the House, which at its best was one of distressed perplexity, and at its worst one of sheer red fury.'[11] One Labour MP, Seymour Cocks, gave vent to this anger. 'I am only a humble back-bencher, and I do not aspire to be anything else; but I would rather this right hand of mine were burnt off at the wrist, leaving a blackened and twisted stump, than sign an order to the British Army to fire on the workers of Greece.' Strong speeches came from Gallacher, Bevan and Shinwell. But Churchill made clear he would not be diverted willingly. 'If I am blamed for this action I will gladly accept my dismissal at the hands of the House; but if I am not so dismissed – make no mistake about it – we shall persist in this policy of clearing Athens and the Athens region of all who are rebels against the authority of the constitutional Government of Greece.' Churchill won his vote of confidence by 279 votes to 30, although only 23 Labour members voted for the Government. 'Do not be disquieted by criticisms,' signalled Churchill to the British Ambassador at Athens. 'I do not yield to passing clamour.... In Athens as everywhere else our maxim is "No peace without Victory".'[12] Halifax reported from Washington that Hopkins had telephoned 'enthusiastic approval' of Churchill's speech, and the Prime Minister sent his thanks next day; but according to Hopkins's account he told Halifax on the 9th that 'public opinion about the whole Greek business in this country was very bad and that we felt the British Government had messed the whole thing up pretty thoroughly'.[13]

Nor could British troops in Athens hope for easy progress in clearing this mess. Most of the rebels were in plain clothes and managed to hide their arms during an area search; insufficient numbers of British troops prevented full patrolling by night, and the guerrillas slipped back into districts previously cleared. 'Increased activities on the part of the rebels and widespread sniping limited progress during the fighting which continued throughout yesterday,' reported Scobie on the 8th. Churchill signalled to Wilson on the 9th: 'You should send further reinforcements to Athens without the slightest delay. The prolongation of the fight has many dangers. I warned you of the paramount political importance of this conflict.' And Scobie wired Churchill next day: 'Fighting may, I hope, be restricted to Athens-Piraeus, but I am ready to see it through in the rest of the country if necessary. It is a pity that tear gas may not be used.'[14] British troops were now forced back into the centre of Athens, heavily outnumbered; Papandreou and his remaining Ministers had lost all authority, and on 10 December the British Ambassador resurrected the previous idea of a Regency being established under Archbishop Damaskinos. Scobie gave him full support, as did Macmillan and Alexander who reached Athens next day, travelling the last few hundred yards in a sealed tank: the rebels now held four-fifths of Athens and the Piraeus together with the surrounding hills, the harbour and one of the two airfields.

In London, Churchill initially approved the proposal to make Damaskinos the Regent, and arranged to see the King of Greece on 12 December to obtain his agreement. Mean-

while the Prime Minister received disappointing news from
Roosevelt concerning his other main preoccupation, the
military state of affairs in north Europe. The President
replied to Churchill's anxious telegram of 6 December, which
had requested an early CCS conference. 'Perhaps I am not
close enough to the picture to feel as disappointed about
the war situation as you are,' declared Roosevelt, 'and perhaps also because six months ago I was not as optimistic as
you were on the time element.' He claimed he had always
believed an advance over the Rhine would be 'a very stiff
job', with his appreciation of the difficulties helped by first-
hand knowledge gained when 'in the old days I bicycled
over most of the Rhine terrain'. The President added: 'Our
agreed broad strategy is developing according to plan', and
the US COS were too busy to attend a CCS conference – they
were 'devoting all of their abilities and energies in directing
their organizations towards carrying out the plans we have
made'.[15] This implied rebuke failed to alter opinions held
by Churchill and the British COS; moreover, Bevin revealed
to the War Cabinet on the 11th that others outside the
Government also believed the military progress to be flagging.
'In Trade Union circles there was an impression that the
position was slipping and was not being properly gripped.
He himself had no information about the present strategy
on the Western Front, but feared that a continuance of the
present position might have serious effects on the Coalition
Government.' Churchill, absent from this meeting, was
informed of Bevin's timely warning immediately afterwards:
he therefore arranged for a special meeting of the War
Cabinet to be held on Wednesday, 13 December, attended by
the COS.[16]

Bevin also played his part in Greek affairs during the day,
carrying the TUC with him in support of the Government's
action. Alexander reported a deteriorating military situation
in Athens; British troops in the city had only six days' rations
and three days' reserve of ammunition. At 6 p.m. Churchill
explained the latest position to the War Cabinet, meeting for
the second time this Monday, 11 December. 'British casualties
were perhaps of the order of 30-40 killed and perhaps 100

wounded. We had on the other hand 1,800 prisoners. Reinforcements were on their way.... The great thing was to
establish order in and around the capital. Thereafter it might
be hoped that negotiations would be set on foot which would
result in the purely Greek Government assuming responsibility.' Despite the TUC support, criticisms were still mounting, at home and abroad, and Churchill thought it 'of great
importance that we should, at the appropriate moment and
in the appropriate way, put our case before the world. Gross
misrepresentations of our attitude were being circulated, and
no attention given either to the fact that we had gone into
Greece at the invitation of the Greek Government, composed of all parties, or to the pains at which we had been to
get such a Government together.'[17] Next day Churchill
and Eden began to exert pressure upon the Greek King to
agree to the creation of Damaskinos as Regent; the Prime
Minister described his efforts to the War Cabinet, hurriedly
assembled at 3 p.m. He and Eden had seen the King at 12.30
p.m. 'The King had reminded the Prime Minister that, a
fortnight ago, he had himself wanted to go to Greece and
stake his life on his crown.... He now agreed that we had
been right and that his presence in Greece would help neither
his dynasty nor the situation. The King had asked for two
hours in which to consider the proposal.' A second meeting
had taken place at 2.45, to which the King brought a written
statement: the King would agree to the appointment of the
Archbishop 'or any other suitable person' as Prime Minister,
but 'the establishment of a Regency would ... be certain to
be interpreted by a large majority of the Greek people as
an abandonment of the struggle by the King'. Eden said the
Monarch's suggestion to make the Archbishop the Prime
Minister had now come too late. 'It would be very dangerous
if the impression got abroad that the new Government had
been nominated by the King.... We had certain obligations
to Papandreou, who was the head of the Government which
had invited us to Greece. It would be undesirable to give
the impression that we had thrown him over. This criticism
Ministers agreed Churchill and Eden should try again, and
would not hold if the Archbishop were made Regent.'

the War Cabinet reassembled at 5.30 p.m. Churchill said
they had put to the King 'as strongly as possible' the Regency
proposal. 'The King had, however, refused absolutely ... and
neither the Foreign Secretary nor he saw any prospects of
moving His Majesty. The King had informed them that he
continued to receive messages from Greece urging him to
stand firm.'[18] The War Cabinet could only agree to report
the lack of progress to Athens; and Churchill's enthusiasm
for this Regency scheme now rapidly waned.

Brooke had snatched a few moments' conversation with
the Prime Minister earlier in the day and had found him
'quite incapable of concentrating on anything but the
Greek situation'.[19] But now, immediately after the 5.30 p.m.
War Cabinet meeting, Churchill hurried to a Staff Conference called to discuss Eisenhower's plans for the Western
Front. The Supreme Commander had flown over with his
deputy, Tedder, and he explained the two main phases of
his future operations to the 6.30 p.m. gathering in the Prime
Minister's Map Room. Phase One would mark the advance
to the Rhine; Phase Two covered the crossing of the Rhine
and the advance into the heart of Germany. The first would
open with an operation to straighten the right flank of 21st
Army Group, to be launched as soon as weather permitted.
After this, Bradley would extend his left flank, to the south
of 21st Army Group, thus releasing four British divisions for
the next important offensive in the north. 'Early in January
it was hoped that 21st Army Group and Bradley's army
opposite Cologne would be able to launch their major attacks
for the clearance of the left bank of the Rhine below Bonn.'
Eisenhower continued: 'It was possible that a major defeat
might be inflicted on the Germans in this area if they decided
to stay and fight it out west of the Rhine. At the same time,
Patton's army would strike north-east towards Mainz, so as
to be in a position to cross the Rhine next spring.' The
Supreme Commander added an optimistic assessment.
'German uncommitted reserves had been reduced and most
of his divisions were weak either in armour or in personnel,
a large proportion of whom were badly trained. Patton was of
the opinion that the army opposite him was on the verge of

cracking.' Eisenhower turned to Phase Two. 'In a normal year the Rhine in January and February would not present an insuperable bridging problem, but it was estimated by the engineers that even if no more rain fell in the watershed this year, the floods early in 1945 would be the worst since 1882. In March and April the bridges would be swept away by ice and melting snow, and it was estimated that it would not be practicable to establish crossings next year until towards the end of May.' Brooke, appalled by this delay, attacked Eisenhower's broad front strategy. 'It seemed that approximately equal forces were to be allotted to the two major thrusts. There was thus a serious danger that neither would succeed.... If the main attack in Phase II was to be in the north, operations to clear the left bank of the Rhine north of Bonn must have overriding priority.' 'Unfortunately,' replied Eisenhower, 'there was a limit to the number of divisions which could be deployed and maintained across the Rhine north of the Ruhr', although he agreed this would be the most important sector. He added: 'The further apart our attacks were made, the more difficult it would be for the enemy, with their lack of mobility, to move forces from one threatened point to another.'[20] The meeting broke up after three hours, with the participants adjourning to a dinner at 10 Downing Street. Brooke left the gathering in the early hours of the morning, intensely dissatisfied and believing Churchill to have given him only half-hearted support. 'Quite impossible to get the PM to understand the importance of the principles involved.' He also wrote in his diary: 'I have just finished one of those days which should have been one of the keystones of the final days of the war. I feel I have utterly failed to do what is required, and yet God knows how I could have done anything else.' The CIGS seriously thought of sending in his resignation.[21]

But next morning Brooke's resilient spirits rose again: Churchill told him that he had felt obliged to support Eisenhower because 'he was one American against five of us.... And also he was his (Churchill's) guest.'[22] Moreover, Brooke was able to present his views at the special meeting of the War Cabinet, called as a result of Bevin's warning on 11

December. The CIGS repeated his arguments against Eisenhower's plans; it was essential that the northern thrust should
have behind it 'sufficient force to ensure the conclusion'.
Brooke believed the meeting 'cleared the air well, and the
Cabinet now know what to expect', adding in his diary that
the May date for the delayed Rhine crossing 'had a profound effect' on Ministers.[23] Ministers met again 45 minutes
later, this time to discuss Greece. A personal message had
arrived from Macmillan to Churchill, strongly urging that
the King of Greece should again be pressed to agree to the
appointment of the Archbishop as Regent. 'Nothing else was
likely to meet the case.' Eden told the War Cabinet that King
George was 'likely to be obstinate', and added: 'The messages which HM was receiving from his supporters in Greece
... might be no more than an attempt to give him what he
wanted to hear.' Ministers agreed the King 'would be free
at any time to dismiss the Regent and the appointment of
the Archbishop would bring the Crown back into the picture.
... It was essential to do something to relax the existing
tension.' The War Cabinet asked Churchill and Eden to make
a further approach.[24] A third meeting with the Monarch
was therefore arranged for the following morning.

British reinforcements were now reaching Athens in a bid
to restore the military situation, and rebel hopes for a rapid
coup had faded, and also on 13 December Roosevelt cabled
moral – though not practical – support. 'I regard my role
in this matter as that of a loyal friend and ally whose one
desire is to be of any help possible in the circumstances....
As anxious as I am to be of the greatest help ... there are
limitations, imposed in part by the traditional policies of the
US and in part by the mounting adverse reaction of public
opinion in this country.' Roosevelt urged the British to obtain
the Greek King's approval for a Regency. Churchill replied
next day, 14 December, and described King George's
obstinacy. He added one jibe: 'The fact that you are supposed to be against us, in accordance with the last sentence of
Stettinius's Press release, has added, as I feared, to our
difficulties and burdens.'[25] Churchill had then to turn to
another diplomatic problem which again caused Anglo-

American upset. Indications had been received that Stalin seemed about to give full recognition to the Polish National Committee, and on 15 December Roosevelt suggested to Churchill that he, the President, might send a message to the Soviet leader proposing action should be delayed until the subject had been discussed at a summit meeting. The Prime Minister agreed, and on the same day added his own appeal in a Commons statement. He called for an immediate meeting of the Big Three, possibly in Britain. Unfortunately, he also disclosed that Britain supported the policy of giving Russia a large slice of eastern Poland, based on the Curzon Line, giving Poland territory from Germany instead. The Poles in London had still to signify their official agreement to this frontier settlement. Almost immediately the statement was seen in America as further proof of Churchill's desire to carve up Europe through secret agreements and to intervene in internal affairs of other countries. Hopkins cabled on the 16th: 'Public opinion here is deteriorating rapidly because of the Greek situation and your statement in Parliament.... I confess I find myself greatly disturbed at the diplomatic turn of events.'[26]

Churchill described other disturbing news to the War Cabinet at 3 p.m. on the 16th – and also announced that the King still refused to agree to a Regency. The latter had repeated his objections at a meeting with Churchill and Eden on the 14th and in memoranda dated the 13th and 14th. Moreover, opposition to the British policy had come from Mackenzie King, Prime Minister of Canada. A telegram late the previous day described his 'uneasiness at the situation which had arisen.... He had given a public assurance that Canadian troops would not serve in Greece without the consent of the Canadian Government.' Ministers agreed a reply to the Canadian leader should say 'he would do a great disservice to the unity of the Empire if he were, as he suggested, to make a public statement disassociating the Canadian Government from the action which was being taken'. The reply would add that no Canadian troops would be sought for the Greek commitment. Churchill had already sent a signal stressing that British troops had been despatched following an invitation from the Greek Government. Mackenzie King eventually agreed not to make any public disassociation. Meanwhile, War Cabinet Ministers at the meeting on 16 December once again wrestled with the Regency problem. Churchill said he had asked the Foreign Secretary 'what action we could take if the King maintained his opposition ... and (if we) reached the conclusion that it was nevertheless essential to appoint a Regent'. Eden had replied that the King would have to be told that 'we should be forced to recognize a Regency, however appointed, as a *de facto* lawful Government ... and to withdraw such recognition from His Majesty'. The question was raised, probably by Churchill, whether the appointment of a Regency was, in fact, the right solution. 'It would be unfortunate if we were to commit ourselves ... only to find that we had asked him (the King) to make the sacrifice involved to no purpose.' Ministers agreed to ask for a fuller appreciation from Macmillan and Alexander.[27] Churchill and Eden saw the King again after this meeting, and once more failed to obtain a result; Churchill's enthusiasm for the Regency idea cooled still further.

But suddenly, with the Greek situation still far from settled, another even more important problem burst into view. German divisions in Belgium, dismissed by Eisenhower just four days before as 'weak' and 'badly trained', launched a desperate and efficient counter-attack, aiming at the weakest part of the allied front in the Ardennes. Rain and fog had reduced Allied air reconnaissance for the past three days; Panzer units now jabbed through the mists to gain complete initial surprise; Allied HQ, and the COS in London, drastically underestimated the threat, and the tanks pushed on.

The advance began early on 16 December under cover of a heavy artillery barrage and V-1 bombs. Overstretched 1st US Army units fought back hard and well during the first day, but this success itself brought dangers: neither Eisenhower nor Bradley, commander of 12th Army Group to which the 1st Army belonged, seemed to realize the extent of the offensive, and believed the enemy instead to be attempting a spoiling attack against Patton's move on the Saar. Only limited steps were taken in Belgium to contain the advance; no special mention of the offensive was made in the Cabinet War Room situation report on 17 December. Yet by then enemy tanks were thrusting through a 50-mile hole in the Ardennes defences. Hitler had ordered three Armies, containing no less than 28 divisions, to strike for Antwerp, Brussels and the Givet-Luxembourg Line. Capture of Antwerp would sever the allied line of supply and would force allied armies north of the Ardennes into a pocket pushed up against the sea: another, and this time fatal, Dunkirk might be brought about. The Führer had overruled all objections from his dubious generals, and Rundstedt had been handed the plan marked in Hitler's handwriting: 'Not to be Altered.' By late 17 December realization at last struck Eisenhower's HQ that, astonishing as it might seem, a full-scale offensive had begun – and by now the Panzers were pushing towards Stavelot, where the allies held large, vital fuel dumps, and farther south had prized open a gap between St Vith and Bastogne. On 18 December Brooke's diary entry revealed growing uneasiness – the Americans 'have no immediate reserves to stem the attack', but he added: 'They ought ultimately to hold it all right and to have an opportunity of delivering a serious counterblow.'[28] Ironically, also on the 18th the British COS returned to their attack on Eisenhower's offensive plans in a memorandum to Churchill.

No special mention of the Ardennes offensive took place at the War Cabinet meeting at 5.30 p.m. on the 18th; instead Ministers considered latest developments in the Greek saga. An appreciation had been received from Alexander, who warned: 'If the present rebel resistance continued, and it might increase, he would be compelled to send another infantry division to Athens, which could only come from the Italian front, with serious results on the battle there.' Churchill informed Ministers of a meeting he and Eden had had with the King of Greece on the 16th. 'The King still saw a strong objection to a Regency, and made it clear that his doubts as to the suitability of the Archbishop as sole agent remained undiminished.... It was plain that His Majesty was under great stress.' Diaries written by Eden and Cadogan reveal that while they remained convinced the appointment of a Regent offered the only visible possibility of a political settlement, Churchill now believed otherwise: the Prime Minister seemed to suspect the Archbishop and became increasingly reluctant to press the King. The War Cabinet minutes for this meeting on the 18th clearly reflect Churchill's opinion. Thus 'the question was raised' whether more evidence should be found 'of the reliability of the Archbishop as sole Regent, and of his previous record', and despite Alexander's warning the War Cabinet agreed 'there would be advantage in postponing any decision as to the line to take for 2-3 days. That would give opportunity for the military situation to clarify itself: we would be in a stronger bargaining position once our control had been re-established.'[29] Churchill informed Alexander of the 'leave it to the military' decision next day, 19 December.

Signals reaching the War Office on the military situation in France seemed sparse and uninformative. 'Eisenhower seems quite confident,' wrote Brooke on the 19th. 'I only hope that this confidence is not based on ignorance.' The Supreme Commander was in fact desperately trying to regain the initiative: the previous night Bradley had cancelled the 3rd Army's proposed attack on the Saar and had been ordered to intervene in strength on the southern flank of the German thrust; during the morning of the 19th Eisenhower ordered the 1st Army to hold the enemy in the north while this southern attack drove towards Bastogne. But by now German armoured units were streaming into Belgium; by the evening German advance units were within 15 miles of Liège. And next morning the seriousness of the situation was at last revealed to the British COS in a telegram from Montgomery. The British Field Marshal, normally so optimistic, began: 'The situation in American area is not – not – good.... There is a definite lack of grip and control and no one had a clear picture as to situation.... I have heard nothing from him (Eisenhower) or Bradley.... My own opinion is that ... the American forces have been cut clean in half.' Brooke rushed a copy of this signal to Churchill and conferred with the Prime Minister in the Map Room at 3.30 p.m. Both agreed Montgomery should be given command of the whole northern wing, and Churchill immediately telephoned Eisenhower; the Supreme Commander had already decided upon such a step: Montgomery would command all elements of 21st and 12th Army Groups, including 1st and 9th US Armies, while Bradley commanded all units from 12th and 6th Army Groups in the southern battle area.

Montgomery immediately briefed his commanders, then hurried over to the northern flank of the German bulge to see the situation for himself: an officer described him arriving at 1st US Army HQ 'like Christ come to cleanse the temple'. He regrouped the 1st Army to face the threat and assembled two reserve forces for a counter-attack. Brooke was informed of his plan late on 20 December, the day Montgomery took over this whole northern command, and formations were frantically reorganized during the night. At dawn on 21 December 12 fresh German divisions, 7 armoured, were flung against the 1st Army area, and the climax of the battle had been reached. American units which had been fighting with tremendous gallantry since the offensive began stood their ground before the Meuse – beyond which lay the open Belgium plain with precious Antwerp only 60 miles away; American fighting spirit, both north and south of the bulge, was epitomized by a US commander's reply after he had been surrounded at Bastogne and ordered to surrender – 'Nuts'.

Untypically, Churchill did not involve himself in this tremendous drama. As Cadogan complained the Prime Minister 'dwelt endlessly' on Greek affairs; and a depressing reply came from Alexander on the 21st: although he might clear Athens, 'this will not defeat ELAS and force them to surrender ... the Greek problem cannot be solved by military measures. The answer must be found in the political field.'[30] Yet the War Cabinet heard on the 21st that the Greek King remained obstinate. Moreover, Eden suspected the King only to be revealing advice received from Athens against a Regency. King George preferred to keep other advice secret.

Thus Eden told Ministers that he had learnt from the Greek Ambassador that Papandreou had actually advised the King to appoint a Regent. But Ministers still believed it might be better to postpone another approach to the King. 'To bring immediate pressure on him to decide in any particular sense would be open to objection on the grounds that we were interfering in Greek internal politics.'[31] This nebulous decision seemed to stem from continuing dislike of the Archbishop by Churchill. Cadogan described the meeting as 'too awful'.[32] Eden commented in his diary: 'W. has his knife into the Archbishop and is convinced that he is both a Quisling and a Communist.' Yet the Foreign Office remained convinced that a Regency provided the only solution, and Eden's position seemed strengthened by a personal letter from Macmillan in Athens: 'I am certain that there is a large amount of sympathy with EAM in Greece, that a moderate, reasonable, progressive policy could detach the vague radical element from the hard, communist core.'[33] Eden intensified his campaign to convince Churchill. 'Went to see W. who was still in bed,' he wrote in his diary on the 22nd. 'After some argument during which he upbraided Leeper and Macmillan, whom he describes as our two "fuzzy-wuzzies", he agreed that we should send for the King.' The meeting took place at 3 p.m.; the King refused to alter his position.[34] And Churchill signalled to Alexander: 'We must ... have a military foundation there on which a Greek Government of some kind or other can function. I have personally great doubts about the Archbishop, who might quite conceivably make himself into a dictator supported by the left wing.' But he added: 'These doubts may be removed in the next few days.'[35] The Prime Minister seemed to have already decided upon the dramatic move which he would reveal to Eden 48 hours later.

The Germans were being held, with Eisenhower acting with a courage and a determination matching the American units in the thick of the fight. An allied line had been wrenched into existence; Brooke's hopes began, cautiously, to rise again. Next day, 23 December, fog and cloud swirled from the battlefield. and allied aircraft stabbed into the

attack to slash the supply line to the German advanced
armour. Also on the 23rd the COS met at 10.30 a.m. to
consider and approve a Joint Intelligence Committee appreciation of German intentions. Mistakenly, the JIC believed
the enemy counter-offensive had been launched with the
support of Rundstedt and other German field commanders,
and judged the German aim merely to be the disruption
of allied preparations for further advance, by causing a
temporary withdrawal. Rundstedt was 'likely to urge a halt
in the advance as soon as he assesses that the allied counter-
attacks are ready. He would then probably be prepared if
necessary gradually to withdraw, assured of having dis-
located the allied plans and of having denied them many
of the resources which they have carefully collected over the
past few months.'[36]

By 24 December the odds in Belgium were lengthening
in favour of the allies; in Athens, the guerrillas were being
held, but a political solution seemed no nearer. And, on this
Christmas Eve, Churchill declared his decision to make a
personal intervention in the Greek situation, on the spot.
The Prime Minister rang Eden during the morning to say he
was considering a mission to Athens; Eden offered to go
instead; Churchill said they both should go. At 5.30 p.m. he
rang again to say the weather seemed good and they would
leave the same night, and Eden permitted himself an exple-
tive in his diary: 'Hell. I was looking forward to a quiet
family Christmas.'[37] The Prime Minister and Foreign
Secretary flew into the dark from Northolt, reached Naples
at 8 a.m., Christmas Day, and touched down at a Greek
airfield at noon. Heavily escorted by armoured cars, Churchill
and his party drove to the coast and boarded HMS *Ajax*,
anchored off the Piraeus. This cruiser, famed for its part
in the River Plate battle, would provide an HQ and a meeting
place for Churchill, Papandreou and Damaskinos. Even
before leaving his aircraft, Churchill and Eden had been
informed by Macmillan of a plan for a gathering of all
Greek political leaders, to which ELAS would be invited.
This suggestion found favour, and at a meeting with
Damaskinos and Papandreou that evening, the Prime Mini-

ster asked the Archbishop if he would preside. Damaskinos agreed. Churchill's suspicions of the Archbishop had soon been overcome; as he reported to the War Cabinet next day, 26 December: 'When he came to see us he spoke with great bitterness against the atrocities of ELAS and the dark, sinister hand behind the EAM. Listening to him, it was impossible to doubt that he greatly feared the communist, or Trotskyite as he called it, combination in Greek affairs.... Generally he impressed me with a good deal of confidence. He is a magnificent figure.... The conference is fixed for 4 p.m.'[38] Eden spent the morning of the 26th successfully persuading American, French and Russian diplomats to attend the talks as observers; Churchill relished the whole drama and personal danger, refusing to stay on board the *Ajax* and, in Macmillan's words, viewing war-torn Athens as 'a sort of "super Sidney Street"'. The various Greek delegates assembled at the Greek Foreign Office, lit by flickering hurricane lamps; the ELAS delegates arrived 30 minutes late, and while Churchill and the others waited they could hear rattling machine guns and snapping rifle fire in the streets outside. Churchill and Eden opened the proceedings, the first stressing British military power, the Foreign Secretary urging conciliation, then the British left the Greeks to their confrontation. Talks continued throughout the evening and late into the night, while skirmishing continued in Athens – and while the German Panzers were being halted in the snowy Ardennes before they could reach allied petrol dumps. In London, suffering the coldest Christmas for 54 years, Ministers awaited news from Churchill in Athens and heard the bombers droning over to cripple the German offensive in Belgium.

Damaskinos reported to Churchill at 10 a.m. on 27 December: the rowdy Greek conference would continue during the day. Another meeting between the Archbishop and Prime Minister took place at 5.30 p.m.: delegates had agreed upon the need for a Regency, and had approved Damaskinos as the choice. But no agreement had been reached over a future Government, and the Archbishop had adjourned the conference – further progress seemed impossible until the Regent had been appointed, and Leeper and Macmillan persuaded Papandreou to advise the King accordingly. Churchill agreed to add his pressure, and arranged to fly home next day, 28 December: if the King continued to refuse, the appointment would be made under a mandate of the three Great Powers, or by a declaration of the Greek Conference, with such a declaration endorsed by the British Government. Churchill's liking for Damaskinos had increased with each meeting; as he wrote later: 'I was already convinced that he was the outstanding figure in the Greek turmoil. Among other things, I had learned that he had been a champion wrestler.'[39] Cadogan, waiting in London, viewed the future with pessimism: 'Prospects of its producing anything definite seem dim.'[40]

Also on the 27th the COS discussed the Belgium situation, and found further grounds for optimism. The Joint Intelligence Committee had added a paragraph to their previous report on German ability to sustain the present offensive: 'The chief limiting factor will be the shortage of sufficient troops to nourish the offensive and to guard the extended German flanks against greatly superior allied forces. It is this factor rather than shortage of supplies which will, in our opinion, govern the German ability to sustain operations.... No major reinforcement of the counter-offensive on the western front from the eastern front appears to have been planned.'[41] And War Cabinet Ministers were told at 5.30 p.m.: 'The enemy must by now be feeling some anxiety about the maintenance of his troops and the risk of counter-attack against the flanks of his force.'[42] Yet in Berlin Hitler remained blindly confident. He assembled his commanders for a conference in his bunker on 28 December: not only would another attempt be made to reach the Meuse, but a new attack would be launched into northern Alsace. 'I have been in very much worse situations,' he boasted. 'We shall yet master Fate.'[43]

Churchill left Greece on the 28th after signalling the COS: 'Great evils will follow here in Athens, affecting our position all over the world, if we cannot clear up situation quickly, i.e. in two or three weeks.' Further reinforcements must be sent, if necessary from Palestine.[44] The Prime Minister reached London soon after 5 p.m. on the 29th; within an hour he was reporting to the War Cabinet. 'He was perfectly satisfied that the advice we had received from our representatives in Athens had been entirely correct. If we had not intervened there would have been a massacre.... He was satisfied that the case for a Regency was decisive, and that the only man for the Regency was the Archbishop.' Churchill asked for War Cabinet approval for a meeting with the King of Greece later in the evening. 'His Majesty would be told of the Prime Minister's appreciation of the situation, and would be informed that we were satisfied that it was necessary for him to appoint Archbishop Damaskinos as Regent without further delay; that if he was not prepared to do so we would have no option but to advise the Archbishop as if he had in fact been appointed by the King.... His Majesty had a great opportunity to make a dignified gesture.'[45] Churchill and Eden accordingly met the King at 10.15 p.m. and arguments lasted until 4.30 next morning. But King George had been placed in an impossible position, and eventually agreed to an announcement that he would not return to Greece 'unless summoned by a free and fair expression of the national will'. Damaskinos was appointed Regent, able 'to take all steps necessary to restore order and tranquillity'. At last a settlement seemed possible, backed by the British military presence. The Archbishop formed a Government and General Plastiras, vehemently Republican, was announced Prime Minister on 3 January 1945, followed by the signing of a military truce on 11 January. Communist guerrillas withdrew from Athens, Salonika and Patras, and Greece was allowed some slight respite, for the moment, from the terrors of full-scale civil war.

But as Churchill reported his success to the War Cabinet on 30 December, and with it the lessening of dangers of a further clash with communism in Greece, East-West confrontation intensified over the other major diplomatic problem, Poland. And this subject would result in Churchill embarking upon yet another wartime expedition, this time for a summit with Stalin and Roosevelt. Ministers were

informed at the 30 December meeting of recent correspondence between Roosevelt and Stalin: the President had sent
his appeal for delay in recognition of the Polish National
Committee; Stalin had replied on 27 December with sharp
criticism of the Polish Government in Exile in London, and
had added that 'if the Polish Committee of National Liberation will transform itself into a Provisional Polish Government, then, in view of the above-said, the Soviet Government
will not have any serious ground for postponement of the
question of recognition'. Churchill told Ministers that this
message was 'far from helpful' and added: 'We ought to
continue to press Premier Stalin not to recognize the Lublin
Government, and tell him plainly that we should not do so,
and that in our view the matter should be for the coming
conference between Stalin, the President and myself.'
Ministers agreed.[46] Stalin proved inflexible. Eden told the
War Cabinet three days later of his concern 'at the extent
to which the Lublin Poles were opening their mouths. It was
satisfactory that British and American policy in this matter
was so closely in line.'[47] Anglo-American accord failed to
prevent official Soviet recognition on 5 January of the Lublin
Committee as the Provisional Government of Poland. This
upset at the very start of 1945 seemed symbolic of the year
to come – the year of the Iron Curtain, when political disillusionment cloaked military glory.

'Well, that's the end of that year,' wrote Cadogan. 'It's been
a good one, but there's lots more to come yet. News is
good.'[48] Brooke reported to the COS on 2 January. 'It looked
as if the Germans had abandoned, at any rate for the time
being, their thrust towards Liège, and were concentrating
their attacks on Le Bastogne salient. A German attack on
the Saar front had been launched the previous day; reports
so far received ... struck a confident note. There were indications that the Germans were trying to collect reserves on the
Upper Rhine for a possible attack against the French.'[49]
Ministers were informed at a War Cabinet meeting on this
Tuesday that Patton's attack had continued in the south
and an attempt would shortly be made to narrow still further

the enemy salient. Next day, 3 January, Montgomery began this attempt with a counter-attack against Houffalize, aiming at a junction with Patton's southern stab; Churchill and Brooke visited the British HQ the following day and the Prime Minister signalled Roosevelt on the 6th: 'I have a feeling this is a time for an intense new impulse, both of friendship and exertion to be drawn from our bosoms and to the last scrap of our resources....'[50] Both sides were in fact stretching these resources to the limit, moreover, the Germans were conjuring up their threat to the French in the Upper Rhine. Brooke wrote after his two-day visit: 'Monty's offensive seems to be progressing very favourably, but I am not at all so certain that matters are all right in Alsace-Lorraine. Alexander is also worrying me by committing more and more troops to Greece.'[51] But Ministers were told at 5.30 p.m. on Monday, 8 January: 'In the Ardennes very satisfactory progress has been made on the north side of the enemy salient and we now hold one of the two east-to-west roads on which the enemy had relied. On the south side of the salient we had also made good progress in the region of Bastogne.'[52] On 16 January Mongomery's and Patton's thrusts linked; enemy divisions had been forced half-way back to their starting line; on the same day Montgomery signalled Eisenhower: 'I have great pleasure in reporting to you that the task you gave me in the Ardennes is now concluded.... We have now achieved tactical victory within the salient. I am returning 1st Army to Bradley tomorrow as ordered by you.'[53] And on 22 January the War Cabinet learnt: 'The German salient in the Ardennes has been still further reduced ... there were also signs of enemy withdrawals.'[54]

Yet Hitler's bold bid had succeeded in disrupting Eisenhower's programme – and had caused about 80,000 US casualties. The Supreme Commander's plan, disputed by Montgomery and the British COS before the German counter-offensive, now became the subject of fresh bickering. A press conference held by Montgomery on 7 January, aimed at stressing allied solidarity, achieved the opposite result – his words were taken by the Americans as showing how

Montgomery believed he had won the recent battle single-handed. Meanwhile, Churchill had approved the COS memorandum dated 18 December, opposing Eisenhower's plans for thrusts both against the Ruhr and the Saar, and this document formed the basis of a signal to the British Mission in Washington on 6 January. 'There are two major issues on which we feel the CCS must reach agreement if further setbacks in Europe are to be avoided. These are a) Concentration of effort on one thrust in the north; b) The command set-up in the north.' With the first, the signal stressed the previous CCS decision to draw Eisenhower's attention 'to the advantages of the northern line of approach into Germany', and continued by saying this 'Octagon' conclusion had not apparently been heeded by Eisenhower. 'There has instead been dispersion of effort as between the North and South.' The COS added: 'In our view one man must be given power of operational control and co-ordination of all the ground forces employed for the northern thrust.' Recent events had strengthened previous British views – 'the quick initial success this attack achieved goes a long way to confirm the misgivings we have expressed'.[55] The Americans gave immediate consent to a British request that Eisenhower should be instructed to submit further plans; the Supreme Commander did so on 20 January, and continued to clash with the view expressed by Montgomery. The British Field Marshal had now drafted a scheme, 'Veritable', which envisaged reinforcing the northern thrust at the expense of a possible offensive by the battle-weakened US 1st and 3rd Armies. Montgomery had believed Eisenhower agreed with this plan, until Eisenhower's report of the 20th indicated otherwise. 'My operations to destroy the enemy forces west of the Rhine must be so designed as to enable me to close the Rhine throughout its length.' Such a statement revived all British fears, even though Eisenhower added: 'In view of the present relative strength I am not in a position to carry out more than one offensive at a time. I am therefore concentrating at the moment on a series of offensives designed to destroy the enemy and to close the Rhine in the north.'[56] Also on 20 January the British COS completed a document which would be put forward to explain their position at the forthcoming summit; the paper, approved by Churchill, contained a draft directive to the Supreme Commander: 'In preparing your plans you should bear in mind our views as follows: a) All resources which can be made available for offensive operations should be concentrated on one main thrust. This thrust should be made in the maximum possible strength with sufficient fresh formations held available to keep up the momentum of the advance.... b) If tactical considerations allow, this main thrust should be made in the north, in view of the overriding importance to the enemy of the Ruhr area.'[57] No progress could be made until the summit opened at the end of the month.

Meanwhile Churchill had searched for some method of speeding military events; the allies had still to regain all ground lost in the German offensive; the date for the ending of the war had slipped back still further. In mid-January Churchill returned to his old idea of floating mines down the Rhine to destroy bridges or, alternatively, a massive bombing campaign should be launched against these Rhine crossings. Both suggestions were turned down by the COS on the 16th: Admiral Cunningham claimed the production of special mines would interfere with the sea mining programme, while Portal said the bombing campaign would need about 14,000 sorties, affecting other commitments.[58] Even Churchill did not react to one idea, apparently received from Stalin and discussed by the COS on the 25th – a possible offensive through Switzerland to turn the Rhine positions, at the expense of Swiss neutrality. The COS sent a minute to the Prime Minister: 'We should oppose operations through Switzerland since they would (a) offer a difficult and comparatively unprofitable approach into Germany; (b) open hostilities with a courageous and stubborn opponent....'[59] Nor could cheer be squeezed from Italian news during this winter wait. At the end of the year the allied line still lay south of Bologna, blocked by the weather, German determination and shortages in strength. Alexander submitted future plans in a report to the COS on 8 January; the armies in Italy must, in fact, pause until spring and continued operations would have to be based on an air offensive. The COS realized this report 'raises big issues'.[60] It marked final confirmation that no spectacular results could be hoped from the Italian campaign.

Discussions during the next few days led to a COS paper proposing the immediate withdrawal of divisions from the Italian to the Western Front: since strength would anyway be insufficient in Italy, these would be better employed in the north; the first of 6 divisions would be ready for operations late in April 1945, if operations in Italy went over to the defensive. Churchill told a staff conference on Tuesday, 23 January, that he had 'with great regret given up hope of a British right-handed thrust into the armpit of the Adriatic', and he agreed in principle to the transfer. Churchill envisaged 6-8 divisions being involved in this switch, but expressed concern over the length of time the movement would take – the Joint Planners estimated it would take $2\frac{1}{2}$ months to transfer each division from Italy to the line in the north-west, and the Prime Minister therefore declared: 'The gain to the Western Front was a small reward for having to give up all hopes of offensive action in Italy and the Adriatic.' After more discussion he said he would give the matter further study; not until the summit had actually begun, on 30 January, did Churchill finally commit himself.[61]

As a background to this depressing discussion, ending so many hopes, the Germans continued to bombard Britain with rockets and flying-bombs. Morrison told the War Cabinet on 8 January that 55 incidents from V-2s had been reported during the previous 6 days. 'This was the highest number yet recorded in any one week.' Seven days later he informed Ministers that 54 attacks had come during the week, and he asked whether 'more could not be done by way of counter-measures against rocket sites and supply routes. He detected signs of restiveness as a result of rocket attack.'[62] The problem received consideration at a special COS meeting next day, 17 January, attended by Sandys. The Crossbow Committee had examined the extent to which the enemy could increase the scale of attack against London: 'If he (the enemy) diverted his entire effort from Antwerp, which was unlikely, and the mean point of impact was centred on Charing Cross, then approximately 120 rockets per week could be launched, of which some 90 would fall in the greater London area.' Sandys added: 'In the East End of London there was some deterioration in morale owing to the destruction of houses and to the cold weather.' But a report by the Air Staff offered little comfort; the COS agreed that while the scale of rocket attack could be reduced by the diversion of a greater air effort to bombing launching sites, 'the results would almost certainly be disproportionate to the cost'.[63] Suffering from V-2s would apparently only cease with the defeat of Germany on the ground in northern Europe. On 23 January Churchill and the COS studied reports by the Joint Intelligence Committee and the Joint Planners on possible dates for the ending of the European war: this might come as early as mid-April, but such a date should be considered as 'a bonus'. According to the Joint Planners: 'The earliest date on which the war is likely to end is 30 June 1945. The latest date beyond which the war is unlikely to continue is 1 November 1945.'[64]

Much depended on continuing successes by the Red Army. On 7 January a signal came from Stalin: 'We are preparing an offensive, but the weather is at present unfavourable. Nevertheless, taking into account the position of our allies on the Western Front, GHQ of the Supreme Command has decided to accelerate the completion of our preparations and, regardless of the weather, to commence large-scale offensive operations against the Germans along the whole Central Front not later than the second half of January.' The offensive began on the 12th. Koniev attacked around Sandomierz in Poland, aiming at Breslau and the upper Oder. Other armies plunged forward. Warsaw fell to Zhukov on the 17th, and he immediately swung west towards Frankfurt – and towards Berlin. Rokossovsky drove towards Danzig and the Baltic coast; southern thrusts were made along the Czechoslovak frontier. War Cabinet Ministers were told on 22 January: 'In the north the German defensive position in East Prussia had been pierced.... East Prussia is also threatened by Russia from the south.' Yet Brooke gave

Ministers a warning: 'At this stage it is impossible to say how far the Russian advance will continue before it loses its impetus. But as and when German territory is reached the difficulties of the advancing troops will be increased.'[65] A week later the War Cabinet received a further report: 'The Russians are reported to be within 4 miles of Königsberg. The thrust north of Warsaw has now reached the Baltic and Russian forces are within 30 miles of Danzig. It is estimated that 15 German divisions are hemmed in between Danzig and Königsberg.... The average Russian advance since the commencement of the offensive is 16 miles a day. The Russian claims for German casualties are 86,000 prisoners and 300,000 killed.'[66] This grim, relentless advance continued: by the end of the month Breslau and Tilsit had fallen; Zhukov had almost reached Frankfurt – and the German frontier defences had been shattered. Red Army units were within 80 miles of Berlin.

Such momentous news eclipsed allied progress on the Western Front, and even obscured excellent reports from far-away Burma. Despite reduced resources, especially aircraft, Mountbatten's forces advanced with all available strength to take advantage of Japanese withdrawals, and the 14th Army burst from the hills of central Burma at the beginning of the year into the plains north-west of Mandalay. On 22 January the War Cabinet were informed that British troops had occupied Akyab; American forces had made 'very good progress' on the island of Luzon.[67] Moreover, US warships were now sailing supreme after the disastrous defeat inflicted upon the Japanese in the Battle of Leyte Gulf the previous autumn.

So shafts of sunlight did penetrate winter gloom. Yet good news, balanced against prevailing depression, proved insufficient to remove the strain in London, and Brooke's diary revealed increasing exhaustion. 'Every day I feel older, more tired and less inclined to face difficulties,' he wrote on 18 January.[68] Cadogan complained over Churchill's reluctance to discuss post-war topics. 'Cabinet at 5.30,' he wrote on the 11th. 'World Organization on Agenda, so PM had got Carton de Wiart in for a talk – so as to put off consideration of WO.'

And next day: 'Cabinet took 2 hours to do what I could have done in 20 minutes.... A. lost patience.'[69] On 19 January Attlee complained to the Prime Minister of lack of method in Cabinet proceedings. 'I consider the present position inimical to the successful performance of the tasks imposed upon us as a Government and injurious to the war effort.' Churchill was accused of showing scant respect for his colleagues on civil affairs, of not reading papers thoroughly, and of not sticking to the point. 'Not infrequently a phrase catches your eye which gives rise to a disquisition on an interesting point only slightly connected with the subject matter.' Three days later Churchill sent a prim reply. 'I have to thank you for your Private and Personal letter of January 19. You may be sure I shall always endeavour to profit by your counsels.'[70]

A break from routine would be beneficial for all concerned. And, after days of complicated arrangements, the British party departed for the last Big Three summit to be held during the war against Germany, code-named 'Argonaut'. Rendezvous point would be Yalta; first would come talks between Roosevelt and Churchill and the CCS at Malta. Churchill reached the island at 4 a.m., 30 January, with a raging temperature which obliged him to remain in bed throughout the day. Roosevelt would arrive on the 2nd; meanwhile the British and American COS began their combined conferences.

After a meeting at noon on the 30th to discuss agenda and times, the CCS assembled at 2.30 p.m. and immediately turned to the most controversial topic: Eisenhower's orders. An explanation was given to the CCS by Bedell Smith, the Supreme Commander's Chief of Staff; surprisingly, this seemed to follow very much the line which the British had always sought, including the incorporation of Montgomery's 'Veritable' scheme. The latter would be launched between 8-10 February, although Eisenhower still believed that 'the short length of river available for the (northern) crossings, together with other limiting factors, made it essential to have an alternative thrust available should the northern thrust be held up. The situation had been eased by Soviet successes in the east, said Bedell Smith, and 'in view of the present diminution of German offensive capabilities in the West, it was essential to get to the Rhine in the north as soon as possible'. He stressed that the Supreme Commander 'intended to put into the northern effort every single division which could be maintained logistically.... The southern advance was not intended to compete with the northern attack, but must be of sufficient strength to draw off German forces to protect the important Frankfurt area and to provide an alternate line of attack if the main effort failed.' All this seemed eminently satisfactory. Brooke expressed his relief and welcomed the explanation; he said the British COS had disagreed with Eisenhower's plan as drafted in his previous report, but 'this however had taken on a different complexion in the light of General Smith's explanation'. The peculiar situation had thereby arisen in which the British approved Bedell Smith's interpretation but not Eisenhower's paper itself. Brooke therefore suggested that the record of Bedell Smith's remarks should be written up in the minutes and should receive further examination next day; in other words, these minutes might receive approval, but not Eisenhower's document.[71]

This tangle stemmed from the acute suspicions bedevilling discussions of these fundamental issues. Brooke had always belittled Eisenhower's military abilities, whilst admiring his statesmanship, integrity and organizing flair; Eisenhower, whilst on good personal terms with Montgomery, clashed over strategic views; the American COS disliked Montgomery's attitude and resented accusations against Eisenhower, who, they said, had shown his abilities through the massive advance made since June 1944. And so, in this sour situation, differences of opinion – not now so far apart – were aggravated by personal distrust. The British wanted a clear statement, in absolute black and white, that the northern thrust would receive maximum priority; Eisenhower took the reasonable view that the northern thrust must not entirely exclude southern operations. Suspicions came to a head next day, 31 January. Brooke and Bedell Smith had successfully redrafted Eisenhower's appreciation to make it conform more closely with the meaning placed upon it at the CCS session. This redraft was despatched to Eisenhower, who immediately accepted the wording, replying on the 31st: 'You may assure the CCS that I will seize the Rhine crossings in the north immediately this is a feasible operation and without waiting to close the Rhine throughout its length.' This was exactly the statement sought by the British. But Eisenhower added one more sentence. 'I will advance across the Rhine in the north with maximum strength and complete determination, as soon as the situation in the south allows me to collect the necessary forces and to do this without incurring unnecessary risk.' The words differed very little from Bedell Smith's exposition the previous day – but they had been written by Eisenhower. Brooke, handed the Supreme Commander's reply at the CCS session at 2.30 p.m. on the 31st, immediately condemned it as 'impossible'. Discussion failed to break the deadlock.

Progress was however made on the question of the future of the Italian campaign. Brooke had conferred with Alexander the previous day, 30 January, and this discussion had led to a revised timing for the transfer of divisions – the whole process would be completed in six weeks instead of the previously estimated ten. Churchill's temperature had prevented him joining the Alexander-Brooke meeting, but the CIGS nevertheless informed his British colleagues on the morning of the 31st that the Prime Minister now agreed to this transfer scheme. Brooke presented the plan to the Americans at the CCS session in the afternoon, and immediate approval resulted. Moreover, the Americans also agreed to a British proposal for future operations in southeast Asia; Mountbatten would now be told: 'Your first object is to liberate Burma at the earliest date. Subject to the accomplishment of this object your next main task will be the liberation of Malaya and the opening of the Straits of Malacca.'[72]

But the directive to Eisenhower still remained the primary source of Anglo-American contention. Both sides returned to the attack next day, 1 February; Marshall suggested the 2.30 p.m. meeting should move into closed session, and the

British agreed. No records are therefore available of the subsequent discussion, but according to some participants, the argument brought out more acrimony than any other in the CCS war dealings.[73] Possibly the British proposal for a changed system of European command received attention: Brooke commented in his diary that the closed session 'allowed Marshall to express his full dislike and antipathy for Monty'.[74] Nevertheless, the meeting saw the required breakthrough. The British finally gave approval to the directive to Eisenhower as redrafted by Brooke and Bedell Smith after the first, optimistic meeting on the 30th, despite suspicions revived by Eisenhower's subsequent signal. Brooke found this agreement easier to give after a meeting with Bedell Smith the previous night: the CIGS's suspicions of Eisenhower did not extend to his Chief of Staff, and Brooke wrote after this late night *tête-à-tête*: 'I think that the talk did both of us good and may help in easing the work tomorrow.'[75] So it proved; moreover, the spectacular Russian successes, combined with deteriorating German morale, allowed greater flexibility in the western plans; thus Brooke wrote: 'It was clear that after the failure of Rundstedt's offensive German morale had deteriorated and that from now on we could take greater liberties. Under these new circumstances an advance on a wider front might present advantages.'[76] The CCS therefore agreed Eisenhower would 'carry out immediately a series of operations north of the Moselle with a view to destroying the enemy and closing the Rhine north of Düsseldorf ... seize bridgehead over the Rhine ... deploy east of the Rhine and north of the Ruhr the maximum number of divisions which can be maintained ... deploy east of the Rhine, on an axis Frankfurt-Kassel, such forces, if adequate, as may be available.' The task of the latter force would be to draw enemy forces away from the north.[77]

At 9.30 a.m. next day, 2 February, President Roosevelt's cruiser moved sedately into Valetta harbour to the strains of 'The Star-Spangled Banner'. 'While the bands played,' wrote Eden, 'and amid so much that reeked of war, on the bridge, just discernible to the naked eye, sat one civilian figure. In his sensitive hands lay much of the world's fate. All heads were turned his way and a sudden quietness fell.'[78] Roosevelt, re-elected President the previous November, had not long to live; he had been warned this journey might finish him; all now agreed he looked extremely unwell. The Prime Minister had recovered from his fever sufficiently to dine with Roosevelt on the USS *Quincy*; the CCS met at noon to settle final points in their interim report to the two leaders. A full plenary session began at 6 p.m., when the report received approval.

Eden had meanwhile been fretting over lack of progress in Anglo-American diplomatic discussion. No top level talks had taken place, despite a dinner organized specifically for this purpose on the evening of Roosevelt's arrival. 'The President was so unpredictable,' wrote Eden later, 'that the Prime Minister and I became uneasy at this void.'[79] Now, late on 2 February, the exodus by air from Malta began. Ahead lay Yalta, and Stalin. Frantic preparations had been made during the previous month by allied advance parties and the Russian hosts to prepare the conference location. Telegrams had flashed to London listing essential items to be brought, down to the last detail – 'plenty of flea powder and toilet paper (to) be issued to all ranks'. Yalta had been devastated by the Germans during the Crimean fighting: over 1,000 Soviet soldiers had been repairing roads, rebuilding and repairing houses, planting gardens. Long lines of railway trucks had clattered from Moscow bringing priceless paintings from the capital's art galleries, and furniture, carpets, bedding, food, drink, chefs, waiters, maids. No detail seemed overlooked. Just before Churchill's arrival the Russians were told he preferred to sleep in a double bed; urgent signals immediately passed between Yalta and Moscow, and a huge bed reached Churchill's room in the Vorontov Palace just before his arrival. This palace provided a superb setting, overlooking the Black Sea, with terraced gardens stretching down to the beach, and a pine forest behind clinging to the slopes of a 4,000 foot mountain. A year before, German officers had enjoyed their Christmas revels in the magnificent palace rooms; now Churchill arrived with his huge staff to discuss the final stages of the war against the Reich and Japan and to open talks on post-war problems.[80]

Stalin called on Churchill at 3 p.m. on 4 February, the day after the Prime Minister's arrival. The meeting proved pleasant, with mutual congratulations, and served as an excellent opener for the first Three-Power session starting at 5 p.m. This dealt with the current military situation, and especially with Russian progress on the Eastern Front. General Marshall described operations in the west, and the meeting agreed that co-ordination of the east and west offensives should receive staff consideration next day.[81] Diplomatic subjects had still to be broached, much to Eden's dissatisfaction; nor was the Foreign Secretary reassured by a dinner that evening. 'A terrible party,' he wrote in his diary. 'President vague and loose and ineffective. W. understanding that business was flagging made desperate efforts and too long speeches to get things going again. Stalin's attitude to small countries struck me as grim, not to say sinister.'[82] British and American COS met their Soviet counterparts at noon next day, 5 February, and Brooke sought Russian assurances that the Red Army would continue to press forward during March and April to help the Western Front offensive. The Russians proved evasive; according to the minutes, 'General Antonov said that, as Marshal Stalin had pointed out, the Russians would continue the offensive in the East as long as the weather permitted. There might be interruptions.... The Soviet Army would, however, take measures to make such interruptions as short as possible.'[83] The British and Americans would have liked a more explicit statement; concern especially centred on the possibility of a thaw softening the ground and hindering Russian armour, hence allowing the Germans to shift resources back to the west.

Conversely, the Russians asked the allies for specific statements on another major topic discussed at Yalta: dismemberment of defeated Germany. Britain declined to enter into a categorical commitment. Agreement had still to be reached between the British Foreign Office and COS attitudes, and Churchill had tried to delay a decision, writing to Eden on 4 January: 'It is much too soon for us to decide these enormous questions.... It is a mistake to try to write out on little pieces of paper what the vast emotions of an outraged and quivering world will be either immediately after the struggle is over or when the inevitable cold fit follows the hot.'[84] Now, at 4.15 p.m. on the 5th, Stalin asked what form the dismemberment of Germany should take, and the Prime Minister replied that the question needed longer study. At Tehran, Stalin had agreed with Roosevelt's suggestion that Germany should be divided into five parts; Churchill had hesitated, and now repeated his tentative belief that the country should merely be split into two, with Prussia detached and with a southern state possibly centred on Vienna. Roosevelt suggested the Foreign Secretaries should consider a plan for studying the question within 24 hours and a definite plan for dismemberment within a month. Stalin and Churchill agreed. The plenary session also decided that the Foreign Secretaries should discuss German reparation; Churchill voiced opposition to huge demands, amounting to 10,000 million dollars, which Stalin declared should be the Soviet share.[85]

War Cabinet Ministers meeting at 10 Downing Street during this evening of the 5th heard latest reports of the military situation in Europe – and already the British and American fears over further Red Army progress seemed justified. 'Russia. A thaw had set in on 31 January. The muddy conditions had increased German resistance and a strained administrative situation had slowed down the Russian advance.'[86] At Yalta, the question of East-West co-ordination received further attention next morning, 6 February, and once again Antonov proceeded cautiously. 'Soviet offensive action had started and would continue. The Soviet forces would press forward until hampered by the weather.' If an offensive were launched on the Western Front in March and April, 'the Soviets would take every possible action on the Eastern Front', although Antonov warned that this period was 'the most difficult season' from the weather aspect.[87] While this discussion took place at Yalta, the Vice-COS were meeting in London in an attempt to delve deeper into Soviet intentions by means of a Joint Intelligence Committee report. This paper, on the likely course of events on the Eastern Front, said there seemed to be two alternative courses of action. First, the Soviets might pause on the Oder down to the Baltic to build up strength; alternatively, they might attempt a continuous drive on to Berlin and beyond. Capture of Berlin would give the Russians added prestige; it would involve the destruction of further German forces; and it would deprive Germany of her largest industrial city. But the further the Russians advanced, the more they would open themselves to counter-attack, and the attempt to capture Berlin – as opposed to surrounding it – would lead to costly fighting in largely built-up areas; moreover, no natural defensive positions would exist to cover communications. The JIC therefore believed the Russians would stop at the Oder.[88]

Also on this Tuesday, 6 February, Eden clashed with Molotov over the question of German dismemberment; the Foreign Secretary wrote in his diary: 'Molotov wished to tie us hand and foot to dismemberment before enquiry was made. I refused to do this and stuck to my point.'[89] Eden's obstinacy apparently proved successful; Molotov dropped the subject at the plenary session held during the afternoon. Instead this plenary meeting turned to the equally controversial subject of Poland. The London Poles had still to agree to the Curzon Line as an eastern frontier. But at Yalta this difficulty tended to be submerged beneath the constitutional and political problem of Poland: Eden and Churchill believed that without agreement on this issue, the frontier settlement would be virtually worthless. Britain still recognized the Polish Government in London, while Moscow recognized the Polish National Committee as the Provisional Government. Eden and Stettinius had already agreed that the only solution lay in the creation of a Provisional Government representing all sections, which would hold power until free elections could take place, and Roosevelt advocated this policy when the plenary session began on the 6th, supported by Churchill – who declared: 'A strong, free and independent Poland was much more important than

particular territorial boundaries.' Stalin replied that a Polish
Government could not be created unless the Poles themselves
agreed to it, and deep hostility existed between the Lublin
Government and the Government in Exile – with the latter
to blame. Discussion continued late into the night, without
results.[90]

No military talks took place next day, 7 February, and
Brooke toured the nearby Balaclava battlefields. The three
leaders met again in plenary session during the afternoon,
and agreed a conference should be arranged to succeed
Dumbarton Oaks. Then they turned to Poland again. Roosevelt had written to Stalin, with Churchill's concurrence,
suggesting two members of the Lublin Government and two
from London or from within Poland should attend the Yalta
conference. Stalin agreed in principle. Should they be unable
to arrive before the conference closed, Molotov had drawn
up proposals for a draft agreement. '1. It was agreed that the
Curzon Line should be the eastern frontier.... 2. It was
decided that the western frontier of Poland should be drawn
from the town of Stettin (which would be Polish) and thence
southwards along the river Oder and the western Neisse.
3. It was considered desirable to add to the Provisional Polish
Government some democratic leaders from Polish *émigré*
circles. 4. It was considered desirable that the Provisional
Polish Government, enlarged as suggested in (3) should as
soon as possible call the population of Poland to the polls....'
Roosevelt and Churchill accepted this declaration in principle, although both objected to the word *émigré*, and
Churchill suggested 'Poles abroad' instead. Once again the
Western leaders disregarded the eastern frontier question in
their desire to reach agreement over the political issue;
Churchill merely expressed fears over the amount of German
territory which Poland would acquire in the west: 'It would
be a great pity to stuff the Polish goose so full of German
food that it died of indigestion.' Six million Germans lived
in this western area – although Stalin observed that they
had now run away.[91] Churchill, according to Lord Moran,
was disturbed by Roosevelt's lack of participation in the talks.
'The President no longer seems to the PM to take an intelli-

gent interest in the war,' wrote Moran. 'To a doctor's eye, the President appears a very sick man. He has all the symptoms of hardening of the arteries of the brain in an advanced stage, so that I give him only a few months to live.'[92] Nevertheless, Roosevelt submitted a revised draft of Molotov's proposals to the fourth plenary meeting next day, 8 February, which rejected the extension of the Polish western frontier to the western Neisse. He also proposed that Molotov should meet the British and American ambassadors to Moscow, to start discussions with the Poles regarding a three-man Presidential Committee. More argument followed, until Churchill asked the direct question as to how soon a Polish general election could be held. Within three months, replied Stalin, and Churchill thought this likelihood of an early date might change the whole situation and enable a compromise to be reached. The three leaders therefore agreed Eden, Stettinius and Molotov should now confer with the British and American ambassadors.[93]

The CCS had met during this Thursday to settle technical matters concerning the European war. And the CCS were informed that Montgomery, on schedule, had launched his assault towards the lower Rhine. Preceded by the biggest barrage of the war, the 1st Canadian Army drove southwards into the Reichswald Forest east of Nijmegen, strongly reinforced by units from the 2nd British Army. The battle for the Rhine and Ruhr had begun. Reports of excellent progress reached London by the time the War Cabinet met at 5.30. The Canadian advance had pushed aside opposition, and would be supported by a converging attack by the 9th US Army from the line of the Roer, to be started within 48 hours.

War Cabinet Ministers then discussed telegrams received from Churchill at the 'Argonaut' conference, dealing mainly with Poland and the dismemberment of Germany. With the first, Ministers felt uneasy over western frontier proposals. 'Public opinion both in Parliament and in the country was increasingly critical of the exaggerated territorial demands which had been put forward by the Lublin Poles. It would be preferable, if possible, to avoid tying our hands at this stage more than was actually necessary.' No mention was made of the eastern frontier along the Curzon Line. With dismemberment, Churchill had informed the War Cabinet that the conference had agreed the Foreign Secretaries would consider how a reference could be inserted into the terms of surrender. Ministers pointed out that 'it was by no means clear what was precisely involved in dismemberment' and the economic and political problems had not yet been considered in Cabinet. Ministers therefore agreed 'it was desirable to avoid any commitments until the matter as a whole could be reviewed'. The War Cabinet met again at 10.30 p.m. and approved a draft telegram to Churchill, despatched next day, 9 February, which outlined the views expressed in discussion.[94] The telegram had still to reach Yalta when Eden attended talks with Stettinius, Molotov and the ambassadors on the morning of the 9th. Stettinius said the Americans had agreed to drop the proposal for a Polish Presidential Committee; Molotov argued that the Lublin Government represented the people of Poland, although he agreed the principal requirement was for a general election. Eden replied that British public opinion would not regard an election managed by the Lublin Committee as being free. Argument spilled over into the afternoon plenary session, with both Roosevelt and Churchill demanding assurances that elections would be free. The Foreign Secretaries met again in the evening, and by now Eden had been handed the War Cabinet's telegram, dealing with both Poland's western frontier and a political settlement. With the first, the War Cabinet suggested the phrase in an 'Argonaut' declaration referring to this frontier should run 'and such other lands to be east of the line of the Oder as at the Peace Conference it shall be considered desirable'. As regards a political arrangement, the War Cabinet stressed that any interim arrangement before free elections should represent a balance of political opinion inside the country. Thus strengthened, Eden declared that unless something on the lines of the British proposals were accepted for the 'Argonaut' declaration, no hope existed of an agreement.[95]

The CCS final report to the President and Prime Minister

received immediate approval at a noon meeting on the 9th. During this Friday, the Germans forestalled the 9th Army advance by flooding the Roer from the last of the dams, thus denying any forward move for a fortnight. Brooke and his colleagues were anxious to return home to be in closer touch with the situation, and accordingly left Yalta next morning, 10 February. Churchill and Eden struggled on with the Polish problem, meeting Stalin and Molotov during the afternoon of the 10th – no Americans being present – and the Soviet leader now agreed that the British Ambassador at Moscow, Clark Kerr, should have freedom of movement in Poland to supervise electoral conditions. Later in the afternoon the three leaders met for the last plenary session, and now accepted a draft settlement on Poland: liberation of the country called for the establishment 'of a Provisional Polish Government which can be more broadly based'; Harriman, Clark Kerr and Molotov would act as a commission in Moscow to consult members of the present Lublin Government and other Polish leaders 'from within Poland and from abroad with a view to the reorganization of the present Government.... This "Provisional Government of National Unity" shall be pledged to the holding of free and unfettered elections as soon as practicable.' The plenary session also dealt with frontiers, with Churchill referring to the War Cabinet opinion. Roosevelt said he preferred no mention of frontiers at all, but Stalin insisted that the Curzon Line should be specified, and the three leaders therefore agreed to a declaration referring to this eastern boundary, adding that the final delineation of the western frontier would await the Peace Conference.[96]

'Argonaut' ended next day, Sunday, 11 February. Many issues were left undecided, including dismemberment of Germany; the related subject of Germany's occupation by the victorious allied armies had received some discussion, and various zones had been agreed in principle, but final arrangements had still to be made – opening the way for possible confusion. Other issues, including Poland, rested upon good faith; as Eden commented: 'It was the execution which mattered.' And this execution depended upon Soviet intentions and Soviet willingness to co-operate. Churchill, when he returned to London, would reveal to the War Cabinet the astonishing amount of trust which he was prepared to place upon Stalin's words. Roosevelt said on his return to Washington: 'The Crimea Conference ... spells – and it ought to spell – the end of the system of unilateral action, exclusive alliances, and spheres of influence, and balance of power and all the other expedients which have been tried for centuries and always failed.' Yet Yalta all too soon indicated an intensification of these evils, and even on 11 February, as the delegates prepared to leave, Churchill and Eden learnt of American 'unilateral action' which flew in the face of Roosevelt's fine words. The day before, 10 February, Roosevelt and Stalin had reached secret agreement on Far East terms, withheld from the British until the 11th although Stalin had previously dropped a hint to the Prime Minister. These terms, proposed by Russia and agreed by the President, were largely at the expense of the Chinese, including the establishment of Port Arthur as a Soviet naval base, acquisition by the USSR of the Kurile Islands, and granting Russia extensive rights in Manchuria. The Russians in return repeated their promise to enter the war against Japan within three months of Germany's defeat. The terms guaranteed fulfilment irrespective of Chinese objections. Moreover, Roosevelt failed to secure a Russian promise that support would be avoided for Chinese Communists. Eden urged Churchill not to sign his approval of the agreement, and an argument broke out between the two men in the presence of Stalin and Roosevelt, but Churchill had his way. The Prime Minister believed the matter to be an American concern, and 'it would have been wrong for us to get in their way unless we had some very solid reason'.[97]

War Cabinet Ministers decided next day, 12 February, to send congratulations to Churchill and Eden 'on the skill and success with which they had conducted the discussions in the Conference and on the results which had been achieved'.[98] On the 13th the Polish Government in London condemned the Curzon Line frontier settlement as 'a fifth partition of Poland, this time carried out by her allies', and

complained of lack of guarantees that any member of a
Provisional Government would in fact be allowed to remain
there.[99] Churchill enjoyed himself touring the Balaclava site
on the 13th, before paying a short visit to Athens, after which
he spent five days in Egypt with Eden. On 15 February he
met Roosevelt again for a brief talk on board the USS *Quincy*
in Alexandria harbour. 'The President seemed placid and
frail,' wrote the Prime Minister later. 'I felt that he had a
slender contact with life. I was not to see him again. We bade
affectionate farewells.'[100] In more ways than one the era of
Big Three wartime decision-making was drawing to a close.

Battle continued in Europe. Zhukov, as the British Joint
Intelligence Committee had guessed, indeed halted on the
eastern bank of the Oder on 10 February. But Canadian
troops under Montgomery pressed forward; the British
Commander, now delighted by Eisenhower's attitude, wrote
to Brooke on the 14th: 'He is giving me two more American
infantry divisions.... He reaffirmed his intention to concentrate all resources, ground and air, on doing one thing
at a time.... I do believe that we are at last all well set with
a fair wind to help us into harbour.'[101] Yet Hitler still
stabbed back at Britain, with Morrison reporting to the War
Cabinet on the 12th that 56 V-2s had landed during the
previous week. 'The Vice-COAS said that Fighter Command
had already been pressed to increase their counter-measures
... and it was hoped to increase the effort by 50 per cent.'[102]
Next night, 13 February, allied strategic bombers intensified
their part in the air war. Dresden had been selected as the
target for concentrated attack. The scale of slaughter reached
new records – yet official documents now hint that results
far exceeded expectations.

No War Cabinet or COS discussion took place prior to the
terrible Dresden raids, which would soon be placed in history
as the ultimate in saturation bombing. The attacks originated
from a plan put forward by Portal to the Air Staff in August
1944, based on a scheme to break German morale, and given
added impetus in February, 1945, by the supposed value of
bombing important centres in the path of the advancing
Russian armies. The original scheme, 'Thunderclap', envi-

saged attacks on Berlin, Leipzig, Dresden and Chemnitz. Portal, in August 1944, had declared: 'Immense devastation could be produced if the entire attack was concentrated on a single big town other than Berlin, and the effect would be especially great if the town was hitherto relatively undamaged.'[103] Dresden was now selected – not by the War Cabinet or the COS. Churchill was far away at Balaclava. Dresden's population of 600,000 had been swollen by refugees. Just over 800 aircraft of Bomber Command clustered over the target on the night of the 13th; 400 aircraft from 8th US Air Force followed on the morning of the 14th; a third attack was made on the 15th by 200 more American bombers. First information received by War Cabinet Ministers came in an undescriptive Cabinet War Room situation report on the 15th: 'On the night of 13/14, 1471 tons of high explosives and 1175 tons of incendiaries were dropped on DRESDEN, 755 tons on Bohlen synthetic oil plant, 96 tons on MAGDEBURG....'[104] The extent of the damage had apparently not yet been realized. Not until Monday, 19 February, would the War Cabinet begin to appreciate the full horror; according to the unemotional minutes of the 6.30 p.m. meeting: 'The COS reported the principal events of the previous week. Bomber Command had flown 3,615 sorties and had dropped 8,000 tons of bombs. The attack on Dresden had practically wiped out the city.'[105] The whole area had in fact been swept by a massive firestorm. Fires raging close together raised the general temperature to such an extent that everything burst into flame; fed by an updraught, flames rushed down the streets faster than men and women could run. Over 135,000 people may have died. Dresden was not the only target selected for concentrated bombing during these weeks: heavy attacks were made on Chemnitz and on Leipzig, and over 1,100 bombers of the 8th Air Force would strike at Berlin on 26 February. During March over 133,500 tons of bombs would be dropped on all types of target by British and American aircraft.[106] As far as the British War Cabinet were concerned, Dresden merely formed part of the overall programme of terror as the Battle for Germany climbed to its climax.

10

End and Beginning

Churchill reached England from Cairo on Monday, 19 February, in time to interrupt the 6.30 p.m. War Cabinet meeting. Ministers had just been informed of the latest military events: Morrison reported a total of 78 V-2 attacks during the previous week; Brooke said Montgomery's offensive had 'advanced from 4-5 miles on a 25-mile front in very bad going. Opposite Aachen, US forces had made small but important progress.' In Burma the island of Ramree had been cleared; Americans in the Pacific had started their attack on Iwo Jima. As usual, the Russians seemed to be having the most spectacular success: Brooke said the Red Army had resumed its advance west of the Oder, and Budapest was firmly in Soviet hands. And, after receiving further congratulations from Attlee, Churchill concentrated on Russia in his startling statement to the War Cabinet.

'So far as Stalin was concerned, he (Churchill) was quite sure that he meant well to the world and to Poland. He (Churchill) did not himself think that there would be any resentment on the part of Russia about the arrangements that had been made for free and fair elections in that country ... almost the whole of Poland had been liberated; in many parts of the country so reconquered the Russians had been warmly welcomed.... Stalin, at the beginning of their conversations on the Polish question, had said that Russia had committed many sins ... against Poland, and that they had in the past joined in the partitions of Poland and in cruel oppression of her. It was not the intention of the Soviet

Government to repeat that policy in the future. He (Churchill) felt no doubt whatever in saying that Stalin had been sincere. He had very great feeling that the Russians were anxious to work harmoniously with the two English-speaking democracies.' Churchill described the 'closeness of contact' and understanding at Yalta. 'Stalin was a person of great power in whom he had every confidence. He did not think that he would embark on any adventure, but he could not deny that much rested on Stalin's life.... As regards Greece, the Russian attitude could not have been more satisfactory. There was no suggestion on Stalin's part of criticism of our policy. He had been friendly and even jocular in discussion of it.'¹ Churchill's glowing assessment of Stalin's personality and intentions bore a remarkable resemblance to an account given by another British Prime Minister to the Cabinet over 5 years before, describing another dictator – Adolf Hitler. Thus Neville Chamberlain had reported to Ministers after his visit to Berchtesgaden in September 1938: 'It was impossible not to be impressed with the power of the man.... Further, and this was a point of considerable importance, he (Chamberlain) formed the opinion that Herr Hitler's objectives were strictly limited.... The impression left on him (Chamberlain) was that Herr Hitler meant what he said. His view was that Herr Hitler was telling the truth.'

General Anders, commander of the Polish forces fighting with the allies in Italy, arrived in London two days later to warn Churchill against trusting the Russians. The Prime Minister apparently heard him sympathetically, but the interview proved non-productive. Anders saw Brooke next afternoon, 22 February, and the CIGS wrote in his diary: 'He said that he had never been more distressed since the war started.... I felt most awfully sorry for him.'² Next day, the 23rd, the Commission set up by the Yalta conference to discuss Poland held its first meeting in Moscow; complications immediately arose. The British and American Ambassadors asked for Mikolajczyk and Romer to be invited to the consultations on a Polish Provisional Administration, but these two were ruled out by the Lublin Poles as being hostile to the Yalta decisions. Another suggested delegate,

Witos, proved to have 'gone into hiding', according to the
Lublin Poles.³ Within 24 hours another upset emerged, this
time in Roumania. A Soviet-sponsored *coup* took place in
Bucharest on the 24th against Radescu's Government; two
days later Vyshinsky entered the country and demanded a
communist-controlled Government.⁴

While these depressing reports reached the Foreign Office,
encouraging signals arrived at the War Office from the
European battle-front. British and Canadian troops struggled
over the sodden fields between the Meuse and Rhine and
managed to take the Goch stronghold on 21 February. Forty-
eight hours later the 9th US Army began its postponed attack
from the Roer, advancing north and north-east to link with
Montgomery's south-east thrust. Also on the 23rd the 1st
US Army joined the 9th in the push across the Roer before
swinging south towards Cologne and Bonn. Montgomery
wrote to Brooke on the 24th: 'I ordered that advance be
pressed relentlessly, and that every legitimate risk be taken
to get forward. The weather is fine and the ground is drying
up.'⁵

Churchill rose in the crowded House of Commons on 27
February to make a 120-minute speech defending the Yalta
decisions. 'The Crimea Conference leaves the allies more
closely united than before, both in the military and political
sphere.... The Three Powers are agreed that acceptance by
the Poles of the provisions on the eastern frontiers, and, so
far as can now be ascertained, on the western frontiers, is an
essential condition of the establishment and future welfare
and security of a strong, independent, homogeneous Polish
State.... Most solemn declarations have been made by
Marshal Stalin and the Soviet Union that the sovereign
independence of Poland is to be maintained.' At one point
Lord Dunglass jumped to his feet. 'I am sorry to interrupt
the Prime Minister, but this point is highly important ... is
there going to be some kind of international supervision?'
'I should certainly like that,' replied Churchill, 'but we have
to wait until the new Polish Government is set up and to see
what are the proposals they make....' Lord Dunglass,
branded as a 'Munich' man, returned to his point in a speech

attacking the Polish agreement. '(This) is the first case, a test
case, in the relationship between a great power wielding great
military might, and her smaller and weaker neighbour....
It is imperative that these elections should be really and truly
free....' On the same day the British Ambassador at Moscow
felt obliged to point out to Molotov that he could not accept
proposed facilities for observers to go to Poland, since,
following the unco-operative Soviet and Lublin attitude, this
acceptance would now be seen as recognition of the Lublin
Government.[6]

The Commons debate continued next day, 28 February;
a critical amendment was defeated by 396 votes to 25 and the
Government remained safe. Yet Churchill took the precaution of instructing the British Ambassador at Moscow
to accept Molotov's 'friendly offer' of facilities for observers,
despite the implied recognition of the Lublin Government.
Clark Kerr and Harriman therefore formally accepted the
offer on 1 March – and the invitation was immediately withdrawn by Molotov because of contemptuous remarks made
by Eden against the Lublin Poles during the Commons
debate, and because the British and Americans had refused
to invite these Polish communists to send representatives to
the Moscow talks.[7] Also on 1 March, President Roosevelt
gave his optimistic report on the Yalta conference to a joint
session of two houses of Congress. The President's health was
clearly failing, and he apologized for having to sit while
delivering his speech. 'I know that you will realize that it
makes it a lot easier for me not to have to carry about 10
pounds of steel around the bottom of my legs, and also ...
I have just completed a 14,000 mile trip.' The occasion
marked the first time he had publicly mentioned his crippled
legs since 1928.[8]

Churchill flew with Brooke to the Western Front on 2
March. 'The battle is going wonderfully well,' wrote the
CIGS, 'and there are signs from all sides of decay setting in
in the Germany Army.'[9] During the day two German officers
appeared in Switzerland from the staff of General Karl Wolff,
SS Commander in Italy, and made tentative approaches to
the British authorities. The 9th Army had accelerated

forward and by 26 February its right had reached the Rhine south of Düsseldorf, and on the day of Churchill's arrival at the front its left entered Venlo. Fifteen German divisions were caught on the west bank of the Rhine between the jaws of Montgomery's twin advance. Troops from the two arms joined hands at Geldern on the 3rd, and during this Saturday Churchill celebrated by urinating on the Siegfried Line, having first told press photographers: 'This is one of the operations connected with this great war which must not be reproduced graphically.' Brooke wrote: 'I shall never forget the childish grin of intense satisfaction that spread all over his face as he looked down at the critical moment.'[10] The tour continued on the 4th and 5th with Churchill arguing to be allowed nearer the fighting. On 5 March centre units in the 9th Army took Krefeld and probed towards the enemy's bridgehead over the Rhine west of Wesel; also on this Sunday elements on the left of the 1st US Army reached the smoking suburbs of Cologne, battered by allied bombers only 3 days before.

'American forces were now in Cologne,' reported the CIGS to the War Cabinet at 5.30 p.m. next day, 6 March, 'and were closing in on the Rhine between Cologne and Düsseldorf. Within the next few days allied troops would probably have reached the Rhine from Nijmegen to Cologne.... The Pacific. The island of Corregidor had been cleared. The Americans claimed that during the operations in the Philippines some 55,000 Japanese had been killed. Russia. The Russians had made very good progress in the north and had now cut off Danzig and were near to Stettin.' But Morrison told Ministers that 71 V-2s had landed during the previous week, and there had been a resumption of V-1 attacks. Churchill said he was considering issuing a warning to the German people. 'This could make it clear that if the Germans prolonged their resistance, particularly past the time of the spring sowing, they would incur the risk of widespread famine in Germany after their final surrender. In those circumstances they could not rely on the allies to feed those who ... had brought famine upon themselves.' War Cabinet discussion turned to distressing news about Poland. Eden said a telegram had just been received from Clark Kerr: the British and American Ambassadors 'had had a very unsatisfactory discussion of 3 hours with Molotov.... Molotov had refused to abandon his claim that, under the terms of the Yalta communiqué ... the Warsaw (Lublin) Poles must be heard first.' Eden advised rejection of Molotov's demand. Bevin reported the strength of feeling in Labour circles over Poland, but suggested Molotov and not Stalin might be responsible for the present unsatisfactory situation. Churchill tried to cover his previous position. 'We had been fully entitled to take the line we had ... since we were bound to assume the good faith of an ally. ... If, however, it became clear that the Russians were not going to carry out the conditions to which he had agreed, it would be necessary to give the full story to Parliament. We could not run any risk of a suggestion that Parliament, in which feeling on this matter was strong in all parties, had been deceived.' Eden was also 'greatly concerned' at the way in which the Russians were handling the Roumanian situation, 'and by the revelation of their attitude which it represented'.[11]

Allied forces closed in on the Rhine. Tanks from the US 3rd Army reached the river north of Coblenz during the 7th and found all bridges destroyed. But on this Wednesday afternoon an advanced force from US 1st Army reached the river further north at Remagen and found a bridge astonishingly left intact. By evening the bridge had been taken; troops raced across – and the allies were on the east bank of the Rhine. Eisenhower immediately ordered Bradley to consolidate this bridgehead with some five divisions. By now, the end of the first week in March, about 50,000 prisoners had been taken, and 40,000 Germans estimated killed or wounded, since the offensive began on 8 February, while British and Canadian losses totalled 15,634 and US casualties 7,478. Brooke warned Montgomery that Churchill might soon pay another visit to the front.

V-2s continued to sting the British capital. The COS were told by Morrison on the 7th that 'the state of morale of the London population was causing ... considerable anxiety. After 5 years of fairly heavy, though intermittent, bombardment, culminating in the flying bomb attacks of last year, the Londoner had been suffering from considerable strain ... as the scale of (V-2) attack had increased, the relapse in morale had been noticeable.' This especially applied to London's crowded East End. Brooke insisted all possible was being done to stop the attacks, but operations in the Arnhem area and seaborne action against the Dutch coast or further north had so far been rejected because of the unpromising terrain and extensive flooding, and the bulk of the launching sites were therefore still intact.[12] Next day, 8 March, a new factor arose which affected this question of V-2 sites and which could influence the advance on Berlin. Churchill forwarded to the COS a letter from the Dutch Prime Minister, Dr Gerbrandy, urging an operation to bring about early liberation of his country, in view of the extensive starvation being suffered. The Prime Minister declared in a covering letter: 'I am of opinion that a military plan should now be concerted to prevent the horrors which will befall the Dutch, and incidentally to extirpate the rocket-firing points.' He supported such an operation, even if it resulted in 'a certain delay ... in the main advance on Berlin'.[13] The COS discussed the problem next day, 9 March, together with a JPS assessment which advised against such a plan on military grounds. The COS agreed however that other factors must be taken into account, and a telegram left for Washington: 'Dr Gerbrandy states that deaths by starvation are increasing, and that if the liberation of Holland has not been completed by May, there will be little population left to liberate ... we feel we must re-examine the possibility of liberating Holland.'[14]

War Cabinet Ministers heard on the 8th of further deterioration in dealings with the Russians. Churchill revealed that the previous Roumanian leader, Radescu, had sought sanctuary in the British Legation at Bucharest. 'The British representative had reported that there was a possibility that the new Prime Minister, Groza, had issued instructions for Radescu to be removed from the Legation, alive or dead.' British officials were determined to resist any such attempt, using firearms if necessary; nor were the

Russians apparently making any attempts to calm the situation. The War Cabinet supported a strong stand being taken.[15] Also on the 8th Churchill sent Roosevelt a draft message to Stalin; in his covering letter the Prime Minister told the President that the Polish question was a 'test case' over the meaning of such terms as 'democracy, sovereignty, independence, representative Government, and free and un-fettered elections'. The proposed message to Stalin therefore declared that Churchill would have to make a statement of 'our failure' to Parliament, unless the Moscow Commission agreed to essential conditions, including the withdrawal of Molotov's claim of prior right of consultation for the Warsaw (Lublin) Poles, and the introduction of observer facilities. Roosevelt sent objections on the 11th. 'I feel that our personal intervention would be best withheld until every other possibility . . . has been exhausted.' Clark Kerr also advised a further delay, and Churchill acquiesced.[16]

'Allied troops are holding the west bank of the Rhine from Nijmegen to the junction of the Moselle,' reported Brooke to the War Cabinet on the 12th. 'A bridgehead on the east bank of the Rhine has been established at Remagen. . . . The enemy will be hard put to it to find sufficient troops to hold the Moselle, defend the Remagen bridgehead and meet possible allied threats further north.'[17] The situation in the centre had exposed the whole of the German flank around the lower reaches of the Moselle and Saar; operations to clear this area, and to secure bridgeheads across the Rhine from Mainz to Karlsruhe, had been assigned to the 3rd and 7th US Armies supported by the 1st French army moving north from Strasbourg. But so successful had 3rd US Army opera-tions been in the Coblenz area that Bradley now urged an earlier move into this second stage of the offensive. Eisen-hower agreed, and on 14 March the 3rd Army crossed the lower Moselle, while the 7th Army pushed forward into the Saar. Within 48 hours the 3rd Army had broken through German defences and tanks were moving fast through the open country towards Mainz and Worms.

Secret meetings had been taking place in Switzerland over the possible surrender of the German army in Italy. Follow-

ing a visit by emissaries on the 2nd, General Karl Wolff
slipped into Switzerland on 8 March with a provisional offer
to which, he stressed, Kesselring had not yet been asked to
agree. He was told that only unconditional surrender would
be accepted. Alexander reported these events to Brooke and
to the CCS, asking permission to send a British and an
American officer from his staff to attend further talks in the
Swiss capital, purely, at this stage, to establish the *bona fides*
of the German approach. The CCS signalled approval on the
12th, and the officers met Wolff on the 15th – only to be
told that Kesselring had now left Italy and his successor,
von Vietinghoff, would have to be approached. Wolff slipped
back over the border. And now the situation led to another
source of conflict with the Russians. Moscow had been
informed of the contact on 12 March and replied the same
day, agreeing the meetings should continue but asking that
3 Russian officers should participate. The allies doubted the
wisdom or necessity of the Soviet presence, and suggested
to Moscow on the 15th that Alexander should merely inform
the Russians of the results. But next day Molotov complained
to the British Ambassador that the exclusion of the Russian
officers appeared 'utterly unexpected and incomprehensible';
talks should be severed and the British Government should
agree to 'rule out' separate negotiations in the future.[18]
Churchill reported this disturbing development to the War
Cabinet on the 19th. Ministers agreed the Russian attitude
might have been based on a misunderstanding: the talks
were only concerned with establishing *bona fides*, and would
anyway only touch upon military matters. The British and
American Ambassadors were instructed to explain the
situation to Molotov to remove the 'misunderstanding'.[19]
Also on the 19th another effort was made to clear up the main
East-West problem of Poland: the British and American
Ambassadors now presented a communication to Molotov
detailing conditions which they felt the Moscow Commission should accept – expressed in less drastic form than
Churchill had proposed in his draft message to Roosevelt
on the 8th.[20]
London and Washington awaited the Moscow reaction

to both these approaches while the armies in Europe continued their momentous advance; the 3rd Army had almost
cleared the west bank of the Rhine from Mainz to Mannheim; Bradley enlarged the Remagen bridgehead; forces in
the north prepared to cross the Rhine at Wesel. On 20 March
these successes and the possibility of German surrender were
linked in a report by the JIC, approved by the COS. 'General
collapse of control and the disintegration of the party
machine now appears more possible than at any stage in the
past.... Nevertheless, the German people, now required to
accept a further all-round cut in their food rations, exhausted
and preoccupied with the personal problem of daily life,
lack the leadership, the political vitality, or the organization,
to stage a revolt.... Many of them in the East would in any
case prefer the hardships of war to the horrors of enslave-
ment in Russia.' War would not end until Germany had
suffered complete military defeat.[21]

Relations with Russia slumped even lower. On Thursday,
22 March came the Soviet reply to the allied note on the
Wolff 'misunderstanding'. 'In this instance,' wrote Molotov
to the British Ambassador, 'the Soviet Government sees not a
misunderstanding but something worse....' Negotiations
had been carrying on 'behind the backs of the Soviet Union,
which is bearing the brunt of the war.... The Soviet Government consider this completely impermissible.'[22] Churchill
told Eden it would be best to ignore the communication,
especially as the Swiss talks seemed to have ended for the
moment.[23] Within 24 hours Molotov replied to the Anglo-
American message concerning Poland; he was 'astonished'
at the intention to send British and American observers into
Poland – 'such a proposal might offend the national dignity of
the Poles'. After another inconclusive discussion on this
Friday, the Moscow Commission adjourned.

Churchill had flown to the battle-front again. He wished
to be there for the kill at the main Rhine crossings; Brooke
had written in his diary the previous night, 22 March: 'I am
not happy about this trip; he will be difficult to manage, and
has no business to be going. All he will do is to endanger his
life unnecessarily.'[24] The Prime Minister and CIGS reached

Montgomery's HQ during the afternoon of the 23rd: the offensive over the Rhine would begin that night on two fronts, the 9th US Army on the right and the 2nd British Army on the left. The Rhine, still swollen by winter floods, lay some 500 yards wide. Already, as Churchill arrived, massed allied artillery had begun the preliminary bombardment. Montgomery went to bed after dinner; Churchill examined telegrams brought to him by special messenger, including one containing Molotov's note about the surrender negotiations. Throughout the night, 15 miles from the Prime Minister's comfortable camp-bed, thousands of allied soldiers fought their way across the Rhine and on to the eastern bank, and by dawn next day, 24 March, the bridgehead had been secured. Churchill watched operations after breakfast, revelling in the roar of the guns and the sight of the gliders floating over his head. The Prime Minister's party drove away, and Churchill fell asleep well satisfied, gradually sliding on to Brooke's knees.[25] Opposition to the allied landings at this Wesel crossing proved weaker than expected, and more units were fed in to swell the bridgehead. And by this Saturday, 24 March, further south the whole of the 1st US Army was deploying east of the Rhine between Bonn and Coblenz, making use of the Remagen entrance. Next day, Palm Sunday, these units swung to the east, while the Prime Minister fulfilled a major wartime ambition and crossed the Rhine himself into Wesel. Shells were landing nearby, snipers were active, and he almost had to be dragged back again. 'The look on Winston's face,' wrote Brooke, 'was just like that of a small boy being called away from his sandcastles on the beach. . . . He put both his arms round one of the twisted girders of the bridge and looked over his shoulder at Simpson with pouting mouth and angry eyes.'[26] Latest military reports were read to the War Cabinet next day, 26 March: 'All enemy resistance west of the Rhine has now ceased, and of 250,000 enemy troops estimated to have been in that area, about 150,000 have either been captured or killed. . . .'[27] Churchill flew back to England while this War Cabinet meeting took place. Brooke commented: 'I honestly believe that he would really have liked to be killed on the front at this moment of success.... I rather feel that he considers that a sudden and soldierly death at the front would be a suitable ending to his famous life and would free him from the never-ending worries which loom ahead with our Russian friends and others....'²⁸ Back in London these never-ending problems with the 'Russian friends' would now be given a sudden extra importance: an issue was about to arise which would dog Churchill to the ending of the war, and which would carry through long into peace: the race to Berlin.

Churchill and the Chiefs of Staff had always had the firm impression that Berlin would, and should, be the primary allied objective. The allies would pluck out the heart of the Reich; the capital had supreme military and psychological importance. In May 1944, Berlin had been defined by 'Overlord' HQ as the ultimate goal of the Western armies; hence the British belief that the main thrust should be in the north, towards this area. CCS discussions at Malta had finally convinced the British COS that Eisenhower would now concentrate on this northern thrust, and a confident Montgomery signalled Brooke on 27 March: 'The situation looks good and events should begin to move rapidly in a few days.... My tactical HQ moves will be Wesel-Munster-Herford-Hanover – thence via *autobahn* to Berlin, I hope.'²⁹ Next afternoon came a complete reversal of all previous expectations. Eisenhower dispatched a startling signal to the Military Mission in Moscow, to be handed to Stalin; not until the evening of the 28th did the CCS receive a copy of this message 'for information only', and no prior consultation had taken place. The signal to Moscow revealed that Berlin would not be the main objective; instead Eisenhower intended to launch the primary thrust further south, to meet up with the more southern Russian advance thus splitting Germany in half. 'My next task will be to divide the remaining enemy forces by joining hands with your forces. For my forces the best axis on which to effect this junction would be Erfurt-Leipzig-Dresden. I believe, moreover, that this is the area to which main German Governmental Departments are being moved. It is along this axis that I propose to make my main effort.'³⁰

Eisenhower based his policy purely upon military factors. He believed the enemy organizational structure had sought safety by moving south, away from Berlin; he believed his plan offered the best chance of bringing about the earliest possible military defeat of Hitler and his armies. And this, no less than the capture of Berlin, was in line with the basic CCS objective. The Supreme Commander took no account of possible diplomatic factors connected with the capture of Berlin; moreover, he rightly believed that the three leaders had already given provisional agreement to British, American and Russian occupation zones in Germany, which, although allowing for the joint occupation of Berlin itself, would place the German capital deep in Soviet administered territory. This arrangement had been accepted in principle in the optimistic atmosphere at Yalta. The British Chiefs of Staff, like Eisenhower, did not concern themselves with diplomatic questions; they now quarrelled with the Supreme Commander on military and procedural grounds, and their attitude was tainted by previous suspicions of Eisenhower's military abilities. Moreover, Churchill initially attacked Eisenhower's plans for exactly the same military reasons, and no more. If the Yalta atmosphere had continued, the Prime Minister would probably have agreed to restrict his opposition to the line taken by the COS. Even now memories of Yalta still lingered. Only gradually, under the pressure of other events, did Churchill adopt an attitude which later earned him credit for his diplomatic foresight; at the time this foresight was by no means instantaneous. It took time for him to start attacking Eisenhower's scheme on the far more fundamental basis of the diplomatic need to reach Berlin before the Russians.

First news of Eisenhower's signal to Moscow reached London early on 29 March. Churchill attached a minute to the telegram and sent it to the COS before their meeting on this Thursday morning: 'This seems to differ from last night's Montgomery, who spoke of Elbe. Please explain.' The COS were unable to do so; as Brooke wrote in his diary: 'To start with, he (Eisenhower) has no business to address Stalin direct ... secondly, he produced a telegram which was unintelligible;

and finally, what was implied in it appeared to be entirely
adrift and a change from all that had been previously agreed
on.'[31] As a result of the COS discussion their secretary sent
a note to the Prime Minister: 'They (the COS) have never
contemplated a direct approach by SCAEF (Eisenhower) to
Marshal Stalin', and the COS could not determine the military merits of the plan from the information given by
Eisenhower so far.[32] Churchill summoned a staff conference
at 5.15 p.m. when Brooke repeated that the COS criticized the
direct approach to Moscow and were 'somewhat alarmed at the
divergences between the plan of operations described in the
telegram and the previously agreed strategy'. He explained
the differences with the aid of maps, and the conference
approved a draft telegram to the British Mission in Washington. Churchill voiced no objections to this signal, which was
accordingly dispatched.[33] Brooke and his colleagues were
chiefly dismayed by possible repercussions along the North
Sea and Baltic if the emphasis of the allied advance were to
be switched south. Their signal stressed the need to capture
German ports as quickly as possible, both as supply inlets
and in order to prevent a renewal of U-boat attacks. Moreover, they wished to end the war in Holland, following the
Dutch Prime Minister's plea concerning the starving population. The telegram continued: 'For the above reasons, the
emphasis placed by General Eisenhower on the main thrust
on an axis Kassel/Leipzig/Dresden causes us much concern.
We are forced to doubt whether there had been sufficient
appreciation of issues which have a wider importance than
the destruction of the main enemy forces in Germany.' By
this 'wider importance' the COS only referred to the military
factors.

Churchill also continued to restrict his reasoning to the
military aspect. He claimed in his memoirs that he disagreed
with some points made in the COS telegram and implied that
this signal did not go far enough; the official minutes of the
staff conference on 29 March do not substantiate this recollection; he agreed at the time that Eisenhower's military
evidence seemed flimsy, and demands were immediately
made to the Supreme Commander for more information.

Similar requests were made by the US COS in Washington. Next day, Good Friday, Brooke left for Hampshire hoping for a long Easter weekend at home away from worries. Churchill remained at 10 Downing Street until journeying to Chequers on the Saturday night. During this Saturday he sent a minute to the COS. This seems to indicate a realization that wider factors were involved, centring on the need to reach Berlin first; and this minute has been used as an example of the Prime Minister's diplomatic foresight. In fact, linked with other documents, the minute shows Churchill still to be thinking primarily along military lines. The COS had not mentioned Berlin, but had restricted their remarks to the need for other military operations in the north; Churchill's minute therefore declared: 'I have considered your telegram, and of course it is a good thing for the military points to be placed before the COS committee. I hope however we shall realize that we have only a quarter of the forces invading Germany, and that the situation has thus changed remarkably from the days of June 1944.... It also seems that General Eisenhower may be wrong in supposing Berlin to be largely devoid of military and political importance. Even though German Governmental departments have to a great extent moved to the south, the dominating fact on German minds of the fall of Berlin and leaving it to the Russians to take at a later stage does not appear to me correct.' Churchill's reference to 'political importance' was linked to German and not Cold War politics: the JIC had already emphasized that the enemy would fight to the death rather than surrender to the rampaging Russians. Thus Churchill's minute to the COS continued: 'As long as Berlin holds out and withstands a siege in the ruins, as it may easily do, German resistance will be stimulated.'[34] The Prime Minister, like the COS and Eisenhower, therefore concerned himself with methods of ending the war in the shortest possible time, rather than seizing Berlin for future value in the East-West confrontation.

Churchill summoned the COS to attend a staff conference at Chequers next morning, Easter Sunday, 1 April. By now signals had arrived from Washington and from Eisenhower.

The latter, in a telegram dated 30 March to the Prime Minister, had given more military reasons for his proposals and stressed the aim of overrunning the important industrial area around Leipzig, and of cutting German forces in half. The Supreme Commander added: 'Once the success of main thrusts is assured I propose to take action to clear the northern ports.... Montgomery will be responsible for these tasks, and I propose to increase his forces if that should seem necessary.' Churchill had replied on Saturday, 31 March, pointing to the resulting overstretch in Montgomery's 21st Army Group and adding: 'Further, I do not consider myself that Berlin has yet lost its military and certainly not its political importance.' This mention of the capital must be presumed to be based on the same reasoning Churchill had used in his minute to the COS, sent the same day; he continued: 'The fall of Berlin would have a profound psychological effect on German resistance.... While Berlin holds out great masses of Germans will feel it their duty to go on fighting.' Eisenhower replied early on Sunday, 1 April. 'I think you still have some misunderstanding of what I intend to do.... In the first place I repeat that I have not changed my plan.... The situation that is now developing is one that I have held before my Staff for more than a year ... namely, that our forces should be concentrated across the Rhine through avenues of Wesel and Frankfurt.... From there onwards the problem was to determine the direction of the blow that would create the maximum disorganization to the remaining German forces and the German power of resisting. I had never lost sight of the great importance of the drive to the northernmost coast, although your telegram did introduce a new idea respecting the political importance of the early attainment of particular objectives.... The only difference between your suggestions and my plan is one of timing.'[35]

The telegram from Washington, received late on Saturday the 31st, gave full support to Eisenhower. The American COS believed the Supreme Commander's direct approach to Stalin had been 'an operational necessity in view of the rapidity of the advances into Germany', and the signal continued: 'General Eisenhower's course of action ... appears to be in accord with agreed major strategy and with his directive, particularly in light of the present development of the battle for Germany....' The telegram added: 'To disperse the strong forces which probably would be required to reach and reduce the northern ports before the primary object of destroying the German armies is accomplished, would seriously limit the momentum of a decisive thrust through the centre.' Thus the American COS did not mention Berlin – but neither had the British; and now, on 1 April, Brooke and his colleagues expressed themselves more satisfied with the military factors behind Eisenhower's proposal, as detailed by the Supreme Commander and reinforced by Washington – although Brooke considered Marshall's signal to be 'rather rude'. As the CIGS commented: 'Now that Ike has explained his plans it is quite clear that there is no very great change, except for the fact that he directs his main axis of advance on Leipzig, instead of Berlin.'[36] The Sunday staff conference discussed a reply to the Americans, and the draft also received Churchill's approval: this merely repeated disapproval of Eisenhower's direct approach to Moscow.[37]

Sometime during this Sunday evening, Churchill's attitude underwent an abrupt change. Now, five days after Eisenhower had sent his signal to Moscow, the Prime Minister suddenly seemed to realize the far-reaching, diplomatic importance of reaching Berlin before the Russians; and with this realization came a reversal of Churchill's attitude towards Russia on the widest possible scale: not only Berlin must be saved from the Red Army, but also Prague, Vienna, north Germany, Denmark.... The Prime Minister's campaign to save East Europe before the Iron Curtain crashed down had taken time to start; it came too late; not even Churchill's massive energy and insistence could stop the Red Army advance from swamping the greater part of this area.

No single reason led to Churchill's conversion. Rather this resulted from an accumulation of evidence received by him during this Easter weekend, culminating in a telegram from

Moscow received late on the Sunday night. Numerous telephone calls with Eden during the day had indicated that
deadlock remained over Poland; above all, reports revealed
that sixteen Polish nationalists, invited to Moscow to talks,
had disappeared. Further signals showed that claims by
Moscow over the extent of popular support for the Warsaw
Government were false, and a general rising might take place
in western Poland within the next few weeks.[38] Other factors
had also arisen; following an agreement between Roosevelt
and Churchill to address separate appeals to Stalin, the text
of the President's message had been received in London,
dated 29 March, and this revealed an extremely courteous
American attitude towards Moscow: 'Having understood
each other so well at Yalta, I am convinced that the three of
us can and will clear away any obstacles which have
developed since then.'[39] At the same time, disturbing reports
had been received over the President's health: Oliver
Lyttelton, who saw Roosevelt on the 29th, signalled he was
'greatly shocked by his appearance'.[40] Roosevelt might be
unwilling or unable to join with Churchill in a united front
against Stalin; and a further report had come from Clark
Kerr, Ambassador at Moscow, which described the overall
situation as 'disappointing and even disturbing'.[41] Finally,
another cable from the Soviet capital revealed that British
and American authorities had passed Eisenhower's original
message to Stalin and Molotov the previous day, and the
cable contained the text of Stalin's reply. The Supreme
Commander's southern proposal 'entirely coincides with the
plan of the Soviet High Command.... Berlin has lost its
former strategic importance. The Soviet High Command
therefore plans to allot secondary forces in the direction of
Berlin.'[42]

The tone of Churchill's telegrams after the arrival of this
Soviet reply seems to indicate that he viewed it in looking-
glass fashion – the words were interpreted in reverse: Stalin
might now go all-out to reach the capital before the Anglo-
American armies. Eisenhower had made no specific mention
of Berlin in his message; Stalin stressed the capital in his
reply. And Stalin could no longer be trusted. So this un-

settled Easter atmosphere led to the final shattering of the
Yalta spirit; and Churchill's disillusionment six weeks after
the high hopes of the Crimea paralleled Neville Chamberlain's transition after Hitler's breach of the Munich agreement. Late on this Sunday, 1 April, the Prime Minister
addressed himself both to Stalin and to the ailing American
President. To Stalin he declared: 'If our efforts to reach an
agreement about Poland are to be doomed to failure I shall
be bound to confess the fact to Parliament.... No one has
pleaded the cause of Russia with more fervour and conviction
than I....'[43] Churchill's signal to Roosevelt at last laid bare
the Berlin issue. 'The Russian armies will no doubt overrun
all Austria and enter Vienna. If they also take Berlin, will
not their impression that they have been the overwhelming
contributor to our common victory be unduly imprinted in
their minds, and may this not lead them into a mood which
will raise grave and formidable difficulties in the future? I
therefore consider that from a political standpoint we should
march as far east into Germany as possible and that should
Berlin be in our grasp we should certainly take it.'[44]

Next day, Monday, 2 April, as the Moscow Commission
met for another sterile session on Poland, Churchill signalled
Eisenhower: 'I am ... all the more impressed with the
importance of entering Berlin, which may well be open to
us, by the reply from Moscow to you, which in paragraph 3
says, "Berlin has lost its former strategic importance." ... I
deem it highly important that we should shake hands with
the Russians as far east as possible.'[45] The following morning
the COS discussed the situation. Unlike Churchill, they considered Stalin's reply at face value: the Russians would
not launch a strong thrust at Berlin. Yet this led the COS
to the same conclusion as the Prime Minister, although for
different reasons: the allied thrust became even more important in view of the Soviet downgrading. Militarily,
Berlin must be taken as soon as possible in order to destroy
the spirit of German resistance. Thus 'it was agreed that the
boundaries laid down by Eisenhower somewhat modified the
views expressed (earlier). On the other hand, the information
contained in Marshal Stalin's reply lent weight to the argu-

ment in favour of maintaining the emphasis on the northern thrust.'[46] At 5.30 p.m. on this Tuesday, 3 April, the War Cabinet met Dominion Leaders, in London for discussions; Brooke began proceedings by describing the latest military progress: 'East of the Rhine, American and British forces had made an average penetration of some 90 to 100 miles on a 200-mile front. The enemy forces in the Ruhr were now encircled and attempts by the 17 weak German divisions in this area to break out had been held. Prisoners had been taken at the rate of 15,000 to 20,000 per day.' Brooke continued: 'The main Russian advance had been in the direction of Vienna. Russian forces had now cleared the whole of Hungary and had crossed the Austrian frontier.' Morrison reported that only eleven V-2s had landed during the previous week, and only four V-1s had reached London – unknown to Ministers, the last V-2 of all had in fact fallen on 27 March and the last V-1 on the 29th. Churchill now addressed Dominion leaders. 'Relations with Russia, which had offered such fair promise at the Crimea Conference, had grown less cordial during the ensuing weeks.... It was by no means clear that we could count on Russia as a beneficent influence in Europe, or as a willing partner in maintaining the peace of the world. Yet, at the end of the war, Russia would be left in a position of preponderant power and influence throughout the whole of Europe.'[47] The COS repeated their military fears in another signal to Marshall next day, 4 April, based on their discussion on the 3rd.

Within 24 hours Churchill's apprehensions over Russia had multiplied. Roosevelt passed to the Prime Minister a reply from Stalin, received on 3 April, which referred to a message Roosevelt had sent the Soviet leader concerning the Swiss talks – these, the President had stressed, had not amounted to full negotiations. Stalin's extremely offensive and outrageous reply declared: 'You insist that there have been no negotiations yet. It may be assumed that you have not been fully informed. As regards my military colleagues, they on the basis of data which they have on hand, do not have any doubts that the negotiations have taken place.' Stalin then made the preposterous allegation that an Anglo-American agreement had been reached with the Germans, 'on the basis of which the German commander on the Western Front, Marshal Kesselring, had agreed to open the Front and permit the Anglo-American troops to advance to the east'. The Soviet leader went even further: 'As a result of this at the present moment the Germans on the Western Front in fact have ceased the war against England and the United States. At the same time the Germans continue the war with Russia....' Roosevelt was by this time gravely ill, and Marshall had therefore sent the American reply in the President's name, denying the 'astonishing' allegation. 'It would be one of the great tragedies of history if at the very moment of the victory now within our grasp such distrust, such lack of faith should prejudice the entire undertaking.... Frankly, I cannot avoid a feeling of bitter resentment towards your informers, whoever they are, for such vile misrepresentations of my actions or those of my trusted subordinates.' The War Cabinet met in emergency session during the day, 5 April, and Ministers agreed upon a draft signal from the Prime Minister to Stalin, together with a message to Roosevelt. The latter began: 'I am astounded that Stalin should have addressed to you a message so insulting to the honour of the United States and also of Great Britain,' and Churchill took the opportunity of returning to the Berlin question, informing Roosevelt that 'the Soviet leaders, whoever they may be, are surprised and disconcerted at the rapid advance of the allied armies in the West and the almost total defeat of the enemy on our front, especially as they say they are themselves in no position to deliver a decisive attack before the middle of May. All this makes it the more important that we should join hands with the Russian armies as far to the east as possible, and, if circumstances allow, enter Berlin.' Churchill continued: 'I may remind you that we proposed and thought we had arranged six weeks ago provisional zones of occupation in Austria, but that since Yalta the Russians have sent no confirmation of these zones. Now that they are on the eve of taking Vienna and very likely will occupy the whole of Austria, it may well be prudent for us to hold as much as possible in the north. We must always be anxious lest the brutality of the Russian messages do not foreshadow some deep change of policy.'[48] Churchill's stiff signal to Stalin mentioned an accusation which the Soviet leader had made in his message to Roosevelt concerning 'the silence of the British' over the Swiss talks. The Prime Minister referred to Molotov's insulting note of 23 March, and declared: 'We thought it better to keep silent ... but you may be sure that we were astonished by it (the note) and affronted that M. Molotov should impute such conduct to us.' Churchill stated: 'There is no connection whatever between any contacts at Berne or elsewhere with the total defeat of the German armies on the Western Front....'[49] Also on the 5th the Polish leader in London, Count Raczynski, called at the Foreign Office to ask Cadogan if the British had any knowledge of the fate of the sixteen Poles who had gone to Moscow and had disappeared. Cadogan said he had no news and did not understand 'what the Russians were driving at'. Raczynski replied: 'We will know soon enough.'[50] Next day, 6 April, the Polish Government in London issued a public statement describing the disturbing story.

Also on the 6th the American COS told the British that Eisenhower's 'sound' scheme must take preference over a race to Berlin. 'Such psychological and political advantages as would result from a possible capture of Berlin ahead of the Russians should not override the imperative military consideration, which in their opinion is the destruction and dismemberment of the German armed forces.'[51] Eisenhower had already issued orders in line with his policy, but he told Marshall on the 7th that he would give way if necessary. 'I am first to admit that a war is waged in pursuance of political aims, and if the CCS should decide that the allied effort to take Berlin outweighs military considerations in this theatre, I would cheerfully readjust my plans.' Marshall saw no reason for him to do so.[52] Churchill did, and cast aside consideration of the provisional agreement reached at Yalta over occupation zones: he told the COS on the 7th: 'If we crossed the Elbe and advanced to Berlin, or on a line between Berlin and the Baltic, which is well within the Russian zone, we should not give this up *as a military matter*. It is a matter of State to be considered between the three Governments, and in relation to what the Russians do in the south, where they will soon have occupied not only Vienna but all of Austria.'[53]

The British COS discussed this delicate subject of occupational zones two days later, 9 April, the same day on which the Russians took Königsberg and thereby virtually ended the Baltic campaign. Eisenhower had considered the zone question during the past few days: the issue involved two considerations, first, immediate zones of responsibility – areas dictated by current military operations – and secondly final zones of occupation. These two types might not coincide: military activities might dictate a shift beyond the boundaries of the agreed occupational areas, either in pursuit of the enemy or to lend assistance to other armies. Contrary to the final occupational zones, no provisional agreement had yet been reached between the allies on the areas of immediate military responsibility, and Eisenhower urged some declaration to avoid the risk of accidents between allied armies arising through mistaken identity. He therefore proposed an approach to the Russians, and suggested armies should be free to move as events dictated until contact with another allied army seemed imminent, and thereafter forces should withdraw into the occupational zones. The British COS, discussing this proposal on the 9th, disagreed, giving reasons in a telegram to the British Mission at Washington. 'A. Military. To approach the Russians on this matter might lead to an attempt by them to restrict the scope of our advance.... B. Political. Withdrawal into zones of occupation is a matter of State to be considered between the three Governments in relation to what the Russians do in the south, where they may soon be in occupation of the British and US Zones in Austria.' The signal therefore reflected Churchill's minute of the 7th, and as the COS told Wilson, head of the British Mission, 'the Prime Minister attaches great importance to this matter'.[54]

Next day, 10 April, Stalin's reply reached Churchill concerning the Swiss talks dispute, and the Soviet leader had clearly moderated his tone. 'Neither I nor Molotov had any intention of "blackening" anyone. It is not a matter of wanting to "blacken" anyone, but of our having developed differing points of view as regards the rights and obligations of an ally.... My messages are personal and strictly confidential. This makes it possible to speak one's mind clearly and frankly....' This reply enclosed a copy of a message sent by Stalin to Roosevelt, again pleading not guilty to the charge of rudeness.[55] On the same day Churchill received a communication from the Soviet dictator concerning the Polish talks: he would use his influence with the Warsaw Government to make them withdraw objections to the participation of Mikolajczyk in the discussions, 'if the latter would make a public statement accepting the decisions of the Crimea Conference on the Polish question and declaring that he stands for the establishment of friendly relations between Poland and the Soviet Union'.[56] Churchill saw some hope in both these signals; with regard to the latter, over Poland, he cabled Roosevelt next day, 11 April: 'We shall have to consider most carefully the implications of Stalin's attitude and what is to be our next step.' Yet despite Stalin's slight flexibility the British Ambassador in Moscow learnt during this Wednesday that the Russians were going to be obstructive over the question of the missing Poles: Clark Kerr received a note from Molotov saying the Soviet authorities were 'overburdened with urgent work' and could not answer enquiries about 'these or those Poles'. The Foreign Office told Clark Kerr to persist in his inquiries; at the same time the Foreign Office began the attempt to gain from Mikolajczyk the necessary affirmation of the Yalta decisions, in order that he might be invited to Moscow.[57] Also on the 11th Churchill signalled Roosevelt about Stalin's attitude to the surrender talks. 'I have a feeling that this is about the best we are going to get out of them....' The President's reply probably marked the last message received by Churchill from his old friend Roosevelt: 'I would minimize the general Soviet problem as much as possible, because these problems, in one form or another, seem to arise every day, and most of them straighten out.... We must be firm however, and our course thus far is correct.'[58]

The COS had been giving further consideration to occupation areas, and told the Americans on the 11th that 'on cessation of hostilities our respective armies (should) stand fast until they receive orders from their Governments'. Marshall and his colleagues agreed with this immediate measure, and discussions continued in London and Washington on a detailed directive to Eisenhower.[59] Meanwhile, allied armies lurched forward again. Bradley's 12th Army Group advanced on Magdeburg, Leipzig and Bayreuth, and, on 12 April, elements of the 9th Army crossed the Elbe and reached a point only 60 miles from Berlin. The 1st US Army moved south of the Harz mountains, while the 3rd Army on its right had taken Weimar the previous day. To the north the 2nd (British) Army pushed towards Soltau and Lüneburg, while another corps pushed north-east towards Bremen. The 1st Canadian Army undertook the clearing of Holland.

Amidst these signals reporting renewed successes came word of Roosevelt's death, late on Thursday, 12 April. Despite the President's illness, this news was completely unexpected in London. Churchill was stunned by the loss – 'I felt as if I had been struck a physical blow.' The Prime Minister had relied upon Roosevelt for over four heavy years, for friendship, stimulation and support. And now Harry Truman emerged from the obscurity of the Vice-President's office, where his duties had been confined to domestic affairs, to be immediately plunged into the maelstrom of the ending of the Second World War and the beginning of the Cold War.

Next day, Friday the 13th, the Russians took full possession of Vienna, and, during a flurry of telegrams and talks over whether Churchill should fly to America for Roosevelt's funeral, the Prime Minister felt obliged to prod once again for the early capture of Berlin. Butcher, a member of Eisenhower's staff, wrote in his diary: 'Ike returned before midnight. The Prime Minister wants him to take Berlin and Ike sees no military sense in it.'[60] Next day Churchill reminded the COS that zones of occupation must be linked with 'political issues operative at that time'[61] and, on the 15th, Truman took up the international reins of his new office with a signal to Churchill on Poland. He included the draft of a message to Stalin, which pointed out that the 'real issue' remained whether the Warsaw Government had a 'right to veto individual candidates for consultation', and Truman proposed that invitations should be sent to a group of Poles, including four from the Warsaw Government and four from London. After discussions with Eden, now in America to attend Roosevelt's funeral on Churchill's behalf, and after amendments in wording, this message was sent to Stalin on the 18th.[62] At the same time Mikolajczyk was persuaded to make a declaration affirming support for the Crimea decisions, and by 22 April and after two public announcements, hopes had been raised in London that progress could at last be made.[63] Meanwhile, surrender talks had been revived by Wolff. The allied offensive had been resumed in Italy on the 9th, and on the 14th a message from Wolff indicated that cessation of hostilities in Italy might be imminent; this time the British and Americans would make all possible efforts to bring in Russian representation.

American, British and Polish forces continued to advance on Bologna and the plains of the Po; to the north the threats on Germany from west and east were intensified. On 16 April the Russians launched their assault towards Berlin, advancing on a 200-mile front – an offensive which Stalin had said would be 'subsidiary' and would not start until 'approximately the second half of May'. On the same day the British COS considered a depressing message from Eisenhower, sent to the CCS in Washington on the 14th, which declared: 'In view of the urgency and importance of initiating operations in north and south, operations to Berlin will have to take second place, and await the development of the situation.... The essence of my plan is to stop on the Elbe and clean up my flanks.' By now Eisenhower's line lapped a few miles over the Elbe – about 50 miles from Berlin. The Russian line on the Oder at Kuestrin lay about the same distance from the German capital to the east. But American and British supply lines were stretched to their limits, and substantial German forces still offered resistance on the northern and southern flanks; as always, Eisenhower rightly restricted his view to military aspects. The British COS agreed with the Supreme Commander's military assessment, but suggested that the CCS might still draw his attention to the desirability of taking any opportunity to advance upon Berlin.[64] Next day, 17 April, as Zhukov, Rokossovsky and Koniev moved forward from the Oder and Neisse, Eisenhower flew to London to confront Churchill; and as the Supreme Commander later wrote: 'So earnestly did I believe in the military soundness of what we were doing that my intimates on the staff knew I was prepared to make an issue of it.'[65] Not even Churchill could shift Eisenhower's resolve, and on the 18th the British approved his proposal, 'with such modifications as may be indicated by the rapid development of the situation'.[66]

Magdeburg fell to the US 9th Army during the 18th, opening the way for another thrust towards Berlin over the Elbe – if resources could have been found. But also on this Wednesday Montgomery's forces took Soltau and Lüneburg in the drive north towards Lübeck, and a telegram from Churchill to Eden on the 19th emphasized the importance of this advance – again because of the Russians. 'A Russian occupation of Denmark would cause us much embarrassment.' The Prime Minister added: 'Our arrival at Lübeck before our Russian friends from Stettin would save us a lot of argument later on. There is no reason why the Russians should occupy Denmark.... Our position at Lübeck, if we get it, would be decisive.' This signal also revealed added reason for continued operations in the south, at the expense of a move on Berlin: 'In this region are the main German installations connected with their atomic research, and we had better get hold of these.' Churchill therefore declared: 'It would seem that the Western Allies are not immediately in a position to force their way into Berlin.'[67] Eden wired his agreement; ironically, the Foreign Secretary had stayed in America to attend the San Francisco conference – called to consider post-war problems.

Two days later, 21 April, an exhausted Brooke left London

for a week's fishing leave. He had written in his diary the previous week: 'The longing for the end of the war becomes almost unbearable at times.'[68] Yet as the CIGS travelled north towards the quiet of the Dee, the war rushed to an end in the theatre which had perhaps given him most concern during the last two years – Italy. Bologna fell on this Friday; on the same day Wolff reappeared in Switzerland to intensify surrender moves. The allies immediately invited Russian representatives to attend any negotiations, and Stalin signalled his cordial agreement. Thus one source of dispute with the Soviets had been removed. Next day, as Hitler made his final decision to stay in doomed Berlin, Eisenhower sought to settle the complications over zones of occupation – and this gave formal recognition of the Anglo-American decision to leave the German capital to the Russians. 'I have chosen the line of the Elbe River–Mulde River on our central front as being identified easily on the ground and desirable as the general boundary between our forces.'[69] But Poland still remained the paramount diplomatic problem, and relations with the Russians over this subject had been further soured by a Soviet treaty with the Warsaw Government, condemned by the British Foreign Office as totally incompatible with the spirit of the Yalta declaration. Eden and Stettinius met Molotov in Washington on 22 April and twice on the 23rd, but could make no progress.[70] Anxiety had also arisen at the Foreign Office over Czechoslovakia, upon which the Red Army was now swooping; Eden asked Molotov for more information, but the Soviet Minister appeared uncommunicative.

Exhilarating military signals continued to reach London. War Cabinet Ministers assembling at 6 p.m. on the 23rd were informed that 'after meeting considerable opposition ... the 1st French and 7th US Armies had made very rapid advances.... Leipzig had been cleared by 1st US Army and the Harz mountain pocket had been eliminated.... The whole of the Ruhr was now under allied control.... British 2nd Army forces had cleared the south bank of the Elbe to the suburbs of Hamburg.... North-east Holland was now practically clear of enemy troops and western Holland had

been virtually sealed.' But Ministers were also told: 'The
Russians are maintaining a very strict security silence with
regard to their advances from the Oder.... The northern
attack had probably reached the suburbs of Berlin; the other
was aimed evidently at encircling the city from the south-
west.'[71] More details of Soviet intentions came in a signal
to Eisenhower next day, 24 April, in reply to the Supreme
Commander's message of the 22nd concerning zones. 'The
immediate plan of the Soviet Command contemplates both
the occupation of Berlin, and also cleaning out the German
forces from the eastern shore of the Elbe River north and
south of Berlin, and the Vltava (Moldau tributary of the
Elbe) river valley....'[72] Yet this would mean not only a
Russian advance to Berlin, as expected, but also the takeover
of Prague. Fears for Czechoslovakia were amply justified.
Moreover, the Russian reference to the Elbe north of Berlin
could indicate a Soviet intention to advance up to this river
line as far as the sea, thus blocking the approach to Denmark.
Yet Montgomery's forces were pushing towards the Elbe,
and he planned to cross the river to reach Lübeck.

Dangers had therefore arisen of a clash on the ground
between British and Russian forces in the north; the Russians
seemed intent on seizing Czechoslovakia in the south; and
they might intend to push into Denmark. And behind the
battlefields in the reeling Reich remained the spectre of
Poland. Next day, 25 April, the Russian Ambassador brought
to the Foreign Office the reply to Truman's proposals of the
18th. Stalin ignored the procedural suggestions, except to
say he would now recommend an invitation to Mikolajczyk.
He stressed that the Russians had a special security interest
in Poland, similar to Britain's interest in Greece and Belgium.
Also on the 25th Red Army units surrounded Berlin and
entered Stettin; Russian troops linked with Americans at
Torgau. And in the early hours of this Wednesday a dramatic telegram reached the Foreign Office from Sir Victor
Mallet, British Ambassador to Sweden: the previous evening
he and his American colleague, Johnson, had met Count
Bernadotte at the Swedish Foreign Ministry, and had been
told that Himmler had asked to meet Eisenhower to arrange

the capitulation of the whole of the Western Front. Mallet and Johnson believed Himmler's refusal to offer the surrender of the Eastern Front seemed a last attempt to split the Western Allies and Russia. Churchill summoned the War Cabinet for an emergency meeting during this Wednesday morning, and Ministers agreed with the Ambassadors' assessment. They decided upon a signal to Truman and to Stalin; the message to Moscow declared: 'There can be no question ... of anything less than unconditional surrender simultaneously to the three Major Powers.'[73] Stalin replied the same day, in a message described by Churchill as 'the most cordial I ever had from him'. 'I consider your proposal ... the only correct one. Knowing you, I had no doubt that you would act in this way. I beg you to act in the sense of your proposal, and the Red Army will maintain its pressure on Berlin in the interests of our common cause.'[74] At the same time, negotiations had now begun in Switzerland, following the arrival of two delegates from von Vietinghoff's HQ the previous day; meanwhile American units reached the Po river during the 25th, and in the evening a 30-vehicle convoy drove towards the Swiss frontier carrying Benito Mussolini in German disguise. A partisan patrol stopped the party before the border; Mussolini was recognized, and within hours a partisan bullet ended the life of the Duce. His body, together with his slain mistress Signorina Petacci, swung head downwards from meat hooks in a petrol station on the Piazzale Loreto. Also on the 25th, as the San Francisco conference opened, Stimson held his first conversation with Truman on the atomic bomb project; the US War Secretary accurately predicted that 'within four months' a bomb would be available for use.

Herman Goering had fled south from Berlin on the 24th. Hitler now had few supporters around him, and, in the shambles of Berlin, few troops remained to face the Russian horde. Soviet shells began to smash the Chancellery on 26 April, and Hitler's bunker shook as massive masonry crashed into the courtyard above. An eye-witness described the Führer: 'His head sagged, his face was deathly pallid, and the uncontrolled shaking of his hands made the message (from Goering) flutter wildly.'[75] The Russians were a mile away. German forces everywhere were being split and splintered, and the allied race for territory continued. Bremen fell to British troops and Montgomery prepared to cross the Elbe. And far to the south, Red Army units were pushing out of the Czechoslovakian foothills towards Brno, about 150 miles from Prague. Churchill signalled Eden on the 26th to urge another approach to Molotov over the Czech situation, and next day he cabled Stalin over zones of occupation. 'Our immediate task is the final defeat of the German Army. During this period the boundaries between the forces of the three allies must be decided by commanders in the field, and will be governed by operational considerations and requirements. It is inevitable that our armies will in this phase find themselves in occupation of territory outside the boundaries of the ultimate occupational zones....'[76] Churchill mentioned the need to reach an agreement 'without delay' on zones to be occupied in Austria. Trieste would be an essential supply port for future Austrian occupation, and Churchill told the American President, also on the 27th, that 'it seems to me vital to get Trieste if we can do so ... and to run the risks inherent in these political-military operations'.[77] Alexander had already been ordered to push forward 8th Army units in this direction.

Montgomery's forces were closing rapidly on the Elbe near Lauenburg; to the south the 3rd US Army had taken Regensburg on the 26th and was now moving towards the Austrian border via Passau, and American forces on the left flank were about to cross into Czechoslovakia. But some Red Army units were already past Vienna, while others were fast approaching Prague. Marshall believed Churchill would soon propose a lightning American advance to liberate the Czech capital before the Russians, and informing Eisenhower of these suspicions on the 28th he added: 'Personally, and aside from all logistic, tactical or strategical implications, I should be loath to hazard American lives for purely political purposes.'[78] On the same day the old Czech Ambassador to London, Jan Masaryk, spoke at the San Francisco conference, and his words could have been an appeal against future suffering: 'My country, Fellow Delegates, has been one concentration camp since 1939....' Eisenhower replied to Marshall next day: 'I shall certainly not attempt any move I deem militarily unwise merely to gain a political advantage unless I receive specific orders from the CCS.'[79]

'I expect the relief of Berlin,' wired Hitler to Keitel during Saturday, 28 April. 'What is Heinrici's army doing? Where is Wenck? What is happening to the 9th Army? When will Wenck and the 9th Army join us?...' A member of his dwindling entourage in the bunker described Hitler as pacing up and down 'waving a road map that was fast disintegrating from the sweat of his hands'. Exhausted German soldiers and young boys were fighting like rats in the rubble above, street by street. And that night a brief Reuter report chattered on the tape-machine in Hitler's bunker – Himmler had contacted the Swedes to arrange peace terms. At about 1 a.m. on the 29th Hitler married Eva Braun and then, while brittle celebrations continued, he walked to his claustrophobic study to dictate his last will and political testament. 'I have preferred death to cowardly abdication or even capitulation.'[80]

Brooke was relishing his fishing by the Dee; Churchill spent the weekend at Chequers, enjoying a stroll in the spring sunshine during the afternoon then staying up late to send a signal to Stalin: 'There is not much comfort in looking into a future where you and the countries you dominate, plus the Communist Parties in many other States, are all drawn up on one side, and those who rally to the English-speaking nations and their associates or Dominions are on the other. It is quite obvious that their quarrel would tear the world to pieces.'[81] As this telegram went over the wires to Moscow in the early hours of the 29th, and Hitler sat in his study in Berlin, British and American troops under Montgomery were heading for Lübeck and the gateway to Denmark.

At noon on the 29th, while black smoke obscured the sun above Berlin, Hitler held his usual military conference in his lamp-lit bunker. Useless maps lay strewn upon the table. The Russians had crept closer towards the crumbling

Chancellery during the night and early morning; ammunition for the defenders was almost exhausted; no information had been received from Wenck's rescue army. Instead, the Führer received one of the last items of news to reach the bunker from the outside world, revealing Mussolini's degrading death. Churchill, still at Chequers, received more updated information from Italy and immediately sent another signal to Stalin. 'I have just received a telegram from Field-Marshal Alexander that after a meeting at which your officers were present the Germans accepted the terms of unconditional surrender presented to them.... It looks therefore, as if the entire German forces south of the Alps will almost immediately surrender.'[82] The end of the war in Italy would take effect from noon, 2 May; the capitulation of Army Group C involved almost one million men, and the Italian campaign, whose primary object had always been limited to strategic containment in support of the main offensive in the north, thus brought about the first act of unconditional surrender by a theatre command.[83] Churchill now urged even greater results from Alexander's armies. He returned to London next day, Monday, 30 April, and revealed his hopes to the War Cabinet. Alexander's forces lay from Como almost to Trieste, and Churchill 'stressed the political importance of exploiting this victory to the full by rapid advances to Trieste and into western Austria'. Ministers were also told: 'The Russians are advancing west of Stettin. Berlin is still holding out.'[84]

Eisenhower made another attempt to explain his intentions to Moscow. 'I am now launching an operation across the Lower Elbe intended to establish a firm operational east flank.... The exact position will be adjusted locally by co-operative action when our forces meet.' This would give the Western allies the entrance to Denmark. But Eisenhower's signal continued by cutting across Churchill's remaining hopes for Prague and Austria. 'My forces will hold initially along approximately the 1937 frontiers of Czechoslovakia.... My plans on the southern flank call for an advance to the general area of Linz.'[85] The Russian reply would signify 'full agreement', and Austria and Czechoslovakia would therefore be exchanged for Denmark. Churchill, unaware of Eisenhower's message, continued his pressure for Prague. 'There can be little doubt,' he wired Truman during this Monday, 30 April, 'that the liberation of Prague and as much as possible of the territory of western Czechoslovakia by your forces might make the whole difference to the post-war situation in Czechoslovakia, and might well influence that in nearby countries.'[86] On the same day Truman concurred with Churchill's proposal that Alexander should push on for Trieste; the British commander should make it clear to Tito that any Yugoslav forces in the area must come under allied command. Alexander doubted whether they would do so – and, on this Monday, Tito announced that his partisans had reached the Trieste suburbs.[87]

These urgent discussions were irrelevant to the struggle against Germany. They flashed above the heads of the sprawling armies. And they had nothing to do with Hitler, now a discarded nonentity. At 2.30 p.m. Hitler and his bride finished their vegetarian lunch and retired to their rooms; moments later a sharp crack echoed down the dim corridors. Hitler lay across his sofa, his face shattered by his revolver shot. His wife had swallowed poison. Moments later the bodies, wrapped in a German army field-grey blanket, were placed in a muddy shell-crater outside the bunker, doused with petrol, and ignited. Mourners headed by Goebbels and Bormann withdrew to the shelter of the entrance to the bunker, hurriedly raised right hands in a last Nazi salute, then darted inside their rat-hole as Soviet shells began to splatter the garden again. On the same day British radio listeners heard the cultured voice of Lord Haw-Haw, William Joyce, for the last time. 'You may not hear from me again for a few months.... *Heil Hitler*. And farewell.' Churchill and his Ministers would hear the news of Hitler's death next day; meanwhile, even more important information reached London from Washington, with Wilson signalling Sir John Anderson: 'The Americans propose to drop a (atomic) bomb sometime in August.... Do we agree that the weapon should be used against the Japanese?'[88] Under the pressure of business Churchill would not find time to answer the question until 21 May.

The British COS would not be involved in this crucial issue; nor, at the beginning of May, were they involved with the immediate activities in Europe – as always they had to look ahead. Brooke had returned from leave on 30 April; on 1 May he chaired a long COS meeting which discussed bomber deployment in the Far East, manpower redeployment for the war against Japan, and naval dispositions in the Pacific.[89] Churchill was asked in the Commons if he had any statement to make on the war situation. 'Yes,' came his flippant reply, 'it is definitely more satisfactory than it was this time 5 years ago.' Harold Nicolson wrote: 'Generally he is good at making this sort of joke. But he was feeling ill or something.' Churchill was preoccupied with other matters; like the COS he had to think ahead. Truman had told him of Eisenhower's plan to stop short of Prague; and Alexander had signalled: 'Tito's regular forces are now fighting in Trieste.... I am quite certain that he will not withdraw his troops if ordered to do so unless the Russians tell him to.'[90] Eden telegraphed from San Francisco to say the Americans believed Stalin should be told they saw no use continuing discussion on Poland.[91] Czechoslovakia, Austria, Yugoslavia, Poland – reports on all were depressing.

Listeners throughout Europe and Britain heard the momentous announcement on the midnight news: 'Unser Führer, Adolf Hitler, ist ... gefallen.' Doenitz, named by Hitler as his successor, broadcast his praise of the dead leader. 'Early he had recognized the terrible danger of Bolshevism and had dedicated his life to the fight against it....' The following day, Wednesday, 2 May, Berlin fell silent. Montgomery received a message at his 2nd Army HQ: German delegates would arrive next day to start surrender talks.

Signals reaching London describing the closing stages of the German war were interspaced by reports from distant Burma. The attack on Rangoon had been launched the previous day; now, on this Wednesday, allied troops found the city evacuated by the Japanese. War Cabinet Ministers were informed of this stepping-stone to Burmese victory in

the situation report issued next morning, Thursday, surely
the most dramatic daily war announcements.

'*Cabinet War Room Record* for the 24 hours ending 0700
3 May 1945. 7th US Army troops are within 15 miles of
LANDECK. Resistance has collapsed in MUNICH and US
forces are reported to have reached the River INN at three
points. The 3rd US Army has crossed into Austria to within
15 miles of LINZ, and further north has continued to advance
into Czechoslovakia on a broad front.... In the LAUEN-
BERG bridgehead, British and American troops have broken
through, and the former are reported to have reached the
Baltic. The German armies in Italy have surrendered....
The Russians claim the complete capture of BERLIN and
the surrender of the garrison.'[92] Yet at 10.30 a.m. on this
Thursday the COS approved a Joint Intelligence report on
Japan's capacity to resist, which gave gloomy indications of
prolonged struggle. 'For the defence of the inner zones, Japan
may deploy by 1 October, 1945, some 96 divisions, with a
total strength of some 3,100,000 men.... The bulk of the
Japanese air force and navy are already concentrated in
the inner zone. These forces will be increasingly used in a
suicide role.'[93]

At 11.30 a.m., while this COS meeting continued in
London, a delegation sent by Field-Marshal Keitel arrived
at Montgomery's HQ, Lüneburg Heath, with the consent
of Admiral Doenitz. The group, headed by General-Admiral
von Friedeburg, C-in-C of the German Navy, stood waiting
for the British commander to emerge from his tent; Montgomery's wireless operators could hear faint clicking on the
command's radio frequency link as the Germans tried to
listen in for surrender instructions. Negotiations began;
Keitel had instructed Friedeburg to offer the surrender of the
three German armies withdrawing in front of the Russians
between Berlin and Rostock; Montgomery replied that these
should surrender to the Russians. Eventually the German
delegation agreed to take a document to Keitel and Doenitz,
drafted by Montgomery, which would cover the unconditional
surrender of German forces in Holland, Friesland, Schleswig-
Holstein and Denmark; Montgomery told them to return

by 6 p.m. next day, 4 May.[94] Meanwhile the advance continued. Hamburg surrendered during the 4th and the US
7th Army took Hitler's 'Eagle's Nest' at Berchtesgaden. And
at this final hour it seemed as if Churchill's hopes for an
advance into Czechoslovakia might yet be fulfilled. Russian
forces were still about 100 miles from Prague, while elements
of the US 12th Army Group were only 60 miles from the
Czech capital. Eisenhower, still thinking purely along military lines, now considered a further thrust to wipe out
German resistance in and beyond Prague, and in the afternoon of the 4th he informed Moscow that 'we are prepared,
if the situation so dictates, to advance in Czechoslovakia to
the line of the Vltava (Moldau) and Elbe Rivers to clear the
west banks of the rivers'. Such a move would have lapped
over the centre of the country; the Russians hastened to
reply. In a telephone conversation with Eisenhower at 6.45
p.m. Churchill 'drew attention to the importance of getting
to Prague first'; according to Churchill's subsequent report
to the War Cabinet, Eisenhower had replied that 'he had this
point uppermost in his mind'.

Ten minutes later, at 6.55 p.m., Churchill had another
telephone conversation, this time with Montgomery. As a
result, War Cabinet Ministers and the COS hurried to 10
Downing Street for a staff conference beginning at 7.30 p.m.
Brooke and his colleagues arrived to find Churchill on the
telephone to the King. Then the meeting began in the
Cabinet Room. Churchill declared: 'Montgomery had
reported that German representatives ... had signed an
instrument of surrender operative at 0.800 BST on Saturday,
5 May, whereby all German armed forces in North-West
Germany, Schleswig-Holstein, Holland, Denmark, the Frie-
sian Islands and Heligoland surrendered unconditionally.'
At 7.15 p.m. Churchill had again spoken to Eisenhower, and
it had been agreed that a communiqué should be issued
almost immediately. 'Eisenhower had told the Russians that
he proposed to tell the Germans that Germans fighting in
front of the Russians should surrender to them and that he
(Eisenhower) would accept the surrender of any forces fighting on British or American fronts.' Churchill added: 'The

surrender already agreed affected German forces totalling some one million men. This surrender might easily ripen into a complete surrender of all German forces.' But the Prime Minister also declared: 'There were many outstanding problems such as the occupation of Vienna to be settled with the Russians. He thought these were matters which should be settled at a conference between Heads of State, which should be held in Germany. British and American forces had penetrated deep into Germany, and occupied territory which fell within the zone which it had been agreed should be occupied by Russians. This was a valuable bargaining counter.'[95]

Firing between German and British forces in the north accordingly ceased at 8 a.m. next day, Saturday, 5 May. Meanwhile the Americans continued to move forward in the south. But also on the 5th came the Russian reply to Eisenhower's signal sent the previous day concerning an American advance beyond Prague. 'The Soviet Command asks General Eisenhower not to move the allied forces in Czechoslovakia east of the originally intended line.... The Soviet Command, to meet the wishes of General Eisenhower ... stopped the advance of its own forces to the Lower Elbe east of the line Wismar-Schwerin-Dömitz. We hope that General Eisenhower in turn will comply with our wishes.' Eisenhower obliged, ordering 12th Army Group to halt before Prague, and sending a superfluous signal to Moscow: 'Presume Soviet forces can advance rapidly to clear up the situation in the centre of the country.'[96] Alexander had managed to sneak New Zealand troops into Trieste, to obtain the surrender of the German garrison before Tito's regulars could arrive in strength, but now a confrontation seemed likely between these Yugoslav troops and the allies, and Alexander reported that he believed Tito would be co-operative – if 'he can be assured that when I no longer require Trieste as a base for my forces in Austria, he will be allowed to incorporate it in his New Yugoslavia'. Churchill replied: 'There is no question of your making any agreement with him about incorporating Istria, or any part of the pre-war Italy, in his "New Yugoslavia". The destiny of this part of the world is reserved for the peace table, and you should certainly make him aware of this.'[97]

Berlin, Vienna and Prague had gone; the allies had Denmark; Trieste remained at issue, and Churchill fully intended to continue the fight, alone, if necessary. Telegrams between Churchill and Truman on East-West relations during these few crucial days now only referred to Poland. No detailed War Cabinet discussions took place on the East-West struggle for European territory; the COS did not extend their brief beyond military aspects. Yet the previous COS attitude over Britain's security in Europe supported Churchill's views; and no Minister spoke in opposition to the Prime Minister when he outlined his position at War Cabinet meetings. Churchill kept Eden fully informed in America: during this Saturday, 5 May, the Foreign Secretary received a long and perceptive telegram which stated: 'I fear terrible things have happened during the Russian advance.... The proposed withdrawal of the US Army to the occupational lines which were arranged with the Russians and Americans ... would mean the tide of Russian domination sweeping forward 120 miles on a front of 300 or 400 miles ... territories under Russian control would include the Baltic Provinces, all of Germany to the occupational line, all Czechoslovakia, a large part of Austria, the whole of Yugoslavia, Hungary, Roumania, Bulgaria, until Greece in her present, tottering condition is reached.' And during the 5th the Prime Minister sent another paragraph: 'Nothing can save us from the great catastrophe but a meeting and a showdown as early as possible at some point in Germany.'[98]

Friedeburg had already established contact with Eisenhower's HQ. Discussions dragged on throughout the 5th, with the Supreme Commander refusing to accept the surrender of German forces facing the Russians in addition to those opposing the Anglo-American armies. Documents had still to be signed on Sunday, 6 May, and uncertainty continued over this surrender of the remaining German forces. 'A quiet Sunday,' wrote Brooke in his diary. 'During the afternoon ... put up hides for nightingale, bullfinch and black-cap nests.'[99] Exhausted German units were laying down their arms piecemeal along the front; American forces from Italy linked with comrades coming down from the north at the Brenner Pass, joining the two theatres. Then, in the early hours of Monday, 7 May, a telephone call from Eisenhower's HQ awoke Churchill to inform him of the end of the war in Europe: at 2.41 a.m. General Jodl had signed the instrument of surrender, to take effect at midnight on the 8th. General Bedell Smith had signed for the Supreme Commander, a Russian officer for the Soviet High Command, with a French officer as witness. The COS met in London at 11 a.m. to 'take note' of the news. The Supreme Commander had recommended a public statement should be made as soon as possible, owing to the certainty that the news would leak out.[100] Almost immediately, East-West difficulties arose on this question of a public declaration, with Churchill reporting the situation to the War Cabinet at 6.30 p.m. He had proposed simultaneous announcements in London, Washington and Moscow at 3 p.m. BST next day, 8 May, and Truman and Stalin had agreed. Eisenhower had however objected, on the grounds that before then the news would have been broadcast by the Germans – this had already happened. Churchill had therefore proposed to Stalin and Truman that the simultaneous announcements should be put forward to 6 p.m., BST that evening, 7 May, but a message had just been received from Washington, from which it appeared that as Stalin did not concur in the proposed change, Truman must withhold his agreement. Bickering amongst the wartime allies therefore even complicated the announcement of peace; the Russians were suspected of trying to steal a little extra territory. Ministers at the War Cabinet meeting finally decided upon a devious solution; the Minister of Information was asked to arrange for this immediate broadcast: 'It is understood that in accordance with arrangements between the Three Great Powers an official announcement will be broadcast by the Prime Minister at 3 p.m. tomorrow, Tuesday, 8 May. In view of this fact tomorrow, Tuesday, will be treated as Victory in Europe Day.'[101]

Ships at Southampton began the celebration proceedings

at midnight on 7/8 May by blaring their sirens, and search-lights flashed out 'V' in morse across the sky. Victorious hordes took over London, jamming the streets and crowding to worship in St Paul's; flags fluttered in the drizzly breeze from bomb-damaged houses; the *Daily Mirror* fulfilled its promise to the troops and displayed its strip heroine, Jane, naked at last; the British COS held their usual morning meeting. Loudspeakers were rigged up in Whitehall for Churchill's broadcast, and as the echoes of Big Ben boomed across the Thames, the Prime Minister began to speak. His words seemed unexpectedly sombre. 'The evil-doers now lie prostrate before us. We may allow ourselves a brief period of rejoicing, but let us not forget for a moment the toil and efforts that lie ahead.' The Prime Minister arrived at the House of Commons at 3.20 p.m. to be greeted by scenes of fervour rarely surpassed in Parliament. 'We have all of us made our mistakes, but the strength of the Parliamentary institution has been shown to enable it at the same moment to preserve the title deeds of democracy while waging war in the most stern and protracted form....' Later, the Prime Minister appeared at a Home Office balcony above the teeming, shrieking crowds in Whitehall. 'This is your Victory! It is the victory of the cause of freedom in every land. In all our long history we have never seen a greater day than this.' Churchill conducted the crowd in 'Land of Hope and Glory' and the people joined him in his tears, while Brooke slipped away to finish his day's work at his cluttered War Office desk.

'Terminal'

War with Japan had still to be ended, and military assessments agreed the struggle would be prolonged; the Cold War had only just begun. And with the latter, Churchill now found he had lost another of the preliminary battles. On 7 May, a few hours after the Germans had signed the final surrender at Rheims, the Prime Minister sent another signal to Eisenhower: 'I am hoping that your plan does not inhibit you to advance to Prague if you have the troops and do not meet the Russians earlier....'[1] Forty-eight hours later on 9 May, as Britain celebrated VE-2 Day and formal ratification of the surrender took place in Berlin, the Russians entered the Czech capital. For a moment Truman seemed to promise support over Trieste, signalling Churchill on 12 May to express concern over Tito's stubborn attitude and urging a policy of determination; two days later he switched to a more cautious policy, urging that allied troops should not take the offensive unless the partisans did so first. The moment for action passed, and Morgan, Alexander's Chief of Staff, eventually agreed with the Yugoslavs upon a temporary demarcation line. Churchill meanwhile warned against premature troop withdrawals from Europe, signalling Truman on the 12th: 'I am profoundly concerned about the European situation.... The newspapers are full of the great movements of the American armies out of Europe. Our armies also are, under previous arrangements, likely to undergo a marked reduction.... Meanwhile, what is to happen about Russia?' He added: 'An iron curtain is drawn upon their front.'[2] Marshall managed to give Eden some reassurance in a meeting on the 14th, but on the same day a new scare arose; Churchill sent a minute to the COS drawing attention to reports that 400,000 Russian troops had been massed in Bulgaria along the Macedonian Frontier. The COS dismissed the rumours as gross exaggeration.[3] Yet Brooke wrote in his diary next day: 'The vultures of Europe are now crowding round and quarrelling over bits of the Austro-German-Italian carcass. Meanwhile they gather round a table in San Francisco to discuss how to establish universal peace.'[4]

Discussion between various Polish representatives at last took place in Moscow during June, resulting in the formation of a Polish National Council with Mikolajczyk amongst the Ministers; but on the day of this announcement, 21 June, the 'missing' Poles were brought to trial in Moscow and found guilty of subversion, terrorism and espionage. Sentences ranged up to 10 years.[5] In this shifting, secretive atmosphere the need for a Big-Three summit had become urgent, and Churchill had increased his pressure in a message to Truman on 13 May, warning that Stalin would not initiate any proposal – 'time is on his side if he digs in while we melt away' – and the President signalled his agreement next day. But Truman also attempted his own method of negotiation: at the end of May he sent Harry Hopkins to Moscow and Joseph E. Davies, ex-Ambassador to the USSR, to London. Davies failed to find favour with Churchill, both as a result of his strong pro-Russian attitude and his revelation that Truman had suggested a meeting alone with Stalin. But Hopkins had secured agreement from Stalin for a tripartite meeting, and Churchill continued to prod Truman; on 4 June, in a telegram to the President on the Polish problem, he once again referred to 'the descent of an iron curtain', and three days later Truman signalled his final agreement for a Three-Power conference to start on 15 July – later than Churchill had hoped. And so the Potsdam meeting, 'Terminal', had been arranged.[6]

Meanwhile unease prevailed, summed up in a JIC report approved by the COS on Wednesday, 23 May. 'Our relations with Russia during the last four years have been governed by the necessity for maintaining Russia's war effort against Germany at the highest possible level.... There is no longer any need for us to continue to be conciliatory at all costs. We can afford to be more tough.' The report continued: 'Relations between the Russians and the British and Americans have recently deteriorated at all levels for the following major reasons: (a) Russian insistence ... on treating Eastern Europe as their exclusive sphere of influence.... (b) Russian failure to fulfil the spirit and in some cases the letter of the Crimea agreement; (c) Russian pique and chagrin caused by the rapid Anglo-American advances after the crossing of the Rhine and the acute suspicions engendered by the Berne negotiations; (d) Russian resentment at finding the British and Americans co-ordinating their policy in matters in dispute with the USSR....' This COS meeting also took note of a grim report by the JIC at SHAEF on the political situation in North-West Europe. 'The events of the past week prove that Germany still does not regard the struggle as over ... this extraordinary country is still fighting with weapons which she forged and used with success during the years 1919-1939: the weapons of political intrigue.... Their policy is quite simple: embroil the allies at all costs with the Russians.... They will take every opportunity of licking the allies' boots in order to make us gradually acknowledge that they are "correct". At the same time they will do everything they can to cheat the Russians, thus engendering in the Soviet mind, quick to be suspicious, that the allies are behind this German trickery....'[7]

On the one hand the COS therefore agreed with a 'tough' policy towards the Russians, yet on the other they agreed an East-West rift would help dissident Germans to ferment trouble. The day-by-day experience of this dilemma fell upon the commanders in Europe, and Eisenhower revealed part of the burden to a staff conference in the Defence Map Room on 16 May. 'Serious difficulties were being experienced by his forces in Germany. The trip through Germany today was the best possible visual lesson of the cost of war.... There were vast numbers of prisoners of war, of displaced persons and of civilians whose homes had been destroyed; all these had to be fed and accommodated. Problems were already arising in connection with feeding this vast number of people.' Eisenhower added: 'Under present conditions the greatest difficulties were being experienced in all matters in which it was necessary to consult the Russians.... This gave rise to interminable delays.'[8] On 10 July Ministers were informed that food shortages were becoming acute; they were also informed that 'the allied occupation of the various zones in Germany had been virtually completed'. Meanwhile the prisoners of war returned: Ministers learnt on 14 May that 'of the estimated total of 180,000 British Commonwealth POWs in Europe, it was estimated that some 163,000 had been recovered and 97,471 brought to this country'. A further 50,000 were brought home during the next three weeks.

The war against Japan still seemed to stretch far ahead. The COS reported to the War Cabinet on 5 June: 'Owing to the onset of the monsoon and the pause following the fall of Rangoon, operations in Burma were restricted to mopping up.... In southern Okinawa the stiff opposition was being overcome.'[9] On 1 July Mountbatten reported his intention to attack Singapore on 9 September, and nine days later Australian and American troops landed in North Borneo. Main fighting on Okinawa ended on 21 June, and on the 29th the President approved plans for the invasion of mainland Japan, scheduled for 1 November, but on 10 July the COS received a JIC report which again stressed the difficulties of this final invasion. 'Japan's greatest strength lies in her armies, the bulk of which have not yet been committed to battle. Their strength in the islands of Japan is steadily increasing. Until such time as battle wastage is incurred, the allied bombing offensive and blockade can restrict but cannot eliminate this continuing accretion of strength.'[10] The COS remained unaware of details of the drastic developments taking place in America. After discussions with Churchill on 21 May, Anderson informed the British Mission in Washington on 2 July: 'The Prime Minister has approved my proposal that agreement to decision to use weapon should be recorded at next meeting of

(Combined Policy) Committee.'[11] On 17 July, the day before 'Terminal' began at Potsdam, an atomic bomb was successfully exploded at Alamogordo, New Mexico. No reference to the atomic bomb appears in the Cabinet minutes; Ministers, like the COS, remained apart from this discussion concerning Britain's agreement to the weapon's use.

By now the War Cabinet had gone. On 23 May the Prime Minister had tendered his resignation to the King, who had immediately invited him to form a new Government, and this National Administration – the 'Caretaker Government' – now provided the Ministers in the Cabinet Room until a general election could be held. Rifts had begun to appear in the Coalition Government back in April as the imminent ending of the war brought closer the prospect of an election, and as political parties in the Coalition began to manoeuvre for position. Especial difficulties arose over post-war subjects which would perhaps be used as electioneering capital or ammunition. Describing the situation in May, Attlee wrote: 'I found ... that it was more and more difficult to get post-war projects before the Cabinet. Agreements arrived at after long discussion by a Committee, in which both parties were fully represented, were blocked by the opposition of certain members of the Government who evinced a quite new interest in subjects hitherto outside their range of attention. It was, indeed, becoming clear that the Coalition Government formed to win the war would not survive its success.'[12] Churchill wrote to Eden in California on 28 April, just after a Conservative defeat at Chelmsford by-election: 'It seems to me most likely that electioneering will begin the moment after the end of the German war.'[13] In view of international events, the Prime Minister wrote to Attlee on 18 May asking for an agreement for the Coalition Government to continue until the end of the Japanese War. The Labour Party Executive, then meeting in Blackpool, rejected the proposal; Attlee told Churchill on 21 May that he would prefer a continuation of the Coalition until a General Election in October; Churchill replied: 'It is not good for any country, and it is impossible for any Coalition, to live for so long a time under the spell of an approaching General Election,

Least of all is this possible in a world where events are so tumultuous and dangerous as now.'[14]

So the Coalition Government departed, and with it the War Cabinet. No Cabinet meetings took place between 18 and 30 May. New Ministers met at 11.30 a.m. on the 30th, to discuss India, War Crimes and the General Election. Polling would take place on 5 July, but to cover the delay whilst soldiers' votes were brought home the declaration of the result would not take place until 26 July. The Caretaker Cabinet would therefore sit for two months: Eden, Anderson and Lyttelton retained their previous War Cabinet seats and appointments. Beaverbrook, Cranborne, Amery, Stanley and Hudson kept their old appointments, but now came fully into the Cabinet. Other Cabinet Ministers were Lord Woolton, who took over from Attlee as Lord President, Butler, who succeeded Bevin as Labour Minister, Sir Donald Somervell, taking over from Morrison as Home Secretary, Brendan Bracken, successor to Alexander as First Lord, Macmillan and Lord Rosebery who became Air Secretary and Scottish Secretary respectively in succession to the Liberal leader, Sinclair, and Thomas Johnston. The Caretaker Cabinet therefore had 16 members, including Churchill, whereas the last War Cabinet only had nine. Among Ministers outside the Cabinet were a number of men who had hitherto been critics of Churchill and the Coalition Government, notably Hore-Belisha, War Secretary under Chamberlain until his resignation, and now Minister of National Insurance. Of the overall Ministers, thirty were Conservative or allies, one was Liberal, eight were Independent, and one was not in Parliament.

Electioneering accelerated. Parliament reassembled on 29 May, and the row in the Commons proved so great that speakers were inaudible; four days before Emanuel Shinwell had declared at the Labour Party Conference: 'Mr Churchill is now engaged searching on the hills, the beaches and the seas – for a Government of men of good will. There can be no Government of men and women of good will outside the ranks of the Labour Party.' Churchill undertook the first party political broadcast on 4 June with a startling allegation: 'I declare to you, from the bottom of my heart, that no socialist system can be established without a political police.' If Labour tried to carry out their full socialist programme, 'they would have to fall back on some form of Gestapo'. Next day Attlee hit back, claiming Churchill 'feared lest those who had accepted his leadership in war might be tempted out of gratitude to follow him further. I thank him for having disillusioned them so thoroughly.' Yet Churchill and Attlee tried to reach a working arrangement with foreign affairs, over which the Prime Minister remained acutely disturbed. Ministers at the Cabinet meeting on 8 June were told that Churchill had written to Attlee on 31 May saying he hoped the present agreement between parties on foreign and military policy would continue. Attlee had agreed to accept Churchill's offer of access to important papers. The Prime Minister also told the Cabinet that he had invited Attlee to go with him to Potsdam 'in order that, whatever the result of the election, the voice of Britain might be united'. This offer had also been accepted. Even this arrangement faltered. On 14 June the newly appointed Chairman of the Labour Party Executive, Harold Laski, declared: 'It is of course essential that if Mr Attlee attends this gathering he shall do so in the role of an observer only.' Churchill immediately wrote to Attlee objecting to this apparent attempt to inject politics into their agreement. Attlee believed the subsequent exchange of letters to be motivated primarily for political purposes, with the Prime Minister attempting 'to show that I was a mere tool in the hands of a non-Parliamentary Body'.[15] Churchill claimed other reasons in his report to the Cabinet on 20 June: he had previously been strengthened by the thought that 'whatever the results of the election, the next Government would honour any commitments'; now, however, he could not be sure how far 'the foreign policy of a Labour Government would be determined by the ex-labour Ministers, or how far it would be dictated by the Executive Committee ... he would not feel that the integrity of his position would be assured'. Churchill therefore proposed the summit should be postponed until after the election. Ministers agreed, but also decided to wait for a possible announcement by Attlee or Laski which would assure Churchill that no divergence of views existed on foreign policy.[16] Attlee managed to give Churchill the necessary reassurance; the Potsdam date remained unchanged. And electioneering continued with Churchill embarking upon a rumbustious triumphal tour in American 'whistle-stop' fashion, while Attlee preferred to travel in his somewhat battered car, driven by his wife.

The election campaign swept Britain while British troops continued their dingy and depressing occupational duties in Germany. Appalling civilian problems had to be solved by troops in 21st Army Group alone: over one million civilian refugees had fled into the region before the Red Army; about one million German wounded lay in the hospitals, without adequate medical supplies; nearly two million un-wounded German troops had surrendered; transport and industry had ceased; the population had to be fed, housed, kept free from disease.[17] Nor were British servicemen safe from the possibility of further active duties, even without being sent to the Far East. Once again conflict had arisen with the French, this time in Syria, and the problem confronted the Caretaker Cabinet on the very day of its first meeting, 30 May. France's liberation had led to a serious crisis in the Levant, increasing the need for a new treaty to define French colonial interests. De Gaulle's Administration refused to start negotiations, and on 17 May additional troops had been sent to Beirut. Riots broke out. A Foreign Office statement on 26 May regretted the arrival of French reinforcements; next day a Paris announcement alleged that the disturbances were artificially provoked, and that British troops in the area had been reinforced without protests by the Syrians or the Lebanese and without French agreement. Firing began in Syria on 28 May, and rapidly intensified. Churchill told the Cabinet at 6.30 p.m. on the 30th: 'There had been a serious deterioration in the last 24 hours and the position was now grave. The French had again bombarded Damascus; and there had been a serious loss of life and destruction of property.' Paget, C-in-C Middle East, had accused the local French commander, General Oliva Roget, of being 'wholly irresponsible' and 'had raised the question of taking control himself of all the troops in the Levant'. Churchill believed urgent action must be undertaken, but it was of the 'utmost importance' that America should give support. Ministers agreed a telegram should be sent to Truman describing orders to Paget to intervene. The Cabinet met again at 11.30 a.m. next day, 31 May. 'The situation at Damascus had grown rapidly worse.... In addition to indiscriminate shelling, French troops were spraying the streets with machine-gun fire.... His Majesty's Minister was isolated in Damascus, his telephone communication with the Lebanon and the HQ of the British 9th Army having been cut.' Churchill telephoned the American Ambassador during this meeting; no reply had yet come from Truman to the telegram sent the previous day, and the Prime Minister told the Ambassador that 'in view of the continued deterioration in the situation in Syria, HMG had no alternative but to act'.[18] British intervention proved immediately effective; the French commander, on instructions from Paris, proclaimed a cease-fire and tension eased, and the incident subsided, despite protests over the British action from Paris. But the episode provided a foretaste of the colonial-type problems soon to become familiar in the post-war world.

Inevitably, these weeks before Potsdam saw a Cabinet preoccupation with the domestic problems of transition from war to peace – reconstruction, industrial and agricultural programming, re-employment, damage repairs, coal production, housing shortages. With the latter, the Health Minister told the Cabinet on 18 July that 'there was an immediate need for over 1 million houses, and that however successful the house-building programme might be, relatively few new houses would be ready for occupation before the spring. Large numbers of men released from the Services would wish to establish homes....'[19] Unoccupied houses in Brighton had recently been seized by 'vigilantes'. The ending of the European war increased the general Cabinet work-load, rather than the reverse. Strain therefore continued, especially felt by those who continued their wartime office. Eden had to be absent from the Foreign Office during June, suffering from a duodenal ulcer. The COS, coping with the host of administrative and personnel problems thrust upon them after the German surrender, could not enjoy a lessening of meetings; Brooke wrote on 6 June: 'I feel very, very weary.'[20] Churchill alternated between high spirits and exhausted depression; Lord Moran described his behaviour on 8 July: ' "I'm very depressed," said the PM, walking into the room before luncheon and flopping into an armchair. "I don't want to do anything. I have no energy. I wonder if it will come back." The election festers in his mind. "Nothing," he said, "will be decided at the conference at Potsdam. I shall only be half a man until the results of the poll. I shall keep in the background of the conference." '[21]

Churchill had flown to France the day before, 7 July. 'I was resolved to have a week of sunshine to myself between the General Election and the Conference.' He established himself in a villa at Henday near the Spanish frontier, scene of Hitler's meeting with Franco on 22 October 1940, and the Prime Minister sunned himself, read and painted. He left his retreat to reach Berlin on 15 July, joined by the Foreign Secretary and the CIGS. The Russians had chosen the Cecilienhof Palace as the conference centre, just outside Potsdam and an oasis in the devastated wilderness. The green park seemed almost untouched, except for rough graves containing bodies of men who had fought hand to hand between the trees – these improvised resting-places lay near small, neat headstones commemorating the life and death of the Crown Prince's dogs and cats.

The British and American COS began their meetings on 16 July; throughout the conference discussion would concentrate mainly on British participation in the Far East war; during the next afternoon, 17 July, Churchill learnt from Stimson of the successful atomic bomb test the previous day. At 5 p.m. on the 17th the first 'Terminal' plenary session began, under Truman's chairmanship, for preliminary discussion of a wide range of problems, many of them interrelated, and including reparations, German-Polish frontiers and an Italian peace treaty. Churchill had a private talk with Stalin, during which the two leaders discussed reports of

Japanese peace feelers; next morning, 18 July, Truman gave Churchill a full account of the atomic bomb development. At 5 p.m. the second plenary session opened with a discussion on European peace treaties before turning to Poland; Churchill then referred to the 'great improvements in Poland during the last two months' since the National Committee had been created, and he 'cordially hoped for the success of the new Government, which, although not all we could wish, marked a great advance and was the result of patient work by the three Great Powers'. A number of issues remained outstanding, he continued. 'The London Government was liquidated in the official and diplomatic sense', but still remained in being; above all, free elections had still to be held. As far as the unfortunate London Poles were concerned, Churchill asked Stalin to put his trust in His Majesty's Government and 'give us reasonable time' for the problem to be solved. And as for free elections, Stalin claimed the Provisional Government had never refused that these should be held; Truman and Churchill agreed with his suggestion that the whole Polish matter should be referred to the Foreign Secretaries.[22]

Truman and Churchill had no room for manoeuvre over Poland; Russian troops were in full control. As with all East European problems, everything depended upon Russian goodwill. Churchill dined with Stalin on the night of the 18th and seemed slightly reassured for the moment: 'We conversed agreeably from half-past eight in the evening to half-past one next morning without reaching any crucial topic.... My host seemed indeed to be physically rather oppressed, but his easy friendliness was most agreeable.' Stalin insisted that 'in all the countries liberated by the Red Army the Russian policy was to see a strong, independent, sovereign State. He was against Sovietization of any of those countries. They would have free elections....'[23] This artificial atmosphere extended to military affairs. Next day, Thursday, 19 July, the CCS agreed that for planning purposes 'the date for the end of organized resistance by Japan be 15 November 1946'.[24]

And so the discussions continued. Charges were met by

counter-charges throughout the 19th, 20th and 21st as the three leaders tried to discuss European questions. Stalin maintained free elections would be held in Poland; he referred to the percentage agreement for East European countries as agreed with Churchill in Moscow; he claimed he had been 'hurt' by the American demand for changes of Government in Roumania and Bulgaria, where 'everything was peaceful'. He accused the British and Americans of stirring up trouble among dissidents. In general, discussions assumed the depressing pattern which would become so clear during the Cold War. Finally, on 22 July Churchill suggested representatives of the Polish National Council should come to the Conference; Stalin and Truman agreed. On this Sunday, Churchill and Eden met Truman and James Byres, now US Secretary of State, and the final decision was taken to drop an atom bomb on Japan if she refused to accept unconditional surrender. Churchill revealed this decision to the British COS at lunch-time next day, 23 July, and Brooke described the Prime Minister as 'completely carried away. (Churchill said) it was no longer necessary for the Russians to come into the Japanese war; the new explosive alone was sufficient to settle the matter. Furthermore, we now had something in our hands which would redress the balance with the Russians.' Brooke said Churchill pushed out his chin, grimaced, and declared: 'Now we could say, "If you insist on doing this or that, well...." And then where are the Russians?' The CIGS tried to calm Churchill's optimism, based on the results of one experiment, and 'was asked with contempt what reason I had for minimizing the results of these discoveries. I was trying to dispel his dreams and as usual he did not like it.'[25] Truman told Stalin of the atomic bomb next day, 24 July; the Soviet leader merely nodded his head and muttered: 'Thank you.'

Polish representatives reached Berlin during the evening of the 24th, and the new Polish President, Bierut, met Churchill next morning to assure him that 'Poland would be far from Communist. She wanted to be friendly with the Soviet Union and learn from her, but she had her own traditions and did not wish to copy the Soviet system....'[26]

Churchill attended one more plenary session during this Wednesday morning, 25 July, urged again that Poland's western frontier could not be settled without taking into account the million and a quarter Germans still in the area, and he then left Berlin for London. 'Here, so far as I am concerned,' wrote Churchill, 'was the end of the matter.'[27] The General Election results would be declared next day. The Prime Minister had told Stalin that Attlee might possibly be returning as British leader; 'I don't think,' said Stalin, 'that Mr Attlee looks like a man who would seize power.'

Churchill reached London during the early evening 25 July. Within 24 hours he had handed in his resignation to the King, defeated by the Labour landslide: 393 Labour seats to 213 Conservative. He told the nation: 'The decision of the British people has been recorded in the votes counted today. I have therefore laid down the charge which was placed upon me in darker times....' At noon next day, 27 July, Churchill held a farewell Cabinet meeting, the minutes of which have still to be revealed; Eden described the session as a 'pretty grim affair.... He was pretty wretched, poor old boy.'[28] Churchill escaped to Chartwell among the Kentish woods, while Attlee and Bevin returned to Potsdam for the remaining six days of the conference. Sessions still hung in futile limbo, suspended between recent military realities and future diplomatic dealings – too close to the former for the second to be possible. And Churchill remained with his sadness while the atomic bomb shattered the future peace of mind of the world at Hiroshima and Nagasaki on 6 and 9 August, and while the Japanese accepted the allied terms on the 14th – fifteen months before the date accepted by the CCS: on this last point of difference between the Prime Minister and his CIGS, Churchill had been right. He remained apart from the VJ celebrations; according to Moran he declared: 'I go to bed about twelve o'clock. There is nothing to sit up for.' A few weeks before, Churchill had talked to his doctor about the British people, his mighty audience of the war years, suddenly silent at the polls; he had summed up the whole situation, and with it the ending of his war: 'I have no message for them now.'[29]

Sources

Note. Cabinet papers used in this book are all to be found at the Public Record Office, London. Unfortunately, difficulties arise through the method of filing adopted by the Secretaries during the war, with especially sensitive material being kept separate and hence having a different file number to the rest of the minutes of the meeting concerned. This applies both to War Cabinet and Chiefs of Staff sessions. In addition the latter were also split between simple COS meetings and COS(O), with no apparent reason for the distinction. This especially applies to 1944. Thus a COS meeting in January 1944 might be found in file number CAB 79/28, or in the very sensitive file, known as the Secretary's Standard file, CAB 79/89, or in COS (O), CAB 79/69.

In an attempt to simplify these source lists I have therefore merely given the basic file number, together with the year. Thus COS material is merely noted as CAB 79. In the same way War Cabinet references are simply given as CAB 65, the Defence Committee is CAB 69, and the Combined Chiefs of Staff comes under CAB 88. Other main files consulted are the War Cabinet Memoranda: CAB 67; Chiefs of Staff Memoranda: CAB 80; War Cabinet Daily Situation Reports: CAB 100; Joint Planning Staff: CAB 84.

Details of papers available are given in *The Second World War; A Guide to Documents in the Public Record Office,* published by HMSO for the PRO. This does not however give the number of the pieces for the particular year. Further details can be obtained in the PRO guide, Part II.

Throughout these sources lists Winston Churchill's *The Second World War* is merely referred to as Churchill IV, V

or VI. The initials OH have been placed after an item if the
work concerned is an Official History. Full details of all the
books mentioned are to be found in the Bibliography.

CHAPTER 1 LIGHTED TORCH

1 CAB 100 (CWR) 8 Nov '42
2 BRYANT, *Triumph in the West*, 22-23
3 NICOLSON, *Diaries and Letters*, 384
4 BRYANT, *The Turn of the Tide*, 552; ISMAY, *Memoirs*, 317
5 BRYANT, *Triumph in the West*, 457
6 CAB 88 (CCS) '42
7 DILKS, *The Diaries of Cadogan*, 490
8 EISENHOWER, *Crusade in Europe*, 116
9 CHURCHILL IV, 582
10 WOODWARD, *British Foreign Policy in The Second World War* (1962 version), 214 (OH); DILKS, *op. cit.*, 491
11 BRYANT, *The Turn of the Tide*, 521
12 CAB 65 (War Cab) '42
13 EDEN, *The Reckoning*, 348
14 MONTGOMERY, *Memoirs*, 143
15 CAB 65 (War Cab) '42
16 CHURCHILL IV, 567
17 DILKS, *op. cit.*, 493
18 CAB 79 (COS) '42
19 CAB 65 (War Cab) '42
20 WOODWARD, *op. cit.*, 211 (OH)
21 DILKS, *op. cit.*, 494
22 CHURCHILL IV, 568
23 CAB 69 (Def Com) '42; BRYANT, *The Turn of the Tide*, 522
24 CHURCHILL IV, 569
25 HOWARD, *Grand Strategy*, IV, 177 (OH)
26 CHURCHILL IV, 582-583
27 EISENHOWER, *op. cit.*, 118
28 BRYANT, *The Turn of the Tide*, 527
29 NICOLSON, *op. cit.*, 262
30 EDEN, *op. cit.*, 351
31 DILKS, *op. cit.*, 496

32   DILKS, *op. cit.*, 496; CAB 65 (War Cab) '42
33   DILKS, *op. cit.*, 496
34   HOWARD, *op. cit.*, 234 (OH)
35   CAB 79 (COS) '42
36   CAB 69 (Def Com) '42; CHURCHILL IV, 584
37   CAB 79 (COS) '42
38   BRYANT, *The Turn of the Tide*, 528
39   CAB 65 (War Cab) '42
40   HOWARD, *op. cit.*, 219 (OH)
41   CHURCHILL IV, 585
42   *Ibid*, 594
43   CAB 65 (War Cab) '42
44   EDEN, *op. cit.*, 353-354
45   CAB 65 (War Cab) '42
46   CAB 65 (War Cab) '42
47   CIANO, *Diary*, 529
48   LEWIN, *Rommel*, 194
49   BRYANT, *The Turn of the Tide*, 532, 533
50   HOWARD, *op. cit.*, 209 (OH)
51   CAB 65 (War Cab) '42
52   CAB 79 (COS) '42
53   CHURCHILL IV, 587
54   CAB 79 (COS) '42; BRYANT, *The Turn of the Tide*, 530
55   CHURCHILL IV, 595, 596
56   CAB 65 (War Cab) '42
57   WOODWARD, *op. cit.*, 212 (OH)
58   CHURCHILL IV, 571; EDEN, *op. cit.*, 354
59   CHURCHILL IV, 597
60   BRYANT, *The Turn of the Tide*, 536
61   WOODWARD, *op. cit.*, 212 (OH)
62   DILKS, *op. cit.*, 499
63   CHURCHILL IV, 572, 573; EDEN, *op. cit.*, 357
64   HOWARD, *op. cit.*, 219 (OH)
65   CHURCHILL IV, 590
66   CAB 65 (War Cab) '42; DILKS, *op. cit.*, 499
67   HOWARD, *op. cit.*, 177
68   WOODWARD, *op. cit.*, 239 (OH)
69   CHURCHILL IV, 600
70   CAB 79 (COS) '42; BRYANT, *The Turn of the Tide*, 535

71 CAB 79 (COS) '42; BRYANT, *The Turn of the Tide*, 535
72 BRYANT, *The Turn of the Tide*, 535
73 CIANO, *op. cit.*, 536
74 CAB 65 (War Cab) '42
75 CAB 88 (CCS) '42
76 HOWARD, *op. cit.*, 182 (OH)
77 DILKS, *op. cit.*, 493
78 CHURCHILL IV, 578
79 EDEN, *op. cit.*, 359
80 CAB 65 (War Cab) '42
81 CAB 69 (Def Com) '42; HOWARD, *op. cit.*, 216 (OH)
82 HOWARD, *op. cit.*, 182 (OH)
83 HULL, *Memoirs*, 1205

CHAPTER 2 CASABLANCA

1 ROSKILL, *The War at Sea*, II, 353 (OH)
2 CAB 65 (War Cab) '43
3 EDEN, *The Reckoning*, 359; BRYANT, *The Turn of the Tide*, 529
4 HOWARD, *Grand Strategy*, IV, 179 (OH)
5 *Ibid*, 175
6 WOODWARD, *British Foreign Policy in the Second World War* (1962 version), 215 (OH)
7 DILKS, *Diaries of Cadogan*, 503
8 CAB 79 (COS) '43
9 CAB 65 (War Cab) '43
10 CHURCHILL IV, 602
11 CAB 79 (COS) '43
12 HULL, *Memoirs*, 1205, 1206
13 *Ibid*, 1207
14 CHURCHILL IV, 825
15 CAB 65 (War Cab) '43
16 MONTGOMERY, *Memoirs*, 153, 154
17 CAB 79 (COS) '43
18 BRYANT, *op. cit.*, 544
19 CAB 88 (CCS) '43
20 BRYANT, *op. cit.*, 544

21 CAB 88 (CCS) '43
22 BRYANT, *op. cit.*, 546
23 CAB 88 (CCS) '43
24 CHURCHILL IV, 547
25 BRYANT, *op. cit.*, 546
26 CAB 88 (CCS) '43
27 BRYANT, *op. cit.*, 548
28 CAB 65 (War Cab) '43
29 WOODWARD, *op. cit.*, 216 (OH)
30 CAB 88 (CCS) '43; BRYANT, *op. cit.*, 548, 549
31 HULL, *op. cit.*, 1207
32 CAB 65 (War Cab) '43
33 CAB 88 (CCS) '43
34 BRYANT, *op. cit.*, 550
35 SLESSOR, *The Central Blue*, 446
36 CAB 88 (CCS) '43
37 CAB 65 (War Cab) '43
38 WOODWARD, *op. cit.*, 217 (OH)
39 CAB 88 (CCS) '43; BRYANT, *op. cit.*, 556
40 CAB 88 (CCS) '43
41 CAB 65 (War Cab) '43
42 CAB 65 (War Cab) '43
43 BRYANT, *op. cit.*, 557-558
44 CAB 88 (CCS) '43
45 MACMILLAN, *The Blast of War*, 249, 251
46 CAB 65 (War Cab) '43
47 CAB 88 (CCS) '43
48 HOWARD, *op. cit.*, 625 (OH)
49 CAB 65 (War Cab) '43
50 HOWARD, *op. cit.*, 625 (OH)
51 SHERWOOD, *Roosevelt and Hopkins*, 696
52 CAB 65 (War Cab) '43
53 CHURCHILL IV, 629
54 HOWARD, *op. cit.*, 327 (OH)
55 CAB 65 (War Cab) '43
56 CHURCHILL IV, 635, 636
57 BRYANT, *op. cit.*, 572
58 HOWARD, *op. cit.*, 637, 638 (OH)
59 *Ibid*, 589, 590

60 BRYANT, *op. cit.*, 578
61 DILKS, *op. cit.*, 513
62 CAB 65 (War Cab) '43
63 CAB 65 (War Cab) '43
64 CAB 65 (War Cab) '43
65 CHURCHILL IV, 666
66 *Ibid*, 667, 668
67 CAB 69 (Def Com) '43; CHURCHILL IV, 668
68 CAB 69 (Def Com) '43
69 HOWARD, *op. cit.*, 332 (OH)
70 CIANO, *Diary*, 554, 555
71 CAB 65 (War Cab) '43
72 CAB 79 (COS) '43
73 HOWARD, *op. cit.*, 398-402 (OH)
74 CAB 79 (COS) '43; HOWARD, *op. cit.*, 366 (OH)
75 BRYANT, *op. cit.*, 583
76 CAB 88 (CCS) '43
77 HOWARD, *op. cit.*, 367 (OH)
78 *Ibid*, 368; CAB 79 (COS) '43; CAB 88 (CCS) '43
79 CHURCHILL IV, 458
80 CAB 65 (War Cab) '43
81 CAB 65 (War Cab) '43
82 CAB 65 (War Cab) '43
83 NICOLSON, *Diaries and Letters*, 283
84 CHURCHILL IV, 657
85 CHURCHILL IV, 682, 683

CHAPTER 3 INTO THE UNDER-BELLY

1 CAB 79 (COS) '43
2 HOWARD, *Grand Strategy*, IV, 351 (OH)
3 CHURCHILL IV, 687
4 BRYANT, *The Turn of the Tide*, 587
5 CAB 65 (War Cab) '43
6 CAB 65 (War Cab) '43
7 CHURCHILL IV, 677
8 CAB 79 (COS) '43
9 CAB 79 (COS) '43

10   HOWARD, *op. cit.*, 369, 370 (OH)
11   *Ibid*
12   CHURCHILL IV, 677
13   CAB 65 (War Cab) '43
14   CAB 65 (War Cab) '43
15   DILKS, *Diaries of Cadogan*, 520, 521; WOODWARD, *British Foreign Policy in the Second World War* (1962 version), 203 (OH)
16   CAB 65 (War Cab) '43
17   CAB 65 (War Cab) '43
18   CAB 65 (War Cab) '43
19   BRYANT, *op. cit.*, 592; HOWARD, *op. cit.*, 362 (OH); CAB 79 (COS) '43
20   CAB 79 (COS) '43
21   CAB 79 (COS) '43
22   BRYANT, *op. cit.*, 602
23   CHURCHILL IV, 849
24   MONTGOMERY, *Memoirs*, 170, 171
25   CAB 79 (COS) '43
26   EDEN, *The Reckoning*, 382, 383
27   CAB 65 (War Cab) '43
28   HOWARD, *op. cit.*, 353 (OH)
29   CAB 65 (War Cab) '43
30   CAB 65 (War Cab) '43
31   BRYANT, *op. cit.*, 604
32   MONTGOMERY, *op. cit.*, 165; CHURCHILL IV, 691
33   CHURCHILL IV, 702
34   BRYANT, *op. cit.*, 608
35   CAB 79 (COS) '43
36   CAB 79 (COS) '43; HOWARD, *op. cit.*, 418 (OH)
37   HOWARD, *op. cit.*, 415 (OH)
38   MATLOFF, *Strategic Planning for Coalition Warfare*, 136
39   CAB 100 (CWR) 8 May '43
40   GOEBBELS, *Diary*, 9 May '43
41   CAB 65 (War Cab) '43
42   CHURCHILL IV, 695
43   ASTLEY, *The Inner Circle*, 94
44   BRYANT, *op. cit.*, 611
45   CHURCHILL IV, 707-709

46 *Ibid*, 697
47 *Ibid*, 698
48 CAB 65 (War Cab) '43
49 ISMAY, *Memoirs*, 296
50 CAB 88 (CCS) '43
51 BRYANT, *op. cit.*, 615
52 HULL, *Memoirs*, 1217-1219
53 CAB 88 (CCS) '43
54 BRYANT, *op. cit.*, 616, 617
55 CAB 88 (CCS) '43
56 CAB 88 (CCS) '43
57 BRYANT, *op. cit.*, 621
58 CAB 88 (CCS) '43
59 CAB 88 (CCS) '43
60 BRYANT, *op. cit.*, 622
61 CAB 65 (War Cab) '43
62 DILKS, *op. cit.*, 532
63 CAB 65 (War Cab) '43
64 CAB 65 (War Cab) '43
65 BRYANT, *op. cit.*, 626
66 CHURCHILL IV, 724
67 BRYANT, *op. cit.*, 628
68 CHURCHILL IV, 729
69 *Ibid*
70 *Ibid*, 730
71 EISENHOWER, *Crusade in Europe*, 184
72 HOWARD, *op. cit.*, 497, 498 (OH)
73 CHURCHILL IV, 734
74 BRYANT, *op. cit.*, 638
75 CHURCHILL IV, 740
76 WOODWARD, *op. cit.*, 221 (OH)
77 CHURCHILL V, 154
78 CHURCHILL IV, 742
79 CAB 65 (War Cab) '43
80 CAB 79 (COS) '43; EDEN, *op. cit.*, 392
81 CAB 69 (Def Com) '43
82 GOEBBELS, *op. cit.*, 22 May '43
83 CAB 69 (Def Com) '43
84 CAB 69 (Def Com) '43

85 POSTAN, *British War Production,* 226 (OH)
86 WOODWARD, *op. cit.,* 221 (OH)
87 CHURCHILL V, 156
88 MACMILLAN, *op. cit.,* 345
89 HULL, *op. cit.,* 1222
90 CHURCHILL V, 156
91 EDEN, *op. cit.,* 384
92 CHURCHILL V, 157
93 CAB 65 (War Cab) '43
94 WOODWARD, *op. cit.,* 221 (OH)
95 MACMILLAN, *op. cit.,* 353
96 WOODWARD, *op. cit.,* 241 (OH)
97 DILKS, *op. cit.,* 536; WOODWARD, *op. cit.,* 241-242 (OH)
98 WOODWARD, *op. cit.,* 242, 243 (OH)
99 *Ibid,* 249
100 DILKS, *op. cit.,* 540
101 WOODWARD, *op. cit.,* 250 (OH)
102 CAB 79 (COS) '43
103 HOWARD, *op. cit.,* 482 (OH)
104 CAB 79 (COS) '43
105 CAB 79 (COS) '43
106 CAB 65 (War Cab) '43
107 HOWARD, *op. cit.,* 467 (OH)
108 NICOLSON, *Diaries and Letters,* 303; DILKS, *op. cit.,* 541; BRYANT, *op. cit.,* 669

CHAPTER 4 SPLINTERED AXIS

1 BRYANT, *The Turn of the Tide,* 669
2 CAB 100 (CWR) 10 July '43
3 CAB 65 (War Cab) '43
4 CHURCHILL V, 157-159
5 EDEN, *The Reckoning,* 597, 598; DILKS, *Diaries of Cadogan,* 544
6 CAB 65 (War Cab) '43
7 CAB 79 (COS) '43
8 HOWARD, *Grand Strategy,* IV, 502 (OH)
9 CAB 79 (COS) '43

10 CHURCHILL V, 34, 35
11 CAB 79 (COS) '43
12 HOWARD, *op. cit.*, 560 (OH)
13 CAB 88 (CCS) '43
14 HOWARD, *op. cit.*, 503 (OH)
15 CAB 79 (COS) '43
16 CAB 65 (War Cab) '43; DILKS, *op. cit.*, 545
17 CAB 79 (COS) '43
18 CAB 65 (War Cab) '43
19 CAB 65 (War Cab) '43
20 CAB 79 (COS) '43; HOWARD, *op. cit.*, 505-506 (OH)
21 BRYANT, *op. cit.*, 672
22 EDEN, *op. cit.*, 399
23 CHURCHILL V, 159-160
24 BRYANT, *op. cit.*, 672
25 CHURCHILL V, 411
26 WOODWARD, *British Foreign Policy* (1962 version), 224
    (OH)
27 CAB 79 (COS) '43
28 HOWARD, *op. cit.*, 545-546 (OH)
29 *Ibid*, 547
30 *Ibid*, 506
31 BRYANT, *op. cit.*, 673
32 CAB 100 (CWR) 25, 26 July '43
33 HARRIS, *Bomber Offensive*, 174
34 CHURCHILL V, 51
35 CAB 65 (War Cab) '43
36 CAB 79 (COS) '43
37 CAB 88 (CCS) '43
38 CAB 69 (Def Com) '43
39 CHURCHILL V, 59
40 *Ibid*, 58
41 DILKS, *op. cit.*, 548
42 CHURCHILL V, 579, 580
43 CAB 65 (War Cab) '43
44 CAB 69 (Def Com) '43
45 CHURCHILL V, 37
46 CAB 79 (COS) '43
47 CAB 69 (Def Com) '43

48 BRYANT, *op. cit.*, 689
49 HOWARD, *op. cit.*, 473 (OH)
50 CHURCHILL V, 91
51 CAB 65 (War Cab) '43
52 HOWARD, *op. cit.*, 521 (OH)
53 MACMILLAN, *The Blast of War*, 359
54 CAB 79 (COS) '43; HOWARD, *op. cit.*, 565, 566 (OH)
55 BRYANT, *op. cit.*, 693
56 CAB 79 (COS) '43
57 HOWARD, *op. cit.*, 562 (OH)
58 STIMSON, *On Active Service*, 228-230
59 HOWARD, *op. cit.*, 563 (OH)
60 CAB 65 (War Cab) '43
61 CAB 79 (COS) '43; HOWARD, *op. cit.*, 567 (OH); BRYANT, *op. cit.*, 705
62 CAB 88 (CCS) '43
63 BRYANT, *op. cit.*, 705
64 CAB 88 (CCS) '43
65 BRYANT, *op. cit.*, 706, 707
66 CAB 88 (CCS) '43
67 BRYANT, *op. cit.*, 706
68 WOODWARD, *op. cit.*, 229 (OH); HOWARD, *op. cit.*, 522 (OH)
69 HOWARD, *op. cit.*, 523 (OH)
70 *Ibid*, 568-569
71 BRYANT, *op. cit.*, 708
72 CHURCHILL V, 58
73 CAB 88 (CCS) '43
74 CAB 88 (CCS) '43
75 HOWARD, *op. cit.*, 554 (OH)
76 CAB 88 (CCS) '43
77 BRYANT, *op. cit.*, 713, 714; CHURCHILL V, 80-81
78 CHURCHILL V, 77
79 BRYANT, *op. cit.*, 712
80 CHURCHILL V, 248
81 HOWARD, *op. cit.*, 524, 525 (OH); WOODWARD, *op. cit.*, 229 (OH)
82 CHURCHILL V, 95, 96
83 MONTGOMERY, *Memoirs*, 191, 192
84 CHURCHILL V, 79

85 CAB 88 (CCS) '43
86 BRYANT, *op. cit.*, 714
87 EDEN, *op. cit.*, 402, 403; HULL, *Memoirs*, 1233
88 CAB 88 (CCS) '43
89 WOODWARD, *op. cit.*, 445, 446 (OH); DILKS, *op. cit.*, 554
90 CAB 88 (CCS) '43; HOWARD, *op. cit.*, 682-692 (OH)
91 BRYANT, *op. cit.*, 718
92 WOODWARD, *op. cit.*, 224 (OH); HULL, *op. cit.*, 1241, 1242
93 DILKS, *op. cit.*, 556
94 MACMILLAN, *op. cit.*, 386
95 CAB 65 (War Cab) '43

CHAPTER 5 TALKS AT TEHRAN

1   CAB 65 (War Cab) '43
2   CAB 65 (War Cab) '43
3   CAB 65 (War Cab) '43
4   CAB 65 (War Cab) '43
5   HOWARD, *Grand Strategy*, IV, 432 (OH)
6   *Ibid*
7   CAB 88 (CCS) '43
8   CHURCHILL V, 182
9   CAB 79 (COS) '43
10 CHURCHILL V, 247-251
11 EDEN, *The Reckoning*, 405
12 CAB 88 (CCS) '43
13 HOWARD, *op. cit.*, 534 (OH)
14 SHEPPERD, *The Italian Campaign*, 128
15 BRYANT, *Triumph in the West*, 42
16 CHURCHILL V, 101
17 CAB 65 (War Cab) '43
18 BRYANT, *op. cit.*, 32
19 SHEPPERD, *op. cit.*, 132
20 CHURCHILL V, 130
21 *Ibid*, 131
22 CAB 79 (COS) '43
23 NICOLSON, *Diaries and Letters*, 323
24 CHURCHILL V, 134

25   CAB 79 (COS) '43
26   CAB 79 (COS) '43; BRYANT, *op. cit.*, 43
27   BRYANT, *op. cit.*, 44
28   CAB 88 (CCS) '43; HOWARD, *op. cit.*, 534, 535 (OH)
29   CAB 69 (Def Com) '43
30   CHURCHILL V, 234, 235, 236
31   CAB 79 (COS) '43
32   CAB 79 (COS) '43; BRYANT, *op. cit.*, 50-51
33   CHURCHILL V, 186, 187, 188
34   *Ibid*, 188-189
35   BRYANT, *op. cit.*, 51
36   CHURCHILL V, 189
37   *Ibid*, 190
38   *Ibid*, 98-99
39   *Ibid*, 193, 195
40   BRYANT, *op. cit.*, 53
41   DILKS, *Diaries of Cadogan*, 564, 565
42   CAB 65 (War Cab) '43
43   HULL, *Memoirs*, 1277
44   CHURCHILL V, 237
45   CAB 65 (War Cab) '43
46   DILKS, *op. cit.*, 565
47   *Ibid*, 568; CHURCHILL V, 237, 238
48   CAB 65 (War Cab) '43
49   CAB 79 (COS) '43
50   BRYANT, *op. cit.*, 74, note 1
51   CAB 79 (COS) '43
52   BRYANT, *op. cit.*, 55
53   ISMAY, *Memoirs*, 324
54   EHRMAN, *Grand Strategy*, V, 107-108 (OH)
55   CHURCHILL V, 220
56   BRYANT, *op. cit.*, 56
57   CAB 65 (War Cab) '43
58   CAB 69 (Def Com) '43
59   CAB 79 (COS) '43
60   CAB 65 (War Cab) '43
61   CAB 65 (War Cab) '43
62   DILKS, *op. cit.*, 571
63   CHURCHILL V, 279, 280

64 BRYANT, *op. cit.*, 59
65 ISMAY, *Memoirs*, 327
66 CAB 65 (War Cab) '43
67 CAB 65 (War Cab) '43
68 WOODWARD, *British Foreign Policy* (1962 version), 355 (OH)
69 CAB 65 (War Cab) '43
70 EHRMAN, *op. cit.*, 73 (OH)
71 CAB 79 (COS) '43
72 CAB 65 (War Cab) '43
73 CHURCHILL V, 221
74 EHRMAN, *op. cit.*, 74 (OH)
75 MONTGOMERY, *Memoirs*, 197
76 EHRMAN, *op. cit.*, 109-111 (OH)
77 BRYANT, *op. cit.*, 67
78 CHURCHILL V, 291-294
79 EHRMAN, *op. cit.*, 120 (OH)
80 SHERWOOD, *White House Papers*, II, 762-763
81 BRYANT, *op. cit.*, 71
82 CAB 65 (War Cab) '43
83 BRYANT, *op. cit.*, 75
84 EHRMAN, *op. cit.*, 162-164 (OH); CHURCHILL V, 294
85 WHITE, *The Stilwell Papers*, 245
86 BRYANT, *op. cit.*, 80, 81; CAB 88 (CCS) '43
87 ARNOLD, *Global Mission*, 220
88 EHRMAN, *op. cit.*, 166 (OH)
89 CAB 88 (CCS) '43
90 CAB 88 (CCS) '43
91 BRYANT, *op. cit.*, 84
92 CAB 88 (CCS) '43
93 BRYANT, *op. cit.*, 79
94 EHRMAN, *op. cit.*, 170, 172 (OH)
95 CHURCHILL V, 299
96 ISMAY, *op. cit.*, 337
97 HOWARD, *op. cit.*, 685 (OH)
98 BRYANT, *op. cit.*, 90-91
99 EHRMAN, *op. cit.*, 173-176 (OH)
100 LEAHY, *I Was There*, 242
101 EHRMAN, *op. cit.*, 571 (OH)

102 *Ibid,* 177-178
103 BRYANT, *op. cit.,* 92
104 EHRMAN, *op. cit.,* 179-181 (OH); CHURCHILL V, 329
105 BRYANT, *op. cit.,* 93
106 CAB 79 (COS) '43
107 CAB 88 (CCS) '43
108 CHURCHILL V, 332-336
109 BRYANT, *op. cit.,* 95
110 EHRMAN, *op. cit.,* 183 (OH)
111 DILKS, *op. cit.,* 580
112 EDEN, *op. cit.,* 427, 428
113 *Ibid,* 429
114 WOODWARD, *op. cit.,* 447, 448 (OH)
115 DILKS, *op. cit.,* 528
116 CAB 79 (COS) '43
117 CAB 88 (CCS) '43
118 BRYANT, *op. cit.,* 104
119 EHRMAN, *op. cit.,* 184-197 (OH)
120 *Ibid,* 186
121 CAB 88 (CCS) '43
122 BRYANT, *op. cit.,* 105-106
123 CAB 88 (CCS) '43
124 CAB 88 (CCS) '43
125 CHURCHILL V, 364
126 BRYANT, *op. cit.,* 109
127 MORAN, *Struggle for Survival,* 137
128 CHURCHILL V, 365
129 CAB 88 (CCS) '43
130 CAB 88 (CCS) '43
131 CAB 65 (War Cab) '43
132 CAB 88 (CCS) '43, '44

CHAPTER 6   WINTER ILLS

1 BRYANT, *Triumph in the West,* 111
2 CAB 65 (War Cab) '43
3 MACMILLAN, *The Blast of War,* 437
4 BRYANT, *op. cit.,* 122, 123

5 CHURCHILL V, 373, 375
6 BRYANT, *op. cit.,* 125
7 CAB 88 (CCS) '43; EHRMAN, *Grand Strategy,* V, 213-214 (OH)
8 CHURCHILL V, 380
9 CAB 79 (COS) '43; EHRMAN, *op. cit.,* 210 (OH)
10 CHURCHILL V, 381
11 CAB 79 (COS) '43
12 CAB 79 (COS) '43
13 CHURCHILL V, 386, 387
14 *Ibid,* 386
15 CAB 79 (COS) '43
16 CHURCHILL V, 390-391
17 ISMAY, *Memoirs,* 343
18 NICOLSON, *Diaries and Letters,* 332
19 MOOREHEAD, *Eclipse,* 18
20 EHRMAN, *op. cit.,* 223 (OH)
21 MACMILLAN, *op. cit.,* 438-446
22 EDEN, *The Reckoning,* 432-433
23 CHURCHILL V, 416
24 *Ibid,* 416, 417
25 WOODWARD, *British Foreign Policy* (1962 version), 278 (OH)
26 CHURCHILL V, 398
27 BRYANT, *op. cit.,* 128
28 *Ibid,* 130
29 CAB 79 (COS) '44
30 CHURCHILL V, 396, 397
31 CAB 79 (COS) '44
32 CAB 79 (COS) '44
33 BRYANT, *op. cit.,* 131
34 CHURCHILL V, 396
35 CAB 79 (COS) '44
36 EHRMAN, *op. cit.,* 235 (OH)
37 CHURCHILL V, 397
38 NICOLSON, *op. cit.,* 346
39 CAB 65 (War Cab) '44
40 CAB 69 (Def Com) '44
41 EHRMAN, *op. cit.,* 435 (OH)

42   CAB 79 (COS) '44
43   CAB 100 (CWR) 23 Jan. '44
44   CAB 88 (CCS) '44
45   CAB 79 (COS) '44
46   CAB 79 (COS) '44
47   CAB 79 (COS) '44; BRYANT, *op. cit.*, 141
48   CAB 79 (COS) '44
49   EHRMAN, *op. cit.*, 238 (OH)
50   CAB 79 (COS) '44
51   CAB 69 (Def Com) '44
52   EHRMAN, *op. cit.*, 240 (OH)
53   BRYANT, *op. cit.*, 145; EHRMAN, *op. cit.*, 240 (OH)
54   CHURCHILL V, 431
55   CAB 79 (COS) '44
56   CAB 79 (COS) '44
57   BRYANT, *op. cit.*, 146, 147
58   CAB 79 (COS) '44; BRYANT, *op. cit.*, 146
59   CHURCHILL V, 432
60   CAB 79 (COS) '44
61   CAB 79 (COS) '44
62   BRYANT, *op. cit.*, 149
63   CAB 79 (COS) '44; BRYANT, *op. cit.*, 150
64   CAB 79 (COS) '44; BRYANT, *op. cit.*, 152
65   CAB 79 (COS) '44; BRYANT, *op. cit.*, 152
66   NICOLSON, *op. cit.*, 348
67   EHRMAN, *op. cit.*, 230, 231 (OH)
68   CAB 79 (COS) '44; BRYANT, *op. cit.*, 153
69   CAB 100 (CWR) 25 Feb. '44
70   CAB 79 (COS) '44
71   EHRMAN, *op. cit.*, 454-455 (OH)
72   *Ibid*, 244
73   BRYANT, *op. cit.*, 160
74   CHURCHILL V, 434
75   EHRMAN, *op. cit.*, 441-444 (OH)
76   BRYANT, *op. cit.*, 161
77   EHRMAN, *op. cit.*, 448-449 (OH)
78   CAB 79 (COS) '44
79   CHURCHILL V, 508, 509
80   BRYANT, *op. cit.*, 162

81 *Ibid,* 163
82 CHURCHILL V, 509, 510
83 EHRMAN, *op. cit.,* 452 (OH)
84 CAB 79 (COS) '44
85 BRYANT, *op. cit.,* 164, 165
86 *Ibid*
87 CAB 79 (COS) '44
88 CAB 79 (COS) '44
89 BRYANT, *op. cit.,* 166
90 CHURCHILL V, 615
91 CHURCHILL V, 511-512
92 BRYANT, *op. cit.,* 168
93 DILKS, *Diaries of Cadogan,* 612
94 EHRMAN, *op. cit.,* 252, 455-456 (OH)
95 CAB 79 (COS) '44
96 DILKS, *op. cit.,* 615; EDEN, *op. cit.,* 449
97 NICOLSON, *op. cit.,* 358
98 BRYANT, *op. cit.,* 175
99 CAB 79 (COS) '44
100 CAB 79 (COS) '44
101 BRYANT, *op. cit.,* 170-171, 175
102 EHRMAN, *op. cit.,* 253 (OH)
103 *Ibid,* 103
104 CAB 79 (COS) '44; EHRMAN, *op. cit.,* 254 (OH)
105 EHRMAN, *op. cit.,* 295-297 (OH)
106 CAB 65 (War Cab) '44
107 EDEN, *op. cit.,* 448-449
108 CAB 69 (Def Com) '44; CHURCHILL V, 466
109 KENNEDY, *This Business of War,* 326
110 BRYANT, *op. cit.,* 180
111 CAB 79 (COS) '44
112 CAB 79 (COS) '44
113 CAB 79 (COS) '44
114 CAB 79 (COS) '44
115 EHRMAN, *op. cit.,* 573-575 (OH)
116 CAB 69 (Def Com) '44
117 EHRMAN, *op. cit.,* 486 (OH)
118 CAB 79 (COS) '44
119 CAB 79 (COS) '44

120   EHRMAN, *op. cit.*, 259 (OH)
121   BRYANT, *op. cit.*, 184
122   DILKS, *op. cit.*, 622
123   CAB 69 (Def Com) '44
124   BRYANT, *op. cit.*, 184
125   EHRMAN, *op. cit.*, 259, 260 (OH)
126   CAB 79 (COS) '44
127   CAB 88 (CCS) '44
128   CAB 69 (Def Com) '44
129   CAB 65 (War Cab) '44
130   CAB 65 (War Cab) '44
131   CAB 69 (Def Com) '44
132   EHRMAN, *op. cit.*, 304 (OH)
133   CAB 79 (COS) '44
134   EDEN, *op. cit.*, 451
135   EHRMAN, *op. cit.*, 263 (OH); CAB 79 (COS) '44
136   EHRMAN, *op. cit.*, 489 (OH)
137   CAB 79 (COS) '44
138   CAB 79 (COS) '44
139   CAB 79 (COS) '44
140   CAB 79 (COS) '44
141   CAB 65 (War Cab) '44
142   CAB 65 (War Cab) '43
143   CAB 65 (War Cab) '43
144   CHURCHILL VI, 65; WOODWARD, *op. cit.*, 292 (OH); HULL,
       Memoirs, 1451-1453
145   BRYANT, *op. cit.*, 196
146   WOODWARD, *op. cit.*, 264, 265 (OH)
147   CHURCHILL V, 529
148   BRYANT, *op. cit.*, 189
149   ISMAY, *op. cit.*, 352
150   CHURCHILL V, 532
151   CAB 79 (COS) '44; DILKS, *op. cit.*, 629
152   WOODWARD, *op. cit.*, 265 (OH)
153   CHURCHILL V, 535, 536
154   CAB 79 (COS) '44
155   CAB 65 (War Cab) '44
156   CAB 79 (COS) '44
157   EDEN, *op. cit.*, 452

158 CAB 79 (COS) '44
159 ASTLEY, *The Inner Circle*, 143, 144
160 MONTGOMERY, *Memoirs*, 248; TEDDER, *With Prejudice*, 545; EISENHOWER, *Crusade in Europe*, 222
161 EDEN, *op. cit.*, 453; WOODWARD, *op. cit.*, 266 (OH)
162 ASTLEY, *op. cit.*, 144
163 BRYANT, *op. cit.*, 205
164 CAB 65 (War Cab) '44
165 DILKS, *op. cit.*, 635
166 BRYANT, *op. cit.*, 206

CHAPTER 7 D-DAY AND BEYOND

1   CAB 79 (COS) '44
2   BRYANT, *Triumph in the West*, 209
3   DILKS, *Diaries of Cadogan*, 635
4   EDEN, *The Reckoning*, 454-455
5   EHRMAN, *Grand Strategy*, V, 266-267 (OH)
6   CAB 65 (War Cab) '44
7   WOODWARD, *British Foreign Policy* (1962 version), 267 (OH); EDEN, *op. cit.*, 455
8   CHURCHILL VI, 65
9   HULL, *Memoirs*, 1454
10   CAB 79 (COS) '44
11   CAB 88 (CCS) '44
12   NICOLSON, *Diaries and Letters*, 381
13   BRYANT, *op. cit.*, 238
14   CAB 88 (CCS) '44
15   BRYANT, *op. cit.*, 211
16   CHURCHILL VI, 65-67; WOODWARD, *op. cit.*, 292, 293 (OH)
17   BRYANT, *op. cit.*, 211
18   CAB 65 (War Cab) '44
19   NICOLSON, *op. cit.*, 382
20   CAB 88 (CCS) '44
21   CAB 65 (War Cab) '44
22   CAB 65 (War Cab) '44
23   CAB 88 (CCS) '44; BRYANT, *op. cit.*, 218
24   CAB 65 (War Cab) '44

25 NICOLSON, *op. cit.*, 383
26 CAB 65 (War Cab) '44
27 BRYANT, *op. cit.*, 220
28 CAB 79 (COS) '44
29 CAB 79 (COS) '44; EHRMAN, *op. cit.*, 347, 348 (OH)
30 CAB 79 (COS) '44
31 MACMILLAN, *The Blast of War*, 506-507
32 HULL, *op. cit.*, 1456
33 EDEN, *op. cit.*, 459
34 CHURCHILL VI, 68
35 CAB 79 (COS) '44; BRYANT, *op. cit.*, 223
36 EHRMAN, *op. cit.*, 349, 359 (OH)
37 EDEN, *op. cit.*, 464
38 CHURCHILL V, 660
39 BRYANT, *op. cit.*, 223
40 CAB 79 (COS) '44
41 CHURCHILL VI, 69
42 WOODWARD, *op. cit.*, 293 (OH)
43 BRYANT, *op. cit.*, 239
44 CAB 65 (War Cab) '44
45 CAB 79 (COS) '44; EHRMAN, *op. cit.*, 352, 353 (OH)
46 EHRMAN, *op. cit.*, 353-355; *Bryant, op. cit.*, 227
47 BRYANT, *op. cit.*, 225
48 *Ibid*, 226
49 CAB 79 (COS) '44; EHRMAN, *op. cit.*, 356-358 (OH)
50 CAB 65 (War Cab) '44
51 CAB 84 (JPS) '44
52 BRYANT, *op. cit.*, 227
53 CAB 79 (COS) '44
54 CAB 84 (JPS) '44
55 CHURCHILL VI, 39
56 CAB 79 (COS) '44
57 EDEN, *op. cit.*, 461
58 CAB 65 (War Cab) '44
59 DILKS, *op. cit.*, 645
60 BRYANT, *op. cit.*, 239, 240
61 SPEIDEL, *We Defended Normandy*, 123
62 CAB 65 (War Cab) '44
63 CHURCHILL VI, 96

64 BRYANT, *op. cit.,* 86
65 CAB 79 (COS) '44
66 CAB 79 (COS) '44
67 CAB 84 (JPS) '44
68 CAB 79 (COS) '44
69 CAB 84 (JPS) '44
70 EDEN, *op. cit.,* 462; EHRMAN, *op. cit.,* 485 (OH)
71 CAB 65 (War Cab) '44
72 BRYANT, *op. cit.,* 234
73 CAB 65 (War Cab) '44
74 SHERWOOD, *White House Papers,* II, 803
75 CAB 65 (War Cab) '44
76 CAB 65 (War Cab) '44
77 BRYANT, *op. cit.,* 243, 244
78 EHRMAN, *op. cit.,* 372 (OH)
79 CAB 79 (COS) '44
80 CAB 79 (COS) '44
81 EDEN, *op. cit.,* 462
82 CAB 79 (COS) '44
83 CAB 79 (COS) '44; BRYANT, *op. cit.,* 250
84 BRYANT, *op. cit.,* 249
85 WOODWARD, *op. cit.,* 299, 300 (OH)
86 CAB 65 (War Cab) '44
87 CHURCHILL VI, 116, 117
88 CAB 65 (War Cab) '44
89 CAB 65 (War Cab) '44
90 CHURCHILL VI, 119
91 WOODWARD, *op. cit.,* 346 (OH)
92 EHRMAN, *op. cit.,* 391 (OH)
93 *Ibid,* 377
94 CHURCHILL VI, 119
95 CAB 65 (War Cab) '44
96 CHURCHILL VI, 101
97 *Ibid,* 120
98 MONTGOMERY, *Memoirs,* 265
99 CAB 79 (COS) '44
100 CHURCHILL VI, 120-122
101 CAB 65 (War Cab) '44
102 CHURCHILL VI, 123, 124

103 CAB 65 (War Cab) '44
104 BRYANT, *op. cit.*, 262, 263; EHRMAN, *op. cit.*, 380 (OH)
105 CAB 65 (War Cab) '44
106 CAB 65 (War Cab) '44
107 CAB 65 (War Cab) '44; CHURCHILL VI, 125, 126
108 CHURCHILL VI, 126
109 CAB 65 (War Cab) '44
110 ISMAY, *Memoirs*, 373
111 CAB 65 (War Cab) '44; CHURCHILL VI, 43
112 CAB 65 (War Cab) '44
113 WOODWARD, *op. cit.*, 305 (OH)
114 CAB 65 (War Cab) '44
115 EHRMAN, *op. cit.*, 384 (OH)

CHAPTER 8   QUEBEC TO MOSCOW

1   BRYANT, *Triumph in the West*, 269
2   *Ibid*, 268
3   CAB 79 (COS) '44
4   EHRMAN, *Grand Strategy*, v, 402 (OH)
5   CAB 79 (COS) '44; EHRMAN, *op. cit.*, 503 (OH)
6   CAB 79 (COS) '44; BRYANT, *op. cit.*, 269, 270
7   CAB 88 (CCS) '44; BRYANT, *op. cit.*, 272
8   BRYANT, *op. cit.*, 272, 273
9   EHRMAN, *op. cit.*, 509, 518 (OH)
10 CHURCHILL VI, 137, 138
11 CAB 88 (CCS) '44
12 BRYANT, *op. cit.*, 374; EHRMAN, *op. cit.*, 531 (OH)
13 BRYANT, *op. cit.*, 274
14 CAB 88 (CCS) '44
15 BRYANT, *op. cit.*, 274
16 HULL, *Memoirs*, 1605, 1606
17 WOODWARD, *British Foreign Policy* (1962 version), 472 (OH)
18 EDEN, *The Reckoning*, 476
19 WOODWARD, *op. cit.*, 472, 473 (OH)
20 CAB 88 (CCS) '44; EDEN, *op. cit.*, 477
21 CAB 65 (War Cab) '44

22 CAB 79 (COS) '44
23 CHURCHILL VI, 127
24 EISENHOWER, *Crusade in Europe*, 336
25 BRYANT, *op. cit.*, 285
26 CAB 65 (War Cab) '44
27 EHRMAN, *op. cit.*, 530 (OH)
28 CAB 79 (COS) '44
29 CAB 79 (COS) '44
30 CHURCHILL VI, 248
31 CAB 79 (COS) '44
32 CAB 65 (War Cab) '44
33 NICOLSON, *Diaries and Letters*, 406
34 CHURCHILL VI, 139
35 CAB 79 (COS) '44
36 CAB 79 (COS) '44
37 CAB 79 (COS) '44
38 CHURCHILL VI, 192
39 EHRMAN, *Grand Strategy*, VI, 47 (OH)
40 EDEN, *op. cit.*, 481
41 CHURCHILL VI, 198; WOODWARD, *op. cit.*, 307 (OH)
42 CHURCHILL VI, 199
43 EDEN, *op. cit.*, 482, 483
44 WOODWARD, *op. cit.*, 307-308 (OH); EDEN, *op. cit.*, 493
45 EDEN, *op. cit.*, 483
46 CHURCHILL VI, 195
47 EHRMAN, *Grand Strategy*, VI, 48, 49 (OH)
48 CHURCHILL VI, 202
49 *Ibid*, 201
50 CAB 65 (War Cab) '44
51 WOODWARD, *op. cit.*, 309-311 (OH); EDEN, *op. cit.*, 486, 487
52 BRYANT, *op. cit.*, 306
53 CAB 79 (COS) '44
54 CHURCHILL VI, 196
55 CAB 79 (COS) '44
56 EDEN, *op. cit.*, 488
57 EHRMAN, *Grand Strategy*, VI, 167, 168 (OH)
58 *Ibid*, 50
59 NICOLSON, *op. cit.*, 412
60 EHRMAN, *Grand Strategy*, VI, 32, 33 (OH)

61 BRYANT, *op. cit.*, 320
62 CAB 79 (COS) '44
63 EHRMAN, *Grand Strategy*, VI, 52, 53 (OH)
64 CAB 79 (COS) '44
65 EDEN, *op. cit.*, 489-492
66 CHURCHILL VI, 250
67 DILKS, *Diaries of Cadogan*, 676
68 CAB 65 (War Cab) '44
69 EDEN, *op. cit.*, 496; WOODWARD, *op. cit.*, 312 (OH)
70 DILKS, *op. cit.*, 683
71 CAB 65 (War Cab) '44
72 CAB 65 (War Cab) '44
73 BRYANT, *op. cit.*, 340, 341
74 *Ibid*, 322
75 ISMAY, *Memoirs*, 381
76 CAB 65 (War Cab) '44
77 NICOLSON, *op. cit.*, 417

CHAPTER 9 COUNTER-OFFENSIVE

1   CHURCHILL VI, 252
2   PARKINSON, *Peace for Our Time*, 193
3   WOODWARD, *British Foreign Policy* (1962 version), 359 (OH)
4   CHURCHILL VI, 253
5   CAB 79 (COS) '44
6   CHURCHILL VI, 234, 235, 236
7   CAB 79 (COS) '44
8   EHRMAN, *Grand Strategy*, VI, 35, 64 (OH)
9   BRYANT, *Triumph in the West*, 349
10 *Ibid*, 348
11 NICOLSON, *Diaries and Letters*, 421
12 CHURCHILL VI, 258
13 SHERWOOD, *White House Papers*, II, 382
14 CHURCHILL VI, 253, 254, 255
15 *Ibid*, 237, 238
16 CAB 65 (War Cab) '44
17 CAB 65 (War Cab) '44

18 CAB 65 (War Cab) '44
19 BRYANT, *op. cit.*, 351
20 CAB 79 (COS) '44
21 BRYANT, *op. cit.*, 351, 352
22 *Ibid*, 352
23 CAB 65 (War Cab) '44
24 CAB 65 (War Cab) '44
25 CHURCHILL VI, 261-263
26 *Ibid*, 263, 264
27 CAB 65 (War Cab) '44
28 BRYANT, *op. cit.*, 356, 357
29 CAB 65 (War Cab) '44
30 CHURCHILL VI, 269
31 CAB 65 (War Cab) '44
32 DILKS, *Diaries of Cadogan*, 689
33 EDEN, *The Reckoning*, 499; MACMILLAN, *The Blast of War*, 622
34 EDEN, *op. cit.*, 500; WOODWARD, *op. cit.*, 361 (OH)
35 CHURCHILL VI, 289
36 CAB 79 (COS) '44
37 EDEN, *The Reckoning*, 501
38 CHURCHILL VI, 272, 273
39 *Ibid*, 274
40 DILKS, *op. cit.*, 691
41 CAB 79 (COS) '44
42 CAB 65 (War Cab) '44
43 BULLOCK, *Hitler*, 763, 764
44 CHURCHILL VI, 277
45 CAB 65 (War Cab) '44
46 CAB 65 (War Cab) '44
47 CAB 65 (War Cab) '44
48 DILKS, *op. cit.*, 692
49 CAB 79 (COS) '45
50 CHURCHILL VI, 242
51 BRYANT, *op. cit.*, 376
52 CAB 65 (War Cab) '45
53 MONTGOMERY, *Memoirs*, 309
54 CAB 65 (War Cab) '45
55 CAB 79 (COS) '45

56 CAB 88 (CCS) '45
57 CAB 79 (COS) '45
58 CAB 79 (COS) '45
59 CAB 79 (COS) '45
60 CAB 79 (COS) '45
61 CAB 79 (COS) '45
62 CAB 65 (War Cab) '45
63 CAB 79 (COS) '45
64 CAB 79 (COS) '45
65 CAB 65 (War Cab) '45
66 CAB 65 (War Cab) '45
67 CAB 65 (War Cab) '45
68 BRYANT, *op. cit.*, 382
69 DILKS, *op. cit.*, 694, 695
70 WHEELER-BENNET, *Action This Day*, 117
71 CAB 88 (CCS) '45
72 CAB 88 (CCS) '45
73 EHRMAN, *op. cit.*, 89 (OH)
74 BRYANT, *op. cit.*, 397
75 *Ibid*, 396
76 *Ibid*, 398
77 EHRMAN, *op. cit.*, 92 (OH)
78 EDEN, *op. cit.*, 511, 512
79 *Ibid*, 512
80 ISMAY, *Memoirs*, 387; ASTLEY, *The Inner Circle*, 175, 183-185, 191; DILKS, *op. cit.*, 703
81 EHRMAN, *op. cit.*, 103 (OH)
82 EDEN, *op. cit.*, 512, 513
83 EHRMAN, *op. cit.*, 103 (OH)
84 CHURCHILL VI, 305, 306
85 WOODWARD, *op. cit.*, 488-490 (OH); CHURCHILL VI, 307
86 CAB 65 (War Cab) '45
87 CAB 88 (CCS) '45
88 CAB 79 (COS) '45
89 EDEN, *op. cit.*, 516
90 CHURCHILL VI, 320-325; DILKS, *op. cit.*, 704
91 CHURCHILL VI, 326, 327; WOODWARD, *op. cit.*, 496 (OH)
92 MORAN, *Struggle for Survival*, 395
93 WOODWARD, *op. cit.*, 496, 497 (OH)

94   CAB 65 (War Cab) '45
95   CAB 65 (War Cab) '45; WOODWARD, *op. cit.*, 498 (OH)
96   WOODWARD, *op. cit.*, 499, 500 (OH)
97   WOODWARD, *op. cit.*, 486, 487 (OH); EDEN, *op. cit.*, 513
98   CAB 65 (War Cab) '45
99   WOODWARD, *op. cit.*, 500, 501 (OH)
100   CHURCHILL VI, 348
101   MONTGOMERY, *op. cit.*, 325
102   CAB 65 (War Cab) '45
103   ELLIS, *Victory in the West*, II, 226 (OH)
104   CAB 100 (CWR) 15 Feb. '45
105   CAB 65 (War Cab) '45
106   ELLIS, *op. cit.*, 227 (OH)

CHAPTER 10   END AND BEGINNING

1   CAB 65 (War Cab) '45
2   BRYANT, *Triumph in the West*, 418
3   WOODWARD, *British Foreign Policy* (1962 version), 502 (OH)
4   *Ibid*, 515
5   BRYANT, *op. cit.*, 419
6   WOODWARD, *op. cit.*, 503 (OH)
7   *Ibid*, 503
8   ROOSEVELT, *FDR*, 290
9   BRYANT, *op. cit.*, 422
10   *Ibid*, 423
11   CAB 65 (War Cab) '45
12   CAB 79 (COS) '45
13   CHURCHILL VI, 359, 360
14   CAB 79 (COS) '45
15   CAB 65 (War Cab) '45
16   WOODWARD, *op. cit.*, 503-505 (OH); CHURCHILL VI, 373
17   CAB 65 (War Cab) '45
18   WOODWARD, *op. cit.*, 123, 124 (OH)
19   CAB 65 (War Cab) '45
20   WOODWARD, *op. cit.*, 505 (OH)
21   CAB 79 (COS) '45

22   EHRMAN, *Grand Strategy*, VI, 124 (OH)
23   CHURCHILL VI, 388
24   BRYANT, *op. cit.*, 432
25   *Ibid*, 434
26   *Ibid*, 438
27   CAB 65 (War Cab) '45
28   BRYANT, *op. cit.*, 440, 440 note
29   *Ibid*, 442
30   CAB 88 (CCS) '45
31   BRYANT, *op. cit.*, 441
32   CAB 79 (COS) '45
33   CAB 79 (COS) '45
34   CHURCHILL VI, 403
35   *Ibid*, 408
36   BRYANT, *op. cit.*, 445
37   CAB 79 (COS) '45
38   EDEN, *The Reckoning*, 526; WOODWARD, *op. cit.*, 506 (OH)
39   CHURCHILL VI, 634
40   *Ibid*, 418
41   WOODWARD, *op. cit.*, 517 (OH)
42   EHRMAN, *op. cit.*, 142 (OH)
43   CHURCHILL VI, 383, 384
44   EHRMAN, *op. cit.*, 142 (OH)
45   CHURCHILL VI, 409
46   CAB 79 (COS) '45
47   CAB 65 (War Cab) '45
48   CAB 65 (War Cab) '45
49   CHURCHILL VI, 395, 396
50   DILKS, *Diaries of Cadogan*, 726
51   CAB 79 (COS) '45
52   EHRMAN, *op. cit.*, 145 (OH)
53   CHURCHILL VI, 447
54   CAB 79 (COS) '45
55   CHURCHILL VI, 396-398
56   *Ibid*, 385
57   WOODWARD, *op. cit.*, 511 (OH)
58   CHURCHILL VI, 398
59   CAB 79 (COS) '45; EHRMAN, *op. cit.*, 152, 153 (OH)
60   BUTCHER, *Three Years with Eisenhower*, 673

61 CAB 79 (COS) '45
62 WOODWARD, *op. cit.*, 508, 509 (OH)
63 CHURCHILL VI, 426, 427
64 CAB 79 (COS) '45
65 EISENHOWER, *Crusade in Europe*, 440
66 CAB 79 (COS) '45
67 CHURCHILL VI, 449
68 BRYANT, *op. cit.*, 451
69 EHRMAN, *op. cit.*, 146
70 WOODWARD, *op. cit.*, 509 (OH)
71 CAB 65 (War Cab) '45
72 EHRMAN, *op. cit.*, 157 (OH)
73 CAB 65 (War Cab) '45
74 CHURCHILL VI, 468
75 BULLOCK, *Hitler*, 788
76 CHURCHILL VI, 450
77 *Ibid*, 480
78 EHRMAN, *op. cit.*, 161 (OH)
79 *Ibid*, 161
80 BULLOCK, *op. cit.*, 794
81 CHURCHILL VI, 433
82 *Ibid*, 460
83 EHRMAN, *op. cit.*, 121 (OH)
84 CAB 65 (War Cab) '45
85 EHRMAN, *op. cit.*, 158 (OH)
86 CHURCHILL VI, 442
87 EHRMAN, *op. cit.*, 129 (OH)
88 *Ibid*, 276, 296
89 CAB 79 (COS) '45
90 CHURCHILL VI, 481
91 WOODWARD, *op. cit.*, 510 (OH)
92 CAB 100 (CWR) 3 May '45
93 CAB 79 (COS) '45
94 MONTGOMERY, *Memoirs*, 334-337
95 CAB 79 (COS) '45
96 EHRMAN, *op. cit.*, 160 (OH)
97 CHURCHILL VI, 482
98 *Ibid*, 438, 439
99 BRYANT, *op. cit.*, 455

100   CAB 79 (COS) '45
101   CAB 65 (War Cab) '45

CHAPTER 11   'TERMINAL'

1   CHURCHILL VI, 422
2   *Ibid*, 498
3   CAB 79 (COS) '45
4   BRYANT, *Triumph in the West*, 468
5   WOODWARD, *British Foreign Policy* (1962 version), 513 (OH)
6   *Ibid*, 520, 523
7   CAB 79 (COS) '45
8   CAB 79 (COS) '45
9   CAB 65 (War Cab) '45
10   CAB 79 (COS) '45
11   EHRMAN, *Grand Strategy*, VI, 297-298 (OH)
12   ATTLEE, *As It Happened*, 132
13   EDEN, *The Reckoning*, 533
14   ATTLEE, *op. cit.*, 135; CHURCHILL VI, 516
15   ATTLEE, *op. cit.*, 145
16   CAB 65 (Cab) '45
17   MONTGOMERY, *Memoirs*, 356
18   CAB 65 (Cab) '45
19   CAB 65 (Cab) '45
20   BRYANT, *op. cit.*, 471
21   MORAN, *Struggle for Survival*, 249
22   WOODWARD, *op. cit.*, 542, 543 (OH); CHURCHILL VI, 565, 566
23   CHURCHILL VI, 548-550
24   CAB 88 (CCS) '45
25   BRYANT, *op. cit.*, 477, 478
26   CHURCHILL VI, 575
27   *Ibid*, 581
28   EDEN, *op. cit.*, 551
29   MORAN, *op. cit.*, 254

Bibliography

Official Histories (OH); HMSO.
Campaigns.
PLAYFAIR, MAJOR-GENERAL, *The Mediterranean and Middle-East*; ROSKILL, CAPTAIN S. W., *The War at Sea*; WEBSTER, SIR C. K. and FRANKLAND, N., *The Strategic Air Offensive against Germany.*

Civil Series.
POSTAN, M. M., *British War Production.*

Diplomatic.
WOODWARD, SIR LLEWELLYN, *British Foreign Policy in the Second World War*, Vols II and III.
——, *British Foreign Policy in the Second World War* (original version published 1962).

Grand Strategy.
Volume IV, HOWARD, MICHAEL; Volume V, EHRMAN, JOHN; Volume VI, EHRMAN, JOHN.

ARNOLD, H., *Global Mission*, New York, 1951
ASTLEY, J., *The Inner Circle*, London, 1959
ATTLEE, CLEMENT, *As It Happened*, London, 1954
BIRKENHEAD, EARL OF, *The Prof in Two Worlds*: The Official Life of Professor F. A. Lindemann, Viscount Cherwell, London, 1961
BROME, VINCENT, *Aneurin Bevan*, London, 1953
BRYANT, ARTHUR, *The Turn of the Tide* and *Triumph in the West*, London, 1957 and 1959

BULLOCK, ALAN, *Hitler: a Study in Tyranny*, London (Pelican), 1962
——, *Life and Times of Ernest Bevin*, Volume II, Minister of Labour, 1940-1945, London, 1967
BUTCHER, HARRY C., *Three Years with Eisenhower*, New York, 1946
CALDER, ANGUS, *The People's War*, London, 1969
CHURCHILL, SIR WINSTON, *The Second World War* (Volume IV, *The Hinge of Fate*, London, 1951; Volume V, *Closing the Ring*, London, 1952; Volume VI, *Triumph and Tragedy*, London, 1954)
CONNELL, JOHN, *Auchinleck*, London, 1959
——, *Wavell, Supreme Commander*, London, 1969
COOPER, ALFRED DUFF, Viscount Norwich, *Old Men Forget*, London, 1953
CUNNINGHAM, LORD, of Hyndhope, *A Sailor's Odyssey*, London, 1951
DILKS, DAVID, (ed.), *The Diaries of Sir Alexander Cadogan*, London, 1971
EDEN, ANTHONY, (Lord Avon), *The Reckoning*, London, 1965
EISENHOWER, DWIGHT, *Crusade in Europe*, New York, 1948
GARDNER, BRIAN, *Churchill in his Time. A Study in Reputation, 1939-1945*, London, 1968
GAULLE, GENERAL CHARLES DE, *War Memoirs*, New York, 1955
GOEBBELS, *Diary* (ed. L. P. Lochner), London, 1948
GRIGG, SIR JAMES, *Prejudice and Judgement*, London, 1948
GUDERIAN, HEINZ, *Panzer Leader*, London, 1952
HARRIS, SIR ARTHUR, *Bomber Offensive*, London, 1947
HULL, CORDEL, *Memoirs*, Volume II, London, 1948
ISMAY, GENERAL LORD, *Memoirs*, London, 1960
KENNEDY, GENERAL SIR JOHN, and FERGUSSON, B., *The Business of War*, London, 1957
LEAHY, FLEET ADMIRAL WILLIAM, *I Was There*, New York, 1950
LEASOR, JAMES, and HOLLIS, GENERAL SIR LESLIE, *War at the Top*, London, 1959
LEWIN, RONALD, *Rommel as Military Commander*, London, 1968
LYTTELTON, OLIVER, *The Memoirs of Lord Chandos*, London, 1962

MACMILLAN, HAROLD, *The Blast of War*, London, 1967

MAISKY, I., *Memoirs of a Soviet Ambassador*, 1939-1943, London, 1967

MATLOFF, MAURICE, and SNELL, EDWIN M., *Strategic Planning for Coalition Warfare*, Army Department, Washington, 1953

MINNEY, R. J., *The Private Papers of Hore-Belisha*, London, 1960

MONTGOMERY, VISCOUNT, of Alamein, *The Memoirs of Field Marshal Montgomery*, London, 1958

MOOREHEAD, ALAN, *Eclipse*, London, 1945

MORAN, LORD, *Winston Churchill : Struggle for Survival*, 1940-1965, London, 1966

MUGGERIDGE, MALCOLM, (ed.), *Ciano's Diary*, 1939-1943, London, 1947

NICOLSON, HAROLD, *Diaries and Letters*, Volume II, 1939-1945 (London, 1967), Fontana edition, 1970

ROOSEVELT, ELLIOTT, *As He Saw It*, New York, 1951

——, (ed.), *FDR—His Personal Letters*, 1928-1945, New York, 1950

SCHMIDT, PAUL, *Hitler's Interpreter*, London, 1951

SHEPPERD, G. A., *The Italian Campaign*, London, 1968

SHERWOOD, ROBERT E., (ed.), *White House Papers of Harry L. Hopkins*, London, 1949

——, *Roosevelt and Hopkins*, New York, 1948

SHIRER, WILLIAM L., *The Rise and Fall of the Third Reich* (London, 1960), Pan edition, 1969

SLESSOR, SIR JOHN, *The Central Blue*, London, 1950

SPEIDEL, GENERAL, *We Defended Normandy*, London, 1951

STIMSON, HENRY, and BUNDY, MCGEORGE, *On Active Service in Peace and War*, New York, 1947

STRAWSON, JOHN, *The Battle for North Africa*, London, 1969

TEDDER, LORD, *With Prejudice*, London, 1966

TREVOR-ROPER, HUGH, (ed.), *Hitler's War Directives*, London, 1964

WHEELER-BENNETT, SIR JOHN, (ed.), *Action This Day*, London, 1968

——, *John Anderson*, London, 1962

WHITE, T. H., (ed.), *The Stilwell Papers*, London, 1949

WINANT, JOHN GILBERT, *A Letter from Grosvenor Square*, London, 1947
YOUNG, KENNETH, *Churchill and Beaverbrook*, London, 1966.

Index